Wholesaling
in marketing
organization

Wholesaling
in marketing
organization

DAVID A. REVZAN

Professor of Business Administration
School of Business Administration
University of California
Berkeley, California

New York · London, John Wiley & Sons, Inc.

Dedicated to
EDWARD A. DUDDY
Professor Emeritus of Marketing
The School of Business
The University of Chicago

Preface

One of the surprising aspects of the supply of existing marketing literature is the paucity of writings in the field of wholesaling. Only one book—Beckman and Engle, *Wholesaling: Principles and Practice* —covers the entire field.* Special studies are available in abundance, of course. But when one considers the quantitative significance of wholesaling in marketing, as well as the challenging problems that arise in this subject matter material, then the lack of writings becomes even more surprising and unexplainable.

This book, in its attempt to overcome this shortage, is designed to give the serious student (in all meanings of the word) a detailed analysis of the whole field of wholesaling. As such it begins with the external view of the field, and then moves from the external aspects to the internal management view. In the external view, new materials are included under basic concepts such as the funnel concept of wholesaling, and linkages and blockages in channels of distribution. In addition, materials on channel structure within marketing organization are integrated into the more orthodox treatment of the various types of wholesale middlemen.

The internal management section introduces several kinds of new materials and approaches. For one thing, there is a complete chapter on "Selection of Type of Wholesale Middleman Operation," in which certain quantitative analyses are introduced. In addition, the discussion of internal management policies and problems stratifies the analysis by type of middleman operation wherever differences in type

* R. D. Buzzell was added as coauthor in the 1959 3rd edition.

account for fundamental differences in organization and policies. The discussion of price introduces new materials on the over-all wholesale price structure. New materials are included, as well, on inventories and inventory theory, and on coordination and control of wholesale middlemen's policies and operations.

All in all, an attempt has been made throughout this book to sharpen the theoretical tools pertinent to an up-to-date treatment of the field. Wherever possible, the treatment has been integrated with the institutional approach to marketing developed by Professor Edward A. Duddy and the author.

DAVID A. REVZAN

Berkeley, California
January 1961

Contents

1

Some Basic Concepts

The field of wholesaling represents by far the most significant segment of marketing based on any or all of several points of view: Annual gross cumulative sales volumes; the variety of types of middleman operations compared with retailing; the range of kinds of business involved; the number of levels and complexity of the transactions involved; or the complexity of the problems involved. It entails as well, cutting across the above, the critical evaluation of the position of primary and intermediate markets. Many of these points of view will be treated in detail in later chapters. The levels of business transactions involved are many, ranging from the extractive industries through basic and secondary manufacturing levels, going on to the service businesses, the various wholesale and retail middlemen, and, finally, to many governmental levels, educational institutions, and other agencies as well. These are only some of the aspects which underlie the importance and complexity of wholesaling.[1]

But however viewed, wholesaling is a part of marketing which emphasizes matters of structural arrangement based upon degrees of specialization of both types of business and kind of transaction. Some aspects, as will be noted in a later section of this chapter, create no questions as to whether or not the transaction involved is wholesaling in nature. But other aspects, because of their relationships with retailing activities, cannot be classified so easily and certainly as wholesaling in nature. Additional differences and difficulties,

[1] One should keep in mind also, at this beginning, additional considerations of the diversities introduced by foreign as well as domestic geographical coverage, and, too, the sharp increases in the volume and variety of goods to be marketed.

1

as will be noticed, arise from variations between the specifications contained in existing forms of legislation; from legal interpretations in cases; from Bureau of the Census definitions; and from other sources. These differences and difficulties can and do lead, in turn, to sharp differences in the quantitative measurement of the importance of wholesaling.

Various Meanings of Wholesaling

Orthodox marketing meanings

The orthodox marketing definition of wholesaling generally stresses, among other things, the nature and motivation of the buyer as the single most important criterion. Based on this criterion, wholesaling may be defined, in the orthodox sense, as that part of marketing in which goods and services move to various classes of buyers (or agents thereof) who will: (1) engage in the resale of such goods and services with profits in mind; (2) use the goods and services in order to facilitate the production of other goods to be sold with profits in mind;[2] or (3) use the goods and services for various institutional purposes (e.g., educational, charitable, governmental).

On this basis, it follows that all remaining sales and movement of goods and services to persons who use these goods and services to satisfy their respective wants and desires represent retailing transactions. These persons can combine, of course, in any form of living-spending unit relationship without affecting the retailing nature of the transaction. Thus, if the total quantitative measure of goods and services is known in any year, the division as between the volume of wholesale and retail sales can be made by using these criteria.

Two refinements need to be introduced into the discussion of the orthodox definition at this point. First, the prices charged for a given product sold at wholesale may or may *not* be lower than prices charged at retail, although a lower price for the wholesaling transaction *usually* is the prevailing situation. But if, for example, a person operating an office buys a single typewriter, he may pay the identical price charged to a student buying the product for his own needs (a retail transaction). Second, the quantity purchased at wholesale *usually* is, but need not necessarily be, larger than the quantity purchased at a single retail sales transaction. Many important variables affect this factor of the quantity purchased at each transaction.

---

[2] Or to be used by governmental agencies in the conduct of their regular and extraordinary functions.

From the preceding discussion, several characteristics or criteria emerge which may be useful in identifying a wholesale transaction: (1) The motive of the purchaser; (2) the quantity purchased at each transaction;[3] (3) the wider varieties of goods offered for sale compared with retail sales; (4) the wider geographical base for wholesale sales; and (5) usually, the lower prices per unit involved. In addition, it may be inferred, because of the varieties of business and other activities involved, that wholesale transactions frequently involve the sale of the same product two or more times; while, on the other hand, retail transactions involve selling the same category of product only once.

The Beckman-Engle concepts

The authors of the only existing complete book on wholesaling have developed what they refer to as the *narrow, middle,* and *broad* views of wholesaling.[4] By the *narrow view,* they mean only that part of wholesaling that involves sales to the various types of retail middlemen. Whether or not this view restricts, in addition, the meaning only to those wholesale middlemen who take title to the goods they sell is open to considerable debate.

The *middle view* coincides with the definition used by the Bureau of the Census:

Wholesale trade as defined in the *Standard Industrial Classification* manual, and as covered in the 1954 Census, includes establishments or places of business primarily engaged in selling merchandise directly to retailers; to industrial, commercial, institutional or professional users; or to other wholesalers; or acting as agents in buying merchandise for, or selling merchandise to, such persons or companies.[5]

The main restriction of this view is tied to the establishment or place of business proviso.

Finally, these authors have the following to say about the *broad* view:

In its broader aspects the term *Wholesaling* includes all activities relating to the purchase or sale of goods at wholesale in the light of the criteria discussed in an earlier part of this chapter. This view recognizes no fundamental distinction between the sale of goods by prime producers, by manufacturers or other processors, by wholesalers, or by any of the functional or non-title taking middlemen engaged in wholesale trade; nor does it differentiate, save

[3] Subject to the qualifications noted.

[4] Theodore N. Beckman, and Nathanael H. Engle, *Wholesaling: Principles and Practice,* rev. ed. (New York: The Ronald Press Co., 1949), pp. 30–33.

[5] U. S. Bureau of the Census, *U. S. Census of Business—1954,* Vol. III, "Wholesale Trade—Summary Statistics and Public Warehouses" (Washington, D. C.: U. S. Government Printing Office, 1957), p. 1.

within the field of wholesaling, between sales of goods to retailers, to industrial customers or to wholesale organizations, so long as the purpose of the customer in buying such goods is not for personal gratification and the quantity, if bought from a concern operating substantially as a retail establishment and not for resale, is materially in excess of that which might reasonably be purchased by an ultimate consumer.[6]

Other meanings

It must be recognized that additional specialized meanings of the term "wholesaling" can arise in connection with the provisions of sales tax laws, the Fair Labor Standards Act, and other legislation, and in the interpretation of these types of legislation in various courts. Except to take note of their existence at this point, little importance need be assigned to them in the study of wholesaling within the complete framework of marketing organization.[7]

Levels of Wholesaling Activities

The various concepts of wholesaling explained in the preceding section make it necessary to discuss the activity levels of wholesaling. These levels call attention not only to the possibilities for the varieties of customers and transactions noted briefly above but also to the variety and complexity of channel arrangements to be discussed in Chapters 5 and 6. Perhaps, the best methods in which to consider these levels is to classify them, in some detail, from producing levels to retail middlemen levels as follows:

I. *Production Levels*
    A. Extractive industries (domestic and foreign).
        1. Agriculture.
        2. Mining (metals, coal, other).
        3. Fishing.
        4. Quarrying.
        5. Petroleum.
        6. Others (not elsewhere classified).
    B. Manufacturing industries (domestic and foreign).
        1. Primary, by kinds of goods.
        2. Secondary, by kinds of goods.

[6] Beckman and Engle, *op. cit.,* p. 31.

[7] However, the reader interested in these should see Beckman and Engle, *op. cit.,* pp. 23–30, and the references cited.

II. *Construction Industry* (domestic and foreign, by type)
    A. Roads, etc.
    B. Factories, commercial properties, etc.
    C. Residential.
    D. Others (not elsewhere classified).
III. *Transportation Industries* (domestic and foreign)
    A. Railroads—passenger and freight.
    B. Local railways and bus lines.
    C. Highway—passenger and freight.
    D. Water—passenger and freight.
    E. Air—passenger and freight.
    F. Pipelines.
IV. *Communications Industries* (domestic and foreign)
    A. Telephone, telegraph, and related services.
    B. Radio broadcasting.
    C. Television broadcasting.
V. *Utilities: Electric, Gas, Oil, etc.* (domestic and foreign)
VI. *Wholesale Middlemen*
    A. Merchant.
    B. Manufacturers' sales branches and sales offices.
    C. Petroleum bulk stations, etc.
    D. Agents and brokers.
    E. Assemblers of farm products.
VII. *Government Agencies*
    A. Federal.
    B. State.
    C. County.
    D. Municipal.
    E. Foreign.
VIII. *Services*
    A. Agricultural.
    B. Business and commercial.
        1. Professional.
        2. Repair.
        3. Others (not elsewhere classified).
    C. Hotels and motels.
    D. Personal.
        1. Professional.
        2. Repair.
        3. Entertainment.
        4. Others (not elsewhere classified).
IX. *Financial Institutions*

X. *Educational Institutions*
XI. *Office and Other Commercial Buildings*
XII. *Retail Middlemen*
   A. Store retailers.
   B. Nonstore retailers.
      1. Mail-order houses.
      2. Direct selling (house-to-house) organizations.
      3. Merchandise vending machine operators.

Thus, as defined above, wholesale sales may be made by wholesale middlemen to any or all of the above groups; or from type of wholesale middlemen to one or more other types of wholesale middlemen; or between separate establishments within the same classification of wholesale middleman.

Functions and Processes

Although it is true to say that wholesaling involves the same group of processes and functions applicable to the whole field of marketing, some special adaptations and applications need to be noted. The term "function" is used at this point in the sense of a group of purposeful activities which are homogeneous in the sense of having common objectives and molding (as well as being molded by) managerial organization units. Since these functions will be discussed in detail in the internal-management section of this book, the following classification scheme will suffice:

I. *Functions of Exchange and Contact*
   A. Merchandising: the function of marketing strategy.
   B. Buying and selling: the tactics of marketing.
II. *Functions of Physical Distribution*
   A. Transportation.
   B. Storage.
III. *Facilitating* (auxiliary) *Functions*
   A. Standardization and grading.
   B. Financing.
   C. Communication and research.
   D. Risk.

Of more importance at this stage of the discussion is an analysis of the marketing *processes*. Processes, in their marketing context, deal with meaningful groupings of functions, as outlined above. These processes may be useful in describing and analyzing the flow-of-commodities aspect of marketing and, in addition, to emphasize the division in specialization between wholesale and retail market levels; i.e., between the primary and intermediate markets, on the one hand, and the final markets, on the other. The discussion which follows will center around the Fred E. Clark concept, the Wroe Alderson concept, and the Vaile-Grether-Cox concept.

The Fred E. Clark concept

The late Professor Fred E. Clark, author of one of the earliest and best marketing textbooks, used a threefold division to describe the marketing processes—concentration, equalization, and dispersion.[8]

It will prove helpful at this point to emphasize the fact that the marketing machinery of today has been built around a two-fold flow of products, which involves three major processes—the concentration, equalization, and dispersion of goods. The first aspect of this flow of products is the process of concentrating the basic raw materials, foodstuffs, and manufactured goods at central points. Concentration is particularly important in the marketing of goods sold in their natural state. . . . Concentration is also important in the marketing of some manufactured products that are used as production goods by other manufacturers.

The second aspect of this two-fold flow of products is the process of dispersing toward the consumer these commodities which have been concentrated in the central markets. Raw materials are dispersed to manufacturers, and products ready for final consumption are dispersed to middlemen for further dispersion to final consumers.

Between these processes of concentration and dispersion occurs the activity which we call "Equalization." Equalization consists of adjustments of supply to demand on the basis of time, quantity, and quality. It is the process by means of which the supply of goods ready for sale is adjusted to the demand for them. . . .[9]

From the above, it is apparent that the processes of concentration and equalization are at the heart of the subject matter of wholesaling, while part of the process of dispersion is also essential. Later discussions of channels will indicate the unequal roles these processes perform in marketing, depending upon the commodity, the types of middlemen, and other structural elements.

Diagrammatically, these processes may be presented in triangular arrangement, as shown in Fig. 1.

[8] For his last statement, see Fred E. Clark and Carrie P. Clark, *Principles of Marketing,* 3rd ed. (New York: The Macmillan Co., 1942), pp. 4–7.

[9] *Ibid.,* p. 5.

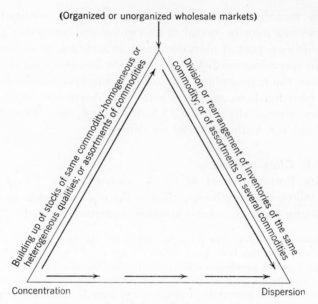

FIG. 1. The marketing processes triangle.

The Wroe Alderson concept

This concept was developed in a series of writings and speeches and has as its beginning the notion of the "radical heterogeneity of markets."

An advantageous place to start for the analytical treatment of marketing is with the radical heterogeneity of markets. Heterogeneity is inherent on both the demand and the supply sides. The homogeneity which the economist assumes for certain purposes is not an antecedent condition for marketing. Insofar as it is ever realized it emerges from the marketing process itself.

The materials which are useful to man occur in nature in heterogeneous mixtures which might be called conglomerations since these mixtures have only random relationship to human needs and activities. The collection of goods in the possession of a household or an individual also constitutes a heterogeneous supply, but it might be called an assortment since it is related to anticipated patterns of future behavior. The whole economic process may be described as a series of transformations from meaningless to meaningful heterogeneity. Marketing produces as much homogeneity as may be needed to facilitate some of the intermediate economic processes but homogeneity has limited significance or utility for consumer behavior or expectations.[10]

[10] Wroe Alderson, "The Analytical Framework for Marketing," *Proceedings—Conference of Marketing Teachers from Far Western States,* Berkeley: (University of California Press), Sept. 8–10, 1958.

From this framework, Alderson then develops his processes of *sorting* and *matching*.[11] Sorting applies either to the practice of breaking down or building up collections of goods in both their quantitative and qualitative aspects. There are four aspects of sorting:

1. *Sorting out*. The breaking of a collection into various types of goods, which results in separate sets of supplies which may be viewed as homogeneous in terms of the classification scheme used by the sorter.
2. *Accumulation*. The building up of larger supplies from a single sorting operation, or to bring together in a single place of products meeting standard specification but drawn from different localities.
3. *Allocation*. The apportionment or breaking down of a large homogeneous supply within single or organizational units or through the market
4. *Assorting*. The collection of unlike supplies in accordance with some pattern determined by demand in order to develop complementarity, and to possess some degree of potency for meeting future contingencies.

Based upon these four aspects of sorting, Alderson develops the following two sets of relationships:

I. *Alternative A*
   A. Sorting out + assorting = qualitative aspects of collections.
   B. Accumulations + allocations = quantitative changes in what is taken to be a homogeneous supply.
II. *Alternative B*
   A. Sorting out + collections = breaking down of supplies.
   B. Accumulation + assorting = building up of supplies.

Matching is then defined as the process which:

. . . aligns a small segment of supply against a small segment of demand. Considering the radical heterogeneity of both demand and supply and the geographical dispersion of the segments which are to be matched with each other, it would not be economically feasible for the pairing to be accomplished one pair at a time. . . . Instead of being carried out directly, matching is the end products of sorting in its various aspects. The goal of marketing is the matching of segments of supply and demand. . . .[12]

[11] This discussion is based upon Wroe Alderson, *Marketing Behavior and Executive Action; A Functionalist Approach to Marketing Theory* (Homewood, Ill.: Richard D. Irwin, Inc., 1957), pp. 199–202.
[12] *Ibid.*, p. 199.

From matching as so defined, the four aspects of sorting became the essential mechanism by means of which the ends of matching are achieved.

The Vaile-Grether-Cox concept

These authors have evolved a concept of marketing processes which seems to be halfway, conceptually speaking, between the Clark and the Alderson concepts. *Collection* is the process by which goods that are available in small lots in the market place are brought together in large lots either by collecting large lots of a single good or by collecting large assortments of varied goods. Although some large collections are passed on in the channel to users "as is," most involve the next process—*sorting*. This process involves the selection from among assorted collections of: (*a*) items of goods sorted into smaller lots, each of which meet written or verbal specifications as to quality, and (*b*) building up assortments of the lots determined under (*a*) so as to have variety. The final process—*dispersing*—involves the dividing or apportioning of the sorted or unsorted collections.[13]

The General Strategy of Wholesaling

To understand something of the importance attached to wholesaling in marketing, it is necessary to emphasize, at this stage of the discussion, the general strategy of wholesaling, wholesale markets, and the various types of wholesale middlemen.

The strategic aspects of wholesaling and wholesale markets

The general strategic aspects of wholesaling in marketing, stem from the following conditions:

1. The development of diversified, large-scale mass production in factories located at a distance from the areas of principal use of the output thus produced.

2. An increase in the volume and proportion of such production made prior to, rather than for, the specified order of users.

3. A corresponding increase in the number of levels of intermediate-user consumption between the production of basic raw materials at the beginning of the channel and the areas of final use at the end of the channel.

[13] Roland Vaile, E. T. Grether, and Reavis Cox, *Marketing in the American Economy* (New York: The Ronald Press Co., 1952), Chapter 6.

4. The increasing need for adaptations of products to the needs of intermediate and final users in terms of quantities, shapes, packages, and other elements of assortments, as well as in pricing arrangements.

5. Continuing increases in both the quantities and varieties of goods and services in relation to the foregoing.

6. The necessity of establishing primary and intermediate markets (organized and unorganized) in which the various stages of wholesale exchange and the establishment of wholesale price levels (systematic and unsystematic) would take place.

Given these forces, then, wholesaling developed in structure as attempts were made by producers and other business firms—mainly in the forces of the various types of wholesale and retail middlemen—to solve the problems of marketing thus created, and to bridge the growing marketing gap between the various types and levels of producers at one end, and the various types and levels of users at the other.

But the bridging of this gap should not be thought of as merely the physical forms of a pipeline or as a series of links. Rather, it should be thought of as a composite of a complex schematic framework which regulates physical flows both as to quantities and qualities in terms of spatial allocations; of locating potential users, or intermediate "users" in the form of middlemen, and convincing them to buy; of establishing the prices at which exchanges would take place in the primary and intermediate markets; and of feeding back various kinds of data to guide the management efforts of the various extractive and manufacturing producing agencies.

From the above discussion, it may be inferred that a considerable segment of wholesaling has to do with a theory of primary and intermediate markets. By primary and intermediate markets are meant the organized or unorganized institutional arrangements within which the prices and other aspects of the wholesale marketing transactions are determined. They exist at the extractive and primary manufacturing industries levels in connection with the concentration process. And they are located at strategically located trading centers in connection with the equalization process. Depending upon channel complexities to be investigated at a later point, they may be found either in single or in multiple combinations. Specialization may exist for a single class of products, or opportunities may be present in the channel for dealing in assortments.[14]

[14] Many of these aspects will be developed in later sections of the book. But interested readers may wish, at this point, to refer to Ralph F. Breyer, *The Marketing Institution* (New York: McGraw-Hill Book Co., Inc., 1934), Chapter V.

The strategic intermediate position of wholesale middlemen

The various types of middlemen that conduct their businesses in these primary and intermediate wholesale markets are, accordingly, the instrumentalities through which the general strategic position of wholesaling is made effective. Figures 2 and 3 show the *combined*

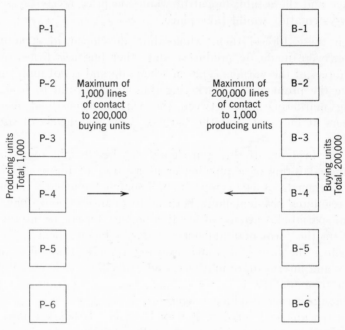

FIG. 2. Wholesaling structure without intermediate markets and wholesale middlemen.

importance of wholesale middlemen under the following set of assumptions: (1) The total number of buying units is 200,000 but with no assumption of equality of buying strength; (2) the *average* purchase per buying unit per unit of time accounts to $100, and consists of 25 *separate* products; and (3) the total number of products handled by each buying unit is 5,000, produced by 1,000 separate producing units, with no assumption of equal producing strength.

Given these assumptions, Fig. 2 shows the generalized pattern of the necessity for the marketing system to provide 200,000 lines of contact from each of the 1,000 producing units, if *all* buying units are potential customers for all 5,000 products and if the producing units assume the marketing initiative in searching for each buyer. Similarly, these will be 200,000 lines of communication from the buying units to each producing unit for each buying transaction *if* the buyers assume the marketing initiative. Thus, given these assumptions, there could be a minimum of 200 million and a maximum of 400 million individual lines of communication for each buying operation. The

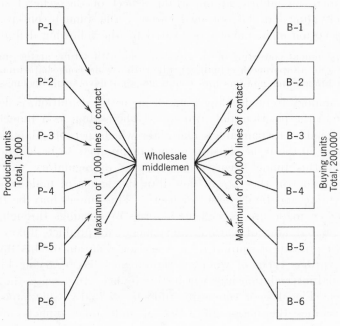

FIG. 3. Wholesaling structure with intermediate markets and wholesale middlemen.

multiplication by the average dollar volume of sales for each purchase, and the number of products involved, gives the total dollar volume of sales and the total physical flow.

With the introduction of wholesale middlemen of various types handling the output of all producing units and selling this output to all buying units, Fig. 3 indicates the reduction in lines of communication that would take place as compared with the 200 to 400 million noted in Fig. 2. The actual reduction would depend on how many business establishments would be involved at the wholesale middlemen's level. In actual practice, of course, there are variable combinations found in the marketing structure depending upon the numbers and types of producing units, the numbers and types of wholesale middlemen, the numbers and assortments of products involved, and the size and variety of the buying interest.

The funnel concept

Given the above analysis of the marketing processes and of the strategic importance of wholesaling, wholesale markets, and wholesale middlemen, an additional important aspect of the general strategy of wholesaling can be obtained through the funnel concept. The general notion of a funnel is indicated by the following definition:

> An instrument consisting of an inverted cone with a tube at the small end (or ends), or a tapering or cylindrical tube with a wide, cone-shaped mouth for pouring liquids and powders into containers that have small openings. . . .[15]

The analogy to be developed, based upon this definition, is designed to explain the position and strategy of wholesaling as a funnel made of stretchable (expandable) materials which permit adaptation to variations in the total physical output of products to be handled. In addition, this funnel incorporates a series of regulatory valves designed to control the rate of flow into the hands of middlemen and intermediate and final classes of users. This funnel may be thought of as being made up, as well, of a series of openings through which the regulated flow of various assortments of products takes place. Figure 4 presents a simplified cross-section diagram of this funnel.

The various types of wholesale middlemen have varying kinds of functional interrelationships within this funnel. In a sense, the funnel shown in Fig. 4 is a composite funnel. Actually, the funnel concept includes the notion of a set of individual funnels for each meaningful grouping of products, and with each having a systematic positioning within the channel pattern. Similarly, these series of individual product funnels have spatial adaptation.

It has been indicated that the funnel in the wholesaling structure is something more than the physical unit of simple dimension outlined in the dictionary definition. The funnel in Fig. 4 acts as a marketing medium through which moves the flow of goods from producers in a fashion designed to match as closely as possible the needs of intermediate and final users in terms of desired quantities, qualities, package, time, and geographical considerations. Furthermore, as has been indicated in the explanation of the equalization process, the prices and terms of sale at which these matchings and exchanges

---

[15] *Webster's New World Dictionary of the American Language* (Cleveland & New York: The World Publishing Co., 1957), p. 587. The unabridged dictionaries usually contain an illustration showing funnels having several different shapes.

take place are negotiated in the funnel. The classification of the
levels of users at which transactions may take place has been discussed elsewhere (pp. 4–6). The variety of channels within which
the funnel operates will be discussed in Chapters 5 and 6.

The notion of the funnel in Fig. 4 as a composite of a series of

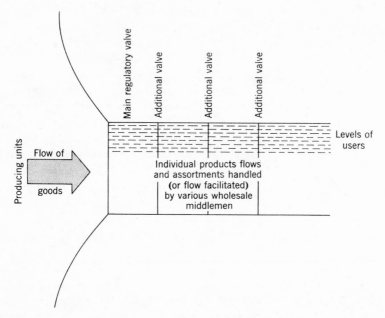

FIG. 4. The wholesaling funnel (composite total form).

individual funnels needs some additional explanation at this point.
Much of this concept of composite and component funnels stems
from the following variables as being suggestive:

1. *The type of product*—that is, whether raw material, semiprocessed, or finished, and whether for example, it has single or
   multiple uses.
2. *The physical volume* of the commodity flow and its time divisions
   within a year's cycle.
3. *The monetary value* of the physical flows in (2).
4. Variations in the *types of middlemen* found in the channels of
   distribution for the product.
5. The *varieties and levels of users* for the product based upon the
   characteristics noted in (1).

6. The *number of assortment combinations*—actual and potential—
   in which the product appears.
7. *Geographical variations* in the commodity flows, channel patterns,
   and types of users.

The Individual Strategy of Each Type of Wholesale Middleman

Before the analysis of the internal-management aspects of wholesale middlemen is undertaken in Chapters 9–21, some introductory
discussion is needed of the individual strategy of each type of
wholesale middleman. Each middleman has his own individual
managerial strategy; and the executive must decide on the degree to
which this individual strategy needs to be adopted to the over-all
strategy of wholesaling as discussed previously. Such strategy involves, among other things, the necessity for each wholesale middleman to determine whether or not he can have effective policies, and, if so, the determination of the content of the pertinent
policies.

One of the most important elements of this aspect of individual
middleman strategy pertains to the decisions as to which type (or
types) of middleman to be, and to include the accompanying product
assortments and functional assortments in this basic set of policy
decisions. The decisions, so far as product assortment are concerned,
may range from complete specialization to complete general-line
activities within a homogeneous commodity grouping, or may cut in
unorthodox fashion across commodity groupings. Similarly, decisions
may range from complete performances of all functions and their
component elements to highly streamlined functional arrangements,
and from routine, orthodox performances to highly individualistic and
differentiated activities.

Building on these functional and product adaptations, each middleman can then base his individual strategy on further refinements of
his decisions pertaining to products and product assortments. As
indicated above, the individual middleman can handle only orthodox
product assortments or he can experiment with many innovations.
These decisions are never permanent. Producing units change and
their products change as they attempt to influence the channel and,
in turn, are influenced by the channel. The meaning of "orthodox"
and "unorthodox" undergoes continual modification in this connection.
The establishment may feature only low-quality levels of products,
within the assortment decision, or it may feature only high-quality

levels or variable qualities. These have important interrelationships upon matters of prices and terms of sale.

The third element of the individual middleman's strategy stems from decisions as to his adaptation to various locational alternatives. From the sum total of these individual management decisions as to where to locate wholesale establishments comes the particular geographical stratifications of the individual funnels by regions, by states, by metropolitan areas and their components, or by the non-urban sections of a state. Finally, the individual strategy of a particular type of middleman originates from the extent to which he possesses a positive differential over his competitors in over-all managerial ability. This individual differential may or may not be accentuated by: (a) pooling together such ability with that of other middlemen, as in the case of the voluntary group and cooperative chains, or (b) a tie-up with the management abilities of the producing unit, as in the case of an exclusive distributorship.

Wholesaling and Marketing Organization Through the Channel

General meaning of marketing organization

Since wholesaling is but one aspect of marketing organization, some discussion is needed at this point of the general meaning of marketing organization. The concept as it is used in this introductory context is not concerned with the internal aspects of particular firms. What is being emphasized here is the way in which many different kinds of individual firms and establishments array themselves in *formal, systematic* manner within various producing, buying, selling, and facilitating agencies in making possible the systematic, continuous movements of goods and services from producing to using units, together with the necessary determinations of prices and terms of sale for their exchange. Depending upon the ideology of the political environment, the maximization of alternatives for final users may or may not result, and the operation of the organization within some framework of "efficiency" may or may not take place.

The marketing organization is formal and systematic in the sense that there has evolved over a long period of time: (a) specialized production units both at the extractive and at the manufacturing levels which account for the highest percentage of all goods produced; (b) a series of specialized wholesale middlemen who, together with integrated types, operate in various types of wholesale primary and intermediate markets; (c) a series of specialized retail middlemen who, together with integrated types, operate similarly in retail markets; and (*d*) many types of facilitating agencies offering services to establishments at all levels, and who act in a buying capacity as well including professional transportation, storage, financial, communication, research, and related facilitating functions.

Thus, to summarize, the marketing organization is a cross-sectional or dissectional study of the agencies and mechanisms of marketing as they array themselves in systematic fashion each to the other in moving goods and services from producing units.

Marketing organization and channels of distribution

Although in Chapters 5 and 6 we will discuss channel structure in detail, it may be pointed out here that marketing organization is made effective through channels of distribution. Since the flow of goods and services through the marketing organization is not an automatic process, what must be recognized at the beginning is that marketing organization involves a complicated network of buying and selling agencies, of varying periods of negotiation, of physical handling agencies and intermediaries, and of facilitating business units of various sizes in various locations, grouped together in varying combinations to link particular producing units with particular using units. In addition, they combine in varying patterns of complexity to account for the over-all movement of particular commodity categories and groups of categories.

The channel thus becomes the linking vehicle by means of which marketing organization takes place and becomes effective. And as the marketing aspects of a nation grow in complexity parallel to the nation's total social and economic development, so do its channel aspects develop into more intricate patterns along functional, commodity, spatial, and control components.

The position of wholesaling in the marketing organization

Viewed in this way from the dual vantage points of marketing organization and channels of distribution, the strategic position of wholesaling is once again reaffirmed. It constitutes the single most important sector of marketing organization, regardless of the measuring standard used. This sector covers a wider variety of goods and services than any other sector of marketing organization. It has more types of middlemen agency operations than does the retail sector; and their combined sales volume exceeds that of any other group in the channel.

In addition, wholesaling, by virtue of the factor discussed earlier, gives more depth, more variety, and more complexities to marketing than any other sector. [Every technological development of production which affects the volume and variety of goods, must be reflected in, and become magnified through the wholesaling sector.] Viewed in this framework, the funnel concept takes on a more complex perspective not apparent if only the purely physical aspects of the funnel are considered. The waves of effects flowing from the wholesaling structure move forward and backward in the marketing channels. These wavelike movements widen, in turn, the interrelationships between marketing organization and the rest of the business economy.

Linkages and Blockages

The meaning of linkages

In the framework of the wholesaling, *linkages* mean the formal and informal connections between the various middlemen themselves, and between the middlemen and other business enterprises. These linkages may be based on negotiating transactions involved in buying and selling; on communication networks other than in negotiating; on a whole variety of facilitating agencies and their functions; or on varying combinations of these. In a sense, linkages furnish the structural mucilage which make possible the intricate channels of distribution patterns, and, ultimately, marketing organization itself.

Linkages stem from relationships which, in turn, have their various origins with the individual marketing establishments. Once these relationships so begin, they accumulate into a broader framework of linkages which involve *groups* of establishments in a wide range of conceivable relationships each to the other. Convenience, tradition, the competitive structure of the industry, the possession of or the search for managerial power, and the search for additional profits, may explain—individually and collectively—the linkages which emerge.

Types of linkages

A distinction may be made between five types of linkages as they relate to the wholesaling sector:

Type 1—direct linkages: These involve only two establishments and two levels—the producing unit and the using unit—as the goods move through the channel.

Type 2—semidirect and indirect linkages: These involve the insertion of one or more links of types of wholesale and/or retail middlemen.

Type 3—competitive linkages: These involve alternative sets of linkages through which producers may market their output of goods, or through which various levels of users may buy their supplies of goods.

Type 4—Facilitating linkages: These linkages insert into the negotiating-price system of linkages, those establishments which may furnish one or more of the following—specialized communication, research, risk bearing, or related types of facilitating functions.

Type 5—Control linkages: These linkages establish the types and level of institutions which have the dominant management position in the marketing organization, so far as decision-making matters are concerned. Such control linkages may be superimposed upon each or all of types 1 through 4.

The meaning of blockages

Once a set of linkages is established, the agencies which are linked together may attempt either individually or collectively, or both, to set up obstructions to the formation of competitive linkages. These obstructions or blockages may be made effective by one or more of the following: by means of exclusive-dealership franchises; by resale price maintenance agreement or other price control measures; legislation barring the free movements of goods; membership requirements; trade association activities; establishment of special fighting brands in the channels; creation of special subsidiaries not identified with the parent organization; or similar devices. Blockages, then, are but one of a series of formal and informal devices originated by marketing institutions to counteract or forestall anticipated marketing changes, except those favoring the institution using the blockage.

Relationship of linkages and blockages to channels

Based upon the above discussion, the grouping together of individual establishments into linkages of all types for a given commodity framework constitutes the foundation for the formation of channels of distribution in the marketing organization for the products involved. There follows a continuous, accumulative process by means of which channels ultimately are created for groups of commodities and then the over-all channel structure which underlies the concept of marketing organization.

The formation of blockages designed to protect existing linkages, to force out competing linkages, or to curb or prevent the formation of new linkages also has very significant meaning for, and relationship to, the channel structural aspects of marketing organization. Further development of these relationships of linkages and blockages to marketing organization is included in the complete discussion of channel structure in Chapters 5 and 6.

Wholesaling and Integration

The role of wholesale middlemen as independent intermediaries in the market channel is a precarious one. As is true of any intermediary, either the originating or the terminal end of the channel may attempt either to eliminate him or to reduce his importance. Thus, the producing level may attempt elimination or increased control by means of vertical integration based upon direct ownership of the intermediary; from restrictive controls by means of contracts or marketing policies; by granting exclusive dealership franchises in return for the middleman's to reduce his buying alternatives and to restrict his area of selling activity; and by indirect pressures resulting from selling and advertising efforts directed at the ultimate user.

Partially to offset these attempts by producers, and partially for reasons of pressure and control, both retail middlemen and users may indulge in reverse or backward vertical integration efforts. These efforts may be based upon direct ownership of either the wholesale middlemen agencies or of the producers, or both. Or they may represent contractual devices designed to secure both price and product identification advantages. Or, finally, they may represent a mutual pooling of retail and wholesale middlemen's financial resources and management know-how into some cooperative agency effort.

The wholesale middleman may do nothing actively in either combatting or joining these attempts at vertical integration. Or he may retaliate in kind against each by moving either backwards or forwards, or in both directions, in the channel in order to control directly or indirectly the business units involved. Or he may strengthen his competitive defenses by incorporating changes in internal organization and policies in other directions, including the pooling of similar wholesale middlemen's resources on a common or wider geographical front.

As a result, these various aspects of integration keep changing the patterns of linkages and blockages in the channel. These changing patterns result, in turn, in ever-changing patterns of channel arrangements. The complexities of these various types of integration will become more apparent in the classification of wholesale middlemen in the next chapter and in later chapters discussing channel structure.

Measures of the Importance of Wholesaling

As a final part of this introduction to the wholesaling sector of marketing, some reference should be made to measures of the importance of wholesaling. Because wholesaling involves a considerable amount of multiple handling and sales of goods, any realistic measure of its importance must include measures of *gross* as well as of *net* importance. These measures of gross importance may be noted here: (1) The total value of all extractive industries' output, *plus* the total value of all domestic manufacturers' output, *plus* the value at wholesale of all imports; (2) the total dollar sales of all wholesale middlemen as reported by the Bureau of the Census; and (3) the ratio of total wholesale sales to total retail sales.

Most of the measures of the *net* importance of wholesaling stem from the program of national income statistics prepared by the Department of Commerce. Of the many possibilities, these are especially useful in the present context: (1) The ratio of full-time equivalent employees in wholesale trade compared with the total number in all industries; (2) the ratio of corporate sales for wholesale trade establishments to the sales of all industries; and (3) the proportion of the national income accounted for by wholesale trade as compared with all industries.

QUESTIONS AND PROBLEMS

1. Do you agree with the statement, "The field of wholesaling represents by far the most significant segment of marketing based on any or all of several points of view"? Upon what evidence do you base your agreement? If you disagree, what is the basis of your disagreement?
2. Differentiate completely between the orthodox and other meanings of wholesaling. Which meaning represents the strongest statement?
3. How is the complexity of the wholesaling sector revealed by the variety of customer levels discussed in the chapter?
4. What pressures make for continuous change in the levels of wholesaling activity? What pressures make for stability?
5. Explain, in detail, why a knowledge of marketing processes is fundamental to the understanding of the functions of the wholesaling sector.

6. What is the relationship of marketing processes to the incidence of whole-sale markets?

7. What is the relationship of the aspects of sorting to the marketing processes?

8. What is meant by "the strategic aspects of wholesaling and wholesale markets?"

9. To what extent does the funnel concept help to explain the complexity and strategic importance of the wholesaling sector? What are the important limitations of this concept?

10. What kind of component funnels are found within the over-all funnel?

11. In what way is marketing organization formal and systematic?

12. Differentiate between marketing organization in its internal and external aspects.

13. What is the position of the wholesaling sector in marketing organization?

14. What contribution does the concept of linkages and blockages make to an understanding of the wholesaling sector?

15. What factors contribute to the origin and use of linkages and blockages?

16. How does integration relate to the wholesaling sector?

17. Discuss the differences between measures of the gross and net importance of wholesaling.

CHAPTER INTEGRATING ASSIGNMENT

To what extent does the sector notion in marketing organization help to improve the professional and analytical points of view of marketing? To what extent does it introduce some serious shortcomings?

2

The Structure of Wholesaling
in the United States:
Agency Structure

This chapter and the four chapters which follow are designed to give the reader a detailed insight into the complex structure of wholesaling in the United States. Together with the later chapters dealing with prices and price structure, they provide a comprehensive institutional view of the wholesaling sector of the over-all marketing organism.[1]

Problems of Definition and Classification

Agency structure describes and analyzes that part of wholesaling which consists of the pattern or design of the various business establishments whose principal concern it is to carry on the functions of wholesaling within the over-all marketing system. In such description and analysis, the major attempt is made to answer such questions as the following: (1) How should wholesale middlemen be classified?

---

[1] For a complete statement of the institutional approach see Duddy and Revzan, *Marketing: An Institutional Approach,* 2nd ed. (New York: McGraw-Hill Book Co., Inc., 1953), Chapter 2 and Appendix C.

(2) Why are there so many types of wholesale middleman operations? (3) What analytical tools are available for establishing meaningful differences between each type? (4) How can these analytical tools be used? and (5) How can such matters as specialization and competition be analyzed? Intensive use of census data is made wherever possible to qualify the characteristics being discussed; and explanations will be made of the significance of the quantitative and qualitative material used.

Definition of middleman

The term "middleman" is very pertinent in marketing because it implies a group of business agencies that exist in the channel intermediate to the producing units at one end and the using units at the other. The basic dictionary concept of the middleman as a go-between or intermediary is especially applicable. Although often viewed in historical perspective as parasites, middlemen are entirely differently evaluated in the modern marketing system. A result of a rapidly evolving economic system in which producer and consumer are separated and unknown to each other in a personal sense, and in which an ever-widening assortment of goods must flow, the middleman is a constantly present example of growing specialization and complexity in trying to match what is being produced with what users need or can be convinced to buy.

In actuality, as shall be developed later in the discussion of channels, the middleman is not a single-level type of intermediary but represents rather several levels of intermediate relationships. These intermediate positions keep changing as business units which have not been intermediaries try to control or absorb such intermediaries, while the middlemen, in turn, frequently develop beyond their roles as intermediaries. Thus, as frequently happens when specialization continues to expand, increasing lines of friction develop between levels and categories of specialists, leading, in turn, to overlapping and confusions. But despite these blurring developments, sight should not be lost of the fundamental meaning of the term middleman.

Criteria for classifying wholesale middlemen

As is true wherever generalizations are attempted, students of marketing have had to develop criteria for classifying wholesale middlemen operations in order to achieve economy and careful analysis. In trying to condense over 200,000 separate establishments

into operational groups meeting the above needs, the following
criteria have been found useful:

1. *Type of managerial operation,* furnishing probably the single
   most important criterion.
2. *Ownership of goods,* emphasizing the main element of differentiation between the merchant and agent middlemen groups.
3. *Sales size and number of employee size,* in order to permit
   groupings according to some meaningful measures of scale.
4. *Range of functions,* permitting differentiation between full-service
   and limited-function middlemen, with some intermediate groupings also possible.
5. *Kinds of commodities* handled, furnishing the basis for kind of
   business classification and the separation of general-line from
   specialized.
6. *Location of middleman,* furnishing the basis for differentiation
   between local, regional, and national middlemen on the domestic
   scene, and foreign-based middlemen.
7. *Integration,* furnishing the basis for integrated versus nonintegrated middlemen.

Problems created by census reports

Many of the textbooks on marketing have based their classifications
of middlemen upon the data and classification schemes presented in
census publications.　Unfortunately, these census reports vary from
base period to base period as to type of operation and kind of business.
These variations obviously interfere with the continuity and comparability of the statistical data.　Accordingly, in the discussion which
follows, the classifications used attempt to include all types of operation regardless of whether or not census data are available.　Necessary
qualifications will be introduced whenever census statistical data are
introduced and the qualifications are needed.

Orthodox marketing classification of wholesale middlemen

Based upon the discussion above, it is accurate to say that the
following classification scheme represents an "orthodox" view as found
in the majority of the literature.

I. *The Merchant Middlemen Group:* (*a*) Regular wholesalers,
   including jobbers; (*b*) cash-and-carry wholesalers; (*c*) industrial distributors; (*d*) converters; (*e*) drop shippers or
   desk jobbers; (*f*) mail-order wholesalers; (*g*) importers; (*h*)

exporters; (*i*) truck or wagon jobbers; (*j*) chain store buying offices and warehouses; (*k*) wholesaler-sponsored, retailer-sponsored buying-pool cooperative chains.

II. *Manufacturers Sales Branches* (with stocks) *and Sales Offices* (without stocks).

III. *Petroleum Bulkplants, Terminals, LP Gas Facilities:* Independent, commission, cooperative, and refinery controlled.

IV. *The Merchandise Agent and Broker Group:* (*a*) Auction companies (terminal and shipping point); (*b*) brokers representing sellers and representing buyers; (*c*) commission agents; (*d*) export agents; (*e*) import agents; (*f*) selling or sales agents; (*g*) manufacturers' agents (with and without stocks); (*h*) resident buying offices; (*i*) purchasing agents; and (*j*) cooperative selling agencies.

V. *Assemblers of Farm Products:* (*a*) Local commission buyers; (*b*) assemblers; (*c*) cooperative marketing associations; (*d*) cooperative purchasing agencies; (*e*) cream stations; (*f*) grain elevators; and (*g*) packers and shippers.

These five groups and subtypes of operation are, in turn, subdivided into 306 trade or kind of business classifications. A cross tabulation of the principal categories for each of the five groups is contained in Table 1. This tabulation reveals the wide extractive industry kinds of businesses found for merchant middlemen, for example, as compared to only manufactured goods for sales branches and sales offices. It reveals, also, the narrow commodity base underlying the petroleum and assemblers groups.

Suggested new classification scheme

Although the classification given above has the distinct advantage of permitting close comparison with census data, it does not provide as meaningful a classification as is needed for purposes of modern marketing description and analysis. The suggested new classification scheme outlined below is designed to overcome some of the disadvantages of the preceding plan.

I. *Merchant Middlemen*
   A. Nonintegrated, full service.
      1. Regular or service wholesaler (including jobbers).
      2. Industrial distributors.
      3. Importers.
      4. Exporters.

TABLE 1

PRINCIPAL KINDS OF BUSINESSES, BY GROUP TYPES OF WHOLESALE MIDDLEMEN

Merchant Wholesalers	Manufacturers' Sales Branches, Sales Offices	Petroleum Bulk Plants, Terminals LP Gas Facilities	Merchandise Agents, Brokers	Assemblers of Farm Products
Grocery, confectionery, meats	food and kindred products	gasolines	grocery, confectionery, meats	dairy, poultry products
Edible farm products, beer, wine-distilled spirits	textile mill products, apparel and related products	distillates	edible farm products, drugs, chemical, paints	fresh fruits, vegetables
Tobacco	furniture and fixtures	residuals	apparel (including footwear)	farm products (raw materials)
Drugs, chemical, allied products	paper and allied products	LP gas	dry goods, piece goods	
Dry goods, apparel	chemicals and allied products		furniture, home furnishings	farm supplies
Furniture; home furnishings	rubber products		paper, allied products	
Paper, allied products	leather and leather products		farm products (raw materials)	others
Farm products (raw materials)	stone, clay and glass products		automotive, electrical, electronic	
Automotive, electrical, electronics appliances	primary metal products		apparatus, equipment and appliances	
Hardware, plumbing-heating	fabricated metal products		hardware, plumbing-heating	
Lumber, construction materials	machinery (except electrical)		lumber, construction materials	
Machinery, equipment, supplies	electrical machinery		machinery, equipment, supplies	
Metals, metalwork (except scrap)	transportation equipment		all other (scrap iron and steel, amusements, sporting goods, toys, books, magazines, newspapers, coal, coke, farm supplies, jewelry, yarns, petroleum products, general merchandise, miscellaneous, not elsewhere classified)	
Scrap, waste materials	instruments and related products			
All other (amusement, sporting goods, books, magazines, newspapers, coal, farm supplies, jewelry, petroleum products, gift, art goods, greeting cards, flower bulbs, plants, miscellaneous, not elsewhere classified)	other manufacturers			

Source: U. S. Bureau of Census, *U. S. Census of Business—1954*, Vol. III, "Wholesale Trade."

    B. Nonintegrated, limited function.
       1. Cash-and-carry wholesalers.
       2. Drop shippers (or desk jobbers).
       3. Mail-order wholesalers.
       4. Truck jobbers (wagon distributors).
       5. Rack jobbers.
    C. Integrated, manufacturer controlled.
       1. Manufacturers' sales branches (with stocks).
       2. Manufacturers' sales offices (without stocks).
    D. Integrated, wholesale middleman controlled.
       1. Converters.
       2. Wholesaler-sponsored voluntary chain.
    E. Integrated, retail middleman controlled.
       1. Corporate chain buying offices.
       2. Corporate chain warehouses.
       3. Retailers' buying pools.
       4. Retailer-sponsored voluntary chain buying offices.
II. *Agent Middlemen*
    A. Nonintegrated, full service.
       1. Commission agents.
       2. Export agents.
       3. Import agents.
    B. Nonintegrated, limited function.
       1. Auction companies: (*a*) terminal; (*b*) shipping point.
       2. Brokers: (*a*) representing sellers; (*b*) representing buyers.
    C. Integrated: manufacturer-controlled.
       1. Sales or selling agents.
       2. Manufacturers' agents: (*a*) with stocks; (*b*) without stocks.
       3. Purchasing agents.
III. *Combination Merchant and Agent Middlemen*
    A. Petroleum bulk plants, terminals, and LP gas facilities.
       1. Independent.
       2. Chain.
       3. Commission.
       4. Refinery controlled.
    B. Assemblers of farm products.
       1. Nonintegrated: (*a*) assemblers and local buyers; (*b*) commission buyers; (*c*) cream stations; (*d*) grain elevators; (*f*) packers and shippers.
       2. Integrated, producer controlled: (*a*) cooperative marketing associations shipping point and terminal; (*b*) co-

operative purchasing associations; (c) cream stations;
(d) grain elevators.
3. Integrated, manufacturer controlled: (a) local buyers;
(b) cream stations.
C. Multiple-type operations.

Why Are There So Many Types of Wholesale Middlemen?

Much of the criticism directed against marketing stems from the lack of knowledge of why there exist in the structure so many types of wholesale middlemen operations. If many critics cannot understand why wholesale middlemen exist at all, they are doubly confused by the variety of types found. This is true especially when the number of types is compared with the number of types of retail middlemen that exist in the present-day structure.

Yet, there are several pertinent explanations to be made of the variety of types of operation found at the wholesale sector. For one thing, the variety reflects the smaller scale of wholesale middleman operations compared with manufacturing activities and the corresponding greater ease of entry. This is true particularly of those middlemen who do not take physical possession of inventories to be sold. A second reason to be advanced is found in the legal bases for agent-principal arrangements by means of which a whole class of middlemen is thus created.

To this must be added the wide variety of goods to be marketed, and the many possibilities in the marketing of agricultural products for specialized middlemen activities, e.g., auction companies, cream stations, and grain elevators. In addition, specialized adaptation is made possible in terms of the differentiation of domestic as against foreign operations. Finally, because of the diversity of goods and the various levels of business and other institutions involved, a wide variety of control can be provided in the channel by varying the type of middleman operation utilized.

Thus, the complexities of the wholesaling sector of marketing as encompassed in the definition of that sector give rise, in turn, to highly varied types of wholesale middlemen operations offering varying degrees of completeness of functions, of product assortments, of managerial control patterns in the channel, and of adaptation to the geographical aspects of wholesaling.

The Criteria of Competitive Efficiency

Given all of the types of middlemen operations classified above, and given over a quarter of a million separate establishments to study,[2] it would be desirable to develop some shorthand methods to facilitate the description and cross-analytical treatment of each type of wholesale middleman operation with every other type. One method which suggests itself immediately is to list in detailed fashion all of the functions and their component elements which wholesale middlemen perform, and then indicate which of these each type of operation performs.

But this cross comparison of each type by function is only a part of the complete description and analysis which is needed. To fill the gap, there is presented here a series of measuring sticks by means of which one type of middleman operation can be compared with another type; or by means of which one particular type can be evaluated completely as to its strengths and weaknesses. These measuring sticks are called *criteria of competitive efficiency*, and consist of the following: (1) The quality of management; (2) the adequacy and effectiveness of the middleman's location; (3) the performance of the merchandising function; (4) the ability to buy favorably; (5) the type, adequacy, and maintenance of the physical equipment and its layout; (6) the ease and completeness of the managerial control system; (7) the ability to use advertising; (8) the range of marketing functions performed; (9) comparative prices and terms of sales; and (10) customer relations.

The meaning of each criterion

In order to understand fully the usefulness of each of these criteria, a summary definition follows.

1. *Quality of management.* As applied in this context to types of wholesale middleman operations rather than to particular managements of particular individual establishments, this criterion includes: (*a*) the general success or lack of success of any type as indicated in trends of sales, number of establishments, etc., in census and other data; (*b*) the general financial size of each type of operation; (*c*) the ability to use specialists in management level positions; and (*d*) whether or not the type's general organizational characteristics facilitate flexibility in decision making.

---

[2] The number of wholesale trade establishments listed in the *1954 Census of Business* was 252,318.

2. *Adequacy and effectiveness of location.* To what extent are there any peculiar features of a particular type of middleman operation which either facilitate or impede the selection of a location in accordance with the pertinent economic factors?

3. *Performance of the merchandising function.* Does a particular type of middleman have any unique advantages in being able to make full use of merchandising strategy? Or, conversely, does the type of operation make it difficult or impossible to include effectively any aspect of merchandising strategy?

4. *The ability to buy favorably* consists of two important aspects. The *quantitative* aspect is a function partially of financial strength in that it pertains to the ability to buy products handled in sufficiently large quantities to be able to get the most favorable prices and terms of sale. The *qualitative* aspect consists of the ability to buy inventories so that the best matching job is done between what the middleman buys, and what, in turn, his customers will buy from him.

5. *The type, adequacy, and maintenance of physical equipment and layout.* This criterion emphasizes the ability of a particular type of middleman operation to secure the best physical equipment needed for its operation and to budget sufficient funds to maintain such equipment and its physical environment in the most effective appearance and working condition. For those middlemen who handle physically the goods they buy and sell, it suggests, in addition, the ability to arrange the physical display of such goods in a manner designed to maximize customer appeal and sales.

6. *The ease and completeness of the managerial control system.* Does the type of middleman operation make use of the most modern accounting, statistical, and budgetary devices (together with modern types of computing machines) in order to create a flow of the kinds of records, data, and other information needed for the regular and special evaluation of past performance and the preparation of expected future goals?

7. *The ability to use advertising* deals with decisions as to whether or not to use advertising. If the answer is in the affirmative, then the criterion further deals with how much to spend, what kinds of advertising to prepare, what kinds of media to use, how often to advertise, and the evaluation of the effectiveness of the advertising.

8. *The range of marketing functions* performed is based upon the alternative method of analysis and cross comparison noted above.

This criterion becomes one of the significant bases used in the classification of types of wholesale middlemen.

9. *Comparative prices and terms of sale.* Where applicable, this criterion attempts to measure the competitive price levels of each type of middleman operation. These levels are related, obviously, to many of the other criteria.

10. *Comparative operating costs.* Available census data permit comparisons to be made of operating costs as a percentage of sales for each type of operation.

11. *Customer relations.* This criterion represents an attempt to get at the differences between types of middleman operations in actually providing for systematic public relations functions with their customers. It has a broader connotation, however, of the extent to which a segment of the general public has very favorable or very unfavorable attitudes toward any particular type of operation.

Evaluation

Obviously, this analytical device of the criteria of competitive efficiency is not completely without shortcomings. Its great merit, as discussed above, is the attempt made to obtain a more meaningful basis for comparing and contrasting each type of middleman operations with every other type, and in permitting the evaluation of the strengths and weaknesses of any particular type. Some of the criteria certainly are more flexible than others in the extent to which they can be used to evaluate types of operation. In addition, not all criteria are on an equal plane so far as availability of meaningful quantitative data are concerned with which to measure the various characteristics; and even meaningful qualitative information may not be available. Finally, the use of these criteria for each type of operation represents merely a cross-sectional average, so to speak. They should not be interpreted as applying with equal force to each and every establishment found within each type of operation.

Basic Definitions of Each Type of Wholesale Middleman Operation: Merchants

To help keep the wide array of middlemen types of operations in mind, brief definitions of each type are outlined below, together with other pertinent remarks. The framework of presentation is to relate each type of operation to the basic most important type—the regular or service wholesaler—and by comparison and contrast with that type to establish the basic identifying characteristics. The order of presentation follows the suggested new classification scheme.

The regular or service wholesaler

This type of operation continues to be the single most important of all the types. Its importance stems from its form of managerial structure which most closely approximates the funnel concept, and the general strategic importance of the wholesaling sector noted above. In this close approximation, the orthodox wholesaler acts as "the eyes and ears of the wholesale market," and performs the widest range of marketing functions of any middleman type. They own the goods which they sell and they maintain complete inventories of most items. They are found in every geographic unit of the United States, although certainly not in equal proportions. More so than any other type of operation, they are found in the widest range of kinds of businesses handling agricultural, industrial, and consumers' goods.[3]

Industrial distributors

This type is sometimes referred to as mill supply houses. It varies principally from the regular wholesaler in (a) specialization in buying and selling functions applied mainly to industrial goods, and (b) being concentrated mainly in the more important manufacturing sections of the United States. Industrial distributors perform generally, within these points of difference, the same range of functions performed by the regular wholesaler.

Importers

This group deviates from the regular wholesaler type mainly in buying such goods as are carried in inventory from foreign-based sources. In addition, they are found in far fewer kinds of business.

Exporters

This group is the reverse of the importer in that it sells mainly to foreign-based buyers.

Cash-and-carry wholesalers

Found mainly in the grocery and drug products fields, this type of middleman may operate as a distinctly separate type or in a department within a service wholesaler establishment. The variety of goods carried in inventory is reduced to those categories having the highest

---

[3] For a detailed description, see Beckman and Engle, *op. cit.*, Chapters 9, 10.

rates of turnover. This type sells mainly for cash, and deliveries usually are not arranged (except, that in a few cases they may be made for a fee). In some cases, also, restrictions may be placed on the minimum size of order accepted.

Drop shippers or desk jobbers

This type of middleman operation is found primarily for such products as sand, clay, coal, and lumber where transportation costs are high relative to the value of the products and where, accordingly, any interruption of deliveries may lead to significant cost increases. Accordingly, the middleman's operational strength lies in his knowledge of the product and of the location and needs of potential customers. Delivery is made directly from producer to customer, but the middleman is billed for the order, and he, in turn, collects from his customers. A significant feature of this type is the flow of valuable market information from the drop shipper to the producer.

Mail-order wholesaler

This is a deviate type found primarily in the general-line consumers' goods category, and is characterized, as the name implies, by almost complete reliance on the mail-order catalog to generate sales. This type has declined sharply in importance with the modern improvements in transportation and communication.

Truck, wagon jobbers

Found in the fresh fruit and vegetable, confectionery and tobacco, and similar kinds of businesses, these middlemen carry their inventories in trucks (or in wagons). Deliveries are made immediately from these stocks. Customers may be visited on a regular schedule or at irregular intervals. The place of business of the owner may be his home or it may approximate a regular business establishment depending on sales volumes realized. Products featured are mainly, but not always, perishable or semiperishable, with rapidly changing daily rates of sale.

Manufacturers' sales branches, sales offices

These middlemen are next in importance as a group to the regular wholesaler. The census definition is self-explanatory.

These establishments differ from merchant wholesalers in that they are owned by manufacturers or mining companies and maintained apart from manufacturing plants, primarily for selling or marketing their products at wholesale. Branch stores selling to household consumers or individual users are classified in Retail Trade. Sales offices located at manufacturing plants or at general administrative offices of manufacturers or mining companies are excluded unless operated as separate establishments. Manufacturers' sales branches are distinguished from sales offices by the fact that the former maintain facilities for the physical storage, handling, and delivering of at least a portion of the merchandise sold. Sales branches frequently install machinery, equipment, and apparatus sold by them and sometimes are engaged in leasing or renting machinery or equipment on a royalty basis.

Separately incorporated sales affiliates owned or controlled by manufacturers and selling the manufacturers' products generally are included here. Exceptions occur in the wholesale electrical goods trade, oil-well supply houses, and steel warehouses where such businesses are generally considered as distributors (merchant wholesalers). Wholesale establishments owned by manufacturers but principally engaged in buying and selling merchandise of other manufacturers are classified, for census purposes, as merchant wholesalers.[4]

Converters

Confined principally to the textile business, this integrated type reflects the historical structure of the industry. Because there is need for many small textile manufacturers to have an intermediary to convert gray goods into the patterns and colors needed for end uses, this type of middlemen evolved to do that function. Thus, in addition to performing similar to the regular wholesaler, the converter either does the dyeing and cutting of the cloth or contracts to have it done. Usually, he employs designers who keep him informed as to trends in patterns, colors, fabric finish, and the like.

Wholesaler-sponsored voluntary chains

As a result of intensified competition from corporate chains in the food, drug, limited-price variety, and hardware business, many regular wholesalers decided to sponsor chains of independent retailers. In addition to regular wholesale functions, this type of operation provides to its membership store layout assistance, advertising materials, store management and control helps, and private brands of merchandise.

Corporate chain buying offices

This type of operation is self-explanatory.

Corporate chain warehouses

These are the local, sectional, or nationally located warehouses used to store the inventories, and to arrange for deliveries to member stores according to regular schedules.

[4] U. S. Bureau of Census, *U. S. Census of Business—1954*, "Wholesale Trade."

Retailer-sponsored voluntary chains

The same conditions which explain the emergence of the wholesaler-sponsored voluntary chain noted above also underlie this type. The main point of differentiation is in the source of motivation and control. In this instance, the independent retailers organize a wholesale subsidiary to function much along the lines noted above.

Retailer buying pools

Highly informal and highly variable as to periods of operation, this type of operation represents an arrangement whereby a group of independent and noncompeting retailers can consolidate their buying resources in order to get more favorable prices and terms of sale. Depending upon the number of members involved and the amount of resources available, the buying may be done by a special staff hired for the purpose, or by the best talent available among the constituent membership. Deliveries may be made from a central facility or on a decentralized business.

Basic Definitions of Each Type of Middleman Operations: Agents

Auction company

As the name implies, this type of operation uses the auction method of catalogs and bona fide bidding to dispose of products owned by patronizing principals. Found primarily at selected central markets for certain fruits and at producing-shipping points for livestock and tobacco, this type of middleman takes physical possession, arranges for display, prepares catalogs, conducts the auction, and arranges for collection of the proceeds of the sale.

Commission agents

This agent middleman type, except for lack of ownership, conforms most closely to the regular wholesaler in functions performed. In addition, another point of difference is found in the restriction of this type of operation mainly to agricultural products and in far fewer additional kinds of business.

Export agents and import agents

These types of middlemen are the agent counterparts of exporters and importers.

Brokers

Representing either buyers or sellers in any given transaction, but not both, brokers are "middlemen's middlemen," the use of which may be classified most typically into one of three marketing situations. They may, on the selling side, handle the entire output of a small producer with limited financial resources in arranging for initial wholesale distribution. They may operate as the key middlemen in buying and selling activities in organized central agricultural commodity exchanges. Or they may arrange distribution initially for large companies such as the sugar producers. They perform no functions associated with physical possession of inventories. Geographically, they operate on local, sectional, national, or international bases.

Selling agents

Wherever manufacturers cannot afford to have their own marketing departments, they may arrange for the services of selling or sales agents. Generally, these agents usually have authority to negotiate prices and to operate without any territorial or total amount of sales limitations. They frequently even extend financial assistance to their principals.

Manufacturers' agents

This type is a restricted form of selling agents. They may or may not carry inventories of merchandise; they are restricted usually to specific sales territories; they are limited as to the proportion of the principal's output they can handle; and they are limited in authority as to prices and terms of sale. Except for those that handle inventories, manufacturers' agents closely resemble brokers. The main differences are that brokers carry on mainly in businesses of foods and agricultural goods, whereas manufacturers' agents are found mainly in textiles and durable goods.

Purchasing agents buy goods on specification for clients who pay their commissions. Quality, prices, terms of sale, and quantities are controlled closely by the principal.

Resident buying offices are integrated with department stores and departmentized specialty stores. They furnish staff assistance to the buyers of these stores when the latter make their periodic buying trips to the fashion centers. In the periods between buyers' trips, they furnish a steady stream of market information and negotiate "fill-in" orders. Their places of business serve as headquarters for the retail buyers during their regular buying trips.

Basic Definitions of Each Type of Middleman Operations: Mixed Groups

Petroleum bulk plants, terminals and wholesale LP gas facilities

This group of merchant and/or agent middlemen represent specialization in receiving, storing, and marketing gasoline, kerosene, distillate and residual fuel oils, liquefied petroleum gases, and other bulk petroleum products at wholesale. The census distinguishes between bulk plants and bulk terminals as follows: (1) Bulk plants possess bulk storage capacity up to 2,100,000 gallons, and receive their supplies principally by truck or rail; (2) bulk tanks have capacities above 2,100,000 gallons, and receive supplies by tankers, barges, and pipelines in addition to truck and rail. Wholesale LP gas facilities sell liquefied petroleum gases in wholesale quantities in bulk or bottles to all types of customers representing industrial, commercial, and government accounts.

Assemblers of farm products

These types are defined by the census as follows:

This group consists of establishments primarily engaged in purchasing from farmers and assembling farm products in local producing markets and in the cities of producing regions. They are engaged principally in contracting farm products on a relatively small scale and assembling larger lots for shipment to central markets. In addition to the actual buying and assembling of farm products, establishments in this group frequently grade, pack, store, and, in some cases, finance the commodity handled.[5]

Multiple-type operations

The definition of any type of middleman represents a sort of average of business practices at any given period of marketing. In classifying business establishments, any establishment is classified as a given middleman type if one-half or more of its sales revenue in a given year originates from that given type of operation. Because of the volatile and competitive nature of wholesaling, it is well established

[5] U. S. Bureau of Census, *op. cit.*

that many middlemen operated during a given period of time as many types of operation.[6]

Relative Importance of Types of Operation: 1954

In the following sections of this chapter and in Chapter 3, special attention will be given to some quantitative aspects of the agency structure of wholesaling as revealed by census data. Unfortunately, these data do not include all of the types of operation classified and defined above, nor are the various census periods completely comparable each with the other so far as coverage of types of operation and kinds of business are concerned. In some cases, however, the Bureau of the Census has made some adjustments. This section will concentrate on the relative importance of each type of operation in 1954.

Table 2 contains the pertinent data of number of establishments and dollar sales, by type of operation, and the component percentages for 1954. Nearly two thirds of all establishments were of the merchant wholesaler group, but these did only 40 per cent of the sales. On the other hand, only 9 per cent of the establishments belonged to the manufacturers' sales branches and sales offices groups, but they did over 29 per cent of the total wholesale trade. Thus, as will be noted, each middleman type shows wide variations in average sales-per-establishment reporting. Petroleum distributors again averaged smaller sales per establishment, but did only 6.8 per cent of the sales. Agents and brokers, on the other hand, generated one sixth of the combined sales with only 8.8 per cent of the establishments. Finally, assemblers did 3.9 per cent of the business with 5.25 per cent of all establishments.

Even within the census coverage, sharp variations in importance are apparent between the individual types of operation for which data are given. Thus, on an establishment basis, the range is from 0.08 per cent for the retailer cooperative food distributors to 59.5 per cent for the regular service wholesaler (wholesale merchants). Based on dollar sales volumes in 1954, the range was from 0.12 per cent for the cash-carry wholesaler to 35 per cent for the regular service wholesaler. Differences in range of functions performed, in the variety of kinds of business to which the type of operation is adaptable, in the size of the potential markets for the commodities carried, and in the degree

---

[6] A special census report, based upon 1929 data, revealed that one out of every $9.00 of sales was done by multiple-type middlemen.

TABLE 2

WHOLESALE TRADE BY TYPE OF OPERATION:
UNITED STATES 1954

	Establishments		Sales ($1,000)	
	No.	Per Cent	Amt.	Per Cent
United States, total	252,318	100.00	234,974,422	100.00
Merchant wholesalers, total	165,153	65.45	101,100,941	43.03
Service wholesalers				
Wholesale merchants	149,284	59.17	80,877,038	34.42
Voluntary group (grocery)	574	0.23	2,463,756	1.05
Retailer coop. food	193	0.08	1,298,175	0.55
Terminal grain elevators	460	0.18	1,796,713	0.76
Importers	2,571	1.02	4,264,999	1.82
Exporters	2,361	0.94	4,355,553	1.86
Converters	817	0.32	1,503,962	0.64
Limited function				
Cash-carry wholesalers	922	0.37	278,574	0.12
Wagon, truck distributors	5,071	2.01	1,393,119	0.59
Other limited function	2,900	1.15	2,869,052	1.22
Mfrs. sales branches, sales offices	22,590	8.95	69,533,784	29.59
Sales branches (with stocks)	14,759	5.85	36,811,238	15.67
Sales offices (without stocks)	7,831	3.10	32,722,546	13.93
Petroleum distributors	29,189	11.57	16,038,372	6.83
Refiner-marketer bulk plants	17,837	7.07	10,976,082	4.67
Other bulk plants, etc.	10,482	4.15	4,832,756	2.06
Wholesale LP gas facilities	870	0.34	229,534	0.10
Merchandise agents, brokers	22,131	8.77	39,250,509	16.70
Auction companies	1,872	0.74	3,353,761	1.43
Brokers				
Representing buyers	449	0.18	1,377,660	0.59
Representing sellers	3,910	1.55	9,372,830	3.99
Commission merchants	3,568	1.41	8,747,728	3.72
Export agents	639	0.25	969,962	0.41
Import agents	271	0.11	730,811	0.31
Manufacturers' agents				
with stocks	2,482	0.98	1,703,787	0.73
without stocks	6,238	2.47	5,450,357	2.32
Selling agents	2,336	0.39	6,151,917	2.62
Purchasing agents, resident buyers	366	0.15	1,391,696	0.59
Assemblers of farm products	13,255	5.25	9,050,816	3.85

of geographical specialization are the most important variables under-lying these wide ranges of relative importance.

Yet, despite the wide number of types of operations and the ranges noted above, there is a high degree of concentration among a few types of operations. Thus three types of operations—the regular service wholesaler, manufacturers' sales branches (with stocks), and manu-facturers' sales offices (without stocks)—accounted on a combined basis for 68.4 per cent of the establishments and 64.7 per cent of all sales. The next six most important types of operations (based on sales) accounted for only 17.6 per cent of the establishments and 19.4 per cent of the sales.

Changes in Wholesale Trade by Types-of-Operation Groups: 1929–1954

Although changes in census coverage make it difficult to trace changes in importance of individual types of operation between 1929 and 1954, comparison can be made with the five types-of-operation groups—merchant wholesalers, manufacturers' sales branches and sales offices, petroleum bulk plants and terminals, merchandise agents and brokers, and assemblers of farm products (see Table 3). There has been a sharp increase in the number of establishments, but the distribution among each of the five groups has shown marked varia-tions. Increases have been consistent for the merchant wholesaler group only, with a resulting sharp increase in relative importance. On the other hand, there has been a drastic shrinkage in the number of assemblers establishments, with their relative importance being reduced from 19 per cent in 1929 to 5.25 per cent in 1954. The remaining groups show variable trends, but the relative importance of their establishments in 1954 was below the 1929 level.

Because of the sharp increase in varieties of goods marketed as well as inflationary price movements, wholesale sales in 1954 were about four times those of the 1929 base. In general, these trends may be noted as follows: (1) The merchant wholesaler group regaining its 1929 level of importance in 1954, after a sharp decline between 1929 and 1939; (2) the combined relative importance of the manufacturers' sales branches and sales office group increasing steadily; (3) the relative importance of the agents and brokers group declining steadily; and (4) the petroleum and assemblers groups showing mixed trends, but with the former at a higher level in 1954 than in 1929, whereas

TABLE 3

WHOLESALE TRADE BY TYPE OF OPERATION: UNITED STATES: 1954, 1948, 1939, AND 1929

Type of Operation	1954ᵃ		1948ᵃ		1939ᵇ		1929ᵇ	
	No.	Per Cent	No.	Per Cent	No.	Per Cent	No.	Per Cent
Merchant wholesalers								
Establishments (number)		65.45		59.75		51.50		47.31
Sales ($1,000)		43.03		42.38		40.57		43.15
Manufacturers' sales branches and sales offices								
Establishments (number)		8.95		10.97		9.42		10.35
Sales ($1,000)		29.59		28.13		26.51		24.74
Petroleum bulk plants and terminals								
Establishments (number)		11.57		13.12		16.19		12.04
Sales ($1,000)		6.83		5.81		7.08		3.66
Merchandise agents and brokers								
Establishments (number)		8.77		8.39		11.07		11.33
Sales ($1,000)		16.70		18.19		21.91		22.21
Assemblers of farm products								
Establishments (number)		5.25		7.77		11.82		18.97
Sales ($1,000)		3.85		5.49		3.93		6.25
Total—all types								
Establishments (number)	252,318	100	216,099	100	190,379	100	162,936	100
Sales ($1,000)	234,974,422	100	180,576,659	100	53,766,426	100	65,378,051	100

Source: U. S. Bureau of Census, *U. S. Census of Business—1954*, Vol. III, "Wholesale Trade," p. 6, Table 1.
ᵃ Limited to establishments with one or more paid employees—excludes milk-bottling plants.
ᵇ Includes establishments without paid employees—excludes milk-bottling plants.

the relative importance of the assembler group in 1954 was substantially below the 1929 level.

Variation in Kinds of Business, by Types of Operation Groups: 1954

The principal kinds of business for each census grouping of types of wholesale middlemen operations have been listed in Table 1. This section will present the 1954 census data of establishments and sales for the principal kinds of business for each group. From these data, a comprehensive picture may be obtained of the current concentration or diversification of groups of wholesale middlemen operations by commodities.

Merchant wholesalers

In the 1954 Census, merchant wholesalers were classified into some 160 kinds of businesses which, in turn, were combined into 56 groups of trade classifications, and further into 32 major categories. This census classification is complicated by the fact that under the food and textile groups are included kinds of business establishments which, in reality, are types of operation: voluntary-group grocery wholesalers, retailer-cooperative food wholesalers, cash-carry food depots, and piece goods converters.

The data show the relative importance of the major groupings by order of sales importance and the principal trade classifications and kinds of business within each. Immediately to be noticed is the wide distribution of merchant wholesalers, as a group, in all kinds of business. The importance of the food group (grocery, confectionery, meat) is apparent with 17.1 per cent of the sales and one eighth of the establishment. But the significant proportions accounted for by industrial goods categories—machinery, equipment supplies, farm products (raw materials), lumber, construction materials, and electrical, electronics, appliances—will come as a surprise to many.

The wide penetration of the merchant wholesaler group into so many kinds of business is a reflection of the historic dominant position of the group: The need for many manufacturers to use a type of middleman who will absorb risks and who, by selling many products, will reduce the cost burden of each manufacturer; the small size and limited financial resources of many agricultural producers and manufacturers; and the wide geographical outreach of the markets to be served. It is a reflection, also, of the organizational flexibility and range. of services of such middlemen, especially the regular service wholesaler.

Manufacturers' sales branches and sales offices

Although the number of sales branches far outweighed the number of sales offices in 1954, only $4 billion of sales separated the two types of operations. On a combined basis, most sales were accounted for by industrial goods kinds of business, except for the food and kindred products group which accounted for one sixth of the total. Especially important among the industrial products were the primary metals, transportation equipment, chemicals, and machinery kinds of business.

When sales branches are compared with sales offices, by principal kinds of business, sharp differences are apparent. Judging from the evidence, the basic generalization would seem to be that, wherever the commodity lines are bulky and likely to incur large transportation costs, or wherever there is likely to be a considerable amount of custom manufacturing, the sales office type of operation predominates because no inventories are handled. Thus, for primary metal products, the sales of the sales offices were over seven times larger than the sales of sales branches. Similar relationships were found in fabricated metals, stone-clay-glass, and paper kinds of business.

On the other hand, the sales-branch type is important where the maintenance of complete inventories of products and replacement parts are important at strategic wholesale centers because of servicing, perishability, adaptation of the unit of sale, and related reasons. Thus, the sales branches have sales importance which far exceeds that of sales offices for the food, transportation equipment, smaller machinery, rubber, and instrument kinds of business.

Agents and brokers

While agents and brokers are found in many kinds of business, they concentrate in far fewer kinds than was apparent for the merchant wholesalers and manufacturers' sales branches and sales offices types. Agricultural products (raw materials and edible) account for better than one third of the groups sales, whereas processed foods account for an additional 20 per cent. Apart from these kinds of business, the areas of greatest importance were textiles in various forms (8.2 per cent), and machinery, equipment, and supplies (5.53 per cent).

Although the census data do not permit a breakdown of sales by each type of agent middleman operation, it is apparent from the knowledge of each type's functions that a high degree of stratification takes place by kind of business. Thus, auction companies and commission agents are highly oriented towards agricultural products, whereas manufacturers' agents and selling agents are highly oriented towards textiles and machinery.

Assemblers

Table 4 demonstrates the high degree of concentration of sales of all types of assemblers in the marketing of certain kinds of agricultural products. Those assemblers handling grain accounts accounted for 35.6 per cent of all assemblers' sales in 1954—by far the single most

TABLE 4

WHOLESALE TRADE—UNITED STATES 1954:
ESTABLISHMENTS AND SALES OF ASSEMBLER
BY PRINCIPAL KINDS OF BUSINESS

Kind of Business	Establishments		Sales ($1,000)	
	No.	Per Cent	Amt.	Per Cent
Total, all kinds	13,255	100	9,050,816	100
1. Farm products (raw materials)	8,669	65.40	6,171,994	68.19
a. Grain	6,613	49.89	3,225,985	35.64
b. Livestock	1,090	8.22	1,771,355	19.57
c. Cotton	281	2.12	623,751	6.89
d. Hides, skins, raw furs	95	0.72	32,849	0.36
e. Other inedibles	590	4.45	518,054	5.72
2. Farm products (edible)	4,080	30.78	2,680,036	29.61
a. Dairy, poultry products	2,087	15.75	1,392,362	15.38
b. Fresh fruits, vegetables	1,993	15.03	1,287,674	14.23
3. Farm supplies	495	3.73	194.713	2.15
a. Feed	372	2.81	147,422	1.63
b. Seed	123	0.93	47,291	0.52
4. Other assemblers	11	0.08	4,073	0.05

important kind of business. The livestock group accounted for nearly one fifth of all sales; while the two kinds of edible farm products were next in importance. The cross relationships between proportion of sales and proportion of establishments for any kind of business reveals that the livestock and cotton assemblers had by far the largest average sales per establishment. On the other hand, the grain assemblers had average sales per establishment far below the groups' norm.

Sales Size of Wholesale Middlemen

A study of sales-size data is useful in correcting some misconceptions about the scale of wholesale middleman's operations. Unfortunately, the census data for 1954 do not cover all types of operation. For that census year, data were available only for all types of merchant wholesaler sales combined. These data are subdivided, in turn, by the principal kinds of business. Data are available for 1948, in addition, to show the sales-size distribution for manufacturers' sales branches, by principal kinds of business.

Sales size of merchant wholesalers

That the small sales-size establishments account for most of the merchant wholesalers' establishments, while the larger sales-size establishments dominate the proportion of total sales, is clearly shown by the data of Table 5. The single most important sales-size group,

TABLE 5
SALES SIZE—MERCHANT WHOLESALERS:
UNITED STATES 1954

Sales-Size Group	Establishments		Sales ($1,000)	
	No.	Per Cent	Amt.	Per Cent
Total	159,687	100.00	99,619,703	100.00
$10,000,000 and over	815	0.51	18,584,598	18.66
$5,000,000–$9,999,000	1,638	1.03	11,223,011	11.27
$2,000,000–$4,999,000	6,609	4.14	19,940,896	20.02
$1,000,000–$1,999,000	11,969	7.50	16,741,594	16.81
$500,000–$999,000	19,663	12.31	13,952,367	14.00
$300,000–$499,000	19,583	12.26	7,656,795	7.69
$200,000–$299,000	17,886	11.20	4,424,833	4.44
$100,000–$199,000	31,174	19.52	4,532,948	4.55
$50,000–$99,000	25,011	15.66	1,857,660	1.86
Less than $50,000	25,339	15.87	705,001	0.70

on the basis of total sales, consists of establishments having a range of sales of $2 to $3 million each in 1954. This group accounted for only 4.14 per cent of all establishments operated on an annual basis, but the cumulative sales represented one fifth of the total. Close in importance was the $10-million-and-over group which had only 0.5 per cent of the establishments, but accounted for 18.7 per cent of the sales. At the opposite end of the scale, 15.7 per cent of the establishments had annual sales of only $50,000–$99,000 each, and accounted for only 1.9 per cent of sales. An additional 15.9 per cent of the establishments each did less than $50,000 in 1954, accounting for only 0.7 per cent of total sales.

Because of limitations of space, it would be impossible to include all of the detailed sales-size data by kinds of business. The 1954 Census gives breakdowns for 162 separate kinds of business. What will be presented here is a summary of the most important kinds of business found in the largest sales-size groups. For the $10-million-and-over group, 17 kinds of business[7] accounted for $11.3 billion of sales out of a total of $18.6 billion for the entire sales-size group. Seven of the 17 kinds of business represent either raw or processed food groups; and of these 7 kinds, the grain merchants and voluntary-group grocery wholesalers had combined sales of $3.8 billion.

In the $5-to-$10-million group, the available data indicated that 16 kinds of business[8] accounted for combined sales of $6 billion, or 55.2 per cent of the sales-size group's total sales. Once again, the dominant kinds of business were in the food field with 6 of the 16 dominant kinds of business so classified. A comparison of the listing with the dominant kinds of business in the $10-million-and-over group reveals that, although the same kinds of business dominate both lists, there are sharp changes in the order of importance.[9]

[7] Grain; cotton; voluntary-group grocery wholesales; wines, distilled spirits; nonferrous metals; piece goods converters; general-line hardware; petroleum; electrical appliances, radio, TV sets; general merchandise; other general-line grocery; other specialty-line groceries; iron, steel, and products; lumber, millwork (without yards); dairy products; general-line electrical appliances; and meats and meat products, in order of declining sales importance.

[8] Wine, distilled spirits; electrical appliances, radio, TV sets; voluntary-group wholesalers; grain merchants; other general-line grocery; general-line drugs; cotton merchants; general-line electrical; tobacco; iron, steel, and products; meat, meat products; general-line hardware; piece goods converters; retailer-cooperative grocery; lumber, millwork (without yards); and dairy products, in order of declining sales importance.

[9] Because of the nature of census data, nine kinds of businesses in 1954 had their sales combined for the $5-to-$10-million and $10-million-and-over sales-size groups. These kinds of business were in order of declining sales importance: coffee, tea, spices; printing and fine papers; food, beverage basic materials; fresh fruits, vegetables; poultry, poultry products; other raw material farm products; specialty-line drugs; automotive parts, accessories; and construction machinery, equipment. Combined sales for these nine kinds of business totaled $3.9 billion in 1954, 17 per cent of the total sales for these two sales-size groups. Again, the importance of the raw and processed foods kinds of business should be noted.

A lesser degree of concentrated importance is evidenced when the $2-to-$5-million sales-size group is analyzed. It is found that 31 kinds of business[10] are significant.

Their cumulative sales in 1954 amounted to $13.7 billion, or 68.6 per cent of the sales-size group's total sales. Once again, the raw and processed foods group, with 11 out of the 31 kinds of business listed, dominates the sales-size group, but to a lesser extent than for the preceding groups. The most important of the group (other general-line grocery) alone accounted for over $1 billion of sales.

TABLE 6

SALES SIZE—MANUFACTURERS' SALES BRANCHES:
UNITED STATES 1948

| | Establishments | | Sales ($1,000) | |
Sales-Size Group	No.	Per Cent	Amt.	Per Cent
Total	15,716	100.00	$29,229,717	100.00
$5,000,000 and over	1,266	8.06	17,367,547	59.42
$2,000,000–$4,999,999	1,845	11.74	5,910,323	20.22
$1,000,000–$1,999,999	1,945	12.38	2,785,237	9.53
$500,000–$999,999	2,305	14.67	1,635,083	5.59
$300,000–$499,999	1,801	11.46	701,512	2.40
$200,000–$299,999	1,448	9.21	355,764	1.22
$100,000–$199,999	2,267	14.42	331,090	1.13
$50,000–$99,999	1,439	9.16	104,981	0.36
Under $50,000	1,400	8.91	38,180	0.13

Manufacturers' sales branches (with stocks)

The census did not tabulate sales-size data for these establishments in 1954, so 1948 data are presented. Because of the integrated nature of this type of operation, it would be expected that large sales-size establishments would predominate, and the data of Table 6 confirm this expectation. In terms of sales, the $5-million-and-over group

[10] Other general-line grocery; wine, distilled spirits; tobacco; electrical appliances, radio, TV sets; general-line electrical; meats, meat products; fresh fruits, vegetables; voluntary-group grocery; iron, steel, and products; general-line drugs; construction machinery, equipment; general-line hardware; lumber, millwork (without yards); grain merchants; cotton merchants; poultry, poultry products; beer, ale; printing and fine papers; other industrial materials supplies; piece goods converters; lumber, millwork (with yards); millwork, plywood; livestock merchants; coarse-paper products; automotive parts, accessories; dairy products; wiring supplies; plumbing fixtures, supplies; other specialty-line grocery; piece goods; and oil well supply, in declining order of sales importance.

TABLE 7

WHOLESALE TRADE—SINGLE UNITS AND MULTIUNITS, BY MAJOR TYPES: UNITED STATES 1954

No. of Establishments in Firm	Merchant Wholesalers		Mfrs. Sales Branches and Offices		Petroleum		Agents and Brokers		Assemblers		Total	
	No.	Per Cent	No.	Per Cent	No.	Per Cent	No.	Per Cent	No.	Per Cent	No.	Per Cent
Establishments												
In single-unit firms		86.67		3.28		28.58		91.18		66.93		71.84
2 establishments		4.76		2.98		2.66		3.52		5.73		4.30
3 establishments		2.08		2.42		0.81		1.55		2.84		1.96
4–5 establishments		1.79		4.26		0.90		1.15		2.73		1.90
6–9 establishments		1.33		7.63		0.54		1.10		3.57		1.90
10–14 establishments		0.67		8.61		0.81		0.73		2.69		1.51
15–24 establishments		0.64		13.05		0.98		0.28		1.99		1.83
25–49 establishments		0.79		14.65		1.21		} 0.50		3.46		2.18
50–99 establishments		0.47		12.97		1.26				3.18		1.79
100 or more establishments		0.80		30.15		62.25				6.88		10.79
Total	165,153	100.00	22,590	100.00	29,189	100.00	22,131	100.00	13,255	100.00	252,318	100.00
Sales ($1,000)												
In single-unit firms		71.57		5.35		22.31		82.06		68.29		50.24
2 establishments		7.28		2.06		.07		4.82		6.42		4.94
3 establishments		3.45		1.90		1.26		2.99		2.77		2.74
4–5 establishments		3.63		2.98		1.15		2.19		3.65		3.03
6–9 establishments		3.57		5.49		0.55		2.64		4.73		3.82
10–14 establishments		1.51		7.02		0.84		3.46		2.78		3.47
15–24 establishments		1.94		12.31		0.96		0.77		1.63		4.74
25–49 establishments		1.98		15.30		0.96		} 1.07		1.54		} 27.04
50–99 establishments		1.08		13.24		3.11				2.51		
100 or more establishments		3.99		34.35		66.79				5.67		
Total	101,100,941	100.00	69,553,784	100.00	16,038,372	100.00	39,250,509	100.00	9,050,816	100.00	234,974,422	100.00

accounted for 59.4 per cent of the total with only 8.1 per cent of the establishments. On the other hand, establishments with less than $50,000 of sales each in 1948 accounted for only 0.13 per cent of total sales with nearly one eleventh of the establishments. Unlike the tendency noted above for merchant wholesaler establishments, the most important clusterings of sales branches establishments were in the $500,000-to-$1-million and the $100,000–$199,999 sales-size groups.

Once again, space limitations permit only a summary presentation to be made of the most important kinds of business for the three most important sales-size groups shown in Table 6. For the $5-million-and-over sales-size group, 16 kinds of business[11] accounted for $11.3 billion of sales, 64.9 per cent of the total for the sales-size group. Each of the first four kinds of business accounted for more than $1 billion of sales. Although the industrial kinds of business are more important for sales branches than for merchant wholesalers, it is significant to note that the list includes seven kinds of food business, reflecting, in part, the integrated operations of such businesses as the large meat packers and the canners of fruits, vegetables, etc.

For the $2-to-$5-million sales-size group, 20 kinds of business[12] accounted for $4.3 billion of sales, 72.8 per cent of the total sales for the group. The meats and meat product group alone accounted for over $1 billion of sales. Although industrial goods are heavily represented, 6 of the 20 kinds of business again were in the food group.

Finally, in the $1-to-$2-million sales-size group, 28 kinds of business[13] accounted for $2.1 billion of sales, or 74.1 per cent of the

[11] Electrical apparatus and equipment; meats, meat products; miscellaneous grocery specialties; industrial chemicals; farm dairy machinery, equipment; piece goods; automotive parts, accessories; wines, distilled spirits; dairy, poultry products; iron, steel, and products; canned foods; tires, tubes; flour; miscellaneous industrial machinery, supplies; nonferrous metals, metalwork; and confectionery.

[12] Meats, meat products; miscellaneous grocery specialties; tires, tubes; industrial chemical; miscellaneous industrial machinery; supplies; farm dairy machinery, equipment; dairy, dairy products; iron, steel, and products; canned foods; drugs, drug sundries; wiring supplies, construction materials; general-line plumbing, heating; electrical apparatus, equipment; automotive parts, accessories; office machines, equipment; flour; electrical appliances, specialties, n. e. c.; floor covering; nonferrous metals, metalwork; and beer, ale.

[13] Meats, meat products; miscellaneous grocery specialties; iron, steel and products; miscellaneous industrial machinery; supplies; office machines; equipment; dairy, dairy products; general-line plumbing, heating; industrial chemicals; electrical apparatus and equipment; canned foods; drug sundries; flour; amusement, sporting goods; beer, ale; paints, varnishes; tires, tubes; electrical

sales-size group total.   The range of sales among the 28 kinds of
business was quite wide.   Once again, the food industry is well represented with 7 kinds of business.

Major Types of Middlemen Operations
by Single Units and Multiunits

Closely related to the preceding discussion of sales-size distribution
of establishments is an analysis of the number of establishments in
wholesale middlemen's forms.   To those who believe that all wholesale middlemen firms are, by definition, one-establishment firms, the
data of Table 7 may come as a sharp surprise.   On a combined basis,
over one tenth of all establishments are accounted for by firms which
each have 100 or more establishments.   This multiunit size of operation was proportionately more important for the petroleum group
and manufacturers' sales branches and sales offices combined.   Generally, this group accounted for significantly higher proportions of
sales than of establishments.

There are two other observations which may be made about the
data in Table 7.   For manufacturers' sales offices and sales branches,
there was a steady increase, with one exception, in the importance of
the multiunit groups as they progressed upwards from the four-or-
more-establishments group.   The other characteristic of interest is
the significant number of multiunit firms among the assemblers, reflecting, no doubt, the impact of cooperative purchasing and marketing
associations.   Also of interest, again because of integration, is the
high proportion of petroleum bulk stations and related facilities
found in the 100-or-more-establishments-per-firm group.

---

wiring supplies, construction materials; confectionery; lumber, millwork; belting,
hose packing; farm dairy machinery, equipment; glass (building); automotive
parts, accessories; oil wells, oil refining supplies; fertilizers, agricultural chemical;
heating (including stoves, ranges); men's, boys' clothing, furnishings, accessories;
and miscellaneous home furnishings.

3

Agency Structure (Continued)

The preceding chapter has dealt primarily with the background definitions, and with some of the census data needed to appreciate the complexity of the agency structure of the wholesaling sector in the United States. This chapter continues and concludes the discussion of agency structure in terms of: (1) completion of the analysis of selected census data; (2) analysis of specialization of wholesale middlemen; (3) analysis of competition between types of middlemen operation; and (4) re-evaluation of the position of the middlemen types in the wholesaling sector.

Additional Measures of Middleman Size for Average Sales per Establishment

Based upon 1954 data, it has been possible to compute the average sales-size of each type of middleman operation and of the kinds of business for each middleman group. These data reveal, furthermore, the high degree of variability noted in Chapter 2.

Variations, by type of middleman

The wide range in the average sales-size of each type of operation is apparent from the data of Table 8. For the six groups, the manufacturers' sales offices had an average volume nearly eight times that

TABLE 8

DISTRIBUTION OF TYPES OF WHOLESALE MIDDLEMEN, BY AVERAGE SALES PER ESTABLISHMENT (IN DECLINING ORDER): UNITED STATES 1954

Type	Average Sales per Establishment
I. *Type of operation group*	
a. Manufacturers' sales offices	$4,178,600
b. Manufacturers' sales branches	2,494,200
c. Merchandise agents and brokers	1,773,600
d. Assemblers of farm products	682,800
e. Merchant wholesalers, total	606,100
f. Petroleum bulk plants, et al.	549,500
Average	$ 931,260
II. *Individual types of operation*	
A. Merchant wholesalers	
1. Terminal grain elevator	$3,905,900
2. Exporters	1,844,800
3. Importers	1,658,900
4. Other limited-function wholesalers	989,300
5. Regular service wholesalers	571,000
6. Cash-carry wholesalers	302,100
7. Wagon, truck distributors	274,700
Average	$ 606,100
B. Manufacturers' sales branches, sales offices	
1. Sales offices	$4,178,600
2. Sales branches	2,494,200
Average	$3,078,100
C. Petroleum bulk stations, et al.	
1. Refiner-marketer plants	$ 615,400
2. Other bulk plants, et al.	461,100
3. Wholesale LP gas facilities	263,800
Average	$ 549,500
D. Merchandise agents and brokers	
1. Purchasing agents, resident buyers	$3,802,400
2. Brokers representing buyers	3,068,300
3. Import agents	2,696,700
4. Selling agents	2,633,500
5. Commission agents	2,451,700
6. Brokers representing sellers	2,397,100
7. Auction companies	1,791,500
8. Export agents	1,517,900
9. Manufacturers' agents without stocks	873,700
10. Manufacturers' agents with stocks	686,500
Average	$1,773,600

for the petroleum bulk plant group, et al., and nearly five times the average for all wholesale establishments. Equally wide variations are apparent for the individual types within each group. The widest ranges are found in the merchant wholesalers group. At one extreme were the terminal grain elevators with nearly $4 million of sales per establishment, compared with only $274,700 for wagon and truck distributors establishments. Almost as wide were the agent and brokers group—from $686,500 manufacturers' agents with stocks to $3,802,400 for purchasing agents and resident buyers. Of interest was the larger sales potential of manufacturers' sales offices without stocks as compared with sales branches carrying stocks.

The sharp variations indicated in Table 8 are associated with several factors. Chief among these are: (1) The sales potential of the trading area in which the wholesale middleman is located for the kinds of products carried; (2) the nature of the marketing arrangements between the wholesale middlemen and the producers; (3) the range of product assortments handled; and (4) the relative importance of the middleman type for the entire channel of distribution for the products involved. This last-mentioned factor is especially important in terms of the size of the average unit of purchase made by customers and the strategic importance of the kinds of products handled.

It will be noticed that 16 types of middlemen averaged over $1 million of sales per establishment in 1954. On the other hand, only three types averaged $350,000 or less per establishment. The remainder, nine types, ranged between $350,000 and $1 million.

Variations, by kinds of business

Detailed data are available for the merchant wholesalers, manufacturers' sales branches and sales offices, and agents and brokers groups to show variations in the average sales per establishment, by detailed kind-of-business breakdowns. In the discussion which follows, these data have been combined to show the average sales per establishment for each major kind of business group as well as the range of averages for each subgroup, where available, under each major group and the number of such subgroups.

Data are available for 33 major kinds of business groups of merchant wholesalers, and for 173 subgroup kinds of business available for 22 major groups. The range of averages for the 33 groups was extremely wide. The largest average was found in the farm products (raw materials) group, $2,396,000. This average size was over 12 times the size found for the gift, art goods, and greeting card wholesalers group. Only six groups,[1] had average sales per establishment which exceeded $1 million each.

On the other hand, 18 of the 33 groups each had average sales per establishment below the average for all merchant wholesalers' establishments. Also of interest is the wide range found in the subgroups for every kind of business group which had more than two subgroups.

The conclusions to be drawn are that the data support previous observations made about the flexibility of the merchant wholesalers' group. In adapting themselves to every kind of business, they have evolved many types of operation of a wide range of sales potentialities. The capital requirements show similar wide variations, and, as shall be seen in later discussions, geographical flexibility is also a characteristic.

Similar data are available for 21 kinds of business groups for manufacturers' sales branches and sales offices separately and on a combined basis. These types of operations, by the nature of the managerial control evidenced, must support considerably larger volumes of sales than do the merchant wholesalers. As a result, average sales per establishment for all groups of business—except instruments and related products, and furniture and fixtures—each exceeded $1 million. And 11 of the 21 groups, on a combined sales branch-sales office basis, each had averages exceeding $3 million in 1954.

The sharp differences in the average sales size between sales branch and sales office establishments are quite significant. In 12 of the 15 groups for which data were available in 1954, the average sales size of sales offices was significantly higher than for sales branches. Especially significant were the differences in the transportation equipment and the fabricated metal products groups. In each of these cases the products have highly individual design characteristics, are very bulky and expensive to ship, and have other characteristics which encourage maintenance of stocks at key producing points.

In the leather and leather products, electrical machinery, and rubber products groups, the sales branches average sales size exceeded that for sales offices. The high degree of standardization of many of the products together with smaller unit sizes and unit values may be the significant factors explaining the reversal of the usual size relationships of sales branches to sales offices.

---

[1] Farm products (raw materials) merchants; food, beverage basic materials distributors; general merchandise distributors; coal wholesalers; tobacco distributors; and metals, metalwork (except scrap) distributors.

Finally, data similar to those for merchant wholesalers are available for 24 kind of business groups for merchandise agents and brokers. The range was lower than for either merchant wholesalers or manufacturers' sales branches and sales offices groups. Sixteen of the 24 groups each had average sales per establishment of $1 million or more. This narrower range is significant especially when viewed against the large number of diverse component types. Part of the explanation is related, undoubtedly, to the characteristic of many of these types of operations as being middlemen's middleman; that is, in selling mainly to other middlemen and users at the wholesale level.

Again, the data available for 72 subgroups reveal the wide ranges in average size for the subgroups comprising any given kind of business group. Especially wide are the ranges for the farm products (raw materials), groceries, confectionery, meats, apparel, paper and allied products, and machinery equipment supplies groups.

No detailed data are available for the petroleum and assemblers groups by kinds of business. But, in these cases, the products are considerably more homogeneous than for the merchant wholesalers, manufacturers' sales branches and sales offices, and merchandise agents and brokers groups.

Comparative Operating Expense Data

The value of operating expensive data in evaluating middlemen operations was discussed in Chapter 2 in the presentation of the criteria of competitive efficiency. Census data are available by types of operation and by kinds of business within each type of operation group. These data are expressed as percentages of the sales data reported by the establishments. Operating expense data reflect variations in functional activity, efficiency of management activity, relation of sales-size position, and locational factors. As a result, wide variations may be expected as between types of operations and kinds of business.

Variations, by type of operation

The relative average operating expense position of each type of operation is shown in Table 9. At the low end of the scale are those middlemen who act as agents and brokers, the merchant wholesalers who perform a relatively narrow band of functions, and the manufacturers' sales offices which carry no physical inventories. At

TABLE 9

DISTRIBUTION OF TYPES OF WHOLESALE MIDDLEMEN,
BY OPERATING EXPENSE RATIOS (ARRANGED IN
DECLINING SALES–SIZE ORDER): UNITED STATES 1954

Sales-Size Rank	Types of Middlemen	Per Cent
	Merchant wholesalers	13.2
1	Terminal grain elevators	4.2
2	Exporters	5.6
3	Importers	6.3
4	Other limited-function wholesalers	8.4
5	Regular service wholesalers	14.2
6	Cash-carry wholesalers	8.8
7	Wagon, truck distributors	14.2
	Manufacturers' sales branches, sales offices	7.7
1	Sales offices	4.5
2	Sales branches	10.5
	Petroleum bulk stations, et al.	10.0
1	Refiner-marketer plants	9.1
2	Other bulk plants, et al.	11.3
3	Wholesale LP gas facilities	26.5
	Merchandise agents and brokers	3.1
1	Purchasing agents, resident buyers	2.1
2	Brokers representing buyers	1.9
3	Import agents	2.6
4	Selling agents	3.6
5	Commission agents	2.3
6	Brokers representing sellers	2.2
7	Auction companies	2.8
8	Export agents	3.2
9	Manufacturers' agents (without stocks)	5.3
10	Manufacturers' agents (with stocks)	6.9
	Assemblers of Farm Products	8.1

the opposite extreme are the full-functioning middlemen. A very
special case is presented by the wholesale LP gas facilities with
operating expenses of 26.5 per cent.

Within each type of operation group there are wide variations reflecting some of the variables noted above. For merchant wholesalers,
the range was from a low of 4.2 per cent for grain elevators to
a high of 14.2 per cent for the regular service wholesaler and the
truck (wagon) distributor. The effect of carrying inventories and
a smaller average sales size is reflected in an operating expense ratio

for manufacturers' sales branches which was nearly 2½ times larger that that for sales offices. In the petroleum group, the range was from 9.1 per cent for refiner-marketer plants to 26.5 per cent for the wholesale LP gas facilities. For agents and brokers there was a wide range from 1.9 per cent for brokers representing buyers to 6.9 per cent for the manufacturers' agents handling stock.

Variations, by kinds of business

A summarization of the detailed data available by kinds of business is presented in this section. Such data are available for the merchant wholesalers group. The range was quite wide from one business to another—4 per cent at the low end for farm products (raw materials) merchants to 24.2 per cent for gift, art goods, and greeting card wholesalers. Although there is some correlation between average sales per establishment and the size of the operating expense ratio, the evidence is not overly impressive. Only eight kinds of business groups[2] had operating expense ratios below 10 per cent in 1954.

Similar wide ranges were to be found in the operating expenses for each subgroup of kinds of business in which there were more than two kinds for the group classification involved. Especially wide ranges were found for the electrical-electronics-appliance kinds of business, the grocery-meats-confectionery subgroups, the lumber-construction-materials subgroups, the paper-allied products subgroups; the machinery-equipment-supplies subgroups; the jewelry subgroups; and the various types of scrap and waste materials dealers. In all of these cases, there are wide variations in types of operations and product assortment alternatives.

While detailed kind of business data are not available for manufacturers' sales offices and sales branches, comparisons are possible for 15 kinds of business groups. It would be expected that sales offices, because of lack of functions affiliated with physical possession of goods, would have a lower operating expense percentage than sales branches. The data reveal that, for paper and allied products, rubber products, and furniture and fixtures, however, sales offices had, on the average, higher operating expense percentages. In the remaining groups, the sharp variations in the relationship of sales-branch-to-sales-office operating expenses are apparent. For the food group, for example, sales branch expenses were only 1.4 times larger than for sales offices, whereas for fabricated metal products the ratio was

---

[2] Farm products (raw materials); food, beverage basic materials; coal; tobacco; miscellaneous products, not elsewhere classified; industrial yarns; grocery, confectionery; meats and poultry.

over six times. Obviously, the weight and bulk of products handled are among the many factors affecting these ratios.

Finally, data are available for 24 kinds of business groups for agents and brokers, and for subgroups in 13 of these. The range between groups was quite wide—from 1.5 per cent for farm products (raw materials) to 10.2 per cent for books, magazines, and newspapers. But two of the groups had percentages under 2, whereas an additional 15 groups had percentages between 2 and 5. As compared with the merchant wholesalers group, the range was quite narrow for the subgroups of kinds of business found within each group. In many instances this represents a far more homogeneous group of types of operations than is found for the merchant wholesalers group. In addition, it reflects fewer variations in sales size than is found for that group.

Relation of operating expenses to sales size of establishments

Detailed analyses will be made in the discussion of the internal management of wholesale establishments and costs. But it has been indicated, already, that it would be expected that on the average

TABLE 10

RELATIONSHIP BETWEEN SALES SIZE OF ESTABLISHMENT
AND OPERATING EXPENSE PERCENTAGES FOR
ALL MERCHANT WHOLESALERS: UNITED STATES 1954

Sales-Size Group	No. of Establishments	Operating Expenses, % of sales
Total, all establishments	165,153	13.2
No. operated entire year	159,687	13.1
$10,000,000 and over	815	5.7
$5,000,000–$9,999,000	1,638	9.3
$2,000,000–$4,999,000	6,609	11.5
$1,000,000–$1,999,000	11,969	13.8
$500,000–$999,600	19,663	16.6
$300,000–$299,000	19,583	18.9
$200,000–$499,000	17,886	20.5
$100,000–$199,000	31,174	22.5
$50,000–$99,000	25,011	25.4
Less than $50,000	25,339	31.0
Establishments not operated all year	5,466	14.3

Source: U. S. Bureau of the Census, *U. S. Census of Business—1954,* Vol. III, "Wholesale Trade," Table 2A, p. 2–2.

the larger the sales volume the lower would be the operating expense percentage. That this holds true for all merchant wholesalers establishments is evidenced by the data in Table 10. Without exception, every incremental decline in the sales size is accompanied by an increase in the operating expense percentage. For particular kinds of business, however, the relationship would not always exist because of variations in the representativeness of the establishments included.

Specialization of Wholesale Middlemen

Meaning

Specialization, within the context of this discussion of agency structure, refers to various ways in which middlemen may, by adaptation of product lines, functions, area of operation, or classes of customers, or combinations of these, create a basis for formulating a special kind of middleman operation within any of the given types classified and defined in Chapter 2. The development of specialization within this meaning represents an evolution from a period when a middleman would be expected to perform all functions, to handle all commodities, and to service all classes of customers wherever located with respect to the locational framework of his business. This evolution is part and parcel of the broader pattern of complexity introduced by the development of specialization in all phases of economic organization.

Whenever the volume of output of any category of goods reaches a high enough plane, one basis for specialization is created because this volume level permits minimum sales potentialities sufficient to support a given type of middleman operation. Closely related to this factor is the factor of increase in the variety of goods which has to be marketed. This increase in variety is indeed the principal reason for permitting the development of that class of goods referred to in marketing as "specialty goods"; and this creation of specialty goods permits, in turn, the development of specialized middlemen to market such goods. The development of a large and diversified group of customers also makes specialization possible. Finally, the development of the diversified geographical distribution of production units in relation to customers may be noted in this brief introduction.

Forms of specialization

Four main types of specialization have been noted above: (1) By adaptation of product lines; (2) by functions; (3) by geographical adaptation; and (4) by class of customer. The idea of *specialty goods* applies mainly to manufactured consumers' goods, and its original creation is attributed to Copeland.[3] By definition, these goods have some particular (i.e., *special*) attributes as elements of attraction which reduce, in turn, the strength of the influence of price in their selection and purchase. Such elements of attraction may be design and style, the use of extensive advertising to create mental images of exclusiveness and snobbishness, the use of special packaging, and similar aspects. By concentrating on these specialty products, the middlemen can apply much more thorough and aggressive marketing efforts in direct contrast to those types of middlemen who handle wide varieties and must spread their marketing efforts very thinly. In addition, these specialty goods wholesalers generally would carry more complete assortments in depth. It would be expected that these types of wholesale middlemen would, in turn, cater to a narrower group of customers; namely, to those that specialize, in turn, at the retail level in such specialty goods.

Functional specialization refers to those types of middlemen operations who limit their activities to a much narrower range than would be expected otherwise if the basic, broad definition of wholesaling were to be considered. Thus in the merchant wholesaler group, the drop shipper specializes in selling, leaving the functions of storage and other aspects of physical handling to other agencies. On the other hand, the chain store warehouse specializes in physical handling activities. In the agent and broker group, the census data reveal brokers who specialize in representing sellers or in representing buyers. Limitations of financial resources, characteristics of products, factors of costs, legal limitations, and other considerations underlie the existence of functional specialization of middlemen.

Geographical specialization

Since the area structure of wholesaling will be discussed in the next chapter, only a brief discussion of geographical specialization need be given here. It is sufficient here to indicate that wholesale middlemen may be local in scope, confining their activities to a single city or a single metropolitan area; they may operate on a statewide (or part of a state) basis; they may operate on a regional basis (meaning in two or more states); or they may operate on a nationwide basis. In addition, those middlemen specializing in foreign markets (as

[3] Melvin T. Copeland, *Principles of Merchandising* (New York: McGraw-Hill Book Co., Inc., 1929).

exporters, importers, export agents, or import agents) demonstrate a somewhat different aspect of geographical specialization.

Evidence of specialty wholesaling

The census data permit a comparison to be made between general-line wholesalers and specialty-line wholesalers in the grocery-confectionery-meat, drugs-chemicals-allied products, dry-goods-apparel, electrical-electronics-appliances; hardware, and plumbing-heating equipment and supplies groups kinds of business. In addition, the census also gives data for general merchandise wholesalers, within the grocery and dry goods and apparel groups, further breakdown is possible by commodity specialization or functional specialization.

Several points of importance may be noted. Of six kinds of business groups, only in the dry goods and apparel group did the combined importance of the specialty-line wholesaler exceed that of the general-line wholesalers, wide ranges in relative importance are apparent for general-line wholesalers in the six groups of business, with a low of 16.5 per cent for the dry goods and apparel group to a high of 78.5 per cent for the hardware business. The range of specialty-line wholesalers importance was much narrower within the kinds of business groups indicated. Wide ranges in relative importance are apparent also for the specialized kinds of business within each group.

Such data as are available from earlier census releases would seem to indicate that the relative importance of specialty-line wholesalers wherever found has risen sharply since 1929. The reasons have to do with the rising standards of living, the sharp diversification and expansion of manufacturing activities, and the increased interest of consumers in imported items. In addition, the rise of "miracle drugs" has further accentuated the specialty-line aspect of the drug business.

Competition of Middlemen Types of Operation: General Discussion

Any discussion of competition between wholesale middlemen must begin with a consideration of several general aspects of the subject. To begin with, there is competition between different types of operation with the same general grouping; e.g., the full-service wholesaler versus the cash-and-carry wholesaler versus the voluntary group wholesaler, and so on. This type of competition cuts in several directions as to class of commodities, class of customers, geographical coverage, and type of operation assortment of functions. For purposes of this discussion, this type may be referred to as *intra-agency group competition*. Generally, one type of operation permeates several classification categories so far as kinds of business and geographical areas are concerned, while remaining competing types have many restrictions including those which are commodity in nature, functional in nature, or geographical in nature. Concrete examples will be discussed later.

A second form of competition may be designated as *interagency group competition*. In this form, the various directions of competition noted above now are measured and evaluated as between merchant wholesalers, manufacturers' sales offices, manufacturers' sales branches, petroleum bulk plants, terminals, and LP gas facilities, merchandise agents and brokers, and assemblers of farm products as groups of individual types of operation. This census classification of groups created difficulties because two of the groups—the petroleum and the assemblers—are both highly specialized as to kinds of products marketed. On the other hand, the remaining groups, and especially the merchandise wholesalers group, have very wide coverage so far as kinds of business are concerned. In addition, the use of census data creates problems because there are sharp variations in the amount of detailed kind of business data included.

In addition to these forms of competition, a distinction may be made based upon *single type versus multiple type* of operation broken down by commodity, class of customer, and geographical considerations. Although this is a very significant form of competition, unfortunately such data were collected only for the 1929 Census.[4]

A final form of competition may be designated as *product assortment* competition. This form of competition is characterized by the degree to which different kinds of business within the same type of middleman operation or within the same group handle the same general groups of commodities. The discussion of this type of competition will be deferred in part until Chapter 7 when the entire problem of product assortments is discussed.

There are many complicated problems of measurement associated with these four forms of competition. For example, the census data do not give, as was done in earlier periods, detailed breakdowns of the kinds of business in which the individual types of middlemen operations are found, except for manufacturers' sales branches and

---

[4] U. S. Department of Commerce, Bureau of the Census, *Census of Distribution, Wholesale Distribution* (Special Series): *Multiple Types of Wholesaling,* Publication No. W-25, (Washington, D. C.: U. S. Government Printing Office, 1933).

sales offices. Thus, it is almost impossible to get accurate measurements for current years of intra-agency group competition. Some measure of the kind and degree of interagency group competition may be obtained from such data as are available. But even in these cases, the kinds of business classifications are not completely comparable between the operational groups. The lack of current data of multiple-type operations has been indicated above.

What can be presented, accordingly, in the following sections of this chapter is, first of all, some measure of interagency competition by kinds of business on a national basis. This type of comparison will consist mainly of accumulating for each of the five groups of middlemen types data of number of establishments and sales in 1954 by comparable kinds of business classification as found in the census. Such comparisons will not represent a complete measure of competition since one group may, in terms of channel structure, sell to another group within the same kind of business category.

The main discussion in this chapter will be centered around product assortment competition. In measuring this particular form of competition, two main types of analyses will be presented as follows: (1) A percentage distribution was made, for each kind of business, of sales between the main classes of products constituting that kind of business, those classes of products constituting related lines, and all other products handled; and (2) the percentage distribution of sales product classes of a homogeneous group as between different kinds of business. The details of the *1954 Census of Business* permit such comparisons to be made only for the merchant wholesalers, manufacturers' sales offices, and manufacturers' sales branches groups.

Interagency Group Competition, by Kinds of Business

The 1948 and 1954 Census data make it possible to distribute sales by principal kinds between the five types of operation groups as follows: the merchant wholesalers; manufacturers' sales branches and sales offices combined; petroleum bulk plants, terminals, and LP gas facilities; merchandise agents and brokers; and the assemblers of farm products. To give the analysis a more meaningful form, the census data of kinds of business were grouped, so far as possible, into extractive industry products, industrial goods, and manufactured consumers' goods. Thus, except for sales made directly from producers' places of manufacturing without the use of an identifiable wholesale middlemen's establishments, a meaningful approximation

can be made of the percentage distribution of the total gross wholesales of any kind of business as between the five middleman groups.
From these distribution patterns, a groundwork is prepared for
discussion of channels of distribution in Chapters 5 and 6.[5]

What is importantly significant for the discussion of interagency
group competition is that these comparisons reveal:

1. The extent to which a particular kind of business is the sale
   province of a particular group type of middleman.
2. The extent to which significant divisions of sales of a particular
   kind of business is made between two or more group types.
3. The extent to which producer-controlled middleman groups do
   or do not dominate any given kind of business.

Table 10 contains the pertinent detailed data for 1954, by principal
kinds of business and by subgroups.

Evidence of lack of interagency group competition

For purposes of this analysis, lack of interagency group competition
will be defined as the situation in which 75 per cent or more of
the total sales of any kind of business is accounted for by only *one*
middleman group.　　Table A1 presents such detailed data as are
available for 1954.　　To facilitate the analysis, the kinds of business
have been divided into three groups: the extractive industries, including both basic raw materials and edible products; industrial
goods; and manufactured consumers' goods.[6]　Six kinds of business
groups, and 10 subgroups were included under the extractive industries
classification; 12 groups and 19 subgroups were included under the
industrial goods classification; and 14 groups and 17 subgroups were
included under the manufactured consumers' goods classification.
Thus a total of 78 groups and subgroups of kind of business are
tabulated in Table 10.

The evidence of Appendix Table A1, using the 75 per cent or more
criterion, is that there is a lack of interagency group competition in
only a few kinds of business.　For the extractive industries, there are
only three cases: merchant wholesalers in the flower, bulb, and plant
kind of business; agents and brokers for livestock; and the petroleum

---

[5] As the reader works through the following discussion, he should be aware
constantly of the limitations of census data so far as comparability between types
of operation by kinds of businesses and between benchwork years is concerned.

[6] Since the census data do not always give sufficient breakdown of the data,
it should be kept in mind that some of these divisions are arbitrary compromises
based upon the best knowledge available to the author of the products involved.

group for petroleum. The greatest prevalence is found in the industrial goods classification. Merchant wholesalers accounted for 75 per cent or more of the total sales for the construction machinery, millwork, plumbing-heating equipment and supplies, iron and steel scrap, and waste materials kinds of business. Sales branches and sales offices predominated in similar fashion in the metals and metalwork, industrial chemicals and explosives, textile mill products, rubber products (except tire tubes), and leather and leather products kinds of business. In the manufactured consumers goods category, only the merchant wholesalers accounted for 75 per cent or more of a kind of business. These cases were found for piece goods converters, beer and ale distributors, hardware, jewelry, and gift art goods kinds of business.

The nature of interagency group competition

In the remaining kinds of business, the structure of interagency group competition is highly variable. There are no kinds of business, for example, in which all five groups of wholesale middlemen types account for part of the total wholesale sales. Furthermore, there are only a few examples in which four group types compete: dairy products, poultry and poultry products, and the miscellaneous group categories.

Thus, the main structure of interagency group competition consists of competition between three group types. In the extractive industries classifications, the following patterns exist: (1) For farm products (raw materials) the competition is between the merchant wholesalers, agents and brokers, and assemblers of farm products groups; (2) for petroleum, the competition is between merchant wholesalers agents and brokers, and the petroleum group; (3) for farm products (edible) between all groups, except the petroleum group; (4) for the lumber and forest products and coal categories, between merchant wholesalers, agents and brokers, and sales branches and sales offices groups.

In the industrial goods classification, except for the kinds of business mentioned above where one group is dominant, the type of competition is between the merchant wholesalers, sales branches and sales offices, and agents and brokers groups. Similarly, in the manufactured consumers' goods categories, except for the cases of domination, the competition is between merchant wholesalers, sales branches and sales offices, and agents and brokers groups.

Apart from the evidence of interagency group competition, Appendix Table A1 reveals some other interesting aspects of agency structure.

One of the aspects, and this will be discussed in later chapters, is the surprising strength of the merchant wholesalers' group in the industrial goods kinds of business. It has been assumed, generally, that because direct marketing is so evident in the marketing of industrial goods, that most of the sales would be accounted for by manufacturers' sales offices or manufacturers' sales branches. Yet, on a combined basis, for the kinds of industrial goods business listed in the table, the merchant wholesalers accounted for 41 per cent of the total compared with 50.5 per cent for sales branches and sales offices combined. Conversely, it is interesting to note that sales branches and sales offices accounted for 30.9 per cent of the total sales of manufactured consumers' goods compared with 52 per cent for merchant wholesalers. The other interesting aspect is the larger relative strength of the agent and brokers group in the extractive industries classification compared with industrial goods and manufactured consumers' goods.

Intra-Agency Middlemen Competition

Although the *1954 Census of Business* does not give data of kinds of business sales by individual types of middleman operation, sufficient information is available together with other analytical materials to permit some meaningful observations to be made. Obviously, the competition of middlemen classified under the petroleum group is in the marketing of petroleum and petroleum products, derivatives of this product base, and liquefied petroleum (LP) gas. For the remaining groups, the observations may be grouped under each classification heading.

Merchant wholesalers

Within this group, the regular or service wholesaler is the diversified type of operation, by kind of business, and this, within the merchant wholesalers groups, competes with one or more specialized types, depending upon the kind of business. In the grocery-confectionery-meats category, this type competes with the various voluntary chain wholesale middlemen, cash-and-carry depots, chain store buying offices and warehouses, truck (wagon) distributors, and exporters and importers. In the industrial goods kinds of business, the intra-agency competition is mainly with the industrial distributor (mill supply house). In the apparel and dry goods fields the regular wholesaler competes mainly with piece goods converters. In the farm products kinds of business, the competition is mainly again with the voluntary and corporate chain wholesale middlemen, the exporters and importers, and the terminal grain elevator.

Manufacturers' sales branches and sales offices

The previous discussions have already analyzed the competition between sales branches and sales offices, by kinds of business. On an over-all basis, sales branches had $36.8 billion of sales in 1954 compared with $32.7 billion for sales offices. Each type of operation is found in all kinds of business for which census data were collected. Of 20 kinds of business groups and a miscellaneous category, sales branches had the larger volume of sales in 9 categories.

Merchandise agents and brokers

Certain types of operation within this group are oriented towards very special kinds of business. Thus, auction companies are concerned mainly with fresh fruits and vegetables and livestock, while commission agents are mainly found in the farm products (raw materials and edibles) kinds of business. Brokers are significant in the farm products, grocery-meats-confectionery, and several other categories. Manufacturers' and selling agents are heavily oriented towards the apparel-textile-dry goods and machinery-equipment-supplies kinds of business. Export agents are found in a wide array of businesses, especially in the food, farm products, machinery-equipment-supplies, petroleum and general merchandise groups. Import agents have their largest volume of sales in the grocery-confectionery-meats, edible farm products, metal and metalwork, and the miscellaneous kinds of business groups.

Assemblers of farm products

Some types, such as the assemblers, local buyers, and cooperative marketing associations, handle all types of farm products. Others, such as cream stations and country grain elevators have particular commodity specialization.

The Position of the Middleman Types in the Wholesaling Sector

With the background of Chapter 2 and the preceding sections of this chapter a re-evaluation of the position of each middleman type in the wholesaling sector may be undertaken. This re-evaluation can be made in terms of: (1) relative over-all importance; (2) functional adaptation; (3) kind of business adaptation; and (4) channel position adaptation.

Relative over-all importance

The types of middlemen operations for which census data are available show wide variations in relative importance. Three types— the regular service wholesaler, manufacturers' sales branches, and manufacturers' sales offices—together accounted for 64.9 per cent of total 1954 sales. The remaining merchant wholesalers, eight types, together accounted for only 8 per cent. The agents and brokers ranged in importance from 4.6 per cent for brokers to 0.3 per cent for import agents. All types together accounted for about one sixth of total sales. The petroleum group combined, and all types of assemblers accounted for 6.8 and 3.9 per cent respectively. These wide variations in relative importance highlight, of course, the complex agency structure which has been discussed. Thus, the three major types of operation heavily affect the main pattern of agency structure, but the remaining types introduce the significant shadings of functional and kind of business adaptations.

Functional adaptation

There need only be summarized here what has been discussed before. The wholesaling sector offers a wide variety of middlemen who perform a wide variety of functions designed either to conform to the management needs on the producing side or to management needs on the buying side; or designed to secure for the middleman some feeling of independence at an intermediate level. In addition, a certain proportion of establishments serves as multitype operations, thus adapting their functional activity from transaction to transaction.

Kind of business adaptation

Detailed analyses have been presented already of variations in kind of business adaptations of the various types of operation, ranging from the narrow coverage of petroleum bulk tank stations (and related agencies) to the broad coverage of the regular service wholesaler through all kinds of extractive industry, manufactured industrial goods, and manufactured consumers' goods categories.

What is introduced here, in addition, and as a prelude to the discussion of product assortments in Chapter 7, is a tabulation for the merchant wholesalers and manufacturers' sales branches and sales offices groups of the breakdown of their commodity sales into most important, related lines, and other lines categories (see Table 11). The main purpose of this table is to show the wide ranges between these three categories for various kinds of business. Especially to be noted is that for the merchant wholesalers group, four kinds of

TABLE 11

FREQUENCY DISTRIBUTION OF PERCENTAGE DISTRIBUTION OF MERCHANT WHOLESALERS' AND MANUFACTURERS' SALES BRANCHES AND SALES OFFICES FOR 1954 SALES BY MOST IMPORTANT, RELATED, AND OTHER COMMODITY LINES[a]

Percentage Class	Merchant Wholesalers			Mfrs., Sales Branches, Sales Offices		
	Most Important	Related Lines	Other	Most Important	Related Lines	Other
None	—	14	—	—	4	—
0.1 – 3.9	—	10	9	—	5	9
4.0–7.9	—	12	13	—	1	10
8.0–14.9	—	5	9	—	5	14
15.0–19.9	—	3	10	—	14	7
20.0–29.9	—	2	4	—	11	7
30.0–39.9	—	1	1	—	7	1
40.0–49.9	−1	—	1	5	2	—
50 – 59.9	−2	—	—	9	—	1
60 – 69.9	2	—	—	13	—	—
70 – 79.9	12	—	—	12	—	—
80 – 89.9	15	—	—	4	—	—
90 – 99.9	15	—	—	6	—	—
Total	47	47	47	49	49	49

Source: Author's computations from *1954 Census of Business.*

[a] "Most important lines" are those classes of products which make up a kind of business classification. "Related lines" are those which fall within the same coding group. "Other lines" are unrelated as to coding groups used by the Census.

business had 20 to 30 per cent of their sales accounted for by product lines unrelated to their kinds of business. Similarly, for sales branches and offices, there were seven kinds of business so classified; and, in addition, one kind of business had 50 to 60 per cent of its total sales in unrelated lines. Obviously, these situations reveal the range of functional activity and the multitype of operations referred to above.

Channel position adaptation

Finally, as a prelude to the discussion in Chapter 5, the analysis of agency structure reveals flexibility of the types of operation with respect to channel position. Certain types—the assemblers group, and the petroleum group, for example—are almost completely extractive industry oriented in their channel positions. Other types—manufacturers' sales branches and sales offices, manufacturers' agents, selling agents, and purchasing agents—are manufacturer controlled. The voluntary group wholesalers, chain store buying offices and warehouses, and resident buyers are all examples of retailer-oriented types of middlemen. Finally, the regular service wholesaler, especially, and the brokers as well, are prime examples of multichannel-level-oriented wholesale middlemen.

QUESTIONS AND PROBLEMS

1. What does the word "middleman" connote in its basic sense? in its marketing aspects?
2. Discuss the logic of the criteria used for classifying the various types of wholesale middleman operations.
3. Compare critically the orthodox classification scheme with the suggested new scheme.
4. To what extent does the type of operation depend upon the kind of business? To what extent is the kind of business affected by type of middleman operation?
5. To what extent do you believe that the explanation of "why there are so many types of wholesale middlemen?" has validity. What are your principal areas of disagreement?
6. What is meant by the criteria of competitive efficiency, and how may they be used in understanding the agency structure of wholesaling?
7. From the basic definitions of each type of wholesale middleman, prepare a check list showing the primary and secondary areas of similarity and contrast.
8. To what extent do you believe multitype middleman operations exist in the wholesaling sector?
9. What conclusions can you advance based on the data in Table 2?
10. How do you explain the changes in the importance of type-of-operation groups between 1929 and 1954?
11. What conclusions do you reach by a cross-comparison of type-of-operation groups as to the variety of kinds of business?
12. How do manufacturers' sales offices differ from sales branches so far as kind-of-business characteristics are concerned?
13. Why are there such wide sales-size differences between types of operation and kinds of business?

14. How do you account for the continued large numbers of small and medium sale-size establishments in the wholesaling sector?

15. Why should nonintegrated wholesale middlemen engage in multiunit operations?

16. Write an essay explaining the principal reasons for sharp variations in the average sales per establishment.

17. What, in your opinion, are the main explanations behind the wide variations in operating expenses between the various types of operation and kinds of business?

18. Why are some kinds of manufacturers' sales offices more expensive to operate than sales branches?

19. What is meant by wholesale middleman specialization? What forms does such specialization take?

20. How does the competition between wholesale middlemen manifest itself in its interagency and intra-agency aspects?

21. In your opinion, what are the primary factors influencing interagency competition? intra-agency competition?

22. What conclusions can you present based on the data in Table 6?

CHAPTER INTEGRATING ASSIGNMENTS

1. Summarize the comparative aspects of wholesale middlemen's type of operations, by using the criteria of competitive efficiency in the preparation of a master checklist.

2. Write an essay in which you (a) discuss the general and individual strategy of each wholesale middleman type of operation; and (b) discuss critically and analytically the position of the middleman types in the wholesaling sector.

3. Critically compare an actual wholesale middleman's operation in your city with the basic characteristics of the type as discussed in Chapters 2 and 3. Be sure to explain each basic difference uncovered.

4

The Geographical Structure
of Wholesaling

The preceding discussion of agency structure has developed the framework of the wholesaling sector in its national aspects. But this national accumulative view is, in the same sense as a statistical average, an artificial creation concealing many of the meaningful variations which arise because of geographic factors. None of the economic components of the wholesaling sector are distributed equally per square mile of space. Neither the basic raw materials nor the intermediate stages of industrial goods nor the final purchases of consumers' goods have such geographical symmetry. In addition, wholesale middlemen vary in the extent to which they may be either seller oriented or buyer oriented, or both. Some commodities move through the wholesaling sector only to have additional flows created whereas other products have only one sequence of flow.

The Conceptual Framework of Area Structure

Area structure, in its present context, has reference to the extent to which there are to be found systematic patterns of relationships between the various components of the wholesaling sector and the pertinent spatial units. The initial impact arises from the spatial gaps between where supplies of basic raw materials can be made

74

commercially accessible and the locational patterns of the using manufacturing industries and related business. These initial impacts are enhanced further by the geographic layout of the transportation system by means of which such gaps are bridged. A second level of structure arises in the patterning of spatial arrangements between various components of the wholesale middlemen agency structure. Further spatial arrangements of retailing agencies and of ultimate consumers act as modifying influences at the other end of the commodity flows.

Thus, a series of economic units arise which become oriented and structured in their locational patterns on where raw materials are found; on market-oriented locations; on intermediate locational bases found strategically between producers and markets; on "footloose" or geographical amenities bases; or on multiple-location orientation-pattern bases.[1]

From these preliminary observations, it may be inferred that the geographical exchange of goods will depend basically upon two sets of considerations. First, one area (whatever its economic-geographic size), which finds itself in a *deficit supply* position, must offer either a money price or its equivalent in goods and services, sufficient to generate a flow of the commodity needed from the *surplus-producing* areas. This type of exchange must consider a number of variables: all transportation and related costs; the size and nature of the deficit area's demand based upon the want-need patterns of its population; the impact of total and per capita effective purchasing power; the socio-economic characteristics of the actual and potential consuming population; and differential regional costs of production based, in turn, upon differences in the amount, quality, and relative accessibility of its resources, upon differences in the scale and technology, of production, and upon related factors. It should be noticed, in this connection, that the burdens placed upon the various marketing agencies will vary with the distance of the producing plant from the center of gravity of where the customers for its output are located. There is assumed, of course, a mutuality of wants between areas so that each can obtain the means for paying for its imports in terms of what, in turn, will sell.

Upon the interrelationships of these factors are superimposed the managerial policies of individual businessmen operating in specific types of business situations as these pertain to locational decisions, to selection of types of managerial operations, and to various market-

---

[1] A later section will introduce into the discussion the development of locational theory.

ing decisions involving, among other things, necessary price and nonprice policies. In addition, the patterns of flows of trade reflect the effects of various types of governmental policies as administered and enforced by various levels of government agencies. Obviously, these may serve to promote, to regulate and systematize, or to impede geographic interchange.

A series of wholesale markets arise which are the net resultant of these variables and their interrelationships as well as of accidental factors. As a result, these wholesale markets may be raw-material oriented, as in the case of local agricultural markets. Or, they may develop into strategically located primary centers intermediate between production and secondary wholesale centers or centers of consumption. As will be discussed at a later point, these markets may or may not be designated as organized; and the prices determined in them may be, as a result, systematic or unsystematic in structure. Also geographically arranged channels are created which, in turn, re-enforce the semblance of systematic spatial patterning.

Competition becomes, correspondingly, a matter of rivalry not only between economic units within the same zone of influence of a market but, also between markets and between channels of distribution (or segments thereof) in a geographic framework. Attempts introduced by some managerial agencies to achieve geographic stability are met by vigorous attempts of other management agencies to insure changes in the existing spatial patterns. Thus, the geography of markets becomes a battleground, so to speak, in which much of the management struggle for marketing existence and dominance is crystallized.[2]

The Basic Structure of Extractive and Manufacturing Production in 1954

The wholesaling sector is rooted in the extractive and manufacturing industries both in terms of these industries as initial sources of products to be sold in wholesale markets, and in terms of their importance, as well, as intermediate and final purchases. In this section, some of the basic characteristics of the extractive and manufacturing industries for the United States as a whole will be outlined

---

[2] For the institutional approach in its relation to this discussion see Duddy and Revzan, *Marketing: An Institutional Approach,* 2nd ed. (New York: McGraw-Hill Book Co., Inc., 1953), pp. 26–27 and Appendix C. The relationships between this conceptual framework, the area as a structure, and the economic determinants of wholesale market areas will be deferred until later sections of this chapter.

while geographic variations in the over-all structure of manufacturing will be discussed in the following section.

Structure of Agriculture

Since the agricultural group includes the production of both animals and crops and, within these, variable units of weight are involved, the only common denominator of comparison must be the dollar income received from the marketing of these products together with the value of the products used by farmers for their home consumption. Data for 1954 show that the livestock animals and related products group accounted for over one half of the total receipts of $32.4 billion. Within this group, the meat animals, dairy products, and poultry and eggs categories are the most significant.

All crops combined accounted for 43.7 per cent of the 1954 total receipts. This group is considerably more varied in the component products than in the livestock, etc., category. The single most important crop was cotton, accounting for about one twelfth of the total cash receipts, followed closely by feed crops, feed grains, and vegetables, in this order. Together these four categories (consisting of some 64 separate product classes) accounted for 29 per cent. Fruits, tobacco, and oil-bearing crops were also of significance. Thus, the wholesaling sector must deal with a wide number of agricultural livestock and crop classes having wide variations in physical output and in importance so far as cash receipts are concerned.

Geographic variations in the structure of agriculture

So far as this section is concerned, how did the combined cash receipts from livestock (and products) and crops vary between the geographic divisions and between states? For livestock, the West North Central States (especially Iowa, Minnesota, Missouri, and Nebraska) and the five East North Central States accounted for 54 per cent of the total cash receipts from livestock marketings in 1954.[3] Of importance, also, are California, Texas, Pennsylvania, and New York. Especially interesting is the continued importance of many states which also have, as will be noted later, significant proportions of manufacturing activity. A partial explanation is found in the significance of the dairy industry as mainly market-oriented in its locational structure.

---

[3] It should be kept in mind that nearly $2 billion of livestock and crops were used by farmers for their own home consumption in 1954. The values so used are not distributed geographically in the same relative percentages as for cash receipts.

A much more even distribution exists for the crops as a whole. Five divisions—the West North Central States, the Pacific States, the West South Central States, the South Atlantic States, and the East North Central States—ranged from a high of 18.04 per cent to a low of 14.45 per cent, or a combined position of 78.58 per cent on an individual state basis; wide ranges of importance are apparent from a high of 11.83 per cent for California to a low of 0.04 per cent for Nevada. The California position rests, of course on its very high production of fruits, vegetables, and nuts. The 10 most important crop-producing states[4] together accounted for about 40 per cent of the total receipts from crop marketings. An additional 10 states[5] accounted for nearly one fourth on a combined basis. Again, it is interesting how many of the leading manufacturing states are among the leading crop-producing states.

The mineral industries

The value of all shipments from all minerals industries in 1954 was estimated at $14.9 billion. Nearly two thirds of this value of shipments consisted of crude petroleum and natural gas products and related contract services. Bituminous coal (including lignite) ranked second in value of shipments, followed closely by the nonmetalic, acid-metallic mining industries. Because of the high degree of importance of the petroleum group, the geographical distribution by states is biased. By far the largest percentages were accounted for by Texas, California, Louisiana, Pennsylvania, Oklahoma, and West Virginia. This high degree of geographic concentration has import repercussions, of course, on the locational patterns of the wholesale middlemen handling these products.

The manufacturing industries

The largest and most complicated part of the basic production structure is to be found for the manufacturing industries. Not only are there considerably more categories of products involved than for the agricultural and mineral segments but also the dollar values are several times higher. The basic complexities may be seen, first of all, in the number of industry groups and their component industries, based upon the 2-digit, 3-digit, and 4-digit coding system used by the Bureau of the Census.

[4] California, Texas, Illinois, North Carolina, Iowa, Kansas, Florida, Ohio, Indiana, and Washington, in declining order of importance.
[5] Arkansas Minnesota, Michigan, Missouri, North Dakota, Nebraska, Georgia, Kentucky, Missouri, and Arizona.

From Table 12, it is apparent that the manufacturing industries of the United States may be classified into 21 basic groups (2-digit code) ; and that these 21 groups are further subdivided into 94 3-digit component industries, which may be subdivided again into 445 4-digit

TABLE 12

MAJOR INDUSTRY GROUP CODES, AND COMPONENT
3-DIGIT AND 4-DIGIT INDUSTRIES:
UNITED STATES 1954 (CENSUS OF MANUFACTURES)

Group No.	Major Industry Group	No. of 3-Digit Industries	No. of 4-Digit Industries
20	Food and kindred products	9	42
21	Tobacco manufactures	0	4
22	Textile mill products	7	32
23	Apparel and related products	7	41
24	Lumber and wood products	4	18
25	Furniture and fixtures	5	15
26	Pulp, paper, and products	3	12
27	Printing and publishing	3	16
28	Chemicals and products	9	42
29	Petroleum and coal products	3	7
30	Rubber products	0	4
31	Leather and leather goods	4	12
32	Stone, clay, and glass products	5	27
33	Primary metal industries	5	19
34	Fabricated metal products	6	30
35	Machinery, except electrical	9	41
36	Electrical machinery	3	21
37	Transportation equipment	4	14
38	Instruments and related products	2	10
39	Miscellaneous manufactures	6	38
1900	Ordnance and accessories	0	1

component industries. The food, textile, apparel, chemical, fabricated metals, machinery, and miscellaneous groups have the most complicated classifications of their component industries in terms of 3-digit and 4-digit industry codings.

These 21 industry groups and their component industries operated in 1954 in 286,817 establishments employing 15.7 million persons, and adding an estimated $116.9 billion of value by their respective manufacturing operations. In order to appreciate the geographical structure of these complex groupings, it will be necessary at the outset to visualize the composition of these aggregates. From this dissection process, it will then be possible to investigate the geographical divisions and state patterns as well as the distribution within the more important standard metropolitan areas.

Data are available showing the composition of the manufacturing industries of the United States in terms of distribution of establishments, employment, and value added by major industry groups. Although the detailed data for the 3-digit and 4-digit industries are not included, some comments about them will be included in this section. The data indicate the degree of concentration of importance, with five groups accounting for one half of the value added with only 31.5 per cent of the establishments. The food group, for example, is no longer the single most important industry, yielding that honor to transportation equipment. Nor do the primary and fabricated metals groups rank as high in combined importance as would be expected in a highly industrialized country.

A visual comparison of the percentage of value added by manufacturers with the percentage establishments accounted for gives a combined measure of concentration of large-scale units and the relative value of products for each industry groups. Especially to be noted in this connection were the transportation equipment, primary metals, electrical machinery, and petroleum groups. On the other hand, the printing, apparel, and lumber groups accounted for significantly higher proportions of establishments than of value added by manufacture.

Within the seven most important industry groups, based on value added, the following 3-digit and 4-digit industries were most important:

1. Group No. 37—motor vehicle and equipment, and aircraft and parts industries.
2. Group No. 20—dairy products, beverages, bakery products, and meat products industries.
3. Group No. 35—the metalworking, general industrial, and services and household machinery industries.
4. Group No. 28—organic, inorganic, and drugs and medical chemicals industries.
5. Group No. 33—blast furnaces and steel mills, and iron and steel foundries industries.
6. Group No. 34—structural metal products, metal stamping and coating, and cutlery, tools, hardware industries.
7. Group No. 36—communication equipment, and electrical industrial apparatus industries.

How are these major industry groups distributed by the nine geographic divisions? Two tests of significance may be applied: (1) How the proportion of the United States total value added for each group is distributed within each division, and (2) how important each group is in each division in terms of the division in terms of the division's total value added. On a total basis, the East North Central States and the Middle Atlantic States dominate the manufacturing structure by accounting for 57.2 per cent of the total value added while having only 40.2 per cent of the population and 49.3 per cent of the establishments.

When each division is analyzed in terms of the proportion of the total value accounted for by each industry group relative to the division's over-all average position, the following conclusions may be advanced based on the 1954 data.

1. *New England States:* Leather, textile, rubber, instrument, paper and pulp, and machinery groups.
2. *Middle Atlantic States:* Apparel, electrical machinery, and printing groups.
3. *East North Central States:* Machinery (except electrical), transportation equipment, primary metals, rubber products, and electrical machinery groups.
4. *West North Central States:* Leather, printing, stone, clay, glass, and transportation equipment groups.
5. *South Atlantic States:* Tobacco, textile, furniture, chemicals, and paper and pulp groups.
6. *East South Central States:* Tobacco
7. *West South Central States:* Petroleum
8. *Mountain States:* Lumber and wood products, and petroleum and coal product groups.
9. *Pacific States:* Lumber, transportation equipment, and food groups.

Within each division, relative to its own total value added by manufacture, what were the percentages accounted for each group? In the New England States, the most important were the machinery, electrical machinery, textile transportation equipment, fabricated metals and food groups, in this order. For the Middle Atlantic States the most important were apparel, food, machinery (except electrical), electrical machinery, primary metals, chemicals, printing and publishing, and transportation equipment. The ranking in the East North Central States were transportation equipment, machinery (except electrical), primary metals, food, fabricated metals, electrical machinery, and chemicals. In the West North Central States, food, transportation equipment, machinery (except electrical), chemicals, and printing and publishing were most important. For the South Atlantic States, textiles, chemicals, food transportation equipment, tobacco, primary metals, and pulp and paper were most important. In the East South Central States, the chemicals, food and primary metals groups were very important. In addition, the textiles, fabricated metals, lumber, apparel, pulp and paper and machinery (except electrical), were significant. For the West South Central States, the chemical, food, and petroleum and coal groups were very important, while the transportation equipment, machinery (except electrical), primary metals, and pulp and paper groups were also among the most important. In the Mountain States, the food, primary metals, lumber, chemicals, printing and publishing, and petroleum groups were most significant. Finally, in the Pacific States, the most important groups were transportation equipment, food, and lumber, while in the second level were the fabricated metals, machinery (except electrical), chemicals, primary metals, printing and publishing, paper and pulp, and electrical machinery groups.

While the detailed data presented for the geographic divisions are available by states, it will be sufficient for purposes of this chapter if only summary data are used. New York, Ohio, Pennsylvania, Illinois, Michigan, California, and New Jersey accounted for 5.4 to 12.1 per cent each of the total value added by manufactures in 1954. Their combined importance was 57.8 per cent. As a sidelight, it is interesting to note that, of these several leading industrial states, only California had a percentage of total value equal to its proportion of the population. Only six states—Massachusetts, Connecticut, Indiana, Wisconsin, Missouri, and Texas—accounted for 2 to 5 per cent of the total value added, with a combined importance of 18.3 per cent. This combined importance was about equal to the percentage of population. Thus, even with all of the geographical decentralization of activities which have taken place, manufacturing still continues to show heavy concentrations in these states having significant accumulations of the population.

One final observation needs to be made. Of the states accounting for 2 per cent or more of the total value added by manufacture, only Massachusetts, New York, New Jersey, Pennsylvania, Ohio, Indiana, Illinois, Michigan, and Wisconsin, had significantly larger percentages of total value than of population.

Finally, a brief reference may be made to the concentration of manufactures in urban areas. Table 13 summarizes the distribution

TABLE 13

LEADING STANDARD METROPOLITAN AREAS,
VALUE ADDED BY MANUFACTURE: UNITED STATES 1954

Standard Metropolitan Area	Per Cent of Total Value Added by Manufacture
1 New York-Northeastern New Jersey	11.22
2 Chicago	6.75
3 Los Angeles	4.31
4 Detroit	4.03
5 Philadelphia	3.44
6 Pittsburgh	2.12
7 Cleveland	2.05
8 St. Louis	1.76
9 Boston	1.69
10 Buffalo	1.44
11 San Francisco-Oakland	1.43
12 Baltimore	1.32
13 Milwaukee	1.23
14 Cincinnati	1.13
Total	43.92
50 Additional standard metropolitan areas	20.86
Grand total—64 areas	64.78

of value added by manufacture for the principal standard metropolitan areas. Sharp variations in importance are apparent immediately between the 14 most important areas, with a range from 1.13 to 11.22 per cent each. Together, they accounted for 43.9 per cent of the total value added. Of this amount, 26.3 per cent was concentrated in four areas—New York, Chicago, Los Angeles, and Detroit. The combined 64 standard metropolitan areas accounted for nearly two thirds of the total value added in the United States in 1954.

The Geographic Structure of Wholesaling in 1954: Establishments and Sales

Although a book could be written about the available census data of wholesale trade, this section and the sections which follow will deal only with some of the principal geographic characteristics. The discussion as in the preceding sections will deal only with the 1954 situation as revealed by *Census of Business* data. As in preceding sections, the important geographic units will be the divisions, states, and standard metropolitan areas. This section will deal primarily with the distribution of establishments and sales in 1954.

Distribution, by geographic divisions

More than one half of the wholesale trade of the United States in 1954 was done by establishments in the Middle Atlantic and East North Central States (see Table 14). These divisions accounted for

TABLE 14

PERCENTAGE DISTRIBUTION OF WHOLESALE
ESTABLISHMENTS AND STATES BY GEOGRAPHIC
DIVISIONS: UNITED STATES 1954

Rank (Sales)	Division	Establishments	Sales
7	New England	5.73	4.97
1	Middle Atlantic	23.77	29.23
2	East North Central	19.58	21.73
4	West North Central	12.04	10.11
5	South Atlantic	10.42	9.33
8	East South Central	4.47	4.37
6	West South Central	9.10	7.34
9	Mountain	3.97	2.49
3	Pacific	10.91	10.43
	Total	100	100

only slightly more than two fifths of the population. The Pacific and West North Central States together accounted for 20.5 per cent of the wholesale trade while containing 19.4 per cent of the population.

If comparisons are made in Table 14 between the percentage of establishments accounted for in each division and the percentage of sales, it is apparent that only the establishments in the Middle Atlantic and East North Central States had proportionately higher sales. The establishments in the East South Central States had relatively the same percentages of sales as of establishments. In the remaining divisions, the proportion of establishments exceeded that of sales, especially in the West North Central, West South Central, and Mountain States.

Distribution, by states

It will be sufficient for purposes of this presentation to confine the data to be included to only the more important states. On an over-all basis, the number of establishments ranged from a low of 0.13 per cent in Nevada to a high of 15.06 per cent in New York. Similarly, for sales, the range of importance for the states for which data were available was from 0.19 per cent for New Mexico to a high of 21.01 per cent for New York.

Table 15 presents the data for all states, each of which accounting for 1.5 per cent or more of the total volume of 1954 sales. The high degree of geographic concentration is shown by the top 5 states which accounted for nearly one half of wholesale trade, with only 40.2 per cent of the establishments and 35.5 per cent of the population. At the opposite extreme, 31 states and the District of Columbia accounted

TABLE 15

PERCENTAGE DISTRIBUTION OF WHOLESALE
ESTABLISHMENTS AND SALES BY LEADING STATES:
UNITED STATES 1954

States and District of Columbia	Establishments	Sales	Population
New York	15.06	21.01	9.82
Illinois	6.54	8.68	5.68
California	7.88	7.92	7.76
Pennsylvania	5.97	5.70	6.73
Ohio	4.75	5.37	5.49
Total—5 states	40.20	48.68	35.48
Texas	5.45	4.70	5.25
Michigan	3.74	4.29	4.39
Missouri	3.01	3.49	2.56
Massachusetts	3.14	3.19	3.00
New Jersey	2.74	2.52	3.24
Total—5 states	18.08	18.19	18.44
Minnesota	2.42	2.33	1.94
Tennessee	1.54	1.94	2.09
Georgia	1.78	1.94	2.25
Indiana	2.33	1.87	2.63
North Carolina	1.88	1.78	2.62
Iowa	2.24	1.59	1.65
Wisconsin	2.22	1.52	2.25
Total—7 states	14.41	12.97	15.43
Total 31 states and Dist. of Columbia	27.31	20.16	30.65
Grand total—United States	100	100	100

for 30.7 per cent of the population, but only one-fifth of the sales.

Among the 17 states which accounted for four fifths of all sales in 1954, only 7 had substantially higher proportions of sales than of establishments, and only 4 states had substantially higher proportions of sales than of population. Especially significant in this respect was New York with 21 per cent of sales and only 9.8 per cent of the population. For four states, there was a substantial balance of proportions of establishments and of sales, and of proportions of sales with those for the population. All in all, the geographic arrangements of wholesale trade, by states, show as much concentration of importance as was evident in the preceding discussion of manufactures.

Distribution, by standard metropolitan areas

Because of restrictions on disclosure of data which have been placed on the Bureau of the Census, data of total wholesale sales are not available for every standard metropolitan area. However, such data are available for most of the important standard metropolitan areas. On a combined basis, 168 areas accounted for 84.7 per cent of the wholesale sales, with only two thirds of the establishments.

For the 168 standard metropolitan areas, the following distribution of establishment was found, based on 1950's population sizes: (1) Areas with 1,000,000 or more persons each—37.4 per cent; (2) areas with 500,000 to 999,999 each—10.3 per cent; (3) areas with 300,000—to 499,999 persons each—6.6 per cent; (4) areas with 200,000 to 299,999 persons each—5.7 per cent; (5) areas with 100,000 to 199,999 persons each—5.9 per cent; and (6) remaining areas with less than 100,000 persons each—1.1 per cent.

Table 16 summarizes the percentages of establishments and sales for these standard metropolitan areas accounting for 1 per cent or more of the 1954 trade.[6]

The wide range of relative importance is again apparent from these data, with the New York and Chicago metropolitan areas accounting for one half of the combined sales importance of the 15 most important areas in 1954. All of the 15 areas had significantly higher proportions of wholesale sales than they did of establishments. This is indicative, among other things, of the higher-than-average sales per establishment to be found in these most important trading centers.

---

[6] This excludes those standard metropolitan areas which might have met the criterion, but for which total sales data for 1954 were not disclosed.

TABLE 16

PERCENTAGE DISTRIBUTION OF WHOLESALE SALES AND
ESTABLISHMENTS, STANDARD METROPOLITAN AREAS
ACCOUNTING FOR ONE PER CENT OR MORE OF SALES
IN 1954

	Metropolitan Area	Establishments	Sales
1	New York-Northeastern New Jersey	14.12	20.62
2	Chicago	4.32	7.26
3	Philadelphia	3.64	4.48
4	Los Angeles	2.62	3.91
5	Detroit	1.83	3.15
6	Boston	2.12	2.57
7	San Francisco-Oakland	1.86	2.49
8	St. Louis	1.30	1.94
9	Cleveland	1.24	1.80
10	Minneapolis-St. Paul	0.99	1.76
11	Pittsburgh	1.24	1.51
12	Kansas City	0.83	1.39
13	Cincinnati	0.75	1.33
14	Dallas	0.82	1.27
15	Memphis	0.43	1.05
	Total 15 areas	38.11	56.53
	Total—all standard metropolitan areas	66.99	84.73

The Geographic Structure of Wholesaling in 1954:
Types-of-Operation Groups

Just as for manufactures, wholesale trade consists of a complex
number of types of operation and kinds of business. This section is
concerned with tracing the geographic structure of the major types-
of-groups into which 20 individual types of operation are classified.[7]
Preceding analyses have dealt with the United States cross-sectional
view of the pattern of kinds of business: 160 kinds for merchant
wholesalers; 67 kinds for manufacturers' sales branches and sales
offices; 4 kinds of petroleum group, terminals; 63 kinds of merchandise
agents and brokers; and 10 kinds of assemblers of farm products.

[7] Merchant wholesalers; manufacturers' sales branches and sales offices; petroleum bulk plants, terminals; agents and brokers; and assemblers of farm products.

General variations by type-of-operation groups

Previous discussions have emphasized the geographic variations of middlemen's operations. No better illustration can be given of the urban orientation of some groups as compared with the nonurban orientation of others than by reference to the data of Appendix Table A2. The significant relationships may be summarized as follows:

1. In terms of establishments, the merchant wholesalers, manufacturers' sales branches and sales offices, and agents and brokers show substantially above average concentrations in cities having 100,000 or more persons.
2. On the other hand, the petroleum and assemblers groups show even more bias towards these parts of the United States having fewer than 5,000 persons.
3. In terms of sales, the merchant wholesaler group closely approximates the national average, whereas the sales-office sales-branch and agents and brokers groups are heavily oriented toward cities with 500,000 or more persons each.
4. The petroleum and assemblers groups are heavily oriented toward cities with 5,000 to 24,999 persons or, more important, to the remaining incorporated and unincorporated places.

Thus, the petroleum and assemblers groups, as the definitions of their component subtypes of operations have indicated, are based upon the extractive industries whereas the remaining groups have a more universal kind of business orientation.

Regional variations, by type-of-operation groups

While Appendix Table A2 establishes the basic urban-nonurban aspects of each type-of-operation group, some further treatment of variations by regions and states may be of value. Obviously, the regional and state data are influenced to a considerable extent by the composition of the urban and nonurban areas located within their respective political boundaries. This is true both as to the number and population sizes of the incorporated and unincorporated places. Table 17 contains the pertinent percentage distributions of establishments and sales.

So far as sales importance is concerned, the merchant wholesaler group concentrated primarily in the Middle Atlantic, East North Central, and Pacific States. Only the first two of these divisions dominate the manufacturers' sales branch-sales office group, while the

TABLE 17

WHOLESALE TRADE: 1954 SALES AND ESTABLISHMENTS
BY TYPE OF OPERATION GROUP, BY GEOGRAPHIC DIVISIONS

Division (Sales Ranking)	Merchant Whole- salers	Sales Branches, Sales Offices	Petro- leum Group	Agents and Brokers	Assem- blers	Total
			Sales			
1 Middle Atlantic	30.14	32.00	18.50	31.85	5.48	29.23
2 East North Central	19.13	25.93	20.44	20.52	25.93	21.73
3 Pacific	11.30	9.91	11.28	8.29	12.51	10.43
4 West North Central	8.92	7.52	9.97	13.57	28.49	10.11
5 South Atlantic	8.99	9.04	14.65	8.89	7.92	9.33
6 West South Central	8.76	6.06	8.12	5.76	6.71	7.34
7 New England	5.50	4.89	7.04	3.68	1.62	4.97
8 East South Central	4.72	3.11	5.76	5.00	4.84	4.37
9 Mountain	2.53	1.53	4.23	2.44	6.51	2.49
U. S. Total	100.00	100.00	100.00	100.00	100.00	100.00
			Establishments			
1 Middle Atlantic	28.44	20.58	6.12	27.27	4.14	23.77
2 East North Central	18.86	22.28	20.75	20.21	20.29	19.58
3 Pacific	11.24	12.54	8.67	11.15	8.58	10.91
4 West North Central	8.00	9.88	25.60	9.63	40.29	12.04
5 South Atlantic	10.52	11.67	10.33	11.12	6.16	10.42
6 West South Central	8.73	9.30	12.67	7.46	8.38	9.10
7 New England	6.66	6.39	2.27	5.10	1.61	5.73
8 East South Central	4.34	4.01	5.68	5.44	2.64	4.47
9 Mountain	3.22	3.36	7.92	2.63	7.91	3.97
U. S. Total	100.00	100.00	100.00	100.00	100.00	100.00

South Atlantic, West South Central, New England, East South Central, and Mountain States have above normal proportions of sales for the petroleum group. Above-normal percentages of agents and brokers are found in the Middle Atlantic, West North Central, and East South Central States, reflecting, in part, the agricultural bases of much of these types of operations. Finally, proportionately heavy concentrations of assemblers' sales are found in the West North Central and Mountain States and, to a lesser extent, in the East North Central and Pacific States.

It will be noticed, also from Table 17 that considerable variations are found between divisions as to the proportion of sales for each group relative to the proportion of establishments. At one extreme, the Middle Atlantic States have consistently higher proportions of sales for each type-of-operation group than of establishments. The Mountain States, on the other hand, have exactly the reverse set of relationships. Various combinations between these two extremes exist for the remaining divisions. Thus, the East North Central States have significantly higher proportions of sales than of establishments for 3 of the 5 type-of-operation groups.

Variations, by states

Finally, a summary reference may be made to the variations in percentages of sales by state groupings. The sharp range of variations for each state grouping by type-of-operation group is shown for 1954 in Table 18. Especially to be noted are the proportionately high

TABLE 18

CUMULATIVE PERCENTAGES OF 1954 WHOLESALE SALES, BY TYPE OF MIDDLEMAN GROUPS, BY STATE GROUPS

State Group	Merchant Wholesalers	Sales Branches, Sales Offices	Petroleum Group	Agents and Brokers	Assemblers	Total, 5 Types
Highest 5 states	53.19	60.81	36.01	55.97	45.83	53.38
Next 5 states	17.59	18.37	21.66	18.21	19.38	17.76
Third 5 states	10.07	7.73	13.25	10.46	13.05	10.17
Remaining 33 states (and Dist. of Columbia)	19.15	13.09	29.08	15.36	21.74	18.69
Total	100.00	100.00	100.00	100.00	100.00	100.00

percentages of sales-branch sales-office sales to be found in the highest 5 states group, as compared with the very low percentage of sales for the petroleum group. Conversely, the lowest 33 states and the District of Columbia had very high proportions of the petroleum group, and very low percentages of the manufacturers' sales-branch sales-office group.

Distribution of Principal Kinds of Business: 1954

No attempt will be made to present here the voluminous series data showing geographic variations in the distribution of wholesale trade by kinds of business within each type-of-operation group. Only some of the main tendencies will be summarized.

Merchant wholesalers group, by geographic divisions

In 7 of the 9 divisions, the grocery-confectionery-meats group was the single most important kind of business. Only in the West North Central and East South Central States was this kind of business displaced by the farm products (raw materials) group. The machinery-equipment-supplies kind ranked among the top half dozen kinds of business in all divisions; and the electrical-electronics-appliance group in all except the West South Central States.

In all other cases, the most important kind of business reflected regional specialization. Thus, in New England and especially in the Middle Atlantic States, the dry goods and apparel groups were very important. Metals and metalwork also ranked as very important in the latter division. The lumber and construction materials business ranked among the six most important kinds in the East North Central, West North Central, South Atlantic, East South Central, Mountain, and Pacific States. The raw-materials farm-products business was, in addition to its top importance as noted, also of significance in the Middle Atlantic, East North Central, South Atlantic, and West South Central States. Finally, the edible farm products kind ranked sixth in importance in the Pacific States.

Sales branches, by geographic divisions

Some sharp variations are apparent from the pattern for merchant wholesalers. The food and kindred products group was dominant in six divisions—New England, Middle Atlantic, South Atlantic, East South Central, Mountain, and Pacific States. In the remaining three divisions, the transportation equipment group was dominant. Electrical machinery, and machinery (except electrical) ranked among the most important kinds of business in all divisions as did the chemicals and allied products group. Leather and leather products, and the rubber products group were significant in New England, while the primary metals group was important in the Middle Atlantic States.

Sales offices, by geographic divisions

Because this type of operation does not carry inventories, the geographic patterns of important kinds of business in which they are found vary considerably from the preceding types. In all divisions, except the South Atlantic States, the primary metals group was the most important kind; in the South Atlantic States, the food and kindred products group was dominant. The chemicals and food groups were also among the most significant in all divisions. Other kinds of business ranked among the most important in each division in the following patterns: (1) Electrical machinery in New England; (2) fabricated metals in the Middle Atlantic, East North Central, West North Central, South Atlantic, West South Central, and Pacific divisions; (3) paper and pulp products in the Middle Atlantic,

Mountain and Pacific states; (4) textile mill products in the Middle Atlantic States; and (5) the stone-clay-glass group in the East North Central, West North Central, East South Central, West South Central, Mountain, and Pacific States.

Agents and brokers, by geographic divisions

This group of middlemen are considerably more oriented to farm products than any of the preceding types-of-operation groups. Thus, the raw-materials farm-products group is highest in proportionate significance in the East North Central, West North Central, South Atlantic, East South Central, West South Central, and Mountain States, while ranking among the most important in the remaining divisions. The grocery-confectionery-meat group is most important in the New England, Middle Atlantic, and Pacific States, and ranks among the top kinds of business in the remaining divisions. Other kinds of business groups having particular regional significance were as follows: (1) Machinery-equipment-supplies in New England, Middle Atlantic, East North Central, West South Central, and Pacific States; (2) edible farm products in the New England, Middle Atlantic, East North Central, South Atlantic, and Pacific States; (3) dry goods, piece goods, and apparel groups in the Middle Atlantic States; (4) the automotive group in the East North Central States; (5) and the lumber-construction materials and electrical-electronics-appliances groups in the Pacific States.

Variations in kinds of business, by urban unit

One measure of the variations found in the distribution of wholesale trade in cities is based on the proportion of such trade, by kinds of business, done in cities having 500,000 or more persons each. The wide range of importance of the large cities reflects, among other things, the influence of the following variables:

1. The kind of business in relation to the income levels of the users.
2. The locational patterns of the manufacturing industries producing such products.
3. The locational patterns of the users of such products, including the manufacturing industries and other business establishments.
4. The presence or absence of organized wholesale commodity markets in this size of city.
5. The nature of the channels of distribution used by the kind of business group.
6. The nature and size of the trading area found for these cities for each kind of business group.

The Geographic Structure of Wholesale Trade in 1954:
Sales Size of Establishments

A final view of the geographic structure of wholesale trade may be obtained by studying the distribution of the sales size of merchant wholesalers' establishments by city-size groupings. The following conclusions may be advanced. All population sizes of areas contain a wide range of sales sizes of merchant wholesalers' establishments. Cities having 100,000 or more persons have much higher relative importance so far as representing locations for establishments which had sales of $2 million or more per establishment. Cities having 5,000 persons to 500,000 persons were proportionately much more important for the $1 million to $2 million sales-size group. Cities having 5,000 to 100,000 persons, and the "remainder-of-the-United States" group, are proportionately more important for the less than $1 million sales-size group.

So far as the distribution of establishments is concerned relative to the distribution of sales size for each city-size group, there is a sharp increase in the proportion of establishments as the sales-size category declines. Thus, even in cities having 500,000 or more persons, for example, there were nearly seven times more establishments in the less than $200,000 sales-size group than in the $2,000,000 and over group, although they accounted for only about one twelfth of the total sales.

Types of Theory Available for Analyzing
the Area Structure of Wholesaling[8]

In trying to analyze systematically the wide variety of geographical patterns indicated in the preceding section of this chapter, recourse must be taken to various theoretical and applied tools of analysis. The theoretical tools to be discussed in this section are concerned with the economic theory of the location of manufactures, the economic theory of the law of market areas, and measures of regional trade balances.

[8] No attempt is made here to present the actual theory involved together with the mathematical representation. The reader interested in the theory should refer to the references cited in this section, and for those listed under this chapter in the bibliography at the end of the book.

The economic theory of the location of manufactures

There has been a considerable volume of high-quality literature devoted to the economic theory of location since the beginning of the 20th century. Most critics agree that, although Von Thunen's work in 1826 furnished a very excellent beginning, it was not until the appearance of Weber's work in 1909 that a real framework of a general location theory was provided.[9]

Although there were a few attempts made at improving Weber's framework, the next important step did not appear until 1925 in the writings of Andreas Predohl.[10] Although the Germans continued to dominate this field, with their work appearing in German,[11] the next important advancement was obtained from the translations of the works of August Losch.[12] A further major contribution in integrating location theory with a theory of interregional and international trade came with Bertil Ohlin's work issued in 1933.[13]

Since the development of the writings of the European (especially German) school, three important contributions have been made by American scholars. The first of these appeared in 1948, written by Edgar M. Hoover,[14] based on a series of empirical studies. This study attempted to establish a theoretical framework for analyzing locational preferences and patterns, locational change and adjustments, the locational significance of political boundaries, and the relationships of locational theory and public policy. It is generally

[9] The English translation did not appear until 1929. See Carl J. Friederich (Ed.), *Alfred Weber's Theory of the Location of Industries* (Chicago: The University of Chicago Press, 1929).

[10] Again, while his original writing in German appeared in 1925, a briefer version in English did not appear until 1928 as "The Theory of Location in its Relation to General Economics," *The Journal of Political Economy*, XXXVI (June 1928), 371–390.

[11] See the discussions by Walter Isard in *Location and Space-Economy: A General Theory Relating to Industrial Location, Market Areas, Hand Use Trade, and Urban Structure* (New York: John Wiley & Sons, Inc., 1956), Chapter 2 and the excellent bibliography of writings in foreign languages.

[12] August Losch developed his theoretical framework in writings in German appearing in the 1930's and early 1940's. Reference is made here to "The Nature of Economics Regions," *Southern Economic Journal*, V (July 1938), 71–78. More recently his theory has appeared in book form, *The Economics of Location* (translated by William H. Woglow and W. F. Stalper) (New Haven: Yale University Press, 1954).

[13] Bertil Ohlin, *Interregional and International Trade*, Harvard Economic Studies, Vol. XXXIX (Cambridge, Mass.: Harvard University Press, 1933).

[14] Edgar M. Hoover, *The Location of Economic Activity* (New York: McGraw-Hill Book Co., Inc., 1948).

agreed that this is a general theory and not too applicable to individual management units seeking locations.

The second American contribution was written by Melvin L. Greenhut, and was published in 1955.[15] He reviews and appraises selected contributions, analyzes the most important factors influencing plant location, appraises a selected number of empirical studies, and then advances a general theory of plant location.[16] The following year (1956) appeared the book by Isard, in which he develops his theory around such topics as posing the location and regional problem; some general theories and empirical regularities; transport inputs; locational equilibrium; market and supply area analysis and competitive locational equilibrium; agricultural location theory; interrelationships of location and trade theory; and a general location theory, including a mathematical formulation.

The law of market areas

Two important contributions have been made to a framework of economic theory and the law of market areas. The first formulation was by Frank A. Fetter.

The boundary line between the territories tributary to two geographically competing real markets for like goods is a hyperbolic curve. At each point on this line the difference between freights from the two markets is just equal to the difference between the prevailing market prices, whereas on either side of the line the freight difference and the price difference are unequal. The relation of prices in the two markets determines the location of the boundary line: the lower the price in a market relative to that of a neighboring market, the larger the tributary area.[17]

Based upon this law, Fetter thus establishes the relationships that market territories may vary inversely either with increases of base prices or of freight rates relative to those of their geographical competitors. For buying markets, the higher the relative market price, the larger the tributary area from which sellers are attracted in

[15] Melvin L. Greenhut, *Plant Location in Theory and in Practice: The Economics of Space* (Chapel Hill, N. C.: The University of North Carolina Press, 1955).

[16] For a very excellent article review of both the Losch and the Greenhut books, see E. T. Grether, "The Economics of Space: a Review Article," *The Journal of Marketing,* XXI (January 1957), 369–375.

[17] Fetter's initial statement was stated in "The Economic Law of Market Areas," *Quarterly Journal of Economics,* XXXVIII (May 1924), 520–529; and was repeated later in *The Masquerade of Monopoly* (New York: Harcourt, Brace and Co., Inc., 1931), Chapter 20. On page 284 of the latter reference, he presents a graphic illustration of his law.

competition with other markets. For selling markets, the reverse relationship holds true, namely, that the tributary area from which buyers are attracted becomes larger as a markets' relation price becomes lower.

As will be discussed later, Fetter's law has important meaning for and application to the determination of the boundaries of supply and distribution areas. One of its principal limitations as stated is, of course, its applicability only to a single set of markets, A versus B, rather than to multiple sets of markets and their intercompetitive structure. In addition, the Hysons[18] have demonstrated that Fetter's law is a special statement of a more general law describing hypercircles as follows:

> In summary, the economic law of market areas should be more generally stated as follows: The boundary line between the territories tributary to two geographically competing markets for like goods is a *hypercircle*. At each point on this curve the difference between freight costs from the two markets is just equal to the difference between the market prices, whereas on either side of this line the freight differences and the price differences are unequal. The ratio of the freight rates from the two markets, determine the location of the boundary line; the higher the relative price and the lower the freight rate, the larger the tributary area (p. 324).

Measures of regional trade balances

In addition to the economic theory of plant location and the economic law of market areas, additional progress has been made in developing the theoretical framework by the analysis of interregional trade flows and regional trade balances. The work of Walter Isard and the Federal Reserve District Banks may be noted in this connection.[19] The Isard approach is a useful tool, still in its pioneering stages, in applying the Leontief system of input-output analysis to

[18] C. D. Hyson and W. P. Hyson, "The Economic Law of Market Areas," *Quarterly Journal of Economics,* LXIV (May 1950), 319–327. This article should be consulted for the figures and the important mathematical equations and proof.

[19] Walter Isard, "Regional Commodity Balances and Interregional Commodity Flows," *American Economic Review,* XLIII (May 1953), Papers and Proceedings of the Sixty-Fifth Annual Meeting, pp. 167–198; and Discussion, pp. 199–202.

Guy Freutel, "The Eighth District Balance of Trade," *Monthly Review of the Federal Reserve Bank of St. Louis* (June 1952).

Monthly Review of the Federal Reserve Bank of San Francisco, "Twelfth District Interregional Trade—1950" (September 1952); and "Twelfth District Commodity Trade—1950" (June 1955).

See also: Edward L. Ullman, *Maps of State-to-State Freight Movements for 13 States of the United States in 1948* (mimeographed); and related reports. Stuart Daggett, *Principles of Inland Transportation,* 4th ed. (New York: Harper Bros., 1955), Chapters 10, 11.

the determination of regional commodity flows and net balances. Thus, both the Isard and the Federal Reserve types of studies are the beginnings of useful theoretical tools in linking the locational patterns of the extractive and manufacturing industries with those for wholesale trade as discussed in preceding sections of this chapter.

Empirical Studies of Wholesale Trading Areas: The Case of Organized Wholesale Markets

Two types of empirical analyses will be summarized in this and the following sections. The first type to be discussed in this section is based upon analysis of supply and distribution areas for certain agricultural products where systematic price series are available as the result of the existence and activities of organized wholesale markets. These analyses build, as has been noted, upon the Fetter theoretical framework noted above. The second group of analyses provides for those marketing situations where no systematic price data are available because of the absence of organized wholesale markets.

The determinants of the boundaries of organized wholesale market areas[20]

Since it has been indicated that wholesale trade has a two-directional focus, namely, producer-oriented flows and user-oriented flows, it follows that a wholesale trade area is the net result of the functioning of a wholesale market as a center of gravity to which goods are attracted from single or multiple center points of production and the dispersing center from which goods move to various classes of customers. These modern wholesale markets are, at any given moment of time, based upon a wide variety of evolutionary forces. At the same time, a hierarchy of wholesale markets develops in which the key group—the *primary central markets*—attracts goods from a series of local or concentrating wholesale markets and distributes these, in turn, through a series of secondary or dispersing markets either to industrial or to retail types of customers. Through the application of the tools of analysis, the described areas of *potential* supply and distribution may be determined and compared with actual areas.

[20] Much of the following discussion is based upon the author's work with Professor Edward A. Duddy at the University of Chicago in the period 1930–1943. See the bibliography applicable to this chapter, and Duddy and Revzan, *op. cit.*, Chapter XXIV.

Factors influencing boundaries

Building upon this base, it is very simple to determine actual supply and distribution areas for those organized commodity markets where public agencies and such private agencies as the transportation companies have compiled accurate data of receipts, shipments, etc. But, in interpreting the patterns revealed from the systematic analysis of such data and especially when relating them to the boundaries of the potential areas, the following factors operating either singly or in combination are applicable.

1. *Product weight relative to value.* Where transportation costs are a small percentage of the total value of the product because the products' value is high relative to its bulk and weight, the supply and distribution areas may be expected to have wider boundaries than if the reverse were the case. Low-value situations may be offset, in part, by the existence of special commodity freight rates and, if the movement is by rail, special transit privileges. In the competition between trade centers, as will be noted, it is the differential relationships between these characteristics which are important, and not the absolute relationships.

2. *Relative perishability.* Where such protective devices as canning, fast freezing, and storage are not available, or are *differentially* available, perishability restricts the size of both the supply and distribution areas. The distribution of fresh milk, ice cream, and bread are all pertinent illustrations. Sharp improvements in the speed of transportation may significantly widen the area if the product's value permits. Note in this connection the wholesale distribution of fresh flowers by air cargo express.

3. *Product differentiation techniques.* To the extent that manufacturers are successful through their marketing programs in establishing strong national brands for their products, to that extent will the areas of distribution for these products be widened. Similarly, integrated wholesale and retail middlemen may build wide areas of distribution for their private (distributor-controlled) brands. To the extent that public or private agencies may establish standardization of products, the products so standardized will have wider wholesale distribution than unstandardized products.

4. *Factors affecting plant location.* From the economic theory of plant location (see above) and from many empirical studies,

systematic statements of the factors which influence plant location have been evolved. The net resultant of the operation of such factors is the differentiation of the orientation of plant locations at sites accessible to raw materials sources because of perishability, labor supply, and transportation cost factors, for example; to consuming market sites because of cost factors, size of market, customer preferences for freshness, or for similar reasons; at intermediate locations because of the balancing of inbound and outbound cost factors against the advantages of an intermediate location; or on the so-called footloose basis because of the desire to maximize the amenities aspect of location against the economic factors.

5. *Prices and price policies.* In uncontrolled, organized markets, differential prices become, as in Fetter's law, the primary determinants of potential supply and distribution areas. For unorganized markets, prices and price differentials are much more difficult to determine, and the competitive structure of the industry has a marked effect upon the boundaries of the wholesale trading area.

6. *Transportation rates and services.* The structure of freight rates in terms of the presence or absence of special commodity rates, the type and amount of progression of rates with distance, the relationship between rail and truck rates, the relationship by quantity levels, the relationship between raw materials and finished products rates, and the relationship between rates and transit privileges, all affect the differential relationships between competing markets. In addition, these relationships are affected by whether or not changes in freight rates are made on proportionately equal terms.

Rate relationships may be adversely or favorably affected by the transportation service, including: (a) the layout of the transportation network; (b) the relative speed of travel; (c) frequency of schedules; (d) dependability of service; (e) provision of special heating and refrigeration protective services; (f) provision of special wholesale market facilities such as hold yards, terminals, auction facilities, and warehouse facilities.

7. *Individual firm's marketing methods.* As will be seen from the discussion of managerial policies, the decisions of the individual firms as to marketing functions and channels of distribution either enhance or reduce the significance of particular trade centers.

8. *Auxiliary services.* Finally, the influence of organized wholesale markets is expanded by the use of methods of systematic circulation of price and related market information; by providing specialized physical facilities in which the activities of middlemen may be housed; and by providing for specialized financial and other types of institutions and services.

Market areas of single-product markets under special circumstances[21]

The classic examples to cite here are the various studies of the milksheds of metropolitan markets. Since most milksheds have stringent health board supervision, and either State or Federal regulations of prices, definitions of product classes, and related items, the determination of the market area becomes a special case. The following summary is useful:

According to the research technique, milk and cream zones were developed for each market simultaneously with the development of efficient price relationships. Considering the Northeast as a whole, the fall milk zone assumes a concentric shape from the Atlantic Seaboard, 280 miles from Portsmouth and 350 miles from Boston by truck. In the flush period, comparable distances are 150 and 200 miles. A flat 15 percent increase in the supply causes a contraction of about 80 miles in this arc; a 9.1 percent decline in fluid milk consumption is responsible for a somewhat smaller contraction. . . .[22]

Actual and potential market areas

Duddy and Revzan completed a series of studies between 1930 and 1941 dealing with the delineation of actual and potential supply and distribution areas for several agricultural products. The potential area may be defined as that area in which sales may be made from the wholesale center (distribution area) or from which products may be purchased (supply area) at a return which is larger than that which may be obtained by the wholesale middlemen at other wholesale centers with which the given center is in competition.

The general research procedure used was to obtain data that show the actual geographic origins of the agricultural product received at

[21] For a full discussion of this example see Duddy and Revzan, *op. cit.,* pp. 425–426.

See also: James Stepp, *The Economics of Price in the Milk Industry,* Report of the Bureau of Public Administration, Series, B No. 9 (Charlottesville, Va.: University of Virginia, 1943, mimeographed), Chapter 3.

William Bredo, and Anthony S. Rojko, *Prices and Milksheds of North-Eastern Markets,* Northeast Regional Publication No. 9 (Amherst, Mass.: University of Massachusetts Agricultural Experiment Station), Bulletin No. 470 (August 1952).

[22] See Bredo and Rojko, *op. cit.,* for an excellent statement of the theoretical relationships.

competing centers or that show actual shipments from the market involved. Against this was compared the potential area based upon an extension of Fetter's law. Price differentials were computed on minimum, average, and maximum seasonal bases, and these were then related to differential transportation costs and services. From such analyses, the general shape of the supply area for a given commodity class for the Chicago market was an ellipse with an east-west direction, with the Chicago market as the eastern focus. For the distribution areas, the elliptical shape (with east-west direction) was maintained, but the Chicago market now became the western focus. Where geographical barriers such as mountains or oceans intruded, the elliptical shape took a north-south rather than east-west bias.

When actual and potential supply and distribution areas are compared, the failure of the actual area to conform exactly to the boundaries of the theoretical potential area is evidence of the existence of qualitative factors not assured in the differential price-freight relationships. But the potential area boundaries also serve to provide the wholesale middlemen in the trade center with a guide against which their actual geographic outreach may be measured.

Dynamics of supply and distribution areas

Considering the type of relationship used to determine the boundaries of the potential market areas, it should be clear that any change in either the price or the freight rate part of the relationship will change the boundaries as determined. In addition, changes in the existing technology of transportation will probably work to the disadvantage of existing centers and to the advantage of new centers. The conversion of raw materials into new, higher value products, usually enlarges the outreach of the wholesale market. Where prices change frequently, boundaries may have to be determined according to both seasonal and long-run average differentials.

Empirical Studies of Wholesale Trading Areas: The Case of Unorganized Wholesale Markets

Under conditions of the existence of organized wholesale markets, the determination of trading area boundaries can be based upon the use of systematic wholesale prices which would apply to the entire supply of the commodity marketed and to the middlemen members of the organized market. With the existence of unorganized markets, the determination of trading area boundaries becomes much more an individual management decision and less a group decision. It is true, of course, that as long as various forms of administered price policies exist, the determination does become an industry group affair. It is true, also, that individual managements can decide to use trading area boundaries determined by some private or governmental agency.

Types of trading area situations

Given the characteristic of the absence of an organized wholesale market, the following types of trading area situations may exist: (1) Production of highly specialized industrial goods used by highly specialized classes of customers; (2) widely used and distributed industrial goods; (3) manufactured consumers goods involving highly selective retail distribution; (4) manufactured consumers goods with broad, intensive geographic coverage of retail outlets; and (5) the restricted manufacturing situation in which the owner-manager must assume the bulk of the marketing functions, including actual selling.

In all of these trading area situations, there are certain beginning constants. For one thing, there must be adequate knowledge on the part of management as to how many accounts can accurately and adequately be serviced each working day. Related to this must be adequate knowledge of how many potentially active accounts exist. The relationship between these two items and the addition of traveling and wasted-time allowances give a workable notion of salesman's account productivity per working day and have a fundamental bearing on trading area and salesman's territory considerations.

The highly specialized industrial good illustration

The type of good involved in this case is the capital equipment-accessory equipment example used by a special industry category, e.g., printing presses, steel mill equipment. The basic assumption here is that the users generally are concentrated, so far as geographic location is concerned, in a few parts of the United States. Thus, the 1954 Census listed only 61 standard metropolitan areas having 40,000 or more manufacturing employees each.

Accordingly, given a measure of salesman's daily productivity as outlined above, the management can decide how many salesmen will be needed. Then, the location of every actual and every potential buyer can be spotted on a map. In addition, it must be determined which goods can be carried in inventory and which goods have to be produced only according to individual order. This determines, in turn, whether or not inventories can be decentralized. The reconciliation of all these variables will give an initial approximation of the number and size of the wholesale trading area. In addition, the locational patterns of specialized industrial goods wholesale middlemen might affect such areas.

The widely distributed industrial goods case

An example would be office equipment. Here the underlying assumptions have changed so that the number and location of actual and potential customers have increased substantially. Use may be made in such case of the work of a trade association. Thus, in 1956 the Office Equipment Manufacturers Institute presented a map of the United States dividing the country into 308 basic marketing areas. The formula used was as follows:

1. The principal commercial center in any county having one or more cities above 50,000 population was considered a leading marketing center.
2. In counties having cities between 15,000 and 50,000 population, the principal commercial city was again chosen as a leading marketing center, but only *providing it was beyond certain prescribed distances from larger cities.*
3. No county would be split.
4. No dead-end sales trips.
5. Although state lines should be crossed when necessary, such crossing should be held to a minimum.
6. A disputed county which was approximately *equal distant* between two marketing centers would be given to the *smaller* center in order to build up that center, and because there would be less traffic congestion in moving out of the smaller center.
7. Where the easiest accessibility to a county could not be readily determined from an examination of road maps, the experience of a majority of the companies represented would be used.[23]

Other analytical tools which are useful are those discussed in the cases for manufactured consumers' goods.

The selectively distributed manufactured consumers' goods case

The wholesale trading area analysis involves in this case a two-sided approach. On the one hand, there must be a determination of the locations of the types of retail outlets which are suited to these types of consumers' goods and an estimate of their relative sales

[23] Office Equipment Manufacturers Institute, "The Marketing Areas Map of the Office Equipment Manufacturers Institute," Address by John B. Butler, May 11, 1956.

performance. On the other hand, there is involved the quantitative determination of the relationship between total and per capita sales of the product, and such related geographical factors as income, age, etc. In addition, the relative possibilities of centralized and de-centralized inventories must be explored. A reconciliation of these two sets of variables and comparisons with both salesman's indexes of daily potential coverage should give some beginning approximation of the trading area boundaries.

The efforts of trade associations, government agencies, publications, and individuals in measuring trading area boundaries should be examined closely for possible usefulness. The opinions of wholesale middlemen would be of very great importance. Thus, the U. S. Department of Commerce has made studies of wholesale grocery territories and wholesale dry-goods trading areas based upon actual distribution of middlemen's sales. As noted above, trade associations have made useful studies. The Hearst Magazines have prepared excellent studies from time to time. In addition, wholesale trading areas may be evaluated by combining boundaries of retail trading areas based on Curtis Publishing Company, Rand McNally & Company, and other sources. Excellent studies may be available of single centers.[24] The annual data contained in *Sales Management* may be useful.[25] But, whatever the study used, all the boundaries must be evaluated by each marketing agency in the light of its own channel and related marketing decisions.

The widely distributed manufactured consumers' goods case

In this product situation, comprehensive coverage is required, such as in the case of a canned goods manufacturer. The boundaries of the wholesale trading areas must be based upon: a comprehensive survey of the geographic distribution of retail outlets; of the retail trading areas of which they are a part; the factors influencing total and per capita retail sales; the frequency of retail visits and the marketing policies of the manufacturer as evidenced in the selection of channels and in merchandising strategy relative to intensive versus extensive penetration. The available types of determinations referred to in the preceding section may be the determining feature, or may be used to check the individual manufacturer's or middleman's determination.

[24] See, for example, Rayburn D. Tousley, "Some Aspects of the Spokane Wholesale Market," *The Journal of Marketing*, XVI (January 1952), Part 1, 321–330. For a more complete study, see the bibliography for additional examples.

[25] *Annual Survey of Buying Power* issue appearing on May 10.

Restricted management size situations

Unless the management solves its geographic difficulties by using either merchant or agent middlemen, the problem of trading area analysis becomes of minor significance compared to the executive problem of selecting such areas and types of customers as can be reached in the owner-manager's time schedule. In such cases, the middlemen utilized will have to make the trading area determination.

This section has confined itself to general trading area situations. Chapter 11 will deal with the selection of the individual locations of middlemen's establishments.

QUESTIONS AND PROBLEMS

1. Discuss the general content of the conceptual framework of area structure. How does this conceptual framework relate to the funnel concept of wholesaling?

2. To what extent is a system of wholesale markets a necessary corollary to area structure?

3. Of what value is it to study the basic geographical structure of the extractive and manufacturing industries in order to understand, in turn, the geographical structure of wholesaling?

4. What are the significant regional variations in the production of the extractive goods industries? of the manufacturing industries?

5. How do wholesale sales vary by geographical regions? by states? by metropolitan areas?

6. To what extent are there sharp geographical variations in types-of-operation? To what extent are there some fundamental similarities?

7. To what extent do the geographic variations in wholesale middlemen's kinds of business parallel the variations in production? To what extent are the patterns unlike?

8. Of what value is it to study the economic theory of location in order to understand the area structure of wholesaling?

9. What is Fetter's "Law of Market Areas"? How has this law been modified by the findings of the Hysons?

10. What are the basic differences in establishing the boundaries of wholesale trading areas for organized as against unorganized markets?

11. Evaluate critically the relative importance of each of the determinants of the boundaries of organized wholesale market areas.

12. Of what value to wholesale middlemen is the determination of trading area boundaries?

13. What is meant by "dynamics of supply and distribution areas"?

14. What types of trading area situations exist for unorganized wholesale markets?

15. How can one determine the trading area boundaries under conditions of unorganized wholesale markets?

CHAPTER INTEGRATING ASSIGNMENTS

1. It can be said that the whole foundation of an understanding of marketing organization, especially that sector called wholesaling, consists of an appreciation of the importance of area structure. Discuss *critically:* (*a*) the implications of this assertion for sharpening the conceptual framework for the study of wholesaling; and (*b*) the impact of such understanding upon the managerial aspects of the wholesaling sector.

2. The area structure of any wholesale market consists of a segment which may be called the "heart" or primary zone; a subsequent layer around the heart zone which may be called the secondary zone; and remaining zones which overlap with competing wholesale markets' areas. Of what value is this framework to an understanding of the area structure of wholesaling?

5

The Structure of Wholesaling
in the United States:
Channels

The previous chapters have analyzed the wholesaling sector in terms of the middlemen agencies and geographic structural characteristics. But the "mucilage" which joins these aspects together into some notion of an organizational system was not discussed. It will be the purposes of this and the following chapter to deal with this organizational system. This chapter will be concerned mainly with the general concept of marketing organization through the channel; types of channels of distribution; channel structure, the nature of the commodity, and commodity flows; analysis of sales by class of customer; and factors explaining channel patterns. Chapter 6 will discuss the managerial struggle for control of the channel including some evolutionary aspects of that struggle; orthodox versus non-orthodox channels; the evaluation of channel effectiveness; the relationship of channel structure to area structure; and some final observations.

The Concept of Marketing Organization Through the Channel

Ordinarily, marketing organization would be visualized mainly in its internal aspects: that is, primarily how individual business enterprises engaged in the work of marketing allocate responsibilities among the various personnel in relation to authority; what type of organizational framework is applicable; what span of executive control is visualized; and whether or not decentralization of authority is utilized. These aspects and their relationship to policy formation and functional arrangements are analyzed completely in later chapters.

Within the content of this chapter, marketing organization is studied only in its external aspects. In this perspective, it is concerned with how agencies related directly, semidirectly, or indirectly to the functions of marketing are so intertwined with each other that some semblance of orderly relationship can be detected. The main vehicle for this orderly relationship, as will be seen, is the channel of distribution. But the concept of marketing organization in these external aspects also connotes the existence of systematic relationship in terms of the geographic units involved. In this sense, it has a very close tie-in with the motion of area structure discussed in the preceding chapter. Thus, the external view of marketing organization is a result of the concept of level of business activity, of specialization of labor, and of function and process (marketing) as they relate to structure.

Within this context of marketing organization, the most important factors acting as influencing agents are: The physical and dollar volume of goods and services to be marketed; the varietal composition of the goods and services included in the preceding; the evaluation of specialized management abilities within the marketing framework; the increasing diversification of types of users of products; the increasing diversifications of locations of buyers and sellers; the increasing diversification of the auxiliary marketing functions; the changing sizes and policies of business firms; and the effects of government activities.

The meaning of channel of distribution

The word "channel" has its origins in the French word for canal. It thus connotes, in its marketing application, a pathway taken by goods as they flow from point of production to points of intermediate and final use. But in these flows there is a further connotation of a sequence of marketing agencies; namely, the wholesale and retail middlemen who perform, type by type, various combinations of marketing functions at various points in the channel in order to facilitate such flows. In addition, there is a connotation of a sequence of facilitating agencies which perform auxiliary functions at one or more points within the channel. Some writers view each functional or subfunctional grouping as giving rise to flows. The channel is, therefore, the vehicle for viewing marketing organization in its external aspects and for bridging the physical and nonphysical gaps which exist in moving goods from producers to consumers through the exchange process, including the determination of price.

The channel thus bridges the gap, geographically speaking, between producers and users. In this sense, distance is involved not only in the usual terms of miles (or an equivalent measure) but also in terms of the times involved and the costs of communication and transportation. In addition to time in this aspect, the channel has a function to perform in bridging time gaps in the pure storage sense. Thus, within the channel, certain types of middlemen and certain special agencies arise to carry physical inventories (and to change their physical characteristics) over periods of time. In addition, the channel is useful in bridging gaps in product assortment patterns by matching sellers' inventories—in physical and qualitative aspects— with buyers' inventory intentions. More will be said of this function of channels in later sections. Finally, the channel is a means of bridging gaps in knowledge and in the communication of that knowledge. It becomes, accordingly, a structural arrangement whereby sellers (or their middlemen representatives) search for customer prospects with whom to communicate and to whom sales can ultimately be made, and whereby buyers, in turn, search for sellers carrying the assortments desired from whom purchases ultimately can be made.

The concept of the channel of distribution involves, in addition to these characteristics, sets of vertical and horizontal relationships between various types of wholesale and retail middlemen. As such, it can be used as the keystone for the analysis of various "circuit" and "flow" arrangements centering around these management aspects. Based upon all of these considerations, there can evolve systematic analysis of such problems as: (a) the characteristics of various types of channel structures; (b) the power focus of the management element in each kind of channel structure; (c) comparisons between these as to relative short-run and long-run efficiency; (d) comparative costs of keeping and defending existing channels of distribution as against selecting new types.

From this lengthy definition of the channel and its characteristics, it follows that the channel is composed of the following:

1. A series of more or less complicated connections between business units or groups of business units by means of which the center of

marketing activity is effected; namely, the transfer of legal possession or right or use by means of buying and selling activities.
At the wholesaling sector there may be more than one cycle of
buying-selling relationships in the channel.
2. A pattern of physical flow of the commodity or commodities
   involved which may parallel the business connections in (1) or
   move through different business unit arrangements.
3. Further patterns designed to show flows of other auxiliary
   activities.[1]

The business units involved in channels of distribution, other than
the wholesale and retail middlemen as such, may be classified as
follows:[2]

I. *Extractive Industry Establishments*
  A. Agriculture.
  B. Forestry.
  C. Fisheries.
  D. Mining (metal, anthracite coal, bituminous coal, crude
     petroleum and natural gas, and nonmetallic mining and
     quarrying).
II. *Contract Construction*
III. *Manufacturing Establishments*[3]
IV. *Finance, Insurance, and Real Estate Agencies*
  A. Banking.
  B. Securities brokers, dealers, exchanges.
  C. Finance agencies, n. e. c.
  D. Insurance carriers.
  E. Insurance agents and combination offices.
  F. Real Estate.
V. *Transportation Agencies*
  A. Railroads freight and passenger.
  B. Local and highway passenger.

---

[1] R. Vaile, E. T. Grether, and R. Cox, *Marketing in the American Economy*
(New York: The Ronald Press Co., 1952). These authors speak of *forward
flows* of physical possession, ownership and negotiation; *backward flows* of
ordering and payment; and *combination flows* of information, financing, and
risking.

[2] In this classification scheme, any one of the groups may appear in the
channel as an originating seller; as an intermediate or final buyer; as a provider of
some primary or auxiliary function within the channel; or in a combination of
these.

[3] See the classification used in Chapter 4.

      C. Highway freight transportation and warehousing.

      D. Water.

      E. Air.

      F. Pipelines.

      G. Services allied to transportation.

  VI. *Communications and Public Utilities Agencies*

      A. Telegraph telephone, and related.

      B. Radio broadcasting and television.

      C. Utilities—electric and gas.

      D. Local utilities and public service, n. e. c.

 VII. *Services*

      A. Hotels and other lodgings.

      B. Personal.

      C. Private households.

      D. Commercial and trade schools and employment agencies.

      E. Business services, n. e. c.

      F. Miscellaneous repair services and hand trades.

      G. Motion pictures.

      H. Amusement and recreation (except motion pictures).

      I. Medical and other health services.

      J. Engineering and other professional services, n. e. c.

      K. Educational service, n. e. c.

      L. Nonprofit organizations, n. e. c.

VIII. *Government and Government Enterprises*

      A. Federal.

      B. State.

      C. County.

      D. Municipal.

      E. Foreign.

The channel and linkages and blockages

In terms of physical analogies, the channel has been referred to as a canal in which is contained the variegated physical flow of goods. But in view of the complex array of business units as classified which may be involved in one or all aspects of channel functions, the channel may be visualized also as a chain-link arrangement in which each business is in effect one link. Thus, the channel may be here visualized as a series of linkages which vary as to the number of links, as to the functions to be performed by each link and the entire set of linkages, and according to the "thickness" and strength of each link. Some links are dominant, as will be discussed in the next chapter, whereas others play a subordinate role. Closely related to this is the situation wherein some links are engaged in the primary functions of marketing, whereas others function merely as facilitating or auxiliary links.

It is in the functioning of the channel as a series of linkages that there arises also the phenomenon of blockages. In a sense, blockages may be visualized as the activities of one or more links (business units) in a particular channel to protect the economic status of that channel by placing barriers (blockages) in the way of competing channels. These blockages may consist of such legal devices as an exclusive agency franchise arrangement preventing any links in the channel from handling competitive products; they may consist of various forms of legislation designed to restrict the units permitted to market particular products; they may represent manufacturers control over resale prices; or they may represent collusive activity within or outside the letter and the spirit of the law. Such blockages may have only very temporary success, or they may have elements of permanency, or they may generate their own destruction by giving alternative channels and their own linkages considerably more motivation than might be otherwise expected.

The relationship of the channel of distribution to the "funnel" concept

The channel is the concrete marketing organizational framework in which the abstract concept of the funnel is executed. The funnel depends on one or more of the types of channels to be discussed later to become a reality. Depending upon the channel and the sum total of the functioning of its component links, the funnel concept may or may not be completely realized. The sum total of the functioning of all channels becomes the basis, in turn, for the approximation of the funnel concept in its total abstract meaning.

Types of notation systems for channel diagrams

As a final preliminary to the discussion of types of channels, a word needs to be said about how channel diagrams are constructed. In general, the components of the channel diagram consist of: (a) a box enclosing the title of and the type of agency making up a link; (b) a solid or broken line indicating, accordingly, either physical or nonphysical flows; (c) an arrow indicating the direction of the flow; and (d) a box enclosing the title and type of each using agency at the end of the channel. In addition, notation schemes may be used to indicate and differentiate primary agencies from auxiliary or facilitating agencies. By means of varying widths of lines, the proportionate importionate importance of each segment flow through each agency combination can be shown.

Some simple diagrams may indicate each of these aspects of the notation systems. Figure 5 illustrates some kinds of notation systems which may be used to designate the agencies (links)

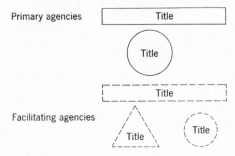

FIG. 5. Notation system for agencies in channel.

involved in channel diagrams. Any geometric design is permissible, although in actual practice there is no hard and fast line of distinction. Figure 6 shows the notation systems typically used for designating the type and direction of flows. Solid lines are the orthodox notational scheme for indicating the physical flow of the commodity or

FIG. 6. Notation system for types and direction of flows.

commodities involved. Broken lines generally denote the nonphysical flows and may be further coded to reflect each type of such flows.

Figure 7 shows a concrete illustration of an actual channel for fresh California tomatoes in which the width of the lines shows the relative importance of the flows based upon the total volume sold. It will be noticed that no detailed breakdowns are given of the agency links; but it should be noticed, also, that the area of each circle is proportionate to the volume handled.

In the absence of any standardized notational system, it is obvious that the numerous channel diagrams available show a wide variety of notational framework found in the discussion of types of channels

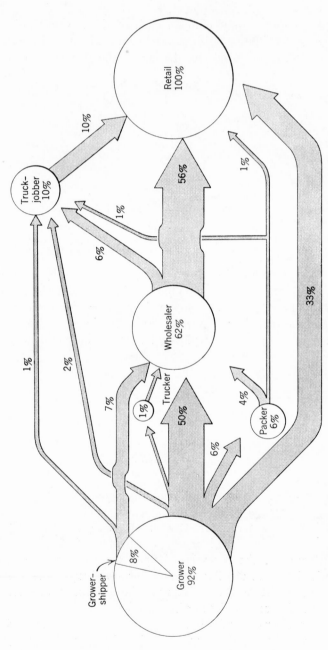

FIG. 7.   Dealer types handling fresh tomatoes sold at retail in northern and central California summer and fall, 1948. (*Source*: Walter D. Fisher, *California Fresh Tomatoes—Marketing Channels and Gross Margins from Farm to Consumer —Summer and Fall, 1948*, University of California, College of Agriculture (Berkeley), mimeographed Report No. 113, June 1951.)

which follows. Any one using channel diagrams ought to be in a position of obtaining from such diagrams the kind of information which may be useful in understanding channel structure.

One other aspect of channel diagram notation may be useful, namely, the indication of the direction and extent of management

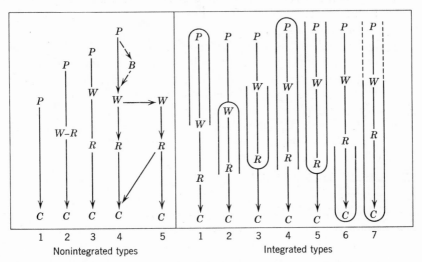

FIG. 8. Progression from simple to complex channels.

P—Producer.
R—Retailer.
B—Broker or selling agent.
W—Wholesaler.
C—Consumer.
Nos. 1 and 4—Producer-owned or controlled.
No. 2—Wholesaler-owned or controlled.
Nos. 3 and 5—Retailer-owned or controlled.
Nos. 6 and 7—Consumer-owned and operated.

control. The form used is by Duddy and Revzan[4] (see Fig. 8) and is used to explain the evolution of more complex forms of channel organization.

Types of Channels of Distribution

There are perhaps five important variables which affect the classification of types of channels: (1) Channels may be distinguished

[4] E. A. Duddy and D. A. Revzan, *Marketing: An Institutional Approach,* 2nd ed. (New York: McGraw-Hill Book Co., Inc., 1953), p. 266.

according to the number of links (intervening business agencies) involved; (2) channels may be differentiated according to their relative level of importance or their position within the entire framework of marketing; (3) channels may be differentiated according to the type of managerial control manifested; (4) channels may be separated according to the breadth of business penetration which may be presented; and (5) channels may be designated according to the types of flows indicated above.

Obviously, this classification format is so cross-related that any collection of channel diagrams may have to undergo multiple assortment. Presumably, a sixth classification basis could emphasize, by evaluating the five types indicated above, the relative degree of simplicity or complexity found in any given channel situation. But this is a far less satisfactory basis for classification than any of the preceding five indicated.

Channels, by number of links

This is the oldest and most orthodox classification scheme used in the marketing literature. Based on the number of links, it distinguishes between direct, semidirect, and indirect channels, and, in addition, has both a commodity and functional aspect. A *direct channel* is characterized by the existence of a single-link pattern; namely, direct contact between manufacturer (or other producer) and user. The producer may assume full responsibility for the marketing functions and for the establishment of communication between himself and the users; or the user may assume full responsibility for the functions and communication. There may be, and usually are, facilitating agencies involved; but the main characteristic is the directness of both the physical and nonphysical flows. The producer may send his salesmen directly to the customers' place of business or residence; the customer may send his buyer to the producer's place of business; or a specialized facility may be used, such as a roadside stand or a mail-order catalog.

Indirect channels represent the opposite spectrum from that of the direct channel. By indirect is meant the insertion between producer and user of more than one type of wholesale middleman if the commodity is of the industrial goods type, and of more than one type of each of wholesale and retail middleman if the commodity is of the consumers' goods category. Indirect channels represent, accordingly, the most complex arrangements from the point of view of both the number of linkages and blockages and the variety of types of middlemen involved.

Semidirect channels represent an intermediate situation between these extremes. Only one type of wholesale middleman may be involved in the case of industrial goods, or only one type of wholesale and of retail middleman may be involved. There is no hard and fast dividing line between the semidirect and indirect channels.

In each of these cases, the characteristics as to number of links are modified by the kinds involved and by the middlemen's adaptations of the functions which need to be performed. For example, both roadside stands and municipal farmers' markets become physical parts of the direct channels for certain kinds of agricultural products. They are not found, on the other hand, in the direct channels either for industrial or manufactured consumers' goods. Again, certain types of organized wholesale market facilities become part of the indirect channels for certain types of agricultural goods but not for the other categories. It may be stated somewhat categorically that the direct channels usually involve the performance of a much wider range of primary and auxiliary functions by the middlemen included than is likely to be the case either for indirect or semidirect channels.

Channels according to level of importance

Where a channel exists which makes use of more than one combination of agencies, a differentiation may be made between that part of the channel which is a primary level of importance and that part which is of auxiliary importance. Thus, in Figure 6, it is apparent that the primary channel for fresh California tomatoes consists of (a) the movement from grower → to wholesaler → to → retailer; and (b) the direct movement from grower → to → retailer. The same diagram shows at least six auxiliary channels which account for substantially minor proportions of the total movement of the product.

Channels, by type of control

This classification scheme introduces the element of managerial integration, and subdivides channels into producer controlled, wholesale-middlemen-controlled and retailer-middlemen-controlled. Subclassifications can be introduced by the type of operation found within each group. However, a much more useful subclassification scheme can be based upon the type of horizontal and vertical integration found in the channel.[5]

[5] The discussion which follows is based to a considerable extent upon Werner Z. Hirsch, "Toward a Definition of Integration," *The Southern Economic Journal*, XVII (October 1950), 159–165, and his longer version of the article in typed manuscript form.

The horizontally integrated channel includes two types. Type A involves a single management which controls a number of units all handling the same general assortments of commodities on the same business plane, *viz.*, production, wholesale market, or retail market. Type B involves a similar arrangement of units, but these units together or separately handle either complementary product lines, or completely unrelated lines, or combinations of both. In both types, the controlling management pursues a unified profit policy.

The *vertically integrated* channel is subdivided into two types, and each of these is, in turn, further subdivided into three groups. Type A represents a channel arrangement in which the vertically integrated firm controls a number of different operations in production and/or marketing of *similar* commodities on successive business levels. This type is subdivided into: (a) the *backward vertical integration* form, in which the controlling business firm is further away from the ultimate consumer in the channel than any other agency link; (b) the *forward vertical integration* form, in which the controlling business firm is further away from the ultimate consumer in the channel than any other agency link; and (c) the form which is a combination of (a) and (b). Subgroup (a) may be termed retailer-controlled for edible agricultural products and manufactured consumers' goods products, while subgroup (b) may be subdivided into producer-controlled or wholesale-middleman-controlled.

Type B of the vertically integrated channel consists of the complementary vertically integrated firm which controls a number of different operations in the marketing and/or production of complementary products on successive business levels. This type also is subdivided into three groups as follows: (a) the *divergent forward variety,* in which a firm begins with one or a few commodities and then divides these into numerous complementary products as they flow closer and closer to the consumer; (b) the *convergent backward variety,* in which a firm "pulls" in numerous raw materials and services in order to manufacture and place in the channel one or just a few commodities; and (c) the *forward parallel variety,* in which firms merely begin with a given number of complementary products and push these along in the channel without any significant change in number.

There are in addition to these groupings two types of a combination of the horizontally integrated and vertically integrated channel. Type A consists of a joint horizontally and vertically integrated firm which controls a number of vertically integrated units all handling *similar* products at successive levels of the channel. Type B consists of the same kind of arrangement in which the controlled vertically integrated units all handle *complementary* products. Each of these types may be subdivided into the same subgroupings as type *B* of the vertically integrated channel.

Some discussion may be pertinent at this point of the main devices used by business firms to achieve complete or partial integration of the forms noted. The most obvious and completely successful device is for the controlling business unit to acquire the direct ownership and management of all units involved in the channel of distribution. Control may also be acquired through ownership of the patents of the basic machinery used in the production process or through legal control over an entire product or family of products. Policies may be dictated through the many-sided forms of interlocking directorates or other financial-organizational controls.

A much more informal but, nevertheless, very effective control may be achieved by aggressive sales promotion by any agency in the channel which is designed to enhance that agency's control over part or all of the channel. These tactics may establish strong brand preferences which may "force" the product through the channel over the opposition of intermediate channel agencies; or they may open other areas of informal integration. Any agency may attempt to secure informal integration by prepackaging policies and by such inventory tactics as full-line forcing. The extension of credit arrangements and the use of such legal devices as exclusive dealer franchise contracts may act as the basis for informal integration. The use of resale price maintenance agreements extends the manufacturer's control through the length and breadth of the channel. Finally, such tactics as sharing-the-market agreements or cartels act as very potent integrating forces in the channel until dissolved by the extension of government regulation.[6]

Channels, by breadth of business penetration

It is obvious that channel structure begins with the individual channel arrangement which exists for the product (or products) produced by a given producing unit. From this beginning arrangement, there may emerge as many such channels as there are producing units. Every change in the number of producing units or in the number and types of products produced can lead to changes, in turn, in the number and format of each of these individual producers' channels.

These individual producers' channels may be combined, in turn, into two different group arrangements. Products of homogeneous marketing characteristics can be grouped together into a *product*

[6] At this point, the reader should keep in mind the relationship between this discussion and the previous discussion of linkages and blockages.

family channel. Thus, all the individual producers' channels for soaps and detergents may be grouped into a soap-and-detergent group channel. Or, using the classification scheme discussed in Chapter 4, individual producer channels may be grouped, in turn, into industry channels, using either the two-digit basis of classification only or adding the three-digit and four-digit subgroupings. Finally, product group and/or industry channels may be further combined into channels for extractive industry products, channels for industrial goods products, and channels for manufactured consumers' goods products.

Channels, by types of flows

It has been indicated that, so far as flows are concerned, most marketing studies separate the physical from the nonphysical flows. But, as has also been indicated, some writers subdivide the nonphysical flows into several component types. Although not much attention will be given to these subdivisions in this book, the reader should be aware that some writers devote a considerable amount of detailed description and diagrammatic representation to these flows.[7]

The Geographic Structure of Channels of Distribution

Although the usual notation systems used for channels of any of the types discussed in the preceding section do not indicate their geographic characteristics, it should be obvious that channels reflect all of the geographic characteristics discussed in Chapter 4. The agencies involved in any channel of distribution represent, among other things, a series of individual decisions by individual business firms as to where to locate a particular establishment. Each establishment in the channel has a geographic zone of influence which represents decisions of some individual firm or group of firms as to what the wholesale and, in the case of consumers' goods, retail trading areas are, measured potentially and in actuality. It has been indicated that these areas change in boundaries with varying degrees of frequency based upon many variables.

Since so much information has to be included in the notation systems for channel diagrams, it should be obvious as to why the geographic aspects are frequently excluded. This exclusion is done for purposes of making the channel diagrams manageable both in physical size and in comprehensibility.

This short section has been included for those readers interested in

[7] Vaile, Grether, Cox, *op. cit.,* Chapters 5, 7.

the full complexity of channel diagrams, and to point out that there is a wealth of complicated geographic data which have not been omitted simply because no notation has been made.[8]

Channel Structure, the Nature of the Commodity, and Commodity Flows

The purpose of this section is to sketch the approach to be taken in succeeding sections in adapting the general outline of channel structure, as discussed in previous sections, to the particular position occupied by wholesale middlemen in channels found in particular commodity situations. It should be apparent that little or no attention can be given here to those types of channels used in marketing the products of individual producing firms.

In the following sections the discussions will center around the channels of distribution for the following industry and product groupings:

I. *Channels of Distribution for Agricultural Products*
   A. Products to be processed.
      1. Moving to industrial users.
      2. Moving to ultimate consumers.
   B. Products moving to ultimate consumers without processing.
II. *Channels of Distribution for Other Extractive Industry Products*
III. *Channels of Distribution for Manufactured Industrial Goods*
   A. Products entering directly into the production of other products.
   B. Products facilitating further production.
   C. Products for nonmanufacturing types of customers.
IV. *Channels of Distribution for Manufactured Consumers' Goods*
   A. Durables.
   B. Semidurables.
   C. Nondurables (except agricultural).
V. *Channels of Distribution for Services*
   A. Business and government services.
   B. Personal services.

[8] R. F. Breyer has a very interesting way in which to diagram a geographic pattern. See his *The Marketing Institution* (New York: McGraw-Hill Book Co., Inc., 1934), Chapter X, and especially Figs. 14–20 therein. But even these diagrams are only suggestive of the complete range of agencies which can be included in a limited representation of the geographic detail. However, the treatment is in the usual highly imaginative and valuable style of Breyer's writings on marketing organization.

In developing the discussion under each subgrouping, it is assumed that the reader has been exposed to the wealth of detail on commodity marketing presented in the better basic marketing textbooks. It is further assumed that he has been exposed to diagrammatic materials which exist for the various commodity and industry channels. With these assumptions in mind, the discussion under each heading will present the following pattern of analysis: (1) The underlying conditions of production which are related to channel structure; (2) the commodity characteristics which bear importantly on the channels of distribution; and (3) the factors that explain the importance of wholesale middlemen in the direct, semidirect, and indirect channels. A final section will deal with the factors that influence the choice of individual manufacturing units for their particular products.

Channels of Distribution—Raw Materials, Agricultural Products

Characteristics of production

Agriculture is a series of industries involved in producing a wide range of edible and inedible products which have, in turn, wide variations in physical characteristics, in volume moving to market, in value characteristics, and in conditions of production. Some of the geographic conditions of production have been indicated in Chapter 4. In terms of producing units, the number of farms in the United States in 1950 totaled 5.4 million, with an average size of only 215 acres. All but one third of these are unimportant as commercial producers; nevertheless, the less important units do contribute variable quantities of agricultural products into the marketing channels. Because of locational dependence upon natural production factors—soil, climate, topography—many farms are at considerable geographic distances from consuming markets. Thus, transportation and storage are of even greater significance than for most manufacturing industries.

Conditions of production range from rudimentary dependency upon manual labor for some crops to a revolutionary increase in the use of machinery at the production and harvesting phases. Fertilizers, medicines, and insecticides, together with various forms of botanical experimentation, have increased sharply the yields of crops per acre and of animals. Yet, the time cycle of production remains relatively rigid, ranging from a few weeks, relatively speaking, for certain truck crops to a period of perhaps 5 years before a citrus fruit tree may reach the maturity period of commercial yield.

It must be emphasized in a discussion of this kind that agricultural production, in a collective sense, is essentially speculative. This is so because of the relative unpredictability of weather conditions (despite recent improvements in forecasting techniques) and, similarly, of such related environmental factors as the presence of plant-destroying insects, and the like. This uncertainty affects both the quality of the crop and animal production involved. Obviously, the shorter the period of harvest, the greater the impact of the risk.

These variables have some very marked effects on the channel structure. For one, a great deal of emphasis must be placed upon the necessity of providing agricultural producers with a variety of alternatives so far as liquidation of output for cash and transfers of ownership are concerned. Structurally, the middlemen in the channel must be attuned especially to the phases of concentration and equalization processes within their respective channel positions. Also, a great deal of specialization must be manifested by these middlemen in the price-determining and risk-bearing aspects of the channel structure. Grading and packaging aspects become magnified in importance, also, as compared with factory production.

Commodity characteristics

The raw-material agricultural products are divided into foods, fibres, and other groupings. The food group has crops and animals as its initial subdivision. The food crops are mainly as follows: The grains (wheat, corn, oats, barley, rye); fruits and vegetables for canning, preserving, and fast freezing; cane and beet sugar; and the vegetable oils—soybeans, cottonseed, etc. The food animals are the livestock group (cattle, calves, hogs, and sheep); and the poultry group (chickens, turkeys, ducks, etc.). In the fibre group are included both animal and vegetable—cotton, wool, hemp. Finally, the "other" category includes the inedible derivatives from livestock, the industrial uses of grains and soybeans; the production of seed crops and breeding animals; and tobacco.

These raw materials have several characteristics which affect the existing channel structures. They vary widely as to the quantities available to be marketed, as to relative perishability, as to susceptibility to grading and standardization, as to the length of the marketing period, as to the variety of producing conditions, and, finally, as to the stage of development of the manufacturing utilization of raw materials. In general, they vary also as to the need which exists for the utilization in the channel of organized as against nonorganized local and central market facilities.

Factors explaining the variable importance of wholesale middlemen

From preceding discussions, the following aspects of the role of wholesale middlemen in the marketing of raw-material agricultural products will have been noted: (1) The existence of certain types of assemblers, such as the grain elevators, local buyers, cooperative shipping associations, which facilitate the performance of the various components of the concentration process; (2) the decision of many agricultural producers to maintain ownership control of their products while using specialists—mainly agent middlemen—to carry on the remaining marketing functions through the channel; (3) the existence of organized central commodity markets which, by virtue of their location relative to agricultural producers, require various types of wholesale middlemen who, as members, represent these producers or represent buyers; (4) the existence of other organized markets with such restrictive membership requirements that more frequently than not wholesale middlemen specialists will be needed; and (5) wholesale middlemen who represent buyers while moving from one agricultural producing area to another.

The resultant of the operation of these forces is a complex mixture of direct, semidirect, and indirect channel arrangements for the same class of raw materials. For the highly perishable raw materials, the role of the nonintegrated wholesale middleman is likely to be at a minimum level because of the necessary close proximity of processing facilities to producing areas. For products such as livestock, there has been an increasing proportion of the output moving through direct channels, but there is a very considerable volume moving through semidirect and indirect channels. In these latter cases, the commission agent, the broker, the cooperative marketing associations, and merchant wholesalers (especially the regular wholesaler) emerge to positions of greatest importance. For export and import trade movements, such wholesale middlemen as exporters, importers, export agents, and import agents assume increased importance. For those commodities sold on the speculative exchanges, the buying and selling brokers assume considerable importance.

Based on the 1954 Census data, it is apparent that, of the total 1954 wholesale sales of raw-material agricultural products, the agent-broker group was most important with 42.7 per cent of the total, duplicated sales volume. The merchant wholesalers group accounted for 34.3 per cent, and the assemblers for the remainder 22.9 per cent. Such integrated middlemen of importance as are found are the cooperative marketing and shipping associations included in the agent-broker and assembler groups. These data do not reflect, of course, the activities of those buyers employed by manufacturers who do not operate separate places of business.

Channels of Distribution—Edible Agricultural Products

Production characteristics

The production characteristics for these commodities are identical with those listed above for the raw-material category. This is especially so for those types of edible products also classified as raw-material types of products.

Commodity characteristics

Most of these edible products are, by physical nature, extremely perishable. At the same time, the variable-quality characteristics, noted above, place a very high premium on sales by inspection. The channel structure must provide, accordingly, for rapid physical flows while still permitting such sales by inspection to take place at any transaction center within the channel.

Highly variable relationships exist as to the length of the marketing season for each category of product. Some fresh fruits such as strawberries may be available for only a few weeks of the year, depending, in part, upon the accessibility of a given market to the sources of supply. Other commodities, by virtue of both their growing seasons and the diversity of producing areas together with their ability to be stored for long periods, may be available in "fresh" condition during every week of the year. Examples of such commodities are potatoes, onions, and apples. There are, of course, several gradations between these two extremes.

The fresh, edible products vary according to weight-value relationships. At one extreme are the bulky products of corresponding heavy weights, such as potatoes and cabbage. Generally, but not always, these have the lower relative prices per pound. At the opposite extreme are the fancy fruits and vegetables, relatively lighter in basic selling weights, and usually commanding relatively higher prices, especially when the first shipments of the season take place. These are, of course, only average tendencies, and there are many exceptions.

These categories of commodities vary widely in susceptibility to packaging. Where the products tend to be of very uniform quality and can be assorted by sizes without affecting quality, packaging may enhance the products' value and facilitate movement through the channel. On the other hand, basic physical characteristics together with highly variable runs of sizes and low unit values may make packaging unsuccessful. As the quality and ingenuity of packages and packaging materials continue to improve, and as the demands of self-service marketing continue to require more and more prepackaging, a larger proportion of these products will appear in some form of packaging, including the use of bindings as for bananas and for some forms of lettuce.

Related to the commodity characteristics as they affect the channel structure are certain demand characteristics. First to be noticed is the existence of an important institutional demand as well as ultimate consumer demand. The nature of the institutional demand stemming from restaurants, hotels, dining cars, hospitals, and the like requires a completely different channel structure than do the movements to ultimate consumers either through retail agencies or by means of direct channels. These institutional buyers have different quality and unit purchase requirements than do ultimate consumers. Obviously, the channel will have less need to provide prepackaging for these customers than for ultimate consumers.

Ultimate consumers, as of the present period, have variable reactions to the purchase of fresh products as against utilizing fast-frozen products. With the design of the modern refrigerator and the use of deep-freeze cabinets, many households prefer to stock fast-frozen products in preference to more frequent purchases of the fresh products. As a result, many ultimate consumers have highly fluctuating demands for the fresh products, and this places considerable stress, in turn, on the various types of food stores handling the perishable produce. There is, of course, some underlying foundation by virtue of the fact that some fruits and vegetables do not have any fast-frozen equivalents.

Factors explaining the variable importance of wholesale middlemen

There are some conditions which are favorable to the marketing of fresh, edible products through direct channel arrangements, but these are relatively unimportant. Quality considerations, freshness, and the availability of specialized farmers' market facilities are among the reasons why direct channels exist and will be used. But, in view of the varying quantities and varieties of the products to be marketed and the widespread geographical distribution of users, such channel arrangements can do only a fraction of the marketing job.

Accordingly, the bulk of these products must move through considerably more complicated semidirect and indirect channels. The wholesale middlemen tend to be classed in the following functional-process positions in the channel.

1. The *assemblers* group, consisting mainly of those middlemen close to the producers, who conform to the marketing pattern of arranging for partial or complete aspects of the process of concentration. Thus, they may be producer-oriented, as in the case of cooperative shipping associations; or they may be wholesale-market-oriented, as local representatives of central market wholesalers; or they may be representatives of the large-scale retailers, as the corporate chain buyers. They may be used to facilitate the producers' continuous control of legal ownership; or they may provide him with the earliest channel opportunity for liquidation of harvestings for cash while providing for the transfer of ownership.

2. The *central market middlemen* group consisting, on the one hand, of the agent middlemen representing the producers. Of these, depending upon the product and whether or not physical possession of inventories is necessary to the channel structure, the more important would be the auction companies, brokers, commission agents, and cooperative marketing agencies. A second group consists of the orthodox wholesalers, the voluntary chain representatives, and related types, all of whom own the fresh products offered for sale. A third group represents, on either an agent or merchant middleman basis, the larger institutional buyers noted above. And a fourth group of wholesaler merchants, especially the orthodox wholesaler and the truck distributor, supply the assortment needed by the nonintegrated or semi-integrated food stores. These middlemen are involved, collectively, in the equalization process and the beginnings of the dispersion process.

3. The final set of middlemen, completing the dispersion process, consists of the various forms of retail and service agencies who sell the products directly to the ultimate consumers or who use the products in the preparation of meals to be served to these consumers.

On a combined basis, the distribution of 1954 sales of edible farm products was as follows: By merchant wholesalers, 49.1 per cent; by assemblers, 21.7 per cent; by agents and brokers, 17.0 per cent; and by manufacturers' sales branches and sales offices, 12.2 per cent. The gross sales value of the products handled was $12.4 billion.

Channels of Distribution—Other Extractive Industry Products

Production characteristics

The main categories of products to be considered are petroleum, lumber and forest products, ferrous and nonferrous ores, and coal and coke. Except for the lumber group, the products involved are all located in mines, or their equivalents, below the surface of the earth or of bodies of water. These deposits are not replaceable, as is the case for lumber. And, as already noted for agricultural products, the quality of the raw-material deposits is not controllable to any extent for the commercial market by human beings. As to where these raw materials are located has a considerable bearing upon where the commercial users will locate.

The extraction of these products, including lumber, involves increasingly the use of machinery; and, because of the depletion factor, considerable attention must be devoted to the extraction of all usable deposits of every commercial gradation so far as quality is concerned. In the case of petroleum, very expensive efforts must be made to uncover the deposits wherever they may be in the world. As a result, increasing percentages of our domestic petroleum requirements are being derived from foreign deposits.

Commodity characteristics

The greater part of these commodities are very bulky and heavy in relation to their values. Thus, the channel must provide a wide range of middlemen devices which reduce the number of times the product must be handled physically. Grading must be done systematically because of the importance of such specifications in the use by various classes and because of the small degree of usefulness these commodities serve in the commercial flows.

Practically all of the categories have experienced distinctly widening varieties of intermediate and final uses, thus increasing sharply the varieties of initial and intermediate users of and customers for the raw materials. Thus, the destructive distillation of lumber yields an increasing number of synthetic-product end uses. In addition to the widening varieties of use for fuel, petroleum, by means of the ever developing petro-chemical industries, is also offering an ever-widening range of uses. Coal, too, in addition to its established use as a fuel, is becoming an important raw-material source for many synthetics. Finally, the metallic ores are becoming the initial ingredients in ever-widening lists of industrial and manufactured consumers' goods products.

Factors explaining the variable importance of wholesale middlemen

For such basic raw materials as petroleum and the metallic ores, the largest initial movements of the raw materials are likely to be controlled by those plants which are part of the integrated manufacturer structure. In such cases, the movements are between units of the same business empire, and the pricing process becomes a matter of internal accounting. For products such as coal and lumber, a wider variety of channel alternatives is available. Although large integrated companies may control the forests, and their sales branches and sales offices may control, in part, the initial flows of lumber, these meet only a fraction of the channel needs.

As a result of the diverse intermediate and end uses, wholesale middlemen are necessary who can: (a) locate and maintain contact on a continuous basis with all classes of users and (b) maintain inventories—in addition to those at the forest lumber mill points— from which size, shape, and quality inventory adaptations can be made. Because of weight and transportation cost factors, much intermediate handling is reduced to a minimum by using drop shippers, sales offices, brokers, and manufacturers and sales agents.

In the case of coal, there are somewhat the same channel considerations as for lumber, but the industrial uses of the product are far more important than lumber. As a result, the mining companies have their own sales branches and sales offices which assume considerably greater levels of importance than for lumber. The broker and sales agents, in addition, assume increased importance.

Based upon 1954 data, the types-of-operation groups handling petroleum and petroleum products were petroleum bulk stations, et al., 89 per cent; merchant wholesalers, 7.9 per cent; and agents and brokers, 3.1 per cent. For the lumber and forest products, the division was as follows: Merchant wholesalers, 72.9 per cent; agents and brokers, 15.9 per cent; and sales branches and sales offices, 11.3 per cent. Finally, for coal and coke, the distribution was: Merchant wholesalers, 40.9 per cent; agents and brokers, 30.1 per cent; and sales branches and sales offices, 29 per cent.

Channels of Distribution—Manufactured Industrial Goods

Production characteristics

Data pertaining to the distribution of establishments, employees, and value added by manufacture, as well as by kinds of manufacturing activity and by geographic divisions, have been presented in Chapter 4. From these data, it was apparent that there are wide ranges of importance depending on the types of products produced and on the difference between the highly geographically concentrated industries and those which are dispersed in location. Furthermore, the manufacturing units range from large numbers of small-size units to such integrated giants as the automobile and steel-producing companies.

In addition, there are wide ranges from those companies producing few products of a relatively homogeneous nature to those producing wide varieties of products classified under more than one category. The products produced have wide ranges of end uses as well, and many have both industrial goods and manufactured consumers' goods characteristics. Manufacturing establishments may concentrate on highly technical products made to complex specifications, as in the case of the missile program; or they may produce highly standardized products, as in the case of electric bulbs; or they may produce varying combinations of both.

Commodity characteristics

The manufactured industrial goods category involves a wide assortment of products. The most useful classification is to distinguish between two categories: (1) those goods which enter directly into, and can be identified in the actual products produced, and (2) those which either facilitate such production or are needed by the various types of institutional customers. In the first category, apart from the primary and secondary raw materials already discussed, would be included the wide array of semiprocessed and fully processed components, ranging in value from a few cents each to thousands of dollars or more; packaging materials which become part of the final products; and directly related services.

In the second category would be included the following: The basic major equipment (or capital goods) and buildings used for the manufacturing, construction, or similar activities; such accessory equipment as small tools, jigs, dies, which are employed in conjunction with the basic major equipment, but which are used up in considerably shorter periods of time; the office equipment needed by any business, government, educational, or other profit and nonprofit units; various kinds of supplies (lubricating, etc.) needed in both the production and the nonproduction aspects of customer activities; such process materials as bleaching chemicals, enzymes, catalytic chemicals; transportation and storage services; shipping containers; stationery, office supplies, etc.; and all types of accounting and statistical machines, including computers.

These commodities may be, as noted, highly standardized, or they may involve manufacturer, buyer, or other specifications. They may be highly technical in nature, requiring salesmen with scientific and engineering training, or they may be of such general nature as to require no such specialized knowledge for selling and servicing. They may be durable and last for decades, as in the case of buildings and railroad equipment, or they may be completely used up by each application. As a result, each category has highly varying periods of customer reordering as compared with other categories. Because of these characteristics, sales negotiations may be of very routine nature, or they may involve, on the other hand, key executives as the negotiating agents and months and even years of negotiation. Technical servicing requirements may range from none to very highly skilled arrangements. Many products are covered by intricate patent and/or cross-licensing agreements, while other types have no such protection. Wide varieties of packaging characteristics are to be noted, together with wide ranges of susceptibility to manufacturer brand identification. Obviously, many products lose their brand identification by being components of other final products.

Factors explaining the variable importance of wholesale middlemen

Generally, the following factors will be of some help in understanding the high significance of direct channels: (1) The small number of potential users for certain types of industrial goods, requiring very close and continuous contact by the manufacturer if no potential or actual sales opportunities are to be overlooked; (2) a large average unit sale which requires long periods of time for completion of negotiations;[9] (3) concentration of actual and potential customers in very compact geographic areas, thus permitting intensive use of a relatively small sales force; (4) the need for considerable technical advice and assistance in making the initial sales, and in the continuous postsales servicing period; (5) the need for providing key executives

---

[9] Visualize, for example, the time periods involved in the sale of jet planes to airline companies, or complete, streamlined trains to the railroads.

on the selling side to match the organizational levels of the buyers; (6) the impact of reciprocity in making industrial goods sales; (7) the impact of the greater incidence of integration among industrial goods sellers and buyers; and (8) the length of time required to introduce buyers either to new uses of existing products, or to revolutionary types of new products (such as electronic computers).

On the other hand, there are many factors which underlie the use of many types of merchant and/or agent middlemen in semidirect and indirect channels:

1. The need for specialized knowledge of and contact with specific markets on a widely distributed geographical basis, thus involving a relatively large force of marketing representatives.
2. The inability of many manufacturers, because of financial and manpower reasons, to perform any or all of the marketing task for their product line.
3. The frequent need for guaranteeing products which originate from relatively unknown manufacturing sources.
4. The existence of a "thin" market in the geographic and sales sense. In order to spread the costs of the channel under such conditions, the use of wholesale middlemen handling competing and/or noncompeting lines of products may well be the only satisfactory solution.
5. The existence of a large, widespread market in which customers place frequent orders consisting of many items needing rapid delivery service.
6. The existence of well-known, standardized products requiring less technical and intensive sales arrangements.
7. The existence of large numbers of small buyers who frequently require financial assistance in making purchases.

As a result of the diversity of characteristics and factors affecting the channel structure for manufactured industrial goods, it is true, undoubtedly, that the relative importance of the direct channels has been overstated. Data for 1954 show that the merchant wholesalers group accounted for better than $2 out of every $5 of total gross sales, and that the wholesalers and agent-broker groups combined were just about equal in importance to the manufacturers' sales branches and sales offices group.

For individual kinds of business, however, much wider variations are apparent. Thus, within the limits of census data, sales branches and sales offices apparently accounted for the distribution of all textile mill products (excluding consumers' goods), instruments and related products (excluding tires and tubes), and leather and leather products. They also accounted for above-average percentages in the chemical and metal products groups. On the other hand, the merchant whole-salers' group was very important in the wholesale sales of scrap and waste materials, plumbing-heating equipment and supplies, and farm supplies. In addition, they had above-average importance for the machinery equipment and supplies, millwork and construction mate-rials, and paper and allied products kinds of business.

Channels of Distribution—Manufactured Consumers' Goods

Production characteristics

It is in this commodity category of channel structure that one finds the greatest diversity of manufacturing units—size ranges, geographi-cal patterns, variety of output, value added, and other measures considered. The producing units range all the way from the numerous individualistic garment manufacturers, with unstable financial struc-tures, unknown brand names, and variable marketing output, to the large, integrated giants. The range of products produced in a single manufacturing plant may consist of one or two to as many as hun-dreds, especially if the variations in brand names and packages also are considered. The time period of production may range from highly concentrated seasonal periods to an annual cycle.

As to location, the plants producing manufactured consumers' goods range from production-point clusterings, as in the case of meat-slaughtering establishments, to ultimate consumer market orientation, as in the illustrations of bread and bakery products, ice cream, and soft drinks. Every gradation of locational preference is likely to be found, and, once again, the marketing channel structure must reflect an adaptation to these wide ranges. The geographical, chronological, and communication gaps between producers and ultimate consumers create very complex problems for marketing organization.

Commodity characteristics

The variety of manufactured consumers' goods moving through marketing channels is staggering. No matter which classification scheme is used, it is not difficult to detect sharp increases in the last decade or so in: (a) varieties of products within existing classification categories; (b) identification (brand) names used; (c) varieties of packages for existing categories; and (d) new classification categories. Among other effects, for example, the impact of the foreign automobiles has been the cause to multiply, suddenly and substantially, the buying alternatives. Similarly, the manufacturing of filter-tip cigarettes, together with standard versus king size, and changes in types of packaging are illustrative of explosions in the variety of existing products. On the other hand, the synthetic-fibre and stereophonic-sound-equipment products are examples of new categories which extend existing categories.

In terms of durability, manufactured consumers' goods have a wide range from very perishable to very durable. To many consumers, a loaf of bread has a life of only one to two days, despite the fact that the product may be placed in a deep-freeze unit for use at later dates. On the other hand, a suite of furniture or a rug may last for two or more decades, especially with proper maintenance. Items such as pharmaceuticals may have dosages prescribed which use up the entire amount of the product within a day or a few days. For the various types of durables, there is no comparable notion of dosage.

So far as units of sale are concerned, there exists, once again, a very wide range. Some products are purchased one at a time, whereas others may be purchased by the dozen, bushel, gross, or some similar measure of quantity. Physically, the unit may vary in weight from a single ounce or less to several thousand pounds. The channel structure receives highly unequal impacts from such variations even so far as the delivery function itself is concerned.

Again, extremely wide ranges in unit product values are apparent. Manufactured consumers' goods range in price from fractional cents per unit to thousands of dollars (as in the case of automobiles, motor boats, or jewelry). Even within the same category of product use, sharp variations in unit values are apparent, e.g., perfumes, women's apparel, and jewelry.

Increasingly, the impact of the channel itself is to magnify the importance of packaging for manufactured consumers' goods. Because of over-all physical size some products, such as automobiles, cannot be packaged. In such cases, it is questionable anyway whether or not the package would have any marketing significance. But, in some cases, startling innovations in packaging materials have led, in turn, to startling innovations in prepackaged products. Two examples may be given: the transparent wrappings for meats and certain other manufactured foods, and the cellophane wrappings for men's white shirts which facilitate self-service retailing.

Closely related to, and affected by, the variations in durability noted above is the characteristic of frequency of purchase. Some products, because they are used up physically in the consumption process, have high rates of frequency of purchase, e.g., meats, toothpaste. Other products, as noted, may last for decades. In one case, accordingly, the channel and the middlemen therein devote considerable marketing efforts to maintain their shares or to increase their shares of existing consumption. They attempt, also, to develop new users. In the furniture case, the channel must devote most of its time in selling those persons involved in the formation of new households while the replacement market assumes reduced importance.

Among the more important characteristics affecting channel structure is the factor of relative weight and bulkiness. Manufactured consumers' goods range in physical size and bulk from the very small sewing needle or tablet of medicine to very bulky items such as refrigerators, certain items of furniture, and automobiles. As a result, once again variable combinations will be found of wholesale middlemen selling with and without inventories of merchandise physically present.

Finally, wide ranges are found in the elasticity of demand for manufactured consumers' goods and in the availability of substitutes. The consumers' goods range all the way from vital necessities to complete luxuries, with corresponding effects on the elasticities of demands. In terms of substitutability, the products range from conditions of having hundreds of brands of direct or semidirect substitutes to conditions of no substitutes, as in the case of a rare gem.

Factors explaining the variable importance of wholesale middlemen

The complexities of the channel structure for manufactured consumers' goods almost rival those already described for agricultural products. With the exception of the assemblers group, opportunities exist for the use of all types of merchant wholesalers and agent middlemen. All forms of channels from the most simple and direct to the most complicated indirect patterns characterize the flow of manufactured consumers' goods.

The importance of direct channels is limited, relatively, to a few cases of specialty items and to such marketing arrangements as the various types of "of-the-month" clubs. In the case of the specialties, the basis for the direct channel is found in the unique nature of the merchandise coupled, as in the case of Fuller brushes, with a desire to control the complete channel. In the case of the "of-the-month" clubs, in addition to the factor of unique merchandise, there may be offered the features of low prices and the expert advice of a board in selecting each monthly choice.

Of much greater importance are the semidirect channels. These channels have two distinct structural patterns. The first consists of those manufacturer-controlled channels where, because of the unique nature of the product, of the variety of goods produced, of service, or because of financial considerations, the manufacturers use sales branches and/or sales offices in selling to the various classes of retail customers. In the second form, the retailers, by virtue of backward vertical integration, contact manufacturers directly.

But by far the most important segment of these channel structures consists of the indirect channels. The explanation lies, in part, in the fact that the marketing task to be performed matches very closely the analysis given in explaining the funnel concept of wholesaling and its strategic importance in marketing. This would include the need of many small manufacturers for brokers or selling agents (or their equivalent) in contacting the orthodox wholesaler and other types of merchant wholesalers. Another aspect is to be found, once again, in the close relationship of this particular problem and the importance of the basic marketing processes. A final explanation lies in the complexity of the geographical distribution of retail and ultimate consumers to be reached.

Data exist showing the relative importance of the three types-of-operation groups. On an over-all basis for selected manufactured consumers' goods, the merchant wholesalers had 52 per cent of the gross wholesale sales, whereas the sale branches and sales offices had nearly twice as much of the remaining compared with the agents and brokers group. The merchant wholesalers were very much of above-average importance in the following kinds of business: gift and art goods; jewelry; hardware; beer, wine, distilled spirits; amusements, sporting goods, toys; and tobacco. The kinds of business in which the manufacturers' sales branches and sales offices had above-average sales were: automotive; drugs; electrical appliances, radios, TV sets; books, magazines, newspapers; and tobacco. Finally, the agents and brokers were relatively most important for the dry-goods and apparel groups, and the groceries-confectionery-meats groups.

Channels of Distribution—Services

A discussion of channels of distribution for services opens a field of discussion which has been hardly touched upon in the existing literature.[10] Many of the personal services are either marketed

---

[10] There are, of course, estimates of expenditures for selected services in the national income statistics and data for selected services in the *Census of Business*.

through direct channels from source to user, as in the case of medical, dental, and legal services, or simply involve the use of a retail-type establishment, as in the case of the apparel cleaning, shoe repairing, and barber and beauty shop kinds of business. Some personal services such as motion pictures and baseball require expensive, highly specialized types of establishments. But the discussion here is concerned mainly with other types of channels which involve a much wider range of channel considerations.

Production characteristics

Most of the types of services being considered here have no concept of production in the ordinary sense in which the term is used for the manufacture of tangible goods. The closest parallel exists in the case of utilities services where there are plants which generate electricity. In most cases, however, the creation of the service is inherent in the professional, semiprofessional, skilled, and unskilled talents of one or more persons. In this sense, also, most of the services cannot be produced in advance of use and stored. The locational aspects of most services becomes, again, a considerably different geographical problem than the location of manufacturing industries.

Commodity characteristics

Although many services are intangible in and of themselves, they become intertwined, nevertheless, in a particular physical environment. Examples are the institutional aspects of the modern commercial and savings banks, the plush offices of advertising agencies and management consulting firms, and the elaborate facilities of storage and transportation agencies. Most services are highly perishable in the sense that the originator cannot, in most instances, store them until they can be marketed. Grading and standardization specifications are nonexistent, and knowledge of quality must depend to a great extent, accordingly, on word-of-mouth promotion. Packaging, at least in the tangible-commodity meaning, is also nonexistent. Pricing and price determination assume far different aspects because of the haziness of what costs are, in most cases, and because of the absence of any systematic price-determining markets.

Factors explaining the variable importance of wholesale middlemen

Because of some of the characteristics noted above, it would be expected that the more professional the type of service considered, the greater would be the impact of direct channels of distribution. This is true, however, only where the marketing area is limited or where codes of ethics prevent any widespread use of advertising, as in the legal and medical professions. But in the case of many types of entertainment, various types of management or booking office services exist to establish contracts with the entertainment places used, to publicize the event, to arrange for transportation of the entertainers, and to handle the financial aspects. In the marketing of securities, there do exist organized stock exchanges which rival the organized commodity markets in structure; and within these exchanges there are the important buying and selling brokers.

For the travel industry, including the hotels as well as the transportation agencies, increasing use is being made of travel agents, as well as of the agencies' own controlled sales office, in reaching the wide array of business, government, institutional, and ultimate consumer customers. For such specialized financial problems as one finds in the textile industry, there exist special middlemen known as *factors* who have had a long history of use both in Europe and the United States.[11]

Many services, however, are based either upon individual proprietorship or upon partnership forms of organizations. In such cases, the business must depend upon the ability of its principals to build up a wide, personal acquaintanceship with potential users. This is true, for example, of many corporation lawyers, public accounting firms, advertising agencies, and management consulting firms. Advertising, except for the strict limitations noted in the professional services, may be used. Great dependency must be placed upon so servicing customers that a very important word-of-mouth reputation is created. Where these agencies are organized on either partnership or corporate bases, the withdrawal of an execution may involve a considerable diversion of business from the existing firm to a newly created firm.

Middlemen's Sales, by Class of Customer

While available census data permit detailed analyses to be made of each type-of-operations group's sales, by class of customers for the most important kinds of business, only summary information can be presented. Table 19 presents the available data for the 1935, 1939, 1948, and 1954 Census periods. In using these data, it must be

[11] The modern factors, such as the Walter Heller Company in Chicago, not only purchase a concern's accounts receivables but frequently offer a quality of professional managerial advice rivaling that of the consulting firms. See the bibliography for appropriate references.

TABLE 19

SALES, BY CLASS OF CUSTOMER: UNITED STATES 1954, 1948, 1939, AND 1935

Type of Operation and Census Year	Total		Total ($1,000)	Percentage Distribution—Reporting Establishment				
	Estab-lishments	Sales ($1,000)		to Re-tailers	to Industrial Users (including Gov't.)	to Whole-sale	to Consumers and Farm	for Export
Merchant wholesalers								
1954	165,153	101,100,941	87,235,929	45.2	32.0	15.1	2.8	4.9
1948	146,518	79,766,589	75,838,020	46.9	31.8	13.7	1.6	6.0
1939	101,627	23,641,924	21,972,974	58.9	23.6	11.6	1.9	4.0
1935	88,931	17,661,691	15,905,271	59.2	24.9	10.2	1.9	3.8
Merchandise agents and brokers								
1954	22,131	39,250,509	33,729,858	13.8	43.7	37.1	2.1	3.4
1948	24,361	34,610,092	28,691,265	16.1	41.8	36.5	0.4	5.2
1939	20,903	11,201,035	9,839,969	16.8	35.8	40.6	0.7	6.1
1935	18,147	8,908,076	6,697,013	21.0	34.9	39.4	0.1	4.6
Assemblers of farm products								
1954	13,255	9,050,816	6,488,377	6.8	45.1	34.6	10.9	2.5
1948	19,268	10,957,893	10,053,170	9.4	32.6	51.8	5.3	0.9
1939	29,122	3,088,571	2,695,058	13.5	21.3	55.8	6.2	3.2
1935	26,515	2,463,011	1,773,011	12.7	29.5	50.0	4.1	3.7
Manufacturers' sales branches, sales offices								
1954			N.A.	N.A.	N.A.	N.A.	N.A.	N.A.
1948	23,768	52,738,577	51,154,221	31.3	42.7	23.0	0.4	2.6
1939	17,926	14,253,609	12,628,980	31.6	43.2	23.1	0.4	1.7
1935	15,830	11,066,088	9,110,062	41.5	37.8	19.4	0.3	1.0
Petroleum bulk stations, terminals								
1954			N.A.	N.A.	N.A.	N.A.	N.A.	N.A.
1948	29,451	9,000,370	56,522,646	64.1	35.9	a	b	a
1939	30,825	2,942,982	1,903,472	74.0	26.0	a	b	a
1935	27,333	2,704,047	1,379,520	73.3	9.9	8.4	8.0	0.4

Source: U. S. Bureau of the Census, *U. S. Census of Business—1954,* Vol. III, p. 18, Table N.

a Included in "to retailers."
b Included in "to industrial users."

remembered that they represent the averages for a wide range found among various kinds of business.

For merchant wholesalers, the main trends have been: (1) A sharp reduction in the percentage of sales made to retailers from 59 per cent in 1935 to 45 per cent in 1954; (2) a sharp rise in the proportion moving to industrial users from 25 to 32 per cent; and (3) increased sales made to other types of wholesale middlemen. For agents and brokers, sales to industrial users and to other types of middlemen account for most of their business. Sales to industrial users have increased steadily since 1935, whereas those made to other types of wholesale middlemen have had irregular movements.

Because of the rise of the fast-frozen food industry, the new and expanded uses of soy beans, and related factors, sales from assemblers of farm products to industrial users have outstripped sales to other types of wholesale middlemen since 1935. Sales to industrial users have risen from 29.5 to 45 per cent, while sales to other types of wholesale middlemen have declined from 55.8 per cent in 1939 to 34.6 per cent in 1954. Reduced proportions of sales to retailers from 13.5 per cent in 1939 to 6.8 per cent in 1954 have been offset by an increase in sales direct to consumers from 4 per cent in 1929 to 11 per cent in 1954, with most of this increase registered between 1948 and 1954.

Data for manufacturers' sales offices and sales branches and for the petroleum group were available on a combined basis only for 1935, 1939, and 1948. For the sales branches and sales offices, sales during this period direct to industrial users have displaced sales to retailers as the most significant. There have been increases, also, in the importance of sales to other wholesale middlemen and for export. Because of the rise of the petro-chemical industry, there has been a sharp increase in the proportion of sales made to industrial users at the expense of sales of gasoline and oil to filling stations. This has taken place despite the sharp increase in the use of the automobile.

Factors Explaining the Use of Particular Channels by Individual Manufacturers

Finally, a summary explanation needs to be given of the factors which help to explain the use of particular channels of distribution by individual manufacturers for their products. These factors are divided into basic external considerations and selective internal considerations peculiar to the individual manufacturer. The division, however, is not a hard and fast one, but is meant to be merely suggestive.

Basic external considerations

These considerations may be subdivided into volume of sales, order, market, product, and channel subclassifications. Volume of sales considerations bring into the channel discussion a marketing research approach: the estimation of total sales potentialities for the product or products to be marketed; the percentage of this estimated total sales which the individual manufacturer can expect to realize, subdivided by product lines and geographic units; and the productivity of various individual channel alternatives in realizing these estimates.

The order characteristics summarize the variables which have been discussed for the various channel patterns. These involve, among other things, the influence of the dollar amount of the average sales order, the relative frequency of ordering, the regularity with which orders are placed, the number of separate product items in each order, and the extent to which solicitation by salesmen may or may not be necessary for repeat sales.

Under market considerations are included all of the pertinent factors explaining the composition of the manufacturers' customers. Included are such factors as: Who are the customers? How many are there? What is the geographical distribution? What are their product dislikes and preferences? What type of person influences the purchase? What is the density of distribution? Is it necessary to have personal acquaintanceships in order to make sales?

The product characteristics include the following: (1) Is the product relatively new in the channel or has it an established marketing position? (2) how rapidly does product style or design change? (3) the relative value of the product; (4) the product's weight in relation to such value; (5) the need for promptness in delivery; (6) whether or not technical knowledge is needed for the sale and in installing and servicing the product; (7) the nature and extent of the repair service required, if any; (8) whether or not the product is standardized; and (9) the type of product involved—industrial or consumers' goods.

Finally, increasing attention must be given by the manufacturer to channel characteristics. Pertinent to this analysis is the use of analytical tools and techniques to determine channel costs relative to the functions performed; the effect of channel alternatives on profits; and the attitude of the middlemen in the channel alternatives towards the manufacturer's product or product line.

Internal considerations

There are, finally, certain selective internal management considerations. One of these considerations involves whether or not the industry, of which the manufacturer is a member, uses orthodox or traditional channel arrangements. If the answer is in the affirmative, then the individual manufacturer must decide whether or not to conform with the industry pattern. In making this decision, he must be guided, in part, by an evaluation of the success achieved by competitors in using nonorthodox channels and, in part, by some of the external considerations.

The manufacturer must consider, also, what functions he needs from the channel; how well his financial and manpower resources will permit him to exercise the degree of channel control he desires; the extent and type of cooperation desired from middlemen in the channel; a critical evaluation of the significant channel trends taking place; and, finally, whether or not there are executive channel preferences or prejudices.

6

Channel Structure (Continued)

The preceding chapter has developed the necessary framework for enlarging the perspective of channel structure from the wholesaling sector point of view. This chapter is designed to broaden the perspective by introducing selected problem areas. This discussion will serve as an introduction to later discussions of internal managerial activities. In this way it is hoped to strengthen the liaison elements inherent in the subject matter contents.

The Continuing Managerial Struggle for Channel Control

From what has been presented already in Chapter 5, it should be apparent that the channel is the specific marketing organizational vehicle in which the abstract theoretical concepts of competition (pure and otherwise) take a concrete application involving specific products, specific types of middlemen, and specific linkages and blockages woven together into channel structural patterns as described. The aspects of this specific competition which are pertinent for a discussion of the wholesaling sector involve an understanding of (a) the managerial struggle for the control of the channel, and (b) some other aspects of competition through the medium of the channel.

The meaning of managerial struggle for channel control

In the absence of a theory of automatic marketing or marketing under the guise of an "invisible hand" arrangement, any notion of competition must involve, in its channel aspects, an understanding of what is meant by the managerial struggle for channel control. What is implied by competition is a sense of the internal structure of a particular channel pattern in which the agencies involved at each stage of the channel must decide whether or not to adopt specific policies which will affect the nexus of management power within the channel. The attempt to establish such nexus of power may result in one level of management achieving success, or it may lead to the countermove by means of which some of the management units may respond by becoming instrumental in creating new channels, thus introducing elements of competition to be discussed in the following section.

The control thus manifested within a particular channel for a particular category of products involves an organizational jousting for channel position which cuts across the element of integration discussed in Chapter 5. It may result in a clear-cut victory for one level within the channel or in a serious stalemate in which no single management unit "wins" or "loses." It may result in strengthening the solidity of the channel or it may generate the seeds of the channel's destruction. Cooperation or anarchy may accompany all such attempts at achieving control.

Thus, the struggle becomes a manifestation of the extent to which the marketing system makes it possible for a given producer to place a cloak of protection over his product lines throughout the channel, or whether it forces an early divorcement between the producer and the marketing destiny of the products he has produced. Because of the nature of the channel, as discussed in the preceding chapter, it becomes the logical center for such management struggles.

Forms of managerial struggles and control devices

From the point of view of a single channel structure, the struggle for channel control involves four sets of management levels: the producer-directed struggles; the wholesale-middlemen-directed struggles; the retail-middlemen-directed struggles; and the facilitating-agency-directed struggles. These may be subdivided, in turn, in any given channel illustration into the particular types of agencies found for each of these four levels. Thus, there is a wide range of individual patterns available within even a single channel structure.

Closely related to this set of struggles within any given channel pattern are the various types of control devices used by the management units.[1] Any of these four levels may achieve successful control

---

[1] This discussion should be coordinated in all aspects with the discussion of integration in Chapter 5.

by acquiring complete ownership of any or all of the remaining levels within the channel. In lieu of direct ownership, however, a series of contractual devices may be used. On the manufacturers' side, this may involve resale price maintenance agreements, franchised distributorship arrangements, or the use of agent-principal contracts establishing the scope of activity of the agent middlemen. In the case of wholesale and retail middlemen, it may involve contracts made with manufacturers for all or part of their output identified with the middleman's own brand or similar form of designation. In addition to these devices, the battling parties may have recourse to all of the professional aspects of advertising campaigns and campaigns designed to counter these. It is impossible to indicate in any given situation which of these devices has the greatest potentiality for success.

Other forms of control devices may be utilized. One involves substituting group control for the struggles between individual management levels in the channel in order to meet other forms of channel competition. Thus, the use of the voluntary chain principle is one pertinent example, while another is the group buying-manufacturing arrangement found among noncompeting department stores. Another example is to be found as a by-product of the quantity of credit extended by means of which the creditor, whatever his channel position and importance, is given a voice in the marketing movements of the products through the channel. In other cases, the producer may attempt to buy channel cooperation by widening the middleman's margin or by granting additional types of price discounts in such forms as advertising allowances or "push money allowances" for a distributor's salesmen.

Objectives of the struggle for control

While the goal of all types of managerial struggle for channel control may be summed up in the clichés, "the search for marketing power," and "improved profits," there are so many aspects of each of these that some additional discussion is necessary. Keeping in mind that each of the following objectives may be subdivided according to the level of the channel, they may be grouped as: (1) an increase in the degree of control exercised by the manufacturer over the marketing destiny of his products; (2) improvements in the short-run and long-run profit positions of any of the agencies in the channel structure; (3) improvements in managements' share of the total market for the products involved at any channel level, market area by market area; (4) the insurance of the success of a given management's marketing policies and marketing program; (5) the development of countermoves at other managerial struggles for control within the channel or against competition from other channels; and (6) increased emphasis on nonprice versus price aspects affiliated with the products as they move through the channel.[2]

Other Aspects of Channel Competition

The preceding discussion of the managerial struggle for channel control has emphasized mainly the *internal* aspects of channel competition; that is, competition between the levels already noted within a particular channel structure for particular products. But there is an important *external* view to channel competition, as well, which needs to be noted. This external competition involves two main classes: (1) that between each pattern within a network of the internal channels, as noted above, which constitute all of the management units involved in moving a product or a group of interrelated products through this composite channel within the highly technical meaning of the term "industry"; and (2) that between management units in the channel for which a given product is a significant item, saleswise, and those management units in a different channel for which the product is of minor significance.

Within the industry channel type of competition (type 1), the struggle for management control becomes superimposed on a broader framework of competition between the competitive strengths of the direct, semidirect, and indirect channels. This cross-sectional competition involves, in turn, competition between various types of operation at both the wholesale and retail middlemen levels in all of the forms described elsewhere. In addition, such forms of competition become increasingly complex by virtue of the variety of geographical aspects in which they may take on concrete form.

In the second type, the complexities of the internal managerial struggles for control and the forms noted above are joined by the channel alternatives found in the nonindustry environment consisting of the agencies handling the products as minor items of inventory im-

---

[2] For an interesting comparison of this view of the managerial struggle with other views, see Ralph F. Breyer, *Quantitative Systemic Analysis and Control: Study No. 1—Channel and Channel Group Listing* (Philadelphia: The Author, 1949), Chapter 3.

David R. Craig and Werner K. Gabler, "The Competitive Struggle for Market Control," *Annals of the American Academy of Political and Social Science,* CCIX (May 1940), 84–107.

portance. Thus, a second array of direct, semidirect, and indirect channels is superimposed upon the first array. Since the products of minor significance have possibilities of achieving increased significance, this type of competition may become quite violent in its repercussions. It may even lead the agencies within the industry channel to invade the minor groups' product lines as one form of retaliatory competitive tactics.

Thus, these forms of channel competition become quite complex in all of their manifestations. These, in turn, may make it very difficult at any moment of time to detect the full incidence of such forms of competition within the entire framework of competition. Furthermore, the channel turmoil thus created is responsible, additionally, for the introduction of new forms of blockage efforts within the channel.

Evolutionary Aspects of Channel Competition

This section will merely point up the analysis, in a preliminary sense, of selected evolutionary aspects. The first of these which needs to be emphasized is tied in with the cycle of development of the various types of wholesale middlemen, beginning with the period of the domination of the orthodox wholesaler and continuing with the factors underlying the development of the deviate types of wholesalers and other types of operations as well. The second evolutionary aspect involves the development of manufacturing production in the United States from one of purely local status to a position of regional and national status. Related to this, also, is the development from a period in which production was of a scale sufficient to meet only existing demands to a period when much production takes place in anticipation of demand. A third set of evolutionary aspects building on the previous aspects includes the rise of branded products. At first, this rise was in terms of the manufacturer-controlled brand, but later it shifted to a combination of such brands and to the wholesale- and retail-middlemen-controlled brands in various combinations of local, regional, and national patterns. The final set of evolutionary aspects involves the evolution of various types of retail middlemen, especially of the large-scale, integrated types.

Apart from these main currents of evolutionary considerations, there are many important types of cross-currents stemming from the evolution of storage, transportation, and related facilitating agencies.

Major aspects in channel competition within the agricultural goods area are the forces behind the origins, the rise in importance, and the decline in importance of organized wholesale markets. Packaging developments, in their relationship to product identification and to self-service retailing, have special significance in selected product examples. The widening array of products to be marketed through the channel has accentuated the industry versus nonindustry type of channel competition noted above.

On the side of government regulation, the development of certain forms of regulatory measures has had great significance for channel competition. Among the more important in this respect to be discussed in detail in Chapters 21 and 22 are: trade-mark and trade-name laws in relation to the increased significance of product identification; resale price maintenance and related legislation concerning channel structure and channel control; corporate chain store tax laws and related regulations; the Robinson-Patman Act; various regulations pertaining to the marketing (especially the prices) of agricultural products; and the various modifications of and amendments to the basic antimonopoly laws.

Finally, there must be mentioned the whole series of advances in the knowledge and art of management, many of which have contributed, by their essential nature, directly or indirectly to channel competition. Closely related to these are the increased attempts to understand the nature of the consumers, and to improve the techniques by means of which advertisers can intensify their influence through the various advertising media.

Orthodox Versus Nonorthodox Channels

The marketing literature dealing with channels of distribution, has termed some channel patterns as traditional or orthodox and others as nonorthodox. In addition, this notation of orthodox channels has been extended to include the entire wholesaling sector. The differentiation is significant for this discussion in at least three ways. First, the concept of orthodox versus nonorthodox channels is related very closely to certain evolutionary aspects already presented. Second, this concept has a very close relationship to the managerial struggle for channel control as discussed in Chapter 5. Finally, this concept has a very important bearing on the whole subject of product assortments in the channel.

The meaning of orthodox and nonorthodox

For the case of a channel for a particular producer's product (or products), or for a particular commodity group, the concept of an orthodox arrangement is that of the most commonly used arrangement, or, coordinately, the channel with the longest tradition of importance by usage. Related to this is the implication of established, traditional patterns of linkages in such channels, including the indirect (facilitating) linkages. These characteristics connote, in turn, that there can be varying channel arrangements which may be designated as orthodox depending on the length of time during which a particular producer's product or a commodity group has been on the market using such arrangements. Thus, orthodoxy achieves its status, in part, by the passage of time.

As has been implied, there is also a much broader aspect to the concept of orthodox channels. For the wholesaling sector as a whole, this designation would be based upon the emphasis placed in marketing upon the dominance of the orthodox wholesaler in the wholesaling sector and upon the resurgence of this type in importance since the end of World War II. In the particular case of agricultural products, orthodox channels imply using organized central markets as pivotal institutions in the equalization-process phase of the channel.

In addition to these points of view, the concept of orthodox may be extended, also, to include the types of product assortments handled by the middlemen agencies. Thus, there is the point of view that orthodox channel arrangements involve not only traditional arrangements of middlemen and linkages but also customary assortments of products at each middlemen's level. This, in turn, is designated by some writers as one aspect of "orderly" marketing, together with the use of the orthodox channel. However, this product assortment aspect of orthodox raises issues of a broader nature than merely the channel implications (see the discussion in Chapter 7).

From these definitions it follows that nonorthodox implies the reverse of what has been designated as orthodox. Thus, the use of a type of middleman not commonly found in a channel pattern within a relatively long period of time implies a nonorthodox situation. Similarly, any significant reduction in the over-all use of the regular, orthodox wholesaler in the wholesaling sector would indicate a basic marketing shift to nonorthodox arrangements. Again, the declining use and importance of organized central wholesale markets would indicate the same tendency. Finally, any basic shifts from the ordinary product assortments would represent a change from "orderly"

to "scrambled" channel arrangements. The nonorthodox arrangements, if proven dominant over time, may achieve ultimately the
status of orthodoxy.

The importance of the concepts

Orthodox versus nonorthodox channels are closely intertwined with
the managerial struggles for control of the channel. They are related,
also, to the general topic of innovation and change in marketing as
opposed to stability. If the managerial struggles move in the direction
of upsetting the dominant middlemen types and linkages in the
channel, they will have the end result of emphasizing the nonorthodox characteristics of the channel as reconstituted. On the other
hand, if orthodox wholesalers or any other dominant type, by virtue
of their counteracting struggles succeed in staving off any attempts
at achieving a nonorthodox channel, then the orthodox channel and
linkages will maintain or increase the preceding level of importance.

In any given product channel situation, the manufacturer must
evaluate very carefully the strength of the orthodox channel elements
in the total marketing picture. If he underrates the orthodox
strength, he may engage in a costly and abortive form of nonorthodox
channel activity which may have the effect of weakening his net position in the managerial struggle for channel control. If, on the other
hand, he overrates the orthodox channel strength, he may find himself in the position of being outmaneuvered in terms of marketing
strategy. Thus, this aspect of channel behavior involves a very
careful analysis by management at the manufacturing level of the
position of the orthodox and nonorthodox channels at a given moment
of time, and the same type of careful analysis of whether there will
be any high probability of change and, if so, in which direction.

But the wholesale and retail middlemen have equally important
roles to play in the evaluation of orthodox versus nonorthodox
channels. If the middlemen are the key agencies constituting the
orthodox channel, they must continually evaluate the strength of
the orthodox channel situation; and they must also decide whether,
in the case of any movement towards nonorthodox channels, to take
active steps to maintain or increase the orthodox aspects, or, on
the other hand, to revise their types of operation to reflect the direction of the nonorthodox changes. If the wholesale and retail middlemen are currently within the nonorthodox channel aspect, then they
must evaluate carefully the probabilities of being able ultimately to
convert their nonorthodox arrangements into the orthodox channel.

The Evaluation of Channel Effectiveness

At the outset, it must be emphasized that far too many writers have viewed the evaluation of channel effectiveness only from the vantage point of the manufacturer.[3] That this view is emphasized should not be surprising since it is a continuation of a narrowness of perspective which all too often is present in the discussion of channels. Actually, the evaluation of channel effectiveness is, and should be, the concern of every primary agency in the channel—producer, wholesale middlemen, and retail middlemen. In addition, there is an over-all point of view which reflects the evaluation of the efficiency of the wholesaling sector within the entire marketing system. The objectives of the evaluation and the types of tools and techniques will vary according to the viewpoint thus indicated.

Objectives of the evaluation

Any discussion of the evaluation of channel effectiveness must take into consideration the objectives of each channel level's view as well as the over-all marketing view as noted. From the manufacturer's level, the principal objectives may be stated as follows: (1) To determine the contribution of the channel alternatives to the achievement of the company's over-all marketing program, in quantitative and qualitative units; (2) to determine, more specifically, the direct and indirect relationship between channel alternatives and the degree of market penetration of the company's product lines, area by area; (3) to determine the contribution of the channel alternatives to customer recognition and acceptance of the company's sales promotional campaigns; (4) to determine the contribution of the channel to the company's complete knowledge of the characteristics of the market it services; (5) to determine the contribution of the channel to the company's favorable or unfavorable cost-profit position, product line by product line, and market area by market area; and (6) to determine the contribution of each channel alternative to the degree of aggressiveness of the company's marketing program. Inherent in each of these are the implications for the managerial struggle for channel control noted above; and each of these may be subdivided into many appropriate subdivisions.

From the wholesale and retail middlemen's points of view, the following constitute the main objectives: (1) The extent to which

[3] See, for example, R. M. Clewett (Ed.) *Marketing Channels for Manufactured Products* (Homewood, Ill.: Richard D. Irwin, Inc., 1954), Chapters 17, 18, and 19.

the channel alternatives maximize the middleman's freedom of managerial activity with respect to products handled, territory covered, and functional activities to be performed; (2) the extent to which the channel arrangement maximizes or circumscribes each middleman's freedom to expand; (3) the extent to which the channel arrangement permits the wholesale or retail middleman to enter the managerial struggle for control of the channel, if he so desires; (4) the extent to which the middlemen are permitted in the channel to maintain their type-of-operation identity, instead of being played off one against the other; and (5) the extent to which the wholesale and retail middlemen are permitted to realize either price spread margins or commissions or fees commensurate with their cost-profit requirements.

Types of management tools available for channel evaluation

Before discussing the general framework of how the management tools may be used to evaluate channel effectiveness, an introductory description of the basic types of tools may be appropriate. The first management tool is the use of comparative sales analyses. These analyses involve the determination of the sales realized by the agencies in a particular channel structure, and the comparison of these results with some sales goals as established by the appropriate management unit. These types of analyses may be instituted by any agency level of the channel, with only the necessary changes of emphasis designed to meet differences in objectives as noted above.

Since much emphasis needs to be placed in the analysis of channel effectiveness on the relation of such effectiveness to cost and profits, it must be obvious that a second tool involves the use of special techniques of distribution cost accounting. In these analyses, distribution cost accounting may be used to evaluate the differential cost elements inherent in alternative channel structures; for measuring, similarly, alternative profit returns; for evaluating the cost of servicing various sales-size classes of customers; or for other types of problems to be discussed later.

A third family of tools may be included under the broad term of "marketing research." This may involve systematic analyses by the manufacturer or middlemen to test: (a) customer attitudes towards products and related services offered in the channel; (b) customer satisfaction or dissatisfaction with existing channel arrangements, and attitudes towards suggested alternatives; (c) the determination of the trading area boundaries of wholesale and retail markets or of specific types of wholesale and retail middlemen; (d) the attitude of middlemen in the channel towards the manufacturer, his marketing policies, and his products; (e) the attitude, conversely, of the manufacturer towards each type of middleman; (f) the establishment of specific sales and cost goals for each agency in the channel. The tools under this heading frequently are combined with the other types to develop complicated marketing potentials to be derived from alternative channel arrangements.

The basic components of channel analysis

Given any particular channel arrangement and any given combination of analytical tools, the following represent the components of a necessary beginning analysis on which can be built a whole series of special studies:

1. The measurement of the size of the potential trading areas, using techniques which have been or will be described in detail.
2. The development of sales potentials for each of these trading areas.
3. The subdivision of (1) and (2) by product lines, if necessary, with accompanying measures of the estimated market penetration ratio of each line.
4. The subdivision of (1), and (2), and (3) by salesmen and salesmen's territories. This involves knowledge, by time-and-duty analyses, of how many customers a given type of salesman can adequately service per working day.
5. The calculation of the cost-of-getting-sales ratios, by product lines, salesmen, territories, etc., in terms of the direct, semidirect, and indirect components based on historical and estimated future bases.
6. The alternative costs, as in (5), for substituting possible channel alternatives.
7. The subdivisions of the cost estimates in (5) and (6) by various size classes of customers.
8. Finally, a comparison of actual sales, cost, and profit results with the budgeted potentials, together with a critical explanation of the reasons why the potentials have or have not been realized.

Specific studies

The basic components outlined above are part of an analytical framework which can be undertaken by any business unit of sufficient sales size, adequate financial resources, and possessing sufficient insight into the marketing perspective so that it can keep its organizational executives well informed of the entire channel. In actual practice, most of these units undertake at any given period of time only those special studies which reflect for each some scale of urgency. Thus, trading area boundary studies frequently are reduced in analytical content and cost by accepting such determinations made by others in the manner already described. The systematic determination of the boundaries of salesmen's territories and related quotas, while done most frequently by the manufacturing agencies, represents another grouping of specific studies in which the wholesale middlemen also can use many of the tools of marketing research in preparing complete studies; they may give the middlemen necessary data with which to check estimates prepared by the manufacturer for the use of the middlemen.

More manufacturers than wholesale middlemen are likely to make systematic cost studies of the contributions to profits and market penetration made by each sales-size category of customer. Yet such studies are very important for middlemen as well as for manufacturers in understanding the alternative yields available from each sales-size class by making selected channel pattern shifts. Again, more manufacturers than wholesale middlemen are likely to use the various techniques of sampling and interviewing in order to get reliable estimates of consumers' attitudes towards products as they move through the channel. This is true all too often even where the wholesale middleman or retail middleman, as the case might be, has his own brand affixed to the products. Sharp differences frequently are present between manufacturers themselves, or between manufacturers and middlemen, concerning the value of studies which present continuing measurement of total and individual product market penetration. The aggregates of such studies can become most valuable evidence in understanding why total budgeted sales may or may not be realized.

Sharp differences also exist between the awareness of individual managements as to the relationship between sales size of customer accounts, the number of invoices per account, the division of assignable and nonassignable items of cost by accounts, and estimated profits. Similarly, wide differences are apparent among management levels in the use of graphic relations between sales volume and profit volume. For manufacturers, careful distribution cost analyses must be made of the variable cost components of alternative channel arrangements if accurate estimates of net additions to profits are to be determined. These must include, as well, realistic estimates of sales, especially if middlemen, formerly used by the manufacturer, represent strong competitive lives in the shifts in channels. Finally, careful cost allocations must be made by all agencies handling multiproduct assortments, in order that realistic calculations may be made of the contribution of each item to gross and net profit.[4]

An additional type of analysis which requires much continuous research is the study of those marketing trends which have some significant relationship to channels of distribution. The appropriate personnel assigned to make such analyses in any organization must be well trained, first of all, in how to detect evidence of the existence of any change. This involves, in turn, professional acquaintanceship with the basic marketing literature; with those publications of the trade press specializing in the reporting of changes; with various statistical studies and professional studies of special aspects; and with provision for a continuous flow of oral and written reports about significant trends from the salesmen and branch executives in the various key centers of trade. From the evidence collected, careful analysis must be made of both the content and implication of each trend presented. The final aspect of such analyses must include careful recommendations as to whether the management can influence the direction of the trend or, on the contrary, can be dominated by the basic changes being generated.

All in all, the marketing organization (channel) aspects of many marketing problems have not been given, it would appear, the importance by the various agencies in the channel that they seem to require in view of the significance of channels. As has been indicated in Chapter 5, and as will be re-emphasized at the conclusion of this chapter, the channel is the managerial battlefield in which marketing strategy and marketing tactic activities of each business unit either succeed or fail. It would seem only logical, therefore, that a great deal of the marketing research being done recognize and emphasize this level of significance, and that the problems be so carefully defined as not to eliminate important channel aspects and implications.

Some Further Observations on the Geographic Aspects of Channels

Some preceding remarks have indicated, in somewhat preliminary fashion, the importance of thinking about channels and channel structure in specific geographic context rather than in abstract non-

[4] These statements are only suggestive of the kinds of analyses which need to be made and the types of analytical tools to be used. The next sections will examine certain aspects of these analyses in more detail in their internal management perspective. The evaluation of the over-all effectiveness of channels will be included in the concluding discussions of the efficiency of the wholesaling sector.

spatial terms. This emphasis is necessary regardless of the type ￼ channel under consideration. There are at least four types of cas￼ in which the geographic aspects of channels and channel structu may be visualized:

1. *Type 1*—emphasizes the locational aspects of the agencies ￼ levels of the producing-manufacturing, wholesale middlemen ar retail middlemen, facilitating, intermediate user, and fin consumer.
2. *Type 2*—emphasizes the complete geographic outreach of tl entire channel.
3. *Type 3*—emphasizes the geographic characteristics of the chaɪ nels involved in terms of urban or rural orientation.
4. *Type 4*—emphasizes the wholesale and/or retail trading ar￼ aspects.

This list is only suggestive, and each type can be subdivided, turn, by the types of channels discussed in Chapter 5. Each of the types will be described more fully below.

Type 1

All discussions of channels must begin, in emphasizing the ge graphic aspects, with certain locational constants; and it is the locational constants which are incorporated in this type. To beg with, whatever the product which moves through the channel, it produced by a given extractive industry or manufacturing un located at given sites either within the United States or in a foreiǥ country. Similarly, each wholesale middleman, retail middlema or facilitating functional agency have specific locations, as do tl intermediate and final users. Thus, a channel is, first of all, a syste of linkages located at specific geographic points, thus creating peculiar spatial pattern which can only be duplicated by anoth channel pattern if it involves identically the same agencies wi identically the same locations. In this important sense, then, channel for a particular make of product has its own uniqʋ geographic structuring.

Type 2

Because of the unique characteristics noted for type 1, some valʋ may be obtained for channel discussion by regrouping the geograph aspects. In this way, the entire geographic outreach of the combin￼ channels for a group of individual products having similar marketiɪ characteristics may be studied. On this basis, channels may classified as: those confined to a local area (as in the case of bre￼

or pasteurized milk); the sectional or complete state outreach; regional channels, encompassing more than one state; national channels; and, finally, as international channels subdivided according to import or export in flow and to the number and locational zone of the country involved.

Type 3

The third classification type distinguishes the geographic structure of the channel according to the urban-rural locational aspects of the agencies involved. It stems, in part, from the spatial patterns developed under type 1. The following subgroupings represent, at least, the more important which may be identified:

I. *Primarily Rural Structure (Producing and Buying)*
    A. Single-centered.
        1. Producing location.
        2. Buying location.
        3. Both (1) and (2).
    B. Multiple-centered.
        1. Producing location.
        2. Buying location.
        3. Both (1) and (2).
II. *Primarily Urban Structure (Producing and Buying)*
    A. Single-centered.
        1. Producing location.
        2. Buying location.
        3. Both (1) and (2).
    B. Multiple-centered.
        1. Producing location.
        2. Buying location.
        3. Both (1) and (2).
III. *Rural Producing—Uniurban Buying Locations*
IV. *Rural Producing—Multiurban Wholesaling, Multiurban Retailing Locations*
    A. Domestic.
    B. Foreign.
    C. Combination of (A) and (B).
V. *Urban Producing—Uniurban Buying Locations*
VI. *Urban Producing—Multiurban Wholesaling, Multiurban Retailing Locations*

Among other uses, this type of subdivision is of valuable assistance in analyzing centralization and decentralization in the channel context.

Type 4

The geographic structure of the channel may emphasize, finally, the physical and nonphysical flows in the channel in terms of the trading areas of the wholesale and/or retail trading centers involved. This structure is based upon the classification scheme outlined for type 3. But to this scheme it adds the analytical pattern for the determination of the supply- and distribution-area boundaries for each of the wholesale trading centers involved, and, similarly, of the intercity trading-area boundaries for each retail trading center. In this manner, it is a further refinement in tracing the series of commodity flows and nonphysical flows which are encompassed in particular channels.

These four types emphasize the main geographic aspects of channel structure. Channels thus become effective as result of a series of management decisions about particular products produced in locations dominated either by raw materials or other locational considerations and balanced by the locational determinants of the consuming markets. *From a geographic point of view, the channel becomes the marketing vehicle which obtains the best equilibrium of a series of individual and/or group management decisions about locational factors.* Changes in any of the basic variables, such as the location of raw materials, comparative transportation costs and services, the location of storage facilities, and patterns of customer location, all affect the geographic structure of the channel.

Some Final Observations

The discussion in Chapter 5 together with the discussions in this chapter have served to bring to the foreground the unique importance of marketing organization through the channel. The channel serves to particularize, in the marketing sense, the physical and associated nonphysical movements of goods from point of production to points of intermediate and final use in terms of particular patterns of linkages and blockages of various levels of business agencies. It becomes, accordingly, the battleground in which the abstract theoretical concept of competition (of all forms) becomes actualized in terms of specific products, specific business units, and specific geographical patterns. It becomes, in an additional sense, the battleground for competition within the channel control previously discussed; and there exists, within the framework of marketing organization as a whole, the various other forms of channel competition discussed above.

By the very nature of wholesaling as examined already in detail, it is obvious that the wholesaling sector is related inextricably with the channel. One cannot investigate channels with any degree of analytical depth without being immersed immediately into the concepts of channel structure, and vice versa. Various marketing authorities in the past have too much subjugated the analysis of channels in favor of discussion of the over-all, abstract marketing viewpoint. Rather, the point of view of the emphasis in this discussion has been that management units cannot take any fundamental marketing actions without creating concurrently a series of important channel-of-distribution effects. This must be so by virtue of the indicated relationships that show that marketing must and does take place within a framework or structure of the various types of channels.

QUESTIONS AND PROBLEMS

1. What is the marketing meaning of the "channel"? How does this meaning vary as between its physical and nonphysical aspects?
2. What kinds of middlemen relationships are included in the concept of the channel?
3. What are the component elements of a channel?
4. Of what value is it to visualize the channel as a series of linkage?
5. How does the "phenomenon of blockages" arise from the functioning of the channel?
6. Where, in the funnel concept of wholesaling, does the channel fit?
7. Of what value are channel diagrams? How are they constructed?
8. Classify channels by types. What are the important characteristics of each type?
9. How is the element of managerial control affected by the type of channel? How is the type of channel the resultant of the element of managerial control?
10. "The channel, in any specific situation, has a geographical structure by virtue of the locational characteristics of the business agencies linked, and by virtue of the geographic distribution of the customers serviced." Critically evaluate this statement.
11. Compare and contrast the underlying factors which influence the type of channels found for extractive industry products, industrial goods, and manufactured consumers' goods.
12. What factors must individual manufacturers consider in selecting particular channels of distribution?
13. What evidence can you show of the continuing managerial struggle for channel control? What forms does the continuing struggle take?
14. "Competition in the marketing sense ultimately takes place within the framework of the channel." Do you agree or disagree? What are the reasons for your agreement or disagreement?

15. Of what importance is the distinction between orthodox and nonorthodox channels?

16. How can a given management unit evaluate the effectiveness of a channel?

17. Differentiate between the four types of situations in which the geographic aspects of channels may be visualized.

18. Discuss critically the implications of the following statement: "From a geographical point of view, the channel becomes the marketing vehicle which obtains the best equilibrium of a series of individual and/or group management decisions about locational factors."

CHAPTER INTEGRATING ASSIGNMENT

Based upon the references or other sources, select a given product or industry as the basis for studying channels. Indicate the basic industry and product factors which form the background for the channels. Discuss fully the channels which currently are utilized, with emphasis on the types of wholesale middlemen utilized. To what extent do the channels match the classic patterns as discussed in the chapters? Explain fully how such channels as are found came to be. What future changes in channels may be expected?

7

The Wholesaling Sector and Product Assortments

Before the discussion of the wholesaling sector in its external aspects can be complete, the subject matter which needs exploration is that dealing with product assortments in the channel. The special role of the wholesale middlemen will be at the center of the presentation. The nature of the commodity aspects of the wholesaling sector has been touched upon at several places in the preceding chapters.

The Meaning of Product Assortments

Basic definition

Product assortments, especially from the viewpoint of the wholesaling sector, can be approached from an internal managerial and an external structural point of view. These are not the only approaches, of course. Product assortments can be viewed as merely a part of the discussion of product policy in connection with the manufacturing and marketing policies of a given producer.[1] From an internal managerial viewpoint, a product assortment is: (a) the particular combination of

---

[1] See Alderson, *Marketing Behavior and Executive Action: A Functionalist Approach to Marketing Theory* (Homewood, Ill.: Richard D. Irwin, Inc., 1957), pp. 199–200, for a different approach to a definition based upon his framework of matching and sorting as the logic of exchange.

individual products found as part of the production and marketing activities of a particular establishment at the extractive industry or manufacturing industry levels, or (*b*) the combination of individual products, item by item and line by line, which are accumulated by given wholesale or retail middlemen in order to execute as effectively as possible the marketing policies of their particular type of operation.

From the *external* point of view, product assortments represent the sum total of the internal product assortments noted in (*a*) and (*b*) above which are needed to meet the requirements of all agencies involved in a given channel of distribution system of linkages for a stated kind of business. This external definition is most important for this section of the book, although reference will be made to the internal aspects as needed for development.

A product, for purpose of this definition, is the result of any specific extractive or manufacturing industry activity which has a particular combination of specific physical and/or chemical characteristics designed to meet a specified need or interrelated series of needs. Each product, in this context, carries its own means of identification. Thus, if a company packs two separate brands (either its own or distributor's) of coffee, each is considered an individual product. The combination of all individual products satisfying a particular need would constitute a product line for a given producer or middleman. An accumulation of several product lines having a common tie of homogeneity within a family of uses establishes the basis for a product family. Thus, one may speak of a line of canned peas and a family of canned vegetables.

Variables in product assortments

Before classifying the types of product assortments and defining each type, it may be well to remember the more important variables in product assortments. One is the basic category of the product as indicated by some end-use designation, e.g., stove, spoon, motor. These end-use designations of products may be further subclassified according to whether the product has a single use, few uses, or multiple uses. Next are such important physical characteristics as model number, physical sizes, weight specifications, or color designations, which lead, in turn, to product multiplication. Other variables include quality specifications, types of package, trade-mark or trade name designations, or price level designations. These variables most frequently affect product assortments by working in tandem, rather than being identified individually.

Types of product assortments: internal management levels

The types of product assortments found under this heading are based upon the levels involved, namely, extractive industry, manufacturing industry, wholesale middlemen, and retail middlemen assortments. Type I, dealing with the extractive industry level, has three subclasses:

Type IA product assortments fixed by the nature of the available natural resources, as in the case of commercial supplies of fish, coal, metal ores, or diamonds.

Type IB product assortments in which some variety and quality range is introduced by virtue of producers' selections of the breeds of animals to be reared or by the botanical varieties of crops to be produced.

Type IC product assortments based upon a multiproduct situation, as in the case of mixed-crop and truck-crop farming.

Again, at the manufacturer's level (type II), several alternative product assortment possibilities are open within the framework of the type itself. Depending upon his financial strength, the ability of the marketing personnel within the firm, the marketing characteristics of the product(s) involved, and the degrees of control desired in the channel, a manufacturer can vary his product assortment policies:

Type IIA. Under a short-line product assortment policy, he may select to create only canned tomatoes, canned peas, and canned corn, for example.

Type IIB. Under a full-line policy, or more correctly a full-product-family policy, the manufacturer would can and market every conceivable variety of vegetables that could be so processed.

Type IIC. Manufacturers producing a product assortment consisting of a family of products with closely homogeneous production and/or end-use characteristics.

Type IID. Manufacturers producing a product assortment consisting of a family of products with highly variable production and/or end-use characteristics.

For each of these four types, a manufacturer can elect to produce the assortments under his own brand(s) names, under distributors' brands, with no brand identification, or on a multiple-brand basis.

Finally, the product assortment alternatives of wholesale and retail middlemen need to be classified and described (types III and IV).

Types IIIA and IVA. The product assortment is determined by each level signing an exclusive distributorship arrangement with the manufacturer. Thus, the wholesale and retail middlemen's assortments are limited to what the manufacturer will produce. In some arrangements, limited, noncompeting lines may be handled.

Types IIIB and IVB. These types represent product assortments in depth, under which the wholesale and retail middlemen take a given homogeneous product family and stock, so far as sales potentials indicate, every possible producer's output.

Types IIIC and IVC. These types of product assortments represent, as defined above, policies of assortments in breadth in which, subject to minimum sales criteria, the wholesale and retail middlemen select a wide range of products based on merchandising policy, end uses of products, and customer characteristics criteria.

Types IIID and IVD. Under very limited circumstances, types IIIB (and IVB) and IIIC (and IVC) may be combined.

Types of product assortments: channel perspective.[2]

The basic description of the various types of wholesale and retail middlemen, together with the types of channels of distribution, furnishes the bases for classifying product assortments according to the channel perspective. Three channel level designations may be indicated, under which each of Breyer's product assortment types could be classified. These channel level designations are as follows:

I. *The Extractive Industry Edible Products Channel Levels*
   Extractive industry producers' level.
   Wholesale middlemen's level—stage 1.
   Wholesale middlemen's level—stage 2.
   Retail middlemen's level.
   Consumers' level.

II. *The Industrial Goods* (Raw, Semiprocessed, and Processed Goods) *Channel Levels*
   Extractive industry producers' level (domestic and foreign).

[2] The classification scheme (with the designation titles) is based upon the system developed by Breyer, *Quantitative Systemic Analysis and Control: Study No. 1—Channel and Channel Group Costing* (Philadelphia: The Author, 1949), p. 61. The channel level groupings are the author's own classification.

Wholesale middlemen's level.
Manufacturers' level.
Wholesale middlemen's level.
Users' levels (domestic and foreign).
III. *The Manufactured Consumers' Goods Channel Levels*
Manufacturers' level (domestic, foreign).
Wholesale middlemen's level—stage 1.
Wholesale middlemen's level—stage 2.
Retail middlemen's level.
Consumers' level (domestic, foreign).

For each of these channel levels, six types of product assortments may be noted as follows:

Type I (band pattern—narrow, medium, broad).   In this type of product assortment there is no change in the composition of the assortment as it moves through any of the channel groupings noted above.   Whatever the composition of the assortment is as generated by the producer is that found, without change, at all subsequent levels in the channel.

Type II (diamond pattern).   Narrow product assortments are found at the producers' level, the widest assortment at the wholesale middlemen's level, and then narrow product assortments, once again, at the retailers' level.

Type III (triangle pattern).   There is a continuous broadening of product assortments at each level of the channel group arrangement.

Type IV (inverted triangle pattern).   There is a continuous narrowing of product assortments at each level of the channel group arrangement.

Type V (picket pattern).   There is a broadening of product assortments from the producers' level to the wholesaler middlemen's level, and a maintenance of the breadth through the remaining levels.

Type VI (inverted picket pattern).   There are broad assortments at the producers' and wholesale middlemen's levels (stage 1), and a narrowing of such assortments at the remaining levels.

These are type case generalizations, of course, and not every type of producer or of every type of wholesale and retail middlemen function in identically the same way so far as product assortments are concerned.   As discussed earlier, these wholesale middlemen who do not take physical possession of products merely establish the contactual bases for building up any of these types of product assortments by other agencies in the channels. The channel groups noted above will change the characteristics of the six types noted above.

General Line versus Specialization in Wholesale Middlemen's Product Assortments

This section is designed to cross-relate the discussion in Chapter 3 with the context of the present framework of product assortments. Middlemen have the management alternatives of featuring any of the pertinent types of product assortment alternatives noted above. The exact product content of each assortment alternative will vary by type of operation and by kind of business. Detailed analysis of the available census data of commodity-line composition of sales will be presented in the following section.

The existence of general-line operations among merchant wholesalers in certain kinds of business is related to the structure of individual products found in any given line of business; to the kinds of retail middlemen who are the customers of the particular kinds of business; to the kinds of customers found for those businesses handling industrial goods; to the presence or absence in any given channel situation of any severe managerial struggles for channel control; and to the total sales potential available from alternative product assortments. In addition, the opportunity for general-line operations may be throttled by virtue of the manufacturers' marketing policies in a given industry. Expansions or contractions in the range of available products, by virtue of changes at the manufacturing level, will have significant effects. Attempts by any level in the channel to improve its marketing margins may lead to changes in product assortments; and, as will be discussed later, a broad development of scrambled merchandising will act as a powerful modifying force.

All in all, the varying importance of general-line versus specialty operations for certain kinds of business at the wholesale level reflects a continuing battle between the pressures noted above. Note that this battle of pressures leading to general-line or specialized operations is part of the broader discussion of pressures making for change versus pressures making for stability. In the Los Angeles wholesale grocery study,[3] one of the competitive tactics used by the orthodox wholesaler

[3] R. Cassady, Jr., and W. L. Jones, *The Changing Competitive Structure in the Wholesale Grocery Trade: A Case Study of the Los Angeles Market, 1920–1946* (Berkeley and Los Angeles: University of California Press, 1949).

in meeting the increased use of direct channels by manufacturers, was to reduce the product assortments offered. Similarly, the emergence of nonfood lines in super markets has had two effects on wholesale middlemen: (1) the creation of sufficient sales basis for the rack jobber specializing in such product assortment; and (2) the additions of such product assortments as new departments within an orthodox wholesaler's type of operation.

It is also interesting to note that, not infrequently, manufacturers' sales branches and sales offices add product assortments beyond those accounted for by the manufacturers in control. The attempt to spread the overhead costs of such branches or sales offices may be the important motivating force; or there may be excess salesmen capacity available during certain months. Other important reasons may be the availability of noncompetitive lines or very favorable terms, and the necessity for a change in policy because of the nature of the customers serviced. In any case, it is important to remember that the inherent nature of such operations does not preclude the possible widening of product assortments.

Certain types of *agent* middlemen may or may not have stability of product assortments as inherent aspects of their type of operation. To the extent that contracts lasting for a season, for a year, or for longer periods restrict the middlemen's freedom of action, to that extent will the nature of the product assortments be made rigid. On the other hand, commission agents operating in wholesale fresh fruit and vegetable markets, for example, may have high variability of product assortments occasioned by variations in producer contacts as well as by seasonal variations in the supply of available products. Volume potentialities may lead, on the other hand, to product specialization in these types of markets, as in the case of brokers specializing in potatoes and/or onions. Certain agent middlemen may operate as multitype wholesale middlemen, thus widening their range of product assortment alternatives.

Finally, it may be desirable to recall those examples of special types of wholesale middlemen operations in which unique forms of rigidity in product assortment alternatives are induced by the nature of the operation. Thus, the major part of petroleum bulk plant and bulk terminal sales consists of petroleum products, although some sales are made of such products as batteries, tires, etc.[4] Likewise, country grain elevators handle primarily assortments in depth of

---

[4] The 1954 Census reported that of total sales of $13 billion by bulk plants and terminals the establishments did $11.9 billion in petroleum products (excluding LP gas).

grain.[5] Finally, the piece goods converter is limited primarily to those product assortments available in this textile category.

Commodity-Line Composition of Wholesale Middlemen's 1954 Sales

Some characteristics of the product assortments found in particular kinds of wholesale business are available from the 1954 Census mainly for the merchant wholesalers and the manufacturers' sales-branches sales-offices type-of-operation groups. For the merchant wholesalers' group kinds of business, the census consolidates individual product items into a commodity line, using a 3-digit coding notation.[6] For the manufacturers' sales branches and sales offices kinds of business, each commodity line is identified by a 5-digit coding notation, thus representing a much more detailed individual product listing.[7]

Of the types of analyses possible from these data, the most important is the indication for each kind of business—under these two types-of-operation groups—of the percentage of the covered sales accounted for by the *most important* commodity lines, *related* commodity lines, and *all others,* including the miscellaneous or unclassified group. The *most important* category includes those code numbers of commodity lines listed by the census in its definition of kind of business.[8] The *related* commodity lines are those whose code numbers fall within a code number range closely related to the main kind-of-business grouping. The "all other" category includes all remaining digit codes, the category of "miscellaneous commodities, not elsewhere classified," and labor, service, and rental receipts.[9] In addition, an important kind of analysis can be presented of an approximation, within the limits of the data, of how many kinds of business handle

[5] Even in this kind of business the 1954 Census stated that reporting establishments had only 76.3 per cent of their sales accounted for by grains, with the remainder spread among 20 commodity lines and an unclassified category.

[6] For example, commodity code 000 includes, under the heading "canned, bottled foods," the following: canned baby foods; canned fruits, fruit juices; canned vegetables, vegetable juices; canned fish, seafood; canned meats; canned milk; and other canned, bottled foods.

[7] Thus, compared with the coding in footnote 6, canned fish and seafood are coded 20310, canned fruits 20331, and so on.

[8] For example, the food group in the merchant wholesalers' group consists of the following code numbers: 000, 010, 020, 030, 040, 041, 050, 060, 062, 070, 080, 090, 100, and 101.

[9] The receipts entry is included because, for some kinds of business, it was not identified separately from the miscellaneous commodities.

a particular commodity line as identified by either the 3-digit or 5-digit code number arrangement.

Before presenting the detailed analyses of the distribution of reported commodity-line sales between "most important," "related," and "all other" groupings, by kinds of business, it might be of value to present a frequency distribution of the percentages as such (see Table 20). For the merchant wholesalers group for the 47 kinds of

TABLE 20

FREQUENCY DISTRIBUTION OF PERCENTAGE OF SALES
OF MOST IMPORTANT, RELATED, AND UNRELATED
COMMODITY LINES: MERCHANT WHOLESALERS' AND
MANUFACTURERS' SALES BRANCHES AND SALES OFFICES:
UNITED STATES 1954

Percentage	Merchant Wholesalers' Kinds of Business			Sales Branches, Sales Offices Kinds of Business		
	Most Important	Re-lated	Other	Most Important	Re-lated	Other
None	—	14	—	—	4	—
0.1– 3.9	—	10	9	—	5	9
4.0– 5.9	—	9	7	—	—	4
6.0– 9.9	—	6	8	—	3	10
10.0–14.9	—	2	7	—	3	10
15.0–19.9	—	3	10	—	14	7
20.0–24.9	—	1	2	—	5	5
25.0–29.9	—	1	2	—	6	2
30.0–34.9	—	—	—	—	4	1
35.0–39.9	—	1	1	—	3	—
40.0–49.9	1	—	1	5	2	—
50.0–59.9	2	—	—	9	—	1
60.0–69.9	2	—	—	13	—	—
70.0–79.9	12	—	—	12	—	—
80.0–89.9	15	—	—	4	—	—
90.0–99.9	15	—	—	6	—	—
Total	47	47	47	49	49	49

business analyzed by the census,[10] nearly two thirds had product assortments in which the most important group fell into the 80 per cent, or more, of total sales frequency groups. Much wider ranges of distribution of importance are shown for the related and other

[10] Restricted only to those establishments furnishing the necessary commodity-line breakdown.

groups. However, for 14 kinds of business there were no sales reported of related commodity-line groups. On the other hand, one third of all kinds of business reported sales of other commodity-line groups ranging from 15 to 50 per cent of covered sales.

Partially because of the more detailed product-line coding procedures used, the percentage position of most important group sales of the manufacturers' sales branches and sales offices kinds of business is quite different from the above distribution (see Table 20). The two most important groups were the 60–69.9 and 70–79.9 per cent groups, respectively, with 25 of the 49 reporting kinds of business. The grouping and range of importance of the related and other categories were much wider than for the merchant wholesalers' kinds of business. These differences in percentage distributions would seem to confirm, in part, two previous observations: (1) that sales branches and sales offices, by virtue of their manufacturer ownership, have much narrower commodity-line possibilities; and (2) that the tendency is offset only, in part, by the handling of noncompeting lines and by the increased tendency towards product diversification among some manufacturing units.

Detailed analyses: merchant wholesalers' kinds of business

Data listing commodity-line sales into the three groups for each of the reporting merchant wholesalers' kind of business show, first of all, that there is a very variable coverage between each kind of business so far as reported commodity-line sales are concerned. The range is from a low of 76 per cent for confectionery wholesalers to a high of 96 per cent for 3 kinds of business. The *most important* commodity-lines groups for 22 kinds of business were represented by a single code number group, whereas in an additional 11 kinds of business only two code groups were involved. Only in the specialty-line grocery, home furnishing and floor covering, construction materials, professional equipment and supplies, and service kinds of business did the most important group involve 4 to 6 commodity-line groups. These variations reflect, among other things, the number of commodity-line groups which are used by the census to define each kind of business.

Of the 33 kinds of business in which related commodity-line group sales were reported, the number of such lines ranged from one for 12 kinds of business to 13 for the general-line grocery wholesalers. Wide variations are apparent, also, in the percentage importance of such sales, with no apparent relationship existing between the number of commodity-line groups and the percentage importance of such sales.

At one end of the scale was the home furnishing and floor covering group with two *related* commodity-line groups accounting for only 0.4 per cent. At the opposite end of the scale, iron, steel and products kinds of business with 6 related commodity-line groups accounted for 38.8 per cent. Product specialization obviously is a highly variable concept from kind of business to kind of business, depending upon the kinds of commodities handled, the total number of commodity-lines sold, and related considerations.

Even wider ranges are apparent for the other commodity-line group. Excluding the miscellaneous group of wholesalers, this category ranged from 1 to 36 commodity-line groups, and from 0.9 to 34 per cent of the reported sales. This upper percentage was accounted for by 22 lines in the hardware kind of business. Among some of the commodity lines included were: kitchen utensils and miscellaneous homewares; toys, games, and athletic goods; iron and steel wire, and wire products; and industrial equipment and supplies. These indicate, for the hardware business as a whole, the broadening of product assortments which has been taking place.

The foregoing data also reveal, on a summary basis, the wide range of product assortments from kind of business to kind of business. It must be remembered, however, that many 3-digit commodity-line groups include several product items or lines, as earlier defined, so that these indicators are only partial approximations. A later section will analyze the extent to which the same commodity-line group is handled by many kinds of merchant wholesalers' business.

Detailed analyses: manufacturers' sales branches, sales offices kinds of business

Data for manufacturers' sales branches and sales offices, with 49 kinds of business categories included, show that percentage coverage of commodity-line sales is much more complete than for the merchant wholesalers' group. With few exceptions, the combination of most important and related commodity lines accounts for higher percentages of reported sales than was true for the merchant wholesalers' kinds of business. It has been indicated already that, partially because of differences in coding, the percentage position of the most important commodity-line group ranks below that for the merchant wholesalers' kinds. Because the coding is much narrower and specific, more commodity lines are included within this category.

For the kinds of business having sales of related commodity-line categories, the numbers of such lines ranged from 1 to 44, and, in percentage importance, from 0.6 to 44.6. Among the kinds of business with larger numbers of related commodity lines were: industrial inorganic and organic chemicals (44); other chemicals and allied products (38); other primary metal industry products (31); general industrial machinery (37); and electrical industrial apparatus (37).

Significantly different from the merchant wholesalers' kinds of business was the small number of commodity lines included in the "other" group. The predominant numbers included were either 1 or 2 commodity lines, with a maximum of 4 (excluding the miscellaneous kinds of business). However, these ranged in importance from 0.3 to 34.9 per cent. This maximum was found for the carpet and rug kind of business, and consisted of commodity lines not elsewhere classified. The next highest percentage, 28.2, was found in the concrete and plaster products kind of business, and represents, again, an unclassified category.

Middlemen's Product Assortments Alternatives

In the context of the discussion so far of product assortments, and from the point of view of individual wholesale middlemen managements, some remarks should be made preliminary to the detailed discussions about some selected managerial policy alternatives which are available and which have important relationships to the subject. In this introductory aspect, these policy alternatives may be conveniently divided into those leading to maximization of product assortments and those leading to a reduction or minimization of product assortments.

Maximization policy alternatives

Inventory policies are of necessity closely related to the types of product assortments as classified and described previously. Specialty-line wholesalers may make policy decisions, by the very nature of the management choice exercised in selecting that type of operation, leading to product assortments in depth within a product line or product family outreach. On the other hand, the decision to organize and operate a general-line type of operation involves policy decisions leading to assortments in depth. Choice of agent middlemen types of operation have other policy implications for product assortments. The sharp expansion in the variety of goods available, and such limitations as those of working capital and available storage space, all serve to have considerable effects on these product assortment decisions. These developments, however, have different influences on assortments in breadth as against those in depth.

Other decisions involve considerations of certain types of pricing and packaging policies. Pricing policies, involving the level as well as the variety of prices, together with matters of price lines, all have extremely important effects on the maximization of product assortments. This is true, also, in the relationship of pricing policies to the decision as to whether or not to add distributors' as well as manufacturers' brands of products.

The many packaging alternatives also have the effect of widening product assortments both in depth and in breadth. Thus, the fruit and vegetable wholesaler who sells carrots and tomatoes in the ordinary farm-to-retailer manner, as well as in his own cello-wrapped packages, has served to increase assortments. Packages may be used by the middlemen to market combinations of products or to widen the number of units of a homogeneous product made available to customers.

Minimization policy alternatives

The pressure of competition from manufacturers and integrated retail middlemen in the struggle for channel control may lead to policy decisions to reduce product assortments. In some cases, the decisions taken may be, as noticed, to change the type of operation as from the orthodox wholesaler to the cash-and-carry wholesaler. In the case of some agent middlemen, this may mean a realignment of contracts with principals. In some cases, the reduction in product assortments may be the result of coordinated manufacturer-middlemen actions, as in the illustration of product standardization and simplification of industrial goods, or of package specifications.

Pricing can be the policy avenue leading to product assortment minimization as well as maximization. Establishment of one-price policies may imply the correlative establishment of a one-quality level of product assortments. Refusal of wholesale middlemen to subscribe to the resale price maintenance philosophy of manufacturers may result in the closing of channel connections for the price-maintained products. Adoption by the wholesale middlemen of a vigorous policy of featuring distributors' brands may result, again, in closing the avenues of supply of certain manufacturers' products. Certain types of integration with retail middlemen may have the end result of minimizing or reducing product assortments.

Similarly, wholesale middlemen may, through their packaging activities, minimize product assortments. This may come about both by restriction of qualities and by standardization and/or simplification of lines handled.

Product Assortments and Channel Structure

Product assortments have, as noted above, various impacts upon the channel. If one includes in product assortments various combinations of ranges of services, then the impact becomes even more pronounced. In a sense, marketing may be said to consist in substantial part in maximizing the range of product-service assortment alternatives found in the entire channel structure and at any given level within the channel. This is, indeed, the most important rationale, if any is needed, for the wide variety of existing middlemen's types of operations and kinds of business. The net resultant, so far as product assortments are concerned, is the complicated classification of product assortment alternatives already discussed.

Except for these middlemen who control manufacturers, and those who are controlled by the manufacturers, there are certain basic conflicts between these two levels. Product assortment policies, especially of wholesale middlemen, may, by the very nature of the diversity created, affect the marketing efforts of manufacturers to secure forecasted market penetration positions for their respective products. On the other hand, the expansion and diversification efforts of manufacturers may result in such heavy pressures on wholesale middlemen to expand product assortments as to lead to significant channel conflict.

Accordingly, partly for these reasons, there arise varieties of middlemen operations, of channel patterns, and of product assortment alternatives already discussed. Assortments may remain unchanged, may increase in complexity in breadth or depth, or may be reduced in complexity and depth as commodity flows are established through the channels. These product assortments may or may not be physically tangent, in part or in total, to the buying and selling activities in the wholesale markets. Middlemen may perform varying ranges of functions within the funnel in adapting product assortments and the rates of flow of such assortments to the needs of customers; and from these stem again, in part, the managerial struggles for control of the channel.

Thus, this concept of product assortments in the channel structure is closely tied in with the whole funnel concept of wholesaling, and, also, is closely related to basic marketing processes as will be indicated in the following section. The end objectives as stated before, are, or should be, the maximization of product assortment alternatives and of the channel structures through which these product assortments flow. An additional objective is to set up alternatives by means of which variable quantities and qualities of raw material, semiprocessed, and processed products can be matched with variable needs of various types of industrial goods and consumers' goods users. In this aspect the objective is a minimum of waste in the degree of perfection of matching, of the time required, and in the use of deceptive and confusing tactics.

Product Assortments and the Basic Marketing Processes

When product assortments are thus viewed in their channel perspective, the earlier statements about the marketing processes take on additional meaning and logic. The process of concentration becomes emphasized, in this perspective, in its role of building up not only physical quantities as such but also increased product assortment alternatives in depth as well as in breadth. This process provides alternatives for packaging activities and for systematically matching quality gradations of raw materials with the inventory needs of the processing industries. Quality control of the seeds used in growing a vegetable, for example, may result in directly linking the entire output of the extractive industry producing units contracted with those of the processing industry units. Product assortments may be diverted from intermediate channel movements in order to raise the quality level of the remaining assortments, with the possibilities of improving, at the same time, the sum total of the price possibilities.

Equalization through a system of organized and nonorganized markets at the wholesale level provides additional funnel mechanisms for: (a) matching existing product assortments and needs without much change in assortments; (b) expanding product assortment alternatives both in breadth and in depth; (c) beginning the narrowing of product assortments, both quantitatively and qualitatively; or (d) providing product assortments which may vary at different time periods. By the establishment of either systematic or nonsystematic price arrangements, further variations in product assortments may be effected. At the same time, this process provides for stratification of product assortment alternatives as between kinds of business and types of channel and middlemen arrangements.

Dispersion may continue the narrowing of product assortments in depth or in breadth, or may broaden the product assortment alternatives, or may continue them unchanged. However, in most cases, there is a reduction in the quantitative aspects; that is, the volume of units involved in each sales transaction is reduced as compared with the concentration and equalization process phases. The dispersion process is, as noted before, the narrow end of the funnel.

One final aspect of these processes may be noted as they relate to product assortments. It is in the inherent nature of these processes in relation to channel structure not only to interact on the quantitative and qualitative aspects of product assortments but also to have strong influence on the time variable. This is accomplished mainly by means of the extent to which these processes maintain separate positions in the funnel and channel in so far as specialization of middlemen activities is concerned or else become merged by virtue of changes in the channel structure and by the obliteration of distinct middlemen's specialization and level position.

Scrambled Merchandising

Definition

Inherent in the relationship between channels, marketing processes, and product assortments has been the pervasive influence of scrambled merchandising. For purposes of this discussion, a distinction must be made between increasing product assortments in depth and/or in breadth within the same product categories and the addition of product categories which either are new, in a complete sense, or which are new to the middlemen and channels involved. Thus, if a given supermarket formerly handled 3,000 separate items and now handles 5,000 items, and if the increase were only in the breadth and/or depth within the same product categories as for the 3,000 items, the change would *not* be called scrambled merchandising. But if, as is currently reported,[11] a supermarket with $1 million annual sales had 5.2 per cent of its sales accounted for by health and beauty aids (381 items), housewares (167 items), magazines (188 items), soft goods (76 items), toys (93 items), stationery (47 items), and phonograph records (94 items), such changes in inventory policy would represent one aspect of scrambled merchandising.

Relationship to wholesale middlemen

Table 20 has indicated already one aspect of scrambled merchandising as it pertains to wholesale middlemen, namely, the variable percentages of reported sales, by kinds of business, accounted for by commodity lines other than in the most important and related cate-

11 *Progressive Grocer,* "Facts in Grocery Distribution," 1959 edition.

gories. Obviously, these are only gross measures applicable to the establishments reporting in an entire kind of business, and they are affected by the quantity and types of products included in the unclassified category. It is apparent from these data that middlemen in all kinds of industrial and consumers' goods kinds of business are engaged in varying amounts of scrambled merchandising. In so operating, they respond in some cases to pressures being exerted from either end of the channel, whereas in other cases they have acted as the generating forces.

There is yet another way in which these census data may be used to indicate the existence of scrambled merchandising at the wholesale middlemen's level. It will be recalled that the commodity-line sales of merchant wholesalers' and of manufacturers' sales branches and sales offices are available for several kinds of business by 3-digit and 5-digit coding groups. If each digit code grouping is studied according to the number of kinds of business reporting sales, another index of scrambled merchandising may be obtained.

Table 21 reveals sharp variations between the number of kinds of business reporting sales of each commodity-line group and the kinds of business included in the merchandise wholesalers' and manufacturers' sales branches–sales offices groups. For the commodity-line groups for merchant wholesalers, the range in kinds of business reporting sales was from 11 for the apparel, dry goods, textile, and farm products and supplies groups to 36 for various kinds of machinery. There seems to be little relationship between the number of individual commodity lines found in the group and the number of kinds of business reporting sales.

The data for manufacturers' sales branches and sales offices reveal 15 commodity-line groups consisting of 6 to 94 individual 5-digit coded lines. Despite the larger number of individual commodity lines, the number of kinds of business reporting sales ranged from 1 for the lumber and wood products group to 10 for the highly varied machinery group. Again, there seems to be no relationship between the diversity of the commodity-line groups and the number of reporting kinds of business.

What conclusions can be drawn from these sharp differences between merchant wholesalers' kinds of business and the manufacturers' sales branches and sales offices kinds of business? In the light of the discussion of pattern assortments and of previous discussions of type-of-operation characteristics, the following seem warranted:

1. That the merchant wholesalers, and especially the orthodox wholesalers, demonstrate a remarkable flexibility of operation

TABLE 21

NUMBER OF KINDS OF BUSINESS SELLING SPECIFIED
COMMODITY—LINE GROUPS IN 1954, AND RELATED DATA

Type-of-Operation Group and Commodity-Line Group	No. of Individual Commodity-Line Groups[a]	No. of Kinds of Business[b]
Merchant wholesalers' group		
Food, beverages, tobacco	21	17
Drugs, soaps, chemicals	6	27
Paper, stationery, office supplies	6	21
Apparel, dry goods, textiles	6	11
Automotive	2	17
Furniture, home furnishings, floor coverings	5	25
Hardware, plumbing, heating	2	25
Electrical	6	22
Scrap, waste materials	12	14
Commercial and other machinery	38	36
Metals, minerals (except scrap)	18	17
Farm products, supplies	13	11
Miscellaneous	27	26
Manufacturers' sales branches, sales offices		
Food, beverages, tobacco	85	8
Textile mill and fabricated textiles	28	2
Lumber and wood products	24	1
Furniture and fixtures	19	2
Paper and allied products	12	5
Chemicals and allied products	79	8
Products of petroleum and coal	14	3
Rubber products	6	3
Stone, clay, and glass products	34	8
Primary and fabricated metals	69	5
Machinery	94	10
Electrical	49	4
Transportation equipment	9	4
Instruments, et al.	22	6
Miscellaneous	25	7

[a] Three digit code for wholesalers, and 5-digit code for sales branches, sales offices.

[b] Includes miscellaneous kinds of business.

in so far as kind of business is concerned, which leads, in turn, to a remarkable flexibility in product assortments.

2. That the manufacturers' sales branches and sales offices have considerably greater product-assortment rigidities by virtue of their integrated nature.

3. That, except where manufacturers have diversified products individually, the merchant wholesalers are more likely to show greater flexibility in scrambled merchandising than the manufacturers' sales branches and sales offices. A further aspect of this is to be found in the greater flexibility of the merchant wholesalers in developing sales by virtue of multitype operations. Manufacturers' sales branches and sales offices are likely, once again, to demonstrate greater (but not complete) inflexibility.

QUESTIONS AND PROBLEMS

1. What is the meaning of product assortment from the internal viewpoint? from the external viewpoint?
2. Differentiate clearly between each type of product assortment at each level of the channel. Give concrete examples of each
3. What is the relationship between product assortments and general-line and specialty wholesale middlemen?
4. To what extent do wholesale middlemen in any kind of business maintain stable product assortments? What variables may lead to unstable assortments?
5. What conclusions about product assortments can be reached from Table 20?
6. How do most important, related, and other product categories vary by type-of-operation group? by kind of business within each group?
7. Based on the general discussion of wholesale middlemen's product assortment alternatives, give concrete illustrations of each type of alternative.
8. What are the various impacts of product assortments upon the channel?
9. To what extent do product assortment policies lead to conflict between the agencies in the channel? To what extent do they serve as a basis for channel cooperation?
10. How do product assortments in the channel relate to the funnel concept?
11. How does the view of product assortments in their channel perspective give "additional meaning and logic to product assortments"?
12. What is "scrambled merchandising"? How does it manifest itself in product assortments?
13. What conclusions can be based upon the data in Table 21?

CHAPTER INTEGRATING ASSIGNMENTS

1. Write an essay on the general topic: the relationships between product assortments, the general logic of channel arrangement, and the strategic importance of the wholesaling sector.

2. Critically examine the relationship between the various types of product assortments, on the one hand, and the incidence and degree of competition in the channel. Include in your examination the extent to which decisions about product assortments tend either to increase or reduce the impact of such competition.

8

Internal Management:
General Organizational and
Policy Considerations

This chapter departs from the preceding pattern of discussion of the wholesaling sector which confined itself to a dissection of the external aspects. In this chapter the dissection process is directed rather to a view of middlemen's organizational, policy, and operating aspects. The interrelationships between external and internal views need no elaboration at this point. Wherever in the treatment of the external aspects there are generalizations which can be made applicable to every type of wholesale middlemen's operations, such generalizations will be presented.

Greater emphasis will be placed, however, on the differences between relationships which have, by their basic nature, differential application to each type of middleman's operation. By so treating the relationships, we hope to emphasize these internal management characteristics of wholesale middlemen and their operations which develop their individualistic nature relative to the internal management characteristics of manufacturing and retail-middlemen businesses.

The topics to be covered are: General organization and policy considerations; the selection of type of operation and kind of business; the selection of the middlemen's establishment location and other spatial considerations; the nature and content of middlemen's merchandising, buying, selling and price policies; the nature and content of the various physical operations of wholesale middlemen; the nature and content of the various auxiliary functions; managerial control of costs and profits; and over-all managerial coordination and control.

Applicability of General Organizational Principles

Most of the available literature dealing with business organization and administration is oriented mainly towards the manufacturing enterprises.[1] From such literature are available some general organizational principles and considerations. But because the discussion here is related to wholesale middlemen, including the wholesaling activities of manufacturer-controlled and retail-middlemen-controlled organizations, special adaptation of the general material is needed. This and the succeeding section are designed to outline and discuss the significant areas of applicability of some of the general organizational materials and some of the necessary qualifications.

Some basic definitions

There are many varying concepts of *organization* and *organizational structure* in the available literature, just as there are significant differences in the component elements. Mooney[2] defines the basic term "organization" as follows:

Organization is the form of every human association for the attainment of a common purpose.

This definition does not mean that all forms of human association are alike, for these are as numerous as the variety of human aims and motives. An investigation of all conceivable human motives is beyond the range of this

---

[1] See the following as representative:

Chester I. Barnard, *The Function of the Executive* (Cambridge, Mass.: Harvard University Press, 1938).

Harold Koontz and Cyril O'Donnell, *Principles of Management: An Analysis of Managerial Functions,* 2nd ed. (New York: McGraw-Hill Book Co., Inc., 1959).

James G. March and Herbert A. Simon, *Organizations* (New York: John Wiley and Sons, Inc., 1958).

James D. Mooney, *The Principles of Organization,* rev. ed. (New York: Harper Bros., 1947).

William H. Newman, *Administrative Action: The Techniques of Organization and Management* (Englewood Cliffs, N. J.: Prentice-Hall, Inc., 1951).

Elmore Petersen and E. Grosvenor Plowman, *Business Organization and Management,* 4th ed. (Homewood, Ill.: Richard D. Irwin, 1958).

[2] Mooney, *op. cit.,* p. 1.

study, but at least it is axiomatic that any motive calling for associated human action must express itself in organization. These forms, of course, will vary according to the nature of the aim; it is only through the finding of certain features essential to all forms that we can justify the claim that we have found a principle. . . .

From this basic definition, he evolves a "logical framework of the principles of organization," which includes the following: (1) The *coordinating principle* which includes authority or coordination, *per se,* the process of possessive coordination, and the effect of effective coordination; (2) the *scalar process,* consisting of leadership, delegation, and functional definition; (3) the *functional effect* through the determinative, applicative, and interpretative functionalism; and (4) the *staff phases of functionalism* involving the informative principle, the advisory process, and the supervisory effect.

Koontz and O'Donnell[3] have a somewhat different emphasis:

The organization function of the manager involves the determination and enumeration of the activities required to achieve the objectives of the enterprise, the grouping of these activities, the assignment of such groups of activities to a department headed by a manager, and the delegation of authority to carry them out. Sometimes all these factors are included in the single term "organization structure"; sometimes they are referred to as "managerial authority relationships." In any case it is the totality of such activity and authority relationships that comprises the organization function.

There are several implications of this concept of organization. In the first place, the one-man business cannot possibly be organized. Since the owner or operator himself performs the sole managerial functions of planning and controlling, he delegates no authority to others.[4] Let him, however, split off the buying activities, delegate them to a subordinate and provide coordination of activity between the buyer and himself, and the enterprise will have become organized. An *organized* enterprise requires at least two *managers* on the same level or in a superior-subordinate relationship.

Thus, an organization is the institutional framework for distinguishing between executives and subordinates, decision makers and the executors of such decisions, and leaders and followers. It becomes the man-made arrangement by which levels of authority and responsibility are defined and allocated to particular persons. Furthermore, it becomes the arrangement by which like functional areas of authority and responsibility may be grouped according to functional divisions. Whether the executive leadership should dominate the organization, or vice versa, has been a problem involving considerable argumentation and wide differences of opinion.

[3] Koontz and O'Donnell, *op. cit.,* pp. 36–37.
[4] This may or may not be so, depending on the number of hours the enterprise stays open and the number of subordinates hired.

An additional word may be said about the meaning and components of organizational structure. Newman[5] states: "Organizational structure deals with the over-all organizational arrangements in an enterprise." In developing this definition, he divides an approach to organizational structure into the following five components: (1) The objectives and activities of the enterprise; (2) *primary departmentation* providing the major divisions into which (1) is best divided; (3) the *forms of organizational responsibility* involving the units and particularly the levels at which most operating decisions will be made; (4) *facilitating units* designed to guide and assist those charged with primary operating responsibilities; and (5) such *structural arrangements* as will add simplicity and consistency to the organization and, in other ways, facilitate its smooth operations.

Levels of organizational authority and responsibility

For purposes of the present discussion, it would seem most useful to visualize the organizational structure as a triangle (see Fig. 9). When

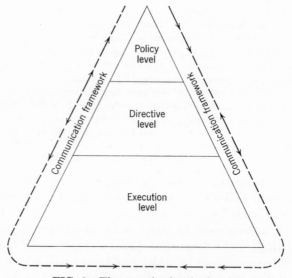

FIG. 9. The organizational triangle.

visualized in this form, several pertinent characteristics are to be noted. The triangular shape reflects the division of the organization into the policy, directive, and execution levels. The *policy* level is

[5] Newman, *op. cit.*, Chapter 16.

the responsibility of the top executives, and the nature of the policy decisions involved will be discussed later. Its position in the triangle reflects both its level of authority at the top and the fewness of the executive personnel responsible. The *directive* level consists of the middle management group who have the responsibility for transforming the general policy statements and the accompanying top executive decisions into the specific working rules needed to spell out specific authority-responsibility roles. These are the key people in the communication network between the policy decision-making levels and the operational levels. Their position in the triangle reflects, also, an intermediate number of personnel. The *execution* level, consisting of the largest number of personnel, is the level of the organization which reflects the operational activities. The personnel involved convert the policies and directives into the day-to-day activities.

The triangle reflects, also, a communication and control network based on interpersonal relationships. By a whole series of formal and informal devices—reports, organizational charts and manuals, meetings, and bulletins, just to mention a few—there evolves a two-way flow of ideas between the top echelon and the remainder of the organization. As the organization becomes larger in terms of number of personnel, and more complex in terms of structure, the complexity and difficulty of the communication network increase almost in geometric proportions.

This dilemma brings in its wake varying notions of how organizational relationships should be established, and the idea of supervisory and executive personnel span of control. Organizational relationships will be discussed below. But the concept of span of control needs further development at this point. The concept refers to the effective relationship ratio between some person in an executive or supervisory capacity and the number of persons (subordinates) who report directly to him and for whom he has designated organizational responsibility. There is no fixed mathematical relationship which is equally effective for all organizations; indeed, there are wide differences of opinion. Much depends on the over-all organizational structure, the nature of the executives or supervisors involved, the kind of personnel being supervised, and other considerations.

Types of organization

The usual classifications of line, line and staff, and others are just as applicable to the organizational arrangements for wholesale middlemen as for any other organization.

A summary view of the types, as reflected in an organization chart, is contained in the following statement:

> While history, purpose, and goal give us many facts about the structure or intended behavior of an organization, the organization chart with its attendant statement of function gives a picture in diagram form that is often useful. It is a graphic presentation which may vary in detail from showing only the major units of the organization to displaying the names of every person on the payroll. In business, industrial, and governmental organizations the chart will likely have lines showing channels of authority. . . .
> The organization chart quickly gives one of the best pictures of intended lines of authority. There are, of course, other charts that show work flow, communication lines, procedures, and processes: all useful guides to executives and other members of the organization. New members of the organization find such presentations useful in getting an early idea of the intended performance. Some persons who are sensitive to status differences prefer to minimize the organization chart. Others will claim that the chart overplays structure and tends to restrict freedom in getting work done. In a small organization, particularly where goals are quite general, the chart may be unnecessary. Structure can be maintained by agreement through discussion. However, anyone working in an organization is entitled to know its purposes, its goals, and other information concerning structure, even though these may be in general terms.[6]

In actual practice, the working relationships and the official and unofficial interpretations may make the "actual" organization chart quite different from the formal, printed version. Many reasons may exist for these deviations: Personality traits of those in superior administrative positions; to rigid adherence to the "letter" rather than the "spirit" of the written organization chart; lack of flexibility in the original planning, and lack of adaptability to foreseen and unforeseen changes. Other causes may stem from organized formal resistance within the organization, and from the ignorance among subordinates as to the nature of the formal organization.[7]

Some Important Organizational Variables

Given the preceding discussion of some general organizational considerations, the extent to which wholesale middlemen's organizational structures will be either simple or complex, standardized or relatively individualistic, depends on a wide range of variables. What can be discussed in this section is only the general range of such variables.

[6] Carroll L. Shartle, *Executive Performance and Leadership* (Englewood Cliffs, N. J.: Prentice-Hall, Inc., 1956), pp. 50–51.

[7] *Ibid.*, pp. 56–63.

The exact weighting and interrelationship in each middleman's situation may show some deviations, of course, or else, in some instances, particular variables may have little or no applicability.

Size of the enterprise

This variable will be discussed also in a later section in connection with policies and policy decisions. It is important here, especially as sales size affects significantly the number of persons involved in the organizational structure. Size, as measured by financial resources, also has important repercussions on the ability of the enterprise to have specialization of executive functions and to use expensive control devices. Finally, size characteristics may affect significantly the extent to which flexibility in decision making and other organizational aspects can or cannot be achieved.[8]

Legal form of the business unit

The legal form of the wholesale middleman's type of operation has considerable interrelationship with the form of internal organizational structure.[9] For one aspect, the legal form frequently is interrelated with the size characteristics previously mentioned. Thus, other things being equal, the individual proprietorship and partnership forms are more likely to be associated with the smaller sales-size operations and, accordingly, with the requirements of less complicated organizational structures. Conversely, the corporations and cooperatives are more likely to involve the detailed and expanded types of organizational structures.

Range of managerial talent

There is a wide range of managerial talent to be found from one wholesale-middleman establishment to another. This wide range of talent has the obvious significant effect on the organizational structure through its relationship to the availability of trained specialists, to the existence of imagination in the range of activities undertaken by the enterprise, and in the quality of the decisions made.

There is another aspect to this variable of managerial talent, namely, the personality of the leadership represented. What are implied here, of course, are the psychological differences among execu-

[8] Note, for example, the relationship of number of executives and staff specialists to the use of the committee system with corresponding effects on the timing of important decisions.

[9] In 1954, the following distribution of establishments was reported: individual proprietorships, 28 per cent; partnerships, 15 per cent; corporations, 51 per cent; cooperatives, 2 per cent; all others and not reported, 4 per cent.

tives which affect the way in which they administer the affairs of an organization and their willingness to delegate responsibility as opposed to dictatorial attitudes. As implied in the last statement, what is being differentiated is the democratic versus the authoritarian type of leadership qualities in the executives involved.

Product assortments

Chapter 7 has discussed in detail the general aspects of product assortments in the wholesaling structure and the individual types-of-operation situations. These product assortments affect, also, the individual enterprise's organizational structure. One obvious relationship which will be discussed in detail later is in connection with the departmentization of sales activities by product lines. Another relationship has to do with the effect on the number and type of salesmen in the organization. A final relationship is that between the nature of the product assortments and the sales size of the enterprise.

Type of middleman operation

The type of middleman operation selected, especially as it relates to range of functions, is a key variable affecting the organizational structure.[10] The presence or absence of any functional group, or of certain elements within a functional group, brings with it a corresponding necessity either to provide or exclude certain functional divisions within the organizational structure. There is likely to be some important relationship between the type of operation and certain geographical characteristics of the organizational structure so far as buying and selling personnel is concerned. Because of the factors of integration, the type of operation will affect the organizational structure as to whether or not it will be free of relationships with the extractive industry, manufacturing industry, or retail middlemen's levels. This variable also has some very important relationships, as has been noted already, with kinds of business and types of product assortments within each kind of business. A more detailed discussion of such relationships will be taken up in the section dealing with divisional organization.

Geographic outreach of the enterprise

Interrelated with many of the variables already mentioned is the *geographic outreach* of the enterprise. Wider geographical coverage

---

[10] Further reference will be made to this variable in conjunction with the discussion of policies.

may have implications for matters of specialization of divisions. Thus, a manufacturing enterprise may geographically structure its organization of sales offices and/or sales branches to reach the geographic segmentation of the market it plans to cover. A multiunit orthodox wholesaler may organize so as to reflect, in part, the geographic structure of such multiunit operations. Certain product-assortment alternatives have implications for the geographic structuring of salesmen by type of market and class of customer. Domestic versus foreign-market locations of customers create further possibilities for stratification and specialization in organizational structure.

Executive freedom

In connection with type of operation, mention should be made also of the variable of *executive freedom*. For a type of operation which, by integration, is controlled either by a manufacturing or a retail middlemen's establishment, the executives, in the wholesale-middleman aspect, may have little or no freedom of organizational activity, except as dictated by the controlling unit. For nonintegrated wholesale middlemen, and within such organizations, there are wide variations in the range of freedom of executives in their specialized divisions. Part of this variation may, of course, depend upon the range of decisions to be made, and upon the scale of difficulty assigned to each decision area.

Network of organizations

A final variable to be mentioned is the *network of organizations* resulting from the position of wholesale middlemen in the channels. Involved are, among other things, the hierarchy of organizations achieved by virtue of the channel and its linkages, and the managerial struggles for channel organization. This is one aspect of organizational structure which is usually overlooked. Another aspect of the network of organization relationships is that involved, again, in the integrated types of wholesale middlemen's operations. In this context, what is involved is the necessity for matching and fitting the organizational structure of the middlemen's establishments with that of the controlling organizational units.

Organizational Divisions for Wholesale Middlemen

Because of the wholesale middleman's position in the marketing channel, the wide varieties of types of operation and kinds of business, and the variables noted above, sharp variations are found in the number and complexity of the organizational divisions. These range, in number, all the way from a single unit arrangement to as many as seven divisions.

Single-division arrangements

This type is somewhat of a misnomer since it represents the type of wholesale-middleman organizational arrangement in which there is no identifiable degree of executive specialization. It is prevalent among the large number of individual proprietorships, and among those small corporate units in which the owner is also the only operating executive. Thus, in part, it is a direct reflection of the organizational nature of many of the small sales-size units. Operating responsibilities may be stratified depending on the number and type of personnel employed. Accounting responsibilities may be handled as a staff assignment or by using the services of an outside agency, and advertising may be given similar stratification. A high degree of flexibility characterizes the assignment of authority and responsibility.

Two-divisional arrangements

Given an expansion in the size and complexity of the organizational structure noted in the preceding section, or given a partnership situation in which the partners share equally in executive responsibilities, the setting may call for a two-divisional organizational structure. Depending on the nature of the middleman's operation, the usual arrangement would be to place all marketing activities in one division (although the divisional box heading may be designated as buying, selling, or both) and to place all of the so-called operating and related activities in the other division. The operating division would include such activities as financing and credit, accounting and statistics, personnel, warehousing and order filling (if the middleman takes physical possession of products sold), and traffic and delivery (if, again, the middleman takes physical possession).

The extent of the subdivision of functions under each division, including the separation of advertising and research under marketing, depends on a number of factors to be discussed in detail in a subsequent section. What is important to note here is that such a two-divisional arrangement may become a permanent aspect of certain types of wholesale middlemen's operations, or it may be merely the first stage in the ultimate expansion of the organization into a multidivisional arrangement.

Multidivisional arrangements

From the arrangements noted above for the two-divisional organization come the roots for the multidivisional arrangements. Several combinations are possible. Selling will continue to be a separate division, whether or not so listed, or it will be combined with advertising and research functions under the heading of a marketing department. Depending again on the type of operation and kind of business, and the degree of organizational complexity, buying may or may not become a separate division, or it may remain coordinated with selling under the marketing department designation.

In connection with selling activities, the complexities of product assortments, as noted in Chapter 7, may lead to organizational stratification of salesmen by product-line groupings. The nature of the location of customers and stratification of customers by basic characteristics (e.g., type of industry, etc.) may lead, similarly, either to geographical stratification of salesmen, stratification by customer groupings, or combinations thereof. Actual or potential sales expectancies may also be important, in such stratifications. The advertising and research functions may be organized as a separate subdivision, or may be assigned a staff position to the executive in charge of marketing, or may be performed by outside specialists.

Any or all of the functional units listed under the operating division for the two-divisional organization have the potentiality of becoming full-fledged divisions or departments. Although the detailed functionings of these divisions will be discussed in subsequent chapters, it should be noted that various combinations are found for wholesale middlemen because of the many variables already noted and others to be given special applicability below. Thus, there may be variations from as few as three to as many as seven functional divisions. The various types of wholesale middlemen categories are so widely conceived and so flexible in arrangement that it would be a mistake to assume that there is only one *best* arrangement of divisions. After all, a drop shipper, for example, has no need for providing a warehousing and order-filling division or subdivision in his organizational structure.

In the case of integrated middlemen, additional divisions should be noted. If the middlemen, as in the manufacturer's sales branches and sales offices, are directly a part of a manufacturing organization, then the additional functional divisions of the manufacturing activities will become very important. If the middleman, in turn, controls the manufacturer's establishment, direct integration of organizational structure will have to be made with that level either by providing for a manufacturing division or by executive liaison with a separate structure. Similarly, integration with the retail middleman's level will require the necessary formal or informal addition of the number of divisions necessary to reflect such integrated types of operation.

Factors influencing the degree of complexity of the divisional arrangements

Several important organizational variables were discussed earlier in this chapter. This section is designed to bring together in more direct and systematic fashion all of the factors which either increase or reduce the degree of divisional complexity.

Variations in *physical possession* of product assortments among wholesale middlemen have several effects on the divisional arrangements. As noted above, warehousing and order-filling divisions or subdivisions may or may not be required. Although this is the most obvious effect, other effects may be noted on the range and extent of the middleman's advertising activities and, also, on the range of packaging and branding activities. In addition, the absence of physical possession may so simplify the work of the traffic unit as to require merely the services of a staff assistant rather than a full-fledged division or subdivision.

The *range of middlemen's services*, other than those associated with physical possession, has similar effects on the divisional setup. A full range of functions may require, in conjunction with the presence of other variables, the most complex seven-divisional arrangement. On the other hand, limited-function types of operations may lead rather to the complete elimination of a given division or its reduction to a simple staff arrangement.[11]

The *difference between general-line and specialty operations*, as discussed under product assortments, has an important bearing upon the divisional organization. One obvious effect is on the presence or absence of specialization among buying and/or selling staffs, by product-line departments. Another is the effect on the differentiation between the product assortments carried by regular wholesalers as against cash-and-carry operations, or, as in the food business, on the departmentation between regular food and the nonfood product lines. Further differentiations may be made between salesmen handling branded as against unbranded lines. To the extent that customer

---

[11] The elimination may require liaison, however, with an outside agency hired to perform the function.

types are associated with product assortments, as noted above, differentiations may be so made in the salesmen's groupings.

Multiple-type as compared with single-type operations

This separation has important effects on divisional organization through the variable of differences in ranges of functions as well as in other directions. Whether or not this variable has a significant effect upon divisional organization is dependent, in part, upon the financial size and the personnel complexity of the organization involved in executing the multiple-type of operation. But it is conceivable that the divisional organization, in some cases, might have to reflect the existence of separate executives each charged with responsibility for specialization as to a particular type of operation.

Considerable importance must be given to the presence or absence of *multiunit operations,* since the presence will affect the extent to which the headquarters' type of divisional organization will have to be repeated for each unit.[12] Or it may imply the necessity for having each functional executive at the headquarters' organization level supervise the corresponding functional division units for each branch. Obviously, the total financial and sales size and strength of the enterprise, and the availability of adequate executive talent, will be significant corollary considerations. Another important related consideration, as noted in the footnote, will be the entire geographical outreach of the complete multiunit operations.

Much has been said already of the effects of integration on the wholesale middlemen's organizational structures. As noted above, one of the main effects is to determine, as a result of the type of integration, which one of the hierarchy of organizational structures becomes dominant and which subordinate. The range of possibilities is from complete independence to complete subordination. In the case of manufacturers' sales branches and sales offices, the result may be the same as that noted above for multiunit operations. In the case of the wholesale-sponsored voluntary chain wholesalers, divisional

---

[12] A case in point is the Crescent Electric Supply Co. of Dubuque, Iowa, a wholesaler of electrical apparatus and equipment, with 30,000 different items obtained from 5,000 separate suppliers. The company's headquarters and warehouse are in Dubuque, and it has branch warehouses opened or scheduled to be opened in Madison, Wisconsin; Sterling, Peoria, and Quincy, Illinois; Mason City, Spencer, Waterloo, Sioux City, Cedar Rapids, Des Moines, Davenport, Ottumwa, and Burlington, Iowa; and Sioux Falls and Rapid City, South Dakota. These units serve the seven states of Wisconsin, Illinois, Iowa, Minnesota, South Dakota, Nebraska, and Wyoming. See: "Expanding in the Face of a Trend," *Business Week* (April 20, 1957), pp. 61 ff.

provision may have to be made for the various services provided for the affiliated independent retailers. Integrated petroleum bulk terminals may have the same organizational dependence on the refinery as the sales branch's organizational structure has in relation to the controlling manufacturer.

Finally, *sales-size variations,* by their varied influences on financial strength, number of employees, availability of capital resources for hiring executives, and relationships to complexity of functional activities, may act to increase or to reduce the complexity of divisional organization.

Concluding remarks

Such evidence as is available would seem to support the conclusion that there is a much higher degree of variation in wholesale middlemen's organization structures and divisional arrangements than in the equivalent for manufacturing establishments. The main reason would seem to be associated with the wider range of wholesale middlemen's types of operations, of sales size, and of complexities in product assortments. Part of it stems from the less rigid requirements of authority and responsibility needed by the middlemen's organizations. Or, to state it somewhat differently, the wholesale middlemen's organizations have greater possibilities for varying the managerial element, and thus require considerably greater flexibility in structure.

The General Nature of Wholesale Middlemen's Policies and Policy Decisions

Given this organizational framework in which to designate zones of authority and responsibility by functional levels, the executives must concern themselves with making decisions pertinent to the area of policies.

Definition of policies

Policies are actions taken by the top executive or executives in an organization which represent the key targets or objectives, in a strategic sense, to be achieved within a stated period of time or over a somewhat less definitely stated time period. In addition, these policies may represent the basic business philosophy of the organization. They may be the resultant of formal, intensive planning development; or they may be informal, depending upon the nature of the organizational structure as discussed earlier. In an important sense, the policies become the guideposts which keep the particular business moving along a well-planned series of "highways," in order to attain the stipulated targets or objectives. These policies may be highly rigid or they may have considerable flexibility, depending, once again, on the particular assortment of executives staff and operating personnel, the type of wholesale middleman operation envisioned, and the complexities, relatively speaking, of the organizational structure involved.

From the managerial point of view, policies become the guides to and the bases for implementing decisions within the organization. These policies have direct and particular impact upon each and every functional division. If they establish, in effect, the "grand strategy" of the campaign for certain business results to be achieved during a stated period of time, they become also the controlling element in the particular tactics to be used in the day-to-day activities. Thus, policies dominate and establish the directives which, in turn, establish the responsibilities and authorities of each individual and each organizational division within this grand strategy. In the course of these tactics there must be the kind of feedback of information which will permit the best day-to-day check on both the accuracy of the grand strategy and the quality of execution.

The area of policies determination has, by its very nature, a close relationship to the planning activities of the organization. Carefully and incisively stated policies can have important beneficial effects on the quality of the budgets used within the organization and, in turn, are affected by such budgets. Similarly, such policies can act as important generating forces on the nature and extent of the research work carried on by the organization. Statements of policies serve also as valuable guides in preparing marketing plans, especially in terms of the management of the sales force. It is in these relationships that the quality of flexibility becomes of salient importance. For, as was stated earlier, policies become the guideposts to the "highways" the organization must travel in order to reach stated goals, then they must be so arranged that provision is made for organizational "detours" if such become necessary; or in establishing the basis for selecting new organizational roads as the need becomes demonstrated.

Classification of middlemen's policies

From the point of view of the various types of wholesale middlemen, the following outline is suggestive of the main types of policy decisions:

> I. *Selection of basic type of operation and kind of business.*
> This policy area establishes the basic management philosophy

as to what kind of business and what type of operation best meet the needs and resources involved. As will be discussed in Chapter 9, the factors involved and the decisions which result, based upon this policy philosophy, are the keys to every other important aspect of the middleman's operation.

II. *Selection of the geographical outreach of the business.* Coupled with, and stemming from, the preceding policy area, this policy area establishes the organizational bases for determining where to locate the enterprise in relationship to the number and kinds of customers expected to be serviced. It has, accordingly, immediate important and direct effects upon estimates of expected sales volumes, numbers and types of salesmen needed, and related matters to be discussed in Chapter 10.

III. *Selection of basic organizational strategy.* Generally overlooked in the available writings are the many opportunities wholesale middlemen have for a basic over-all merchandising strategy. The possibilities must be explored thoroughly before determination of policy with respect to particular strategies and tactics can take place.

IV. *Determination of product assortments.* This policy area involves the extension by the management of the basic considerations discussed in Chapter 7 to its policy decisions in (I) and (II). Involved, among other things, are questions of the breadth and depth of assortments, reactions to the competitive strength of producers versus middlemen's own brands, and related matters.

V. *Selection of the organizational structure.* This policy area involves the considerations already discussed in considerable detail in an earlier section of this chapter.

VI. *Selection of sales strategy.* Given the variables implied in the preceding policy areas, the management must face up to any special implementing policies necessary in its choice of salesmen and in its ability to use advertising. These become especially crucial if, in the determination of product assortments, there is established the policy of featuring distributor's branded merchandise. This policy area is also related significantly to the geographical outreach of the business.

VII. *Selection of company strategy with respect to control position in the channel.* Since the discussion is centering on the actual middlemen agency units which are constituent parts of the channels of distribution as previously discussed, this policy area involves the decisions the individual middleman enterprise has to make as to whether or not to play an active role in the managerial struggle for control of the channel. Involved also, as a corollary to this, is the middlemen's position with respect to an active or passive role in generating change in the channel.

VIII. *Selection of price policies.* Once again, within the framework of the decision made in connection with type of operation, kind of business, and product assortments, the individual middleman enterprise must establish, through its policy decisions, how far it can and should go in having price policies to begin with and, if the decision is in the affirmative, what kinds of policies it can have within the available range of freedom of choice.

IX. *Remaining policy areas.* Given the main policy areas enumerated above, the management must deal also with such matters as the following: Postsales service policies; its relationship to the significant area of government control; the determination of whether to play an active or a passive role with respect to its adaptation to important marketing trends; and, finally, the evaluation of the effectiveness of its policies, including all efforts made at coordination and control.

The determination of each of these policy areas is at the heart of the managerial decision-making process. The management must evaluate within the limits of its own and staff abilities how far each area involves factual, statistical probability, or other quantitative or qualitative judgment aspects in reaching final decisions.

Applicability of the concept of policies to wholesale middlemen

Much of the general literature on organization, administration, and policies, as has been noted, evolved in relationship primarily to the manufacturing establishments. Accordingly, all definitions, classifications, and other materials pertinent to policies have this manufacturing establishment bias. But, given the definition of policies and the classification scheme just presented, it is apparent that these have important significance for wholesale middlemen as well. To the extent, of course, that certain types of wholesale middlemen operations are merely special integrated organizational appendages of the manufacturing establishments, the relationship to the orthodox literature is direct and obvious.[13]

---

[13] The orthodox aspect of these manufacturer-controlled middlemen organizations is apparent in the treatments found in the available sales management textbooks.

But what are being emphasized here are both the general applicability of these basic organization and policy materials to all types of wholesale middlemen—not merely the manufacturer-controlled—and the necessity, as well, for considering special factors. It is assumed, far too often, that the giant manufacturing corporations can and do dictate policies throughout the length and breadth of the channel. To offset this, the discussion is designed to introduce a broader perspective which will serve to indicate how limited in scope and accuracy such a view is in actuality. After all, giantism in manufacturing frequently is offset by giantism among the customers with whom the manufacturers have to deal. In addition, the strategic importance of such middlemen types has been examined, in part, in an earlier chapter. It has been noted in connection with the general discussion of channel structure and the managerial struggle for channel control that there are other effective restrictions on the large-scale units in addition to some aspects of government regulation.

There is one additional perspective of wholesale middlemen's policies which needs to be presented, namely, the effect of the network of organizations in the channel structure, as has been mentioned previously. Not too much has been written about, or is known of, this phenomenon. What are implied here are the general relationships which exist throughout the channel by virtue of the accumulation of individual enterprise organization structures. The second aspect is the effect of the individual policy framework working within this network of organizations. Thus, policy decisions at one level in the channel may inhibit or promote coordinative or competitive policy decisions at any or all remaining levels in the channel. Furthermore, there usually will be an overlapping of the network organizations for a particular product moving through a particular channel and all the individual channels which constitute, in turn, the group channel for the industry. Also involved in this complicated network concept are the roles played by the respective dominant executives within the individual organizations.

Wholesale middlemen having policies by virtue of ownership of goods

Legal ownership of the product assortments being handled by the wholesale middleman in the channel brings with it the possibilities of some important policy determinations by the management of the types already discussed. Except for the case of organized wholesale agricultural goods markets and other extractive industry examples, ownership brings with it degrees of freedom regarding the sources and quality of the products to be purchased. Ownership also has very important repercussions on the matter of pricing and pricing policies. Furthermore, it may bring with it important decisions concerning classes of customers to be solicited and serviced, and the policies listed for sales promotion. If the wholesale middlemen elect to identify the product with their brand names, they may or may not elect, also, to accompany such brands with their own guarantees.

In addition, legal ownership may carry with it policy implications regarding the struggle for channel control. A decision by the middleman to own the goods sold may be the direct result of a battle in the channel between brands, revolving purely around matters of channel position or taking on the form of competitive retaliatory tactics. Middlemen's brands and the so-called manufacturers' fighting brands may have the same policy implications. Ownership may or may not carry with it additional responsibilities for the formulation of inventory policies. To the extent also that ownership results in the formulation of price policies, important credit and other financial policies will have to be formulated.

Wholesale middlemen having policies by virtue of type of operation

Enough has already been said about this variable to justify only a few summary remarks at this point. Every type of middleman operation, except for the producer-controlled or retailer-controlled types, has a high degree of freedom in selecting its type of operation and the kind of business therein. These decisions are, as has been indicated, policy decisions in and of themselves. But once made. important policy repercussions are felt in other directions: Whether or not to be single type or multitype in operation? Whether or not to have legal and/or physical possession of goods? The range of services to offer customers? What is the geographical outreach of the business? And others already discussed. What is important to recognize is that the particular policy decision made about type of operation and kind of business only opens up a whole group of related policy decisions rather than freezing the situation to a very narrow pattern.

Wholesale middlemen having other policy decisions

The kind of marketing organization found for particular products and kinds of business has important effects upon such policy areas as prices and terms of sale. Thus, in the organized wholesale grain markets, the rules of the various Boards of Trade, within the framework of existing government regulations, serve very well to exclude the possibility of individual middlemen members having price policies.

Other kinds of government regulations may affect either in positive or negative fashion the product, promotional, and pricing policy decisions. Attempts at informal as well as formal forms of integration may generate many policies for the controlling middlemen involved in the integrated setup while reducing the policy decision initiative of the integrated subordinates.

The scale of middlemen's operations, as discussed below in more detail, affects the need for formal policies by influencing the nature and complexity of the organization structure. The quality of the top executive managerial ability affects the nature and extent of policy formation since policy formation, in the sense previously discussed, requires imagination, analytical ability, and determination, among other executive abilities. These are only suggestive of the wide display of variables which affect the kind and complexity of wholesale middlemen's policies.

Wholesale middlemen without or with only very limited policy initiative

It probably is not completely accurate to report that there are types of wholesale middlemen without policy initiative. The closest approximation would be the extent to which producer-owned or retailer-owned middlemen were given no freedom at any stage in the initial formulation and later adaptation of policy decisions affecting such establishments. For all remaining types of operation, there is a minimum of policy initiative, at least at the outset, in the determination of the type of operation and kind of business. Once this policy decision has been made, however, the remaining areas of initiative may be severely reduced or almost eliminated. Thus, many types of agent middlemen operations, by the very nature of the selection of a particular type of agent middlemen, may waive all initiative in the remaining policy areas; while other agent middlemen types, as in the case of some brokers and sales agents, may have considerable areas of policy initiative and responsibility. *It would seem that the range of policy possibilities and combinations at the wholesale middlemen's level far exceeds the range for manufacturing enterprises.*

Effects of Scale of Operations on Policies

Several references have been made in preceding sections to the relationship between some measures of wholesale middlemen's scale of operations and the nature of the organization structure. This section will attempt to establish a similar relationship between scale and policies. The special emphasis, apart from the preceding discussion of variables and factors, is caused by the peculiar nature of scale in wholesaling. All manufacturing establishments are engaged in physically producing products, so there is a homogeneous base of output which can be used as the beginning of the measurement of scale. As wholesale middlemen do not uniformly physically handle product assortments, the homogeneous base found for the manufacturing establishments is lacking. In addition, the varying types of integration and the resultant varied effects have fluctuating relationships in the measurement of scale of wholesale middlemen's operations. Is the scale of the manufacturers' sales branch, for example, that of the manufacturer-owner? Or should its scale be measured by itself?

Previously, several measures of size, as a partial measure of sale, have been presented, by type of operation and kind of business: average sales per establishment; sales-size distributions; multiunit versus single-unit operations; and employment size. The wide fluctuations in scale, as evidenced by these measures, reflect, in turn, wide variations in financial strength, in the ability to use specialists at the executive level, and in related matters—all of which lead to high degrees of variability in organizational structure within and between types of operation and kinds of business. In addition, the possible high incidence of multioperations among wholesale middlemen has been referred to on several occasions.

The chain of causation with respect to policy may be summarized as follows: High variability in scale of operations leads, in turn, to high variability in the financial strength and complexity of operations, as between types of wholesale middlemen's operations, by kinds of business; this high variability of financial strength and complexity of operations then leads to high variability in the number of personnel, especially executives and specialists; and this leads, finally, to high variability in organizational structure. This chain of events then helps to explain, in turn, the wide range of policy attributes from the very initial choice (in simple fashion) of type of operation and kind of business to the most complex classifications.

Again, as noted in Chapter 7 for product assortments, it may be concluded *that, regardless of scale, those wholesale middlemen who are controlled either by extractive industry, manufacturing industry, or retail middlemen's establishments will have far less freedom of policy formation and, accordingly, less flexibility and complexity than for other types of operations.* This is perhaps the key, in the last analysis, as to why the orthodox wholesaler and affiliated types have had the resurgence to previous 1929 levels of sales importance.

In any case, the highly variable characteristics of scale as between types of wholesale middlemen, coupled with the other factors noted, help to explain why their organization structure and accompanying policy formation decisions cannot be standardized so readily, as in the case of manufacturing establishments. Even the retailing sector does not appear to show the kaleidoscopic effects that have been noted for the various types of operation composing the wholesaling sector. Similarly, the variabilities and complexities are transferred to the network of organizations resulting within the channels of distribution. Much more systematic analysis is needed of this phase, and the resultant findings would add very valuable knowledge to the study of organization and administration (both in theory and practice) as applied to wholesale middlemen.

QUESTIONS AND PROBLEMS

1. To what extent are the basic definitions of organization and organizational structure applicable to wholesale middlemen's businesses? To what extent do these basic definitions need to be modified?
2. Of what value is the organizational triangle?
3. What are meant by the "components of organizational dimensions"?
4. Explain each of the variables which may have significant effects on wholesale middlemen's organizations and organizational structure.
5. How important is the concept of "network of organizations"? How do these networks evolve from the channel?
6. Distinguish between the single-divisional, two-divisional, and multi-divisional organizational arrangements.
7. What factors make for simplicity of the organizational structure? for complexity?
8. Do you agree with the statement, "Such evidence as is available would seem to support the conclusion that there is a much higher degree of variation in wholesale middlemen's organization structures and divisional arrangements than in the equivalent for manufacturing establishments"?
9. To what extent can wholesale middlemen have policies? How are such policies classified?
10. How do wholesale middlemen's policies vary by type of operation? by functions performed?
11. Discuss the validity of the statement: "It would seem that the range of policy possibilities and combinations at the wholesale middlemen's level far exceeds the range for manufacturing enterprises."
12. To what extent does large-scale organization lead to increased complexity of policies? to less complexity?

CHAPTER INTEGRATING ASSIGNMENTS

1. Visit a wholesale middleman establishment in your locality. Compare and contrast this establishment's organizational structure with the generalized discussion in the text.

2. Relate the discussion of product assortments in Chapter 7 with the discussion of organization. In your discussion, indicate under what conditions product assortments lead to complexity of organizational structure. Be sure to discuss, as well, some of the alternative organizational devices used to solve these product assortment effects.

3. Prepare a tabular arrangement in which you indicate the principal effects on organizational structure of each type of wholesale middleman's operation and the component functions performed.

9

Selection of Type of Operation
and Kind of Business

All too often it is assumed by many individuals that the easiest way to make a living, if not more substantial success, is either by owning and operating a wholesale or a retail middleman establishment. These two avenues of economic livelihood become the green pastures for the trained and the untrained who, tired of working for and being bossed by others, visualize and capitalize on the joys of being their own bosses. There is a great deal of the romantic, of the noble "Horatio Alger rags-to-riches tradition" in this view. These broad psychological and sociological drives should not be underestimated in the process of selection of type of operation and kind of business

But there are some stern economic realities which need to be faced by persons contemplating starting some kind of wholesale middleman business. Increasingly, the complexity of the marketing organization through the channel, and changes therein, makes it imperative that the economic variables be given proper evaluation and weighting before the final selection is made of the most desirable type of operation and kind of business. Increasingly, the tempo of competition among the various types of wholesale middlemen makes it less likely that the noneconomic factors, in and of themselves, will secure success.

In following the framework of description and analysis in this chapter, the necessary relationships must be kept in mind with the previous chapters dealing with classification and definition of types of operation and with the analysis of census data showing trends by types of operations and kinds of business. In addition, the discussion of the selection process presented in this chapter must be related with the discussion and analysis of the factors involved in the selection of a location to be discussed in Chapter 10. Finally, it must be remembered that the discussion here represents, to some extent, a cross-sectional picture. There are far too many individual situations to permit any analysis to be all-inclusive in treatment.

Availability of Necessary Managerial Ability

Because the mortality statistics of business indicate clearly that inadequate managerial ability is the single most important reason for failures of wholesale middlemen, or at least ranks among the most important reasons, it follows that the problem of the availability of necessary managerial ability should be discussed early in this chapter. The emphasis here is placed on analysis by the prospective executive involved. The noneconomic views noted at the beginning represent additional reasons for such prime emphasis on the availability of the necessary managerial ability.

Types of managerial abilities

The varied types of middlemen operations already classified and defined call for and require many kinds of managerial ability. In addition, the range of considerations already noted in Chapter 8 in connection with the discussion of organization structure serves also to broaden the range of kinds of managerial ability needed. It is against this broad backdrop, accordingly, that each potential managerial group must be evaluated before beginning a particular type of operation and kind of business.

Perhaps the single most important type of managerial ability needed for wholesale middlemen's operations is that of *flexibility*. If the type of operation selected is going to be one of the non-integrated group, this ability of managerial flexibility will be reflected mainly in the adaptability of operations, functionally speaking, to maximize customer appeal. But it will be evident also, as previously discussed, in the approach to product assortments. In addition, it means the ability to adapt policy decisions in rapid fashion to the changing competitive structure of the channel.

For the integrated middlemen types, the ability of flexibility carries with it a somewhat different connotation. If the type of integrated operation is producer-controlled, flexibility calls for the ability of the top management to free its marketing decisions, especially as they pertain to the channel, from the rigidities of the production aspects of the controlling organization. This requirement may lead, in its fullest execution, to giving the executive a considerable degree of organizational autonomy in the operation of the integrated wholesale middleman unit. If the integrated middleman type is retail-middleman-controlled, the attribute of flexibility may require rapid adjustment of the wholesale middlemen operations to the rapidly shifting competitive structure and needs of the retail operations.

A second important ability is that associated with the necessity for many executives in the wholesaling sector to be willing to be both executive and the chief person in charge of operations. Because the concept of scale in wholesaling, as noticed in Chapter 8, is quite different from that in manufacturing, the top executive in a great many organization structures must assume responsibility for operations as well as for policy making and control. This has the advantage of placing the executive on the firing line, so to speak, and thus leads to a more realistic coordination of policies and day-to-day operations. It may have the distinct disadvantage of causing the executive to spend so much time in operations that he fails to devote enough time to the coordination and control aspects of the business as well as to an evaluation of trends both for his business and for the wholesaling sector as a whole.

For certain kinds of business, especially those handling agricultural products in organized wholesale markets, a third attribute is that of *trading* ability. Since a considerable degree of success of these middlemen is associated with (*a*) the skill with which contacts are established with farmers for the sale of their products, (*b*) the skill with which contacts may be established with buyers to represent them in the markets, and (*c*) the ability to sense the trading pulse of a particular trading session in the organized market, it follows that, in the decision to enter such type of operation and kind of business, these aspects must be carefully evaluated.

A final special attribute of executives in charge of various types of wholesale middlemen operations is that of the degree to which such middlemen executives are willing or unwilling *to assume risks*. Obviously, one aspect of a decision to be a certain type of agent middleman is related to the factor that the executives are not then concerned with the risks stemming from ownership. Thus, the type of executive involved in such type of operations is emphasizing other attributes of his executive ability rather than those associated with the willingness to assume ownership.

Measurement of managerial abilities

What has been suggested in the preceding section is that the executive of a type of wholesale middlemen operation requires both the usual traits of executive ability together with some of the special attributes noted. In beginning the analysis of which type of operation and kind of business to select, it may be suggested that a checklist of such requirements be prepared. The checklist might be divided as follows:

1. *Basic executive qualities required.* Such a list would be of the types included in the basic texts, with some kind of rating scale assigned as from 1 to 10, or from "very poor" to "outstanding."
2. *Special executive abilities required for each type of operation and kind of business.* This would represent the executive's evaluation, by means of some rating scale, of the kinds of abilities discussed in the preceding section.
3. *A preliminary budget* of the percentage of the executive's time to be allocated by him in stated areas of responsibility.[1]

From the analysis of the ratings assigned in (1) and (2), the persons involved should be able to get some concrete notion of how well their executive talents measure up to certain norms. These ratings can never be so conclusive as to be the only way in which to measure potentialities for the wholesale middleman's operation. At best, these ratings serve merely, as the title checklist suggests, as a device to make sure that the potential executive does not overlook certain vital considerations.

A failure to evaluate carefully and completely the management potential may be, as noted, the single most important cause of subsequent bankruptcy or, at least, for the sale or termination of the business. The data in Table 22 show the recent failure record in wholesale trade.

[1] See C. L. Shartle, *Executive Performance and Leadership* (Englewood Cliffs, N. J.: Prentice-Hall, Inc., 1956), Chapter 4.

TABLE 22

THE FAILURE RECORD IN WHOLESALE TRADE, BY
SELECTED KINDS OF BUSINESS: UNITED STATES 1957, 1958

Kind of Business	Number		Liabilities (millions)	
	1957	1958	1958	1959
Total, all kinds	1,431	1,236	$82.0	$77.9
Food and farm products	330	283	20.9	18.7
Apparel	62	43	2.7	2.5
Dry goods	46	34	1.5	1.4
Lumber, building materials, hardware	175	154	12.8	9.1
Chemicals and drugs	50	45	1.3	1.9
Motor vehicle equipment	67	72	2.3	3.2
Miscellaneous	701	605	40.5	41.1

Source: Dun's Review and Modern Industry (February 1959), p. 16.

General Factors in Selection of Type of Operation

Although the selection of a type of operation cannot, in actuality, be divorced from the selection of a kind of business, it will be well at this point to separate the discussion before indicating how integration may be accomplished in making the final selection. In actuality, it must be remembered also that matters of available financial resources and the pressure of time will weigh heavily in influencing how carefully and how far the evaluation process may be carried. What is presented here is perhaps an idealized version of all the important variables. The particular persons making the evaluation must then judge to what extent it is necessary and possible for them to secure the necessary data for any of the required categories. In following this procedure, extreme care must be taken not to be so narrow-viewed in perspective that matters of immediate economy are permitted to curtail the extent of the analysis, only to have heavy penalties result at a later date.

Sales performance trends

The basic data of the sales performance of each type of operation are available from the Bureau of the Census data for 1929, 1935, 1939, 1948, 1954, and 1958 as analyzed in Chapters 2 through 4. Unfortunately, there are a few types of operation which have not been included, but these are of minor importance in the total picture of wholesale trade. These data may be used as the beginning point of the analysis by serving as a basis for the following:

1. The rank order of importance of each type of operation in the United States for each census benchmark period.
2. Changes in the relative importance of each type of operation between census benchwork periods.
3. From (1) and (2), an indication of each type of operation in terms of increasing, stable, or declining importance, or of variable positions of importance.
4. The range of establishments by sales size, and the average per establishment, for each type of operation.
5. The geographical distribution of the principal types of operations in terms of regions, states, metropolitan areas, and principal cities.
6. Changes in the relative importance of each type, by the geographic units in (5).
7. Geographic variations in the range of and average sales size per establishment, for the principal types of operation.

These types of analyses give a particular potential management unit the necessary broad historical perspective. The results thus obtained must be correlated with the other types of factors to be considered in this and succeeding sections.

Cost performance trends

While Chapter 19 will discuss the costs of wholesale middlemen, and the variables in such costs, the analysis needed here is to direct managerial attention to operating costs (as a per cent of net sales) in relation to each type of operation. The framework of the analysis is very similar to that indicated for sales performance: (1) The rank order of types of operation from low cost to high cost in relation to services performed; (2) any significant changes in the percentage relationships; (3) geographical variations in operating costs, by type of operation, and (4) variations in operating costs in relation to sales-size groupings.

Size of inventories

The census data show, for the types of middlemen having physical possession, the size of the inventory at the end of the year for each benchwork period. These data may be related to sales in order to get stock-sales ratios. Changes may be computed as between benchwork periods, and as between establishments located in various types of geographic units. From such data, the potential management may be expected to get first approximations of working capital requirements for inventory as well as requirements for warehouse space.

Basic knowledge of each type of operation

Given these basic census data, the management should review the basic marketing literature explaining in qualitative terms the generalized picture of what each type of operation actually does or is expected to do. Such information should be evaluated in the light of each type's relative position as revealed by the census data and by considering the fundamental strengths and weaknesses of each type. In addition, such information may aid the particular management in showing various ways in which its own operations may deviate from the standard composition of activities.

Evaluation of the information

If the management involved is contemplating a nonintegrated type of operation, these initial data must be correlated as follows:

1. The relationship of each type, in view of the preceding discussion, to the person's managerial ability.
2. The estimates of preliminary financial requirements of each type of operation in relation to the potential management's actual financial resources.
3. The relationship of such information to expected sales volumes.
4. Finally, the relationship of each type of operation to the potential management's estimates of the degree of freedom desired in the channel, and of expectation of survival against the competing types.

It must be emphasized, once again, that these analyses are only the first approximations. Succeeding sections will introduce additional analyses, and each of these, in turn, will act as a refinement of the first approximations. They may even lead in a few selected cases to a complete reversal of the divisions based on these first approximations.

If the type of operation contemplated is an integrated firm, then additional basic analyses are required as follows:

1. The competitive strengths and weaknesses, in general, of the types of operation contemplated.
2. Special evaluation of the extent to which the particular type of operation will improve the management's position in the struggle with other managements for control of the channel.

3. The effects of type-of-operation alternatives on expected costs and profits.
4. The effects on other middlemen's acceptance of the company's product lines in view of the integrated middlemen's setup.
5. Does the integration serve as the initiator of change in the channel? Or is it, rather, a defense against some other changes already in existence?
6. Does the enterprise have the available marketing executive ability within the firm to operate these contemplated integrated types? Or, conversely, can such talent be recruited from outside manpower supplies?

General Factors in Selecting the Kind of Business

This section of the analysis begins the process of refining the basic analysis outlined above by bringing into focus the kinds of product assortments to be featured. The background materials of Chapter 7 are important to this analysis. In addition, careful coordination must be made of the findings obtained in the first stage of the analysis outlined above with the results obtained from the following analyses.

Production trends

The management involved must begin its analysis either by evaluating the production of every product handled in the channel or by pin-pointing its analyses to the components of particular product categories. Government trade associations and selected trade magazines together with selected research studies contain the basic data from which the detailed or group data analyses can be derived. The analyses, as made, should include the following as an absolute minimum:

1. The absolute physical level of output of each product item, or product class, by years or other appropriate chronological periods.
2. The relative importance of the output in (1) in relation to group production totals and all production.
3. The dollar value of such output.
4. If a consumer's good, the trend of per capita consumption or use, and the price-elasticity and income-elasticity characteristics.

These data will reveal those products and industries which are experiencing growth phases as compared with those experiencing stability or decline. When related to directories of manufacturers, the

potential management can find the number and geographical distribution of potential suppliers.

Wholesale establishments' sales

The census reports will reveal the sales performance position and
benchwork trends for each kind of business under the type-of-operation
groups. Although the detailed data for each type of operation would
be more useful, the available data, where related to production trends,
will reveal many useful things. The importance of each kind of
business has been noted earlier. Variations in average sales per establishment may be computed as well as distribution of establishments
by sales-size groups. In addition, valuable data are available, as in
Chapter 7, showing the breakdown of sales by commodity lines.

The above analyses refer to a United States base. Many similar
analyses can be derived for the regional state, metropolitan area, and
larger city bases. These give the necessary adaptations for later study
of the particular locations for the type of operation and kind of
business selected. The combination of these analyses with the above
yields classification of products and kinds of business into both growth-
and declining-trend groups, with geographic variations.

Operating costs trends

The same kinds of analyses of operating costs noted above for
types of operation can be prepared for kinds of business as well. Then
the two sets of data can be correlated.

Scale analyses

In addition to the sales-size analyses, other analyses of scale can
be made for various kinds of business, e.g., employment-size distributions and single-unit versus multiunit operation. These permit the
prospective manager to evaluate the kind of competition found in each
kind of business as well as the range of potential sales volumes. In
addition, various degrees of detailed scale data, by kind of business,
are available by geographic units.

Evaluation of the information

The same type of evaluation noted for the type-of-operation data
need to be made for the analyses included for the kind of business
data. In addition, interrelationships of the two groups of analyses
must be made so that, in the final evaluation, the prospective manager
can classify types of operation by kinds of business from most fertile
to least fertile possibilities.

With the completion of these two groups of plans, the potential managers have at hand the basic background against which to measure the decisions to be made about the selection of a *particular* kind of business in relation to a *particular* type of operation. The factors to be considered in order to make these *particular* decisions are discussed in the following sections.

Factors Involved in the Purchase of An Existent Business

Once the decisions have been reached as to the most favorable type of operation and kind of business, the next decision which has to be made is whether to purchase an existing business or initiate an entirely new business. This section will deal with the factors involved in the purchase of an existing business.[2]

Sales performance trends

From the authenticated business records of the enterprise, the analysis made by the management must first establish the following three things about the firm's sales performance:

1. Within the length of time of the firm's existence the long-run total sales trend, the cyclical fluctuations in total sales, and month-to-month variations.
2. Breakdown of the total sales in (1) by each product-line subdivision, and computation of the changing relative importance of each.
3. The total market penetration of the firm, and for each product division, by time periods.

Given these three sets of information, the firm's performance should be compared with the basic trends available from the preceding types of analyses of census data. Finally, a total-evaluation score should be computed, so far as sales performance is concerned.

Analysis of the firm's financial statements[3]

Given the sales performance picture of the firm, the next series of analyses involve careful investigation of the firm's financial statements. These analyses involve both *static* and *dynamic* aspects. Static in the sense of a cross-sectional view taken at any given date, and of analysis of changes between financial statement dates.

---

[2] The closely related question of "where" is discussed in the next chapter.

[3] This analysis is based completely on Roy A. Foulke, *Practical Statement Analysis,* 4th ed. (New York: McGraw-Hill Book Co., Inc., 1957).

Since so many wholesaling establishments are of small size, as measured both by sales and net worth, certain special ratios may be used:

1. Cost of goods sold as a per cent of annual net sales.

2. $\dfrac{Cost\ of\ goods\ sold\ +\ net\ profits}{Net\ sales}$ = income to meet merchandise obligations.

3. 100 per cent *minus* per cent in (2) = income needed to cover all gross expenses.

4. Yearly net sales converted into monthly net sales.

5. Cash on hand (date of statement) *minus* average monthly income needed to cover all expenses = excess cash on hand.

6. Accounts payable (date of statement) *minus* excess cash on hand = accounts payable after crediting excess of cash on hand.

7. *Balance in* (6) = number of months needed to balance in (2) to liquidate the remaining accounts payable.

In addition to these, the prospective buyer should obtain the latest Dun & Bradstreet credit rating for the firm.

For the larger firms, a much more intricate type of analysis of the applicable financial statements is possible through the evaluation of the following ratios:[4]

1. *Current assets to current liabilities* (or, as a special version, ratio of cash marketable securities and receivables to current liabilities). This ratio is an indicator of the ability of the firm to meet its current obligations, as of a given date.

2. *Current liabilities to tangible net worth.* This ratio indicates the margin of safety for creditors in that the higher the ratio, the less the protection, and vice versa.

3. *Total liabilities to tangible net worth.* This ratio, for many enterprises, will be the same as (2).

4. *Funded debt to net working capital.* This ratio gives a measure of whether or not the entire capital of the firm is tied up in "slow" assets.

5. *Depreciated fixed assets to tangible net worth.* Foulke[5] indicates that, if the firm has tangible net worth of $50,000 to $250,000, the condition indicated by the ratio should be analyzed care-

[4] These ratios must be interpreted very carefully. In and of themselves, they possess no particular magic. One of the author's colleagues points out that, to many, these ratios seemed to be and, indeed, are used as a form of modern witchcraft.

[5] Foulke, *op. cit.,* p. 294.

fully if it exceeds two-thirds. Where the tangible net worth exceeds $250,000, careful analysis is needed if the ratio exceeds three-fourths.

6. *Net sales to inventory.* With special attention given to the influence of the method used for inventory valuation and the date of the inventory in relation to the seasonal composition of sales, this ratio gives an important clue to the amount of stock needed to generate given volumes of sales. It will indicate, also, whether too much inventory is being carried relative to the firm's net sales volume.

7. *Inventory to net working capital.* If the wholesale middleman's firm has a tangible net worth of $50,000 to $250,000, great care must be exercised if the ratio exceeds three-fourths, *even* if the ratio of net sales to inventory is satisfactory. If the net worth exceeds $250,000, the inventory should not *exceed* net working capital.[6]

8. *Average collection period.* For the wholesale middlemen selling in open-book account, Foulke[7] suggests that the average collection period should not be over one-third above the net selling terms. Thus, given terms of 2/10/n/30, the average collection period should not exceed 40 days. If the average relationship exceeds this one-third excess, then he suggests obtaining sufficient additional information to ascertain if sales bulked more than normally during the 30 to 60 days preceding the statement date, and what percentage of the receivables are past due, and for what length of time.

9. *Net sales to tangible net worth.* A high ratio may indicate that an excessive amount of business was obtained on a thin margin of invested capital. This may lead, in turn, to a resultant over-use of credit. In larger enterprises, with more conservative financial policies, the reverse situation may be found. Thus Foulke states the maximum: If the ratio is more than twice the median for the line of business, overtrading is taking place.[8]

10. *Other significant ratios.* Five additional significant ratios may be found useful: (*a*) Net sales to net working capital; (*b*) net profit to tangible net worth; (*c*) net profit to net sales; (*d*) net profits to net working capital; and (*e*) current debt to inventory.

These 14 types of ratios are available for 24 lines of business for wholesalers in 1955 for the upper quartile median and for lower

[6] *Ibid.*, p. 354.
[7] *Ibid.*, pp. 385–86.
[8] *Ibid.*, p. 412.

quartiles of the reporting firms.[9] In addition, median ratios are available for 21 lines of business for each year, 1951–1955. In addition to these data, trade associations of wholesale middlemen may have additional median figures against which comparisons can be made for the particular firm in question.

In any case, these ratios merely are indicators. They need to be evaluated carefully in the light of the particular kind of business involved. The time factor is equally important since the ratios reflect a situation as of the date of the statement. If the kind of business is characterized by wide swings, the median figures may be of little value.

Strengths and weaknesses of location

In the light of the analysis to be presented in Chapter 10, the prospective buyer must evaluate whether or not a significant advantage to be obtained from the purchase of an existing business is the unique locational position. This advantage is increased in importance if the middleman takes physical possession. The rental terms and other cost obligations must be weighed carefully against the size and quality of the trading area serviced. Other factors to be considered will be deferred until Chapter 10.

Owner's reasons for selling the business

The prospective purchaser of an existing business must be very much aware of the reasons for the sale. In the light of the reasons given by the owner, the analysis of financial statements suggested above must be done with special care in order to determine whether any serious weaknesses exist. A sampling of customers' opinions may be undertaken to determine the general reputation of the firm. If the firm is in sound financial position, the prospective buyer would be well advised to make certain that the owner is precluded, in the contract of sale, from opening a competing business in the same trading area within a stipulated number of years.

A special aspect of this part of the analysis is the determination of whether or not key personnel will remain with the enterprise in the event of its purchase by the prospective buyer. Any unwillingness of key executives and salesmen to remain, depending on the size of the business, would be a serious roadblock to the purchase. This roadblock would be doubly serious if the personnel were considering opening a competing wholesale middleman business.

[9] *Ibid.*, pp. 648–651.

Strengths and weaknesses of product assortments

Finally, the prospective purchaser must carefully evaluate the product assortment base of the existing firms' sales. Are these sales realized by virtue of having exclusive agreements with manufacturers? Are such agreements transferable in the event of the firm's sale? Does the enterprise have strong distributors' brands of its own? Is the inventory based on assortments in depth? Or is it based on assortments in breadth? Have the assortments been changed to meet the changing needs of the firm's customers? Has the firm moved in the direction of scrambled merchandising in its assortments? These are merely suggestive of the types of more important questions for which complete answers must be secured.

Of very key significance in this connection is the unearthing of information about (a) any unusual element in the composition of the product assortments which will lead to benefits in sales or (b) any aspect of the firm's product assortments which, conversely, may help to explain existing weaknesses in the firm's sales records. Closely related is the necessity for determining whether or not there will be any disruption of relationships with the sources of product assortments if the business is sold.

Factors in the Initiation of a New Enterprise

General advantages

Obviously, only a limited number of fertile opportunities exist at any one time for the outright purchase of a successful middleman enterprise in the type of operation and kind of business desired. Accordingly, the management must examine the alternative of beginning a new enterprise. There are many advantages accruing to the owners from such decision. The management may be able to transfer previous valuable experience without resistance from the personnel. Opportunities may exist, similarly, for a fresh approach in terms of the trading area to be developed, the assortment of functions to be performed, and the kinds of product assortments selected. There is always the advantage of beginning with a clean slate and being free to make one's own mistakes.

In addition, existing manufacturers may have had some unwelcome business experiences with the established types of wholesale middlemen. Or an aggressive new manufacturer with interesting and unorthodox product ideas may wish to have an entirely new team of wholesale middlemen linkages rather than battling with existing inflexibilities and traditions among the already established wholesale middlemen linkages.

Limitations

The opportunities for the fresh approach and highly profitable operations do not exist in all kinds of business and for all types of operations. The cream trading areas may be unavailable because of existing competition, and the better exclusive agreements may be assigned already, leaving only the marginal potentialities available. Choice locational sites may be too expensive compared with the financial strength of the firm, or simply may not be available at any cost. Competition may prohibit the realization of carefully planned sales; or the development period may exceed expectations. The expected managerial abilities and knowledge may simply fail to materialize. Finally, legal restrictions may place too heavy financial burdens upon the new firm.

Evaluation of available product assortments

Except for those extractive industry products sold on organized wholesale markets, middlemen have varying degrees of relationships with producers so far as availability of product lines is concerned. The following list is suggestive of the kinds of pertinent questions each prospective middleman will want to have answered before buying such lines or acting as a type of agent middleman for the manufacturer.[10]

1. *Questions about the product.* Is the line well established in the market? What is the extent of users' acceptance of the line in the contemplated trading area? What is the manufacturer's sales position in his industry? What is his penetration ratio in the contemplated trading area? Are there any problems of limited supplies in relation to sales? Is the product highly technical in nature? Will the product line fit into the management's contemplated type of operation and kind of business? What are the important marketing characteristics of the product? Is the

[10] This list is based, in part, on the following articles: "What Distributors Want to Know Before Taking on a Line," *Sales Management* (October 1, 1951), pp. 76 ff. "Why Our Sales Policies are Built Around Manufacturers 'Reps,'" *Sales Management* (October 1, 1950), pp. 117 ff. W. M. Yogerst, "What Can a Manufacturer Do to Keep His Agents Prosperous and Happy," *Sales Management* (June 1, 1950), pp. 52 ff.

products' packaging convenient and attractive? Is the product guaranteed by the manufacturer?

2. *Sales potentialities.* What is the relationship of forecasted sales to the middlemen's expectations? Will the manufacturer help the middleman in estimating sales potentials? What are the competing products distributed in the trading area? Are the sales highly seasonal in their distribution? Or are sales more regularly distributed throughout the 12 months? Have the sales of the product lines been expanding or contracting during the history of the manufacturer?

3. *Prices, profit margins, etc.* Does the manufacturer follow a policy of resale price maintenance? What margins and discounts does he give merchant middlemen? What brokerage fees, commissions, etc., will he pay the agent middlemen? What is the profit margin in relation to selling expense? In relation to stock turnover? In relation to the inventory value?

4. *Manufacturers' channel policies.* How many other middlemen (in terms of numbers, types of operation, and locations) are selling the manufacturer's line of products? Does the manufacturer have a stated policy concerning channels? If the manufacturer sells direct to the middleman's customers, will he credit part or all of such sales to the middleman's account? What are the sales experiences of other middlemen handling the line? Will the manufacturer sign a contract with the middleman?

5. *Manufacturer's cooperation with the middleman.* Does the manufacturer have specific requirements for channel cooperation from the middlemen? How much inventory (if any) must the middleman carry? Does the manufacturer follow a policy of full-line forcing through the channel? How rapidly are the middleman's orders filled? Will the manufacturer accept returns of slow-moving items, or make adjustments? Does he have field representatives to work with the middleman? Does he offer technical help and such services as installation and repairs for the highly technical products? Does he conduct worth-while sales and technical training meetings for the middleman's personnel? What is the nature of the manufacturer's advertising campaigns and aids for the middleman's salesmen? Has the manufacturer followed a consistent policy of displacing middlemen with his own sales branches and/or sales offices after sales volume reaches a desired level? Finally, has the manufacturer followed a continuous program of squeezing the middlemen's margins?

6. *Other questions.* What is the manufacturer's financial rating? Has the manufacturer's position in the industry been expanding or declining? Will the manufacturer produce products with the middleman's brand? Or, conversely, does the manufacturer follow a strict policy of using only his brand name? Will he permit the middleman to add his guarantee to that of the manufacturer? Will he accept financial aid from, or give such aid to, the wholesale middlemen?

Throughout the evaluation process of the product line and the manufacturer, in terms of these types of questions, the middleman must determine as accurately as possible the behavior of the manufacturer in the channel. If the manufacturer has had a history of active battling for control of the channel, then the middleman must decide what the effect will be on his own plans of channel position. The middleman must watch carefully for indications of the presence or absence of "fair" treatment in the kinds of contractual agreements the manufacturer is willing to sign with middlemen. Finally, the middleman must determine from those already in business whether or not the manufacturer, in his struggle for channel control or position, has pressured the middlemen by such devices as resale price maintenance, full-line forcing, and the continuous squeezing of margins.

Availability of favorable locations

One of the complexities of beginning a new business is that of selecting a favorable location. Once again, the discussion of the variables involved must be delayed until Chapter 10.

Financial requirements

The lack of adequate financial resources is one of the more important reasons explaining the failure of wholesale middlemen. Accordingly, the prospective management should prepare a careful budget of the financial requirements for the first year or two by quarterly periods. Sharp differences in the amount of the financial requirements will be dependent especially on whether or not the middleman takes physical possession of inventories, and on the expected scale of operations. If physical possession of inventories takes place, careful allowance must be made of the investments required for the average size of inventories, additional allowances for inventory depreciation, and the fixed and variable expenses related to warehousing and order-filling operations.

Additionally, the management must carefully estimate the components of expenses which will be incurred, and which must be met during the early period of the business when sales may be sporadic and, perhaps, below expectations. The management must decide, also, whether or not it will restrict its remuneration during the first year of the business in order to conserve scarce financial resources until sales revenue materializes.

For the middlemen who do not take physical possession, equally careful financial budgeting is necessary, but the components will be sharply different, especially as far as the overhead cost items are concerned. But, despite these differences, the philosophy should be the same, namely, careful estimates of the unescapable, partially escapable, and variable cost elements during the first years of the business and by quarters, and the most careful estimates of revenue expectations during the same periods.

Channel position

The various types of wholesale middlemen have widely different positions of importance in the channel. In selecting a type of operation, and a particular kind of business, it behooves the management to weigh carefully these varying degrees of importance in the channel. Although the data available from the census give the general analysis, each management must evaluate such data in the light of the particular assortment which it contemplates handling. This is especially the case, once again, when choosing between the integrated and the nonintegrated types of operation.

Other factors

The preceding discussion having outlined the main factors applicable to beginning a new business, some attention should now be given to an analysis of the factors operating in certain special circumstances. There are types of wholesale middlemen in the agricultural goods markets who must register with the Secretary of the United States Department of Agriculture. Many of the same types, if operating in such organized markets as the grain Boards of Trade, will have to meet membership screening successfully as well as pay the applicable membership fees.

Middlemen operating in foreign trade kinds of business may have to meet bonding and custom house licensing requirements. Also, in certain states, middlemen handling wines and liquors may have to acquire special licenses from state boards. There may be such licenses available, or they may have to be acquired through purchase at rather high price. Finally, middlemen, in order to acquire exclusive franchise agreements, may have to meet rather sizable financial standards.

The Final Selection Process

Although it is recognized that individuals, in arriving at decisions as to type of operation and kind of business, use all conceivable processes from pure hunch to very refined scientific methods, the process discussed in this section may minimize the probability of mistakes due to hasty and incomplete decision making.

Step 1. On the basis of the preceding discussions, select the applicable factors or variables, and classify them into two groups —the quantitative and the qualitative. Some factors may have to be classified in an in-between zone, but great care should be taken to prepare as detailed a list of each as possible, with a very careful division between the quantitative and the qualitative factors.

Step 2. In this step, care must be taken to obtain the most up-to-date and complete data for measuring each of the applicable quantitative and qualitative factors. The care and completeness with which this data-collecting process is executed will depend upon the personal characteristics of the executive involved, the amount of financial resources available, and the kind of personnel available for assignment either within the projected organization or from outside research agencies.

Step 3. This step consists of the pertinent analysis of these data as collected in step 2.

Step 4. This step involves the assignment—to each quantitative and qualitative factor—of pertinent weights indicating the relative position, as analyzed by the appropriate methods in step 3.

Step 5. This step involves the accumulation of the individual weightings, as determined in step 4, for each of the quantitative and qualitative factors.

Step 6. This is the final step in which executive judgment must be applied to an interpretation of the final results obtained in step 5. From this is prepared a statement of the final conclusions together with any qualifications that may be needed.

This six-step process has the value of forcing the management to adhere to a systematic procedure designed to improve the quality of its analysis and decisions as to type of operation and kind of business. Some management groups may use it in the form of a simple checklist, with the added refinement of the weighting process noted above. Others, of a research-minded nature, with adequate resources and well-trained research personnel, will execute the six-step procedure in a very scientific manner. Finally, the remaining management groups will fall somewhere in between these extremes in their own procedures. In each of these cases, the great value in the procedure outlined lies in the existence of a more careful type of analysis than mere hearsay or hunch in making an important decision. Once completed, the management is then ready to arrive at a decision as to where the type of operation and kind of business should be located. This analysis will be discussed in the next chapter.

QUESTIONS AND PROBLEMS

1. To what extent is the operation of a wholesale middleman establishment so simple as to require no particular managerial abilities?
2. What specialized managerial abilities are required in order to be a successful wholesale middleman? How may these abilities be measured?
3. How important are each of the general factors discussed in the actual selection of a particular type of operation? of kind of business?
4. Discuss completely the advantages and disadvantages of purchasing an existing business. Under what circumstances do the advantages outweigh the disadvantages?
5. Of what value is the wide array of financial ratios in the decision of whether or not to purchase an existing business?
6. What are the advantages and limitations of initiating a new wholesale middleman enterprise rather than purchasing an existing business?
7. How should the general information on product assortments in Chapter 7 be used in deciding what assortments should be handled in your own wholesale middleman operation?
8. Of what value is the suggested six-step selection process?

CHAPTER INTEGRATING ASSIGNMENTS

1. Suppose a rich uncle willed you $500,000 (after payment of all applicable taxes), with the proviso that you must use this money in operating a wholesale middleman business. You are asked to submit a proposal to the executor of your uncle's estate in which you analyze the following:
   a. The general value of establishing a unique type of operation as against the more popular types.
   b. The extent to which you would feature manufacturer-controlled product assortments as against your own branded assortments.
   c. Whether or not to purchase an existing business?

2. Make a survey of the leading wholesale middlemen in your locality. In this survey, secure as reliable answers as possible to the following:
   a. What were the leading factors which led them to select their present type of operation and kind of business?
   b. If they had it to do over, would they select the same type of operation and kind of business? If the response is "No," ascertain which type of operation and kind of business they would select, and the supporting reasons.
   c. What, in their opinion, are the most important reasons for starting a business from scratch? for purchasing an existing business?

10

Selection of
Middlemen's Locations

Given the managerial decisions outlined in the preceding chapter pertinent to the selection of the type of middleman operation and kind of business, a closely related group of decisions must next be made about where to locate the establishment (establishments) involved. The basic framework for this type of locational analysis was developed in Chapter 4 based upon the writings of Weber, Greenhut, Isard, Loesch, and Fetter, et al. This chapter, based on Chapter 4, deals with the specifics which have to be considered by the management of the individual middleman unit in selecting a particular geographical area and a particular site within an area for its type of operation and kind of business.

General Relationship of Discussion with Chapter 4

The discussion of location theory in Chapter 4 contains, as was indicated, the basis for an understanding of some of the aspects involved in the geographic structure of wholesale trade. The writings of such authors as Weber, Hoover, Loesch, Isard, Greenhut, and Fetter, et al., have their main orientation toward the problem of the location of manufacturing industries rather than of wholesale middlemen. Despite this orientation, these writings serve the function of furnishing a backdrop against which to measure the broad geographic rationale of wholesale trade. To the extent that the locational patterns of certain types of wholesale middlemen operations are interlinked with the locational patterns of manufacturers, to that extent do these writings have even greater applicability.

In the materials on trading area analysis—both in Fetter's law and the Hysons' restatement, and in the empirical analyses referred to—may be found a basis for analyzing the selection of locations which is much more closely related in pertinency to the analysis in this chapter. The Fetter-Hyson statements pertinent to the trading area boundaries of wholesale markets (organized) and the Duddy-Revzan empirical supply area and distribution area analyses furnish the analytical tools with which to determine the geographic outreaches of such markets. They furnish the individual middlemen in these kinds of business, accordingly, with an important set of data pertinent to the selection of a given organized market in a given city in which to locate. From the determination of such boundaries can come the necessary calculations by means of which estimates can be made of potential physical and dollar volume sales.

Similarly, the analytical framework suggested in Chapter 4 for the determination of trading area boundaries of nonorganized wholesale markets, and of the component salesmen's territories therein, can furnish individual wholesale middlemen with an estimate of sales potentials. These can be used, in turn, as one indicator of the potential ranking of each wholesale center in terms of its desirability as to the city in which the wholesale middleman ought to locate. They furnish valuable data as well on the number of competing wholesale trading centers, the potential zones of primary competitive advantage for each, and the overlapping zones where two or more centers have proportionately equal potential drawing power in attracting supplies or strength in making sales to customers.

As will be seen from the following discussion, individual middlemen have varying degrees of influence on the general geographic structure of wholesaling. For the organized wholesale markets, it seems safe to conclude that each individual wholesale middleman must conform to the broad forces which serve to influence the location of these markets. Each middleman's freedom of locational choice would appear to be limited to (1) the selection of the organized market, if any, in which he prefers to locate, and (2) to the selection of a particular site within the facilities of the market.

For middlemen operating in nonorganized wholesale markets, a wider range of influence is apparent. At one extreme, the wholesale middleman may prefer to be of the "lone wolf" type; that is, he may prefer to locate away from any related or unrelated types of operation and kinds of business. At the opposite extreme may be found examples of locational clustering similar to the patterns existing for the organized wholesale markets. Factors of sales size, of degree of integration, and of kind of business are very important in determining the degree to which any individual type of wholesale middleman does or does not exercise any considerable influence over the geographical structure of wholesaling.

In tracing the decision-making process by wholesale middlemen for selection of a city (or other unit of space) and specific sites, the following sections will present one stratification of analyses showing the differences between organized and nonorganized wholesale market situations. An additional stratification will be presented comparing those types of operation which have physical possession of the products handled with those which do not. By means of these stratifications it is hoped that the range of locational variables can both be recognized and kept in orderly focus.

Locational Criteria and Factors: Wholesale Middlemen Operating in Organized Wholesale Markets[1]

Definition and types of organized wholesale markets

An organized wholesale market, for purposes of this discussion, consists of a specialized group of wholesale middlemen operating under specified and codified membership and trading rules and under certain government restraints in specialized marketing and facilitating functional facilities. As will be remembered from previous material, the wholesale middlemen vary in types and numbers according to the type of market, the kind of agricultural products involved, and the nature of the channels. The nature of the physical facilities vary, also, depending on whether or not the products have to be sold by inspection, on the kinds of products involved, and on the relative degree of perishability of the products. These markets operate to establish *systematic* wholesale prices, i.e., prices that reflect accurately changes in the evaluation of underlying economic determinants by the buying and selling interests, and which array themselves by logical differen-

---

[1] Some repetition will be found here in the definitions and classification of types of organized markets with material presented earlier. Such repetition seems to be desirable if the structure and perspective of this section are to be preserved.

tials according to some formal system of grades. Finally, the organized wholesale market must provide for the formal preparation and circulation of complete market news throughout the trading hours for each trading day.

The organized wholesale markets may be classified as follows:

I. *Producing and Shipping Point Local Markets*
   A. Local markets servicing processors (e.g., livestock, grain, cotton, dairy).
   B. Local auction markets (e.g., livestock, tobacco).
   C. Assembling local markets (e.g., fruits and vegetables, eggs).
II. *Primary Central Markets*
   A. Sales by inspection or by sample.
      1. Fruit and vegetable markets (including terminal auctions).
      2. Cash grain markets.
      3. Livestock markets.
      4. Others.
   B. Sales by description: grain futures markets.
III. *Secondary Central Markets*
   A. Interior secondary markets.
   B. Seaboard secondary markets.

The *producing and shipping point local markets* are, as the name suggests, those wholesale markets which are located in strategic proximity to the centers of important commercial production of particular agricultural products. These types of markets act either as mechanisms for determining the prices at which the products are sold to those processing plants located within their respective trading areas or as a link in the channel between producers and central wholesale markets in connection with the concentration process; or they act to establish the prices at which processing plants or large urban integrated retailers located at some distance may obtain products via direct channels from the producers. Such markets vary sharply in the degree to which they conform to the generalized definition of an organized market as given, as well as in the size and specialized characteristics of their marketing and auxiliary facilities. As will be noted later, these local markets, especially in the case of hogs, have reduced substantially the importance of the primary central markets. For those types of markets classified as local auction markets, a special feature is the use of the auction method of bidding and selling.

Primary central wholesale markets are those types of markets at which the key wholesale price barometers are established in connection with the equalization process.[2] Depending upon the type of agricultural goods handled, these types of markets may have either large bodies of consuming groups located within their respective trading area boundaries or significant numbers of manufacturing industries and institutional buyers. In addition, where the product is physically received and handled, these markets reship considerable percentages of the inbound commodity receipts either to the secondary markets or to processing industries not located at the central markets.

The physical facilities of these markets vary widely according to type of product, method of sale, and the physical volume of goods received. Livestock markets, for example, require pens and sheds for the display of the animals to be sold, special weighing and feeding arrangements, and related facilities. Fruit and vegetable markets require special railroad facilities for holding inbound cars until inspection and unloading or reshipments can be arranged, stores for middlemen taking physical possession to display the fruits and vegetables stocked, necessary storage facilities, and related financial and other auxiliary facilities. Grain markets have trading floor arrangements on which tables may be used to contain samples of the cash grain offered for sale, and trading floors or pits classified by commodity. In addition, the building houses office facilities for middlemen and for facilitating agencies.

These markets vary in number according to type of agricultural products handled. As will be discussed later, each product group classification has been affected differently so far as the effects of decentralization are concerned; and, apart from decentralization, each has differing impacts from the shift from rail to motor truck transportation. The discussion of the factors determining the exact location of these markets and the shift in such locations over time will also be examined in a later section of this chapter.

The *secondary wholesale markets* may be located either at interior or seaboard cities. These markets are designated as secondary because of the following conditions: (1) They do not ordinarily receive the same physical volumes of products directly compared with the primary markets; (2) a part of their inbound supplies usually originates as reshipments from primary markets; (3) they do not themselves reship to other wholesale markets; and (4) their price levels do not act as barometers in the same way as do those determined by trading at the primary central wholesale markets. In connection with the last point, their price levels usually are coordinated with the primary market prices. Finally, these secondary markets do not offer the same degree

[2] See Chapter 1 for a definition of this process.

of organization or specialization of facilities as compared with those of the primary markets.

General factors determining the location of local markets

In discussing the location of the local markets in terms of the selection of a city or some other geographic unit, and the specific site within the geographic unit, only the factors applicable to the more important markets will be included. Basic to any understanding of the locational structure is the geographic pattern of the commercial production of the agricultural products handled. Products like live-stock and grain show much more geographic concentration of production than do the various fruit and vegetable crops and the dairy industry. To the extent that the processing involves questions of perishability, as in the canning and fresh milk industries, to that extent will the local markets cluster near the important production centers. The patterns of motor truck connections on inbound movements and of motor and rail facilities for, and the structure of, freight rates on outbound movements will have important bearing also on the actual geographic unit selected for the location of the local market.

For markets handling fresh fruits and vegetables, the selection of a particular city or other geographic unit will be dictated mainly by: the physical volume of fruits and vegetables to be handled; the importance of the central wholesale markets in handling any particular variety of fruit or vegetable; the nature of the outbound transportation facilities and the structure of freight rates, and the extent to which the assembling process is important for the particular class of product. In some cases, government aid may have been significant in establishing key local market facilities in certain places.[3]

Within these localities, the site of the actual market will be a function of: (1) the total acreage of space needed to house the facilities designed to accommodate the estimated physical volumes; (2) whether or not storage and physical display facilities are needed; (3) the location and number of inbound and outbound motor truck arteries, rail facilities, and water facilities (where applicable); (4) the nature of facilities, including physical size, needed by the wholesale middlemen and by the market auxiliary agencies; (5) the proximity of the site to processing plants; (6) land and/or rental costs; and (7) applicable zoning restrictions, if any. Since the kinds of potentially favorable localities range from rural towns to fairly large cities,

---

[3] Note, for example, state aid in establishing local farmers' markets at places such as Benton Harbor, Michigan.

in population size, any discussion has to abstract, of necessity, from the number of minute, individual considerations.

General factors determining the location of primary central markets[4]

Some mention has been made already in Chapter 4 relative to the factors involved in the location of primary central markets. In view of the wide variety of primary central markets in terms of age of market accessibility to adequate inbound and outbound rail facilities, and variations in importance, only generalizations can be advanced for certain types of locational conditions. The impact of decentralization and direct marketing will be discussed in the last section of this chapter.

If the livestock markets are considered, the following factors help to explain the origins and rise of the central markets. Before 1850, as has been noted, the need for concentrating livestock surplus supplies which were scattered geographically over a wide area, in order to facilitate their economic movement over long distances, gave rise to key central markets at Albany, Buffalo, Pittsburgh, Detroit, Cleveland, and Cincinnati. As human population expanded in the eastern sections, and as the extension of railroads on an east-west axis continued, the process of shifting production in the more sparsely settled areas to the West was repeated in several stages. The mainly north-south arrangement of central markets existing before 1850 had shifted by 1890 to an east-west arrangement. From 1890 to 1920, the pattern of market locations so established was continued unchanged until the effects of direct marketing became important.[5]

The shifting locational patterns of the meat-packing industry in relation and addition to the expanding railroad network attracted additional organized central markets as well as local markets. With the expansion of the railroad network, a system of livestock freight rate and transit privileges emerged which fixed the competitive relations of the central markets to each other and to their respective supply and distribution areas. Of importance also were the changing

---

[4] Much of this discussion is based upon the Duddy-Revzan studies of the Chicago and competing fruit and vegetable, grain, and livestock markets. See the bibliography pertinent to this chapter for full references.

[5] The dates of the development of centralized organized markets were as follows: 1865—Chicago; 1871—Kansas City; 1872—St. Louis; 1884—Omaha; 1886—Denver and South St. Paul; 1887—Wichita; 1893—Fort Worth; 1894—Sioux City; and 1895—St. Joseph. See Edward A. Duddy and David A. Revzan, *The Changing Relative of the Central Livestock Market,* Studies in Business Administration, Vol. VIII, No. 4 (Chicago: The University of Chicago Press, August, 1938).

relationships between rail freight rates on the movement of live animals versus dressed meats and related by-products. By 1916, the existing organized central markets began facing pressures which assumed major significance after 1920. These pressures were, on the one hand, from the older Eastern Seaboard markets which began to by-pass the central markets in the competitive search for livestock supplies, and, on the other hand, from the newer central markets developing along the Missouri River and from the increased local markets resulting from the decentralization of the meat-packing industry and the early effects of the motor truck.

The primary central markets for grains are not expected to be as numerous as for fresh fruits and vegetables or for livestock. Because they do not physically handle the grains, the facilities are designed primarily for buying and selling transactions in cash and future contracts. The type of city selected is located, generally, in the midwestern section of the United States intermediate to producing areas in West North Central and West South Central States to the West (as well as Montana and Washington), and to the larger milling operations adjacent to the cities, as well as to the export ports in the East. Because of the highly organized nature of such markets, they number fewer than one dozen compared with the large numbers of fruit and vegetable and livestock markets. The prices established at these key centers become the basis for transactions at the local and secondary markets, with the necessary adjustments for rail or truck freight rate differentials.

So far as the actual location of these markets within a city is concerned, the Chicago markets for fresh fruits and vegetables and grains will be used as illustrations. The presence of some unique locational circumstances will be recognized. First, consider some of the factors in the location of the fresh fruit and vegetable market. Because of the size and complexity of this market, there existed, at the time of the relocation of the Old South Water Market (immediately to the north of the Loop), a conflict in attitudes between those types of wholesale middlemen who took physical possession of the fruits and vegetables sold and those middlemen, on the other hand, who either did not have physical possession in the complete sense or only sold in car-lot or truck-load quantities directly from the inbound transportation facility.

The attitude of the first group may be summarized as follows: (1) The all-important consideration was the availability of storelike facilities in which displays of produce and the related product handlings could take place; (2) relative freedom from congestion caused by the inbound transportation vehicles and from the trucks of customer-buyers; (3) minimization of travel in relation to the location of the institutional buyers and the retail store customers; and (4) only secondary consideration of the accessibility of inbound and outbound rail and motor truck facilities. For the second group, the nature and capacity of the terminal-rail facilities were of utmost importance, especially so far as specialized facilities for holding, inspection, and reconsignment were concerned, as well as the auction facilities for the sale of selected fruits.

Building upon these conflicts of views, certain physical factors influenced the market's ultimate location and capacity. The products to be handled show varying degrees of perishability ranging from those which can be stored for months (e.g., apples, potatoes) to those requiring immediate sale upon delivery (e.g., strawberries). Similarly, the wide variations in bulk and the absence of standardization in the products have significant repercussions. Certain products, such as bananas and tomatoes, require special handling and ripening facilities. Other products may be prepackaged for supermarkets at the wholesale market. As noted, certain fruits (especially the citrus) may be sold at the terminal auctions. Finally, variations in the volume of tonnage between products as well as fluctuations in the supplies of each daily and weekly have significant repercussions. Important related considerations have to do with the increased interest of corporate and voluntary chains in receiving shipments of fruits and vegetables directly in their own warehouses as opposed to the nonintegrated retailers' and institutional buyers' continued use of the organized wholesale market facilities.

The actual reconciliation of these factors resulted in a location which, although not served directly by the railroad team track and siding facilities, was accessible to the main facilities—the Chicago Produce Terminal and the Wood Street Terminal. Similarly, accessibility was maintained to motor truck facilities and to the key arterial streets connecting with highways, although the ultimate size of inbound trucks and trailers together with the growing volumes of truck movements created congestion within the market. The location selected was accessible to necessary cold-storage facilities, and, at the same time, was favorably adjusted both to the restaurant and hotel trade in the Loop (the downtown shopping district) and the population and retail store distributors in the neighborhood areas within the city and the adjoining suburbs. The "suburban surge" in recent years has destroyed this latter adjustment.

The location of the Chicago Board of Trade, on the other hand, in

the Loop adjoining the financial district, reflects primarily the characteristic that no physical handling of the product takes place within
the organized market. Accordingly, the location of the organized
facilities need have no relation to any of the factors outlined above.
The downtown location selected reflects, accordingly, access to important financial agencies and to the offices of important processing
customers. In addition, it shows the multiple use of the office-type
skyscraper for middlemen and related agencies participating in the
market and for other business firms as well.[6]

As indicated, each of these organized central market locations includes in its physical facilities either office buildings or storelike
facilities in which the various types of wholesale middlemen may
locate. Relative rental costs and the prestige position of the middlemen determine whether to rent office space in the market-owned
facilities or in buildings immediately adjacent. The assignments of
pens in the organized livestock markets or stores in the fruit and
vegetable market are under the jurisdiction of the proprietors of the
market. The clustering aspects will be discussed in a later section.

General factors determining the location of organized secondary wholesale markets

Except for the distinguishing features noted in the definition of
the two types of secondary markets, it would be expected that the
same factors determine their locations within a city as those applicable
to the primary central markets. The variations in the physical
volumes of goods handled will affect the physical size of the space
required; but every city of about 100,000 persons or more, except
those operating as organized primary central markets, is large enough
to qualify as a secondary market for fresh fruits and vegetables.
Many of these will qualify, also, as organized livestock markets,
depending upon whether or not any significant volume of meat packing
takes place. The opportunities for grain are far more limited,
involving mainly those cities located near the producing centers or
operating as export parts.

Again, the actual locations of the wholesale middlemen operating
in these secondary markets will be related to the location of the
market facilities in the same manner as has been discussed for the
primary central markets. *Thus, it may be concluded that the factors*

---

[6] In addition to these uses, the building in downtown Chicago provides an
observation tower on the roof. The central location makes possible, also, a
visitors gallery adjoining the trading floor so that valuable public relations may
be obtained by attracting thousands of visitors each year.

that influence the actual location of the organized wholesale market facilities also serve to set the locational patterns for the wholesale middlemen operating in such market facilities.

Locational Criteria and Factors: Wholesale Middlemen Operating in Nonorganized Wholesale Markets

The nonorganized wholesale markets represent by far the most significant percentage of total wholesale trade recorded in any given year. These markets are characterized by the absence of the specialized facilities and the trading rules and procedures noted for the organized markets. In addition, no highly developed system of market news is available for interested members of any given industry, nor do the resulting price structures which evolve reflect the systematic stratifications characterizing the operations of the organized markets. The discussion which follows is divided in terms of those factors involved in the selection of a geographical area and a specific within this area as between those types of wholesale middlemen which have physical possession of inventories and those types which do not.

Middlemen Taking Physical Possession

Factors influencing selection of particular geographical areas

The types of wholesale middlemen who take physical possession of inventories are quite diverse, as has been noted. They run the gamut, as well, from the regular wholesaler found in every kind of business in wholesale trade to those specialized types found in only a single kind of business or for specific categories of goods. As a result, the locational possibilities, so far as a particular area is concerned, fall into the following classes: (1) The central city of a metropolitan area; (2) the satellite-urban sections of the metropolitan area, both incorporated and unincorporated; (3) the independent cities which are not included as a part of any standard metropolitan area; and (4) the remaining rural and nonurban areas.

For many kinds of industrial goods where the users are themselves geographically concentrated, the wholesale middlemen involved in the channels obviously will be restricted, in turn, to those areas having close proximity to part or all of the concentrated markets. In some product cases, such as the petroleum bulk station and LP gas terminal group, the middlemen will be oriented, so far as the initial wholesale movements in the channel are concerned, to the location of the petroleum wells. The remaining segment will have its location influenced by the strategy of the layout of the domestic pipe lines and interior waterway facilities and movements, and by the directional flows of inbound supplies from foreign countries. Other wholesale middlemen, such as the converters in the textile business, are highly oriented toward the locational structure, once again, of the manufacturing units.

Every metropolitan area and its incorporated and unincorporated cities become potentially favorable location possibilities for those types of wholesale middlemen who buy and sell widely and intensively distributed manufactured consumers' goods. Other wholesale middlemen, requiring strategically balanced locational points between manufacturer and customer, will select those areas in which the total volume of wholesale sales and the intermediate locational position hold the strongest possibilities.

Given some of these basic characteristics and considerations, the following represent the more important specific variables in evaluating the competitive position of particular areas:

1. *Evidence of the importance of the area as a general and specific wholesale trade center.* This evidence may be measured by data showing the trend in the area's total annual wholesale trade, by types, and by kinds of business, relative to trends in areas of comparable population size. In addition, very careful attention should be given to the kind-of-business composition of sales and of any significant changes therein.

2. *The industrial structure.* This will be measured by such data as employment and value added by the manufacturing industries, by kind of product. Two types of analyses are important. First, to what extent does the industrial structure of the area re-enforce its position as a wholesale trade center? Second, if industrial goods are involved, to what extent will the industries be active or potentially important customers for the middlemen's kinds of business? Trends relative to other industrial areas of the same population and manufacturing importance should be measured carefully.

3. *Population characteristics.* Of importance are the data measuring the area's growth characteristics and/or the basic foundation for the area's manufactured consumers' goods sales. In addition, the analysis should include labor force characteristics both as

they contribute to the income position of the area and, particularly, as they affect the personnel needs of the middlemen.

4. *Number and characteristics of competing types of wholesale middlemen in the area.* The variable is self-apparent.

5. *The nature of inbound and outbound transportation facilities and rates.* Not only is it important to measure the quantity and quality of the transportation facilities but also the nature of the freight rate structures, transit privileges, and scheduled traveling times from sources of supply and to the customers' locations. Where applicable, the middlemen should determine whether or not the area has the additional benefit of being a rate-breaking point.[7]

6. *Availability of warehouse facilities, or building sites for warehouses.* This general inventory is of special importance in conjunction with the later discussion of specific sites. Included could be consideration of breakdown by public versus private and type of cold storage, where applicable.

7. *Presence or absence of special governmental control factors.* Included are zoning restrictions, taxes, licensing agreements, and the like.

8. *The nature, trend, and structure of retail trade sales.* Where the wholesale middlemen sell to retail stores, the analysis of these data in terms of trends and changes in composition becomes very important.

9. *The nature and types of facilitating agencies.* Included would be such agencies as financial, packaging, advertising, and the like.

10. *The general reputation of the area.* This would be measured by opinions obtained from the area's residents and business men, and from the industry members in general.

Factors influencing the choice of a specific site

Once the above variables have been subjected to the suggested qualitative and quantitative analyses, a weighted ranking should be obtained for each potential area. Next, the site possibilities of the more important areas should be analyzed in terms of the following as suggestive of the more important.[8]

1. *The volume of warehouse space, by type.* This variable includes an exhaustive analysis of the merits and demerits of one-story,

---

[7] By rate-breaking point here is meant the strategic relationship between inbound t.l. or c.l. rates, and outbound l.c.l. or l.t.l. rates.

[8] This discussion excludes the analysis, already discussed, of the alternative of purchasing an existing business.

extensive warehouses versus multistory buildings (to be discussed in a later chapter). It includes, also, any special needs for cold-storage or heated types of warehouses. Of importance, also, is whether or not expensive internal transportation devices are needed as well as side-track facilities externally.

2. *The numbers, types, and locations of potential customers.* In regard to time and costs, how does the potential site's location rate in relation to the geographical distribution of potential customers? This involves, among other things, a trading area analysis of the city or other geographic unit, the pinpointing of locations on a map, and the determination of salesmen's traveling times and delivery times, where applicable.

3. *Rental and related costs; or equivalent construction costs.* The relative merits of the middleman's own architectural specifications must be weighed carefully against rental of an equivalent number and type of square feet of space.

4. *The relative merits of clustering with other wholesale middle-men (related or unrelated) versus isolated locations.* This variable will be discussed in detail in the following section.

5. *The effects of integration.* If the wholesale middleman is controlled by a manufacturer or, in turn, controls the manufacturer, the selection of a specific site may have to be coordinated with the locational characteristics of the type of manufacturing. On the other hand, wholesale middlemen integrated with other middlemen may have to consider carefully the relationship of the location of the wholesale middleman's establishment to that of the retail middlemen. This becomes, in effect, a special case of variable 2 above.

6. *The location of inbound and outbound transportation facilities.* For many kinds of wholesale middlemen, the location and capacity of railroad team track, freight station, and side-track facilities are of key importance in selecting a site. The existence or absence of adequate terminal switching facilities may be significant. Of related importance are the location and number of streets, highways, and freeways for facilitating inbound movements of purchases, and the rapid and economical delivery of customers' orders.

7. *Specific zoning restrictions.* Of key importance are those influencing the type and location of warehouses and related facilities.

8. *The locational proximity of pertinent facilitating agencies.*

9. *The locational proximity, where applicable, to the necessary labor force.*

Middlemen Without Physical Possession

Factors influencing selection of particular geographical areas

Generally, wholesale middlemen who do not take physical possession of the products bought and sold have certain underlying character- istics affecting the selection of locations. Some, like brokers, by being in effect "a wholesale middleman's middleman," have considerable orientation toward the key population centers. The subsequent resale operations will be handled by other types of wholesale middle- men. In other cases, such as for the drop shipper for bulky products, prime knowledge of the location of and contact with the types of customers for such products (e.g., coal, sand, lumber) dictates the locational characteristics of the geographical area selected. Finally, for such types of operations as resident buyers, the nature of the fashion-goods markets will cause them to concentrate mainly in New York City. In addition, some agent middlemen, such as the manu- facturer's agent, may have the area specified in the contract arranged with his principal.

Given these characteristics as important background, the following variables are of key significance in the selection of a particular geo- graphical area:

1. *Determination of trading area boundaries, and the number and types of potential customers within such boundaries.* Utilizing the applicable method outlined in Chapter 4, the geographic outreach of each potential area can be estimated. Once these boundaries have been established, the number of customers can be estimated, and their respective locations can be pinpointed on a map.
2. *Estimated potential sales.* Given the trading area boundaries and the numbers and types of potentials located therein, two sets of estimates can be prepared. One would represent estimated total sales for the kind of business under consideration. The other would involve the percentage of this total which the type of operation can expect to realize.
3. The remaining variables involve all those outlined above for middlemen taking physical possession, except those specifically related to physical possession.

Factors influencing choice of a specific site

Although this class of wholesale middlemen do not require warehouse space for themselves, each component type of operation may have varying responsibilities for supervising inventories consigned by the producer to public warehouses. Accordingly, accessibility of the middlemen's specific sites to the locations of such public warehouses may or may not be important determining considerations. As will be discussed later, depending on the type of operation and kind of business, these middlemen may place variable emphasis upon clustering with similar or unrelated types of operations and kinds of business. The following are the more important variables:

1. *The number and type of personnel to be housed in the office space.* These types of wholesale middlemen have variable ratios of executive and secretarial staffs to selling staffs. In addition, the size of the offices may or may not be influenced by customer visits.

2. *The number and location of potential customers.* It may be stated axiomatically that these wholesale middlemen without physical possession will have to travel longer distances, all other things remaining equal, in reaching customers than will wholesale middlemen who have physical possession. Of course, sharp variations will exist according to kind of business. Thus, the value of a central location in the trading area's central city may become emphasized in importance.

3. *Prestige value of the site.* A nationally established manufacturer's sales office may need space in well-known office buildings for prestige purposes compared with other types of wholesale middlemen who do not have such national reputations.

4. *Office rental and related costs.* These costs would include rental costs, length of lease, utility costs, and maintenance and remodeling costs, if any.

5. *The relative merits and demerits of clustering with other types of wholesale middlemen.* This variable will be discussed at some length in the following section.

6. *Availability of pertinent facilitating agencies.*

7. *Availability of transportation facilities for salesmen.* With the declining importance of the railroad, this factor involves primarily the availability of adequate air transportation or of highways designed to minimize travel time to customers' locations.

Locational Clusterings of Central City Wholesale Middlemen Establishments[9]

The study of locational clusterings is essential to any understanding of the selection of wholesale middlemen's locations because it introduces the important element of whether or not any given middleman should locate in a wholesale district. The advantages of specialized facilities for clustering, such as merchandise marts for the display of goods, possibilities of comparative shopping, pooling of transportation facilities, possible interchanges of inventories for the clustering firms, the building of a trade associational *esprit de corps*, as well as all of the advantages noted for the organized wholesale markets, may be offset by certain disadvantages. Among these disadvantages may be the lack of adequate space for the construction of modern-designed warehouses, traffic congestion, and the inferior location of the wholesale district involved in the clustering to the shifting locational patterns of the middlemen's customers.

Introductory aspects

Human activities of all kinds tend, as society becomes more urbanized, to form clusters in greater and greater profusion. If the reader stops to consider this phenomenon as it applies to business activities, he may recall several examples: the grouping together of retail stores in downtown and other shopping sections of a city as well as on the "string" streets; the necessary clusterings of docks and warehouses along an ocean, lake, or river waterfront; and the large number of related businesses in a single office building.

As the number of establishments carrying on any economic activity

[9] The materials presented in this section are part of a broader research study of the locational clusterings of selected economic activities and services in San Francisco-Oakland and Los Angeles for 1920, 1929, 1939, 1948, and 1953. The data are based upon the classified sections of telephone directories, and their collection was financed by the Real Estate Research Programs, Bureaus of Business and Economic Research, University of California, Berkeley and Los Angeles.

In presenting this summary, the author makes no assumption that the findings are representative of any relationships other than for the geographical areas included. It includes only the types of wholesale trade analyzed. For some broader aspects, the reader may be interested in the author's, "Locational Clusterings of Manufacturing, Retail, Service, and Wholesale Establishments," in *The Broadening Perspective of Marketing,* Proceedings of the Golden Triangle Conference of the American Marketing Association (Pittsburgh, June 20–22, 1956), pp. 90–96.

increases, and as the types of operation and kinds of business increase, the necessity for considering a clustering aspect of locational choice emerges. Under such locational evolution, not all of the establishments of a given type can have the *single best location*. For many kinds of activity, the combined attractive and competitive strength of the clusters may well exceed the locational strength of having only one establishment. In addition to the general advantages already noted, the cluster may have such strength by virtue of: (1) providing a basis for attracting more patronage proportionately than could any single establishment in the cluster by itself; (2) furnishing a basis for complementarity and/or integration of economic relationships; (3) making possible a more systematic basis for conducting marketing transactions, as in the case of organized wholesale markets, once again; and (4) sharpening the competition between similar kinds of business in the cluster. In addition, the cluster may lead to better facilities and their more efficient use than would be the case for a single unit.

Meaning of intracity locational clusters

By an intracity locational cluster is meant the tendency for the managements of establishments of any type to select locations which concentrate on the same streets and/or in the same blocks in the related section of a city. This definition implies the exact opposite of a purely random distribution of the physical establishments of the activities being analyzed. Rather, it stresses the presence in a large number of cases of a kind of "gravitational pull" which causes nonrandom or purposeful clusters of these types of establishments to appear.

In effect, what is being stated is that, if one were to take a bird's eye view of a city, one would expect to find, in the absence of physical locational clusters, an even distribution of establishments per unit of geographical space. What is found, in actuality, is a definite bunching or clustering of activities on particular streets and blocks therein, and the infrequent or complete absence of clusters on other streets and blocks therein.

Accordingly, any meaningful analysis of clusters must begin with the street as the basis of the fundamental clustering unit. It is the nature and layout of a street in the city which serve, in the first instance, to attract or repel locations of activities; then, *and only then,* do the attractive powers of particular blocks serve to influence the further clusterings along the street.

Types of intracity locational clusters

From the concepts given above, it would seem to follow that intra-city clusters may include, first of all, only activities of the same functional level, e.g., manufacturing, wholesaling, or retailing. These types may be further classified, in turn, either as independent or complementary in their relationships to each other. Alternately, the clusters may include activities only of the same type, such as department stores, beauty parlors, or new-automobile dealers; activities of related types such as furniture and radio stores; or stores handling specialty and shopping goods, or establishments handling both automobiles and parts and supplies; activities which are directly competitive; and, finally, activities which may be unrelated *except* as to land-use patterns or similar characteristics.

By a section of a city referred to in the definition is meant any group of streets and/or blocks in such streets located in close geographical proximity to each other in the city. These may correspond with the boundaries of a community area; or they may carry a title such as a "stockyards" district. Under such areas would be included: (1) A downtown shopping area encompassing several districts; (2) an organized or nonorganized manufacturing district; (3) a neighborhood or a regional shopping center; (4) organized wholesale markets of the types noted above; and (5) other types of accumulations of block and street clusters. Most of these categories would include possible sites for wholesale middlemen's establishments.

Based upon the foregoing discussion, the following outline is suggestive of the types of wholesale locational clusters.

I. *As to Geographic Coverage*
    A. Section of a city: community area, zoned area, etc.
    B. Street clusters; principal (or dominant) and secondary.
    C. Block clusters.
    D. Office building clusters.
II. *As to Type of Wholesale Activity*
    A. Organized markets or districts.
    B. Specialized buildings.
    C. Other types.
III. *As to Size of Cluster*
    A. Based on number of establishments.
        1. Large.
        2. Medium.
        3. Small.

 B. Based on percentage concentration.
   1. Large.
   2. Medium.
   3. Small.
IV. *As to Trend*
 A. Expanding.
 B. Stable.
 C. Declining.
 D. Unstable or mixed.

Number of establishments, by type

Based on data obtained from the classified sections of telephone directories, Table 23 lists the numbers of wholesale establishments, by type, in Los Angeles, Oakland, and San Francisco for the benchmark periods indicated. In Los Angeles, the covered wholesale trade categories increased from 681 in 1920 to 3,596 in 1948 and to 3,597 in 1954. Not all of the categories show similar patterns of growth. Building contractor and materials establishments quadrupled between 1920 and 1948, and then declined. Drug establishments rose from only 14 in 1920 to 192 in 1948, and then declined. Fruit and vegetable establishments have shown no substantial growth since 1929. Finally, wearing apparel establishments had significant increases (113 to 368) between 1920 and 1939, and then a sharp gain of 636 establishments between 1939 and 1948.

The steadily increasing importance of Oakland as a wholesaling center is evident from the marked increase in covered establishments from only 98 in 1920 to 462 in 1953. Substantial gains were registered from benchmark period to benchmark period, except between 1948 and 1953. These significant increases were registered by the building contractors and materials, electrical contractors and goods, fruits and vegetables, and steel distributors categories.

In San Francisco, the total number of covered wholesale establishments more than doubled, rising from 785 to 1,889 between 1920 and 1948, and then falling off sharply to 1,700 in 1953. The sharp decline between 1920 and 1929 reflects, undoubtedly, problems of coverage based upon the type of data used. Within this over-all trend, the largest growth has taken place in the grocery and wearing apparel categories; but the building contractors and materials group has grown also by significant amounts. The wholesale establishments of the drug, electrical contractors and goods and steel distributors kinds of business have shown far more moderate rates of expansion. Finally, fruit and vegetable middlemen establishments have shown mixed trends, with

TABLE 23

NUMBER OF WHOLESALE ESTABLISHMENTS, LOS ANGELES, OAKLAND, AND SAN FRANCISCO: 1920, 1929, 1939, 1948, 1953

City and Type of Activity	1920	1929	1939	1948	1953
Oakland					
Building contractor and materials	51	118	138	220	248
Drugs	4	8	5	17	16
Electrical contractor and goods	14	10	44	78	77
Fruits and vegetables	18	30	18	59	62
Groceries	7	4	8	12	9
Steel distributors	0	12	17	34	40
Wearing apparel	4	0	1	10	10
Total	98	182	231	430	462
San Francisco					
Building contractor and materials	366	206	379	600	526
Drugs	26	14	74	98	96
Electrical contractor and goods	128	59	141	247	256
Fruits and vegetables	118	96	118	141	111
Groceries	45	16	168	284	303
Steel distributors	39	31	73	83	88
Wearing apparel	63	86	168	436	320
Total	785	508	1,121	1,889	1,700
Los Angeles					
Building contractor and materials	243	578	671	1,008	978
Drugs	14	36	88	192	182
Electrical contractor and goods	56	73	176	432	435
Fruits and vegetables	186	400	218	409	426
Groceries	38	89	208	406	377
Steel distributors	31	99	113	145	128
Wearing apparel	113	163	368	1,004	1,071
Total	681	1,438	1,842	3,596	3,597

Source: Classified Section, Telephone Directories.

the 1953 level of 111 establishments being slightly below the 1920 level.

Some summary measures of locational clusterings

Table 24 contains data for each city showing the following measures of locational clusterings: (1) The gross (duplicated) number of streets on which the types of wholesale middlemen establishments were located; (2) the range of average number of wholesale establishments

TABLE 24

SELECTED INDICATORS OF LOCATIONAL CLUSTERS,
LOS ANGELES, OAKLAND, AND SAN FRANCISCO:
1920, 1929, 1939, 1948, 1953

Indicator and City	1920	1929	1939	1948	1953
Gross (duplicated) no. of streets					
Los Angeles	255	501	608	1,034	1,064
Oakland	58	112	152	258	279
San Francisco	244	213	352	567	568
Range of average no. of establishments per street					
Los Angeles	1.46–4.23	1.41–5.26	1.54–7.83	1.88–9.21	1.64–9.83
Oakland	1.00–6.00	1.14–4.29	1.00–3.00	1.06–3.47	1.07–4.77
San Francisco	1.63–5.62	1.35–6.00	1.83–6.94	1.93–7.15	1.96–6.17
Range in total no. of establishments per street per activity					
Los Angeles	1–80	1–82	1–82	1–196	1–222
Oakland	1–16	1–16	1–10	1–26	1–25
San Francisco	1–108	1–41	1–58	1–129	1–66
Range in percentage clustering					
Los Angeles	54.4–80.2	45.2–79.4	31.8–78.0	27.6–76.4	26.1–75.3
Oakland	26.3–73.8	28.6–74.8	22.7–74.0	24.4–71.1	39.7–68.1
San Francisco	39.3–89.0	49.0–80.5	63.3–87.3	58.0–82.1	56.3–84.6

Source: Author's calculations.

per street; (3) range in total number of establishments per street; and
(4) the range of percentage clustering of wholesale trade establishments on principal streets.

Based upon these data, the following conclusions may be advanced:

1. Sharp increases are to be noted in the gross number of streets,
   but the net increase in San Francisco was far below that in
   Oakland and Los Angeles.
2. Significant differences are to be found between the three cities
   in the range of average number of establishments per street.
   Only in Los Angeles, however, was there any consistent widening
   in the range since 1920.

3. Similarly, wide variations are apparent in the range of wholesale establishments per street. Although a general increase in the range is apparent, the pattern for each city is quite different.

4. Finally, there was a general tendency for the percentage clustering of wholesale establishments to decline between 1920 and 1953.

Although space does not permit presentation of the detailed data, a few additional conclusions may be presented:

1. By far and large, most streets appeared in only one of the five benchmark periods, although for individual kinds of wholesale trade several streets appeared in 4 or 5 benchmark years.

2. For the same type of activity, sharp variations were to be found in the locational clusters as between cities.

3. The principal clustering streets vary in location and importance for each type of wholesale trade in each city between benchmark periods.

4. Changes in locational cluster demonstrated "finger" movements along principal arterial streets; zone movements in concentric and nonconcentric circles; sectional movements; circular movements; and irregular patterns.

Principal factors underlying locational clusters

The following may be advanced tentatively as underlying reasons helping to explain the patterns of locational clusters:

1. The availability of transportation facilities within the city is of great significance. This availability must be measured in terms of the general layout of the automobile and truck arteries and the public transit lines; the quantity of such facilities; the quality of the facilities and services furnished by the transit companies; and the costs of such services.

2. The changing trends of importance of the types of wholesale middlemen's operations and kinds of business.

3. The extent of manufactured consumers' goods handled by the wholesale middlemen in relation to the number of population and the geographical distribution within the urban area.

4. Whether or not each of the activities, on its locational patterns, utilizes extensive as against intensive types of buildings on the land occupied is related in part to the factors of land values and construction costs.

5. The supply of available physical facilities is significant relative to the type of middlemen.

6. Certain types of middlemen's activities (e.g., fruit and vegetable middlemen) find it necessary, from each middleman's point of view, to cluster either with related or competing kinds of business.
7. The introduction of and changes in both zoning laws and city master plans are causes as well as results of locational clusters.
8. Changes in competition and in methods of operation affect locational clusters.
9. Speculation, realty activities, and construction developments all need to be studied.
10. The effects of changes in the structure and design of the metropolitan area and of its component geographical units are of significance.
11. Finally, the effects of general urban locational pressures leading toward geographical centralization, decentralization, and dispersion (as discussed below) cannot be overlooked or underestimated.

Indicators of Centralization and Decentralization

The location or relocation of wholesale middlemen's establishments is related ultimately to the centralization and decentralization of wholesale trade.[10] Generally, wholesaling is characterized as an urban activity, as earlier data have indicated. But important exceptions have been noted earlier also in connection with selected types of operation and kinds of business. This section will be confined to special aspects of centralization and decentralization, namely, the incidence of direct marketing as an indicator of decentralization among agricultural goods markets, and the changing distribution of wholesale establishments and sales of the standard metropolitan areas in the central cities.

Meaning of decentralization

The two aspects to be discussed in this section point out the difference in the meaning of decentralization of wholesale trade. In the case of the organized agricultural goods markets, it refers to the shift in the sale of livestock and meat-slaughtering operations from locations in cities having organized primary central markets to the cities having interior local markets. The second group of cities containing these local markets are not included in the same standard metropolitan areas containing the first group of cities.

[10] This section should be read in conjunction with the applicable sections of Chapter 4.

In the case of decentralization as it applies to wholesale trade in total, the meaning involves: (1) the reduced importance of the central city's (or cities') total wholesale trade and establishments relative to the total for the standard metropolitan area of which it is a part; or (2) the reduced importance of wholesale trade in the larger urban centers compared with the small urban centers and nonurban places. Emphasis will be placed upon the first in this discussion.

Decentralization in agricultural goods markets

With the rise of the motor truck and the shift in the production of feed crops began the rise of direct marketing and the type of decentralization as defined above. Although the effects were felt most importantly for hogs, they also affected other species of livestock. The new competition thus created was no longer only between primary central markets located in different regions but also between such markets and the local interior markets at concentration yards or at packing plants located nearby the sources of livestock.

Five sets of reasons may be advanced for explaining the *lesser* incidence of such decentralization for cattle, calves, and sheep than for hogs: (1) The supplies of these species are drawn from a much wider supply area than for hogs in order to ensure economical plant operation; (2) the varying yields of dressed meats and by-products from each species, and the varying relative freight relationships of each; (3) the scale on which slaughter must be performed if the recovery of by-products is to take place economically; (4) the varying locations and characteristics of the markets for the varying types of fresh meats and the edible and inedible by-products; and, finally (5) the problem of moving dressed meats quickly into consumption (especially of the meats designed for the kosher demand).

The reasons for the growth of decentralized marketing may be summarized as follows. One cause was the natural consequence, already noted, of the trend of corn and hog production in a north-westerly direction, a trend that was accelerated after 1920. The local packers, partially by virtue of the effects of World War I, became better known to domestic market consumers. In the postwar period, the general freight rate increases of 1920–1921 of 35 to 40 per cent coincided with both the drastic price deflation of livestock and the growth in importance of the motor truck. Livestock cooperative shipping associations shifted marketing policies to permit sale in any type of market, thus contributing to the disorganization of the price-making process. A great many practices of the central primary markets—deceptive and otherwise—had resulted in increased dissatisfaction among country shippers of livestock. The extension of the federal-state market news service to the local markets, via radio broadcasts, widened the circle of effective communication.

In addition, differentials in costs between central and local markets became increasingly favorable to the local markets in terms of: wage costs per 100 pounds of livestock slaughtered; railroad freight rate structures since 1920 favoring the eastward shipments of live hogs from Missouri and interior Iowa points over Chicago; the system of pro-portional freight rates on livestock movements to the East penalizing the Chicago and East St. Louis stockyards; certain markets east of the Mississippi River being refused equal application of certain transit privileges applicable to markets and concentration points west of the Mississippi River; the comparative rate structure from the Missouri River and interior Iowa points favoring the shipment of dressed hogs to Chicago rather than live hogs; and finally, interior Iowa plants having rate advantages in shipping dressed meats direct to Cleveland and New York rather than via Chicago.

The fruit and vegetable markets have not suffered from this type of decentralization. To some extent, they have lost importance because corporate and voluntary group chains located in urban centers have purchased more and more varieties direct from the producing regions rather than from the wholesale markets. But the fresh fruits and vegetables, while shifting in channels utilized, still continue to flow into the facilities of the key market cities even if not into the markets. Of more importance is the growth of direct shipments by motor trucks to cities which formerly purchased from the larger organized central fruit and vegetable markets. The declines, such as they are, do not compare with those for the organized central livestock markets.

Decentralization in selected standard metropolitan areas

Data are available which compare the relative importance of estab-lishments and wholesale sales in 33 central cities in 1948 and 1954 for standard metropolitan areas having 500,000 or more persons each in 1950, as well as the percentage importance for wholesale trade with that for retail trade.

First, to be noticed, is the generally high concentration of wholesale trade in the central cities. In 1954, for areas in which data were available, 12 had central cities accounting for over 90 per cent of establishments and/or sales. An additional 5 central cities accounted for 85 to 90 per cent of the establishments, while an additional 7 central cities accounted for 85 to 90 per cent of their respective standard metropolitan area total sales. From a sales point of view, only

Minneapolis-St. Paul, Indianapolis, and Columbus had comparable proportions of retail sales.

In general, the proportion of wholesale sales accounted for by the central cities in 1954 showed reductions from the 1948 levels, except for St. Louis, Portland (Oregon), and Birmingham. But the range of the declines was quite variable. If the decline in percentage points accounted for less than 5 per cent of the 1948 base, and if such declines were labeled as "minor," then the declines in 18 central cities might be so characterized. The most significant evidences of decentralization were to be found for the central cities of Philadelphia, Detroit, Boston, San Diego, and Albany-Schenectady-Troy, in order of declining population importance of the standard metropolitan areas. Finally, it should be noted that, with few exceptions, the decentralization of retail trade in these areas was far more significant than for wholesale trade.

QUESTIONS AND PROBLEMS

1. To what extent is the proper selection of location the most important factor in the success of a wholesale middleman's operation?

2. What positive contributions can the literature of the economic theory of location make in the selection of a particular location?

3. Why is it important to separate the selection of locations for wholesale middlemen in organized markets versus those in nonorganized markets?

4. How do local markets usually locate where they do? primary central markets? secondary central markets?

5. Evaluate the statement, ". . . . . that the factors which influence the actual location of the organized wholesale market facilities also serve to set the locational patterns for the wholesale middlemen operating in such market facilities."

6. What is the general relationship between the geographic structure of wholesale trade and the selection of the location for a wholesale middleman's establishment operating in a nonorganized wholesale market?

7. What characteristics of a particular city influence its attractiveness for wholesale establishments? What characteristics create a negative atmosphere?

8. What characteristics affect the relative attractiveness of a particular site?

9. What is the relationship of type of operation and kind of business to the characteristics discussed in (7) and (8)?

10. What is meant by intracity locational clusters? What types of such clusters exist?

11. Of what influence are locational clusters in selecting the location for a particular wholesale middlemen's establishment?

12. What factors influence the presence, absence, and the type of locational clusters?

13. To what extent is wholesaling an integral part of the metropolitan centers of the United States? of the satellite cities of metropolitan areas? of the unincorporated areas within and outside of standard metropolitan areas?

14. Do you believe wholesale trade is centralizing or decentralizing? What are the reasons for your answer?

CHAPTER INTEGRATING ASSIGNMENTS

1. Take the most recent telephone directory for your city. From the classified section, tabulate the addresses of a certain type and kind of wholesale middleman operation. Place these addresses on a map, and analyze the ensuing distribution in the light of the chapter's discussion of locational clusters.

2. Make a survey of the wholesale establishments tabulated in (1) in which you attempt to get explanations of the reasons why each is located where it is.

3. In connection with integrating assignment (1) in Chapter 9, prepare a careful analysis of where you would locate the business, giving the supporting reasons and data.

11

Merchandising Policies

The next several chapters deal with the basic policies which may be both formulated and executed by the various types of wholesale middlemen, or which may be merely executed by them. In addition, the discussion will include those operations which are necessary auxiliaries to the policy areas. Importance will be attached not merely to the content of each policy area as such but also to the variations in the degree to which the formulation and execution may take place among the various types of wholesale middlemen. These policies and operations fall into three broad groups: Those policies which serve as the bases for merchandising strategy; those policies and operations serving as the tactical bases of buying and selling, including a separate treatment of pricing; and those policies and operations which involve the auxiliary areas including especially warehousing and inventory handling, delivery, and related topics.

Definition and Component Elements of Merchandising[1]

Basic definition

The heart of the concept of merchandising as the function of marketing strategy is contained in the following quotation:

. . . merchandising may be defined as that function of marketing which emphasizes the use of strategy by either sellers or buyers (other than the ultimate consumer), or by both working together (in coordination), in order

[1] The materials discussed in this section are based completely upon the author's ideas as presented in E. A. Duddy and D. A. Revzan, *Marketing: An Institutional*

253

to secure the advantages of innovation. By strategy is meant the superiority of mental power in planning the combinations of marketing variables with the purpose of outmaneuvering the competition. It means the establishment of a definite and conscious master plan to deviate from routine and traditional marketing operations in order to secure competitive advantages. From merchandising (in connection with other marketing functions) stem the marketing tactics, the methods or procedures (or manipulations), used to accomplish the objectives of the master plan created by the merchandising strategy. The ideas inherent in having the right products at the right place, at the right time, in the right amounts, and at the right prices and terms of sale, are all included. The main emphasis of the definition given here, however, is placed upon the degree to which the determination of what is "right" depends upon its close relation to a consciously conceived plan of strategy. The execution of such a plan will usually, but not always, be assigned to specialists.[2]

Building upon this statement, the definition then proceeds to discuss the following:

Merchandising, thus defined, emphasizes the skill of the management in supplementing the ordinary physical routine of moving goods and services from producer to ultimate consumer with a program of coordinated actions designed to increase the marketing success of the firm. The recognition of the merchandising function, in this strategical sense, results in an awareness of the differences between the passive acceptance of doing what everyone else does in the bedrock functions of buying and selling, and a philosophy of actively trying to outplay the opposition.

The function of merchandising as thus defined should not be thought of as an attempt to secure competitive benefits by illegal or extralegal means. Sellers or buyers, through the use of merchandising, may or may not secure the benefits of monopolistic competition as defined by the economist. Whether or not such benefits will accrue depends, in part, on what the management attempts to do in performing the merchandising function. One firm may emphasize product differentiation and everything related to it, while another firm may employ the strategy of emphasizing price factors in pulling away from competitors, and a third may use a skillful combination of both.[3]

Component elements

From the point of view of wholesaling and of wholesale middlemen, merchandising consists of the following component elements: (1) Product and product-service strategy; (2) organizational structure and functional division strategy; (3) pricing strategy; (4) sales promotional strategy; (5) strategy in the managerial struggle for control of the channel; and (6) physical arrangement strategy. Each of these components, so far as they involve policy aspects, will be discussed in

---

Approach, 2nd ed. (New York: McGraw-Hill Book Co., Inc., 1953), Chapter III. This is the only source which seems to develop in detail the concept of merchandising as a function of strategy. Some adaptations are made here to wholesaling.

[2] *Ibid.,* pp. 36–37.

[3] *Ibid.,* p. 37.

rather complete detail in later sections. It will suffice, for purposes of this section, merely to define each of these elements.

If the broad concept of wholesaling is kept in mind in reading this chapter, then it will be recognized that product and product-service strategy involve both the efforts of producing units as such and the independent or related activities of the wholesale middlemen. The whole range of efforts by these managements at differentiation is involved in this form of merchandising strategy, including uniqueness of original product development, product specialization versus product diversification by both manufacturers and middlemen, product branding, product packaging and labeling, and product guarantees and servicing. The strategic aspect of each will be illustrated in the appropriate section at a later point.

Organizational structure and functional division strategy involve ingenious planning by the executives of the divisional organization, functional divisions, and product-line departmental organization in such ways as to secure, where possible, the benefits of innovation. It may involve either expansion or contraction of functions in such ways as to run counter to the forms of traditional organization found in the industry. Or it may involve organizational coordination with one or another aspect of product strategy as outlined above. Finally, it may involve the clearly planned aspect of combining two or more types of wholesale middlemen's operations under one over-all organizational structure.

Many writers and practitioners overlook the merchandising strategy aspects of pricing (including terms of sale). Modern management has varying amounts of leeway, especially at the wholesale level, with respect to how much policy emphasis it can place on developing a strategy of using price either in a highly competitive or in a non-competitive role. These wide ranges of price strategy policies, when skillfully combined with other merchandising policies, may give the wholesale middlemen their choice of accentuating or reducing price competition, at least during the short-run period. Sales promotion strategy especially will be of key importance in strengthening the strategic values inherent in pricing. As has been pointed out:

. . . the merchandising element of price in relation to product strategy is nowhere more apparent than in selecting the mental requirements of "right price," or more often a series of "right prices," in relation to a product or line of products. Who can deny the strategic success of certain mail-order companies, corporate chains, department stores, or aggressive independent retailers in their strategic use of prices? And, of course, the importance of strategy in the use of terms of sale should not be overlooked.[4]

4 *Ibid.*, p. 42.

In the example cited in the quotation, the dependency of the strategy involved is closely related to the wholesale pricing strategy as well.

Sales promotional strategy frequently is the "magic key" that increases the over-all effectiveness of many aspects of merchandising strategy. Unless the advertising and personal selling aspects emphasize the strategy elements inherent in changes in products, product branding and packaging, the merchandising impact may be all but lost. In fact, many so-called types of product changes are mainly the result of skillful promotional strategy; note the examples found in changes in cigarettes and cosmetic products. But in addition to these, what are meant here are the innovational steps taken in the format of the advertising, in promoting the advertising campaign itself, and in stimulating salesmen.

Stemming from many of these merchandising strategy areas are the coordinated efforts designed to secure, for a particular type of wholesale middleman, a position of dominant, or at least improved, control in the channel in relationship with other middlemen. The general nature of this managerial struggle has been examined elsewhere. What needs to be discussed in this context is the individual wholesale middleman's timing of when to move for control in relation to other policy objectives.

Finally, it should be noticed that, for wholesale middlemen who take physical possession of goods offered for sale, there are some limited opportunities to use some elements of strategy in the physical layout of the warehousing facilities. These opportunities, limited though they may be, are applicable especially where the buyers visit the middleman's place of business and buy on the basis mainly of inspection. One special form may be secured by the clustering of many wholesale middlemen in a "merchandise mart" or "furniture mart" type of building, or buildings.[5]

Factors Influencing the Importance and Complexity of the Merchandising Function

Managerial skill

Because of the diversity of types of operation and kinds of business involved at the wholesale level, it is true, although not susceptible of formal statistical proof, that the possession of superiority of managerial skill is the single, most important, factor in merchandising strategy.

[5] These examples as well as the Florist Mart and Apparel City in San Francisco will be discussed in a later section.

Those executives who have demonstrated superiority can be shown to possess some or all of the following characteristics: (1) Strong intuitive skill in the knowledge of what their customers want or can be "convinced" to buy; (2) adaptation of product assortments and their physical and nonphysical characteristics to such wants; and (3) a frame of mind best characterized as a willingness to risk marketing changes, wherever necessary, in order to get a competitive headstart over the traditionalists in the channel.[6]

Considering the composite characteristics underlying superiority of merchandising skill, it is safe to say that it is not the sole property of executives found in any given type or scale of wholesale middlemen operations.

Nature of competition

The structure of competition at the wholesale level is affected by the factor of managerial skill already discussed; by production characteristics and institutional factors; and by many other elements. As the tempo and intensity of competition become magnified, the necessity arises for any given management to secure better understanding of and knowledge as to how to use merchandising strategy. Given these stimuli, there has been further emphasis on securing research knowledge of and training in the merchandising function. Thus, there is created, to a certain extent, an ever-widening circle of possibilities for merchandising strategy.

Costs

Given the increased possibilities for sharpening the analysis of market costs through the use of evolving distribution cost accounting techniques, and the improved professional content of marketing research, management can secure a more realistic appraisal of the value of merchandising. This appraisal may consist of analyzing the indirect and direct costs associated with merchandising; or of determining differential sales; or of the estimated effectiveness of alternative courses of merchandising action.

Product factors

As a result of the interplay of technological and marketing developments, there has been an accumulation of an increasingly com-

---

[6] From the author's own experience, these merchandising "geniuses" have the uncanny ability of playing hunches whenever necessary, and of basing merchandising practices on sound research knowledge whenever feasible.

plex assortment of goods and services to be handled by wholesale middlemen.

When to these developments are added, for example, improvements in packaging techniques and packaging materials, one can see the evolution of a series of increasingly complex want-satisfying things, which are referred to as "goods and services." Added experience with grading and standardization have increased the range of alternative methods by which sellers aim to secure product differentiation. Production factors, increasing sharply the physical volume of goods to be marketed, likewise have had marked effects on the importance and urgency of the merchandising function.[7]

Legal factors

Only certain aspects of the ever-widening effects of government regulation can be mentioned here. For one thing, the government promotion of certain pricing policies, while prohibiting others, has stimulated the search by management of securing the benefits from certain strategic policies while staying "within the law." Similarly, government controls on packaging, and the use of certain types of tax policies, have had to be considered. While increasing governmental protection of trade-marks and other product identification devices have stimulated their use in product strategy, it probably has stimulated the merchandising efforts of those who cannot use such identification devices as well. Finally, government-executed or sponsored research has and will continue to contribute to increasing product complexities, and thus, in turn, to increasing needs for better merchandising.

Product and Product Service Strategy

The discussion here is concerned mainly with those aspects of product development and service which offer the most fertile potentialities for the use of strategy. Accordingly, discussion is unnecessary for those circumstances under which the management of manufacturing establishments as such, or in relationship with wholesale middlemen, merely produces a product or a group of products which attempt to duplicate what is already available in one or more types of channels of distribution. The aspects of primary concern here are, of course, those attempts to create a feeling of newness or innovation by means of originality as to what to produce or stock, and by later modifications of the original ideas. In the discussion which follows, some distinction will be maintained between producer-controlled and non-

[7] Duddy and Revzan, *op. cit.*, p. 45.

integrated-middlemen-controlled merchandising aspects. These product development and service areas are perhaps the most important of all the merchandising strategy possibilities.

Product development[8]

At the manufacturer's level, the initial strategy element may be derived from the discovery (in both the formal and informal sense) of an invention. The invention may represent an entirely new category of product; or some kind of variation of an existing category; or some change or improvement of a component; or the uncovering of a new area of use; or combinations of two or more of these. The development of the invention, in the broad sense discussed, may be the result of pure accident or the culmination of a long period of highly organized expensive research activities.

Within the manufacturing organization, the existence of excess production capacity may stimulate the search for a strategically new product. In addition, or as a separate venture, the search may center around developing uses for by-products from existing production which, presently, are being wasted; or the search may be conducted to seek a marketing change from existing products in which price competition may be severe and the resulting profit margin entirely unsatisfactory. Additional incentives to new product development may be created by the presence of an unfavorable secular trend of demand for existing products which has failed to respond to ordinary or even extraordinary marketing programs. Occasionally, a brilliant suggestion from company personnel other than product specialists may open an entirely new vista. In any event, emphasis here is placed upon those forms of product developments which emphasize the element of innovation and not merely routine duplication of competitors.

Superimposed upon these, and coordinated with them, are a series of stimulants which may originate from the channel. The various types of middlemen and/or ultimate users of the product may uncover previously untapped needs or uses. Competition from other channels may so cut into the producer's share of the market as to create a basis for serious concern. The desires of wholesale and retail middlemen, in their struggle for the control of the channel, may center upon

---

[8] The merchandising strategy aspects of product development are only a part of the complete discussion as contained in the sales management literature. See, for example, D. M. Phelps, *Planning the Product* (Homewood, Ill.: Richard D. Irwin, Inc., 1947); and Gustav E. Larson, *Developing and Selling New Products: A Guidebook for Manufacturers,* 2nd ed. (Washington, D. C.: U. S. Government Printing Office, 1955).

the addition of product lines carrying their respective distributor's brands. Finally, changing marketing structures may exert additional pressures upon existing product situations. Ultimate consumers may request products unavailable at a given time period in sufficient volume to warrant attention; or, negatively, they may register sufficient dissatisfaction with existing product offers to require the sources of such products either to eliminate such products or to make significant changes. Occasionally, a government decision may force changes.[9]

At the wholesale middlemen's level, the nature of product development—except for distributor's brands to be discussed later—is concerned with the strategy of product assortments. The assortment strategy may manifest itself by virtue of: (1) Exclusive distributorships of established or new products; (2) uniqueness of assortments in width or depth as discussed in Chapter 7; (3) the unique use of scrambled assortments; or (4) the use of a custom order department. These aspects of product assortments sooner or later involve the wholesale middlemen in other forms of product strategy, as discussed later. In addition, the advantages which may accrue to the strategy of one or another form of product development may be strengthened or weakened by other categories of merchandising strategy.

Product specialization versus product diversification

Not all aspects of this type of product policy involve what may be called correctly "merchandising strategy." In its strategy characteristics, this type may involve for the manufacturer elements of broadening the base of acceptance already established for a given brand. It may furnish the manufacturer with a basis for securing better utilization of existing channels or for justifying a shift from indirect to direct channels. Or, even without changing channels, product diversification may secure the advantages of "full-line forcing," although this may bring in its wake considerable middleman resentment. Diversification may serve, also, to make the manufacturer less dependent upon any single stratum of demand. In addition, it may be expensive to implement and may lead, ultimately, to overly complicated organizational structural problems.

At the wholesale middleman level, the analysis involves, in part, the problem discussed earlier of assortments in depth versus assortments in breadth, and both versus scrambled assortments. It involves, as a related consideration, the determination by the middleman manage-

---

[9] Note recently, for example, the decision against future use of coal tar dyes in lipstick.

ment of a policy of whether to depend upon a single source of supply or to diversify its risks. Concentration of purchases may secure advantages both in price and terms of sale, and in available varieties of goods and rapidity of delivery. On the other hand, it prevents the middleman from offering product assortment alternatives to customers; and, in addition, he may find his marketing strategy initiatives sharply reduced by the ever-existing threat of the manufacturer to choke off suppliers unless certain conditions are fulfilled. Also, he may have overly ambitious quotas to reach, and he may have to stock slow-moving items in order to receive supplies of widely accepted products.

Important to both manufacturers and middlemen are the stresses which product diversification places on respective advertising and personal selling programs in terms of expense as well as dilution of individual product impact. Especially critical is the question of whether or not the element of strategy can be maintained if many products have to be marketed. It is not always clear, for example, that diversification permits as close control over product quality as does specialization. Equally important is whether or not each company (either manufacturer or middleman) has sufficient executive talent and research and control devices to evaluate successfully what is happening from the strategy point of view. In an atmosphere of continuing marketing structural changes and of ever-changing products in the foregoing meaning, the manufacturer and middleman who do not diversify find themselves increasingly in the position of having to rationalize their marketing philosophies.

Product diversification[10]

Both the manufacturer and the middleman have variable possibilities of using trade-marks and/or other identification devices to secure or enhance the benefits of product strategy. The general importance for strategy stems from the key advantages of such identification devices in (a) permitting differentiation in the channel and thus securing segmentation of the market, and (b) in crystallizing other forms of strategy, including both pricing and advertising. Thus, in relation to pricing strategy, trade-marks can be used either to accentuate or to reduce the effects of price competition.

Whether or not an individual manufacturer will attempt to use his own brand (or brands) for product strategy purposes depends upon a number of variables: the size of his area of distribution; the propor-

[10] For the reader who is unacquainted with some of the background fundamentals of trade-marks and trade names, reference should be made to any standard book on sales management.

tion of the total industry sales he endeavors to secure; the relative competitive strength of existing brands; the financial resources needed to establish the brand name; and the manufacturer's existing or proposed product lines. Of significance, also, are the circumstances under which alternative identifications can be reached. In addition, the price structure and the available margins of profit will carry considerable influence.

If the evaluation of these factors points toward the establishment of his brand, the manufacturer must then weigh identification alternative in terms of the opportunities for strategy. Should he use a single brand if he produces a single product, or should the brands be stratified by price-quality levels? A single brand permits concentrating the marketing strategy and the necessary "ammunition" on launching and establishing the brand name. Technical problems in the selection of a satisfactory brand name and the legal protection of it may be minimized. On the other hand, diversification of brand names, by price-quality levels, may permit one brand to secure nonprice protection in the channel.

Product expansion from internal reasons as discussed creates problems of strategy of whether or not to use the same brand name (a family brand name for each product). Much depends on whether the products have the same use characteristics, the same level of quality consistency for each item, and the same relative price positions. Obvious economies in advertising can result from a single brand name; and the older well-established products may help pave the way for the new products in the channel. In addition, quick transfer of identification by the customer can be obtained at the point of sale.

On the other hand, if the products are quite diverse in use characteristics and type-of-customer adaptation, cross identification may be undesirable, if not ruinous. In addition, if the brands have been inherited from previous mergers, the controlling manufacturer may wish to protect the market acceptance of each brand; and intramanufacturing product competition in their respective marketing spheres may prove to be healthy. Note, in this connection, the value which General Motors gets from a family of products identified both as a GM product and as an individual brand name.

Strong brand strategy and promotion by the manufacturer may bring strong retaliation from the middleman in the channel in the form of a search for strong distributor's brands for each middleman or for groups of middlemen operating in some form of integrated operation. The general competitive structure may act as an accentuating influence. The middlemen may have established, at the very outset, a merchandising policy of featuring their individual distributor's brands; or the policy may result from certain developments in the channel. A broker handling part or all of a food canner's output may find that, by placing his brand on the product, it will carry more marketing appeal than the brand name of a weak, unknown canner. Manufacturers, by attempting to reduce the margins of wholesale middlemen, may be instrumental in generating distributor's brands priced perhaps at equivalent levels, but yielding higher margins or permitting more aggressive pricing. The struggle for channel control accentuates a distributor's willingness to establish his own brand. Once the use of a distributor's brands becomes widespread in given kinds of business, each individual middleman may have to sharpen his brand strategy, not only in relation to manufacturers' brands but also in relation to other distributors' brands as well.

Borden[11] establishes certain considerations which affect the managerial decisions as to whether or not distributors' brands will or should be used: (1) The market position of the manufacturer's brands, i.e., the proportion of total sales controlled; (2) the conditions under which the middleman can secure his branded products from a manufacturer, price, quality, and length of time considered; (3) the middleman's feeling of satisfaction with the existing manufacturer's margins, and anticipation as to the future course of such margins; (4) closely related to (3) is the extent to which the manufacturer places channel pressure on the middleman through the use of exclusive franchise and resale price maintenance agreements; (5) the distributor's estimates of the potential sales for his branded products, and the costs of obtaining such sales volumes; (6) the number of manufacturers' brands, and the strength of competition between each; and (7) the manufacturer's pricing policies in relation to the middlemen's pricing policies. The middleman's answer to these considerations will decide, in turn, his product assortment strategy as to whether to handle only manufacturers' nationally advertised brands, distributors' brands exclusively, or strategic combinations of both.

Product packaging and labeling

These offer further opportunities for strategy to both manufacturers and distributors apart from the necessary protective and physical handling aspects. The close coordination between this strategy aspect and brand strategy aspect is obvious. Until the brand policy is made effective by the application of the brand to a product, mainly con-

[11] Neil H. Borden, *The Economic Effect of Advertising* (Homewood, Ill.: Richard D. Irwin, Inc., 1942), pp. 589–602, 631–639.

tained in some type of package, it will be a considerably weaker policy from the strategy point of view. Wholesale middlemen may use packaging to identify and increase in value products otherwise sold in bulk. Combinations of products in packages which otherwise are sold separately may lead to increased volumes and types of use.

In visualizing the possibilities for the use of strategy in package design and labeling, a broad managerial perspective is necessary. Apart from those types of containers used to protect the product in transit, the inner container must be viewed from its merchandising impact on the level of the buyer involved in the channel for the particular type of product. Thus, the package may have unique value in its position in the warehouse; or by virtue of its point-of-sales appeal; or by virtue of its usefulness after the product has been removed. In addition, the quality and design may enhance the appearance of the product, especially from the prestige angle.

One of the most important strategy aspects is the atmosphere which the package furnishes for the brand name of the product, and for the related message accompanying the brand name. In addition, the quality of the package may have either favorable or unfavorable effects on the product strategy. Thus, the development of highly visible and durable wrapping materials was important to the marketing of precut meats and certain frozen food products. Relative ease of opening and closing are necessary package features where the contents are not consumed within a single period of use. Wholesale middlemen may be able to contribute to their channel strategy by adapting the size of the package to the varying requirements of their customers.

Sometimes poorly designed packages may backfire and harm product strategy by creating the illusion of containing lesser amounts in appearance than is true in actuality, and by causing wastes in damage because highly irregular shapes result in the product falling from shelves. Two other relationships of the package and label to product strategy may be mentioned: (1) The use of special containers for such gift-giving holidays as Christmas and Easter, and (2) using the package and/or labels to exploit new uses.

Product guarantees and services

This form of merchandising strategy may imply superiority in the terms of the warranty given to a product by its manufacturer, the wholesale middlemen in the channel, the retail middlemen (if it is a consumer's good), or combinations thereof. It includes, additionally, the relative quality of the technical skill involved in installing and servicing both technical industrial goods and technical consumer's goods. But what is frequently overlooked under the heading of services is the strategy of certain wholesale middlemen in adapting merchandise and assortments to their customers' needs. Four cases may be cited as illustrations of such strategy:

Case 1. The pioneering rack jobber furnished special product assortments and accompanying display facilities to food supermarkets in order to implement a policy of "scrambled" merchandising. This type of operation may be an independent establishment or it may be a division of an existing middleman's operation. It should be noted that this rack jobber functioning comes under the heading of a form of merchandising strategy only in the period of unique use in the channel.

Case 2. Whenever the manufacturer or the wholesale middleman adapts the unit of sale or the shape of the package, or both, to the needs of such agencies as limited-price variety stores or vending machines, the initial action attempts one form of product services strategy. In some cases, the middleman, by special adaptation, may obtain the vending of a product by machines which were not previously so handled.[12]

Case 3. In this instance, the steel distributor's warehouse, a type of industrial distributor, will bend, cut, or otherwise adapt its inventory of steel products to the needs of its customers. Similarly, in the plastics business, some 10,000 items consisting of different colors, grades, shapes, may be carried.[13] To the extent such operations become a custom-type service, they approximate, once again, a form of merchandising strategy.

Case 4. Finally, there is the case of the converter in the textile field. The merchandising aspects of this type of middleman operation center in the professional skill of the converter in anticipating uniqueness of colors, designs, or fabrics in connection with the end uses of the converted textiles.

In connection with the strategy of guarantees, mention may be made briefly of the initial success of Graybar in adding its guarantee to that of the manufacturers'. This, indeed, is one of the classic examples of such strategy.

---

[12] Note, for example, the handling of hot beverages, soups, and of selected shopping goods.

[13] See the description of the warehousing operations of the Cadillac Plastic & Chemical Co. of Detroit in servicing 25,000 customers, "Middlemen in the Plastics Trade," *Business Week* (Aug. 10, 1957), p. 92.

Final observations

In the preceding discussions, a great deal of emphasis has been placed on the possibilities for the use of product strategy not only by the manufacturers as the beginning of the funnel aspects of wholesaling but independently or through integration by the middlemen as well. The rise in the prevalence of distributors' brands in many kinds of industrial goods and manufactured consumers' goods business has accentuated the possibilities. In addition, the increased flux of product assortments among channels has served to widen the possibilities.

As the spiral of these merchandising strategy possibilities broadens, through the medium of the product, increased complexities are introduced as to how long the initial effects of the strategy can be maintained, and as to how to measure the effectiveness of the strategy and to related matters. The expansion in recent years in both the number and types of such strategy leads ultimately to sharp increases in cost of establishing such strategy. But the very pervasiveness and past successes of such strategy also place considerable pressure on the middlemen in the channel to try and utilize some form of product strategy wherever feasible. After all, the product (including services) is the key organizing aspect of the channel.

Organizational Structure and Functional Division Strategy

The earlier discussions of types of wholesale middlemen's operations and of their organizational structures have indicated some of the key variations which distinguish one type of middleman from another. It will suffice here to state that the key variations between each type of operation have their strategy aspects when the range of functions is either narrowed or widened by a given management in order to improve its position in the channel. Of key importance is the role of the middleman in originating and transmitting key communications about fundamental marketing aspects either to the producing or to the using side of the channel, or to both. Included in this, also, are the effects of the various forms of formal and informal integration as previously discussed. Of additional importance are the qualitative nuances by which one middleman establishment differentiates his functional combination from competitive establishments.

In addition to these classes of variations between different types of operations and between the different establishments in the same type of operation, other aspects of strategy may manifest themselves within the organizational structure itself. One type reflects the use of a separate division within the regular organization for such special operations as were noted before, e.g., cash-and-carry and rack jobber operations. A second such division may reflect special emphasis given to selected product assortments. The last illustration pertains to the strategic use by an establishment of multitype operations, or to special geographical adaptation through multiple establishments. In all of these examples, the shift in types of operation stems, generally, from types of merchandising strategy made effective in other directions. Rarely can these types of strategy originate and be made effective by themselves.

Pricing Strategy

Apart from the use of pricing strategy by the managements of manufacturing establishments, the opportunities for the use of pricing strategy by other wholesale middlemen arise under highly variable circumstances. The manufacturers may secure advantages from strategic pricing policies by calculated shrewd deviations from generally accepted industry practices. These may involve, in turn, considerable judgment or insight as to when to extract prices "at what the traffic will bear," contrary to the pricing policies of the rest of the industry. Many illustrations to the point are readily available; Reynolds' policy in pricing the original ball point pens; the pricing of Rolls Royce and Bentley automobiles; the pricing of exclusive models of fashion apparel; and, finally, the pricing of so-called deluxe models relative to the standard models.

But manufacturers may follow the reverse price strategy also, namely, of featuring highly competitive prices compared with the general level of the industry. Again, many case illustrations come to mind: Scripto pencils and ball-point pens; paperback versus standard hard-cover books; "fighting" brands versus standard brands; and lower prices resulting from the use of direct channels. In addition, manufacturers may feature lower prices via a twice-a-year clearance sales policy.

Both sets of examples given above pertain to the manufacturer's level. But many types of wholesale middlemen have some opportunities for the use of pricing strategy. These advantages may stem, as noticed, from the relationship of the prices of their controlled distributors' brands; or the structure of assignable costs may permit a higher than normal margin. The strategy in other cases may be the featuring of aggressively competitive prices, especially of those brands controlled by the corporate chains, with correspondingly aggressive price equivalents. Or, the wholesale middlemen may express the exclusiveness of their respective distributors' brands by pricing at "what the traffic will bear" price levels similar to those for the manufacturer's policies.

A different form of middlemen's pricing strategy may be evident with respect to the movement of "distressed" or close-out merchandise through the channel. Such assortments may consist of regular manufacturers' brands, or distributors' brands, or both, or unbranded products available only at infrequent or irregular time intervals. Other assortments may represent regular movements of broken and/or slightly damaged assortments. Or, finally, the assortments may consist completely of "dogs," i.e., products below acceptable minimum quality levels or originating from various unknown manufacturing sources.

In the instance of a new product in the channel, highly ingenious pricing devices may be used to give it initial channel impetus. Two-for-one deals, coupon deals, tie-in sales "skimming the market cream," are all illustrative of particular price policies which assume varying conditions of elasticity of consumer demand, frequency of purchase, size of purchase, and related factors. Under certain conditions, the pricing of a very popular product may be contingent upon the purchase of the slower selling parts of the product line.

But whatever the price strategy used by a given manufacturer or wholesale middleman, its incidence is directly on the wholesaling sector as reflected in the marketing channel. The particular forms of pricing strategy at the wholesale level may operate independently from other forms of strategy. In most cases, however, the strategy of pricing will be interrelated ultimately with one or more additional forms of merchandising strategy.

Sales Promotional Strategy

The general possibilities of manufacturers developing one or another form of sales promotional strategy are well recognized through the skilled coordination of advertising and personal selling. As will be seen from the later discussions of the advertising and personal selling components, the effectiveness of all other forms of merchandising strategy can be realized only by the skill with which they are communicated through the channel by means of the campaign and the quality of the salesmen's presentations. From a strategy viewpoint, much more is involved in advertising than mere routine preparation of copy and its presentation in one or more media. Skillful use of technical data may be necessary in well-presented case studies in order to "push" an industrial good through its channel. The manufacturer of a consumers' good in a highly competitive industry may very well have to depend on carefully prepared combinations of advertising and salesmanship to establish and/or expand his control in the channel. Even such agricultural goods as oranges have had skillful advertising campaigns to secure the benefits of primary and selective demand creation.[14] In these connections, the whole gamut of advertising, as it is used to develop nonprice competition, is of significance.

Because it is so frequently forgotten that middlemen, other than those integrated in the marketing departments of manufacturers, may have important relationships to product strategy, as discussed above, their role in sales promotion is correspondingly underestimated. If these types of middlemen are developing strong distributors' brands, for example, then it follows that well-planned and well-executed sales-promotional programs are an integral accessory to the initial strategy. Similarly, an important aspect of the success of one or another type of voluntary chain is the extent to which the sales promotional programs can establish the unique elements of product assortments, price policies, store layout, and other aspects of the chain's competitive strength. The relationship to wholesaling is evident in the responsibility of the wholesaler in sponsoring one type of such a voluntary chain.

Apart from the usual aspects of personal selling, the wholesale middleman can secure the benefits of merchandising strategy through the coordination of special missionary salesmen's efforts with other aspects of the middlemen's marketing program. Thus, the testing and establishing of new products in the channel may require the services of such salesmen. Again, similar coordination may be required to give special advertising efforts the necessary point-of-sale push. Pricing strategies, including such forms as the two-for-one deals, frequently are made more effective by concentrated sales efforts, once again, at the point-of-sale by these special salesmen or by special assignments given to members of the regular sales force. Another aspect frequently overlooked, but of key importance, is feeding back

[14] See Borden, *op. cit.*, Chap. XIII.

suggestions to the executive management for improvements in existing products and/or additions to new products. Finally, these salesmen may be key links in the evaluation of the success of every merchandising strategy effort undertaken, and in the relative position of such efforts compared with those made by competitors.

One final aspect of sales promotional strategy may be noted here, namely, the efforts made by manufacturers or agricultural producers to prepare advertising copy and other sales promotional kits for wholesale middlemen. Correspondingly, wholesale middlemen may assume similar responsibilities for their retail middlemen customers regardless of whether or not they are integrated in organizational structure and operations.

Channel Strategy

What are to be emphasized here as merchandising strategy are the decisions of either the individual middlemen links in particular product channels, or of several such middlemen, about the relative merits of actively seeking to obtain channel control. What gives this active seeking its strategic benefit is to be found in the particular form it takes and the particular timing. Once again, it is the uniqueness of both the form and timing, in relation to the traditional distribution of channel control, which gives the activity the merchandising designation.

This type of merchandising strategy involves, once again, the integration of many segmented forms of strategy. The main managerial device for securing, or attempting to secure, control of the channel is the use of formal and informal types of integration. Without repeating what has been discussed earlier, but keeping such materials in mind, the important part of such efforts in this connection are the approaches used by individual managements, not only the normal benefits accruing to each integrating device but also the combined advantage of directing these toward the additional goal of channel control. It is this multiple objective characteristic of so much merchandising strategy which makes this particular form so complex.

One other characteristic of the channel control strategy should be noted. Historically, in marketing, the strategic use of formal and informal types of integration has led, in turn, to some strategic forms of control reprisal. Such integrated institutional types in the channel as the voluntary chain wholesalers and cooperative marketing associations have had their roots in the retaliation of independent producers and middlemen to pressures originating, in their respective channels, from corporate chains and the actions of brokers and commission agents which affected net proceeds realized from sales.

Physical Layout Strategy

Three examples may be presented here to show the applicability of this type of strategy to wholesaling, although many more illustrations can be found at the retailing level. The first example, illustrated by the General Electric Supply Co.,[15] involves the use of a type of warehouse layout in which customers can serve themselves for certain electrical products which may be shelved in a manner very similar to that used in retail supermarkets. Obviously, this form of unique warehouse layout can only be used where: (a) the bulk and weight of the products are sufficiently limited; (b) the quantities purchased permit the customer to move the products physically; and (c) there are some kind of price and service inducements for the customer to participate on a cash-and-carry basis.

The second example, which will be discussed in detail in Chapter 17, involves the use of the new discoveries in electronic computers and materials handling equipment in order to get the benefits of more rapid and accurate order filling, reduce average inventory requirements, sharply reduced costs of filling orders, and much improved control in terms of both timing and completeness.

The final example is a form of group middlemen's strategy, and represents a deviation from the definition of merchandising as given. In a sense, it is a deviation from the earlier discussion of locational clustering. The grouping together of middlemen in the furniture trade in the National Furniture Mart in Chicago, and in regional marts in High Point, North Carolina, Dallas, Los Angeles, Atlanta, and New York, is one illustration.[16] A second illustration is to be found in the grouping together of dress designers, manufacturers, and distributors, as in Apparel City in San Francisco. A final illustration is the grouping together of wholesale florists in one physical facility, as in the case of the California Flower Market in San Francisco. Apart from the advantages, already described, to be obtained from clustering,

---

[15] This company is the wholesale subsidiary (sales branch) of General Electric for the distribution of certain types of electrical products.

[16] See "Placing Furniture Marts," *Business Week* (January 24, 1959), p. 71.

the examples given show how the middlemen involved get a partial form of an organized wholesale market, e.g., as found in the agricultural goods markets.

Resumé of Wholesale Middlemen's Merchandising Strategy

It may prove useful, at this point, to recapitulate each of the broader merchandising strategy areas under the six classification headings used in the preceding discussions. In making this presentation, the orientation of this treatment is once more emphasized, namely, the inclusion of the producer's activities by virtue of their direct participation in middlemen's activities; by their exercise of control over the channel in other ways; and by the backward-vertical integrated control of some types of middlemen over the producing levels. Viewed in this manner, the following outline represents a tool for bringing together pertinent information about the merchandising functional activities of any individual middleman establishment, type of middleman operation, or groups of establishments.

    I. *Product and Product Service Strategy*
      A. Product development.
        1. Research on new products.
        2. Research on changes in styles or models of existing product lines.
        3. Research on new uses.
        4. Advice relative to (1), (2), or (3).
        5. Information on user complaints.
        6. Information on product performance.
      B. Product assortments.
        1. Assortments in depth.
        2. Assortments in width.
        3. Combinations of (1) and (2).
        4. Scrambled merchandising.
      C. Product identification.
        1. Manufacturer's brands: national, regional, local.
        2. Distributor's brands: national, regional, local.
        3. Individual product brands versus family product brands.
        4. Insertion of dealer's brand in addition to manufacturer's name.
      D. Product packaging and labeling.
        1. Adaptation to producer's needs.
        2. Adaptation to wholesale middlemen's needs.

3. Adaptation to retail middlemen's needs.

4. Adaptation to user's needs.

E. Guarantees and services.

  1. Guarantees.

  a. Producer.

  b. Wholesale middleman.

  c. Retail middleman.

  2. Services

  a. Installation and maintenance.

  b. Displays.

  c. Adaptations of forms, shapes, sizes, et al.

  d. Style and fashion advice and adaptations.

II. *Organizational Structure and Functional Division Strategy*

A. Strategy of each type of operation.

B. Insertion of special services divisions.

C. Multitype operations versus single-type operations.

D. Advice to integrated units.

  1. On organizational structure.

  2. On marketing policies.

  3. On accounting and statistical controls.

III. *Pricing Strategy*

A. Producer originated and controlled.

B. Wholesale middleman originated and controlled.

C. Retail middleman originated and controlled.

D. Multiple-level strategy efforts.

IV. *Sales Promotional Strategy*

A. Advertising.

  1. Producer originated and controlled.

  2. Wholesale middleman originated and controlled.

  3. Retail middleman originated and controlled.

  4. Producer's materials and services to wholesale and retail middlemen.

  5. Wholesale middlemen's materials and services to retail middlemen.

B. Personal Selling.

  1. Competitive strategy of producer-controlled versus middlemen-controlled salesmen.

  2. Producer services to middlemen.

  a. Training.

  b. Quota determination.

  c. Product information.

  d. Salesman's kits.

        3. Wholesale middlemen's service to retail middlemen.
         a. Training.
         b. Quota determination.
         c. Product information.
   V. *Channel Control Strategy*
     A. Producer-directed channel control strategy.
       1. Formal.
       2. Informal.
     B. Wholesale middlemen-directed channel control strategy.
       1. Formal.
       2. Informal.
     C. Retail middlemen-directed channel control strategy.
       1. Formal.
       2. Informal.
  VI. *Physical Layout Strategy*
     A. Self-service warehouses.
     B. Mechanized warehouses and electronic inventory controls.
     C. Furniture marts and similar clusterings.

Reasons for the Increasing Importance of Merchandising in the Wholesaling Sector

Although the reasons for the increased importance of the merchandising function in the wholesaling sector cannot be separated from the reasons applicable to marketing as a whole, some special emphasis can be given here.

The growing impersonality of marketing transactions

Producers are no longer able to claim having an intimate knowledge of who buys their respective outputs and of having any very widespread personal relationships in the day-to-day buying and selling transactions. The shift from a form of production according to customer specification to much production in anticipation of such demand (except in the more technical forms of industrial goods) places ever-increasing burdens upon channels to provide opportunities for outmaneuvering the competition, *especially since no alert marketing agency can have exact knowledge of what their customers want and when they will buy.*

Production technology

The continuing revolution in production technology leads to many pressures for greater emphasis on merchandising. Automatic production places more and more emphasis upon the manufacturer to produce standardized products in increasingly large quantities. But the pressures placed upon the competitive position of such standardized goods lead increasingly to merchandising efforts to induce product differentiations either by actual physical changes or by shrewd emotional appeals, or by combinations thereof. The alert link in the channel must be aware, always, of the extent to which the available products may fail to meet the needs of any significant numbers of customers.

Increased marketing knowledge

As the sum total of marketing knowledge improves, as evident in the improved quality of the available literature, and as the quality of professional marketing research improves both in perspective and in scope, it could only be expected that some of the improved knowledge would be related to wholesaling and to the strategy involved in that sector.

Increased channel pressures

Finally, the continuing managerial struggle for channel control places a considerable premium on the ability of individual managements to evolve more effective forms of merchandising strategy. Thus, the complicated array of possible forms contained in the preceding section's outline resumé is the result. As more and more middlemen begin to search for aspects of merchandising strategy to use, the problem of initiating and/or maintaining the initiation through innovation and outmaneuvering the competition becomes more and more complex.

QUESTIONS AND PROBLEMS

1. Wherein does the concept of merchandising as the function of marketing strategy differ from the ordinary meanings of merchandising in the marketing literature?
2. What are the component elements of merchandising strategy?
3. How do you explain the increasing importance and complexity of the merchandising function?
4. What are the opportunities of wholesale middlemen to use various types of product and product service strategy?
5. Differentiate between opportunities for strategic product development by manufacturers as opposed to wholesale middlemen.
6. What are the relationships of product diversification and product specialization to merchandising strategy?
7. Under what conditions should a wholesale middleman use his own brands as against manufacturers' brands?

8. What are the various relationships of the product's package and label to the effectiveness of the product strategy?

9. Evaluate the four cases of strategy of wholesale middlemen in adapting merchandise and assortments to customers' needs.

10. To what extent does the type of middleman operation offer opportunities for merchandising strategy?

11. To what extent does the middleman's pricing strategy hinge on the producers' strategy? To what extent is it independent?

12. Discuss, in detail, the various components of sales promotional strategy.

13. What is the relationship between wholesale middleman's channel strategy efforts and channel structure?

14. To what extent are the various forms of the managerial struggle for channel control related to managerial efforts at channel strategy?

15. Explain how physical layout may offer opportunities for strategic efforts.

CHAPTER INTEGRATING ASSIGNMENTS

1. Develop a scale by means of which you rate the comparative merchandising strategy potentials of each type of wholesale middleman operation for each component merchandising element.

2. Discuss critically the extent to which the evolution of certain types of wholesale middleman (*e.g.*, the cash-and-carry wholesaler, the voluntary cooperative wholesaler, and the rack jobber) was based upon elements of merchandising strategy.

3. In your opinion, will the future strategic importance of the wholesaling sector be based upon a greater need for, and use of, merchandising strategy? or will the opportunities be drastically reduced?

12

Buying Elements
and Policies

The breadth and complexity of buying elements and policies in the wholesaling sector have been generally underestimated both by the writers in marketing and by the businessmen themselves. In many cases, as has been discussed, buying at wholesale involves a multiple chain of transactions in the channel rather than a single transaction.[1] The range of products involved includes every conceivable type produced, ranging from the smallest in size and value to the largest. Every conceivable size and type of business and nonbusiness organizations are involved either directly or indirectly. The range of buying skills involved shows a related width and breadth beyond anything required elsewhere in the marketing channels.

Despite the efforts of the personnel involved in purchasing to establish themselves as a separate professional group, the entire range of activities included under the heading of purchasing (or procurement) is encompassed under the buying function in the wholesaling sector.[2] The measure of the importance of the function in dollar terms, as has been indicated earlier, amounts to hundreds of billions of dollars in terms of total gross sales.

Because of the tremendous scope and complexity, this discussion of

[1] This is taking, of course, the over-all view rather than that for a single transaction for a particular commodity.

[2] The reader interested in one example of the present content of purchasing and purchasing policies should consult George W. Aljian (ed.), *Purchasing Policies* (New York: McGraw-Hill Book Co., Inc., 1958).

buying elements and policies is confined mainly to those situations in which the types of wholesale middlemen, as previously classified and defined, have some significant responsibility. Accordingly, no attempt is made to include the activities of purchasing departments of various types of organizations—manufacturing and otherwise—although many of the component elements will be discussed as they pertain to the wholesale middlemen. In this chapter and in the next, the discussion will include: types of buying situations; the content and aspects of each component element of buying; selected buying policies; and, finally, variations in buying elements and policies by types of wholesale middlemen.

Throughout the scope of this discussion, constant attention must be given to the variable positions of influence which each type of wholesale middleman exerts on the buying function in terms of whether or not he occupies a position of initiative or, conversely, one of merely following orders as the buying function is executed. Much of the managerial struggle for control of the channel first becomes evident in the various roles of responsibility in buying either assigned to or assumed by the various middleman linkages in the channel. In the execution of the buying function, the wholesale middlemen, keeping in mind the range of responsibilities, may or may not be able to show much ingenuity in relating such activities to the possibilities for merchandising strategy discussed in the preceding chapter.

Types of Buying Situations

Because the variety in the type of buying situations at the wholesale level has a direct bearing upon the complexity of the component elements of the function, some discussion is needed at this point of the more important classification groupings. The following outline will serve as a useful guide to the discussion which follows:

I. *End-Use Characteristics*
  A. Buying for resale.
    1. Resale to other wholesale middlemen.
    2. Resale to retail middlemen.
    3. Combinations of (1) and (2).
  B. Buying for organizational end use.
    1. Buying for production purposes.
    2. Buying for purposes of equipping and operating other forms of business.
    3. Buying for purposes of equipping and operating various governmental units, including all aspects of the military.

    4. Buying for purposes of equipping and operating various professional units.

    5. Buying for equipping and operating all remaining forms of nonbusiness and nongovernmental agencies.

II. *Number of Transactions*

    A. One wholesale transaction in the channel.

    B. Two to three wholesale transactions in the channel.

    C. Four or more wholesale transactions in the channel.

III. *Time Factor*

    A. Organized wholesale markets: cash versus future transactions.

    B. Nonorganized wholesale markets.

        1. Immediate purchases.

        2. Forward buying.

IV. *Physical Versus Nonphysical Possession*

V. *Buying Bases*

    A. Sale by inspection.

    B. Sale by sample.

        1. Seller's sample.

        2. Buyer's sample.

        3. Third party's sample.

    C. Sale by description.

        1. Seller's description.

        2. Buyer's description.

        3. Third party's description.

End-use characteristics

The categories of buying for resale and buying for organizational end use, outlined above, affect every component element of the buying function at wholesale. They influence those product assortments which will or will not move through the channels, thus affecting what will be bought. Each end-use buying transaction creates its own peculiar institutional composition and, accordingly, its own influence on the pattern of channels to be expected. The varieties of these characteristics affect the competitive structure of the channels and the degree of complexities involved in the entire marketing arrangements. Finally, they affect the extent to which organized wholesale markets may or may not function.

Number of buying and selling transactions

Related to the above classification is that pertaining to the number of buying and selling transactions involved in the wholesaling sector. The total gross sales volume of the wholesaling sector is affected by the extent to which the same category of products may be bought or sold only once or bought and sold two or more times. The factors influencing the choice of channels underlie the extent to which there will be single or multiple transactions. Finally, speculative factors will affect, in addition, the number of transactions.

Time factors

What are mainly implied here are the influences of two kinds of time factors. One is present in the organized wholesale agricultural goods market and involves the differentiation between cash and future transactions.[3] This introduces the whole element of speculation and hedging, and the differentiation from the point of view of the present situation is closely hinged to the time factor. For some product situations, where no organized wholesale commodity exchanges are available, an equivalent type of time treatment may be obtained through forward buying.

Physical versus nonphysical possession

Under certain types of wholesale middlemen operations, as in the case of buying brokers, manufacturers' sales offices, and drop shippers, buying activities take place in which these middlemen do not take physical possession of inventories. This characteristic changes the composition of the component elements of buying as compared with those types of wholesale middlemen who do take physical possession, especially so far as questions of inventory policy and delivery of purchases are concerned.

Many types of agent middlemen do have physical possession of inventories, but do not engage in the technical sense in buying. Instead, they search wholesale markets for those principals who are willing to give them the necessary agency contracts.

Buying bases

Finally to be noted are the variations in buying situations stemming from variations in the bases upon which buying and selling may be executed. Although these have been discussed before, some repetition may be useful within the present context. For those products which cannot be easily graded or standardized as they move through the channel, or for those products for which the quality condition cannot be determined except by close investigation at time of purchase, buying

---

[3] See the discussion in Chapter 13 in connection with inventory policies, and Chapter 16 in connection with pricing and price policies.

on the basis of inspection of the available inventory will be the guiding rule. At the wholesale level, this characterizes much of the trading in perishable agricultural products.

Wherever grading and standardization of products become well established, buying may take place either on the basis of samples or of description. The samples may be representative of a whole commercial lot being offered for sale, as in the case of grains or wearing apparel or many types of industrial goods, or may represent a proposed model prepared by the seller, buyer, or some third party. In the examples of future contracts in the speculative grain exchanges and of highly specialized industrial goods, the complete buying transaction may be based upon written descriptions or specifications prepared by buyers or their representatives, by sellers or their representatives, or by interested third parties.

From the foregoing, it is apparent that wholesale middlemen in the channel have some leeway as to the choice of bases on which they can execute their buying activities. For agricultural products, these middlemen may or may not utilize organized wholesale markets. Accordingly, the buying bases will vary, depending upon whether or not such markets are used and, if such markets are used, as to particular type. Purchase of livestock at central markets will have the basis of inspection, but at auctions both sample and inspection will be utilized. Similarly, fresh fruits may be bought on the basis of inspection or of samples. Depending upon the type of merchandising strategy being utilized, provision of samples and/or descriptions may be a significant part of the attempt made by the wholesale middlemen to differentiate significantly the products involved in the buying and selling transactions. A given buyer, with a distributor's brand policy, may use a government grade as a basis for his labeling. Or, in the case of highly technical and differentiated types of industrial goods, the description may be based upon one or more patents.

Earlier discussions have indicated the relationship between these buying bases and the determination of wholesale prices and the price structure.

Component Elements of Buying

Building upon the preceding discussion of merchandising, it may be advantageous at this point to outline completely the component elements of buying at the wholesaling sector level before each is discussed in detail and related to selected buying policies. The following outline arranges the component elements in the order to be followed in subsequent sections.

    I. *Determination of Product Assortments to Buy*
- A. Influence of end-use characteristics.
- B. Influence of wholesale middleman's merchandising strategy.
- C. Influence of channel structure and of the managerial struggle for channel control.
- D. Influence of other variables.

    II. *Determination of the Source of Supply of Product Assortments*
- A. Types of source determination situations.
- B. Determination of particular sources.
- C. Continuity of source versus use of changing sources.
- D. Multiple versus single sources.
- E. Foreign versus domestic sources.

    III. *Determination of How Much to Purchase*
- A. The influence of the merchandise budget.
- B. The influence of the middleman's inventory policies.
- C. The influence of financial factors.
- D. The influence of the speculative factors.
- E. Leasing versus outright purchase.

    IV. *Determination of Product Branding*
- A. Resumé of reasons for brands.
- B. Selected technical problems.
- C. Factors influencing branding.

    V. *Negotiation of Prices and Terms of Sale*
- A. Types of pricing situations.
- B. Influence of selected product characteristics.
- C. Influence of selected channel characteristics.
- D. Influence of bargaining power characteristics.
- E. Influence of selected legal factors.

    VI. *Delivery Arrangements*

    VII. *Other Elements*
- A. Negotiation of legal transfer of title and related legal factors.
- B. Installation and servicing.
- C. Post-sales relationships.

Determination of Product Assortments

The determination of which products the wholesale middlemen will purchase is primarily a decision as to the product assortments which, in turn, will be offered for sale. Of key significance are the end-use characteristics of the product involved, the existence (or lack thereof) of merchandising strategy, and the influence of channel structure and channel competition.

End-use characteristics

The end-use characteristics of the product have an important, immediate influence on what is purchased. If the product is an industrial good, and is to be used in further production either as a basic raw material or as a semiprocessed or fully processed component, the determination of what to buy is fairly well linked to the production specifications of the manufacturer involved. The tie-in is accentuated, of course, by the degree of control the manufacturer exercises over the buying wholesale middleman through one or another form of integration.

If the industrial good involved is a major installation equipment, the buying is dominated mainly by (a) technical ordering according to specification and by (b) some form of capital budgeting on the part of the using business. For all other types of industrial goods, the buying aspects of product assortments are very closely related to the basic conditions outlined in Chapter 7 so far as choice of specialization versus general line is concerned, and assortment in width versus assortments in depth.

For agricultural goods, the selection of product assortments by buying wholesale middlemen is dominated, in the initial instance, by what the combination of technical skill, natural resources, and the weather conditions make available. Except for an occasional exception of where a cannery, through careful plant breeding, may be able to develop a particular strain of fruit or vegetable for canning or freezing, the buying middleman must make decisions, given the quantity and quality of available output, in terms of which farmer's output to handle, how many varieties to handle, the quality levels to be featured, and, where applicable, whether or not to introduce or adapt the type of packages involved.[4] Certain categories of agricultural products permit more assortment specialization than do other categories. The grains, livestock, poultry, dairy products, tobacco, and the fibres are all obvious examples of products permitting specialization. Because of the volume of sales involved, certain vegetables such as potatoes and onions permit specialization.

[4] To the extent that the products are to be processed, the discussion of basic raw materials in the preceding paragraph becomes applicable.

But for most fresh fruits and vegetables, in general, the considerations underlying assortments in depth versus assortments in breadth once more becomes applicable. Under certain conditions, middlemen may influence assortments by dealing exclusively with certain producers. This type of exclusive representation becomes dominant when related either to selected quality factors or to the existence of cooperative marketing associations at both shipping and terminal market points.

The widest range of possible product assortments exists in connection with manufactured consumers' goods moving through wholesale channels. On the one hand, because of the manufacturer's desire to control the entire channel for reasons already discussed, there exists the exclusive marketing agreements whereby, in any given trading area, only a single wholesale middleman may handle the brand of product in question. At the opposite extreme there exist opportunities for wholesale middlemen to buy wide assortments because of the frequency with which such products are purchased and because of the number of actual or potential customers. In between exists a wide range of product assortment combinations building on these two extremes. As a result, wholesale middlemen have to consider many factors either already discussed in Chapter 7 or to be discussed later under buying policies.

Important in the selection of assortments is the extent to which the wholesale middleman already in business maintains accurate data pertaining to the product during past sales periods.[5] In addition, it is to be assumed that he would have accurate records as to the volume of sales lost because of failure to carry selected product items in stock. Included in such records would be a listing of products requested by customers but which the middleman did not stock. To such data dealing with past experience must be added such available knowledge as to future expectancies, both as to continued rate of customer acceptance of existing product assortments and as to the availability and expected customer acceptability of new products. All of this assumes, where applicable, that each wholesale middleman has accurate knowledge of his customers and their product assortment needs. For the wholesale middleman entering a type of operation and kind of business for the first time, some of the considerations discussed in Chapter 9 are applicable.

One final aspect of this element of product assortments in relation to end use should be noted, namely, the differentiation between the

---

[5] This discussion should be related to the later section in this chapter dealing with merchandise budgets.

roles of the wholesale middleman in intermediate use and final use position. The intermediate end-use product assortments represent the more complex aspects illustrated in the funnel concept. In this position, the wholesale middleman frequently plays an anticipatory role in the product assortments purchased and offered for sale. His success is measured, accordingly, by the extent to which the decisions made about product assortments maximize sales potentialities.

Product assortments in the final end-use position take on two distinct forms. In the first form, by reasons of vertical integration in the channel, product assortments immediately are related to, and become a function of, the production schedules, as noted before, which utilize them either as primary or secondary raw materials, or as semiprocessed or fully processed components. In the second form, by reasons of backward vertical integration, retail organizations are able to relate directly product assortments purchased at the wholesale level to the needs of the respective component retail units as related, in turn, to past and/or anticipated demands of each unit's ultimate consumers.

Influence of merchandising strategy

The extent to which any given wholesale middleman, in executing the buying function, shows innovative as against static tendencies in product assortments is an indication of his attitude towards the function of merchandising in its product strategy aspects, as discussed in the preceding chapter. The range of alternatives in product strategy, including the packaging aspects, is also included in that discussion. These considerations affect this element of buying only to the extent that the individual wholesale middleman concerned elects to engage in one or more forms of such product strategy.

Influence of channel structure

The relationship between channel structure and product assortments also has been discussed before. Integrated channels, involving control by the producing link, invariably restrict the product assortments offered to those which the producing unit has elected to produce.[6] The indirect channels, on the other hand, offer all the possibilities of product assortments described in earlier discussions. The competitive struggle for managerial control of the channel invariably brings in its wake widened product assortments through the increase in the types of alternative channels. This is true especially by means of

[6] In a few instances, noncompeting items produced by other firms may also be stocked.

distributors' brands and scrambled product-assortment arrangements. Accordingly, the decisions of particular wholesale middlemen about channels and channel control do influence, in turn, decisions about type of product assortments.

Influence of other variables

Not infrequently, wholesale middlemen's product assortment decisions are influenced by the availability of "special buys." These special buys usually consist roughly of two types: (1) Those represented merely by the availability at very favorable prices and terms of purchase of product assortments already stocked; and (2) those represented by the availability of brands and of quality levels ordinarily not included in the middlemen's product assortments. The policy aspects involved will be discussed in a later section.

Another variable which may have rather important consequences on product assortments involves the decision of wholesale middlemen to engage in multitype operations. The decision to engage in multitype operations has two important effects on the performance of the buying function, especially in the determination of product assortments:

Effect 1. It may introduce the buying function for part of the middleman's multitype operation; e.g., as in the case of an agent middleman also becoming a merchant wholesaler for some transactions.

Effect 2. It may either broaden or narrow product assortments for part of the middleman's multitype operation.

The broadening aspects in effect 2 originate from the entry of the middleman into multikinds of business by virtue of multitype operations. The narrowing aspects originate from a situation such as the operation of a cash-and-carry division within a regular grocery wholesaler's establishment.

Finally, legal and governmental factors may affect directly the middleman's decisions about product assortments apart from the influence on brands through trade-mark legislation. One such influence may arise from the legal restrictions on products which may be sold. Such restrictions may be absolute in that they may provide for the sale of such products as alcoholic beverages and narcotics only through licensed and bonded distributors; or the restrictions may provide for a complete government monopoly in the channel. Another illustration is represented by the use of government rationing, quota, and price controls for strategic goods during emergency periods. Payments to agricultural producers to reduce or restrict volumes of output of particular products, or the regulation of quantities shipped, represent a third aspect. From the positive side, government research or encouragement of research may be an important contributory factor both in the discovery of new products and in the improvement of existing ones.

Determination of the Source of Supply of Product Assortments

The determination of product assortments to purchase may or may not solve simultaneously the problem of source. In addition, some wholesale middlemen in the channel may or may not be faced with the necessity of evaluating the alternatives of buying directly from the source as compared with purchases from one or more types of wholesale middlemen. For certain kinds of products, the nature of the product and its channel structure may permit only one source arrangement. The problem of determination of source is complicated by the extent to which the channel structure, in relation to the kind of product, does or does not permit individual sources to be maintained through the channel.

Types of source determination situations

Before discussing the process of actual evaluation of particular sources of supply of product assortments, it may be valuable to outline and discuss briefly the various types of source-determination situations. These situations may be outlined as follows:

I. *Determination by Direct Channel Connection with Producer*
   A. Producer's initiative.
      1. Direct selling through manufacturers' sales branches, manufacturers' sales offices, cooperative marketing associations, etc.
      2. Use of exclusive wholesale-market franchise agreements with middlemen.
   B. Middlemen's initiative.
      1. Direct purchase from producer.
      2. Integration with manufacturer from production of distributors' brands.

II. *Determination by Indirect Channel Connections with Producers*
   A. Organized wholesale markets.
      1. Merchant wholesale middlemen contacts.
      2. Agent wholesale middlemen contacts.
   B. Unorganized wholesale markets.
      1. Merchant wholesale middleman contacts.
      2. Agent wholesale middleman contacts.

Under each of these headings, variable situations exist as to the extent to which the products assortments involved may or may not be effective source identification. In the case of agricultural products, identification of source may be accomplished by virtue of the channels utilized as well as by the labeling of containers, etc. For the special case of grains, quality determinations may replace source identification in importance. For semimanufactured and manufactured goods, identification as to source centers in the use of brand names affixed to the product. In unusual cases, such as petroleum and petroleum products, identification may be maintained through the transportation medium, e.g., barges and pipelines, until further processing and identification take place.

Determination of particular sources

Given the above types of source-determination situations, the individual middleman has the problem, then, of evaluating particular sources and reaching a final decision as to which source to use. The evaluation process for a new wholesale middleman has been discussed in detail in Chapter 9. All that has to be added at this point is the need for wholesale middlemen to continue this evaluation process at frequent intervals. As their experience with sources accumulates, and as they watch the entry or exit of sources, the middlemen will find it necessary to reappraise their earlier evaluations.

Continuity of source versus use of changing sources

Where exclusive franchise agreements exist, the middleman, for reasons discussed elsewhere, has obviously committed himself to a policy of continuity of source. In the absence of such agreements, a middleman may continue to have continuity of source by favoring a policy of stocking only well-known manufacturers' brands or by featuring his controlled distributors' brands (provided he maintains continuity of source and quality).

A quite different situation is found where, as in the case of grain, producer identification is subordinated to grade specification. In many instances, wholesale middlemen will have, accordingly, highly changing relationships with sources. Whether or not continuity of ultimate source is maintained, in the case where one type of middleman obtains his purchases from other wholesale middlemen, depends, in part, on the policies of the selling middlemen. Emphasis upon "best buys" may lead, ultimately, to purchases from ever-shifting sources.

Continuity of sources, apart from the exclusive arrangements noted above, depends also on the presence or absence of aggressive producer selling activities in the channel. The use of highly successful advertising, together with other marketing tactics, may so establish a source in the channel as to secure a wide and continuing patronage of buyers. Similarly, the use of resale price maintenance by the manufacturer may secure the continuing patronage of those wholesale middlemen who subscribe to such pricing policies. But the existence of these pricing conditions may stimulate other groups of buying middlemen, on the other hand, to locate alternative sources (including distributors' brands) wherever possible. Rapid change in producers' marketing policies, other than those mentioned, may further stimulate changing sources among buying wholesale middlemen.

Multiple versus single sources

The question of purchases from multiple as opposed to single sources is closely related to the preceding discussion. Involved are questions such as the following:

1. What are the comparative ranges of alternatives open to the middlemen?
2. What are the comparative reputations of the alternative sources?
3. What will be the effects of diversifying as against concentrating purchases on prices and terms of sale?
4. What are the effects on continuity of stocks and stability of quality specifications?
5. What effects will concentration on a single source have on the type of product assortments and on estimated potential sales?
6. Will there be any effects on the managerial struggle for channel control?

Multiple sources offer greater possibilities to wholesale middlemen for variety in product assortments, for wider alternatives as to prices and terms of sale, and for securing more varied adaptations to future channel situations. They permit the buying middlemen to exercise more positive control actions in the channel. For these substantial benefits, the buying middleman must give up the security which goes with the use of a single source, as well as the tie-in with the reputation and market position of the producer. If the volume purchased from a single source is significant, the buying middleman may secure such additional benefits as priorities in times of stock shortages, and special marketing assistance.

Foreign versus domestic sources

This factor has great variability of effect depending on the type of product, the stage of market development and penetration, the extent of government barriers to imports, and the attitude of domestic producers. In some business instances, the use of foreign supply sources is standard, namely, those of importer, import agent, or the manufacturers' sales branches and sales offices of foreign producers. For some domestic middlemen, the use of foreign sources may leave the avenue open in the channel for broadening or extending in depth product assortments. A case in point would be imported grocery items, especially specialty items. For other middlemen, the foreign source may be the strategic instrument for capitalizing on a current aspect of the fashion cycle, e.g., certain types of modern furniture and clothing. In still other cases, it may become the device of a wholesale middleman to secure entry into the channel because of the exclusive distributorship policies of certain domestic producers (note the foreign automobiles as a classic example).

Many times, the availability of imports is instrumental in furthering the use of either highly price-competitive products, at one extreme, or of highly unique products, at the other extreme.[7] Increasingly, in the industrial goods area, foreign sources have been securing entry into the domestic market on the basis of competitive prices, quality levels, and the availability of the products. In some cases domestic ownership of foreign manufacturing facilities has served to open domestic markets to foreign products.[8] In some cases, superior workmanship and lower prices of foreign components lead to their incorporation into the domestic finished products, e.g., camera lenses, scientific instruments, and watch movements.

[7] French wines represent both categories depending on the variety, the shipper or distributor, and the age of the wine.

[8] Note, for example, General Motors distributorship of the Opel Rekord automobile; Chrysler Motors distributorship of the French Simca; and Ford's distributorship of the English Ford.

Determination of How Much to Purchase

Certain policy aspects of this buying element will be discussed separately in later sections. This section is designed to develop a prelude to such policy discussions based on the influence of the merchandise budget; on the influence of middlemen's inventory policies; on the influence of selected financial factors; on the influence of the speculative factor; and on the alternatives of buying outright versus leasing.[9]

The influence of the merchandise budget

The determination of how much to purchase, following the determination of product assortments and sources, involves the assignment, primarily, of quantitative weights to the qualitative elements involved. Whether or not the merchandise budget will be used in a formal sense depends, in part, on the availability of accounting and statistical data and, in part, on the type of wholesale middleman operation and the temperament of the management involved. Middlemen operating in organized wholesale markets would be expected to have far less use for formal merchandise budgets than those operating in other types of wholesale markets. Middlemen acting as exclusive distributors, and with quotas determined by the producing source, would have far less need for formal budgets than other types. Finally, those wholesale middlemen with complicated product assortments would appear to require more extensive merchandise budgets than those with highly specialized or simple assortments.

Where applicable, the merchandise budget encompasses, in its fullest form, the following:

I. *Data of Past Sales*
   A. Total sales: by daily, weekly, monthly, and annual increments.
   B. Breakdowns of (*A*).
      1. By product lines, where necessary.
      2. By geographical divisions, where necessary.
      3. By customer-size categories.
      4. By profitability positions.
      5. By market penetration positions.

[9] It is recognized that the last component involves important legal aspects as well as marketing aspects. But its main marketing impacts need to be considered with this element.

C. List of products requested but not stocked.

D. Estimates of sales volumes lost because of failure to stock items or because of out-of-stock conditions.

II. *Data of Past Inventories*

A. Average inventories, with appropriate dates.

B. Stock turnover data.

C. Sales-stock ratios.

D. Relationship of (*B*) and (*C*) to performance data in (I).

III. *Estimated Future Sales*

A. Products presently stocked, by the same categories as in (I *A*) and (I *B*).

B. Products expected to be added, by the same categories as in (I *A*) and (I *B*).

IV. *Establishment of Purchase Budgets*

A. By product categories and price, style, color, size, etc.

B. By sources of categories (*A*).

These components of the merchandise budgets give each wholesale middleman's management a basis upon which to give direction to, and control of, the firm's buying activities. An important characteristic of the use of such budgets is the reconciliation of actual sales experience with each set of estimates, corresponding upward or downward adjustments of purchases as warranted by such analysis, and an explanation of the relationships as found. Important, too, is the control element inherent in such budgets, especially as the number of products to be purchased increases and as the number of personnel involved in the buying function expands. Finally, all of these aspects serve the important role of sharpening the management's analysis and reformulation of buying policies.

Much of the accuracy and detail involved in these merchandise budgets are dependent upon the nature of the middlemen's accounting system, the presence or absence of up-to-date systems for compiling detailed statistical data of the types noted above, and the availability of personnel with adequate technical training who can execute the types of forecasts and analyses needed. In addition, greater or lesser use of such budgets will depend on the philosophy of the management.

The influence of the middlemen's inventory policies

Where the wholesale middleman takes physical possession of the products purchased,[10] an important determinant of how much to buy is the middleman's management of inventories. This subject is so

[10] Or, in the case of certain types of agent middlemen, of goods to be sold.

complicated that discussion will be deferred until the appropriate sections of the next chapter.

The influence of financial factors

The merchandise budget is a guide to the financial arm of the wholesale middleman's operation as to how many dollars of working resources will be needed at stipulated time periods to make purchases, and how rapidly these capital resources will be replenished by the rate and amount of anticipated sales.   Financial considerations will govern the extent to which buyers can take full advantage of special buys or of purchases in quantity lots as against small lots.   Furthermore, financial considerations will be one of the elements to consider in whether or not to resort to speculative buying from time to time.

The influence of the speculative factor

Certain types of organized wholesale markets arrange for the systematic buying and selling of speculative contracts.   In addition, the combination of spot (cash) and future contracts may make it possible to use hedging in relation to the management of inventories. For other types of organized and nonorganized markets, anticipated price changes and/or product shortages may accentuate the use of forward buying or other speculative aspects.   In addition, the availability of adequate storage space has an important influence.   All of these, again, are so complicated and involve such important policy decisions that a more detailed discussion will be deferred until later.

Leasing versus outright purchase

This problem arises mainly in the purchase of certain types of major installation (capital) and accessory equipment.   Certain standardized considerations favoring the use of each have been advanced as follows:[11]

  I. *Considerations Favoring Leasing*
     A. May be more economical than outright purchase, depending upon the terms of the lease and the length of period of use.
     B. Permits product experimentation in use until its suitability is determined.
     C. Bridges an interim period of need pending availability either of an expected new product or of an improved design of an existing product.

[11] Aljian (ed.), *op. cit.,* pp. 15–19 ff.

    D. Permits activities to take place under circumstances where the lack of adequate financial resources may prohibit outright purchase.

    E. Possible tax advantages.

II. *Considerations Favoring Outright Purchase*

    A. Because of the leasing arrangements, equipment may have to be returned on short notice or at a critical time period; extension of lease may be very costly or impossible.

    B. Avoids extra transportation costs and dismantling and loading costs.

    C. Capital investment aspects of outright purchase may have important favorable financial and tax aspects.

Other factors should be noted. Where the producer has been given a monopoly, and in the absence of government intervention, leasing of equipment may be the only alternative open to the prospective user. The lessor, under certain circumstances, may attempt to minimize his union problems by leasing, e.g., delivery service arrangements; and better, if not cheaper, equipment servicing may result from leasing as against ownership. On the other hand, the advantages of leasing may be offset, in part, by purchasing used products rather than new ones. Note, in this connection, the availability of wholesale middlemen dealing in such used equipment.

Determination of Product Branding

Apart from certain policy matters either discussed earlier or to be discussed in the next chapter, there are certain general considerations which need to be noted. If the wholesale middleman involved is controlled by the producer, the matter of product branding becomes related completely to the producer's branding policies. The factor of branding is influenced significantly by whether the product is a component of some other product or is a final use product in its own right; the relative value and frequency of use of the product; the degree of channel control reflected in terms of the brand involved; and the number and importance of brands of the product category already on the market.[12]

[12] Although the usual marketing arrangement is to emphasize branding in relationship to selling elements and policies of producers, the sequence of the discussion of the wholesaling sector requires a reversal of the orthodox sequence.

Resumé of reasons for brands

From the viewpoint of the buying function of wholesale middlemen, there are two significant aspects of branding: (1) The influence of well-established producers' brands on the middleman's selection of product assortments, and (2) the purchase of products which contain, instead, the distributors' brands, or some integrated equivalent of these. The manufacturer's use of brands[13] reflects the basic marketing objectives of control over the market through the channel and/or greater freedom of and control in price determination through the channel. With respect to control over the market through the channel, the usual motivations include: the extent to which branding insures steadier demand, which leads, in turn, to economies of planned and steady production; making effective the company's advertising and personal selling programs through product identification; aiding the manufacturer in maintaining contacts with consumers throughout the channel, including the use of customer brand preference as a leverage device for exerting influence in the channel.

So far as the pricing aspects are concerned, the following motivations may be advanced from the producer's point of view: (1) To the extent that producer branding achieves successful product differentiation in the minds of users, some price advantage will accrue to the producer; (2) customer preference for any brand may lead, in turn, to attempts by the producer to keep wholesale middlemen's margins at a minimum; (3) producers may not always change the prices of branded items as frequently as for unbranded products; and (4) branded products can only qualify for resale price maintenance protection under existing Federal legislation.

Some of the above objectives are applicable, also, to distributors' brands. A large-scale corporate chain may have decided to adopt distributors' brands from the very beginning of its business history. Similarly, a broker or an orthodox wholesaler may have used distributors' brands since his earliest operations. But, in many cases, as has been noted in the discussion of the managerial struggle for channel control, the wholesale middlemen's use of distributors' brands frequently is in retaliation to the type of control either sought after or actually obtained by the producer. The policy implications will be discussed in a later chapter.

---

[13] The term "brand" is used here in its marketing sense to reflect any better word, name, symbol, or device, or any combination of these used to identify the source of manufacture or distribution of a product, or the source of a particular service.

Selected technical problems

Apart from important policy implications, there are certain technical problems which affect the use of brands and trade-marks in the wholesaling sector.[14] Some of these problems involve such communication recognitions as shortness, simplicity, ease of recognition, pronunciation and recall by the reader or purchaser, and adaptability to presentation in company advertising. Other problems concern the extent to which the brand serves the purposes of (a) distinguishing the product through the channel; (b) identifying the producer and/or manufacturer; and (c) where applicable, identifying a family of products. A third set of problems centers around the ability of the brand's owner to protect the brand as a trade-mark either under Federal or state law. Again, the policy implications of some of these technical problems will be deferred until a later section.

Factors influencing branding

In concluding this element of buying, brief mention should be made of some selected factors which influence wholesale middlemen's decisions about branding. To the extent that either producers' or distributors' brands constitute an important part of a wholesale middleman's product assortment strategy, to that extent will his buying activities be affected. The nature of the product affects its adaptability to branding, especially as the wholesale middleman's position in the channel is concerned. As noted, if the product is a component of some other product, greater difficulties may be related to branding efforts than otherwise would be the case. If the product does not reach the ultimate user in its original package, then branding may be less effective than in the case where the package is preserved throughout the entire channel. The importance of the product to intermediate and final users may affect brand effectiveness. Finally, under product factors, the marketing history of the product may affect the future effectiveness of its brands.

In addition to these considerations, price and the nature of the channels utilized affect both the possibilities of using brands and the choice between producers' and distributors' brands. Finally, the market area in which sales are realized, the total volume of expected sales, and the financial strength of the producer and/or wholesale

[14] For a full discussion of these as well as other parts of the problem, see D. M. Phelps, *Planning the Product* (Homewood, Ill.: Richard D. Irwin, Inc., 1947), Chapter V.

middlemen will affect the use and development of brands by the amount of dollars that will be available for intensive promotion.

Negotiation of Prices and Terms of Sale

Types of pricing situations

From the point of view of the buying activities of wholesale middlemen, a wide range of pricing situations is to be found as follows:

I. *Determination of Prices in Organized Wholesale Markets*
   Buying wholesale middlemen engage directly in price negotiations and determination.

II. *Producer-Determined Wholesale Prices*
   A. Through resale price maintenance.
   B. Through legal monopolies.
   C. Through monopolistic structure of the industry, including patent controls.
   D. Through use of exclusive distributorships.
   E. Through other price policies as discussed in Chapters 15–16.

III. *Wholesale-Middleman-Determined Wholesale Prices*
   A. By product specifications.
   B. By brand control.
   C. By superiority of bargaining position.

IV. *Retail-Middleman-Determined Wholesale Prices*
   A. By product specifications.
   B. By brand control.
   C. By superiority of bargaining position.

The detailed discussion of the above will be integrated with the later discussion of pricing, price policies, and terms of sale.

Influence of selected product characteristics

First among the product characteristics to be discussed are the general quality-level factors. Assuming that the wholesale middleman has any policy whatsoever regarding quality, it would be expected that, in the determination of wholesale prices to be paid, some arrangement of systematic price differentials would result according to quality levels. Where the determination of prices takes place in organized wholesale markets, these systematic relationships would be more apparent than under nonorganized wholesale market price determinations.

For industrial goods, other than those susceptible to grade determinations, the use of technical specifications may be assumed to
result in prices which bear some relationship to costs involved plus
some concept of mark-up. Highly patented goods introduce elements
of monopolistic pricing which may bear no relationship at all to
quality and cost factors. Consumers' high-style goods have some of
the same elements inherent in their prices. Other aspects of product
characteristics must be delayed until the complete discussion of
pricing.

Influence of selected channel characteristics

Assuming the movement of a product or family of products in interstate commerce, with a given pattern of channel structure, and further
assuming compliance of all linkages in the channel with the Robinson-
Patman Act, buyers at the wholesale level will have available a series
of wholesale discounts from a basic producer's price applicable to
quantities purchased, functions performed, qualities and brands
purchased, and related variables.

On the other hand, the use by the manufacturer of a completely
controlled channel will result in a series of prices similarly controlled
by the manufacturer. *Accordingly, the nature of the channel is the
dominant feature which determines how much freedom wholesale
buyers or their representatives have in negotiating satisfactory wholesale prices.* Those buying wholesale middlemen desiring greater
pricing freedom will adjust, accordingly, to appropriate channel positions. Conversely, if security and other benefits are desired rather
than pricing freedom, the buying middlemen will make alternative
channel arrangement decisions.

Influence of bargaining power characteristics

If much buying price determination is the result of the relative
bargaining power strength of the buying and selling linkages in the
channel, it follows that the personal characteristics of these bargaining parties are important. In an auction market for agricultural
products, the auctioneer matches his knowledge of market conditions
and of the individual characteristics of each potential buyer present
against the reverse matching process by each buyer of the auctioneer
and of the competing buyers present.

The buyer representing a department store or a mail-order company,
when negotiating with a manufacturer or his representative, must know
when to use the pressure of the money appeal by placing a pile of
"greenbacks" on the desk, so to speak, and when to use the "soft"

approach in order to maintain important supplier goodwill and continuity-of-supply relationships. Under many buying situations, as already noted, there may be little or no opportunity for effective use of competing bargaining power positions. Rather, the monopolistic structure of the industry, as evidenced in the channel, will lead to inequality of bargaining power positions. But even in these cases, the parties with superior bargaining power positions must be careful that such power does not lead ultimately to middlemen's dissatisfactions, and resulting upheavals in channel structures.

Influence of selected legal factors

Apart from the basic law of contracts and agencies, government control is evident at many points in the determination of wholesale prices. Pending fuller discussion in later chapters, these may be listed as follows: (1) The pricing control aspects of the basic antitrust laws; (2) the important specific effects of the Robinson-Patman Act; (3) "fair trade" and "unfair trade" practices laws; (4) regulation of organized wholesale markets; (5) government agricultural price-support and marketing-agreement programs; (6) government patent and franchise monopolies; and (7) government grading, standardization, and technical product specifications programs.

Delivery Arrangements

Brief mention should be made of certain aspects of delivery as they affect buying at wholesale. One pertains to the variable arrangements affecting the assumption of transportation costs and related drayage and unloading expenses. Wide ranges in responsibility are to be found, and the negotiations of terms of purchase are very significant in this respect. A second aspect pertains to the influence of the quality of delivery service on the quality of the product upon its arrival. This is obvious, of course, in the movement of perishables, but it is equally important in the shipment of highly technical industrial goods. Note, for example, the highly technical and costly delivery problems involved in the shipment of the 200-inch telescopic lens from point of manufacture in Corning, New York, to point of installation in the Mt. Palomar Observatory in southern California. A final aspect has to do with the relationship of the delivery arrangements to inventory policies of wholesale middlemen (as these are discussed in the following chapter).

Other Elements

Negotiation of legal transfer of title and related legal factors

The briefness of this discussion should in no way diminish the importance of this component element. Many wholesale transactions in organized markets do not involve written formal sales contracts, but the importance of the supporting legal aspects is not thereby reduced. In the sale of expensive industrial goods with highly complicated terms of sale, especially in the use of short-term, intermediate, or long-term financing, the best of legal knowledge will have to be used in preparing contracts of sale. Similarly, expert legal knowledge is necessary in the preparation of leases or in purchases made according to lowest written bidding procedures.

But these are the legal aspects related to contracts of sale and the related terms. Legal advice will be necessary in the selection, registration, and protection of trade-marks involved, especially where the distributor is making purchases as the basis for his brands. The legality of prices and terms of sale under the Robinson-Patman Act or other government controls usually requires specialized expert opinions.

Installation and servicing

For highly technical and mechanical products, the responsibility for installation and servicing becomes an important function in buying. The wholesale middleman acting as an intermediary between producer and ultimate user has a delicate problem of deciding (*a*) whether or not the producer's supposed superiority in know-how should be the dominant factor in installation and servicing, and (*b*) whether or not to add his guarantee to that of the producer. These alternatives may be modified greatly by the producer's inability to do the complete job of installation and servicing, and by the wholesale middleman's policies of featuring his own brands of products. Another important element, apart from direct installation and servicing, is the function of the wholesale middleman to maintain adequate inventories of repair and replacement parts.

Post-sale relationships

Wholesale middlemen have two sets of post-sales responsibilities. On the one hand, they have to provide for their producers a continuous flow of information about market performance of products purchased or otherwise handled by them in the channel. Types of information included in this category are receptivity towards design, suggestions for improvement, complaints, and the like. When the middlemen sell to customers, in turn, the various products purchased or handled on an agency basis, they create a second group of post-sales relationships with these customers. In addition to the installation, servicing, and maintenance of stocks of parts, as discussed previously, such post-sales relationships may include information about new uses, new designs, and related items, as well as securing customer reactions about prices, quality, and performance of products.

QUESTIONS AND PROBLEMS

1. Why, in your opinion, have the breadth and complexity of buying policies and elements in the wholesaling sector been generally underestimated and not completely understood?
2. Of what do the breadth and complexity of buying policies and elements consist?
3. Do you agree with the classification of types of buying situations presented in Chapter 12? What are the salient characteristics of each type?
4. What are the significant variables which determine the selection of product assortments by wholesale middlemen?
5. How are the variables you have discussed in (4) related to the discussion of product assortments presented in Chapter 7?
6. Describe, in detail, each type of source of supply determination situation.
7. Under what circumstances should a wholesale middleman depend upon continuity of source? upon the use of changing sources?
8. What are the relative advantages and disadvantages of multiple versus single sources of supply?
9. There has been much argument in the business press of late of the purchases of foreign goods (especially industrial goods) by American businesses. What is the source of the aggravation? What is your position in the argument?
10. What are the main distinctions between the quantitative and qualitative aspects of how much to purchase?
11. What is a merchandise budget? How is it formulated?
12. What other forces besides the merchandise budget influence how much to buy?
13. Why should wholesale middlemen prefer to have their own branded merchandise in preference to the manufacturers' brands?
14. How do decisions about branding affect the general framework of buying decisions? To what extent are the branding decisions influenced by the general framework of buying decisions?
15. What are the various types of pricing situations from the buying point of view?

16. Critically evaluate the following: "Accordingly, the nature of the channel is the dominant feature which determines how much freedom wholesale buyers, or their representatives, have in negotiating satisfactory wholesale prices."

17. What other factors besides the nature of the channel influence pricing arrangements from the buying point of view?

18. Under what circumstances do the remaining elements of the buying function assume significance? minor importance?

CHAPTER INTEGRATING ASSIGNMENTS

1. Based upon the discussion in the chapter, prepare a comprehensive list of the component elements of the buying function. On the basis of this list, indicate for each type of wholesale middlemen: (a) whether or not the type ordinarily assumes responsibility for the element; (b) whether, if the type does assume responsibility, the performance is complete or partial; and (c) whether or not the type of middleman is able to be a major factor in the negotiations.

2. Relate the detailed types of buying situations, type by type, to the nature of the funnel in the wholesaling sector and to the nature of the channel structure.

3. Compare critically the relative complexity of the buying function under conditions of one-phase versus multiphase buying operations in the channel.

13

Buying Elements and Policies (Continued)

The preceding chapter has presented and discussed in detail the component elements of the buying function as it is related to the wholesale middleman's level. The groundwork was established for the discussion of buying policies to be included in this chapter. Only a summary statement of buying policies as they relate to product assortments and brand policy need be presented here in view of the preceding discussions. Accordingly, the main substance of this chapter will be a discussion of the management of inventories by wholesale middlemen.

Summary Statement: Product Assortment Policies[1]

The main components of product assortment policies which need to be summarized here concern the question, first of all, of whether or not to handle product assortments. If the policy determination is in the affirmative, then additional decision has to be made about specialization versus breadth in assortments; assortments in width versus assortments in breadth; and unorthodox assortments versus traditional assortments.

[1] The framework upon which this summary statement is based is contained mainly in parts of Chapters 7 and 11. The meaning of policies as used in this chapter is based upon the pertinent section in Chapter 8.

Assortments versus no assortments

In its basic sense, that is, whether or not the wholesale middleman handles inventories, the fundamental policy decision is made identically at the same time the entrepreneur involved reaches a decision as to the type of operation and kind of business to enter. All of the factors mentioned in Chapter 9 are applicable. The benefits of exclusive dealership arrangements also are applicable here and should be kept in mind as previously discussed.

Of significance also in the formulation of the policy decision is the extent to which the availability of grade specifications (as in the case of grain marketed in organized commodity exchanges) reduces the possibilities of varied product assortments in favor of the skill of wholesale middlemen in negotiating satisfactory pricing arrangements either on the buying or selling side. In the case of many other types of agent middlemen and of drop shippers, the product assortment offered will be identical with and representative of the assortment decisions of the producer represented.

Specialization versus breadth in assortments

Some aspects of this policy decision are related closely to the preceding. But there are other aspects, as evidenced in the discussion of specialization of wholesale middlemen in Chapter 3, in the discussion of general line versus specialization in Chapter 7, and in the factors influencing selection of types of operation and kind of business noted already in Chapter 9. As noted in Chapter 7, general-line operations are related to such variables as the structure of individual products found in any given line of business, to the types of wholesale middlemen's customers and their assortment needs, to channel structure, and to the total sales potential available from alternative product assortments.

Specialization, on the other hand, is related to predominance of brand position, to benefit from nonprice as against intensive price competition, to possible territorial protection from other wholesale middlemen in the channel by the producer, and to special point-of-sale adaptation of advertising. However, not all attempts at specialization of product assortments imply necessarily the existence of exclusive wholesale distributorship arrangements. Specialization may also stem from depth-of-market considerations as well as from attempts, through product assortments, to differentiate one type of wholesale middleman operation from another.

Breath versus depth in product assortments

Again, breadth versus depth in product assortments is related closely to the preceding discussions. Margin considerations, the nature of the customers serviced by the middleman, the traditional channel arrangements for the products involved, and the range of available products in the particular kind of business are among the most important influencing variables that have been discussed. Financial costs of carrying large-scale inventories and the ability of salesmen to sell adequately all items stocked also are significant. In particular kinds of business, such as food, the changing structures of customer needs and buying habits are of great importance.

Scrambled versus traditional assortments

At the wholesale middlemen's level the continuous battle between the orthodox and the unorthodox is carried on so far as product assortments are concerned. It is the wholesale middleman who acts as the important catalytic agent in preserving or changing product assortments, with various types of operation having highly varying roles of influence within this general role of importance.

Brand Policy

The essence of the policy aspects of branding has been presented in detail in the preceding chapter. All that needs to be repeated here is the role of the buying wholesale middleman in accumulating product assortments, either in acting as a "passive" transmitter of brands controlled by producers or retail middlemen through the channel or by being an active force in establishing and marketing his own brands through such channels, or compromising by incorporating combinations of producers' and distributors' brand categories. In making such policy decisions and weighing the variables discussed previously, the wholesale middleman must consider also the effects on product assortments.

Inventory Management: General Aspects

General nature of wholesale middlemen's inventories and inventory position

The strategic importance of wholesale middlemen's inventories are related to several factors: (1) The strategic intermediate importance in the channel as discussed in Chapter 1; (2) the various aspects of the funnel concept as related to this strategic intermediate importance; (3) the complex array of buying situations as outlined in the preceding chapters; and (4) the various aspects of product assortments. Especially important are the various types of products and product assortment situations as outlined in Chapter 7.

For purposes of the present discussion, the main point of emphasis has to do with buying situations involving only those types of whole-sale middlemen who actually own and physically possess inventories. It excludes the purchasing activities of manufacturers having directly owned and controlled purchasing departments, and those types of agent middlemen who take physical possession of product assortments to be bought and/or sold for the accounts of others.[2] Within these restrictions, the following inventory situations may be distinguished:

A. Time Variations

Type I—daily exhaustion of inventories. This type of inventory problem is to be found for wholesale middlemen stocking such highly perishable commodities as fresh fruits and vegetables, bakery products, etc. The essence of the inventory situation is such that the wholesale middlemen must estimate closely the size of daily inventories in order to eliminate carryovers so far as possible. Customer knowledge of carryovers will result either in absolute refusal to buy (as in the case of stale bakery goods), or in reduced price valuations for the carryovers (as in the instance of fresh fruits and vegetables). Wherever repricing or other aspects of aging enter into the inventory situation, the pressures of daily exhaustion of inventories are sharply reduced.

Type II—variable time rate exhaustion. This type of inventory situation results from the partial or complete elimination of the perishability factor, and from the introduction, in addition, of one or another type of product assortment situation with highly variable actual or potential rates of sale. The essence of the problem is the determination of: (*a*) the experience as to the varying time rates involved for each product category, and (*b*) the sizes of inventories needed to realize expected sales volumes and to prevent loss of sales because of out-of-stock condition.

Type III—variable time rate exhaustion, single-product category. This type is really a special case of type II, and occurs most

---

[2] Their inventory characteristics, however, may very well fit into the classification scheme used.

frequently when given product assortments have highly variable seasonal rates of use. Among other inventory problems, this type involves decisions as to whether or not to stock the product in "slow" seasons, and how far in advance and in what quantities to accumulate inventories for peak seasonal sales conditions.

B. Product Change Situations

Type IV—products sold without change. In these types of inventory situations, it is assumed that the wholesale middlemen involved in the channel do not change the names of the products, the packages, or the physical forms in which the product assortments are handled in the channel. Thus, the principal role of the wholesale middlemen becomes one of deciding on the product assortments to be carried, and to act as a regulating valve in the funnel so far as rates of flow are concerned.

Type V—products sold with change. In these inventory situations, the reverse of type IV takes place. Singly or in combination, the wholesale middlemen may change brand names, the nature of the package, or the characteristics of the product in some fundamental manner so far as shape, flavor, size, or related variables are concerned. The effect here is to increase the number of product assortment situations to those included in the classification scheme adopted in Chapter 7. In addition, it creates inventory problems as to how much of such changes to accomplish in advance of sales, and how much, conversely, to make to order.

Type VI—adaptation of inventory quantities. Apart from the alternatives noted in types IV and V, there is one important additional situation, namely, decisions as to whether or not to change the quantities in which product assortments are sold at wholesale. One subtype within this grouping assumes no change in the unit of sale, whatever that unit may be, although there may be time adaptations in the funnel. The other subtype assumes that the wholesale middleman will reduce the unit of outbound sale-per-product item below the unit of inbound purchase.

Where no changes are permitted to be made in the unit of sale, the effect is to simplify the inventory problem because split packages or loose goods are nonexistent, and because warehouse and order-filling handling times are thereby expedited. On the other hand, the unwillingness to adapt quantities sold reduces the range of product assortment alternatives and the varieties of customers that may be serviced.

Many of these types exist in a mixed situation so far as wholesale middlemen are concerned, so that no simple conclusions may be drawn about their inventory situations. When the varieties of product assortment situations are introduced, the complexity of the inventory situations becomes quite staggering. In addition, further complexities may be introduced when the range-of-customer and types-of-channel situations are considered.

Middlemen's inventory situation versus manufacturers' inventories

Many recent writings have dealt with a quantitative form of inventory theory applicable mainly to production situations. Since most of them are of book length, it obviously is impossible to do more than make passing references to them at this point in the discussion. What is of importance is to contrast some of the characteristics of the underlying manufacturers' inventory situations with those facing the wholesale middlemen. In the case of the quantitative models applicable to production inventories, assumed conditions consist mainly of one or a few products, systematically planned production schedules, and related information including such items as warehousing costs, production costs, inventory carrying charges, and a theoretical reference to waiting time and queuing.

For wholesale middlemen there are, to begin with, no production schedules. There may be available, as a partial substitute, more or less systematic schedules of demand, although the timing is in no way comparable to that involved in production schedules, and certainly less manipulatable by the middleman. Inventories built up for production schedules involve, typically, fewer categories of products than the inventories built up for wholesale middlemen, although there are some significant exceptions on both sides. The flow of inventories into a production schedule generally is at a constant rate and with specified quantities and qualities of product components. In the great majority of the wholesale middlemen situations, these conditions are highly exceptional. Finally, so far as some of the more significant differences are concerned, the inventory composition of a manufacturer is likely to remain fixed during a given model cycle. But, in the same time period, the inventories of wholesale middlemen usually undergo several product-assortment changes.

Meaning of inventory management

Inventory management by wholesale middlemen involves a combination of policy decisions and the coordinated use of inventory control devices designed to insure so far as possible, for each management unit, a planned relationship between the quantity and product composition of inventories and the management's merchandising policy objectives. It involves, among other things, systematic policies with respect to quantities to purchase; establishment of policies with respect to quality factors; and decisions about whether or not to use hedging or other forms of forward buying in relationship to the speculative elements involved in inventory accumulations. Finally, it involves the use of accounting and statistical tools for purposes of measuring the quantity and value of inventories at stipulated intervals, the rates of stock turnover, past and estimated, and the estimated relationships of stocks to sales.

From these policy decisions and control devices come the bases for securing a concept of budgeted balanced relationship between what is carried in stock and the realization of estimated sales and other marketing goals. These types of relationships furnish management with a guide to what is taking place, and how these are related to certain preconceived norms. In addition, they furnish a basis for discovering the salient reasons for any significant differences between actual and preconceived relationships.

Inventory Policies: Quantities to Purchase

The emphasis in the remainder of this chapter is on the policy aspects of inventory management from the point of view of the type of wholesale middlemen indicated in previous discussions in this chapter. From time to time, references may be made to useful techniques, but, in the main, these will not be discussed in any great detail.[3]

Determinants of purchase quantities

There is no fixed formula for determining how much inventory to purchase at any given time. Sharp differentiation is necessary, depending upon the type of wholesale middleman. For the manufacturers'

---

[3] References to some basic readings in which these techniques are discussed in detail are to be found in the pertinent bibliography.

sales branches where, technically, there is no real buying, the quantity ordered by any single sales branch at any given time is a function of: (1) its assigned sales quota for the time period; (2) the actual rate of sales; (3) the amount of warehouse space available; (4) delivery from the controlling manufacturer's factory (or factories) to the sales branch; and (5) the division of sale between standardized and made-to-order items. In addition, the controlling organization must determine how much money it plans to invest in inventories relative to alternative uses, and what the estimated value of orders are which may be lost because of incomplete inventories at any given point of time. If the products involved are mechanical in nature, an additional factor is the availability of repair and replacement parts in terms of service to customers. The integration between production schedules and sales branch inventories is highly important, but very much within the control of the management. The allocation of inventories between sales branches is affected, in addition to the variables noted above, by the number of producing points.

Now consider the illustration of the nonintegrated, orthodox, regular wholesaler. A further refinement involves differentiating between the problems of the grocery business and industrial goods kinds of business. From the point of view of the first case—that of the orthodox grocery wholesaler—the problem of purchase quantities is affected by variables stemming from the source side and those related to the customers' side. From the source side, the following determinants are of key importance: (1) The number of product items carried in stock; (2) the number of sources of such items, their locations and delivery schedules; (3) producer's policies as to full-line forcing; (4) pricing policies and terms of sale; and (5) minimum order sizes and sizes of shipping containers.

From the customers' side, the important variables are: (1) The frequencies of purchase of each product item or of product class groups; (2) average dollar size of orders and average number of product items per order; (3) delivery times and costs; and (4) number and frequency of fill-in orders. In addition to these two sets of considerations, the orthodox grocery wholesaler must consider his financial resources, the physical capacity of his warehouse, and whether or not to concentrate only on those product categories the sales of which meet certain minimum dollar-size or physical-size specifications. The structure of inbound and outbound transportation costs may be of some influence as well. In addition, the frequency with which new products appear is significant, as well as the policy of the middleman towards scrambled merchandising.

The introduction of the illustration of industrial goods involves some additional considerations by virtue of the nature of the product. First, the infrequency of purchase of some of the more expensive product lines leads to a policy of handling such items strictly on a consignment or on a drop shipment basis. This type of inventory handling will be influenced also by the prevalence of any significant amount of special order items. Second, the need for product servicing is assumed by the individual wholesaler, and involves the correlative responsibility for maintaining an adequate stock of repair and replacement parts as well as the willingness to handle emergency requests which may involve emergency air freight shipments from the manufacturing sources. Related to this second consideration is the question of how long to maintain reserve stocks once a given industrial good has ceased to be manufactured.[4]

Finally, a brief mention should be made of the similarity of exclusive franchise agreements or of agency middlemen arrangements to the sales branch example noted above. Mention should be made, also, of the special case of manufacturers' sales offices (without stocks). In such cases, two inventory policy possibilities may result: (1) The manufacturer can concentrate all stock at the factory (or factories) with the above influencing factors applying, or (2) strategic inventories of standardized products may be located at key public warehouses adjacent to sales offices, and orders for such items may be filled from these stocks.

Quantity versus small-lot purchases

Not all buying situations require a policy determination of whether or not to purchase in quantities. Although it is true that the funnel concept established the adaptation of quantity as an over-all characteristic, it was pointed out that, for certain types of wholesale middleman operations, no significant changes in quantity may be involved. Thus, in the case of very expensive, infrequently sold products, quantity purchasing would generally prove to be uneconomical. Additionally, custom-order products prohibit the use of quantity purchasing. Perishability, in certain cases, may prevent quantity purchasing, whether the element of perishability involves only a one-day use period or a fashion good with a limited time period of exclusiveness.

Nevertheless, once such special cases are eliminated, there are numerous instances where the wholesale middlemen involved in maintaining inventories have to take rather definite policy stands on the

---

[4] This consideration would apply as well to mechanical consumers' goods.

matter of whether or not to buy in quantities. The classical set of circumstances favoring quantity purchases by wholesale middlemen rests upon the following advantages:

1. The possible availability of quantity discounts, thus lowering unit costs, provided the capital invested, the carrying costs involved, and the risks of obsolescence do not offset such savings.
2. The wholesale middleman establishes himself as an important customer for a given producer's output by concentrating purchases and by securing such additional benefits, accordingly, as advertising allowances and/or help, preferential scheduling or order filling, and preferential delivery schedules.
3. The advantages arising from (1) and (2) may strengthen the competitive position of the wholesale middleman in the channel from the selling side.
4. Such quantity purchases may be a basic requirement for securing distributor's brands or other items in a given manufacturer's product assortment.
5. Some reductions in buying costs may accrue by virtue of reduced paper work and a lessening of the number of orders which have to be placed.

In addition, quantity purchases may facilitate the use of mechanical methods in the physical handling of inventories within the middleman's warehouse.

On the other hand, there are some types of weaknesses which may support a policy of small-lot purchases. As has been indicated, the advantages of quantity discounts may be offset by handling and storage costs. Periodic overcapacity conditions may result unless seasonal rental of additional warehouse space is contemplated. Dependency upon fewer sources may increase the middleman's future channel risks either because the source ultimately attempts to squeeze margins or by virtue of the source's sudden withdrawal from production. Unless the product is a staple, carryover of old models may take place, with possible reductions in prices. Also, the quantity size may be so expensive as to require either overbuying on fill-in orders or out-of-stock conditions after initial quantity purchases. Warehouse space and financial-size restrictions may limit the possibilities of quantity purchases. Reaction to quantity purchases may depend, to a considerable degree, upon the unit size of the quantity-purchase relation to the typical sales-size unit and total expected sales. In some

instances, accordingly, a case or a gross may be considered a quantity purchase whereas, in other instances, a truckload or a car-lot unit may be considered the quantity unit.

The reconciliation of the question of policy depends ultimately on matters of type of operation, kind of business and the nature of the channel structure as well. A wholesaler in an organized commodity exchange buys and sells in the minimum trading unit (or multiples thereof) established in that market. A truck jobber (wagon jobber), by the very nature of his type of operation and kind of business, deals in small-lot purchases and sales. In addition to the variables mentioned, the channel strength of particular producers and whole-sale middlemen, and of producers' brands versus distributors' brands, have great importance. The sales-size and product-assortment characteristics of the wholesale middlemen in particular channels cannot be overlooked.

Not infrequently, the question of quantity purchases is closely related to the availability of "special buys" regularly or at specific times. Since the main issue involved usually pertains to matters of quality and to the relationship of such buys to product assortment policies rather than to the favorableness of the prices and terms of sale alone, a full discussion of this policy aspect will be delayed until a later section.

Determination of maximum inventory positions

Assuming that a particular wholesale middleman has some form of merchandise budget in use, the determination of his maximum inventory position usually begins with some estimate of sales for each product item (or, at least, the significant product groups) by applicable time periods. Based upon inventory control information to be discussed later, data are also available pertaining to rates of stock turnover and to the volume of stock needed to attain an estimated sales volume (stock-sales ratios). These furnish, in addition to data of warehouse space, an estimate of the maximum dollar level of inventories needed at the beginning of each sales period for each particular product item or group. This level must include, in addition, allowances for a cushion against unpredictable changes in rates of sales and for any speculation against possibilities of price increases or declines. In addition, the maximum level must take into account the ease, rapidity, and costs of acquiring inventory replenishments. Also, the six types of inventory situations mentioned in an earlier section are of importance.

Determination of order point and safety inventory levels

Given the maximum inventory levels as determined above, by product lines and for the total accumulation, the establishment of order points and safety inventory levels involves the addition of certain data usually obtained from the merchandise budget and other sources. Reduction in stocks by daily sales can be accumulated on both an actual and a planned (estimated) basis, product item by product item. Experience and knowledge of the buying staff are instrumental in indicating the length of the time period between the time when an order is placed and when it is actually received in the middleman's warehouse and made available for orders to be moved, in turn, to customers. Thus, the order or reorder minimum is reached when the number of days has caused the maximum inventory level to shrink to the level where the number of days remaining equals the average experience as to the total procurement time. By the time purchases actually arrive at the warehouse, sales will have caused the inventory to have dropped to the *safety level*, i.e., the level below which stocks of a given product cannot be permitted to move if the customers are to be serviced according to the middleman's policies. With the arrival of the purchases, the inventory position rises once again to the planned maximum level.

Through the use of correct calculations, accumulated sales and inventory experience, and graphic analysis, the buying executives can establish flexible standards relating to maximum, order point, and safety inventory levels for each meaningful product category and for the total product assortment to be stocked. These standards, when properly used, can be of much value to management in establishing merchandising strategy and related buying policies. In addition, they may be of help as bases for costing out inventory activities. But they are, or should be, subordinate to the merchandising strategy and buying policies. Due allowances need to be made for unpredictable changes in the daily-rate stock depletion, in the availability and strategy of acquiring special buys, or in the merchandising skill with which product assortments are otherwise changed. These are, as stated, standards and not straitjackets meant to contain and dominate management action.[5]

[5] For the mechanics involved maximum-minimum inventory level calculations, and for excellent graphic illustrations, see G. W. Aljian (ed.), *Purchasing Policies* (New York: McGraw-Hill Book Co., Inc., 1958), Section 13, pp. 13–13 to 13–29.

Influence of assortments

The influence of special buys has been mentioned briefly in connection with quantity versus small-lot purchases. For certain middlemen, such buys may become both important in a time and percentage meaning. Accordingly, they have to be included in regular assortment strategy and planning. But product assortments affect policies with respect to quantities in other ways. Concentration on a few products in contrast with many categories increases the possibilities of larger purchases at any given order period. In addition, simplicity of assortments reduces the complexities of determining maximum, order, and safety-point calculations.[6] The related policies of sources, brands, and concentration of purchases likewise are simplified. Similarly, a simplification of the paper work involved in buying procedures should result. But, again, these advantages should not be permitted to dominate management thinking as compared with the advantages already noted which stem from assortments in depth and/or breadth, even though inventory policies and procedures may be complicated in the process.

Inventory Policies: Quality Factors

A very important buying policy of wholesale middlemen is related to the determination of quality in the inventory to be stocked. It is apparent, once again, that this type of inventory policy is related closely to preceding discussions of merchandising policies. In addition, middlemen's policies with respect to quality must discuss the meaning and measurement of quality, and the relationship of quality factors to source of purchase.

Relationship to merchandising policies

The merchandising policies of wholesale middlemen with respect to product assortments and branding strategy set the general framework of quality within which the buying policies and activities must operate. The specific inventory policies with respect to quality factors bridge the gap between the abstract strategy level and the concrete necessities of insuring that the quality factors are made available to cus-

[6] It permits the use, as noted, of certain quantitative models developed recently in inventory theory applicable to production situations.

tomers in actual inventories of particular product assortments. The actualities of the inventory quality situation may reinforce the merchandising strategy in every respect or may lead to significant modifications. There may be such powerful merchandising strategy considerations, however, in individual middlemen situations that the inability to obtain products to meet stipulated quality levels may result in their elimination from product assortments in order to protect uniformity of quality. The implications may lead ultimately to distributor's brands.

Meaning of quality

In order properly to understand quality as a buying policy, it is necessary to understand, in turn, the basic meaning of quality, and variations in quality in relation to different channel situations. Considering the wide range of products moving through the wholesaling sector, the most workable concept of quality for a given or intended use, or for a given class of customers, is to emphasize the combination of physical, chemical, and mentally induced properties which are characteristic of a particular product or of its component parts. All three groups of properties need not be applicable to every product. Technical products emphasize physical and/or chemical properties, whereas fashion goods or products such as perfumes may depend for quality characteristics almost completely upon mentally induced impressions.

Thus, most classes of products encompass a range of quality factors falling within these properties. In a very few instances, products may have only a single level of quality. In addition, the nature of the package, of related services, and the name and reputation of the producer may influence quality-level evaluations. Given these bases for quality variations, it follows that the responsibility of wholesale middlemen in accumulating inventories is to determine which quality level or levels can best maximize their respective sales potentials. It does not follow automatically, accordingly, that the *right* quality in any given buying-selling situation *need always be*, or *need ever be*, the highest available quality level.

There are varying degrees of freedom possessed by wholesale middlemen in the formulation of quality policies. At one extreme, the wholesale middleman's quality requirements may be dominated by the superior position of the producer in the channel. At the opposite extreme, the ultimate user or the intermediate customer may issue specific quality needs or expectations. In between, the individual wholesale middleman has ample and varied opportunities to influence sharply what is the *right* quality level (or quality levels) to meet particular channel needs.

Keeping in mind, then, the wide range of adjustments of quality to particular products, particular channel linkages, and particular users, the following list is suggestive of particular quality properties in a few commodity examples.

1. *Edible products:* appearance; color; maturity; ripeness; size; sugar content (where applicable) ; age; freshness; finish.
2. *Wearing apparel:* design; durability of materials; tailoring quality; color fastness; shrinkage; washing or cleaning characteristics.
3. *Raw materials:* workability; uniformity of chemical properties in order to permit a high degree of standardization of final product; uniformity of physical properties; appearance in finished form relative to use to be made of final product.
4. *Machinery and related accessories and equipment:* length of economical working life; costs of installation and operation; economy in use from point of view of time and labor requirements; output per man-hours or some equivalent standard; and frequency and cost of maintenance and repair.

These and other quality characteristics of various types of products are related closely to the bases of purchases discussed in the preceding chapter. They affect, to a very considerable extent, the meaning of quality inherent in a brand name. Grades and standards incorporate these properties in their specifications. The wholesale middleman, given these quality properties and considerations, has several different inventory quality policies as alternatives. Under circumstances where the wholesale middleman has full control over the product in the channel, he may link his merchandising strategy to superior quality levels, to the lower ranges of available qualities, to some concept of average market quality, or to various combinations. The wholesale middleman must use his best knowledge and judgment of products, customers, competition, and strategy in selecting the most profitable quality mix.

At the other extreme are those channel circumstances in which the manufacturer exercises considerable or complete control over the quality levels. Much depends on the availability and costliness of quality control methods as to whether high rate of uniformity is ever obtained. In the case of the extractive industries, much quality control is beyond the reach of the producers. Instead, well-developed systems of grading by both governmental and private agencies have emerged. Where, in addition, such products are highly perishable, sales by inspection become necessary, as noted, in order to insure the effectiveness of point-of-shipment grading throughout the channel.

Under special circumstances, product quality may be standardized regardless of producer or middleman individual quality policies. Thus, in the case of pharmaceuticals, a government manual such as the *U. S. Pharmacopoeia* establishes a common specification basis;[7] or, the work of an agency, such as the Bureau of Standards, may create uniform processes for dyes and a wide range of other products. In addition, partial quality uniformity may result from legislation.[8]

It should not be imagined that brand names are, by any stretch of the imagination, synonymous with uniform quality. Much depends on the type of product being branded. Many perishable edible products which are branded have variable quality ranges from season to season, or even within the same season. For other types of products, much depends, as noted, on the effectiveness of quality control within the manufacturing phase. Excessive costliness of such control may prohibit or restrict its effective use; or the nature of the components may make close quality tolerances impossible. Then, too, the management itself may simply elect to use a variable quality policy.

Finally, it should be noticed that, for certain types of manufactured consumers' goods, the retail middlemen may play a very important role in the quality-level policy determinations. This is true especially in those cases where these middlemen utilize their own brands of products or family of products. But it is effective, also, in the purchase of perishables for premium operations and in the area of "special buys." These retail middlemen may make effective use of rigorous merchandise quality testing in order to measure the conformity of manufacturers' products with stipulated quality specifications.

Measurement of quality

Depending upon the type of product and the complexity of the quality measurement problem, there are available various methods of measuring quality, and various types of agencies to do the work.

[7] On occasion, a strong producer or middleman may be able to develop effective brand differentiation.

[8] Note, for example, the effects of the Meat Inspection Act; the Wool Products Labeling Act; the Wheeler-Lea Amendment to the Federal Trade Commission Act; and the stipulations of minimum butter fat content for fresh, grade A, market milk.

Where chemical properties are of predominant importance, competent chemists employed by the manufacturer, government, or specialized testing businesses are the determining experts, utilizing all the theory and technique of chemical qualitative and quantitative analysis. Apart from these agencies, these experts, in special instances, are part of such consumer advisory services as *Consumers' Research, Inc.*, or *Consumers' Union*.

Similarly, quality control experts within or outside the manufacturing establishments are engaged in measuring quality through such physical tests as tensile strength, electrical qualities, elasticity, or conformity to certain tolerances or thread counts. In addition, for agricultural products, much governmental participation is available through the U. S. Department of Agriculture for grading livestock, grains, fruits and vegetables, meats, eggs, and canned goods, to mention just a few categories. The consumer advisory services mentioned, together with such magazines as *Parents'* and *Good Housekeeping* (with their seals of approval), represent additional sources of quality measurement. In some product instances, valuable testing information may be given to users by means of special statements attached to the product or its container, or in separate pamphlets.

Quality in relation to source of purchase

One final aspect of quality in relation to inventory management needs to be mentioned here. Given all of the variables inherent in the quality level or range of quality levels for a particular type of product, it follows that the selection of source is a vital factor either in insuring highly standardized quality levels, or highly variable quality characteristics. Besides placing considerable responsibility on the source to meet such quality specifications as may have been stipulated in the original purchase agreement, the buying agency may have to provide for rigorous inspection of the entire shipment or of samples to secure necessary conformity if its policy is one of rigid quality-level conformity. Whatever the situation, decisions by wholesale middlemen as to quality affect, in turn, the decisions as to source of purchase.

Inventory Policies: Speculation and Hedging

No attempt will be made in this section to discuss every aspect and operational detail of this complicated subject. Rather, three aspects will be presented only in sufficient detail to furnish a basis for relating hedging to wholesale middlemen's buying policies. These include basic meanings, the relationship of hedging to organized wholesale markets, and the role of wholesale middlemen.[9]

Basic meanings

Differentiation is necessary here between the orthodox and the newer concept of hedging. The orthodox definition may be summarized as follows:

> . . . Hedging is a use of the futures market which has as its purpose the minimizing of the price risk that is inherent in a commodity market in which prices are constantly fluctuating. Hedging, therefore, is a means of protection against inventory loss by offsetting a purchase or a sale of commodity by a counterbalancing sale or purchase of an equivalent amount of futures contracts. If a grain buyer purchases cash grain, he subjects himself to the risk of price declines, but if at the same time he buys the cash grain he sells an equivalent amount of futures in the same grain, he is protected. If subsequently the price of cash grain does decline, his loss on the cash transaction is offset by the buying-in of his short sale of futures, the future price having also declined in sympathy with the cash price.[10]

A sharply revised concept of hedging has been developed by Holbrook Working,[11] after years of research at the Food Research Institute, Stanford University. Abstracting from this path-breaking study, the following quotations are of importance in understanding this newer concept of hedging:

> First, contrary to common impression, hedging of the sort here considered is not properly comparable with insurance. It is a sort of arbitrage. We shall consider later an example of conditions under which hedging may in fact be profitably compared with insurance, but such conditions obtain for only a small proportion of the hedging that is done on futures markets. Most hedging is done in the expectation of a change in spot-futures price relations, the change that is reasonably to be expected being often indicated quite clearly by the current spot-future price relations.
>
> Secondly, hedging does not eliminate risks arising from price variability. Risk is less than on stocks held unhedged, but it still exists. When the commodity involved is of quite different quality than that represented by the future, or in a location remote from that to which the futures price relates, the risks assumed by hedgers tend to be much larger than is suggested by the examples given here.

[9] For some of the background and detailed operational workings of hedging see E. A. Duddy and D. A. Revzan, *Marketing: An Institutional Approach*, 2nd ed. (New York: McGraw-Hill Book Co., Inc., 1953), Chapter XXI and XXII, and the references cited therein.

[10] *Ibid.*, p. 389. See this page, also, for a statement of the systematic relationship between cash and futures prices upon which the success of hedging relies.

[11] Holbrook Working, "Futures Trading and Hedging," *The American Economic Review*, XLII (June 1953), 314–343.

And thirdly, hedging is not necessarily done for the sake of reducing risks. The role of risk-avoidance in most commercial hedging has been greatly over-emphasized in economic discussion. Most hedging is done largely, and may be done wholly, because the information on which the merchant or processor acts leads logically to hedging. He buys the spot commodity because the spot price is low *relative* to the futures price and he has reason to expect the spot premium to advance; therefore he buys spot *and* sells the future. Or in the the case of a flour miller, he sells flour for forward delivery because he can get a price that is favorable *in relation* to the price of the appropriate wheat future; therefore he sells flour *and* buys wheat futures. (Here the arbitrage, it may be noted, is between two forward prices, that for flour and that for wheat.)

. . . To put it briefly, we may say that hedging in commodity futures involves the *purchase or sale of futures in conjunction with another commitment, usually in the expectation of a favorable change in the relation between spot and futures prices.*[12]

One final aspect of Working's concept needs mention, namely, the relationship of hedging to control of commodity stocks. Holbrook Working states the relationship as follows:

. . . Merely by supplying simultaneously quotations applying to various subsequent dates, futures trading tends to promote economically desirable control of stocks; and futures markets, through their use for hedging, make the holder of stocks sharply aware of any losses that must be expected from carrying unnecessary stocks in times of relative shortages of supplies, and provide assured returns for storage over periods where there is a surplus to be carried. A merchant or processor with warehouse facilities will undertake storage in response to prospect of a 10-cent per bushel gain from carrying hedged stocks about as readily as he will undertake storage in response to an increase of 10 cents per bushel as a fee for storing government-owned grain. Indeed he may undertake storage for the return promised by hedging more willingly than for the fee, because the stocks that he holds hedged need be carried only as long as he wishes, and can be a source of convenience or profit in connection with his merchandising or processing business. The argument often made that management of reserve stocks of commodities should be a governmental function rests in large part on ignorance of the effectiveness with which the hedging facilities of futures markets assure private carrying of stocks in about as large a volume as can be justified on purely economic grounds.[13]

The role of organized wholesale markets and wholesale middlemen

Only a brief reminder need be inserted here of the fact that the cash and futures prices which are related so closely to the hedging control of stocks are determined by wholesale middlemen operating in organized commodity exchanges known as Boards of Trade. The characteristics of these organized markets have been discussed in

[12] *Ibid.*, pp. 325, 326.
[13] *Ibid.*, pp. 326, 327.

Chapter 5.[14] While there are many types of merchant and agent middlemen operating in the cash and futures markets, attention need be directed here only to the primary role played by the buying and selling brokers.

Inventory Policies: Other Forms of Forward Buying

Basic meaning

Apart from the use of futures contracts in organized commodity exchanges, other forms of forward buying take place for other than agricultural products. Whenever a purchase of commodity or service is made for delivery at a future date which exceeds normal timing in order to secure the maximum inventories relative to estimated ordinary rate of sale, then an aspect of forward buying is introduced. It is expected that prices and performance conditions usually are stipulated. The difference between the forms to be discussed here and hedging is the absence of organized commodity exchange facilities as well as a system of cash and futures prices leading to the stock control and risk aspects noted above.

Reasons for forward buying

There are certain basic reasons usually advanced to explain the existence of the types of forward buying being discussed here:

1. To insure an adequate inventory of basic raw materials of the necessary quality, especially during periods of anticipated shortages.
2. Closely related to (1) as a form of special cases is the situation faced by year-round production in relation to seasonal supplies.
3. Forward buying may be in anticipation of sharply increased prices affecting the cost of obtaining basic inventories, whether of raw materials or merely of stocks needed for other than production types of business. This is related closely not only to the question of adequate inventory assortment necessary for the conduct of the type of business but to the expectations of speculative profits as well.

Types of forward buying

The preceding discussion has indicated forward-buying transactions in cash and futures contracts on organized commodity exchanges.[15]

---

[14] See also Duddy and Revzan, *op. cit.,* pp. 345–48, 370–81.

[15] The following list is indicative of the wide range of commodities involved in such transactions: wheat; corn; oats; rye; barley; soybeans; cotton; butter;

One additional form consists of forward buying within fixed production or wholesale selling schedules, but at rates which exceed periodic maximum inventory requirements. The second involves forward buying in quantities which go beyond such production and sales schedule expectations.

Policy aspects

In addition to the obvious relationship to other buying policies, this inventory policy raises some additional important considerations. One has to do with the policy question of whether to use forward buying as a regular policy or whether, on the contrary, to restrict its use to irregular intervals. A second policy question concerns making provision for the financial resources necessary to purchase the larger-than-average stocks, to cover the additional associated handling costs, and to provide reserves for the possibilities of either physical or economic depreciation. A final aspect involves the assignment of responsibility within the buying organization for the analysis of the pertinent internal and external data of production, prices, and demand on which decisions as to forward buying need to be based.

Inventory Control

The final aspect of the management of inventories has to do with the provision by management of inventory control. The meaning and systems of control used, the methods of inventory valuation, the use of stock-turnover calculations, and the use of stock-sales ratios will be discussed mainly as they affect the managerial point of view.[16]

Meaning of inventory control

The available literature shows a definite and sharp division of opinion as to whether inventory control is a management-controlled activity or a procedural device. The confusion is unfortunate because, in our opinion, inventory control is an important accessory to merchandise budgeting as discussed in the preceding chapter. *It consists*

---

eggs; pork products; tallow; cottonseed oil and meal; soybean oil and meal; silver; tin; copper; lead; zinc; hides; crude rubber; raw silk; coffee; cocoa; sugar; molasses; peanuts; pepper; crude oil; gasoline; potatoes; onions; and wool tops.

[16] For a detailed description of the mechanics involved, see T. N. Beckman, N. H. Engle, and R. D. Buzzell, *Wholesaling: Principles and Practice,* 3rd ed. (The Ronald Press Co., 1959), Chapters 20, 25.

of provision by management of systems and personnel designed to provide certain accounting and statistical data and related analyses as guides to buying and buying policies.

Apart from the details to be discussed later, these data supply the following kinds of information: (1) How much of *each product* currently is in stock; (2) how much is on order; (3) dates of delivery of each item on order; (4) at what inventory-level point each product item should be reordered. The types of information provided become important in merchandise budgets, as guides to actual day-to-day buying activities, and in furnishing the explanations for conditions of understocking or overstocking if and when they exist.

Not all types of wholesale middlemen who actually take physical possession of inventories need equally complex and costly forms of inventory control. The more complicated and costly systems are found under such circumstances where product assortments involve many categories of component items with highly varying turnover rates, where assortments are not sold in regular amounts frequently each day, and where financial resources are sufficient to support both the initial cost of installation and operating costs.

Systems of inventory control in use

Wholesale middlemen may secure control of inventories by physical inventories, through the use of accounting and statistical records, or by combinations. The physical inventory may be subdivided in either complete actual physical counts taken one or more times each year, physical inspections to determine where low stock conditions exist, or so-called continuous stock-taking consisting of counts of goods only in original containers and without the need of extending counts by unit values in order to secure total dollar value. The so-called control by means of accounting and statistical records consist of: (1) the purchase record system of control; and (2) real perpetual inventory systems using punch card, Kardex-type files, McBee Keysort systems, electronic-computer equipment, or other installations.

None of the accounting and statistical record systems can be effective without at least one complete physical inventory each year, especially if an accurate measurement of leaks and stock shortages is to be available to management. More frequent complete physical inventories obviously increase the degree of such managerial control. In complicated, time-consuming inventory situations, statistical sampling serves to reduce both the time and records needed without any significant sacrifice in accuracy. Under conditions where no inventory items are knowingly permitted to be out of stock, fill-in data of inventory condition between complete physical inventories can be obtained by physical inspection of stocks and from the preparation of lists of products in low inventory condition; i.e., below established or arbitrary reorder points.

The accounting and statistical records build on the data obtained from the complete physical inventories. Depending upon the completeness and costliness of the system, and the rapidity with which data can be compiled, the following may be obtained: a running balance in physical and/or dollar units of every item carried in inventory at a given beginning time period; the amount ordered as obtained from copies of purchase records; cancellation of orders, or parts of orders, where applicable; actual receipt of items ordered based on invoices or receiving department reports; order items canceled by the seller; goods returned for credit by the wholesale middleman; and a complete record of sales, and when each order was filled and shipped.

As indicated earlier, the main reason for discussing these methods is to emphasize the availability of data useful to management in the control of inventories, and the nature of such control uses, rather than the details of how these inventory methods are executed. These management aspects will be further investigated in the remaining sections of this chapter.

Systems of inventory valuation

Some mention needs to be made here of the cost bases upon which inventories may be valued. Apart from income tax and other tax purposes, the determination of the cost base affects the value turnover of inventory and the calculation of prices.[17] The more rapid the changes in buying prices, the more difficult it becomes to determine accurately the landed cost of each lot of merchandise in stock in the middleman's warehouse. The following methods suggest the more important open-to-management uses by wholesale middlemen.

1. *Lifo, or last purchase method.* This method emphasizes the unit purchase price of the last purchase lot as the basis for valuation. When used accurately, it may tend to minimize the effects of rapidly fluctuating purchase prices for the wholesale middlemen.

2. *Fifo, or first-in, first-out.* This method requires maintaining accurate records of the exact cost of each purchase of inventory in stock. The unit cost applicable to the total inventory at any

---

[17] The topic of inventory valuation is very complicated. For detailed analyses, see the appropriate bibliography for selected references.

given point of time, accordingly, is that which the records indicate was paid for the oldest purchase lot in stock. Depending upon the direction and rapidity of changes in commodity, prices will depend on whether such valuation policy has inflationary or deflationary effects.

3. *Current market or replacement cost.* As the name indicates, the cost of the inventory at any given time is determined by the then applicable effective seller's price, *regardless* of whether or not the wholesale middleman has made any purchase at that price. It has the effect, accordingly, of valuating inventories at the highest point or level of prices in an inflationary period, and at the lowest level in a period of rapidly declining prices.

4. *Weighted average cost.* One compromise between the three valuation methods noted is to calculate the total landed cost (at warehouse) and quantities involved in each purchase lot, and then to secure the average cost of the purchase lots in stock by dividing the total amount of such landed costs by the total units in the purchase lots.

5. *Weighted moving-average costs.* If prices are changing rapidly, the use of (4) results in an average cost which may be significantly behind the current level or significantly above, depending upon the direction of change. One method which corrects for this is to maintain a running record, or moving average, of purchases made and of sales at each weighted average point, and then recalculate the weighted average for each successive amounts of purchases and sales.

Thus, the nature and frequency of wholesale purchase prices, the accuracy of the middlemen's purchase records, and the rapidity with which the wholesale middleman wishes to reflect changes in purchase prices in his selling prices are important management considerations in the selection of a valuation method (apart from the tax considerations already mentioned).

The measurement and control of stock turnover

As is true in all buying and selling businesses, the relationship between sales and inventories is an important matter. The relationship states the rate at which a representative inventory moves through the wholesale middleman's warehouse, within a stated period of time. The following conditions need to be noted:

1. The rate of stock turnover may be stated as annual, semiannual, or even more frequently, depending upon the nature of the

business. If the rate is annual, the average inventory is computed as one-half of the opening and closing inventories for the business year used. If the rate is semiannual, the inventory base is the average of the opening, midyear, and closing inventory amounts, and so on. Thus, the formula for an average inventory is

$$\text{Average inventory} = \frac{\sum(\text{inventories})}{\text{No. of inventory periods}}$$

The inventory may be stated either in physical terms or in dollar values of cost price or selling price.

2. The physical or dollar sales are then computed for the equivalent time periods.

3. The *stock turn* or *turnover rate* may then be stated as follows:

$$\text{Turnover} \begin{cases} \text{annual} \\ \text{semiannual,} \\ \text{etc.} \end{cases} = \frac{\text{Sales} \begin{cases} \text{physical units} \\ \text{cost-price units} \\ \text{selling price units} \end{cases}}{\text{Average inventory}}$$

It should be noted that physical stock turnover rates can be computed only for *homogeneous* product classifications, whereas sales-value turnover may be computed both for homogeneous classifications and the cumulative inventories.

The advantages of higher stockturns, *other things remaining equal,* fall under the following: (1) Reductions in the amount of working capital tied-up in inventories; (2) reductions in such related expense items as warehouse space expense, interest on investment, taxes, insurance costs, and costs of obsolescence; (3) more rapid adjustment of inventory costs to changing wholesale prices; and (4) fresher stocks (physically, fashionwise, modelwise) of goods for customers. In addition, stock turnover rates furnish certain standards. *When used with care and judgment,* these standards have significance in determining maximum, order, and safety-inventory-point position for each important product-item category.

But there are definite and important limitations to each wholesale middleman's search for higher stock-turnover rates and for the total channel aspect in any kind of business. If the turnover rate is increased too rapidly, certain customer orders may be lost either because particular goods may be out of stock or because assortments may be incomplete. Such savings in high turnover as have been noted may be offset in part or in whole by the increased costs of placing more frequent orders and by the costs of maintaining adequate inventory control methods. Opportunities for advantageous quantity purchases and special buys may be lost. In addition, the wholesale middleman has to weigh the advantages of speculating on the possibilities of inventory value appreciation because of price increases against the advantages of more rapid stock turnover as noted. Much depends on the margins which can be secured. Without careful management supervision the search for high turnover may cause chronic overselling of the middleman's customers. Finally, policies related to the use of distributor's brands may or may not affect policies related to stock-turnover rates.

Accordingly, stock-turnover rates are a very valuable tool, but only a tool, for the wholesale middlemen establishing inventory policies. Each middleman must compare his inventory situation with that applicable to the kind of business of which he is a part *before* using common turnover rates as a standard. The benefits of wider assortments or assortments in depth, as discussed earlier, must be weighed carefully against the advantages to be obtained from streamlined, simplified inventory assortments resulting from the search for higher stockturns.

Stock-sales ratios

Of great value in planning inventories, especially in relation to the managerial aspects of merchandise budget, are the ratios of stocks, at the beginning of a sales period, for a product category and in total to the planned sales expected during that period. The formula would be expressed as follows:

Stock-sales ratio (month, etc.) =

$$\frac{\text{Beginning stocks (at cost price or at selling price)}}{\text{Planned total sales (at cost price or at selling price)}}$$

These ratios became extremely useful guides in: (1) making certain that the wholesale middleman secures a balanced inventory which will insure that sales will not be reduced by the failure to have such assortments on hand in sufficient time; (2) alerting the buying personnel, accordingly, to budget accurately for the proper assortments; and (3) acting as a corrective, on the one hand, to too much managerial "worship" of rapid stock turnovers, while securing monthly and seasonal flexibility by the frequency with which such ratios are calculated and analyzed. An important aspect of the analysis is why actual sales experience did or did not match the expectancies indicated by the stock-sales ratios.

QUESTIONS AND PROBLEMS

1. What are the wholesale middlemen's policy alternatives so far as product assortments are concerned?
2. What are the important factors affecting the choice of the policy alternatives discussed in question 1?
3. What is meant by "inventory management"? To what extent does the scope of inventory management by wholesale middlemen differ from that for the manufacturer?
4. Define each type of wholesale middlemen's inventory situations.
5. Indicate the important determinants of purchase quantities. How do these determinants vary according to (a) type of wholesale middleman operation and (b) types of products handled?
6. How is the problem of inventory management affected by manufacturer-controlled wholesale middlemen operations? by retailer-controlled wholesale-middlemen operations?
7. Discuss the comparative merits of quantity versus small-lot purchases from the middleman's point of view.
8. What is the effect of channel structure upon quantity versus small-lot purchases?
9. Reconcile the discussion of quantity versus small-lot purchases with the funnel concept.
10. Define: maximum inventory positions; order point levels; safety inventory levels. How do these relate to the whole problem of inventory management?
11. What should be the attitude of wholesale middlemen to "special buys"?
12. How important are quality of product factors in inventory management?
13. To what extent are quality factors underestimated in discussions of the buying function? To what extent are they overemphasized?
14. How do quality factors affect quantity to purchase considerations?
15. Compare and contrast the newer concept of hedging with the orthodox concept.
16. What is the significance of hedging for inventory management?
17. What other forms of forward buying are available to wholesale middlemen in addition to hedging? How do these affect buying policies?
18. Differentiate between the managerial and the procedural aspects of inventory control.
19. How is stock turnover measured? What important variables affect the rate of turnover?
20. Compare stock-sales ratios with stock-turnover ratios. How would you expect these ratios to vary by kinds of business?

CHAPTER INTEGRATING ASSIGNMENTS

1. In this chapter, greater emphasis has been placed on matters of inventory management. To bring the managerial aspects of inventory management to the fore, develop a critical comparison and contrast between the fol-

lowing wholesale middlemen situations: (*a*) the H. J. Heinz Company selling its complete line of canned and bottled food products through its sales branches, and (*b*) a regular wholesaler in the grocery business stocking 25,000 product items.

2. Given the background of the discussion in Chapters 12 and 13, write an essay in which you discuss the following: (*a*) the relative complexity of the buying function under conditions of single sale and multiple sale channel situations; and (*b*) the integration of inventory management in the channel under conditions of multiple wholesale sales. In addition, indicate how, in your opinion, the quality of the performance of inventory management affects the competitive position of the wholesale middleman.

14

Selling Elements and Policies: Nonprice Aspects

Although there are many parts of selling elements and policies which represent, in a manner of speaking, a reversal of the direction of emphasis of the elements as discussed in connection with buying, this is not the complete picture. For one difference, the discussion of the elements and policy aspects of selling must include many types of wholesale middlemen who, as has been noted, have no responsibilities for buying but do have considerable responsibility for selling. This difference alone is significant enough to warrant considerable discussion.

But there are certain component elements and policy areas, in addition, which are not discussed in any detail under buying, namely, demand-creation activities involving both advertising and the management of the sales force. In other instances, only brief mention need be made in this chapter of certain elements and policies in order to provide adequate coordination with preceding discussions of merchandising and buying.

Except for the detailed discussion of prices, price policies, and terms of sales to be given in Chapters 15 and 16, the general pattern of this chapter follows much the same format used in the preceding discussion of buying.

Types of Selling Situations

The matching side of the beginning aspects of the selling function with that of the buying function is the variable nature of the selling situations facing wholesale middlemen. Depending upon the nature of the channel and upon the types of product situation, the selling aspects may originate at any point in the entire wholesale movement of products through the channel, or they may originate in conjunction with the types of buying situations outlined and discussed in Chapter 12.   '

Types of customers

Three selling situations may be distinguished according to types of customers. One situation is based upon a sharp distinction between the types of customers for industrial goods as compared with consumers' goods. Closely related to this, but not in a complete fashion, is a distinction between those customers who "consume" products sold to them as compared with those customers who use such products as raw materials, or fabricating components, or facilitating agencies in further production. The third type of situation is a distinction between selling to establishments which are businesses as against such nonbusiness agencies as governmental units, educational institutions, hospitals, and doctors.

The main value to be derived from this type of classification is its usefulness to wholesale middlemen in making possible more systematic classifications of their customer for detailed analysis. In addition, it focuses considerable attention on the varying complexities of the selling situation of wholesale middlemen viewed in an entire channel context.

Single versus multiple selling transactions

This type of selling situation is the one which underlies the gross importance of the wholesaling sector. As discussed in Chapters 5 and 6, dealing with channel structure, many types of products sold by wholesale middlemen involve two or more transactions at the wholesale level of the particular channel involved. Obviously, the whole nature of the selling function is affected, accordingly, by this characteristic as compared with the situation which would exist if all commodities moving through the wholesale section of the channel were sold only once. There is a very interesting interplay between the number of selling transactions and the complexity of the channel structure:

1. One direct-selling channel arrangement may involve other types of channels in selling transactions, as there is a continuous flow of raw-material products to the finished-product stage within the wholesale level; or
2. the product, at a single stage at the wholesale level, may involve several degrees of channel complexity and several wholesale selling transactions.

Time factors

This type of selling situation involves the complementary side of the forward-buying situations discussed in detail in the preceding chapter. In addition, the time factor also introduces the use of the consignment sale in lieu of outright sale in order to reduce the risk elements inherent in the prospects of the sales to be made at a later time period in the channel, especially of new, untried products. A final aspect of the time factor involves sales made in which certain products such as cheeses, wines, and tobacco are withheld to permit proper aging to proceed. In addition, certain time aspects to price and terms of sale quotations will be discussed in subsequent chapters.

Legal ownership versus agency arrangements in selling

This type of selling situation is one of the really important identifying characteristics of the wholesaling sector. It involves in the selling situation the whole range of agent wholesale middlemen—already classified and described—as well as the various types of merchant middlemen who own the products involved in their respective selling situations.

Except for those types of agent middlemen operating in the grain markets, most of the selling types have product assortments dominated by the product assortments which their principals make available to them. As noted, within this arrangement, certain types of agent middlemen restrict themselves completely to the products produced by their principals. But others may handle either noncompeting or even competing product assortments, depending upon their authority designations and power position in the channel. These wholesale middlemen are, accordingly, specialists in selling as a result of the types and depths of customer contacts they have developed in particular trading areas for particular products.

Physical versus nonphysical possession

Both agent and merchant middlemen show operational variations and adaptations so far as physical possession of product assortments is concerned. The same range of bases—inspection, sample, and description—applies here as in the buying situations. In addition, the presence or absence of organized wholesale markets, together with the use of commodity grades, causes sharp variations in the incidence of physical inventories, and thus in the selling tactics utilized.

Thus, at any given time period, the selling aspects of the wholesaling sector represent a highly complex and varied situation. For any given product channel arrangements, there is a series of buying-selling transactions in both a vertical and horizontal sense. *Vertically*, these buying-selling transactions reflect the various numbers of customers at a given agency point within the wholesaling part of the channel. *Horizontally*, the channel may reflect the existence of multiple wholesaling selling transactions representative of the types of selling situations noted above. When the perspective is expanded to include all product channels and the variations caused by the other types of selling situations, the complexity becomes apparent. It is at this point in the analysis that the values of the funnel concept, of the classification of channels, and of the marketing processes—as systematizing influences—become increasingly apparent.

General Outline: The Component Elements of Selling

Paralleling the outline used for the buying function, the general outline of the component elements of the selling function of wholesale middlemen is presented as follows, preceding any detailed discussions of each component element.

    I. *Determination of Product Assortments to be Sold*
       A. Coordination with merchandising and buying functions, where applicable.
       B. Types of product-assortment situations for the selling wholesale middlemen.
       C. Branded versus unbranded product assortments.
          1. Factors influencing choice of unbranded product assortments.
          2. Factors influencing choice of branded product assortments.

      3. Factors influencing choice of producers' versus distributors' brands.
   D. Relationship of product assortments to sources.
II. *Determination of Customers for Product Assortments*
   A. Relationship to types of selling situations.
   B. Differentiations in element between existing customer and new customer categories.
   C. Measurement of basic characteristics of each customer category.
      1. Numbers and size characteristics.
      2. Geographical distribution.
      3. Buying characteristics.
      4. Relative profitability of each customer's account.
      5. Relationship to selling middleman's position in the channel.
      6. Estimated future importance.
III. *Determination of How Much Can be Sold: Sales Budgets*
   A. Data of past sales.
      1. Total.
      2. Breakdown of (1) by principal product categories.
      3. Breakdown of (1) and (2) by appropriate time periods.
      4. Classification of (2) and (3) by profitability categories.
   B. Computation of inventory relationships (see Chapter 13).
      1. Stock-turnover ratios.
      2. Stock-sales relationships.
   C. Estimated future sales, by the same categories as in (*A*).
   D. Relationships with buying budgets, where applicable.
IV. *Coordination with Other Institutional Elements in the Channel*
   A. Relationship to preceding channel discussions.
   B. Relationship to producers and to producers' marketing policies.
   C. Relationship to other wholesale middlemen as sources of product assortments.
   D. Relationship to other wholesale middlemen as customers.
   E. Relationship to other types of customers.
   F. Relationship to facilitating agencies in the channels.
V. *Demand-Creation Activities*
   A. Advertising.
      1. Determination of whether or not to advertise.
      2. Budgeting aspects: how much to spend.

        3. Problems of objectives and choice of types of advertising.

        4. Media selection and evaluation.

        5. Coordination with personal selling.

        6. Evaluation of advertising effectiveness.

    B. Personal selling.

        1. Determination of whether or not to use salesmen.

        2. Budgetary aspects.

        3. Recruitment and training of salesmen.

        4. Territorial and quota aspects.

        5. Remuneration.

        6. Evaluation of personal selling effectiveness.

    C. Relationship of (*A*) and (*B*) with producers' demand-creation activities.

        1. By direct integration.

        2. By use of advertising allowances.

        3. By producers' training methods.

  VI. *Determination of Prices, Price Policies, and Terms of Sale* (see Chapters 15, 16)

  VII. *Legal Aspects*

    A. Sales versus leasing arrangements.

    B. Other legal aspects.

  VIII. *Delivery and Postsales Servicing*

    A. Determination of responsibility.

        1. For delivery service.

        2. For delivery costs.

    B. Product installation (where applicable).

    C. Product repairs and continuing service (where applicable).

    D. Postsales services other than (*B*) and (*C*).

    E. Effects of delivery and servicing on sales.

Determination of Product Assortments to Be Sold

Since this topic has been discussed adequately in Chapter 7, and in relation to merchandising and buying, only an abbreviated discussion of this selling element needs to be presented here. The component parts have been outlined in the foregoing. Accordingly, all that remains to be emphasized are two particular points arising by virtue of the relationship with selling. The first emphasis is the aspect of product assortments in which certain types of agent middlemen secure their respective assortments by virtue of the contractual arrangements they are able to effect with extractive industry and manufacturing industry producers.

The second aspect concerns the extent to which such agent middlemen, by virtue of their positions of importance in the channel, can convince their principals to permit them to brand the products with the distributors' brands.[1]   Such broker-branding arrangements are well known in the grocery and drug businesses.

An additional aspect, which has been noted already for the buying middlemen, is the extent to which those middlemen primarily oriented to the selling side can affect product assortments by the following methods: by changing packaging arrangements, including changes from bulk to package; by repricing or aging products; by adjusting sizes and shapes;[2] or by any other means changing the channel characteristics of the product so as to constitute changes in product assortments.   This aspect, indeed, is one of the significant areas which explains why these selling middlemen continue to play such an important part in the wholesaling sector.

Determination of Customers for Product Assortments

Just as the buying side of wholesale middlemen's marketing operations involves careful evaluation of the sources of product assortments, so does the selling side involve a careful determination of the customers who can be convinced to buy part or all of a certain product assortment from a particular type of wholesale middleman, or who generate the search for particular assortments by backward vertical integration in the channel.   The types of selling situations discussed at the beginning of the chapter set the background to which all subsequent analysis must be related.

Differentiation between existing and new customers

The determination of potential customers for a given product assortment involves differentiating the analysis as between a new middleman and one already in business.   The problem for the existing wholesale middleman further includes making a distinction between new and existing customer categories.

[1] This is separate and distinct from any distributor's brands created either by virtue of ownership of goods and/or from integration arrangements in the channel.

[2] As in the case of steel warehouses, plastic supply houses, and similar operations.

With respect to a new middleman's operations, the determination of customers for the product assortments to be sold involves, in part, the initial analysis on which the decision was made to enter the type of operation and kind of business. Thus, given the choice of a particular trading area from which customers can be selected, the analysis involves measurement of customer characteristics (based on the categories to be discussed below) in terms of the potentialities offered by the given product assortments.

With respect to an existing middleman's operation, the determination of potential customers for product assortments consists of the measurement of characteristics of *existing* customers also in terms of the categories to be discussed. The emphasis here is on the extent to which there are any basic changes from previous measurements which will affect the total sales (and the product composition) to be secured from these "regular" customers. Such analysis would include, also, any changes in the profitability position of each account. In addition, the middleman must estimate to what extent new categories have entered the trading area of the types which can be considered potential buyers of his product assortments. Comparisons need to be made to the extent to which the new categories of potential customers are similar to existing categories, so that careful initial estimates of potential sales can be prepared.

Measurement of basic characteristics

Given the above differentiations, the next step is to measure the basic characteristics of the existing and new customers in terms of such categories as the following:

1. *The number and size distribution of the various pertinent customer classifications.* Size characteristics may be measured in such terms as sales volume, physical output, and number of employees, depending upon the type of customer classification involved.

2. *The geographical distribution* of these customer categories in order to determine the density of such distribution, and the bases for routing salesmen. It has an important subsidiary relationship in determining sales quotas as well.

3. A careful determination needs to be made for each class of customer *of the buying motives influencing purchases.* Depending upon both the nature of the products and the types of selling situations involved, these may approximate the classic patterns of rational buying motives attributed to customers for industrial

goods; the more emotional types of motives associated with buying of consumer's goods; or combinations of the two groups in terms of particular components.

4. The next aspect of measurement involves in conjunction with the preparation of sales budgets, to be discussed next, estimates of how much each account will buy in a given time period, and the relative profitability of these sales to the wholesale middleman.

5. The next step in the customer analysis is related to the type of selling situations, namely, the position occupied by each customer category in the channel.

6. The final step in the measurement of customer characteristics is to determine to what extent each category will show increasing importance in the future, stabilized levels of importance, or declining trends.

Not all types of wholesale middlemen will be able to afford the expense of thorough, professional analysis. Some will have such simplified composition of customer accounts that the analysis will be unnecessary. Others will have neither the personnel nor financial resources. Still others may not have available the flow of accounting and statistical data. But, increasingly, as will be seen later, these analyses are but part of so-called scientific control of the wholesale middleman's operations.

Determination of How Much Can Be Sold: Sales Budgets

The preceding customer analysis sets the basis for the preparation of careful estimates of expected sales volumes. If the wholesale middleman operation is completely new, no recourse can be had to past experience. Accordingly, the preceding six types of measurement must be relied upon by the management to furnish the raw materials for initial sales estimates until experience can be used to refine such calculations. To the extent that the new middleman's sales force and executives have had experience in the same kind of business, the initial estimates may have considerable more validity than if they are new recruits. For the wholesale middleman with a considerable picture derived from past experience, the following pattern of sales budget calculations is applicable.

Data of past sales

From the accounting and statistical data available, the middleman can obtain data of past gross and net sales of value in preparing sales budgets. These records would provide, first of all, data of total net sales subdivided into the time periods appropriate for the type of operation and kind of business. Further refinements of the total sales data are necessary to supply the following types of information, where needed:

1. Per cent of sales accounted for by each important product category, for the same time periods as in total sales.
2. Breakdown of total sales by accounts, and the average sales per account for the same time periods.
3. Product composition of each account's sales.
4. Estimated gross and net profits realized per account, by important product categories.

Inventory relationships

Reference need be made here to the appropriate sections of Chapter 13 for the calculations of the stock turnover and stock-sales ratios. The use of the ratios in the present context is in terms of furnishing bases for the estimation of future ratios in relationship to expected sales volumes.

Estimated future sales

Given the customer analysis above, and the data of past sales together with the inventory relationships, the wholesale middleman must next extend these data into forecasts for stipulated time periods. Forecasts of business conditions applicable to the particular trading area, trends of business and personal income, together with trends of other indexes, may be used as the bases for extrapolating the middleman's expected sales. In addition, key manufacturing sources of product assortments may have useful estimates of the sales outlook for particular products. Where the middleman has an exclusive distributorship arrangement, the manufacturer may actually provide expected quotas for each product category. Much valuable research and expected business-outlook materials may be available from government agencies, banks, and other research agencies.

Depending upon the research resources and orientation of the wholesale middleman, these measurements can be used to make the sales forecasts with the same degree of component detail for which the data of past sales were compiled. Once these forecasts have been made, the wholesale middleman is in a position to formulate his sales budgets. These act as guides for remaining selling activities. In addition, they give the management a realistic basis against which (*a*) to measure actual performance, and (*b*) to adjust marketing policies if such adjustments are necessary to secure better performance.

Relationship to buying budgets

For those wholesale middlemen who have relatively large amounts of responsibility for buying product assortments which, in turn, are to be resold, brief mention only needs to be made of the extent to which these sales budgets are interrelated closely with purchase budgets.

Coordination with Other Institutional Agencies in the Channel

Except for those producer-dominated or user-dominated examples of direct channels, the wholesale middleman is involved in an interlocking series of agency relationships in the channel. A significant element of selling, accordingly, involves coordination with the other agencies found in the channel. Although some aspects of this coordination, especially in connection with demand-creation activities, will be discussed in more detail in a later section, some over-all aspects can best be discussed in this section.

Relationship to producers and to producer's marketing policies

In those channel examples where the wholesale middleman either is controlled by the producer or controls the producer, the relationship of the middleman's selling policies and activities with those of the producer is self-apparent. But even in the case examples of other types of middlemen, the influences of the producer through his marketing policies may be manifested in at least two directions. First, the producer may use, especially if sales-size and financial strength permit, the price-formal or informal type of integration already discussed in connection with the managerial struggle for control of the channel. Where successful, these types of channel control efforts will result, once again, in a close relationship with the producer and his marketing policies. But these tactics may engender the second situation— a series of offsetting efforts by the wholesale middleman to maintain channel position. In such cases, the close relationship between producer's marketing policies and middleman's selling policies and activities may be broken completely, or may even be reversed so far as the controlling level is concerned.

Relationships with other wholesale middlemen as a product assortment source

Because wholesale transactions frequently involve buying-selling arrangements between wholesale middlemen, it is important to note this relationship in connection with the element of the selling function. Many of the wholesale middlemen who become intermediate product sources participate in the channel in connection with the concentration process. Others, by virtue of organized wholesale market arrangements, become intermediate sources in connection with the equalization process. In either case, those middlemen who purchase the product assortments and sell, in turn, from such wholesale middlemen have a different coordination problem than if the product assortments were purchased directly from the producer as such.

Relationship to other wholesale middlemen as customers

This relationship is, in part, merely a reversal of the preceding arrangement. It differs in only one respect; namely, it includes all the selling arrangements in which the wholesale middlemen get product assortments from the producer as well as from other wholesale middlemen. In addition, there are included in this coordinating relationship the maintenance of a system of channel relationships and the strategic element of managerial struggle for channel control.

Relationship with other types of customers

The types of selling situations referred to earlier indicate the wide range of customers, other than wholesale middlemen, who buy from the selling types of wholesale middlemen. The relationships with these types of customers may involve product installation and servicing, as will be noted; coordination of their product needs with the product assortments which are available in the channel, and with many other valuable forms of marketing information. Depending upon the channel arrangements and the type of product, the wholesale middleman may have closer arrangements to the customers he services than to the sources of product assortments.

Relationships with facilitating agencies in the channel

There should be noted, in conclusion, the varying relationships which exist in any channel arrangement between any particular selling wholesale middleman and the agencies which facilitate the buying-selling arrangements. Especially to be noted are: Specialized warehousing agencies; the various transportation agencies involved in the inbound and outbound product movements; various financial agencies; advertising agencies; market news agencies; and risk-bearing agencies. Wholesale middlemen may be employing these agencies on a fee basis, or they may receive the effects of such activities in usual channel methods other than by fee arrangements.

Demand-Creation Activities: Advertising

Although most of the elements of buying already mentioned have repercussions on any discussion of the selling function, it is in the area of demand creation that selling introduces a relatively unique element.[3] Once again, the main emphasis in the following sections is placed on the wholesale middlemen as such.[4]

Determination of whether or not to advertise

There are far too many misconceptions about the role of wholesale middlemen in the use of advertising. Although it is true that a much larger proportion of wholesale middlemen is of local and regional significance so far as advertising outreach, influence, and number of dollars to spend are concerned relative to powerful producer and large-scale retail middlemen units, this *does not* preclude the use of advertising by wholesale middlemen. The types of advertising positions of wholesale middlemen and related underlying factors may be summarized as follows:

1. *Conditions underlying complete advertising campaigns similar to those of producers.* This advertising situation exists where the wholesale middleman has widespread regional, multiregional, or national distribution of his own brands of goods; where opportunities exist for the creation of primary demand, as in the case of cooperative marketing association activities in agricultural products; because of opportunities arising from backward or forward vertical integration with retail middlemen; and by virtue of adequacy of financial resources in relation to the preceding.

2. *Conditions underlying advertising to special groups, by means of special media.* There are several variations of the middleman advertising situation. One example involves the distribution of

[3] This is *not to say* that demand creation has no repercussions on buying but, rather, that there is no complementary element in buying.

[4] For the reader interested in the general over-all aspects of advertising and the producer's responsibilities, some basic references are included in the pertinent bibliography.

specialized industrial goods in which such advertising as has potential for effective results will appear in specialized business publications having, in turn, specialized industrial readers and specialized geographical circulation. A case in point would be the distribution of textile machinery. A second example involves advertising the availability of certain products of a highly seasonal nature, as in the case of a wholesale middleman selling car-lot quantities of lettuce or potatoes. In both examples, the advertisement might contain detailed descriptions of the product, or announce the arrival of new models (or new crops), or offer highly technical materials in the form of brochures, catalogues, or output studies.

3. *Conditions underlying advertising highly specialized copy to special groups of readers.* Examples of these conditions may be found, first of all, in the case of those types of wholesale middlemen operating on the organized grain exchanges. In such examples, their main form of advertising might very well be a specialized market-news letter circulated both to existing and potential customers. A second example would be copy dealing with ethical drug products being circulated among members of the medical and dental profession. A third example might consist of the periodical circulation of a catalogue of available product assortments, including order blanks.

4. *Conditions underlying special coordination with producers' advertising campaigns.* In this situation, the wholesale middleman is in the position of being dominated by the producer in the channel. In one example, the wholesale middleman merely redistributes the advertising materials of the producer to his customers, or he may be identified as a distributor in the producer's advertising. In the second example, the wholesale middleman, as an exclusive distributor for the producer, may be integrated completely into the advertising campaign of the producer. In both situations, the wholesale middleman exercises neither initiative in preparing the advertising material introduced into the channel nor control.

5. *Conditions under which the wholesale middleman, directly or indirectly, engages in no advertising.* There are two important sets of conditions under which the wholesale middleman may not engage in any advertising. The first exists for many kinds of wholesale middlemen who have no distributors' brands, and who act mainly as contactual middlemen in the channel. In addition, the products involved may be so standardized as to secure little or no benefit from product differentiation through adver-

tising. The second example exists where the manufacturer has established a brand preference so successfully through advertising, and so exercises such other forms of channel control as to give the wholesale middleman little need or leeway for his own advertising.

Budgeting aspects: how much to spend for advertising?

Given the four sets of conditions under which wholesale middlemen can use advertising profitably, the determination of how much to spend for advertising is no different, basically, from the budgeting methods used by other forms of advertisers, except for the smaller financial resources generally available. These budgetary methods may be classified roughly into the *aggressive* and *conservative* types.[5] The aggressive types of advertising budgets may be divided, in turn, into the following: (1) The *task method*, in which the objectives and the tasks of the campaign are determined, the effective copy and accompanying media are planned, and the related direct and indirect costs are determined; and (2) a derivation of the first method, which may be called the *intensive* coverage method, which involves planning the cost necessary either to penetrate effectively the competitive market or to increase the wholesale middleman's share of such market.

Some of the more important types of conservative budgeting applicable to wholesale middlemen are: (1) An arbitrary fixed absolute amount determined either by the chief financial executive or by committee action; (2) some fixed percentage of past sales representing either an arbitrary determination, a concept of average cost experience, or some concept of the experience for the kind of business and type of operation; (3) an adjustment of (2) by basing the percentage on estimated next year sales rather than on past sales; or (4) some combination of (2) and (3), with arbitrary additions if sales exceed estimates, and a reduction if sales fall below the estimates.

A budgetary method rarely used either by producers or wholesale middlemen is that of countercyclical budgeting; namely, a plan of expenditures which reduces the intensity of the advertising campaign during periods of prosperity and increasing the intensity during periods of depression. This may be accomplished by varying the tasks and objectives underlying the task method; or by varying the percentage of sales; or by building up advertising budget funds as reserves

[5] Except for the classification scheme, for a full discussion of each method see any standard advertising textbook and, especially, Albert W. Frey, *How Many Dollars for Advertising* (New York: The Ronald Press Co., 1953). The emphasis in these methods is placed on the manufacturer's point of view.

during periods of prosperity for expenditure during periods of depression. The logic of these countercyclical methods rests upon the assumption that more aggressive advertising by any individual middlemen during a period of depression can offset the effects of a general business decline. This logic is effective only where wholesale middlemen have an experience background in the use of advertising, as well as a position of importance in the channel. It is doubtful whether a middleman with only token or no advertising experience can suddenly achieve success in a depression by a suddenly expanded advertising campaign.

Objectives and types of advertising

Based upon the types of advertising situations outlined above, wholesale middlemen can have many objectives in their advertising. These may be summarized as follows:

1. To establish a primary demand for a given product category.
2. To establish a selective demand for the distributor's brand in a trading area (or trading areas) and/or to increase the share of the available total sales.
3. To establish the reputation and the special services offered by the middleman in given trading area (or trading areas).
4. To announce the availability of highly seasonable merchandise.
5. To publicize the range of product assortments and related aspects.
6. To prepare advertising copy to be used by integrated retail middlemen.
7. To publicize price information, especially in the form of market news letters.
8. To coordinate with the advertising materials of the producer or producers supplying the middleman's product assortments.

Given this wide range of possible objectives, it follows that wholesale middlemen can and do use all types of advertising, although, because of factors mentioned at the beginning, not necessarily in the same relative distribution as for producers or retail middlemen. The classification which appears to be most useful for wholesale middlemen is as follows:

1. *Method of presentation*—written, spoken, or combinations, and live versus recorded.
2. *Size* (as applied to written advertisements)—parts of columns; columns; fractional pages; page (or multiples thereof).

3. *Frequency of insertion or presentation.*
4. *Time factors*—(*a*) length of time of presentation; (*b*) seasonal versus all-year.
5. Types of media (see following section).
6. *Illustrated versus solid copy.*

Media problems and evaluation

The specialized aspects of much of the advertising efforts of wholesale middlemen, as compared with both producers and retail middlemen, place considerable importance on the selection of advertising media and the evaluation of their relative effectiveness. Before discussing the variables that are important in the selection of media, some attention should be given to the classification of the more important groups of media.[6]

1. *Newspapers*—daily, Sunday, rural.
2. *Magazines.*
    a. General—weekly, biweekly, monthly, home service.
    b. Women's—service, class, small-town and farm, motion picture, chain-store circulated, and specialized group.
    c. Class—general and specialized.
    d. Sporting and outdoor.
    e. Specialized—general, literary, parents.
    f. Scientific and mechanical.
    g. Association—fraternal, religious.
    h. Men's.
    i. Newspaper magazine supplements.
    j. Business and financial.
    k. Juvenile.
    l. Wood pulp.
    m. Farm—national, sectional, state, specialized.
3. *Outdoors*—posters, panels, billboards, electric and electric spectaculars, miscellaneous.
4. *Radio*—network, local; A.M. or F.M.
5. *Television*—network, local.
6. *Car cards.*
7. *Middleman-controlled*—catalogues, brochures, market news letters, salesmen's aids, point-of-sale displays, etc.

For wholesale middlemen the most fertile opportunities, as a general rule, lie in the business and financial magazines, and in the use of

[6] This classification is based, in part, upon Ben Duffy, *Advertising Media and Markets,* 2nd ed. (Englewood Cliffs, N. J.: Prentice-Hall, Inc., 1959).

their controlled media. This does not mean that opportunities do not exist for the use of other types of media by some middlemen. What is implied, however, is that given some of the advertising situations noted, most wholesale middlemen have too restricted trading area, financial, and kind-of-business orientations to use most media other than those indicated as the most fertile.

Against this background, what considerations should influence a given wholesale middleman's choice of advertising media?[7] Given the complex list of media noted above, and the thousands of individual publications, each potential advertising middleman must go through a highly selective process in which he decides between the broad groups first (i.e., newspapers versus magazine versus radio, and so on). From this priority ranking of these groups, considering the advertising budget, the middleman must then decide on the order of preference of the subgroups. If he decides to select magazines, in other words, which of the many subgroups is best? The final step in the initial process is to make a choice of particular media by name and owner.

In making these decisions, the wholesale middleman should be guided by the following factors:

1. *The nature of the product.* What kind of a product is it, how widely is it distributed geographically, and what are the channels?
2. *The users of the product.* This analysis, building upon the classification of customers discussed elsewhere, determines whether a general, widely circulated medium will be most effective, or whether some special interest medium holds better readership possibilities. In addition, analysis will reveal whether or not particular levels of executives within an organization can best be reached through certain types of media. For this reason, certain types of business publications and the middleman-controlled media have high appeal, as noted before. Where the middleman is pushing his own brands of widely used consumers' goods through the channel, use of so-called mass media may be justified.
3. *The type of advertising.* The relationship to type of media is self-apparent and requires no additional explanation at this point.
4. *The objectives of the advertising.* At many points, as noted in the preceding discussion, the middleman's advertising objectives exert controlling influence on the medium; e.g., circulation of market news, or technical news about a mechanical product.

---

[7] Part of this discussion is based upon Duffy, *op. cit.,* Chapter 3.

5. *The traditional media pattern for the kind of business.* This factor is self-explanatory, especially in promoting particular categories of products.

6. *Quality of the media's circulation.* This requires careful evaluation of authenticated circulation data, with careful breakdowns of the special groups reached wherever that is possible or applicable. Frequently, the more important media will make valuable marketing-research studies available to wholesale middlemen advertising in these media.

7. *Costs of insertion.* Given a particular advertising budget, the cost of placing an advertisement in a given medium will influence, in part, how often and how many insertions will be made. Especially important also is the relationship between the cost of insertion and the number of readers, listeners, or viewers reached. This relationship is needed both on a total circulation basis and, where available, for the number who actually read or listen to the middleman's particular advertisement. If sales can be attributed to particular advertisement, then the cost of obtaining an order by advertising can be calculated. These calculations are necessary especially for the middleman-controlled media.

8. *Evaluation of the medium's effectiveness.* Apart from sales generating effectiveness as measured by orders, other marketing research tools may be used by the media themselves, by the research departments of the wholesale middlemen (where available), or by the media research units of the advertising agencies to determine both general and specific media effectiveness. Whenever such studies are available, they need careful evaluation by the middleman in scheduling his advertising campaign in particular media. Availability of financial resources and the importance of the advertising effort of the middleman will certainly influence how detailed and expensive will be this evaluation phase.

Coordination with personal selling

At the wholesale middleman's level, coordination of advertising and personal selling can best be obtained: (1) by sales meetings in which part of the agenda is devoted to a presentation of forthcoming advertising campaign plans; (2) by furnishing salesmen with copies of advertisements as they have appeared or will appear in noncontrolled media; and (3) by using the salesmen to generate requests for, or to circulate, the various types of middlemen-controlled media. Part of this coordination may be secured by using salesmen to aid the researcher in evaluating the over-all marketing effectiveness. In those cases where the middleman is promoting his own brands of products, salesmen can be used effectively in arranging retail dealer's displays or in distributing point-of-sale material.

Evaluation of over-all advertising effectiveness

Apart from the media evaluation referred to above, and depending upon the available research resources—both financial and personnel—the evaluation process would include the following: (1) Pretesting of advertising copy prior to actual use and insertion in the media; (2) evaluation of effectiveness in the media, including experimentation with the effectiveness of alternative format and copy in the same medium; (3) determination of direct and indirect effects, if any, on sales; and (4) determination of the effects, if any, on profits.[8]

Demand-Creation Activities: Personal Selling

The management of the sales force of the wholesale middlemen is a subject which is covered in part by the personnel management literature and, in part, by the sales management literature. Because of this breadth of subject matter, only the general outline of the material can be discussed in this section.

Determination of whether or not to use salesmen

There are very limited marketing circumstances under which wholesale middlemen do not have to use salesmen. One such situation exists under conditions in which the wholesale middleman makes a decision to operate a strictly mail-order type of business. The opportunities for this, as noted before, are not too numerous. A second situation exists where the wholesale middleman operates principally as a buying middleman. A third situation exists where a considerable proportion of sales may be made as an order-taking operation in connection with cash-and-carry middlemen receiving many orders by phone. A final situation may be found in which a cooperative marketing association, in using fruit auctions, assigns the selling responsibilities to the auctioneer.

In the great majority of wholesale middleman situations, personal selling is necessary, but wide variations of practice are found both

---

[8] The reader interested in the various statistical, psychological, and other research tools, and in representative studies, should consult the basic advertising and marketing research textbooks.

as to numbers and types of salesmen to be utilized. So far as numbers are concerned, the small-scale independent proprietorships embrace a large number of establishments in which the owner probably doubles either as the only salesman or, at least, the principal one. At the opposite extreme are to be found the large sales-size and multiunit establishments, employing large numbers of salesmen, with possibilities of both the territorial and product specialization.[9] Many size variations, so far as sales force is concerned, are to be found in between these extremes.

Within these wide variations of both personal and nonpersonal selling situations are to be found many variations so far as types of salesmen are concerned. At one extreme of the range of possibilities are the salesmen employed by such types of operations as the orthodox grocery wholesalers, in which no distributor's brands are carried in inventory. The variety of products to be sold is so large, and the coverage retail middlemen so intensive, that a salesman can function but little better than an order taker. When, however, this type of middleman adds a line of his own brands of products, more opportunities may be offered to the salesman for creative selling.

For highly technical, complex, and very expensive types of industrial goods, the salesmen may have to negotiate with potential buyers for as much as a year, or even longer, before the order is obtained. He may have to utilize a team of engineers and other specialists to work with him during the course of the negotiations. In addition, he is faced with the pressure of the knowledge that if the sale is lost, a significant percentage of the estimated years' total sales may disappear. Under such circumstances, it is not surprising to find that the type of salesman utilized represents high-calibre talent, is paid among the highest salaries, and may be of executive level within the wholesale middleman firm.

Very closely related to this situation are those salesmen who sell products for which the wholesale middleman has been given an exclusive distributorship. Somewhat different selling skills are needed by those salesmen employed by the types of wholesale middlemen who operate on organized grain exchanges. In these selling situations, the main ability needed is to negotiate transactions at the most favorable price conditions. The products' virtues cannot be given any oral puffing since every party to the transaction has available the results of either government or private-agency grading. Contacts with other

---

[9] See the previous discussion of organizational aspects in Chapter 8 in this connection: The general sales-size and employee-size characteristics were discussed in Chapters 2 and 3.

wholesale middlemen may be of great value, especially in highly critical market conditions.

Under some product-selling circumstances, the salesmen of the wholesale middleman may have to cooperate closely with the missionary salesmen employed by the manufacturer, especially if any sales are to be credited to the middleman's account. In the case of wholesale distribution of certain pharmaceuticals, the middleman's salesmen may have to cooperate with the producers' detail men visiting doctors and dentists, or they may have to function both as a detail and sales person.

Budgetary aspects

Given such wide variations in selling situations and in types of salesmen needed, it is no wonder that the selling expenses of wholesale middlemen (as a per cent of sales) would show wide variations. In addition, wide variations in methods of remuneration used will have important effects on the amounts budgeted.

Recruitment and training aspects

Within the range of specifications for salesmen, based upon the range of the situations discussed, the recruitment and training of salesmen have no distinctive features compared with any salesmen in other kinds of business. Wide numbers and types of recruitment devices are available: the middleman's nonselling employees; want ads; requests to producers; professional employment agencies, etc. Sources of recruitment may be the following: personnel employed by the company; competitors' employees; product sources, customers; noncompeting middlemen; university graduates; and miscellaneous. With such wide range of talents required, training methods may range from the highly informal on-the-job type to lengthy, formal programs. Training may be conducted by the company's employees, by outside experts, by the producer's staff, or by varying combinations thereof.[10]

Territorial and quota aspects

Except for the most simple selling situations, the wholesale middlemen have to allocate part of their trading areas to individual salesmen, and to assign estimated quotas (total and by-products lines) to each salesman. The territorial assignments to salesmen stem from the determination of trading area boundaries as discussed in Chapter 4. Given these boundaries, the total number of customers can be de-

[10] See the basic personnel-management and sales-management literature for detailed discussions.

termined from previous sales budget analysis, together with data of time needed per call and travel times between each call. Coupled with estimated time amounts needed for reports and other indirect selling activities, the total number of salesmen can next be calculated. Except for special selling allocations, the bases are then established for subdividing the trading area into component salesmen's territories.

Given the total sales budgets estimates discussed earlier in the chapter, and given the allocation of customers based upon the trading area analysis, the bases are available, also, for subdividing the total sales budgets into quotas for each salesman. Special allowances may have to be made for the sales accounted directly by the headquarter's staff. Apart from setting each salesman's goals in relation to total sales expectancies, these quotas may be of importance in determining salesmen's compensation.

Remuneration

The variations in the methods of compensating wholesale middlemen's salesmen match the variations in types of selling situations and types of salesmen employed. Depending upon the difficulty of the sales task, the period of negotiation, the margins of profit, the risk involved, and the nonselling objectives provided by management will be the nature of the remuneration plan. Especially important will be the salesmen's attainment of their respective quotas and the profitability of such orders.

Within these variables, then, the wholesale middleman can pay straight salaries, straight commission plans, combination of salary and commission, and various additions including various types of bonus plans. In addition, variable arrangements may be made for traveling expenses.[11]

Evaluation of salesmen's effectiveness

Parallel to the evaluation of advertising effectiveness is the necessity for the careful evaluation of each salesman's effectiveness. One measure of effectiveness is, of course, the salesman's actual sales performance in relation to his assigned quotas. Another is the profitability of the accounts sold. Other factors include quality of the servicing of accounts, the types of products sold, and the achievement of certain nonselling activities. This topic will be discussed in further detail in Chapter 20.

[11] The characteristics of each remuneration plan and the conditions under which each may be used are discussed in D. M. Phelps, *Sales Management* (Homewood, Ill.: Richard D. Irwin, Inc., 1951), Chapter XXVIII.

Demand-Creation Activities: Relationship of
Wholesale Middlemen to Producers

Whereas the preceding discussion of demand-creation activities has centered almost completely on wholesale middlemen as such, it must be recognized that, because of the channel conditions discussed earlier, there are many important relationships of these activities to those of producers. Three situations will be mentioned briefly: by direct integration; by the use of advertising allowances; and by the producers' training activities.

Relationship, by direct integration

Under circumstances of producers' control of the wholesale middleman through direct integration, it follows of necessity that the middleman's demand-creation activity is derived from and is completely dependent upon the producers' activities. All of the brand-preference creation is executed by the producer, as well as other advertising objectives. The main demand-creation activity of the wholesale middleman is to extend all such efforts to the territory assigned to his salesmen. The range of product assortments, similarly, will be curtailed to those permitted by the producer under the integration agreement. In many cases, the producer usually assigns quotas to each middleman.

Relationship, by advertising allowances

Where underlying channel conditions do not permit of producer control by direct integration, the producer may attempt to influence the wholesale middleman's demand-creational activities by granting to him advertising allowances for cooperative advertising. While used more frequently for large retail customers, product assortment conditions and the necessity of compliance with the Robinson-Patman Act may force producers to extend such allowances on proportionate terms to wholesale middlemen.

Relationship, by producer's training activities

Especially where highly technical products are concerned, producers may achieve coordination with wholesale middlemen by training their salesmen on an annual or more frequent basis. If formal or informal integration exists, such training may be so complete as to make it unnecessary for the middleman to provide any further training. Under conditions of the managerial struggle for channel control, these producer's training activities may be a shrewd device to attempt to influence the direction of successful channel control. In other cases, the producer may assign his own salesmen to work the middleman's territory with the middleman's salesmen.

Legal Aspects

Apart from the contractual elements involved in the law of sales[12] and the law of agencies as it applies to the duties and responsibilities of agent middlemen, an important legal aspect frequently overlooked is the negotiation of technical leases under those circumstances in which highly technical and expensive equipment and buildings used for business purposes are leased instead of being sold outright. In addition, the legal aspects must be prepared in a professional manner for the complicated financing arrangements which may accompany the sale and/or leasing of many expensive industrial and consumers' goods.

The legal aspects of other elements of selling must be evaluated properly as they apply to wholesale middlemen operations. Protection of distributors' brands under existing trade-mark laws requires technical legal advice wherever any complicated product and geographical protection situation is involved. Similarly, careful legal protection may have to be provided for package designs whenever and wherever used. Legal advice will be required, also, under those circumstances where the middleman's pricing policies and other activities involving selling cut across the provisions of important Federal and state legislation. Middlemen involved in operating on wholesale organized markets for agricultural products are required to register with the Secretary of the U. S. Department of Agriculture.

Delivery and Post-sales Servicing

These elements of selling are exactly the same as their counterparts in the function of buying. They reappear in connection with the discussion of selling because of the variations found between buyers and sellers in assuming responsibility. The elements involved will be listed here, but the details necessary for discussion are identical

[12] For a complete treatment, see George G. Bogert and William E. Britton, *Cases on The Law of Sales,* 3rd ed. (Brooklyn: The Foundation Press, Inc., 1956).

with those already discussed under buying. One such element is the determination of responsibility for delivery of products sold, and for the delivery costs related to such services. In the case of mechanical-type products, selling assumes responsibility both for initial installation and continuing post-sales servicing and repairs. For other types of products, post-sales services include advice as to new uses and other aspects of utilization, including information about competing products.

Nonprice Selling Policies

The main policy aspects of the selling function are those related to price policies, and these will be discussed in detail in the two chapters which follow. Certain nonprice policy aspects have either been discussed in relation to merchandising and buying or have been inferred in the preceding sections of this chapter. Accordingly, only brief discussion will be presented here of policies relating to product assortments, brands, demand creation, guarantees, and size of order.

Product assortments
Product assortments have both a buying and selling perspective for wholesale middlemen. It is sufficient to note here that all of the preceding characteristics and policy aspects of product assortments apply as well to selling as to buying.

Brand policy
The relationships already noted for merchandising and buying apply to the policy aspects of brands as they are involved in selling.

Demand-creation policies
It is in connection with advertising and personal selling that wholesale middlemen can introduce some new policy aspects not already discussed. To be sure, some of these policies do stem from other policies adopted for product assortments and distributors' brands. Given, in other words, a strong policy of featuring distributors' brands, it follows that the wholesaler must feature, correspondingly, a policy of strong advertising campaigns and aggressive personal selling to secure necessary product "push" through the marketing channel. This would assume, in turn, the use of aggressive rather than conservative budgeting methods.

In addition, wholesale middlemen may feature aggressive advertising in conjunction with such special selling services as cash-and-carry operations, rapid delivery, market news services, and order aspects such as mixed shipments. The salesmen become the wholesale middleman's chief contact in the channel for making effective all of these merchandising strategy policies and the related price and nonprice aspects of selling.

Guarantee policies

Apart from guaranteeing their own brands of goods, wholesale middlemen can adopt variable policies with respect to guaranteeing producers' product assortments. It has been indicated that the use of these "double" guarantees may represent a type of merchandising strategy, and that the selling policies help to crystallize the advantages of such strategy through customer contacts in the channel. In addition to explicit guarantees, there may be implied guarantees in accordance with the law of sales and where wholesale middlemen purport to sell specified grades of products. Finally, where wholesale middlemen perform installations and postsales repairs and servicing, they may adopt policies of additional guarantees for these aspects.

Size-of-order policies

Increasingly, in the attempt to increase profits, wholesale middlemen have adopted critical reviews of the relationship for each account between size of order and profitability. As a result of such studies, and especially where highly varied product assortments are made available, middlemen may adopt a policy of using minimum order quantities. This policy, when used, must then be vigorously publicized both in the wholesale middleman's advertisements and through the salesmen. Price policies may have an important relationship.

QUESTIONS AND PROBLEMS

1. To what extent is the discussion of buying merely a reversal of the discussion of selling? To what extent is it considerably different?
2. How is the complexity of the wholesaling sector reflected in the types of selling situations?
3. What are the vertical and horizontal perspectives of the buying-selling situations in the channel?
4. What is the scope of the selling function viewed in its complete wholesaling sector perspective?
5. Recapitulate the extent to which the determination of product assortments reflects a selling emphasis.

6. What does customer analysis involve so far as selling in the wholesaling sector is concerned?

7. What is the nature and value of sales budgets?

8. What is, or should be, the relationships between sales budgets and purchase budgets?

9. What is the relationship of the sales budgets of a given wholesale middleman to the sales budgets of other wholesale middlemen in a multiphase channel arrangement?

10. Of what basic value is advertising to those wholesale middlemen who are not controlled either by the producer or, in the case of consumers' goods, by the retailer?

11. To what extent does the problem of advertising by a wholesale middleman assume major significance in relation to selling?

12. How do the media problems of a wholesale middleman differ from those for producers and retail middlemen?

13. What are the variations in the types of salesmen needed by wholesale middlemen?

14. What are the special spatial problems faced by wholesale middlemen in allocating salesmen's efforts?

15. How do the selling policies and activities of wholesale middlemen interlock with those of the manufacturers? with those of retail middlemen, for consumers' goods?

16. How important are the legal aspects of selling?

17. To what extent may successful selling be contingent upon the quality of delivery and postsales servicing elements?

CHAPTER INTEGRATING ASSIGNMENT

This chapter has attempted to give the reader something of the variety and complexity of the selling function in the wholesaling sector apart from matters of price and terms of sale. In order to demonstrate your grasp of the variety and complexity, you are asked to do the following: (1) Excluding matters dealing with pricing, enumerate in detail the component elements of the selling function; (2) critically compare and contrast the relative importance of these, in tabular form, for each of the more important selling types of wholesale middlemen. Based upon this, indicate the incidence of the selling function under various types of channel considerations, and explain the role of the management unit in each.

15

Prices, Price Policies, and Terms of Sale

In view of the wide body of basic books and research studies available which deal with this subject, the discussion in this and the next chapter can only serve to point up certain aspects which emphasize the viewpoint of the wholesale middlemen. Within this point of emphasis, two broad divisions of subject matter have been made. This chapter deals primarily with the wholesale price structure in its external aspects. Chapter 16, after a brief review of the manufacturers' price policies, emphasizes in detail the extent to which wholesale middlemen have price policies, and the types of such policies which result.[1]

General Nature and Strategy of Pricing in Wholesale Markets

Meaning of price structure

Underlying this entire discussion of pricing and price policies is an understanding of what is meant by price structure.[2] This discussion

[1] In view of the breadth of available literature, the bibliography pertinent to this chapter can only be suggestive and not comprehensive in its coverage.

[2] The presentation which follows is based upon the author's ideas contained in E. A. Duddy and D. A. Revzan, *Marketing: An Institutional Approach*, 2nd

of price structure is divided into two parts—the general concept and the concept more closely related to the view of the wholesaling sector. The general concept has been stated as follows:

A general price structure represents the unification of the prices of individual goods and services into an over-all price series reflecting interrelationships of demand (competing, completing, complementary, etc.) according to degree; interrelationships of time factors; institutional factors in terms of type of operation and the level thereof; of spatial relationships; varying degrees of managerial and governmental controls; and the presence of erratic forces. The concept of a price structure is useful in showing the effects of various variables on price as it works to effect the coordination of buyers and sellers.

The concept of price structure has back of it the assumption that individual prices are the fibers from which an entire price fabric is knit. Accordingly, individual prices have real meaning only in relation to the over-all price structure. Stated another way, if the present economic order in the United States is primarily one of individual exchange cooperation working through a system of markets and prices, then the price structure is a concept useful in explaining the degree to which there are systematic relationships present sufficient to constitute an over-all pattern of price movements which can be called a structure.[3]

When the price structure is viewed additionally in relationship to the marketing structure, the following concept is applicable:

A price structure, viewed as one part of the marketing structure, may be said to be the resultant of the basic nature of the products involved, the nature of the buying interests for the product in a definite market area, the competitive relations of buyers and sellers in the respective market areas for the product, the competitive relations of the commodity to other commodities, and legal regulations.[4]

Given these background concepts, the last part of the discussion needs to emphasize variations in the complexity of price structure when subdivided by commodities.

From a marketing viewpoint commodities vary with respect to the degree of complexity of their respective price structures. A list of the forces which are at work to affect this degree of complexity must necessarily include the following. Commodities with multiple uses seem to be characterized by more complex structures than those commodities with but a single important use or with few important uses. Furthermore, the type of selling base appears

---

ed. (New York: McGraw-Hill Book Co., Inc., 1953), Chapter XXV, and in D. A. Revzan, *The Wholesale Price Structure for Oranges, with Special Reference to the Chicago Auction Market,* Studies in Business Administration, Vol. XIV, No. 1 (Chicago: The University of Chicago Press, January 1944), pp. 1–5, 59–69.

[3] Duddy and Revzan, *op. cit.,* pp. 444–45.

[4] Revzan, *op. cit.,* p. 4.

definitely to affect the nature of the price structure. On the one hand, those commodities sold on the basis of personal inspection by buyers or their marketing representatives give rise, because of these types of transactions, to price quotations which are highly unstandardized, except where attempts have been made to establish grading of the commodities on a commonly accepted basis (either by government authorities, members of the commodity group, or both). On the other hand, selling and buying transactions involving commodities sold on the basis of description or samples—buyer's, seller's or those from some outside source—give rise to more "systematized" prices based on more widely accepted qualitative standards.

The susceptibility of a product to factors affecting consumers' demand evaluations, such as branding by shippers and producers; variations in the physical size; the use of containers as opposed to shipments in bulk, together with variations in the types of containers when used; the use, in addition to containers, of individual inner wrappings or special containers per sales unit; and the presence or absence of the use of advertising—all these factors increase the complexity of the analysis.

Moreover, the wider the geographical area of distribution and the more numerous the types of wholesale and retail middlemen involved in that distribution, the more complex will be the price-structural elements. Similarly, the greater the number and types of markets utilized, the more complicated will become the resulting study. The presence of both cash and futures transactions will operate to affect the price structure in a similar manner. A greater degree of complexity is introduced, also, with longer marketing seasons and with larger volumes of commodities to be marketed during such seasons. Again, a highly competitive market and very elastic demand for a product increase the number of component elements in the price structure which may have to be studied. And the more the marketing of a particular commodity is subjected to legislative control or to programs of government experimentation, the more difficult will it be to describe, in simple terms, the nature of the price structure for that product.[5]

The component elements of the price structure

As a prelude to the later discussion of the factors influencing the nature of the over-all price structure and its segments, the following outline indicates the range of component elements.[6]

A. Competitive factors.
B. Management and other administrative controls.
C. Government regulation and administration.
  1. Promotion of competition and use of competitive price.
  2. Government price controls and price decisions.
  3. Government recognition of monopolies.

[5] *Ibid.*, pp. 60–61. For a somewhat different discussion and classification, see Jules Backman (ed.), *Price Practices and Price Policies* (New York: The Ronald Press Co., 1953), Chapter 3.

[6] Based upon Duddy and Revzan, *op. cit.*, pp. 446–57.

D. Product factors.
1. Different classes of the same product.
2. Interproduct relationships.
    a. Relationships between prices of competing and complementary goods.
    b. Relationships between prices at different stages of production.
    c. Relationships between prices at different channel positions.
E. Time factors.
1. Short-run, seasonal, cyclical, and secular changes.
2. Cash-futures price relationships.
3. Measures of price flexibility and inflexibility.
F. Spatial factors.
1. Delivered prices varying according to transportation costs.
2. Delivered prices uniform to all buyers within the boundaries of specified market areas.
3. Delivered prices varying unsystematically.
4. Varying combinations of (1), (2), and (3).

Diagrammatic representations of the component elements of price structure

Based upon the preceding outline of component elements, it may be useful to consider how sets of diagrams might be better employed to visualize their relationships. The first set of diagrams would have reference to particular vertical and horizontal price structure relationships for a single product produced by a particular producer. In its vertical aspect, the diagram would show by a bar or a similar graphic device the price as it increases from beginning production to levels of intermediate and final use, by margins paid for the performance of particular functions, and/or the margins realized by each and every agency performing such functions. The horizontal set of diagrams introduces the additional element of geographic variations in these prices (margins). One final aspect would be to show how these vertical and horizontal relationships change over time.

The second set of diagrams would present the relationship which exists horizontally and vertically, as above, between the particular product of a particular producer and all other products of the same kind. Similarly, sets of diagrams would be used to show the interrelationships of measures of demand elasticity and product substitutability. In addition, a third set of diagrams, closely related to the preceding sets, would introduce the price relationships between the product and the family of interrelated products of which the individual product is a part (e.g., apples and all fruits and vegetables; neckties and all boys' and men's wearing apparel and accessories).

The final sets of diagrams would weave the relationships over time between the price of the particular product and the over-all price structure of which it is a part. Thus, depending upon whether the product was an industrial or a consumers' good, an appropriate measure of the over-all price structure would be, respectively, the wholesale price index and the consumers' price index of the Bureau of Labor Statistics. An additional part of such diagrammatic representation would be the importance of each product's price in the over-all structure.

The incidence of pricing initiative in the channel

Any logical discussion of the role of wholesale markets in pricing must include an analysis of the incidence of pricing initiative in the channel. The connotation of pricing initiative here is one of the existence of such degree of individual or group managerial control of the market as to make possible the effective use of price policies in the channel.[7] Thus, the present discussion excludes the example of no-managerial initiative—or very little initiative—in establishing prices.

The first example of pricing initiative is the classic case of the producer-initiated pricing situation. This illustration reflects every nuance and type of producer control from the pure monopoly example, at one extreme, to the use of informal integration technique, at the other, which permit the use, in turn, of a variety of price policy alternatives of the types to be reviewed briefly in the next chapter. Such prices which are the resultant become strategic elements in each producer's attempt to secure successfully managerial control of the channel(s) for his product(s).

In the second example, the wholesale middleman—or a combination thereof—assumes the position of importance as the price policy originator in the channel. This position of dominance may arise from any one, or a combination, of the following:

1. The use by the wholesale middleman (or the group) of distributors' brands under his production and/or marketing control.

---

[7] The term "price policy" here refers to the absence of such conditions of a truly competitive market as to permit management to take a planned course of action in effecting varying degrees of control over the exact price or prices of products in the channel. See Edwin G. Nourse, "The Meaning of Price Policy," *Quarterly Journal of Economics,* **55** (February 1941), 175–209.

2. The delegation of specific pricing authority to the wholesale middleman by the producer, as in the case of selected selling brokers and manufacturers' sales agents.
3. The special case of (2) in which several agricultural producers may form a cooperative marketing association with authority to establish specific price policies.

Finally, under conditions of the use by retail middlemen of distributors' brands, or by virtue of the volume of goods purchased, the retail middleman may supplant both producers and wholesale middlemen as the point of price-policy initiation in the channel.

Where the channel viewpoint is not confined to a single product category, but rather is broadened to include all competitive aspects, all forms of pricing-policy initiative may be competing with each other in the channel. Indeed, as has been noted in earlier discussions, the same wholesale middleman may accept the price-policy initiative of some producers for part of his assortment while acting as a price-policy initiator for other parts of his product assortment. This give and take of the nexus of price policy initiative power is a very significant aspect of both channel structures and the whole strategy of pricing in the wholesale markets.

Review of Price Determination in Organized versus Nonorganized Wholesale Markets

As has been indicated earlier, the existence of organized wholesale markets is one of the unique characteristics introduced into any discussion of pricing in the wholesaling sector. When found for agricultural and other extractive industry products, these markets furnish a much closer approximation of price determination under conditions approaching the competitive norms as compared with determination in the nonorganized markets. Such competitive aspects are manifested in: (a) the lack of any significant identification of any producer's products in terms of the trading arrangements, with the possible exception of the auctions; (b) the frequency with which prices change over time in relation to basic underlying factors; and (c) the general inability of any single buyer or seller, except under the exceptional conditions of a corner, to control or establish prices as a result of particular policies. These competitive characteristics are accentuated additionally by the trading rules of the organized markets applicable to the buying and selling middlemen members.

Of a level of importance almost equal to that of the competitive norms are the systematic price structures resulting from trading operations in organized wholesale markets.[8] The characteristics of these systematic price structures may be summarized as follows, based upon the previous discussions.

1. Relationships between prices between each product grade level which reflect some concept of normal spread, and the requisite that higher prices do not exist for lower quality levels. The stability of these spreads over time is one salient characteristic as long as basic underlying factors do not change.

2. Similar spread relationships are expected between size units, from premium to discount positions based on the nature of the product.[9]

3. Again, spread relationships are expected, where applicable, between varietal types. These varietal premium preferences may be expected to show variations from market to market while maintaining consistency within each market.

4. Some pattern of spreads may be expected between competing markets which reflect the effects of transportation cost factors and related variables.

5. The availability of basic price and related data to interested buyers and sellers in widely circulated government and private market news reports.

6. Finally, the existence of spreads between cash and futures prices in the same market and between markets which are meaningful for speculative and hedging transactions.

These characteristics generally are absent either in part or in whole from prices as determined on nonorganized markets. Apart from the failure to use grade specifications (although brand designations may be used instead), these markets also lack any evidences of failure of buyers and sellers to have insignificant size positions and widely circulated market news reports.

With the declining importance of the organized wholesale markets (for reasons already noticed), and with the increasing evidence of the existence of imperfect competitive conditions in the channel, it may be stated as a basic generalization that systematic price structures have declined sharply in importance in the last 25 years or more. As a result, pricing in the wholesale sector has become much more complex,

[8] For one example pertaining to fresh oranges, see Revzan, *op. cit.*

[9] Sizes of oranges and weights of livestock are pertinent examples.

with many more policies used at each level of agencies in the channel. In addition, many types of backward vertical integration have removed many transactions from the realm of these organized wholesale markets even where they exist. The changing role of the organized wholesale markets has been noted in the previous discussions of the buying and selling functions.[10]

Price Relationships: General Statement

The opening discussion has presented both the general and the marketing concept of price structure. The next sections discuss, in both theoretical and applied fashion, aspects of price relationships as they are found within the price structure. At the wholesale level, these price relationships can be discussed within the types of whole-sale-level transactions involved. If the nature of the available price data permitted, these price relationships might be expressed in terms of the kinds and levels of customers involved, based upon the earlier classifications.

In the absence of such price information, the most workable statement of price relationships within the wholesaling sector may be in terms of the following types of movements:

Type 1. Movements of wholesale prices according to degree of flexibility; i.e., flexible, inflexible, and neither flexible nor inflexible categories.

Type 2. Movements of various wholesale prices of groups of basic raw materials, semifabricated products, and completely fabricated products (i.e., by economic sectors, or stage of processing).

Type 3. Movements of the wholesale prices of the most important kinds of products within each category in type 2.

Type 4. Relative movements of wholesale and retail prices.

If available, on any varied basis, supplementary analysis of whole-sale prices at each stage of the channel of distribution would be of value. But very few useful examples are available. The analysis in type 4 represents a partial approximation.

Given a discussion of these price relationships, the final discussion in this chapter will include an analysis of the factors affecting the

---

[10] For a vigorous presentation of the decline of these markets and the necessity for new versions, see Vernon Mund, *Open Markets: An Essential of Free Enterprise* (New York: Harper Bros., 1948).

wholesale price relationships. The analysis will emphasize those factors contributing to increased flexibility as contrasted with those factors leading to increased rigidities; those factors contributing to more complicated relationships as against those contributing to more simplified relationships; and, finally, factors contributing to more systematic as against nonsystematic price relationships.

Price Relationships: Structural and Cyclical Flexibility

Basic definitions

If the previous discussion of price structure is kept in mind, then the discussion of price relationships in terms of flexibility character-istics will refer to the degree of responsiveness of price to changes in the basic factors related to it. Two types of price flexibility may be distinguished. *Structural price flexibility* refers to the degree of responsiveness of price for a single commodity to the hierarchy of prices. Such flexibility reflects, as will be discussed later, technological, competitive position, elasticity, and production quantity and capacity factors. *Cyclical price flexibility* refers to the responsiveness of individual prices to the movement of general prices during the phases of the business cycle. Hansen[11] indicates three types of responsive-ness: (1) the tendency for prices of agricultural products to diverge from those which are administered and/or government-regulated; (2) the tendency for prices of raw materials to diverge from those of finished products; and (3) differentiation of cyclical movements of prices between sensitive and insensitive groups of commodities.

Price relationships, by degrees of flexibility

Data are available from 1926 to 1939 and from 1946 to 1950 to show changes in groups of wholesale prices according to flexible, in-flexible, and neither flexible nor inflexible categories (see Table 25). These data reflect one aspect of degree of cyclical flexibility. In the 1926 to 1939 period, the inflexible wholesale prices as a group reached a low point during the depression of the 1930's, which were only 16 per cent below the 1926 level and less than 13 per cent below the 1929 level. The flexible wholesale price group declined, on the other hand, by more than 50 per cent between 1929 and 1932. Prices for

---

[11] A. H. Hansen, "Price Flexibility and the Full Employment of Resources," *The Structure of the American Economy: II. Toward Full Use of Resources* (Washington, D. C.: National Resources Planning Board, June 1940), pp. 27–34.

TABLE 25

WHOLESALE PRICES OF COMMODITIES, BY DEGREE OF
FLEXIBILITY GROUPS: 1926–1951
(1926–29 = 100)

Period	Inflex- ible	Neither Flexible nor Inflexible	Flex- ible
Annual			
1926	101.9	102.9	102.7
1927	100.3	99.9	97.8
1928	99.5	99.1	99.8
1929	98.3	98.2	99.8
1930	96.4	91.4	82.4
1931	92.6	80.2	63.2
1932	87.3	71.4	49.6
1933	86.0	73.9	57.1
1934	90.1	81.4	68.6
1935	90.2	80.8	73.5
1936	90.7	82.1	76.0
1937	94.5	89.0	83.6
1938	N.A.	N.A.	N.A.
1939	95.1	85.9	72.6
Quarterly			
1946: June	112.6	120.4	133.9
September	115.9	127.5	147.0
December	123.0	141.1	182.5
1947: March	129.4	147.4	197.2
June	131.6	146.3	183.3
September	135.2	150.8	189.7
December	137.3	156.7	203.4
1948: March	140.6	161.1	192.0
June	142.4	162.2	196.2
September	147.7	167.0	191.3
December	148.3	167.3	187.2
1949: March	150.5	164.8	178.7
June	148.8	158.9	168.3
September	147.4	157.5	171.1
December	147.6	157.1	173.2
1950: March	149.0	158.7	171.9
June	149.0	159.3	178.1
September	152.7	172.6	200.6
December	164.3	186.5	211.8
1951: January	168.2	187.4	213.5

Source: *Survey of Current Business,* **31** (April 1951), 10.

the in-between group averaged a 27-per-cent decline between 1929 and 1932.[12]

In the post-World War II inflationary period, significant differences were apparent in the degree of price increase on an over-all time period basis and in fluctuations between component time periods. Between June 1946 and January 1951, prices of the inflexible group increased by 49.4 per cent as compared with 59.4 per cent for the flexible group, and 55.6 per cent for the in-between group. Two interesting aspects of the behavior during inflationary periods should be noted: the more rapid increases as compared with the declines during the depression period and the closer relationship between the increases for the three groups than for the declines. The removal of price controls and later reinstatement during the post-World War II period, followed once again by removal, must be considered.

Price relationships, administered versus other prices

Some very significant wholesale price relationships may be computed by comparing the size of relative changes in administered prices with such changes in other prices. Means[13] has defined administered prices as those in which, "a company maintains a posted price at which it will make sales; or simply has its own prices at which buyers may or may not purchase." A somewhat different concept has been advanced by Nourse,[14] in which he states that administered prices are

. . . found in those situations in which a seller is a sufficiently important factor in the market and has sufficient control over productive resources to make it possible for him to adopt and carry out a price-and-production program.

In studying the frequency of price changes of 747 items in the wholesale price index of the Bureau of Labor Statistics between 1926 and 1933, Means found the following:

191 items had one change or less than one change every 10 months
183 items had changes at the rate of less than one per 4 months, but more than once every 10 months

[12] It should be remembered that these are group averages of many individual commodity prices. Within each group there was, accordingly, a range of percentage declines.

[13] Gardiner C. Means, "Industrial Prices and Their Relative Inflexibility," *Senate Document No. 13*, 74th Cong., 1st Session (Washington, D. C.: U. S. Government Printing Office, 1935).

[14] Edwin G. Nourse, *Price Making in a Democracy* (Washington, D. C.: Brookings Institution, 1942), Chapter 1.

192 items had changes at the rate of more than once per 4 months, and less than 3 times every month

181 items had changes at the rate of at least 3 times every 4 months[15]

More recently he has made comparisons of wholesale price movements between 1942–1947 and 1953–1957, by product groups according to whether or not the industries were concentrated, highly competitive, or the "mixed" or "in-between" group (see Fig. 10).[16] Compared with the changes in the 1942–1947 period, he sought to show that the price inflation of 1953–1957 was due to the increase in the concentrated industries. On the other hand, wholesale prices increased by only small amounts or actually declined in the highly competitive industries. Whether the conflicting patterns are due to the incidence of administered prices, or because of different patterns of cost increases (especially labor) and pressures of increased demand, has been vigorously debated.

Price Relationships: Component Segments of the Wholesaling Sector

In the myriad of thousands of individual wholesale prices for particular products, which change at variable rates and amounts over time, any semblance of systematic analysis can be obtained only by having recourse to some commodity-group price averages. This section of the discussion of wholesale price relationships, in striving for such systematic analysis, stresses differential movements of prices in terms of commodity groups as such, in terms of economic sectors (i.e., stages of processing), and in terms of relationships between movements of raw materials prices and prices of closely related finished goods.

Relationship, by commodity groups

Two aspects of wholesale price changes, by commodity groups, can be given for purposes of illustrating the diversity of movements. In using these data, one must be aware that among the important factors which influence such changes, and which are to be discussed later, are differences in the quantities of such products sold through the marketing channels and in the seasonal patterns of such marketing flows. The first comparison (see Table 26) shows changes in the prices of 1,641 commodities, by major groups, between July 1953 and

---

[15] Means, *op. cit.*

[16] "Debate on 'Administered Prices'," *New York Times,* March 22, 1959, p. E-7.

GARDINER MEANS' THEORY ON PRICE RISES

Means says recent inflation is not due to an excess of demand over supply. He says it is "administered" inflation caused by large non-competitive industries raising their prices regardless of market conditions. Height of bars in Means' charts shows rise in wholesale prices by commodity group. Width is importance of each group in price index. Means says in previous inflation excess demand pushed all prices up, especially in competitive industries, the most sensitive to the market.

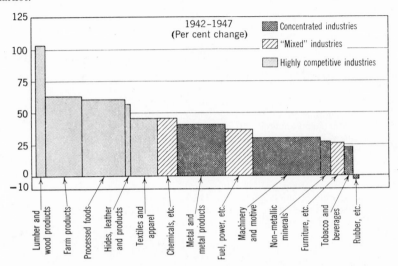

But in the most recent inflation (below), he says, price rises came primarily in industries dominated by a few companies where there was little competition. At the same time there was a decline in prices in some competitive industries. He says this shows inflation was caused by "administered" price rises, not excess demand.

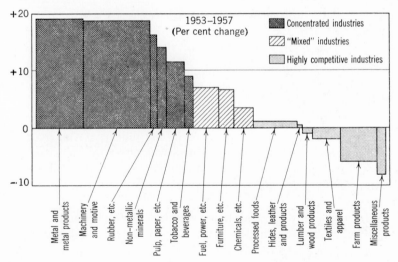

FIG. 10. *Source:* "Debate on 'Administered Prices'," *New York Times,* March 22, 1959, p. E-7.

TABLE 26

WHOLESALE COMMODITY PRICES—CHANGES IN 1,641 INDEXES BY MAJOR GROUPS: JULY 1953 TO JANUARY, 1954 (1947–49 = 100)

Item	July, 1953 Index	Jan., 1954 Index	Changes in Indexes			
			Total No.	Higher	Lower	Unchanged
All commodities	110.9	110.8	1,641	533	432	676
Farm products	97.9	97.9	93	41	45	7
Processed foods	105.5	106.2	138	57	51	30
All other commodities	114.8	114.5	1,410	435	336	639
Textile products and apparel	97.5	95.5	193	22	97	74
Hides, skins, leather products	100.0	95.2	48	8	28	12
Fuel, power, lighting	111.1	110.6	39	11	16	12
Chemicals and allied products	106.2	107.2	230	64	30	136
Rubber and rubber products	124.6	124.8	38	17	9	12
Lumber and wood products	121.1	117.0	63	15	32	16
Pulp, paper, allied products	115.8	117.1	54	21	5	28
Metals and metal products	129.3	127.1	1,176	63	44	69
Machinery and motive products	123.4	124.3	375	144	41	190
Furniture, other household durables	114.7	115.2	87	33	22	32
Nonmetallic structural minerals	119.4	121.0	33	19	2	12
Tobacco mfrs., bottled beverages	115.6	118.2	18	3	0	15
Miscellaneous, n.e.c.	95.3	101.1	56	15	10	31

Source: Charles A. R. Wardwell, "Structure and Trends of Wholesale Prices," *Survey of Current Business,* **34** (March 1954), 13.

January 1954, in terms of those whose index increased, those which were lower, and those which remained unchanged.[17]

Many features of Table 26 should be noticed. On an over-all basis, the stability of prices in these two months reflected the balancing effects of no changes in the indexes for 676 commodities which offset increases in 533 indexes and declines in 432 indexes. And by groups, stability in the prices of farm products was offset by increases in the average for all processed foods of 0.7 percentage points, and a decline of 0.3 percentage points for the average of 1,410 other commodity indexes.

For farm products, over-all index stability resulted from the stability in 7 indexes offsetting higher prices for 41 indexes and lower prices

[17] Other aspects are also discussed. See Charles A. R. Wardwell, "Structure and Trends of Wholesale Prices," *Survey of Current Business,* **34** (March 1954), 13–19.

for 45 indexes. On the other hand, although the prices of 30 processed foods remained unchanged, the size and importance of the increases in 57 indexes more than offset the declines in 51 other indexes. For the remaining 1,410 commodity price indexes, despite no changes for 639 indexes, declines among 336 more than offset the higher prices registered for 435. Similar variations can be found among the 13 subcategories composing this group of 1,410 commodities. In every case, despite significant numbers of unchanged price indexes, the commodity groups registering increases or declines were important enough to cause similar changes for the group as a whole.

The effects of three different types of post-World War II recessions on the average prices of selected commodity groups are shown in Table 27. Especially to be noted were the following: (1) The large

TABLE 27

PER CENT CHANGE IN MAJOR CATEGORIES OF
WHOLESALE PRICES: FIRST ELEVEN MONTHS,
1948–1949, 1953–1954, 1957–1958 RECESSIONS

	Per Cent Change		
Commodity Group	Nov., 1948 to Sept., 1949	July, 1953 to May, 1954	July, 1957 to May, 1958
All commodities	−6.1	0	+1.1
Farm products and processed foods	−7.7	+1.6	+6.8
All other commodities	−5.2	−0.3	−0.3
Crude	−12.7	−7.0	−9.6
Intermediate	−6.3	−0.9	−0.8
Finished	−3.2	+0.3	+0.6
Producers	+0.2	+0.7	+2.4
Consumers			
Nondurable	−5.9	−0.1	−1.2
Durable	−1.5	+0.6	+1.5

Source: Harold Wolozin, "Wholesale Price Movements in Three Recessions," *Monthly Labor Review*, **81** (August 1958), 888–890.

price declines in the 1948 recession (an average of 6.1 per cent) compared with over-all stability during the 1953–1954 recession, and a 1.1 per cent increase during the 1957–1958 recession; and (2) the sharp deviations during each recession of the price movements for the component commodity groups from these average changes. Particularly striking in these respects is the contrast between prices of farm products and processed foods, on the one hand, and those for all crude products, reflecting the depressed condition of the latter group in all recessions, while certain cost rigidities actually resulted in price increases for farm products and processed foods during the 1957–1958 recession.[18]

Relationships, by stage of processing (economic sectors)

Beginning with October 1955, data have been made available which show wholesale prices of commodities by stage of processing (economic sector) since 1947.[19] The main stages represented by the data are crude materials—further processing; intermediate materials, supplies, and components; and finished goods. Appendix Table A3 presents the subclasses under each of these stages together with measures of selected changes between 1947 and 1958. Keeping in mind the variations noted previously in terms of the variability and flexibility of wholesale prices, the following conclusions may be noted:

1. The wholesale prices of all commodities as a group in each of the periods 1949, 1953, and 1958 were higher than the level in 1947.
2. There was a very small increase in the combined price index of all crude materials between 1947 and 1958, compared with the increases for the intermediate materials, supplies, and components group and the finished goods group.
3. The main reason for the relative stability of the wholesale prices of crude materials was due to a decline of 8 per cent in prices of foodstuffs and feedstuffs, which offset price increases of 11 to 49 per cent in the remaining subclasses.
4. Within the intermediate materials-supplies-components group, sharp variations in movements were apparent. For example, a 30 per cent decline in the prices of supplies for animal feeds was offset by over-all stability in the wholesale prices of intermediate materials for manufacturing, and of a range of increases from 3 to 69 per cent in the prices of other subclasses. Additional evidences of variability are to be found in the year of peak price index, the year of the over-all low point in the index, and

[18] The interested reader may wish to refer to Wardwell, op. cit., for similar comparisons of price movements of raw materials versus finished products; of natural versus synthetic materials; and of agricultural products prices versus those for nonagricultural goods.

[19] See the initial presentation and summary discussion in the Monthly Labor Review, 78 (December 1955).

variations in the directions of movement in the intermediate years between 1947 and 1958.

5. Within the finished-goods sector, wholesale prices of producers' finished goods increased an average of 62 per cent over 1947 compared with an average of only 17 per cent in the prices for consumers' finished goods. While the peak of producers' goods prices was reached in 1958, those of consumers' goods were recorded in 1951, 1952, 1957, or 1958 depending on the subgroup.

Price relationships: raw materials and related finished products

Depending upon the percentage relationship between raw-material prices and the prices of related finished goods, of the percentage importance of inflexible labor costs, of the ratio of transportation costs to product value, of government-price controls, and of related factors, wide variations will be found to exist in the movements of wholesale prices of raw materials relative to movements of wholesale prices of related finished goods. Table 28 confirms these variations based upon these factors for several categories of agricultural, industrial, and consumers' goods for the periods December 1949–March 1951, and March 1951–February 1952.

From these data, one may hypothesize that, where raw material prices are a significant percentage of the final value of the finished product, both sets of prices change in close relationship each to the other. Thus, for example, the index of wholesale meat prices moved in close relationship to variations in wholesale livestock prices. On the other hand, the wholesale prices of rubber tires and tubes have fluctuated much less than the prices of crude rubber; and the prices of leather footwear increased at the same time that the index of hide and leather prices was being halved. In addition to the factors mentioned above, these variable movements are related, also, to the administered-price hypothesis discussed in an earlier section.[20]

Price Relationships: Wholesale Price Structure Relative to Retail Price Structure

One final type of price relationship remains to be analyzed, namely, the relative movements of wholesale prices compared with retail prices on an over-all basis. It may be useful to compare, in addition, the relative movements for two significant commodity segments—food and

[20] For a somewhat lengthier discussion, see "Recent Price Developments," *Survey of Current Business,* **32** (April 1952), 4–9.

TABLE 28

RELATIVE MOVEMENTS OF SELECTED RAW MATERIALS
AND FINISHED PRODUCTS WHOLESALE PRICE INDEXES:
1949–1952 (1947–1949 = 100)

Group	March, 1951, as Per Cent of Dec., 1949	Feb., 1952, as Per Cent of March, 1951	Feb., 1952, as Per Cent of Dec., 1949
All commodities	119	97	115
Farm food products	128	95	121
Processed foods	119	98	116
Livestock	145	86	125
Meats	134	94	126
Milk for manufacturing	123	102	126
Dairy products and ice cream	111	108	119
Grains	117	102	119
Cereal and bakery products	112	100	112
Plant and animal fibres	184	70	129
Apparel	110	97	108
Raw cotton	149	89	132
Cotton products	130	85	111
Apparel wool	285	41	118
Wool products	163	70	113
Raw silk	189	89	167
Silk products	162	89	144
Hides and skins	150	48	71
Footwear, leather	121	95	114
Petroleum, crude	101	100	101
Gasoline	111	99	110
Fats and oils, inedible	220	45	98
Other chemicals and products	119	94	112
Paint materials	125	96	120
Prepared paints	111	101	112
Crude rubber	249	81	202
Tires and tubes	132	100	132
Footwear, rubber	135	90	122
Lumber	129	95	123
Millwork	123	97	118
Wood household furniture	117	97	113
Nonferrous metals	137	100	137
Machinery and motive products	112	103	115
Household appliances, radio, TV	104	100	104
Leaf Tobacco	111	100	111
Cigarettes	103	102	104

Source: Survey of Current Business, **32** (April 1952), 7.

apparel. Table 29 shows these comparisons by utilizing the Wholesale and Consumers' Price Indexes of the Bureau of Labor Statistics.

So far as the over-all indexes are concerned, it is evident from the data that, beginning in 1949, consumers' goods prices generally have advanced more rapidly relative to a 1947–1949 base than have whole-

TABLE 29

COMPARISONS OF COMBINED WHOLESALE AND
RETAIL PRICE INDEXES AND FOOD AND APPAREL
INDEXES: 1947–JUNE 1959
(1947–49 = 100)

Year and Month	Wholesale Price Index			Consumer Price Index		
	All Commodities	Processed Foods	Textiles and Apparel	All Items	Food	Apparel
1947	96.4	98.2	100.1	95.5	95.9	97.1
1948	104.4	106.1	104.4	102.8	104.1	103.5
1949	99.2	95.7	95.5	101.8	100.0	99.4
1950	103.1	99.8	99.2	102.8	101.2	98.1
1951	114.8	111.4	110.6	111.0	112.6	106.9
1952	111.6	108.8	99.8	113.5	114.6	105.8
1953	110.1	104.6	97.3	114.4	112.8	104.8
1954	110.3	105.3	95.2	114.8	112.6	104.3
1955	110.7	101.7	95.3	114.5	110.9	103.7
1956	114.3	101.7	95.3	116.2	111.7	105.5
1957	117.6	105.6	95.4	120.2	115.4	106.9
1958	119.2	110.9	93.5	123.5	120.3	107.0
Jan. 1959	119.5	108.7	93.3	123.8	119.0	106.7
Feb. 1959	119.5	107.6	93.7	123.7	118.2	106.7
Mar. 1959	119.6	107.2	93.9	123.7	117.7	107.0
April 1959	120.0	107.2	94.1	123.9	117.6	107.0
May 1959	119.9	107.7	94.5	124.0	117.7	107.3
June 1959	119.6	108.1	94.9	124.5	118.9	107.3

Source: Monthly Labor Review, Bureau of Labor Statistics (Washington, D. C.: U. S. Government Printing Office).

sale prices. This is a reflection, in part, of some of the trends noted earlier in discussing wholesale price relationships; e.g., the greater diversity of price movements because of the wider variety of commodities than would be expected for consumers' prices. An additional factor, undoubtedly, is the compounding of increases at the wholesale level into the retail price structure by virtue of the system of mark-ups widely employed by many retail middlemen.

These diversities of rates of relative increases between wholesale and retail prices become even more apparent when comparisons are made for the foods and wearing-apparel categories. For foods, the average wholesale prices in 1958 were 11 per cent above the 1947–1949 base, compared with a 20.3 per cent increase in consumers' prices. In addition to what has been said in partial explanation, it must be remembered that the wholesale price components of many consumers' goods have variable relationships to the final value. Even more striking than the foods price comparisons is that for wearing apparel. Apart from an abnormal bulge in 1951, wholesale prices by 1958 averaged 6.5 per cent *less* than those of the 1947–1949 base. Consumers' prices, on the other hand, averaged 7 per cent higher.

Factors Affecting Wholesale Price Relationships

Apart from brief references to factors affecting price relationships, no complete analysis (or the outline of such analysis) has been presented. The more complete analysis and discussion in this final section are divided into four parts: (1) Factors affecting the general level of wholesale prices; (2) a classification of the basic factors affecting the wholesale price structure in its important component aspects; (3) a restatement of the importance of channel consideration; and (4) a summary breakdown of the factors in terms of their effects on flexibility versus rigidity, complicated versus simplified structure, and systematic versus nonsystematic price structures.

Factors affecting the general level of wholesale prices

Although the earlier discussion of the meaning of price structure has indicated some of the environment of related factors, no attempt was made to develop any measure of systematic relationship. However, a careful study of the quantitative and qualitative factors affecting the general level of wholesale prices indicates that six economic factors have been associated most closely with changes in the general level of wholesale prices since 1921. These have been determined by Lynip to be:[21]

1. The demand for industrial goods and main-featured consumers' goods as measured by the Federal Reserve Board's, *Index of Industrial Production.*

[21] This discussion is based upon B. F. Lynip, "Factors Affecting the Wholesale Price Level," (San Francisco: California and Hawaiian Sugar Refining Corp., Ltd., July 1950).

2. The size of the total labor force based upon the data of the Bureau of the Census and of the Bureau of Labor Statistics.
3. The productive capacity of all manufacturing plants as measured by data of steel plant capacity (Iron and Steel Institute).
4. The price of gold (constant since 1933 at $35 per Troy ounce).
5. The total dollar value of the outstanding public debt.
6. The total dollar value of the outstanding private debt.

Using these six factors, Lynip has calculated their relationship to the general level of wholesale prices in the following formula:

$$Pw = 0.215P + 3{,}470\,\frac{1}{C_s} + 10{,}500\,\frac{1}{C_L} + 1.26p_g + 0.331D_g + 0.452D_p - 298$$

where

Pw = Bureau of Labor Statistics, *Wholesale Price Index*
P = Federal Reserve Board, *Index of Industrial Production*
C_s = Iron and Steel Institute, *Measure of Steel Production*
C_L = labor force (in millions)
p_g = price of gold (dollars per Troy ounce)
D_g = government debt (billions of dollars)
D_p = private debt (billions of dollars)

The accuracy of this forecasting formula is affected by such qualitative factors as the occurrence of wars, government price controls, social upheavals, inventions, acts of God, and other unpredictable vagaries of nature.

Basic factors affecting the wholesale price structure and its component segments

There are, as has been stated earlier, a myriad of wholesale prices, each clothed in its own institutional environment and, yet, a part (of varying importance) of the fabric of the entire price structure. While some mention has been made of causal factors from time to time in the preceding sections, it would seem useful to present at this point in the discussion a more systematic classification of the more important factors. The outline which follows is the result.[22]

I. *Characteristics of the Product and Industry*
   A. Product characteristics related to demand structure.
      1. Volume of production.

[22] This outline is based in part upon materials contained in the following sources: Backman (ed.), *op. cit.*, Chapter 3. Joe S. Bain, "Price and Production Policies," in Howard S. Ellis (ed.), *A Survey of Contemporary Economics*, (Philadelphia: The Blakiston Co., 1948), Chapter 4.

    2. Degree of durability and perishability.

    3. Type of product: extractive industry, industrial good, consumers' good.

    4. Stage of processing: crude or raw material, semiprocessed, or fully processed.

    5. Elasticity of demand: price and income elasticity.

    6. Sales-promotional characteristics: degree of standardization, differentiation, or uniqueness.

    7. Use characteristics: single versus multiple.

    8. Seasonality of movement to market.

  B. Buyer characteristics.

    1. Type: producer, middleman, institutional, ultimate consumer.

    2. Numbers.

    3. Locational characteristics including density of distribution.

    4. Purchasing habits—reasons.

    5. Frequency of purchase.

    6. Size of each purchase.

  C. Cost factors.

    1. Ratio of raw materials prices to finished product prices.

    2. Transportation costs as a per cent of raw materials and finished products prices.

    3. Nature and relative importance of labor costs.

    4. Other cost characteristics.

II. *Market Structure*

  A. Price determination in organized versus nonorganized markets.

  B. Markets with many sellers, free entry.

    1. Consumers' goods, differentiated products, many buyers: durable and nondurable goods.

    2. Producers' goods, unimportant product differentiation: many or few buyers.

  C. Markets with few sellers in general.

    1. Consumers' goods, differentiated products, many buyers: moderate or high degree of concentration.

    2. Producers' goods: moderate or high degree of concentration.

III. *Channel Structure*

  A. Type of channel.

  B. Presence or absence of organized wholesale markets (see also IIA).

    C. Incidence of channel control: producer, wholesale middleman, retail middleman, or combination.

    D. Incidence of sale versus leasing.

    E. Incidence of multiple sales versus single transactions in the channel.

    F. Presence or absence of trade habits and customs.

 IV. *Government Control*

    A. Resale price maintenance and unfair trade practices legislation.

    B. Agricultural products price controls and marketing agreements.

    C. Franchise monopoly rates and prices.

    D. Robinson-Patman Act.

    E. Effects of wages and hours legislation.

    F. Tariffs.

    G. Patents and copyrights.

    H. Trade mark protection.

Importance of channel considerations

The wholesale price structure in its over-all and component segment aspects, and the pricing activities and policies of producers and wholesale middlemen cannot be divorced realistically from channel characteristics and considerations. It is necessary to remind readers, accordingly, when studying the factors affecting wholesale price relationships, to refer back to the earlier discussion of pricing initiative in the channel. Especially important is the nexus of managerial control in the channel, and the extent to which the channel structure either expands, restricts, or eliminates pricing and policy alternatives.

Factors affecting flexible versus rigid wholesale price relationships

Given the preceding evidence of degrees of flexibility of wholesale price movements, which of the factors outlined above tend to create rigidities in wholesale prices, and which tend to foster flexible prices? The extent to which union controls and other institutional factors lead to high relative labor costs, which remain unvarying over long contract periods, may result in rigid prices, in turn, particularly if other conditions are present. One such additional factor involves the degree of sensitivity of the price of component raw materials, especially if they represent a significant per cent of the products' final value. The structure of the market (as noted above) in terms of monopolistic *versus* competitive elements is a very important set of variables resulting, correspondingly, in either rigid or flexible price relationships.

This is true particularly when accompanied either by organized or nonorganized wholesale markets.

Additional factors affect this rigid *versus* flexible characteristic of wholesale price relationships. The fostering of producer-controlled prices through permissive legislation coupled, as well, with the existence of government-controlled prices leads, of necessity, to increased rigidities. On the other hand, government news activities, regulation of organized markets, and the enforcement of provisions of the Robinson-Patman Act may all lead to more flexible price relationships. The relative speed with which visible supplies can be increased during short periods of time is important: the greater the speed, the more inflexible will be prices, especially if accompanied by frequent fluctuations in demand. Rigidities of short-run supply, accompanied by frequent demand changes, tend to have the opposite effect. Finally, perishability, other things remaining equal, tends to lead to more flexible prices, *except* where some form of effective storage may exist to regulate supplies to demand.

Factors affecting the degree of complexity of price relationships

Simple price structures are formed primarily under monopolistic conditions (perfect or imperfect) where relatively few products exist in available assortments, where such products have comparatively narrow ranges of use, and where there is a marked predominance of direct channels. Complex price relationships exist where there is relatively high degree of freedom of entry of producers; where semidirect and indirect channels predominate; where many differentiated products are found in any given category; where multiple users and types of users are found; and where flexibility exists so far as frequency of change is concerned. In addition, existence of bargaining-power pressures in the channel, within or in violation of existing laws, will create greater complexities. The earlier discussion of the marketing concept of price structure suggests additional factors.

Factors affecting systematic versus nonsystematic price relationships

These have been discussed in detail in the materials dealing with organized and nonorganized wholesale markets.

QUESTIONS AND PROBLEMS

1. Evaluate critically the concept of price structure presented in the chapter.
2. What are the principal variables which shape the marketing structure?

3. What is meant by "variations in the complexity of the price structure" when subdivided by commodities?

4. Take some particular commodity, and use the price data to illustrate what is meant by the diagrammatic representations of the component elements of price structure.

5. What is meant by the incidence of pricing initiative in the channel?

6. Compare and contrast price determination in organized versus unorganized wholesale markets.

7. In connection with question 6, differentiate between systematic and unsystematic price structures.

8. Of what value are the four types of price relationships as presented?

9. Differentiate between structural price flexibility and cyclical price flexibility.

10. What conclusions can be advanced based on the data in Table 25?

11. What is meant by "administered prices"? What is their relationship to the discussion of price flexibility?

12. What do the data of Table 26 reveal about wholesale price relationships?

13. What is the relationship between the stage of processing (economic sector) and wholesale price movements?

14. How may wholesale prices be expected to fluctuate relative to retail prices for related product categories?

15. Why are the range of factors which affect wholesale price relationships so varied and complex?

CHAPTER INTEGRATING ASSIGNMENT

This chapter has emphasized the external aspects of wholesale prices, price policies, and terms of sales. A fundamental aspect of this is the presentation of the concept of a price structure. You are asked to write an essay in which you relate this wholesale price structure to the funnel concept and to channel structure. In addition, include an analysis of the complexities introduced into the concept of wholesale price structure by reason of multiple sales of the same product categories.

16

Prices, Price Policies, and Terms of Sale (Continued)

The preceding chapter has emphasized, in the main, the external environment in which are found the price structure and wholesale price relationships, although some internal implications could not be avoided. The orientation of the discussion in this chapter is to shift the frame of reference to the individual management unit (or groups thereof), the internal environment in which the individual prices of particular products are established.[1] This orientation emphasizes, accordingly, the "myriads of prices" to which reference has been made from time to time in the preceding chapter. The main approach will be to emphasize the individual and group price-determining activities of producers' and wholesale middlemen's managerial units although the presentation will not be detailed.[2]

Producers' Price Policies: General Classification

To understand the price-determining activities of producers, it may be well to outline the pertinent policies which they follow when acting

[1] The only individual prices which are not the concern of this chapter are those which are determined within the institutional framework of the organized wholesale market, as previously discussed.

[2] The pertinent bibliography for this chapter contains a wealth of references dealing with producers' price policies. In addition, the reader will find that most basic marketing textbooks contain large sections of applicable materials.

either as individual management units or as part of groups of such units.[3]

I. *Group Price Policies*[4]
   A. Price leadership.
   B. Sharing the market.
   C. Basing-point systems.
      1. Single basing point.
      2. Multiple basing point.
   D. Delivered price systems.
      1. Uniform.
      2. Nonuniform.
   E. Trade association activities.
      1. Cost exchange and standardization.
      2. Open-price systems.
   F. Patent controls.
   G. Cooperative marketing association activities.
   H. Miscellaneous policies (n.e.c.).

II. *Individual Price Policies*
   A. Time differentials: guarantees against price declines.
   B. Spatial differentials.
      1. Systematic.
         a. Mill base prices.
         b. Delivered prices.
      2. Nonsystematic.
   C. Product differentials.
   D. Cost-price relationships.
      1. Market plus positions.
      2. Market positions.
      3. Market minus positions.
   E. Discount policies.
      1. Channel position.
      2. Quantity.
         a. Cumulative.
         b. Noncumulative.
      3. Type of product use.
      4. Advertising allowances.

[3] This outline follows the scheme used in E. A. Duddy and D. A. Revzan, *Marketing: An Institutional Approach,* 2nd ed. (New York: McGraw-Hill Book Co., Inc., 1953), Chapter XXV.

[4] This list includes policies of historic interest as well as those currently in effect.

5. Brokerage.
6. Functional.
7. Price stabilization.
   a. Resale price maintenance.
   b. Unfair trade practices acts.
8. Datings and anticipations.

The main characteristics of each type will be described in later sections. Mainly, the presentations will be aimed at sufficient detail to relate these policies to the preceding concepts of price structure.

Individual Producers' Considerations in Establishing Prices

The following discussion centers around three main subjects: (1) A statement of the basic objectives underlying each producer's initiation and administration of a price policy; (2) the criteria used by each producer in evaluating what will constitute a satisfactory selling price under a given policy; and (3) additional considerations to be used in establishing particular prices.

Price policy objectives[5]

Companies, depending upon their relative sales-size position, product-line complexities, the nature of the industry structure of which they are a part, and the level of available executive talent, may use a range of devices varying from the highly mathematical to that of intuition and trial-and-error in formulating particular price policies and accompanying particular prices. But whether such policies are based upon rational or intuitive methods, and whether or not there are formal, written statements of the objectives of such policies, a framework of executive action at the producers' level may be assumed to include the following:

1. *The achievement of certain stated or implied profit objectives.* These objectives may be visualized as ranging from maximization by means of some monopolistic position at one extreme to a notion of "competitive average" at the other. It may assume some target percentage of return on investment; or it may have the opportunistic note of "the best any given market conditions can yield at any given time period." Stability of level and/or return may

[5] See A. D. H. Kaplan, Joel B. Dirlam, and Robert F. Lanzillotti, *Pricing in Big Business: A Case Approach* (Washington, D. C.: The Brookings Institution, 1958), Chapter 2, for the source of some of the ideas used in this section. See also, based on this study, Robert F. Lanzillotti, "Pricing Objectives in Large Companies," *The American Economic Review,* **XLVIII** (December 1958), 921–940.

be dominant in executive thinking, or an aggressive competitive tone may prevail. Short-run conditions may force an individual management to have very modest profit expectations during the first few years of marketing experience, compared with long-run expectations. In certain regulated industries, however, the profit objectives may have to conform more or less with the norms established by government policy, and the pertinent judicial interpretations and modifications of such policy.

2. *Stability of prices may be the compelling objective.* This may be because of attempts at "discipline" within an industry; or it may represent a tacit, gentleman's agreement to eliminate the possibilities of recurring price wars. It may represent one form of management philosophy consistent with the availability of some form of "protection" under resale price maintenance laws. The elimination of the hours of effort involved in the sheer mechanics of constructing and changing intricate price lists may be a significant motivating feature. Or, finally, there may be some form of superstitious belief in the magic of price stability so far as effects on profits are concerned.

3. *Every producer is faced with the problem of having to define in more or less quantitative terms objectives of market penetration.* The penetration goal may be stated in terms of absolute dollar volume of sales; in stated percentage increases over preceding sales performance; or in stipulated realizable percentages of existing or estimated total sales available for given product categories. Spatially, this latter percentage calculation may involve a single trading area; some regional combination of trading areas; or a combination, in turn, of the regional combinations approximating a "national" market. The penetration, or market-share percentages, may be uniform as between trading areas, or may vary sharply from trading area to trading area. Aggressive pricing may be related to a management's effort to open up or to penetrate a new area, or to the maintenance of an existing market share.

4. *Individual producers may vary prices to meet changing pricing conditions* in those industries in which highly competitive conditions are a continuous characteristic. This consideration exists separately from the existence of the group policy of price leadership as practiced in any industry.

5. Related to (2) above, but introducing separate considerations as well, are those situations *where the producer prefers to emphasize nonprice competition policies to emphasis on price considerations.* The reasons may stem from efforts to introduce "snob appeal"

into the product, e.g., a Rolls-Royce, or perfume, or jewelry, or special whiskies. In the case of industrial goods, the high units of prices initially and the accompanying inelasticities of demand may make certain ranges of price changes ineffective at best. The effectiveness of advertising and of other forms of sales promotion, and the existence of patent controls and other economic rigidities, may re-enforce the emphasis on nonprice competition.

Criteria of satisfactory selling price

Given the above policy objectives, which the individual producer-seller may adopt singly or in some combinations, attention needs to be directed next to what constitutes a satisfactory selling price.[6] Three basic criteria of satisfactory selling prices may be advanced: (1) that the particular price be high enough to yield the profit and return rates consistent with those of the above objectives selected by management; (2) that the particular price be low enough so as to yield expected market penetration percentage (or range); and (3) that the price be low enough to maximize consumption of the product at the particular profit-return objectives desired, thus preventing any unexpected diversion of sales to competitors which would reduce, in turn, the level of expected market penetration ratios.

The dilemma created by this set of criteria of a satisfactory selling price is that no single pricing policy can adequately meet all taken together. Each management must act, accordingly, to assign necessary weights to each objective in order to get the best reconciliation with the policy selected.

Additional considerations in the computation of actual selling prices

The above-stated objectives and criteria delimit the environment of management thinking so far as selling price policies are concerned. The additional considerations which follow are those which an individual producer must (or, at least, should) use in the process of transforming policy considerations into actual selling prices.[7]

1. Scientific or rule-of-thumb estimates prepared by the individual producer of the total volume of sales available to all firms in the industry. These estimates may be group determined (as by a

---

[6] These criteria and the additional criteria to be discussed in the next section owe much to ideas presented by Howard C. Greer (former Professor of Accounting, The School of Business, The University of Chicago) in unpublished materials.

[7] In this connection, the interested reader may wish to review Alfred R. Oxenfeldt, *Industrial Pricing and Market Practices* (Englewood Cliffs, N. J.: Prentice-Hall, Inc., 1951), Chapter 4, for a discussion of methods used by specific sellers to set prices.

trade association) or determined by the individual producer. Generally, these estimates, however prepared, should pertain to the total area reached by the producer as well as to component trading areas.

2. Similarly, scientific or rule-of-thumb estimates should be made of the percentage of the over-all total, and of each trading area's total, which the individual producer views as his marketing objective.

3. The determination of the detailed cost structures applicable to these estimated volumes.

4. The calculation of fluctuations in the components of (3) as related to variations in the expected sales volumes.

5. Based on (3) and (4), the relative composition of the individual producer's costs and relative position in the cost structure compared with that applicable to the industry.

6. If the relative position of the individual producer in (5) is too unfavorable, what possibilities exist for reducing those particular cost segments which appear to be out of line.

7. Calculation of a particular price (or range of prices) based upon the policy objectives, and the weighing of the above considerations.

8. The determination, as best as possible, of the expected effects of the particular price decision on the pricing decisions of the producer's competitors.

9. Finally, any necessary readjustments in the particular selling price(s) based upon (8).

Producers' Group Price Policies

Barring the existence of very special circumstances, the basic characteristic underlying the various types of producers' group price policies is the presence of varying degrees of imperfect competition. Each example to be discussed below deals with an industry situation in which monopolistic features are to be found in varying degrees of completeness. In some instances, the monopolistic elements in an industry have succeeded in obtaining governmental support for a particular type of group price policy.

Price leadership

This group price policy is found generally in those oligopolistic industries in which large, fixed investments are found in productive plant equipment, and in which chronic overcapacity may be found at varying time periods. In addition, the proportions of the productive capacity and of the industry's sales are not evenly divided between the existing firms. Generally, one or two firms have dominant shares of sales and of capacity as well as disproportionate positions of financial strength.

As a result of these characteristics, these firms usually, but not always, take the initiative in announcing price increases. By virtue of superior financial resources and share of the industry's productive capacity, such firms carry the veiled threat of price-war retaliation if their price leadership is rejected. However, these bases for "discipline" do not always succeed in keeping the larger firms as the leaders in announcing price reductions. In times past, steel, petroleum, and tobacco are some of the industry examples in which the group policy of price leadership has been effectively used.

Sharing of the market

By means of cartel arrangements, or by means of other collusive devices, domestic or international combinations of firms have succeeded in sharing markets effectively for varying periods of time. The principal objective is to increase each member firm's opportunity to secure the advantages of prices approaching most closely a true monopolistic level. These collusive schemes may assign large geographical segments of markets for particular products to a single firm on a protected basis; or buyers, presumed to be competitors, may band together to buy only at controlled price bids or in predetermined quantities and quality proportions. Alleged fixing of prices may result.[8] Certain types of exclusive distributorships may also become the key device through which there may be accomplished a systematic sharing of the market.

Basing-point pricing systems

This form of group price policies has been introduced into this discussion mainly because of its historical value. An additional reason is related to the wide range of views concerning the effects of such policies. The policy is so complex and technical that the brief presentation here can only be considered as an introduction designed to give the main characteristics and a perspective for this section of the discussion.[9]

---

[8] Such an allegation has been made in connection with the pricing of Salk vaccine by five producers [see "Drug Probes," *Business Week* (October 24, 1959), 140–41].

[9] For excellent discussions see the following:

Fritz Machlup, *The Basing-Point System* (Philadelphia: The Blakiston Co., 1949).

The essential features of this price policy may be summarized as follows:

1. Establishment of a single basing point, or a system of multiple basing points, from which prices are determined which are applicable to all plants of the industry regardless of whether or not they are located at basing points. The essential formula is to add to the artificial basing-point(s) price or prices the freight rates from the basing point to any buyer's location, *regardless* of the actual freight rate applicable from any given producer's location.

2. Thus, each producer's plant is given an area of exclusive marketing advantage, except for instances where a competitor uses either freight absorption, or cross-hauling, or nonprice-competition tactics. The structure of the industry (e.g., steel, cement) is such, however, that the threat of retaliatory tactics keeps such deviations in check.

3. In addition, each producer's plant, by virtue of the characteristics noted above, receives a variable net yield from different categories of customers, based on the relationship between actual and basing-point freight rates, and his f.o.b. prices and the basing-point prices.

4. Long-range effects may be noted in terms of restrictions of freedom of entry into the industry, the providing of a price umbrella regardless of cost position, the difference between actual geographical distribution of plants and some calculated distribution of "what should have been," and the consistent uniformity of quoted prices despite variations in underlying cost structures and applicable freight rates.[10]

5. Since this policy represents a sharp deviation from competitive practices, the necessity for industry cooperation is evident in the choice of basing points, in the selection of the basing-point prices and decisions as to changes, and in the industry discipline necessary to enforce the policy.

Corwin D. Edwards, "The Effect of Recent Basing Point Decisions upon Business Practices," *The American Economic Review,* XXXVIII (December 1948), 828–42.

Frank A. Fetter, *The Masquerade of Monopoly* (New York: Harcourt, Brace & Co., 1931).

Jules Backman (ed.), *Price Practices and Price Policies: Selected Writings* (New York: The Ronald Press Co., 1953), Chapter 7.

[10] See Machlup, *op. cit.,* Chapters 6 and 7 for a complete discussion.

Delivered price systems

With the declaration of the basing-point system as illegal, members of the industries involved generally converted to a system of uniform delivered prices used in other cases. The utilization of this type of policy may present very little solace relative to the group action found in basing-point pricing. Cost structures may still be so determined as to yield completely uniform delivered prices between so-called competing firms. In other instances, a single delivered price may be quoted as applicable over a wide geographical area. As a result, production-point yields may be highly variable, depending on structure of the transportation costs and their relative importance in the final selling price. Occasionally, a particular seller may upset the group control by resorting to the same type of freight absorption which was used under basing-point systems.

Trade association activities

In varying degrees of success, trade associations, by means of exchanging cost data in order to establish standard costs, and by means of open-price systems,[11] have had quite serious effects on the existence of competition among members on the domestic scene. Additional activities in product and package standardization, and in control of rate of innovation, may have further effects on pricing. In regard to foreign trade, trade associations may permissively form monopolies within the provisions of the Webb-Pomerene Act.

Patents and patent controls

These may have group price policy repercussions under conditions. (a) of cross-licensing arrangements which involve adherence to rigid prices or leasing terms; (b) of industry patent pooling, by means of which the rate of product innovation is controlled, thus permitting a much longer time in which to extract price returns from existing patents, as well as acting as a continuous price-stabilizing device; (c) where systematic pricing under royalty systems are used, as well as higher-than-competitive levels of prices for repair parts and services; and (d) which permit extraction of other control benefits through threats of withholding of patented devices in strategic production-use

---

[11] By an open-price system is meant the following: (1) the trade association acts as an agency for the collection of price information from its members; and (2) such information is interchanged between members with the purpose of establishing a common base for price quotations and the elimination (or at least reduction) of price cutting.

circumstances, unless price terms are agreed to. In some cases, such as in the pharmaceutical industry, there appears to be evidence of the existence of gentlemen's agreements under which competitors do not act to depress the price of a new "miracle" drug until the discovering firm has had sufficient time to recover its exploratory and developmental costs.

Cooperative marketing association activities

Except for the limiting factor of perishability of product, cooperative marketing associations of agricultural products may hope to increase price controls to members by close control over the quantity produced; by regulating daily and weekly shipments to markets; and by branding. In addition, they may exert pressures designed to secure favorable government regulations. Such control may be only partially effective because of the existence of product perishability already noted; because of the availability of a wide range of substitutes; because of insufficient control over percentage of total output; and because of failures of members to conform completely with the group's policies. In some cases, the nature of government policy and the existence of organized markets in which prices are determined may act as additional limitations.

Producers' Individual Price Policies

The existence of a climate of group policies sets an important limitation to the extent to which individual producers may establish price policies. In other structural situations, the individual producers may have a wider range of policy initiative. The incidence of few or all of the policies outlined below in any particular channel situation is a function of some of the variables to be discussed in a later section.

Time differentials

Under product circumstances where sales may be concentrated to a high percentage in certain seasons, wholesale and retail middlemen may refuse to place orders if there is any strong belief that price declines can be expected in future weeks or months. If economies of production and marketing are likely to be obtained by scheduling and delivering orders in larger quantities, a producer may obtain an important advantage by guaranteeing all orders placed early against all or part of any subsequent price reductions. If such price declines do

materialize, the producer may make the adjustments by cash allowances or deductions, or through delivery of additional quantities of
the merchandise.

Spatial differentials

There are several kinds of geographical price policies, apart from
the group policies discussed above, which individual sellers may use.
By means of f.o.b. pricing policies, the producer obtains uniformity of
quoted prices at point of production or shipment, with the delivered
prices varying according to differences in transportation and related
costs. On the other hand, the producer may use a policy which may
establish uniform prices for the United States; or for two sections—
east of the Rocky Mountains, and slightly higher prices west of the
Rocky Mountains; or, finally, prices which are uniform within several
zones.

Apart from the group policy consequences, an individual producer
may use uniform delivered price policies for any one of the following
reasons:

1. To obtain the benefit of being able to use advertising in which a
   single price (or perhaps two prices) can be featured, with the
   prices remaining unchanged for significant periods of time.
2. To avoid the necessity, as in very low-priced products, of using
   fractional prices to reflect transportation costs.
3. To compete on more favorable terms with regional or local producers who may have more favorable locations and freight rates
   to such regional or local markets.
4. To influence where wholesale middlemen will locate in relation to
   key distribution of his product.
5. To reflect the consequence of the presence, or possible presence,
   of selected group price policies.

Product differentials

Apart from differentials which may reflect variations in quality
levels, producers may establish other systematic or arbitrary price
differentials between products. These differentials may reflect assignable cost considerations, channel considerations, attempts to counteract price cutting, the use of pricing formulas under existing legislation,
or other considerations. Producers, by using deluxe as well as standard models, frequently stratify prices to extract maximum revenue
possibilities. In such cases, the existence of sharp differences in the
elasticity of demand may lead to highly competitive prices, per unit,

for that model category with the more elastic demand. Finally, differences in packaging may be used as a basis for price differences.

Cost-price relationships

Individual producers may couple with other pricing policies reflections of underlying cost considerations in varying relationships with selling prices designated as *market plus, market,* and *market minus* pricing.[12] Under *market plus* pricing policies, the emphasis is placed on a high degree of product differentiation. As a result, selling prices are not keyed at all to applicable cost bases. Thus, the snob appeal, the specialty-product aspects, and the monopolistic elements in selling prices are emphasized. The closest relationship of cost to selling price is found in policies of pricing *at the market*—the nearest approximation to the concept of economic theory dealing with pricing under conditions of workable competition.

Market minus pricing is followed most frequently by producers in introducing new products with estimated mass-market appeal; or during short periods of price wars; or in connection with authentic discount and other forms of sales. In the introduction of new products (in the meaning used elsewhere), the established price may be moderately below the announced "regular" price or below the going price for comparable products; or at approximately half price (including two-for-the-price-of-one) for a limited period of time; or even at no charge.[13] The sharp reductions in gasoline prices are illustrative of the price-war phase of *market minus* pricing. In some cases, the use of this pricing level may reflect the incidence of very competitive pricing elsewhere in the channel.

Where a given producer has a broad product assortment together with a wide range of quality variations, he may find it feasible to use all three levels by stratification of product lines.

Discount policies

Within the framework of existing legislation, the individual producer may or may not follow a systematic pattern of offering various classes of buyers discounts (reductions) from base prices. These discounts, while representing terms of sale, must be considered as being illustra-

[12] See Arch W. Shaw, "Some Problems in Market Distribution," *Quarterly Journal of Economics,* **XXVI** (August 1912), 703–65, for the earliest statement of these.

[13] For example, Hills Bros. introduced its coffee in the Chicago market by mailing a ½ lb can *free* to every mailbox householder. More recently, this policy has been used for dentifrices, instant coffees, and all-purpose detergents.

tive of pricing strategy. They may reflect the position of each middle-man in the channel, and the existence of traditional margins for each; e.g., 40 per cent off list price for regular wholesalers, and 25 per cent off for retailers.

Discounts may be based, also, upon the size of each purchase, thus reflecting supposed production and marketing economies; or they may be cumulated during a given period of time, thus reflecting additional economies presumed to be associated with concentration of purchases. Again, discounts may reflect the type and importance of each use to which a product or category of products may be adapted. And, for certain types of consumers' goods, producers may grant advertising allowances in order to get benefits from the wholesale middleman's reputation, from their more cooperative attitude in sales promotion, and, possibly, from lower media rates. A special form of channel discount may be found in the granting of discounts to *bona fide* brokers.

Closely related to some of the preceding forms of discounts are those based upon the range and quality of functions performed in the channel. Other discounts may be based upon the arbitrary judgment of the producer in connection with the use of resale price maintenance; or by virtue of the umbrella protection of margins under existing un-fair trade practice legislation. Some types of discounts are merely continuations of long traditions. As an example, the ordinary cash discount terms of 2/10/n/30 give purchasers a rate of interest of 36 per cent for paying the invoice within 10 days of its date. This rate of interest could not be obtained from either ordinary savings or even from very successful investments.

Other discounts based upon such *datings* as upon receipt of goods (r.o.g.), or end of month (e.o.m.) may represent unusual shipping arrangements, peculiar industry problems, bargaining power positions, or perpetuation, once again, of customs and traditions. Anticipations represent an additional form traditionally received by department stores. Thus, a buyer may be given an additional discount based on such terms as 2/10/n/30 if he pays his bill on the first day of the discount period instead of on the last day.[14]

From the wide array of discounts in use, it follows that, except for the controls exercised under existing legislation, many may reflect merely bargaining power balance between producer and his customers, actual price discrimination, or the continuation of tradition and custom.

[14] This discount would be calculated at 9/360 of 6 per cent.

Price stabilization devices

To the extent that individual producers find themselves as part of an industry in which some type of group price stabilization policy is in use, to that extent will the individual producer find himself under compulsion to tailor his individual price policy actions in harmony with the group price policy. In other instances, the existence of patents, other forms of monopoly position, or of successful product differentiation, coupled with the cover of permissive legislation, may yield an individual price policy of stabilization for considerable periods of time. This is true especially of resale price maintenance of producers' nationally advertised products in the light of the objectives discussed in a preceding section. Thus, the search for sales and profit stability may be dominant in the use of such policies by producers. In addition, the policy becomes an important weapon in the struggle for managerial control of the channel. Price stability may result, in some cases, from the large spread between costs and selling prices. And, interestingly, the selling price need not always be high. Thus, the price of chewing gum has remained stabilized for many years— with no apparent reduction either in weight or quality. Custom may lead to price stability, also, until significant changes in costs may force either increases or reductions to new levels which will, in turn, become customary.

Factors Influencing Individual Producers' Pricing Policy Activities

Individual producers, in formulating and establishing their price policies and actual prices as outlined above, must function within the boundaries set by the discussion of price structures and the factors affecting such structures, as discussed in the preceding chapter. However, within this framework, the individual producers have varying degrees of freedom in determining how much weight to assign to alternative combinations of factors in relation to their pricing activities. There is, in other words, a kind of "give-and-take" arrangement in which the individual producer operates within the restraining boundaries of the price structure, but may, in turn, influence these boundaries by the very nature of his decisions to the weighing of particular factors and the price policies and pricing actions which ensue.[15]

[15] In the discussion which follows, the general organization and content has been influenced by the discussion in Kaplan, et al., *op. cit.*, Chapter 4.

The importance of the individual producer's marketing objectives

In the sequence of causal occurrences, the single, most important set of factors affecting each producer's price policies and pricing activities would appear to be the nature of his marketing objectives. These objectives have considerable influence on, and relationship to, the pricing objectives discussed earlier in the chapter. Emphasis on non-price competition is one illustration. Thus, many unique types of industrial goods as well as many types of consumers' durable goods (e.g., jewelry, furniture, appliances), and some consumers' nondurables are marketed by producers with emphasis upon matters of design, exclusiveness, and the like. The objective of such nonprice emphasis is to minimize the necessity of featuring price. The same emphasis upon the objective of nonprice competition may result from regular policies of introducing new products, new uses for existing product assortment, identifiable or highly subjective product "improvements," or from the quality of product services in connection with initial installation, continuous repairs, use adaptation, and postsales relationships.

A second group of marketing objectives, related to the preceding, has to do with the producer's use of brands for product identification. Such identification may be used not only to give the producer's product (or complete product assortments) a position of strength in the channel but also to emphasize the nonprice competition objectives outlined above. In addition, branding may introduce elements of strong price competition by means of fighting brands while protecting, it is hoped, the nonprice position of the speciality brand of the same product category. A somewhat different aspect of relation to price competition may result from, or be the cause of, a producer supplying distributors' brands to middleman agencies in any given channel situation.

The producer already in business has a different marketing objective in connection with a new product. One aspect is a careful estimate of the time period involved in developing the full market prospects. This involves, in addition, a careful evaluation of the two-way relationship with the pricing policy pursued and the actual prices established. Selection of prices at too high a level may well lead to serious time delays in realizing sales potentials. A price, on the other hand, pitched at too low a level may well ruin all profit expectations. In addition, these interrelationships must be closely measured in order to secure accurate levels of production quantities in relation to cost structures.

Finally, each producer must determine accurately what his market penetration position is to be, trading area by trading area, and the level and stability of prices will significantly affect the penetration ratios. In addition, the alternative virtues of service and quality versus price must be debated closely in establishing this marketing objective.

The influence of the individual product characteristics

Given the general discussion of product characteristics presented earlier, each producer must consider very carefully how important individual product characteristics affect his pricing activities. Where the influence of the structure of the industry begins, and where that of the individual product ends, is very difficult to ascertain. For example, does the stabilized price quotations for crude oil and steel more nearly reflect the structure of the industry, or the durable and controlled output character of the products, or both? The influence of organized wholesale markets in establishing changing raw materials prices may affect, in turn, the ability of the producer of the finished product to stabilize selling prices. Little may be done if the product is highly perishable; but effective results may be obtained by means of hedging operations.

It may be argued, further, the more varied the end uses of a particular product, the more variable will be its selling prices, especially if it is sold on a wide domestic, or on an international, geographic scale. Conversely, the existence of bulkiness and resulting high transportation costs may give regional producers of such products the advantage of securing and protecting regional price "pockets." All highly differentiated products, and especially those which are newest in the channel, may give the producer more policy initiative than would be possible for highly standardized products. The initiative in pricing new products at higher prices is further enhanced if the product has few or no substitutes and cannot be quickly imitated or copied by competitors. Finally, the range of uses of a product is related directly to policy possibilities of varying prices accordingly. Much depends, of course, on whether or not a given product loses its identity in such uses (as in further processing).

The influence of the producer's product assortments

Many of the preceding observations have to be modified under considerations where a producer manufactures a line of products. The following represent some statements of tendencies:

1. The relationship of prices between individual products in the product assortment will be more systematic if the products com-

pete in similar types of channels, and if they are bought by more
homogeneous customer classes than would be true under conditions of greater diversity.

2. Prices on part of the composition of a product line may be set
   more aggressively if only one or few products account for bulk
   of the sales and profits than would be true otherwise.

3. Depending on the price-making authority in a given producer's
   organization, especially as to product autonomy, price policies
   may lead either to highly standardized or highly diversified arrangements.

4. If the diversity of product lines in an assortment originates from
   joint raw material and joint cost situations, the pricing of each
   product probably will be based upon the rationalization of some
   cost-accounting procedure for allocating such costs.

5. Price relationships will reflect, finally, whether or not any significant amount of demand leakage will take place between each
   product item in the total product assortment, especially in terms
   of trading up and trading down considerations. This is true
   especially if the producer uses uniformity of channels, family
   brands, and uniform packaging tactics.

Other factors

The influence of specific legislation is significant here, as in general
price-structure analysis. Apart from detailed discussions later, especially to be noted are: the antitrust legislations (the price discrimination provisions of the Sherman, Clayton, and Robinson-Patman Acts);
the resale price maintenance laws; government price-fixing activities;
and restrictions on freedom of entry. Custom and habit may be in-
fluential in product situations, as has been noted; and weight has already been assigned to the importance of the structure of industry
characteristics where group price policies have emerged.

Wholesale Middlemen's Price Policies:
General Statement and Classification

General statement

The price policy and pricing activities of individual wholesale
middlemen may resemble closely the group and/or individual activities
of producers, as noted above, under conditions of ownership control,
or other forms of direct and indirect integrated control, over the manufacturing activity. Apart from the establishing of prices in organized

wholesale markets, certain types of wholesale middlemen may waive any pricing authority and responsibility under given channel conditions; e.g., by selection of agent middleman operations, by accepting an exclusive franchise dealership under stipulated pricing conditions, or by agreeing to a producer's resale price maintenance agreement. But, in addition to these situations, there remains an important variety of circumstances under which wholesale middlemen can assume varying degrees of price policy and pricing initiative. These will be classified here and discussed individually in the following sections.

Classification of wholesale middlemen's price policies[16]

The following outline gives the range of wholesale middlemen's group and individual price policies in form comparable to that presented for producers.

I. *Group Price Policies*
   A. Cooperative buying and selling plans.
   B. Trade association activities.
II. *Individual Price Policies*
   A. Cost-price relationships.
   B. Price uniformity.
      1. As to territory.
      2. As to class of customer.
      3. As to position in the channel.
   C. Gross margin and mark-up policies.
   D. Customary prices.
   E. Product differentials.
   F. Price stabilization policies.
   G. Policies related to customer price policies.

Individual Wholesale Middlemen's Considerations in Establishing Prices

The discussion which follows parallels that presented for individual producers in an earlier section. Similarities and differences will be emphasized.

Price policy objectives

In discussing the price policy objectives of individual wholesale middlemen, it is necessary to remember certain important character-

---

[16] Based on Duddy and Revzan, *op. cit.*, pp. 447–48.

istics which differentiate their pricing activities from those of producers: (1) Differences in degrees of managerial freedom in which the producer generally has a wider range of freedom than does the wholesale middleman; (2) differences in both the average sales size of establishment and the range of sizes, in which those of wholesale middlemen usually are smaller than for manufacturers; (3) the wider range of product assortments which have to be priced by wholesale middlemen (usually) as compared with producers; and (4) the narrower geographic outreach of wholesale middlemen, on the average, compared with producers. In addition, the existence of certain legislation may further reduce the middleman's pricing freedom by facilitating the extension of the producer's managerial pricing control.

Within the framework of these differences, the pricing objectives of wholesale middlemen may be stated in a fashion similar to that presented for the producers:

1. The wholesale middleman may have his profit level determined by producer's pricing control as indicated, or he may have a considerably wider range of freedom. He may have carefully estimated profit level and amount objectives; he may, depending upon the nature of his product assortments, either stratify or unify his profit margin levels; or, finally, he may seek stability. The impact of being so frequently in an intermediate position of policy action probably serves to narrow the extent to which these objectives can be realized. Similarly, he may be less able to stratify profit objectives geographically because of his more limited outreach.

2. Wholesale middlemen are more likely to have a flexible point of view towards prices than producers. To state this somewhat differently, wholesale middlemen are less likely to be consistent proponents of price stability than are producers. This is evident in no more positive illustration than in the frequency with which distributors' brands may be used to yield attractive margins to the wholesale middleman while stimulating price competition within the channel.

3. Despite the generally narrower geographic boundaries of the wholesale middlemen's buying and selling operations, it is to be expected that, within such boundaries, they too, would seek a stated penetration percentage or series of percentages. Such market penetration objectives may be derived from the producer's quota determinations; or they may represent the middleman's independent policy determination. Refinements may be, and

usually are, necessary by product categories reflecting, in their use, either aggressive or conservative pricing and related marketing policies.

4. Wholesale middlemen may, under certain circumstances, implement producers' objectives in very instrumental fashion in their preference of nonprice emphasis as against vigorous price competition.   In addition, some wholesale middlemen may be interested in using nonprice tactics for their own distributor brands, paralleling the producers' activities.

5. A special case, so far as pricing objectives are concerned, is to be found in the pricing activities of sales agents.   Despite their agent middleman status, they frequently have been given complete authority by their principals to negotiate effective prices and terms of sale.   Under such circumstances, it is to be expected that there will be very close coordination of principal's and agent's objectives, or that the sales agent may be dominant in formulating such objectives.   This will be the case especially since his remuneration will depend, in part, on the skill with which the pricing policy objectives maximize his sales and, thus, his percentage fee returns.

Criteria of a satisfactory individual middleman's selling price

With only a slight change in perspective, the wholesale middleman's criteria of a satisfactory selling closely resemble those noted above for the producer: (1) that the particular prices determined for the product assortments be high enough to yield a final profit and percentage rate consistent with the preceding objectives; (2) that the prices be low enough to give the middleman his planned percentage of the pertinent sales potentialities in his trading area (or areas); and (3) that his prices be low enough to prevent any significant diversion of sales to competing channel alternatives.

Additional considerations in the computation of actual selling prices

Given the complexities of the product assortments and of the intermediacy of his decision position in the channel, as noted above, a given wholesale middleman may assign importance to the following factors in establishing particular prices:

1. The determination of the total sales potentials for each product line in his product assortment in his trading area (or areas).
2. The determination of his percentages of (1) consistent with his market penetration policies.

3. The presence or absence of specific producer's price controls on any product line in the assortment.
4. In the case of complicated product assortments, some type of allocation of costs of a common nature to each product line over and above the delivered cost of each at his place of business.
5. The relative importance of each product line in generating sales and profits, and the possible effects on these of the cost allocations in (4).
6. The possible influence of the wholesale middleman's customers in terms of their price policy objectives (to be noted later).
7. Testing individual prices as established, in terms of their consistency or lack of consistency to policy objectives, to the product assortment as a whole and in terms of comparability with competing, alternative-channel pricing arrangements.
8. The possible necessity for reducing costs in the light of the considerations in (5), (6), and (7).
9. Finally, the relationship of the prices as established to the policy objectives of the wholesale middleman to establish a reputation as a price cutter or as a source of quality merchandise, etc.[17]

Middlemen's Group Price Policies

Mainly because of sales-size and geographical restrictions, most types of wholesale middlemen do not have the range of opportunities for engaging in group price policies similar to those available to producers as members of oligopolistically or monopolistically structured industries. There are always some exceptions, of course, and mainly for those wholesale middlemen who control the production of their distributors' brands. As a result, the discussion will deal only with cooperative buying and selling associations, and trade association group price policies.

Cooperative buying and selling association policies

There are two examples of this kind of group price policy which may be cited. One is a reflection merely of the pooling of buying strength which may be used to obtain larger quantity and other types of discounts from producers. These may be used, in turn, to support very aggressive selling prices by each member of the pool. Frequently, also, this policy involves integration with retail middlemen, although

---

[17] The reader should keep in mind the relationship of all of these objectives and considerations to the discussion of price strategy in Chapter 11.

such integration (backwards or forward in control) is not a fundamental requirement for its success.

The second form does reflect a more formal type of vertical integration in the channel. It is found in the sponsorship of a cooperative retail chain by a group of wholesale middlemen, especially in the grocery business. An important part of such cooperative action involves the activities of groups of wholesale middlemen (as in the case of the Independent Grocers' Alliance) whereby aggressive wholesale prices can be advanced in the channel to retail members by pooled purchases and aggressive use of distributors' brands. An important auxiliary is the preparation of accompanying sales-promotional materials.

Trade association activities

In addition to the usual direct and indirect pricing activities of trade associations, noted above, for producers, there are two additional types of activities which have particular relevance for wholesale middlemen. One concerns their activities in promoting the passage of unfair trade practices acts and in acting, after their passage, as the agencies for collecting pertinent cost survey data.[18] In addition, to the extent trade associations act as codifying agencies in establishing recommended uniform mark-ups, margins—or for agent middlemen, brokerage and commission fees—they may have some very important effects upon prices and price policies.

Individual Middleman Price Policies

Cost-price relationships

In the channel situation of merchant middlemen, under conditions where complicated product assortments are featured and where producers do not apply a policy of resale price maintenance, the individual middleman is faced with the dilemma of not being able to allocate many common costs to each of the component product lines except by some arbitrary method inherent in distribution cost accounting.[19] Accordingly, in establishing cost-price relationships, the following must be considered: (1) The relative past and expected sales importance

[18] See, in this connection, Robert Tannenbaum, *Cost Under the Unfair Practices Acts,* Studies in Business Administration, Vol. IX, No. 2 (Chicago: University of Chicago Press, 1939).

[19] The question of costs and distribution cost accounting will be discussed in a later chapter.

of each line in the total product assortment; (2) the relative marketing age (or newness) of each such line; (3) the degree and type of existing and anticipated sales volumes and profits; (5) the degree to which any product line may have to be priced at "market plus" levels so as to "subsidize" other product lines which can be sold only at lower margins; and (6) the costliness of trying to develop an accurate distribution cost accounting system.

Experience may dictate the necessity of using these considerations, past sales experience, and something of the industry experience to classify product lines according to both cost level groupings and price and profit margin level positions. But despite experience, especially difficult is the problem of determining whether or not product-line-price relationships will serve to increase both the average purchases per customer and the number of product lines purchased. The determination of cost-price relationships will be affected, also, by the frequency with which price changes have to be made in any marketing time period.

Despite all of these complexities, many types of wholesale middlemen use this basis for establishing prices, partially because of custom and habit, partially because of inertia, and partially because of the apparent ease of calculations, if marketing strategy and accuracy of analysis do not become overriding considerations. These tend to be true, particularly, if the middlemen use, in their calculations, historical costs and cost relationships rather than anticipated costs and cost relationships.

Price uniformity policies

To avoid too frequent price changes and the accompanying marketing turmoil, some wholesale middlemen adopt a policy of price uniformity. These attempts at uniformity may apply to a territorial base, to class of customer groupings, to channel position, or to combinations thereof. Although originally based on one of the types of policies already discussed, or to be discussed, the uniformity may be continued with the same absolute or differential relationships, for the reason noted. It may be the opinion, also, that problems of compliance with the Robinson-Patman Act and the unfair trade practices acts may, thereby, either be eliminated or else reduced.

Gross margin and mark-up policies

Two aspects of this policy may be noted as it applies to wholesale middlemen. One concerns the use of rigid margins and mark-ups which may be based upon past experience, upon industry experience, or both. Under this policy, any given product line in an assortment is screened in terms of its potentiality for reaching the desired mark-up and margin levels, especially if the product is new to the assortment or is being analyzed for possible addition.

A somewhat different approach is to use a flexible margin and mark-up policy under the following conditions:

1. Each product line is assigned, initially, to a given margin and mark-up grouping based upon an analysis of the best evidence at hand.
2. The margin and mark-up grouping in (1) is used to determine the initial selling price.
3. Actual sales experience and resulting margins and mark-ups are compared with the estimated goals.
4. The initial mark-ups may have to be revised either up or down in the light of such analyses.

Such flexible margin and mark-up arrangements not only permit the middlemen to adjust margin and mark-up mistakes as soon as they are discovered but, in addition, furnish the middlemen with an important managerial device for evaluating, as indicated, whether to broaden or narrow existing product assortments. For, by arriving at decisions as to expected margin and mark-up levels, he can relate the apparent effects of such levels to actual sales, profits, and cost experience. In addition, the individual middleman so armed can obtain more responsive decisions as to significant changes in margin and mark-up levels as the channel competition warrants.

Customary prices

On occasion, a given product at a given stage of its marketing history may reach a point where its price becomes a matter of custom or tradition, as well as the margins realized by each agency in the channel. Under such conditions, an element of rigidity is introduced into the freedom of pricing policy of the wholesale middlemen affected.

Product price differentials

Just as the manufacturer of many product lines must watch closely the relationship of prices established for each product line, so, too, must the middleman who handles wide product assortments or many lines in assortment depth. Complementary and competing product-line relationships must be watched carefully, especially in terms of whether to base profits on the price of the initial product, on the sale of related supplies and accessories, on the provision of product servicing, or on combinations thereof. Shifting of sales may take place between competing lines which may not have been expected. And prices of newly added product lines must be watched in terms of whether they contribute additional sales or merely divert sales from existing product lines.

In some instances, as for manufacturers, wholesale middlemen may stock product assortments which are stratified according to channels, thereby formulating price relationships designed, perhaps, to maximize nonprice competition in one channel and price competition in another channel. He may use, in connection with his nonprice efforts, the price umbrella of a producer's national brand to yield higher than average margins on his distributor's brands.

Under some product assortment situations, the wholesale middleman may use aggressive pricing on some lines which are only of minor importance in their contributions both to sales and to profits. In some circumstances, the wholesale middleman may follow the producer's lead in differentiating prices according to category of use. Related problems must deal with the question of whether or not preferential price treatment should be given to those product lines which are newest in the total assortment mix.

Price stabilization policies

These policies parallel those already noted for producers and require no additional elaboration here. They may involve, however, the wholesale middleman to enter into formal relationship with the producer's policies, as noted already for resale price maintenance activities. It should be pointed out, however, that the wholesale middleman probably has far more difficulty in securing the advantages of price stabilization by himself as compared with coordinating such objectives with the producer's attempts.

Policies related to customer's price policies

Two examples may be given of this policy aspect. The first concerns the large-scale retailer who, in establishing a policy of a fixed price or set of prices at which to feature a particular product line, succeeds in effect in "rolling back" the related prices at preceding levels within the channel. This may be viewed as a retailer-controlled pricing situation in the channel.

The second example transfers the control to the wholesale middleman. He is confronted with the situation in this connection in which: (a) he is able to provide retail middlemen with a continuous flow of merchandise which can be featured by them at very aggressive prices; and (b) he is able to supply retail middlemen with "special buys" or "fill-ins" to be featured in special sales at what may be represented as very attractive prices. It should be noted, also, that there are certain categories of industrial goods for industrial buyers involving the same use of aggressive pricing policies. In these cases, as for retail middlemen, the wholesale middleman must relate his price policies and pricing activities to the industrial goods customers' search for best buys.

Factors Influencing Individual Wholesale Middlemen's Pricing Activities

Apart from those channel situations in which wholesale middlemen control manufacturing units by means of formal or informal backwards vertical integration, the factors influencing wholesale middlemen's pricing activities would seem to take on a different perspective than those noted for the producers. For one thing, it is not to be expected that wholesale middlemen would be able to exercise the same degree of monopolistic or oligopolistic controls as those manifested by producers. And, for another thing, the initiating of much wholesale pricing activity must begin, by the very nature of marketing organization through channels, with the producer even if subject to modification by the wholesale middleman.

The influence of the producer

For many wholesale middlemen, based on the preceding, the initial factor in their individual pricing activities originates with the extent of the pricing influence of the producer and of his related marketing objectives. To the extent that the individual producer is able to make these (as discussed earlier) effective in the channel, to that extent is the pricing freedom of the wholesale middleman significantly curtailed. To the extent, however, that the wholesale middleman can challenge effectively this control position in the channel, to that extent is the range of pricing initiative of the wholesale middleman correspondingly increased.

The width of product assortments[20]

Apart from the obvious element of service to the customer, it has been noted that both the width and the depth of a wholesale middle-

[20] The reader should review the contents of Chapter 7.

man's product assortment has a very important effect on his price policies and pricing activities. In one direction, the wider the product assortment, the greater will be his managerial ability to resist the control attempts of the producer in the channel, as noted above. In another direction, the wider and deeper the product assortment, the greater will be the ability of the wholesale middleman to stratify his pricing policies according to the marketing objectives outlined below. Another effect, as has been noted above, is the emphasis placed upon some arbitrary allocation of common costs in actually determining the cost-price relationships of each and every product line in the assortment.

The middleman's marketing objectives

Those wholesale middlemen, particularly of the merchant type, generally have more of a regional than of a national outlook in terms of locations and distributions of customers to be serviced. Accordingly, their marketing objectives, in terms of market-penetration ratios, may be separated into the following groups: those middlemen who specialize in the product lines of only one or a few producers, and who are likely to have their penetration ratio determined for them by these producers; and those middlemen with product assortments in such width and/or depth that they are more likely to establish their own estimates of trading-area penetration ratios, and the relationship of price to such shares.

A second aspect of the middleman's marketing objectives has to do with the whole question of distributor's versus producer's brands. In recalling the previous discussions, the main theme applicable here is the extent to which a policy of using distributor brands influences the wholesale middlemen's pricing objectives, as noted, while becoming an important management tool in the whole struggle for channel control. In some instances, the wholesale middleman may take an opportunistic point of view in the matter of product assortments, distributors' brands, and the whole question of level of penetration of a trading area by simply stocking any and every product line he can obtain.

The nature of the channel

Only brief mention need be made here of the influence of the nature and type of channel. One aspect concerns the relationship of the wholesale middleman as compared with every other type of agency link in terms of scale of importance in the marketing of the commodities involved. The second aspect relates to the complexity of the channel in terms of few versus multiple wholesale pricing decisions. The final aspect relates to the managerial struggle for channel control as discussed at various points.

Other factors

The same relationship of government control mentioned for producers is pertinent, also, for wholesale middlemen, as well as the role of custom and habit, noted above, in relation to price policies and actual levels of prices.

Some Final Observations

Given the complex array of group and individual managerial price policies operating to establish wholesale prices of products, within the environment of the price structure, the following outline presents some of the more important patterns to be noted as these management units cooperated and compete within the framework of the channel.

I. *Ranges of Pricing Freedom of Management Units*
 A. Wholesale prices linked to channels functioning with organized wholesale markets: a sharp limitation on the existence of producer and middleman price policies.
   1. Direct determination of prices by operation of the organized market.
   2. Indirect influence: organized market-price quotations used as a base for the negotiation of prices in private sales.
 B. Government price fixing: elimination of management policies.
   1. Regular price-fixing activities: milk prices; utility rates; price-support programs, etc.
   2. Emergency price-fixing activities.
 C. Producer-controlled wholesale prices.
   1. By monopolistic control: single-firm and group action.
   2. By the oligopolistic structure of the industry.
   3. By legalized resale price maintenance and related policies.
   4. Through control of the channel: direct and indirect integration.
 D. Wholesale-middleman-controlled wholesale prices.
   1. Through control of the channel: direct and indirect backwards and forward vertical integration.
   2. Through group price policy action.

E. Customer-controlled wholesale prices.
  1. For industrial goods.
     a. By specification ordering.
     b. Through control of the channel: direct and indirect backwards vertical integration.
  2. For consumers' goods.
     a. By retail middleman's specification of final price or "best buy," etc.
     b. Through control of the channel: direct and indirect backwards vertical integration.
II. *Levels of Wholesale Price Determination*
  A. Direct producer-to-user determination: single-level channel pricing activity.
  B. Indirect price determination: multiple-agency channel pricing activity.
     1. Pricing of raw materials separated in the channel from the pricing of semiprocessed and fully processed related products.
     2. Multiple wholesale pricing of the same product based on two or more wholesale sales in the channel and upon use of multiple channels.
  C. Combinations of (*A*) and (*B*).

In this summary classification, the importance of the channel as the vehicle for pricing decisions and activities is once again emphasized.

QUESTIONS AND PROBLEMS

1. Differentiate between manufacturers' individual and group policies.
2. Evaluate, in detail, the price policy objectives of individual producers.
3. How do the objectives in (2) affect the individual producer's criteria of a satisfactory selling price? the computation of actual selling prices?
4. Compare and contrast the principal identifying characteristics of each type of producers' group policies.
5. To what extent can individual producers have price policies? What types of price policies can be used under these circumstances?
6. What is the difference between a discount and a dating?
7. How do you array in importance the various factors presented which affect the individual producer's price policies?
8. To what extent are the price policies of wholesale middlemen dependent upon and derived from producers' price policies? To what extent are they complementary? To what extent competitive?
9. What are the pricing policy objectives of wholesale middlemen?

10. To what extent is the computation of actual selling price by wholesale middlemen comparable to that outlined for producers?

11. Compare the range of individual wholesale middlemen's price policies with those for individual producers.

12. What is meant by gross margin and mark-up policies?

13. Discuss critically the factors which influence the price policies of individual wholesale middlemen.

14. What are the ranges of pricing freedom of management units in the channel?

CHAPTER INTEGRATING ASSIGNMENT

Chapters 15 and 16 have presented a discussion of the wholesale price structure in terms of external and internal aspects. You are asked to prepare a paper in which you discuss the following points: (1) To what extent are the internal aspects overriding in importance as compared with the external aspects? (2) what rationale takes the myriad of individual price decisions of wholesale middlemen and producers and molds them into a wholesale price structure? and (3) what forces act to prevent the wholesale price structure from being completely systematic at any given time period and over time?

17

Storage and Warehousing Operations

Although this chapter will deal with the warehousing activities of wholesale middlemen in considerable detail, especially of the non-manufactured-controlled types, a very important section will discuss the incidence of storage activities throughout the entire wholesaling sector. In this twofold treatment, the discussion will deal, accordingly, with both the external aspects of storage and the internal aspects of warehousing. Although the distinction may appear to be a form of hair splitting, it is significant, nevertheless, within the context of marketing organization.

Storage, in the external sense used here, refers to the incidence of the time-bridging function in the channel within the framework of the funnel concept. It refers to interruptions in the physical flow of goods in the channel, together with other component elements, for reasons to be discussed in the following section. Warehousing, on the other hand, is the assumption of responsibility for the adaptation of storage in this external aspect to the internal organizational framework of a given middleman or facilitating agency. The building in which the warehousing may take place[1] can be owned by these middlemen or facilitating agencies, or merely leased. More than one organization may participate in the utilization of space within a

[1] Although it should not be thought that all warehousing is confined to formal structures called buildings.

414

single warehouse; or a single agency may occupy the entire quarters. Also, the warehouse structure may contain space and facilities for other than warehousing activities.[2]

Given these distinctions, the emphasis of this chapter will be less on the purely mechanical aspects of storage and warehousing, including order filling, and more on the relationships existing between the function and nature of the associated physical facilities and the position of the wholesaling sector in marketing organization. Where detailed treatment is given to certain aspects of the physical facilities, the reason will be mainly because of the effects of type, design, and layout of such facilities on costs and efficiency.

Resumé of Principal Reasons for the Importance of Storage and Warehousing in Marketing

A complete understanding of the impact of storage and warehousing in the wholesaling sector as presented in the remainder of this chapter is impossible without a knowledge of the reasons for the importance of the external aspects (storage) and internal aspects (warehousing) of the function. Therefore, a resumé of the principal reasons is presented below.

Reasons inherent in the nature of production

There are several component parts of reasons inherent in the nature of production. One concerns the use of storage as regulatory arrangement (the series of valves in the funnel) for systematizing the physical flows of goods through the channel when (a) either environmental conditions or (b) the economies of time-concentrated production lead to seasonal peakings of available inventories of products. Closely associated with this aspect is the relationship which exists between the regularization of physical flows and the reduction in the range of price fluctuations, especially if the product is highly perishable. In addition, storage may complete the production phase of the product, as in the aging of wines, tobacco leaf, and cheeses, at the same time increasing (it is to be hoped) the market price to a level which exceeds the total costs involved in such storage.

On the other hand, storage may permit production to be spread out in time by pinpointing resulting inventories in key warehouse facilities spatially related to the location of highly seasonal purchases. Also, the relationship between storage operations and physical flows

[2] The types of warehouses will be discussed in a later section of this chapter.

of goods through the channels must be remembered, as they move in interrupted fashion—timewise—between intermediate and final users. In these examples, storage becomes intricately interwoven with the production schedules of the enterprises involved, if the products are industrial goods.

Finally, for this set of reasons, attention should be directed to the extent to which the warehouse facilities of individual wholesale middlemen act as assembling and concentrating facilities in which each wholesale middleman can build up accumulations of product assortments from several producers or other wholesale middlemen. These accumulations facilitate, at one central place, buying activities of these customers in accordance with the policies and accompanying functional details already discussed. They function to permit producers either to maintain substantial inventories in their warehouse facilities, depending upon existing and forecasted price-supply relationships, or such intermediate inventories in the hands of middlemen may permit the producers to operate on hand-to-mouth basis. These inventories may be so strategically located in the channel, relative to transportation costs and delivery times, that only a few days' supply of goods may be actually carried in stock at the point of production.[3]

Reasons inherent in the nature of the product and of product assortments

Cutting across the preceding set of reasons and, yet, closely related are those inherent in the nature of the product and the product assortments. Of the characteristics of the product which appear to be most important, one may note the following: (1) Perishability features which may require protective storage (heated or refrigerated) for variable time periods; (2) as already noted, products which acquire additional economic value by virtue of aging in special warehouse facilities; (3) products which have certain emergency characteristics in use such that key inventories must be available at strategic locations (e.g., pharmaceuticals, certain types of repair parts); (4) products which, because of possibilities of significant variations in quality, have to be sold on the basis of inspection; and (5) products which may have to undergo physical form changes at the point of wholesale sale (e.g., adapting pipes, structural metals, and plastics to certain shape and size needs, or packaging bulk goods).

Enough has been said of the role of product assortments in preceding chapters to reduce what has to be included in the present context.

[3] As in the case of the Milpitas, California, plant of the Ford Motor Company.

What mainly has to be discussed here is the role of individual management's warehouse facilities in accumulating adequate quantities and assortments of products on the inflow side; and their role in regulating outward flows to the pace and composition of orders as received. Further refinements in assortments may result from all of the physical changes in the products which may take place in these warehouses, as already noted. The sum total represents then the complexities of product-assortment flows relative to time which are fundamental to the funnel concept.

Reasons inherent in types of wholesale middlemen's organizations and operations

Again, we refer to Chapter 2 for the detailed discussion of each type of wholesale middleman operations. Three aspects of these types of operation need to be noted here: (1) Those types of wholesale middlemen who, by the nature of their full-function operations, reduce the incidence of the storage burden for the producers from whom they obtain product assortments, and for the customers to whom they offer such assortments; (2) those types of middlemen who, by eliminating those activities associated with the physical possession of products, transfer the storage burden either to producer sources, to customers, or to combinations of both; and (3) those types of middlemen who, by the streamlining of functions, restrict their storage responsibilities either to selected categories of fast-selling products or to stipulated minimum sales-size units.

In addition to these classifications, attention needs to be directed, once again, to the existence of storage facilities furnished by specialized facilitating agencies, such as railroad terminal facilities, trucking terminal facilities, and port facilities, warehousing facilities controlled by organized wholesale markets, and the various kinds of public warehouses available for rental use.

Reasons inherent in customer organization and types of operations

To the extent that customers are producers, the observations already noted above are pertinent. To the extent that customers represent other forms of business and institutional enterprises, in the classification sense noted in Chapter 1, the following observations are in order.

1. The wholesale middleman's individual warehouse facility may serve merely as a regulatory valve in the sense of building up reservoirs of a given controlling producer's product assortments

in such facility, and then filling orders as received from such assortments.[4]

2. The storage facilities may be a fundamental part of the price-determining process, as will be noted below.

3. The wholesale middleman's warehouse facility may be used by his customer as the place from which delivery may be made ultimately to this customer's customers.

4. The warehouse facilities and their time and place accessibility may permit the wholesale middleman's customers to operate on a hand-to-mouth inventory basis by virtue of the frequency with which the middleman will make deliveries and his willingness to make split-package orders despite their effect on lowering the average unit sale. These considerations also apply to perishable produce and the adaptation of the unit of sale for the customer in order to insure freshness.

5. Part of the strategy of backward vertical integration in the channel involves the use and control of warehouse facilities geared to the operations of the controlling agency.

6. Finally, part of the strategy of wholesale middlemen's storage operations may be related to the complementary relationships of products, as in the example of having to stock operating supplies and repair parts in order to service adequately sales of basic equipment.

Reasons inherent in the nature of the channel

Apart from the wide range of reasons noted above, the channel becomes the crucial focal point within which the incidence of the storage function becomes related to matters of price determination and to the individual and group managerial struggles for control of the channel, as discussed earlier. The incidence of the storage function in the channel, and especially the wholesaling sector, requires such detailed discussion that only a beginning mention of it will be made here pending more complete discussion in the following sections.

The channel, through its linkage aspects, tends to crystallize inventory relationships and responsibilities for the agencies involved in such linkages. At the same time, these inventory relationships may be threatened (a) by the competitive efforts of other middlemen handling other product assortments to displace these given product assortments, so far as market shares are concerned, and (b) by the entire assortment weight of one channel competing with the totality

---

[4] This is the case especially for a manufacturer's sales branch.

of assortments in other channels. The breadth and width of the product assortments, and the price relationships of their inventories at various storage locations, become intimately related to the preceding considerations.

Only the very briefest of mentions need be made here of the effect of the channel on the dynamics of both what is in storage (quantitatively and qualitatively) and where such storage facilities and the inventories are located. These dynamics, as well, will be discussed in more detail in a later section.

Reasons inherent in the existence and functioning of organized wholesale markets

Some types of organized wholesale markets cannot function without the actual physical presence of the product assortments to be bought and sold. Accordingly, such markets may have a considerable proportion of their physical facilities in the form of specialized storage arrangements; e.g., auction facilities, livestock pens, or fruit and vegetable stores. Within such organized markets, the individual middlemen may jockey to place their respective facilities and inventories in the best locational proximity to potential buyers or sellers.

In other kinds of organized wholesale markets, sales do not involve the presence of more than a sample of the available product assortments, or no inventories whatsoever. However, the actual location of the available warehouse facilities in which the quantities and qualities of the available product assortments are contained have very important repercussions both on the determination of prices and upon actual deliveries of the products as required.

Auxiliary aspects

Although the main reasons for the existence and the importance of these storage functions in the wholesaling sector have been outlined above, some other auxiliary aspects need to be noted. One of the more important of these is the relationship between stocks in storage and the availability of financing by means of warehouse receipts or other financial instrumentalities. Another aspect is the relationship to certain government activities, as in the case of the agricultural price support programs, where the warehouse facilities act both as a protective device and as a depository to keep stocks out of commercial channels. Finally, the relationship between storage and transportation need only be suggested: accumulation (concentration) of quantities at shipping points for economical units of transportation;

protection of commodities moving under transit freight rate arrangements; and the relationships to price determination at particular markets, and the price relationships between competing markets.

The Incidence of the Storage Function in the Wholesaling Sector: External Aspects

Prior to a discussion of the characteristics of the present-day supply of storage facilities, and some aspects of their internal management, it would appear to be of some value to discuss the incidence of the storage function in the wholesaling sector. The discussion is divided into two aspects—the external and the internal. This section emphasizes the external aspects in terms of meaning; the relationship to the funnel concept; the relationship to the concept of marketing organization through the channel; and the forms taken.

Meaning

The discussion of the incidence of the storage function in its external aspect places emphasis on an analysis of each type of wholesale middleman's responsibility—direct, semidirect, or indirect—for the performance of this function in relationship to his linkage position with a channel.[5] Accordingly, this perspective views not only the importance attached to the physical movements of goods, as such, in accordance with the processes of concentration, equalization, and dispersion, but places considerable emphasis, as well, upon the relationship to the strengthening or weakening of the middleman's control efforts in the channel. Thus, the analysis of the incidence of the storage function in its external aspects introduces into the framework of analysis the relationships existing between the type of middleman, his product assortments, the physical location of such assortments, and the middleman's position in the channel.

Relationship to the funnel concept of wholesaling

From the above meaning of the incidence of storage in its external aspects, it follows that, through the performance of the storage function, the physical flows of goods may be affected by: (1) stopping such flows for varying periods of time; (2) permitting changes to take place in the qualitative nature of the flows as in the case either of building up or breaking down the product assortments; and (3) adapting the rate of inflow of goods into the storage points as

[5] All forms of integrated and nonintegrated wholesale middlemen are included.

compared with the rate of outflow into either customer's hands or into other storage points.

Storage takes place, accordingly, throughout the funnel from its broad-mouthed opening oriented towards the sources of supply (producers' establishments) to the narrow ending oriented towards intermediate or final customers. Thus, the incidence of storage gives rise to both the quantitative and qualitative aspects of the product flows through the funnel. The reasons behind such storage operations are, of course, those discussed in the earlier section of this chapter.

Relationship to the concept of marketing organization through the channel

Related to the funnel discussion above, but introducing additional aspects as well, is the perspective of the storage function as here considered within the framework of marketing organization. What is implied here, first of all, is the patterning of channels of distribution with linkages and blockages for individual products, groups of products, etc. Within this pattern there is established a sequence of storage operations and responsibilities from point of origin to the end of the channel, either in the middleman's business establishments or in specialiazed agencies.

There is implied, secondly, not only the mere physical sequence of such storage operations at specified storage facilities but also a definite relationship of these to the struggle for managerial control of the channel as already noted. In addition, the incidence of the function and the places within the channel at which the function is performed has very important repercussions many times on the determination of prices (both immediately and in the future in any time sequence). Finally, the incidence of the function may generate, in turn, very significant changes in the structure of the channel itself.

Thus in the continuous struggle for managerial channel, the position and qualitative nature of the storage function may shift sharply from link to link in the channel. Producers may find it more strategic to have inventories carried at warehouses which are part of their establishments rather than at intermediate or final points in the channel. In some cases such decisions may be made reluctantly, or actually may be forced on them by middlemen streamlining functions or indulging in hand-to-mouth buying. In other cases, the position of the storage function in the channel may remain unchanged but the controlling agency will shift. Thus, the shift from the warehouse located in an orthodox wholesaler's establishment to that in a manufacturer's sales branch is a case in point. In still other cases, the location of the storage function in the channel may not change, but there may be drastic shifts in the quantities handled.[6]

In all of these relationships, there is an ebbing and flowing of sequential patterns. Under some conditions, the shifting of storage arrangements may be the causal trigger which sets off a series of shocks (changes) varying in intensity throughout the channel. The shifting of storage arrangements, in other cases, may simply be the net resultant of a time sequence of pressures originating from other functional changes and then, finally, triggering the storage function. One such example may involve a changing transportation situation. Another may be linked to such significant series of changes as the relocation of manufacturing and its effect on the channel.[7]

Forms of incidence of the storage function in the wholesaling sector of marketing organization

Given the above materials, it follows that the forms or patterns or incidence of the storage function are much more complicated than ordinarily might be considered. The following, while merely suggestive, is an outline which is self-explanatory so far as the main headings and subdivisions are concerned.

I. *As to the Location of the Function in the Channel*
   A. Storage at point of production or extraction.
      1. For assembling or concentration process activities.
      2. For immediate processing (intermediate and/or final) at point of extraction.
      3. For aging, conditioning, ripening, etc.
      4. For speculative purposes.
      5. For physical protection, pending reshipment.
      6. For ordinary order-filling activities.
      7. For storage of government-owned commodities in relation to price-support activities.
   B. Storage in connection with sale by inspection and/or sample at organized wholesale markets.
      1. Warehouse facilities of wholesale (buying and selling) middlemen having physical possession of inventories.
      2. Warehouse facilities of specialized transportation agencies.

---

[6] Two examples may be cited: that of hand-to-mouth buying already noted; and that of storage of apples at shipping points, cutting down the quantities stored in wholesale markets.

[7] A good example would be the movement of cold-storage facilities accompanying the decentralized locational structure of the meat-packing industry.

       3. Warehouse facilities of the organized wholesale markets.

  C. Storage in connection with sale by sample and/or description at organized wholesale markets.

       1. Warehouse facilities of wholesale (buying and selling) middlemen having physical possession of inventories.

       2. Warehouse facilities of specialized transportation agencies.

       3. Warehouse facilities of the organized wholesale markets.

  D. Storage in connection with production.

       1. At intermediate wholesale market locations.

       2. At final market oriented locations.

  E. Storage in connection with sales to other classes of industrial goods customers.

  F. Storage in connection with sales to retail middlemen.

       1. Producer-controlled warehouse facilities.

       2. Wholesale middlemen controlled facilities.

       3. Retail middlemen-controlled facilities.

       4. Other types of public and private warehouse facilities.

  G. Special storage facilities associated with import-export activities: customs and bonded warehouses, etc.

 II. *As to Position of Importance of Function*

  A. Key significance in buying and selling of products.

  B. Intermediate significance in buying and selling products.

  C. Low level of significance in buying and selling of products.

III. *As to Ownership of Products in Storage*

  A. Producer.

  B. Wholesale middlemen.

  C. Retail middlemen.

  D. Facilitating agencies.

  E. Government agencies.

  F. Other types of owners.

IV. *As to Type of Storage Facility*

  A. Availability of space.

       1. Public warehouses.

       2. Private warehouses.

       3. Combination of public and private.

  B. As to type of warehouse service.

       1. General merchandise.

       2. Household goods.

       3. Refrigerated goods.

       4. Food locker plants.

       5. Farm products.

       6. Special.

       7. Freight trucking and railroad terminal warehouses.

       8. Multiple types: various combinations of (1) to (7).

   C. As to control of facility.[8]

The Incidence of the Storage Function in the Wholesaling Sector: Internal Aspects

Meaning

This section merely serves to introduce subject matter which will occupy most of the remaining half of the chapter. By the incidence of the storage function in its internal aspects is meant the sum total of decisions which are made by managements of each agency performing the storage function with respect to: the type of warehouse facility to operate; where to locate such facilities; and the particular assortment of component elements to include in the storage function. The question of schedule of charges may become an important decision area as well. In this sense, then, the internal aspects of the incidence of the storage function involves a "boring down" in the detail of the operations of each and every business unit controlling such facilities, and building upon the preceding classification scheme. The sum total of these decisions for any given product or group of products helps to establish the pattern of the incidence of the storage function in the channels for particular products when viewed from the external aspects.

Forms taken

Since the internal aspects stem from the decisions of individual managements, it follows that the initial decision as to whether or not to perform the storage function originates from the decisions pertaining to type of operation. Once the decision has been made to assume responsibility for the storage function, then additional decisions must be made as to the following:

   1. Whether to own or to lease the facilities.

   2. Selection of the type of facility either to own or to lease (see part IV of the preceding classification).

   3. Where to locate the facility if to be owned and operated by the middlemen.

---

[8] See classifications based upon location of the storage facility in the channel. The discussion of field warehousing as a type will be deferred until Chapter 18 because of its close relationship to the financing function.

4. If the storage facility is to be designed as a single-story (extensive) or a multiple-story (intensive) type of building.
5. The range of functional elements to be included.
6. Relationship of the storage function to such activities as order filling.

The more important of these will be discussed in several of the remaining sections.

Factors Influencing the Location of Warehouse Facilities

In general, it may be stated that the location of warehouse facilities in nearly every instance is the resultant of forces stemming from other considerations which serve to bend the warehouse locations to these considerations rather than by permitting the warehouse facilities to be located on the basis of independent considerations. Several case illustrations may be given to underscore the validity of this observation:

Case 1. Warehouse facilities are an integral part of the wholesale middleman's operations, and thus are located wherever the middleman locates the establishment, in accordance with the factors outlined in Chapter 10.

Case 2. Warehouse facilities are an integrated part of an organized wholesale market, and are located, accordingly, as part of wherever the market is located.

Case 3. Warehouse facilities are an integral part of the processing activities (manufacturing or extractive), and are located, accordingly, where the processing activities locate.

Case 4. Warehouse facilities, in this situation, become auxiliaries of transportation agencies, and their location in conjunction with the transportation facilities depend upon their type. A grain elevator owned by a railroad will be located along its right-of-way, at sites where alternative uses of the space are not highly competitive and where land costs, accordingly, are relatively low. Other railroad-owned facilities may be attuned in location to the place of the organized wholesale market.[9]

Case 5. Public refrigerated warehouse facilities may become oriented in location towards the periphery of an organized wholesale fruit and vegetable market.

[9] Note that the time interval in which freight cars may be parked on a train track facility represents one form of warehousing.

Having made the above generalization, together with the accompanying case illustrations, a few special exceptions may be noted. One such special case is the "merchandise mart" and "furniture mart" type of combination office and warehouse building which services wholesale middlemen with both types of space. Under these circumstances, the principal locational determinants become: (1) accessibility to the central business district or downtown section of a city; (2) arrangements for incoming and outgoing movements of both goods and services; and (3) the availability of sufficient space, at workable land costs, to accommodate the necessary area needed for the building and accessory facilities.

A second type of exception involves a public warehouse facility which simply must orient itself to the zoned sections of a city which permits the construction of the commercial type of structure needed for such operations. At the same time, the proposed site must be favorably located both with respect to rail facilities and inbound and outbound roads, or at least to the key arterial city streets connecting with such roads. These facilities may have direct communication linkages with middlemen operating from office facilities located in the more central and congested sections of the city. Presumably, under such conditions, the choice of city in which to locate is influenced by its relative importance as a wholesale trading center, and by a favorable relationship between inbound c.l. and t.l. freight rates and l.c.l. and l.t.l. freight rates on outbound shipments.

A third type of location situation closely related to the preceding involves the location of a warehouse designed to serve several retail member stores of a corporate or voluntary cooperative chain. While the location of a warehouse handling dry groceries is influenced in part by the considerations just discussed, an important additional consideration is the centrality of its location, in terms of distance and time, to the stores to be serviced. If the stores are located in a single city or in a single metropolitan area, the location of the warehouse will tend generally towards one of the important commercially zoned sections of the central city, or even towards a light manufacturing zone. In either case, adequate railway receiving facilities and adequate highway connections must be adjacent. On the other hand, if a warehouse is designed to serve a much wider area, a location in the less congested incorporated or unincorporated sections of the standard metropolitan area outside of the central city would be logical, or even in locations outside the standard metropolitan area.[10]

---

[10] Note that warehouses handling such perishables as fruits, or vegetables, or bread would have more limited radii of service and, accordingly, more central locations.

A final, very important, exception applies to the manufacturing company which produces wide lines of products, and which uses either direct channels of distribution exclusively or assumes a significant share of the initial distribution at the wholesale level. Under such arrangements the company may establish four to seven regional warehouses, for example, which may service, in turn, either their sales offices or other types of wholesale middlemen, or both, depending upon the types of channels utilized. The locations of these regional warehouses may reflect an administrative decision so that none of the accounts serviced may be farther from any regional warehouse than three to four days delivery time. Depending upon the products produced and the specialization aspects of each plant's operations, the company may be able to ship either straight or mixed car-lot shipments by rail to each warehouse, except where either custom or semicustom production is involved. Teletype communication and electronic data-processing systems become valuable linkages between the production headquarters centers and the regional distribution warehouses.[11]

The shifting incidence of the storage function in the channel, as discussed earlier, places a great deal of importance on flexibility in the use of warehouse facilities by any link in the channel pattern. Increased use of self-service at the retail level, coupled with large increases in the space requirements of specialty and convenience goods stores, places much more stress on how much inventory can be carried at the point of ultimate consumer sales contact as compared with inventories carried in warehouses located elsewhere. Too much dependency, on the other hand, on "split second" integration of transportation with business operations (whether production or selling) may result in serious and costly bottlenecks at various time periods. Management can alternate, accordingly, between changing its storage arrangements and varying its selling policies and practices to achieve the best balance commensurate with its position in the channel.

Selected Characteristics of Existing Warehouse Facilities in the United States

This section is designed to present selected data of existing warehouse facilities in the United States as reported in the *1954 Census of Business: Wholesale Trade*. Included are data pertaining to the number of establishments, square feet of occupiable space, and related data. These apply to facilities owned by certain types of wholesale

---

[11] See the discussion in, "New-Fangled Routes Deliver the Goods—Faster and Cheaper," *Business Week* (November 14, 1959), 108 ff.

middlemen as well as to public warehouse facilities. In addition, some data of geographical variations in space will be presented, as well as the distribution of space in certain types of warehouses as between single-story and multiple-story building.[12]

Warehouses operated by wholesale middlemen

The census data permit some description to be made of warehouses operated by certain types of wholesale middlemen as of the end of 1954. Table 30 contains the basic data for the United States for those

TABLE 30

WAREHOUSE OCCUPIABLE FLOOR SPACE (500 FT^2 OR MORE) OF WHOLESALE MIDDLEMEN GROUPS: UNITED STATES, 1954

Item	Merchant Whole-salers	Mfrs. Sales Branches	Agents and Brokers	Assemblers of Farm Products
Number of all establishments	165,133	14,759	22,131	13,255
Number reporting floor space	95,992	10,105	3,785	6,371
Per cent reporting	58.1	68.5	17.1	48.1
Sales of all establishments ($1,000)	$101,100,941	$36,811,238	$39,250,509	$9,050,816
Sales of reporting establishment	61,152,387	23,929,532	4,820,463	3,998,747
Per cent reporting	57.6	65.0	12.3	44.2
Occupiable floor space (1,000 ft^2)*	1,015,965	136,411	67,673	73,076
Sales per 1,000 ft^2	$60.19	$175.42	$71.23	$54.72
Per cent space in single story bldgs.*	53.6	56.4	N.A.	68.4

Source: U. S. Bureau of the Census, *U. S. Census of Business—1954*, Vol. III (Washington, D. C.: U. S. Government Printing Office, 1957).

* Buildings with 500 ft^2 or more each.

types of operation groups who reported warehouses with 500 ft^2 or more of occupiable space.[13] Especially to be noticed are the sharp

[12] These data are reported in *U. S. Census of Business 1954:* Vol. III, *Wholesale Trade*—Summary Statistics and Public Warehouses (Washington, D. C.: U. S. Government Printing Office, 1957), Chapters 5 and 11.

[13] Those reporting less than 500 ft^2 were merged with establishments not reporting.

variations in the percentage reporting between each type-of-operation group. The other significant feature of the summary data as presented is the sharp variations in the sales per square feet of occupiable space from $54.72 for assemblers of farm products to $175.42 for manufacturers' sales branches. Such variables as have been discussed elsewhere affect these variations: the range of types of middlemen included under each group; variations in kinds of business; variations in the sizes of trading areas reached; and variations in the average sales size of each establishment as between operations. Finally, the importance of the single-story type of building should be noted.

Sharp variations are to be expected in the ratio of sales to occupiable warehouse floor space by kinds-of-business within each type-of-operation group. For the merchant wholesalers, as a group, the range was from $20.18 per square foot for the scrap and waste materials business to a high of $164.07 for tobacco distributors. Only one other kind of business—beers, wines, distilled spirits—exceeded $100 per square foot. For manufacturers' sales branches, the range was from $61.94 for fabricated metal products to $297.15 for electrical machinery. The majority of the kinds of business exceeded $100 per square foot. The range for agents and brokers was from $39.92 for farm products (raw materials) to $250.30 for automotive, with nine kinds of business exceeding $100. Finally, for assemblers of farm products, the range was from $22.32 for the miscellaneous group to $109.36 for the dairy and dairy products kind of business.

The variety of products handled in the warehouses, their bulkiness, variations in stock turnover and value per physical unit, and variations in the relationship of transportation costs relative to bulk and weight would seem to be among the more important variables influencing the average sales per square foot of occupiable warehouse space.

Sharp variations exist, also, in the per cent of occupiable space in warehouses of 500 square feet or more located in a single-story building. For the merchant wholesalers group, the range was from 25.9 per cent for dry goods and apparel to 83 per cent for metals and metalwork. For manufacturers' sales branches, the range was from 8.6 per cent for leather and leather products to 54.5 per cent for transportation equipment. The range for assemblers' warehouses was from 47.6 per cent for the miscellaneous group to 74.7 per cent for raw material farm products.

Public warehouses

In analyzing some of the data of public warehouse space, the discussion will present first the over-all picture for the United States and the relative distribution among the more important states. Succeeding sections will deal with the basic characteristics of each of the more important subgroups. Table 31 indicates the predominant importance of public warehouse space in 1954 for farm products and general merchandise and, to a somewhat lesser degree, for household goods. The first two types also have a considerably larger-than-average space size per establishment. Food locker plants have, on the other hand, by far the smallest average space size per establishment.

TABLE 31

PUBLIC WAREHOUSE SPACE, BY TYPE OF WAREHOUSE:
UNITED STATES, DEC. 31, 1954

	Establishments		Floor Space (1,000 ft^2)	
	No.	Per Cent	Amt.	Per Cent
Total	7,565	100.00	305,830	100.00
General merchandise	1,197	15.82	108,315	35.42
Household goods	1,816	24.00	50,695	16.58
Refrigerated	577	7.63	10,122	3.31
Food locker plants	2,467	32.61	2,696	0.88
Farm products	1,081	14.29	121,962	39.88
Special	270	3.57	9,740	3.18
Freight trucking terminals	157	2.08	2,300	0.75

Sharp variations are apparent from data for the distribution of the space in these seven types of public warehouses among the 20 most important states. Thus, general merchandise warehouse space clusters most importantly in the states of Pennsylvania, New York, Illinois, Ohio, Massachusetts, New Jersey, Virginia, and Michigan. Spaces in farm products warehouses cluster mainly in establishments located in Texas, Minnesota, Mississippi, Arkansas, Tennessee, Louisiana, and Alabama. Surprisingly enough, California, despite its ranking as one of the top two states in farm income, has a very small proportion of farm products warehouse space. Although the 20 states accounted for only slightly more than two-fifths of the food locker plant space, about 33 per cent are in New York. The implications of these data must be, in part, that there is a highly variable incidence of private warehouse space relative to the public warehouse space from state to state for these product categories.

General merchandise warehouses

A more detailed statistical view of the general merchandise warehouse is available from the data in Table 32. Two aspects are empha-

TABLE 32

GENERAL MERCHANDISE WAREHOUSES AND GEOGRAPHIC DIVISIONS: UNITED STATES, 1954

Geographic Division and Age of Building	Warehouse Buildings		Gross Floor Space 12/31/54		Per Cent Single Story
	No.	Per Cent	(1,000 ft^2)	Per Cent	
United States—total	3,043	100.0	141,386	100.0	25.5
5 years old or less	243	8.0	7,864	5.6	81.4
Over 5 years old	2,800	92.0	133,522	94.4	22.3
New England	242	100.0	11,431	100.0	10.9
5 years old or less	12	5.0	107	0.9	100.0
Over 5 years old	230	95.0	11,324	99.1	10.1
Middle Atlantic	730	100.0	48,189	100.0	16.9
5 years old or less	40	5.5	1,329	2.8	52.5
Over 5 years old	690	94.5	46,860	97.2	16.0
East North Central	645	100.0	25,548	100.0	20.8
5 years old or less	40	6.2	1,360	5.3	81.5
Over 5 years old	605	93.8	24,188	94.7	17.5
West North Central	357	100.0	16,629	100.0	18.6
5 years old or less	31	8.7	983	5.9	84.6
Over 5 years old	326	91.3	15,646	94.1	13.9
South Atlantic	370	100.0	12,944	100.0	70.9
5 years old or less	34	9.2	1,014	7.8	85.7
Over 5 years old	336	90.8	11,930	92.2	61.4
East South Central	187	100.0	5,808	100.0	39.4
5 years old or less	23	12.3	456	7.9	90.8
Over 5 years old	164	87.7	5,352	92.1	35.1
West South Central	240	100.0	9,228	100.0	41.8
5 years old or less	27	11.3	942	10.2	86.1
Over 5 years old	213	88.7	8,286	89.8	36.2
Mountain	56	100.0	1,712	100.0	23.6
5 years old or less	6	10.7	167	9.8	95.2
Over 5 years old	50	89.3	1,545	90.2	16.5
Pacific	216	100.0	9,897	100.0	33.7
5 years old or less	30	13.9	1,506	15.2	94.0
Over 5 years old	186	86.1	8,391	84.8	21.1

sized by geographic divisions. The first is the proportion of space by age of buildings. For the United States, only 8 per cent of the buildings reporting at the end of 1954 were five years old or less; and these buildings contained only 6 per cent of the gross floor space. The range, by geographic divisions, was from only 0.9 per cent of the space in the New England States to slightly more than 15 per cent in the Pacific States.

The second aspect is again related to one part of the later discussion of the essentials of warehouse design; namely, the proportion of space in single-story versus multiple-story buildings. Taking all 1954 public merchandise warehouses, regardless of age, about one-fourth of all space in the United States was found in single-story type of buildings, with a range from 11 per cent in the New England States to 70.9 per cent in the South Atlantic States. As would be expected, the ratios are much higher for the newer buildings (5 years old or less) than for the older buildings. In the United States as a whole, the single-story warehouses 5 years of age or less accounted for 81.4 per cent of the total space in all warehouse buildings of such age distribution. The range was from 52.5 per cent in the Middle Atlantic States to all of the space in New England States warehouses. Of all general merchandise warehouses in 1954 over five years of age, 22.3 per cent of the space was in single-story buildings, with a range from 10.1 per cent in the New England States to 61.4 per cent in the South Atlantic States.

Public refrigerated warehouses

A more meaningful analysis of public refrigerated warehouse space can be made by using cubic feet rather than the square feet shown in Table 31. Available data on the distribution of establishments and space on such basis for 1954 show that three states—New York, California, and Illinois—together accounted for better than two-fifths of the total space. On the other hand, nine states reported no public refrigerated warehouses in 1954.[14] Of the three most important states, Illinois had the highest average space per establishment.

A second aspect of the public refrigerated warehouse space is the breakdown of utilization by principal product categories. The general-line products refrigerated warehouse was the most important in the United States in 1954 with about 40 per cent of the establishments and nearly half of the occupiable public space. These types of warehouses were proportionately more important in the northeastern and southern regions than in the rest of the United States. Of about equal importance, in the proportion of space, were those refrigerated warehouses handling the dairy products-poultry-egg group and frozen fruits and vegetables. More space in warehouses in the North Central States was used for dairy products, etc., than in warehouses in other regions,

[14] Vermont, Massachusetts, District of Columbia, South Carolina, Mississippi, Wyoming, Colorado, New Mexico, and Nevada.

whereas those in the western states had proportionately more space used for frozen fruits and vegetables. Nearly one-eleventh of all public refrigerated warehouse space in 1954 contained meats and meat products, but the ratio was considerably higher in warehouses in the North Central and Southern States than in the remaining regions.

Farm products warehouses

Finally, a word of description might be introduced about farm products warehouses. Of some 121.9 million square feet of occupiable floor space available in 1,081 establishments in 1954, about 80 per cent contained cotton, with about one-eighth additionally holding grain. Slightly more than 4 per cent contained tobacco.

Essentials of Warehouse Design

One of the revolutions in warehouse design since 1939 has been the shift in the design of warehouse buildings from multiple-story to single-story levels, with accompanying changes in the internal design to accommodate mechanical and electronic devices for moving inventories and filling orders. At the same time, under the pressure of increased use of single-story buildings, great strides have been made in modernizing older multiple-story buildings. This section will be directed mainly towards the first phase of these changes—the factors influencing the choice of single-story as against multiple-story buildings, and the factors affecting the internal layout of the available space. In reading this section, the reader should keep in mind the characteristics discussed in the preceding section.

Factors influencing the use of single-story warehouses[15]

The single-story warehouse has had a long and interesting history in the United States. Originally, all warehouses in the United States during the Colonial and Revolutionary periods were one-story buildings with relatively low ceilings and odd-shaped wall arrangements.[16] As cities grew in size, and the wholesaling sector became more complicated, the urban-type warehouses shifted mainly to multiple-story-

[15] The quantity of literature dealing with this subject has increased by leaps and bounds as the use of the single-story warehouse has increased rapidly. In addition to the references contained in succeeding footnotes in this section and in the bibliography, the interested reader will find much current material in such periodicals as *Distribution Age.*

[16] See Clyde E. Phelps, "An Ancient Industry Goes Modern," *Distribution Age* (August 1956), 48 ff.

building arrangements due to factors to be discussed later. But with the evolution and development of mechanized materials-handling equipment, new architectural concepts, increased use of motor trucks, increased urban congestion, and new theories of inventory management, there has been a sharp shift beginning in 1939, and especially since 1945, towards the single-story warehouse building. Besides the above considerations, the factors behind such shifts may be summarized under the following headings:[17]

1. Evolving theories of warehousing and inventory control, especially the Davidson method developed in the late 1920's, for using punched cards and tabulating machines; palletization or unit-load practices; and the concept of the selection line.[18]

2. Business establishments handling highly uniform products so far as types of containers and quantity lots are concerned to provide adequate utilization.

3. Construction of floors of sufficient strength to support the weights and wear of the mechanical materials-handling equipment, especially fork-lift trucks, tractors, etc.

4. Economy in quantity-lot handling by using unit-load devices for stacking merchandise in high fashion, especially if ceiling heights of 20 ft or more are provided.

5. Inventory situations involving load weights of certain types of products exceeding stipulated weight limits such that the floor strength of existing multiple-story warehouse buildings was found to be below acceptable standards, and could not be strengthened at all, or at reasonable costs.

6. Where rapid inbound and outbound movements are characteristic of the wholesale middleman's type of operation and/or kind of business.

7. Where large receiving and shipping platforms (for both rail and motor truck shipments) are needed.

8. To secure the important benefits of flexibility of internal operations, and the availability of adequate sites at competitively low land costs.

9. Where proximity to customers does not require location in more central locations; or where communication techniques permit

[17] See Clark C. Wright and John P. H. Perry, "The Trend to One-Storied Warehouses," *Distribution Age* (April 1948), 34 ff.

[18] See John R. Bromell, *Modernizing and Operating Grocery Warehouses*, Domestic Commerce Series No. 26 (Washington, D. C.: U. S. Government Printing Office, 1951).

the physical separation at least of the buying-selling functions from the warehousing operations. This factor's influence has been strengthened considerably by the transportation mobility offered by the motor truck and the automobile.

There is much controversy as to whether the single-story warehouse yields as large differential-cost advantages as were estimated by the earlier advocates. Whereas it is true that land costs usually will be much lower than for multiple-story buildings, such savings may be offset by higher foundation and roof costs; higher costs for installing heating, plumbing, and electrical facilities by reason of long horizontal runs; possible higher fire and insurance protection costs because of methods of construction and lack of fire departments in unincorporated areas; and certain increased maintenance costs for roofs, ventilation, and illumination. In addition, failure to anticipate rate of growth may require expensive additions. But the factors discussed above, coupled with important labor cost savings, and more rapid and accurate order filling are important offsets.

Factors influencing the use of multiple-story warehouse buildings

Despite the sharp trend towards the single-story warehouse building for the reasons noted above, there are some important factors which help to explain why multiple-story warehouse buildings exist and will continue to be used:

1. Certain types of wholesale middlemen's operations and kinds of business, as were discussed earlier, have locational requirements which result in the selection of sites in the more congested areas where land costs are likely to be too high to permit extensive utilization.
2. The wholesale middleman may not be able to build or lease an entire warehouse for himself and, accordingly, may have to share space with other tenants. Under such situations, the multiple-story warehouse building offers more flexibility in rental arrangement, especially since the inventories handled are likely to be highly variable and subject to change.
3. Because of variability in seasonal needs, the wholesale middleman will require flexibility in handling highly diversified product assortments, with fluctuating size, weight, and height stocking requirements.
4. Limitations on the economic length to which horizontal movements of goods and personnel may take place in single-story warehouse buildings.

5. Limitations on the extent to which the singe-story building may be extended if future expansion in sales and assortments exceed the best space-needs forecasts.

In addition, Bromell[19] indicates several ways of modernizing (streamlining) multiple-story buildings. He states the objectives of such modernizing to: (1) provide the best available means of transporting goods between functions or within a single function, whether horizontally or vertically; (2) reduce the number of functions to a minimum; (3) provide the best available means of reducing the number of piece handling; and (4) provide the best practicable facilities in and by which (1), (2), and (3) may be accomplished. He then indicates in detail that the productivity of labor can be increased by scientific layout and location of inventories; the use of chutes and conveyors and ramps; and the use of materials-handling equipment of the type to be discussed below.

Warehouse layout: single-story and multiple-story buildings

It may be stated categorically at the outset that there is no single best way of designing a warehouse internally from the point of view of layout and stock location. The main reasons are as follows. Some types of middlemen need warehouses which actually resemble retail stores in the sense that customers come to these facilities in order personally to make selections either by inspection or sample. In such cases, the system of layout must provide access ways for customers and probably the separation of types of warehouse space so that the customers run no risk of physical injury from mechanical materials-handling equipment or any other causes.

The depth and width of assortments, and changes therein, vary widely from kind of business to kind of business and between types of wholesale middlemen, creating wide differences, in turn, in space allocations. Similarly, there are sharp differences in the lengths of time for which inventories will remain in warehouses; e.g., note the differences between products held for aging or speculation and those held only for rapid sale. Physical shapes of buildings will vary, as well as the location of receiving and shipping platform facilities. Some types of wholesale middlemen may break the original shipping containers and adapt the unit of sale to the needs of the customers, whereas others may sell only in the original containers. Finally, products vary in their adaptability to be stacked and moved by mechanical methods.

[19] Bromell, *op. cit.*, pp. 6–40.

The following discussions then must be recognized as a series of generalizations from which individual warehouse situations represent important deviations. Meserole[20] has developed some of the more challenging ideas for layout of space in a single-story warehouse building. First, he states that the maximum warehouse economy will be a resultant of

... (1) supplantation of muscle by machinery progressively as output grows, and (2) the use of the arts of cubage use, layout, and placement (spatial relations of the merchandise departments) to secure the least transportation in the handling of the largest tonnage.[21]

He next indicates the factors influencing the number of variable warehouse-cost dollars spent as:

... (1) volume, (2) the way in which the user of labor employs it, and (3) by certain commodity characteristics. The commodity characteristics which make variable warehouse cost vary are but four in number. They are:
1. Velocity of sales
2. The weight of the package
3. The bulk of the package
4. The number of items in the merchandise department.[22]

Given the variables, a graphic arrangement can be made to show their interrelationships in order to determine warehouse commodity position designed to yield the lowest variable cost (see Figure 11). This diagram ultimately permits commodities to be classified as *shelf-stock items*, consisting of the smallest items in bulk, the lightest in weight, and the most in number; *order-pick-line items*, consisting of those product items which range from light to above-average in weight, etc.; and *shipping-platform items*, which have fast velocity, the largest bulk, the heaviest weight, and the smallest number of items.

The multi-story warehouse building creates much more difficult problems of layout. Three layout possibilities can be noted, depending upon the number of floors in the building and the available space on each floor in terms of both square and cubic feet.

Possibility 1. Allocate stocks so that orders are picked on each floor except the ground floor. The ground floor space would then be subdivided into space for truck and rail receiving; for outbound

[20] W. H. Meserole, "Organization of Wholesale Operations for Low Cost," *The Journal of Marketing,* XIV (September 1949), 192–97.
[21] *Ibid.,* p. 94.
[22] *Ibid.,* p. 194.

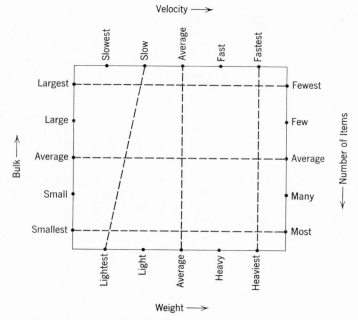

FIG. 11. Use of commodity characteristics to determine warehouse layout. (*Source:* Meserole, *op. cit.*, p. 195.)

shipments; and for order selection lines. The upper floors would each have stocks divided into fast-, medium-, and slow-moving categories. These would. be so arranged, in turn, that the fastest moving items would be closest to elevators or other order moving equipment.

Possibility 2. The first floor would be as indicated in Possibility 1, but order-selection lines would be placed as well on each of the remaining floors, with the rest of the space divided into active- and reserve-stock areas.

Possibility 3. Where the middleman sells both in case lots and broken case lots, the upper floor or floors may be used for the broken-case inventories while the lower floors carry the case lots with the heavier volumes of movements.

In deciding which of the possibilities to use, much depends on the age of the building, the type of goods-conveying equipment, the number of floors in the building, and the volume and variety of product assortments.

Physical Aspects of Warehousing Operations[23]

This section will mainly discuss certain aspects of materials-handling equipment, the process of inventory receiving, and order filling. Although some aspects of each of these have repercussions on warehouse design and are, in turn, affected by warehouse design, they have additional basic features which warrant separate discussion. Some of the interrelationships, however, will be noted.

Materials-handling equipment

The mechanization of warehouse operations has been a phenomenon of the post-World War II period, although some of the types of equipment have been in existence and use for longer periods of time. The incidence of mechanization has varied from establishment to establishment, depending upon the type of building as discussed in earlier sections; whether or not the warehouse operation is interrelated with production which, in turn, has been highly mechanized; whether or not the product assortments are narrow or broad, and homogeneous or heterogeneous; and finally, whether financial resources are available. In addition, the sharp increases in the physical volumes of goods which have to be moved through the channel, coupled with increasing managerial awareness of the advantages more rapid movement of inventories (in a time sense) through the warehouses, have placed a premium upon the increased utilization of mechanical materials-handling equipment.

In general, materials-handling equipment deals with such activities as hauling, pushing, carrying, lifting, and stacking. To accomplish these activities, the following types of equipment are indicative of the sharp advances being made.

1. Devices for increasing the maximum size of unit load which one can handle with the benefit of some type of mechanical equipment. The devices on which a unit load may be placed in order to accomplish this objective are: pallets; pallet boxes; skids; tote boxes; racks; pallet racks; containers; trailers; baskets; and wheelbarrows. Some of these devices may be used

[23] The treatment here will not attempt to include detailed descriptive materials. Those readers interested in such detailed treatment are referred to the references included in this section and to Beckman et al., *Wholesaling: Principles and Practice*, rev. ed. (New York: The Ronald Press Co., 1959), Chapters 23 and 24.

not only for movements into and out of warehouses, and for stacking within the warehouses, but also for stacking within the railroad freight cars on motor trucks.[24]

2. Interrelated with these are mechanical equipments of many types used for moving the unit load devices in (1) within the warehouse, and from within the warehouse to and from receiving and shipping areas. These types of equipment include overhead devices such as cranes, conveyors, and monorails. In addition, there are types of equipment which can stack, push, haul, or turn; e.g., fork trucks (including rams, cranes, grippers, claws, and scoops), and mechanized hand trucks. Available, also, are tractors and pallet-loading machines.[25]

Building upon the use of these types of materials handling equipment, but incorporating as well the use of punch-card equipment, electronic computers, and the work of specialists in inventory theory, there is evolving the semiautomatic and fully automatic warehouse. Many of these have their origins initially in the inventory pressures resulting from the use of automatic production lines coupled with the bottlenecks of nonmechanical warehouses. But increasingly, with the equipment and techniques noted, the same principles of automation are being used in warehouses located at other places in the channel.

Several examples can be given. The Hickok Manufacturing Co. at Lyon, New York, places its lines of men's belts, garters, and suspenders on inclined planes, so that one man can now fill as many orders in three hours as was done formerly by three men working one full day. H. J. Heinz Co., at its Pittsburgh warehouse, use a conveyor network system to sort 6,000 cases of certain products in an hour, and then place them on stacking machines, which move them to double-decked wooden pallets for loading and stacking. Increasingly, beer brewery warehouses are using electronically controlled devices to fill orders. Judy Bond, Inc., in New York City, has a computer-controlled system which is so designed that orders for as many as 3,600 blouses can be filled in one day, or some 6,000,000 blouses a year. Finally, portable mobile devices have been used in Italy and elsewhere which permit order fillers to select single items

---

[24] One drawback in the use of pallets in railroad cars has been the practice of charging shippers the same freight rate for the weight of the pallet as for the products loaded on the pallet.

[25] "Materials Handling: The New Word in Industry," *Fortune*, XXXVII (June 1948), 96 ff.

from widely separated warehouse areas without walking, and from unit loads located in bins from floor to ceiling.[26]

Inventory-receiving procedures

Some attention now needs to be directed to the component elements of inventory-receiving procedure involved for warehouses not connected physically to particular producing facilities.[27] The procedures include accepting incoming shipments from source of supply and the transportation agency involved; accepting merchandise returned by customers for credit or adjustment; transporting, by one of the materials-handling methods described above, incoming shipments to specified receiving areas; unpacking and checking for quality, amount, and physical condition; transporting goods to designated warehouse spaces in accordance with the layout principles noted above; and handling necessary records such as invoices. The control of these operations may be centralized under an operating unit, or may be decentralized. Necessary records may involve the use of modern electronic equipment or less expensive means.

Order filling

Bromell[28] differentiates between consecutive order filling and simultaneous order filling as follows:

Under consecutive filling (a) one picker fills the order completely or (b) work stations are set up and a person in each station or department fills a portion of the order and passes it on to the next station or department. Under the consecutive system the completed order reaches the shipping department as a unit, there is no assembly problem, and only one copy of the total order given by the customer is needed for order filling.

Under simultaneous order filling each department fills a portion of the order and sends it to the shipping department where all the parts are brought together in one complete shipment. This system entails two additional operations which are not necessary in consecutive filling: (1) The preparation of a shipping ticket to notify the shipping department that specific departments are assembling merchandise on each order, and (2) the assembly of the various parts of each order in the shipping department. Simultaneous filling also requires that a separate order be written for each department or a separate copy of the order be supplied to each department.[29]

[26] See "The Push Button Warehouse," *Fortune*, LIV (December 1956), 140 ff.; and "Automatic Order-Filling—Six Million Blouses a Year," *Distribution Age*, (March 1957), 34 ff.

[27] For a more detailed statement, see Beckman et al., *op. cit.*, pp. 432–39.

[28] John R. Bromell, *Dry Goods Wholesalers' Operations* (Washington, D. C.: U. S. Government Printing Office, 1949), pp. 57–67. See also, Beckman et al., *op. cit.*, Chapter 24.

[29] Bromell, p. 57.

The selection of consecutive versus simultaneous order filling is dependent upon the type of warehouse building, its internal layout, the materials-handling methods installed, the type of accounting devices used, the depth of managerial experience, the average number of separate products per order, and the traditions of the wholesale middlemen for the kind of business. It should be noted that some wholesale middlemen use a combination of the two methods in filling orders. And, depending upon the factors noted above, orders may be filled from: (1) *outside lines*—which usually are the longest in length, and which serve to increase the average order-picking time; (2) *inset or horseshoe-shaped lines*—which result usually in the shortest walk; (3) *center lines*—which offer the shortest possible order-picking line; (4) *double lines*—a combination of outside and center lines; (5) *multiple-loop lines;* (6) *twin lines;* and (7) *worm lines* used in conjunction with push trucks.

Some Final Remarks

The discussion of the storage function and of the warehouses in which the function may be centered gives perspective to the physical flow aspects associated with the funnel concept. The sum total of individual management decisions about their individual responsibilities for the storage function gives the over-all funnel its characteristic, as described earlier, of a series of "regulatory valves" which may serve either to adapt the physical flows from faster to slower or to divert partial supplies for varying time periods; or to permit change in the product; or, finally, to permit changes in assortments. In these ways, the storage function has important repercussions on prices and price levels.

For the individual wholesale middleman decisions about the storage function have important repercussions on his position in the channel and upon his attempts, if any, at increasing his struggle for more control of such channels. As a result, the complicated patterns of the incidence of the storage function emerge as indicated in the elaborate classification presented in this chapter. The physical design of warehouses and the extent to which such warehouses have been mechanized serve to influence the extent to which the supply of space does not have to increase commensurate with the large increases in the physical volume as well as the variety of goods. These elements have important effects also upon increasing the speed and accuracy of order filling, while reducing, in many cases, the average cost per dollar of sales.

One final observation may be in order. All through this chapter it has been continuously observed that there is no single best place in the channel where the storage function may be performed. In addition, there appears to be no single best way to design and equip warehouse buildings or to set up order-filling procedures. Although the developments in mechanization and automation have lagged behind those in production, the rate and degree of lagging have been substantially reduced. But even in the adaptation of these developments, it is obvious that there is no simple best system. Forthcoming improvements in the speed and form of transportation will bring, as has been the case historically, very many possibilities for dramatic changes in warehouse locations and operations. But, with all these developments, the individual management unit will have the task of selection; and it involves no crystal ball to predict that several alternative choices will be made rather than a single best choice.

QUESTIONS AND PROBLEMS

1. What is meant by "the incidence of storage activities throughout the entire wholesaling sector"?
2. Explain why storage and warehousing are so important in marketing, especially in the wholesaling sector.
3. What are the fundamental differences between the external and internal aspects of the incidence of the storage function in the wholesaling sector?
4. What are the relationships of the channel and funnel to the external aspects?
5. Indicate the complexity of the forms of incidence of the storage function.
6. To what extent is the problem of locating warehouse similar to the location of a middleman's establishment? to what extent different?
7. Summarize the principal characteristics of existing warehouse facilities in the United States.
8. How does the nature of the product affect the type of storage and warehousing facility?
9. Compare the conditions under which multiple-story warehouses become feasible; single-story warehouses.
10. Why has the use of the single-story warehouse increased so markedly in recent years?
11. What is the essence of the layout problem for warehouses?
12. Why are the physical aspects of warehousing operations increasing in importance?

13. What is the essence of the revolution in the mechanization of warehousing operations?

14. Discuss the important components of inventory-receiving and order-filling procedures.

CHAPTER INTEGRATING ASSIGNMENT

Given the discussion of storage and the wholesale middlemen's responsibility in the channel, develop in complete form (including diagrams) the strategic importance of the incidence of storage in the channels on physical flows.

18

Auxiliary Functions:
Financing

The present chapter concludes the discussion of those auxiliary functions which have special relationships or forms of adaptation to the wholesaling sector.[1]

The Universality or Pervasiveness of the Financing Function in the Wholesaling Sector

It may be said without fear of exaggeration that the financing function cuts across *every transaction* in the wholesaling sector in either complete or incomplete fashion, or in direct or indirect relationship. Even in the case of the cash-and-carry wholesaler, it may be said that he is able to conduct his sales for cash in most cases[2] only

[1] There are, to be sure, some aspects of personnel management which could have been included. But the basic textbooks of personnel management contain much of the scope of what is included in this function from a marketing point of view. The basic textbooks of sales management also include pertinent materials dealing with the management of the sales force. See, also, Beckman, et al., *Wholesaling: Principles and Practice*, 3rd ed. (New York: The Ronald Press Co., 1959).

[2] As will be noted later, even this type, by virtue of multitype operations, is likely to have some credit sales.

because the financing function has been conducted effectively by other agencies in the channel which precede his position; or because his customers have been financed in other forms so that they are able to pay cash for such purchases as are made from him. In a sense, what is being said is that every wholesale sale has back of it either in some direct or indirect meaning (as will be discussed below) one or another form of informal or formal credit base. These forms may range from the simple to the complex; they may involve specialized commercial banking agencies, or tradesmen, or other auxiliaries; and they may have varying time lengths.

The complexity of this network of credit interrelationships, in its gross sense, nowhere has been completely and satisfactorily explored so far as the author's knowledge of available literature is concerned. Although some parts of the network will be discussed here, there is no assumption that this treatment can do any more than scrape the surface of a very complex topic. While the network of credit-financing relationships can be investigated by dissecting it as of a single time period, the dissection treatment can only make qualitative observations about the extent to which the network builds on a series of credit relationships which extend into the past for varying periods ranging from a few weeks to many years. At the same time, the network, as of the dissection time period, will have repercussions also on credit relationships projected into the future with similar wide variations as to time lengths.

A different aspect of the financing network would deal with the variety of the institutions involved in the credit-financing arrangements. Although these will be outlined more fully in the section dealing with the incidence of the function in the wholesaling sector, mention may be made here of differences between members of the commercial banking business; between other primary and secondary financial institutions (in the sense of relative importance); between the marketing agencies themselves; between types of auxiliary agencies; and between types of government credit and financial agencies. These would be linked in the network schematic in terms of originating or facilitating positions, and would be connected by lines which would indicate the direction of the origination of the flows of credit and the performance of the financing aspect.

The two-way form of the network

From the above discussion, and from the point of view of explaining the financing function in the wholesaling sector, the two-way form of the network should be explained, although it has been inferred in the previous discussion. The first aspect is to call the attention of the financing activities by wholesale middlemen of other wholesale middlemen in the channel; of other agencies in the channel preceding the particular middleman's position in the channel; and, finally, of other agencies in the channel which follow the particular middleman's position in the channel. The agencies involved run the entire gamut of these which have been classified in the discussion at the beginning of the book.

The second aspect merely reverses the connecting links in the network to emphasize the flow of credit and financing *to* the wholesale middleman rather than *originating* with him. The supporting of the one by the other, in a time-sequence manner as suggested above for the cash-and-carry wholesaler, must be remembered throughout these discussions.

Indirect financing in the credit network

In further developing the complex nature of the credit-financing network, attention must be given to both the indirect and direct relationships to wholesale trade. The direct relationships will be discussed in the following section. The indirect relationships call attention to the delayed effects which result from the credit mechanism as such, or from the use of other financing devices. Thus, the use of either or both instrumentalities for the expansion of production will have a varying time effect on sales in the wholesaling sector through purchases of all types of industrial goods needed either for a new building or for the extension or remodeling of existing facilities; on the various types of basic production equipment and accessories needed; and on the various types of primary and secondary raw materials needed for the expanded production schedules, or new product production schedules. These may have repercussions, in turn, on direct financing as discussed below.

Of a somewhat different relationship are the credit and financing arrangements extended to customers who do not produce tangible products but originate rather a stream of business and nonbusiness services in both the professional and nonprofessional groupings. But some of these services will be marketed through channels involving middlemen in patterns similar to those existing for tangible goods. In all cases, these agencies will have to purchase varying amounts of products directly and indirectly related to the creation of the flow of such services. These agencies may be involved, in turn, in financing the "purchase" of their services by the varied groups of customers.[3]

---

[3] Note, for example, the wide range of devices which may be used: Open-book credit by medical practitioners; loans by educational institutions; instalment credit by various types of service agencies; and the wide use of various types of credit cards for both business and private travel.

Direct financing in the credit network

One final part of the discussion of the complexity of the credit network is oriented towards its direct relationships to wholesale sales. These relationships subdivide themselves, in turn, into two forms. The first are those credit-financing arrangements made available either by wholesale middlemen or other agencies by means of which customers can immediately purchase products in the channel without having the available money amounts in cash.

The second set of relationships has a delayed time effect. It consists of a series of devices whereby ultimate consumers can purchase varying amounts of consumers' durable, semidurable, and nondurable goods on credit. These sales have repercussions, in turn, backwards through the channel on sales at the wholesale level. Inventories of product assortments have, or may have, accumulated in the channel in anticipation of such sales; or replacements may have to move through the entire channel to replace such assortments as have been made.

Component Elements of the Financing Function

In outlining the component elements of the financing function, two restrictive assumptions necessarily have been made: (1) the function is discussed as it is practiced by a marketing agency in the channel; and (2) because of the marketing orientation, the viewpoint of the discussion is toward its use as an adjunct to buying and selling.

The component elements

Given these two assumptions, the financing function may be subdivided into the following component elements:

1. The policy determination of whether or not to make sales for credit.
2. If the policy answer to (1) is "yes," the determination of the type of credit to be given to customers.
3. The relationship between the type of credit in (2) and pricing policies.
4. Procedures to be used in screening applicants for credit.
5. Liberal or conservative collection policies?
6. Organizational responsibility for administration of the financing function.
7. The costs of performing the financing function.

The final section will discuss certain aspects of these component elements.

Types of financing

Based upon the outline of component elements, certain types of financing may be distinguished as they relate to the wholesaling sector.[4]

The following outline is suggestive:

I. *Financing of Corporate Expansion* (*Intermediate and Long-Term*)
A. Term loans.
B. Through issuance of securities.
1. Stocks.
a. Common.
b. Preferred.
2. Bonds.
II. *Negotiated Forms of Short-Term Credit*
A. Commercial bank loans.
B. Commercial paper markets.
C. Finance companies.
D. Factors.
E. Private lenders.
F. Customer advances.
G. Suppliers' credit.
H. Bankers' acceptances.
I. Special governmental sources.
III. *Borrowing Against Receivables*
A. Discounting notes receivable.
B. Borrowing.
1. Accounts receivable as collateral.
2. Business inventories as collateral.
3. Fixed assets as collateral.
4. Corporation securities and life insurance as collateral.
IV. *Special Governmental Agencies for Agricultural Credit*
V. *Other Special Forms*
A. Leasing arrangements.
1. Of durables.

[4] This outline excludes, of necessity, the various forms of credit made available to the ultimate consumer, although these have important indirect relationships in the network.

   2. Of warehouses.
   3. Of other types of building facilities (including lease-back arrangements).
   B. Equipment trust certificates and debentures in purchase of major installation equipment.

The ideal measure of the volume of such credit arrangements would be the addition of all *gross* amounts outstanding, establishment by establishment. Unfortunately, only a *net* flow-of-funds into and out

TABLE 33

FLOW OF FUNDS IN CREDIT AND EQUITY MARKETS:
1957–1959
(Billions of Dollars)*

	1957		1958		1959†
Flow-of-Funds Sector	1st Half	2nd Half	1st Half	2nd Half	1st Half
Funds raised, total	12.1	24.6	16.4	28.8	25.0
Government	−3.7	9.5	3.9	11.3	4.3
Federal	−6.1	7.1	0.3	9.1	1.3
State and local	2.4	2.4	3.6	2.2	3.0
Private, domestic	15.2	14.2	11.4	16.2	20.1
Consumer	5.4	6.3	4.3	7.7	8.9
Business	8.7	6.3	6.0	8.1	8.5
Financial institutions	1.1	1.6	1.1	0.4	2.7
Rest of the world	0.6	0.7	1.1	1.2	0.6
Funds advanced, total	12.1	24.5	16.7	28.7	25.0
Commercial banking	−2.4	6.7	9.7	7.4	−1.1
Other financial institutions	9.3	8.4	9.9	9.9	12.6
Others	5.2	9.4	−2.8	11.4	13.5
Consumer	6.0	3.7	1.4	1.6⎫	9.0
Business	−3.5	2.5	−4.4	5.8⎭	
Government	2.6	2.7	1.3	2.9	3.7
Rest of the world	0.1	0.5	−1.1	1.1	0.8

Source: "Saving and Financial Flows," *Federal Reserve Bulletin* (August 1959), p. 826. (For earlier data, see the October 1955 issue, pp. 1085–1124).

* *Funds raised* is the excess of borrowing through market instruments over repayments, etc.; *Funds advanced* is the excess of lending through market instruments over repayments, etc. The two totals may differ because of statistical discrepancies.

† Preliminary estimates.

of this complicated structure of financing devices may be obtained from Table 33. The following comments about these data may be made:

Much of the nation's savings and investment is effected by the flow of funds into and out of credit and equity markets. The major part of financing among sectors goes through these markets, either in the form of direct flows between ultimate lenders and borrowers or in the form of flows through financial institutions. In 1958 net funds raised in such markets (that is, the excess of borrowings over repayments) totaled $45 billion, a postwar high. The $9 billion, or 25 per cent, increment over 1957 was equal to the increase in government, almost all of which was by the Federal Government.

In the first half of 1959, funds raised in credit markets, according to preliminary estimates, reached $25 billion, a postwar high for the first half of the year. More than half of the increment over the year-earlier amount was in consumer borrowing. Funds raised by other private sectors were also larger, while total government borrowing was little changed.

The record amount of borrowing in the year 1958 is attributable to strong private credit demands as well as the increase in government borrowing. Increased borrowing by consumers and foreigners offset decreased borrowing by the nonfinancial business and financial institutions sector. The maintenance of private borrowing contrasted with the $14 billion reduction in private capital outlays and the $9 billion increased in private saving in financial form.

Mortgage borrowing by consumers rose sharply in the second half of 1958 and was at high levels in the first half of 1959, as already indicated. The increase in mortgage debt in the second half of last year was much greater relative to consumer purchase of new houses than in 1957. Mortgage credit has become more readily obtainable, and FHA-insured loans were made on existing houses at double the 1957 rate.[5]

The Incidence of Financing in the Wholesaling Sector

From the previous discussion, it is obvious that the financing function is pervasive throughout the entire length and breadth of the marketing organization. Use may be made of highly formal legalistic credit instruments which have their basic roots in such formal credit institutions, in turn, as the commercial banks. Or, on the other hand, the financing may be rooted in the channel structure itself through the use of less formal types of trade credit. But the structure of trade credit in and through the channel merges with the formal credit mechanisms and institutions to the degree—and it is a highly significant amount— that the credit-granting policies of the middlemen and facilitating

[5] "Saving and Financial Flows," *Federal Reserve Bulletin* (August 1959), 825–26. For an explanation of the flow-of-funds system see, "A Flow-of-Funds System of National Accounts Annual Estimates, 1939–54," *Federal Reserve Bulletin* (October 1955), 1085–1124.

agencies are based, in turn, upon the receipt of credit from the more formal institutions.

In discussing the incidence of financing in the wholesaling sector, three divisions of materials will be used: (1) The extension of credit to the extractive industry and manufacturing industry producing units; (2) the extension of credit to wholesale middlemen; and (3) the extension of credit to the customers of wholesale middlemen other than the producers included in (1).[6]

Extension of credit to extractive industry and manufacturing industry producing units

Keeping in mind the types of credit instrumentalities outlined above, three forms of extension of credit may be noted. First, there are the types of credit originating in the government-controlled credit agencies. These may be special institutions for granting agricultural credit such as the Banks for Cooperatives; or they may be special agencies designed to extend financial help to small business; or there may be special financial programs designed to extend financial aids to those producers (including subcontractors) engaged in national defense programs. In addition, there have been such agencies at the RFC (Reconstruction Finance Corporation) which was depression-oriented, but which during World War II extended aid to industries engaged in war production. By 1953, at the time of its termination, it had loaned a total of over $12 billion to businesses of all sizes. Finally, under this grouping, payments to agricultural producers under various types of legislation may be included because of their effects on the demands of such producers for other forms of credit.

A second type would include the use by producers of all the short-term, intermediate, and long-term loan facilities of the commercial banking and money market structures.[7] Finally, the third type includes the various forms of trade credit extended to producers by wholesale middlemen, retail middlemen, and various facilitating agencies in the channel.

Extension of credit to wholesale middlemen

In a manner comparable to that presented in the preceding section for producers, wholesale middlemen may obtain various types of credit for varying lengths of time from the types of government-controlled

---

[6] As indicated earlier, the final section of this chapter will deal with some aspects of credit policies of the individual wholesale middlemen.

[7] Although the major types have been outlined in a preceding section, the interested reader should refer to the basic literature in corporation finance and commercial banking for detailed definitions and discussions.

credit agencies already noted.[8]   There are, secondly, various forms of credit which may be extended by agencies which precede the particular wholesale middleman in the channel.   These may be grouped under the following originating agencies: (1) The producing agency; (2) the assembling-process type of wholesale middleman; (3) specialized commercial banking and sales finance companies dealing directly with the wholesale middleman; and (4) credit stemming from other auxiliary agencies.

Similarly, wholesale middlemen may obtain credit either directly from other agencies which follow any given type of wholesale middleman in the channel, or in indirect fashion from such agencies that may extend credit to one linkage in the channel, and this credit becomes the basis, in turn, for that linkage to extend credit to the particular type of wholesale middleman.   Again, four sets of situations may be visualized: (1) Trade credit extended by equalization-process and/or dispersion-process types of wholesale middlemen to concentration-process types of wholesale middlemen; (2) trade credit extended by retail middlemen to wholesale middlemen, principally by means of backward vertical integration; (3) specialized commercial banking and sales finance companies dealing with middlemen agencies which then extend credit, in turn, to the wholesale middleman in question; and (4) credit stemming in like fashion to that in (3) from auxiliary agencies in the channel.

Extension of credit to customers (other than producers) of wholesale middlemen

The customers of wholesale middlemen may secure financial aid from the wholesale middlemen with whom they deal in the channel, or by means of other financial arrangements from other agencies.   In these other arrangements, the customer may secure credit from government-controlled agencies; from commercial banks and sales finance companies; and from auxiliary agencies.

Special Types of Financing: Case I—Field Warehousing

Before discussing some characteristics of credit sales importance by wholesale middlemen's types of operations and kinds of business, and some aspects of their financing policies, two types of financing by specialized agencies in the wholesaling sector need to be discussed— field warehousing and factoring.   This section will deal with the mean-

---

[8] This becomes true especially if the wholesale middleman also controls manufacturing facilities.

ing, functions, growth, and operational characteristics of field ware-housing, and an example of its use in the food canning industry.[9]

Meaning

There are two kinds of definitions of field warehousing which indicate both its meaning and purpose. The first kind (the more complete) states:

> As the term is ordinarily used, "field warehouse" simply means a public warehouse established by a bona fide public warehouse on the premises of a business concern for the purpose of acquiring custodianship of commodities owned by that concern. Field warehouses are distinguished from "terminal" or other public warehouses in two respects: first, the field warehouse exists only for the purpose of receiving deposits of commodities belonging to a single depositor; second, the warehouse is physically located on the premises of the depositor. The field warehouse is "brought to" the commodities, in contrast to the terminal warehouse, to which commodities are transported for deposit.
>
> The purpose of establishing a field warehouse under the custody of a public warehouseman is invariably to enable the warehouseman to issue warehouse receipts, which may then be used by the concern depositing merchandise in the warehouse as collateral security for a loan. In effect, field warehousing enables the depositor to make "bankable" his inventories of raw materials, semi-processed, or finished goods. The warehouse receipt acquired by the lender as a result of the establishment of a field warehouse on the borrower's premises conveys to the lender legal title to the goods, providing the field warehouse has been properly established, and thus increases the assurance of the lender that the loan will be repaid.[10]

A somewhat briefer definition states:

> Field or, as it is sometimes called, custodian warehousing, is really an in-strument of credit rather than storage as strictly defined. Briefly stated, field warehousing is the establishment of public warehouse branches through which negotiable or non-negotiable warehouse receipts are issued to cover products held in storage on the owner's premises, but actually and legally under the custodianship of a bona fide warehouseman.[11]

Economic functions

Generally, the use of field warehouse receipts as a basis for loans, is to be found under conditions where (a) the business firm cannot

---

[9] The presentation which follows is based mainly upon Neil H. Jacoby and Raymond J. Saulnier, *Financing Inventory on Field Warehouse Receipts,* Finan-cial Research Program, Studies in Business Financing (New York: National Bureau of Economic Research, Inc., 1944).

[10] *Ibid.,* p. 10.

[11] John H. Frederick, *Public Warehousing: Its Organization, Economic Services and Legal Aspects* (New York: The Ronald Press Co., 1940), p. 98.

qualify for a loan on an unsecured basis; or (*b*) where seasonal variations in sales give rise to working capital needs which fluctuate quite widely, and the business firm cannot economically use the short-term money market. In a sense, the basic question may be asked as to the alternatives to field warehouse receipts open to the firm in which the lender can limit his loss in extending credit to a borrower possessing a stock of commodities.[12]

In answering this question, the shortcomings of chattel mortgages as an alternative are the requirements that the inventory be described in detail in the mortgage; that care be taken to register the mortgage properly; and that no change be made in the composition of the inventory without the express consent of the mortgagor. Thus for most business firms with ever-changing inventories, the costs and inconveniences of adapting the chattel mortgage make it entirely too impractical. Again, if a borrower attempts to secure funds by pledging his inventories to the lender and by physically placing them in his hands, two basic problems arise: (1) The lender usually does not have adequate storage facilities; and (2) by using public warehouse facilities separate from the business, interference would be created in the conduct of the firm's normal production and/or marketing functions. Trust receipts involve, among other serious shortcomings, significant difficulties in the case of bankruptcy.

Thus, the field warehouse offers a basis for securing a loan which overcomes most of the shortcomings of alternative methods as noted above while avoiding the creation of significant new problem areas. In addition, it may prove to be the least costly method of financing. And, by reducing the physical movements of inventory, savings may be realized in storage costs, in freight costs, and in costs arising out of possible physical damage.

Factors affecting growth[13]

Several factors have affected the growth of field warehousing—working both from the demand and supply sides. On the demand side, the principal factors may be summarized as follows:

1. The effect of the depression of the 1930's in reducing business firms' available working capital due to the prevalence of serious operating losses. As a result, there was a growing pressure to pledge inventories in order to secure loans.

[12] See Jacoby and Saulnier, *op. cit.*, pp. 10–12.

[13] *Ibid.*, pp. 12–15 contain a discussion of the existing field warehousing companies and selected organizational aspects.

2. The effects of the changing structure of corporate taxes on the firm's ability to accumulate the necessary supply of working capital.

3. The effects of World War II on product shortages, thus requiring firms to invest more money in inventories of strategic raw materials and other components.

4. Increased importance of the differentials between cash and time prices.

5. Savings on purchases of raw materials and components in car-lot quantities.

6. Stability of production rates on an annual basis because of rising labor costs with resulting seasonal increases in inventories.

On the supply side, three sets of factors appear to be most important: (1) Higher banking and credit standards as an aftermath to the banking crisis which existed between 1931 and 1933; (2) the successful use of the Uniform Warehouse Receipts Act in many states,[14] and the legal clarification of the warehouse receipt as a security device; and (3) the active promotion of the field warehousing services.

Some operational characteristics of field warehousing

A wide variety of commodities have been carried in field warehouses, among which the most important were (in declining order of importance): canned goods; miscellaneous groceries; lumber, timber, building supplies; coal and coke; seeds, feeds, grain, and flour; fuel oil, gasoline, and petroleum; wines, liquors, beers; textile products and wearing apparel; iron, steel, and products; household machinery and equipment; miscellaneous agricultural products; paints, drugs, chemicals; paper, wood, pulp; industrial and commercial machinery and equipment; cotton; and wool.[15] Nearly two thirds of the businesses using field warehouses were manufacturing establishments, whereas 32 per cent were in marketing. The main types of lenders were banks, with varying other combinations[16] accounting for the remaining 15 per cent.

An example of lending operations

An example of field warehousing operations for tomato canning may be quoted from Jacoby and Saulnier:[17]

---

[14] The law was first adopted in New York in 1907. See Frederick, op. cit., Chapter 12 and Appendix E.

[15] Based upon 1941 data reported in Jacoby and Saulnier, op. cit., pp. 35–37.

[16] Banks and trade suppliers; trade suppliers only; banks and other institutions; warehouse companies only; finance companies; and all others.

[17] Jacoby and Saulnier, op. cit., pp. 77–78.

During the late winter or early spring months the canner comes to the bank and outlines his prepared plan of operations for the ensuing season. This plan includes a decision as to the number of acres of tomatoes that he will contract to purchase from farmers or he will plant himself. From knowledge of the average yield per acre the approximate number of cases of canned goods requiring financing can then be estimated. Because the selling price of the canned product is variable the banker usually commits himself to advance 60 to 80 per cent of the canner's *cost* of the product against field warehouse receipts. This is equivalent to an advance of from 50 to 65 per cent of the *selling* price of the product. As the tomatoes mature during the mid-summer months they are delivered to the canner who cans them and places the cases of unlabeled cans in a field warehouse. Meanwhile, a broker who acts as agent for the canner and who receives a 2 to 4 per cent commission of the selling price for his services, will probably have found a buyer for the product. The buyers are mainly wholesale grocers or large chain retail grocers, who will design labels bearing their own brand names.

The amount of the canner's outstanding bank credit usually starts rising about the beginning of August, when the canning season gets under way, and reaches its peak about mid-October, after which sales of canned products enable the canner to withdraw goods from the warehouse and to reduce his loan balance. The bank normally expects the canner to "clean up" his loan by the following March 1st, although it may carry him over into the next canning season if it believes that a distressed market condition exists temporarily.

Costs

Finally, a word should be said about costs. The total cost is made up of three components: (*a*) *Component 1*—a $350 to $600 annual minimum charge for installing the field warehouse; (*b*) *component 2*—a percentage of the merchandise value or of the loan value; and (*c*) *component 3*—bank loan rates. The combination of (*a*) and (*b*) may amount to 1½ to 2 per cent of the loan. Bank loan rates usually range from 3½ to 6 per cent. Thus, the aggregate costs may range from as little as 4 per cent of the weighted average annual credit to as much as 10 per cent or more, with the probable majority at 5–8 per cent.

Special Types of Financing: Case 2—Factoring

A discussion paralleling that for field warehousing may be presented for factoring as a special type of financing.[18] In addition, some part

[18] The discussion which follows in this section is based mainly on the following sources:

Carroll G. Moore, "Factoring—A Unique Form of Financing and Service," *The Business Lawyer,* XIV (April 1959), 703–727.

Clyde W. Phelps, *The Role of Factoring in Modern Business Finance,* Studies in Commercial Financing, No. 1 (Baltimore: Commercial Credit Co., Educational Division, 1956).

of the discusion will be directed towards a comparison of factoring as a financing device with accounts-receivable financing.

Meaning and functions

The essence of factoring in its present-day usage is to be found in its functional aspects.

The essence of factoring is to be found in the twin characteristics of transfer of the credit and collection function by manufacturer or other businessman to a factor, and sales of receivables outright (i.e., without recourse to the sellers for credit losses).

Modern factoring involves a continuing agreement under which a financing institution assumes the credit and collection for its client, purchases his receivables as they arise without recourse to him for credit losses, and because of these relationships, performs other auxiliary functions (usually financial or advisory in nature) for its client.[19]

From this definition, the following list of functions may be considered most typical of the factor's operations:

1. The purchase of all accounts receivable of the principal for immediate cash.
2. The maintenance of all necessary accounting records and accounting functions related to (1).
3. Provision for collection of all accounts receivable purchased.
4. The assumption, without recourse, of all credit losses originating in those accounts receivable which were purchased.
5. The provision of additional seasonal or term loans—as needed and approved—on open credit, or on the basis of inventories, fixed assets, or on some other security bases.
6. Servicing of the principal with professional financing, marketing, and production advice as needed.

Trends in factoring

The earliest origins of the factor appear to be found in the Near Eastern countries which had developed foreign trade long before the emergence of Europe. In this environment, the factor actually was a type of itinerant agent-trader who was entrusted with merchandise belonging to his principals in the originating nation. However, the period of significant development for modern-day marketing appeared to have been in Europe during the 15th and 16th centuries. With the golden era of exploration and colonization by the Atlantic Seaboard European nations, the factor filled one vital marketing need by arranging for the sales and distribution of goods originating in the mother

[19] Phelps, *op. cit.*, pp. 12, 14. The italics are the author's.

country to customers located in the colonies. The factor maintained his residence in a colony; provided extensive storage and delivery facilities; became for his principals an important source of advice and information pertaining to products, prices, etc.; and made sales to those customers who appeared to meet stipulated financial standards. At a later period, he began to advance loans to his principals on the basis of the security of their respective inventories. It should be noted that the factor was free in most instances to serve several principals simultaneously.

In the textile industry, the factor evolved in a somewhat different pattern.[20] His prime functions were, first of all, domestically rather than foreign oriented; and he resembled most in his operations the sales or manufacturer's agent of today. In other kinds of business, he may be considered the predecessor of the commission agent.

Beginning around 1900, the factor has been moving gradually and steadily in the direction indicated above in the definition and the list of functions. He began to service more and more manufacturing and middlemen concerns of the types to be listed later. With the emergence of the present-day vast array of types of middlemen, and with the evolution of the manufacturers to the marketing stage where they set up their controlled marketing departments and integrated channels, the factor could no longer serve as a vital and integral middleman in the performance of merchandising, selling, and storage functions. As a result, the factor was transferred from his earlier key role as an agent wholesale middleman, to his present role as a specialized financial and advisory agency performing the functions already noted.

Since 1900, then, sales covered by factoring operations have increased steadily as their role has shifted. In 1917, the estimated covered sales volume was $200 million, and by 1930 it had jumped to $0.5 billion.[21] By 1936 the volume had grown to $0.75 billion, and reached the billion dollar level at the beginning of World War II. More recently, in the postwar period, the volume reached $1.6 billion in 1945, and over $4 billion in 1958.[22]

In these sharp increases, the range of customers has shifted from mainly textile mills, textile sales agents, and piece goods converters to a list which now includes manufacturers (and, in some instances, their wholesale and retail customers) in such kinds of business as:

---

[20] Ray B. Westerfield, "Middlemen in English Business," *Transactions of the Connecticut Academy of Arts and Sciences,* XIX (New Haven: Yale University Press, 1915).

[21] Phelps, *op. cit.*

[22] Moore, *op. cit.*

bedding, chemicals, cosmetics, dry goods, fertilizers, electrical appliances and supplies, furniture, textiles and their end products, paints, paper, and plastics.

Costs

The charges for the factoring services consist of: (a) commissions on the net amount of the sales assigned to the factor for credit and collection; (b) commissions for purchasing the clients' accounts receivables, and thus freeing the client from recourse for credit losses; and (c) interest charges for discounting the client's invoices. The combination of (a) and (b) usually range in amount from ¾ per cent to 1¾ per cent, while the usual discounting rate is 6 per cent per annum.

Given these costs, these business establishments which have their entire credit based on some acceptable form of security, whose customers have well-established credit ratings, and who have strong cash resources or bank lines of credit would hardly ever have to use the services of a factor. On the other hand, the factor would rarely be attracted, considering the structure of his risks, to these businesses which: (a) had working capital resources of less than $50,000 and/or annual sales volume below $250,000; (b) had unprofitable sales trends, with no immediate good prospects for the reversal of such trends; and (c) had product lines of such poor quality characteristics as to lead, in turn, to excessive customer complaints and returns.

Factoring versus accounts-receivable financing

Finally, Moore[23] makes the following distinctions between factoring and accounts-receivable financing:

1. Accounts-receivable financing is nothing more than a method of financing in which the business concern uses its accounts receivables to obtain a supply of cash on a continuing, revolving basis.
2. The customers are not given written notification that their accounts have been pledged to a financing concern.
3. Under accounts-receivable financing, the business concern *and not the lender* collects all accounts.
4. Since the lender assumes no responsibility for credit losses, the borrowing concern must continue to operate its credit and collection departments. This involves, in turn, critical decisions about certain types of policies to be discussed in the section which follows, as well as recruitment of special personnel.

[23] *Ibid.*, pp. 724–25.

5. Finally, the average duration of this form of financing relationship is only about 18 months, compared with several years for the factoring relationship.

Selected Internal Credit-Granting Aspects of Wholesale Middlemen's Operations

The preceding sections have emphasized, in their respective discussions, the pervasiveness of financing in the wholesaling sector; the credit-receiving and credit-granting aspects; the chain of multiple financing relationships which characterizes the incidence of the function in the wholesaling sector; and two special cases of financing. This section is designed to discuss some of the characteristics of wholesale middlemen as credit-granting agencies. In addition to coverage of some policy aspects with respect to credits and collections, it includes a presentation of certain pertinent census and Dun and Bradstreet data.

The extent of credit sales, by type of wholesale middleman

Unfortunately, the census data do not provide continuity of coverage of credit sales, by type of operation, in the years covered since 1929. What can be presented, however, are data from the 1930 Census which show, for 1929, that every type of operation included establishments which sold varying proportions of their total net sales on credit. For the classification of types of operation included, the range was from 3.1 per cent of line grain elevator sales to 91.6 per cent of the converter's sales in 1929. Within the merchant wholesalers and agents and brokers groups, similarly wide ranges are apparent. For the types of merchant wholesalers listed, cash-and-carry wholesalers did 15.5 per cent of their business on credit due, in part, to multiple type of operations by some establishments. The converters, as indicated above, were at the opposite end of the scale. For the various types of agents and brokers, the range was from only 11.3 per cent for auction companies to 91.4 per cent for those import agents who functioned as manufacturer's agents.

Apart from variations in lengths of time for which credit may be extended, and the degrees of formality of the credit arrangements extended, certain factors may be mentioned which would influence these percentage variations in credit sales: (1) The average dollar volume purchased with each order; (2) the frequency with which orders are placed; (3) the kinds of credit policies established by each firm;

(4) the financial stability, relatively speaking, of each wholesale middleman's array (composition) of customers; and (5) the traditions and customs common to the type of operation.

Variations in merchant wholesalers' credit sales, by kinds of business: 1954

By 1954, the merchant wholesale middlemen had, as a group, expanded credit sales in one form or another until 88 per cent of all net sales were granted on a credit base. Table 34 indicates the variations in the importance of credit sales, by kinds of business. At one extreme were the cotton merchants, whose credit sales amounted to less than one-half of their total net sales. At the opposite extreme were 19 kinds of business each of which had credit sales accounting for 95 per cent or more of total net sales. An additional 20 kinds of business had credit sales ranging, respectively, from 90 to 94.9 per cent. The sharp expansion in the percentage importance of credit sales for all kinds of merchant wholesalers business between 1929 and 1954, as already noted, is another illustration of the pervasiveness of the financing function as discussed earlier.

Variations in manufacturers' sales branch credit sales, by kinds of business: 1948

The only other group of wholesale middlemen for which relatively recent credit sales data are available, by kinds of business, are the manufacturers' sales branches. Table 35 contains a grouping of the data for 1948. Once again, there has been some increase in the overall importance of credit sales since 1929, although not nearly so marked as for merchant wholesalers. The range, by kinds of business, is much narrower as well—from 66.6 per cent of total net sales for the edible farm products group (dairy products establishments) to 99.7 per cent for the clothing-furnishing-footwear group. The majority of kinds of business listed in Table 35 had credit sales amounting in 1948 to 90 per cent or more of net sales.

Variations in length of collection periods: 1958

Table 36 contains recent Dun and Bradstreet data (1958) showing variations in the lengths of the collection periods for 24 kinds of wholesale business. Two aspects of the data should be noted. First, there was a wide range in the median length from a low of 11 days in the meat and poultry business to a high of 58 days in the men's, women's, and children's shoe business. Obviously, the rapidity with which in-

TABLE 34

FREQUENCY DISTRIBUTION OF CREDIT SALES AS PER CENT OF TOTAL NET SALES OF REPORTING MERCHANT WHOLESALERS, BY PRINCIPAL KINDS OF BUSINESS: UNITED STATES, 1954

95–100 per cent
  General-line drugs
  Industrial chemicals, explosives
  Clothing, furnishings, footwear
  Drygoods (general line)
  Drygoods (specialty line)
  Piece goods converters
  Home furnishings
  Floor coverings
  Coarse paper and products
  Printing and fine paper
  Raw wool, wool tops, mohair
  Electrical apparatus, supplies
  Lumber millwork
  Construction materials
  Industrial machinery, equipment
  Industrial materials, supplies
  Iron, steel, and products
  Books, magazines, newspapers
  Coal
  Leather goods

90–94.9 per cent
  Drugs (specialty line)
  Paint, varnish
  Furniture (household, office)
  Stationery, office supplies
  Wallpaper
  Electrical appliances, radios, TV sets
  Hardware
  Plumbing-heating equipment, supplies
  Construction machinery
  Service establishment supplies
  Nonferrous metals
  Iron, steel scrap dealers
  Waste materials
  Amusement, sporting goods
  Jewelry
  Petroleum
  Forest products (except lumber)
  Music instruments, sheet music
  Industrial yarns
  Bags, bagging, burlap

85–89.9 per cent
  Fish, seafoods
  Meat, meat products
  Grocery (specialty line)
  Poultry, poultry products
  Wines, distilled spirits
  Farm products, other raw material
  Air cond., commercial refrigeration
    equipment
  Commercial machines, equipment
  Transportation equipment
  Gift, art goods
  Flowers, bulbs, plants
  General merchandise

80–84.9 per cent
  Grocery (general line)
  Fruits, vegetables (fresh)
  Tobacco (leaf)
  Automobile equipment, tires, tubes
  Farm supplies
  Food, beverage basic materials

70–79.9 per cent
  Tobacco
  Hides, skins, raw furs
  Motor vehicles
  Electronic parts, equipment
  Farm-garden machinery, equipment

60–69.9 per cent
  Confectionery
  Livestock (except horses, mules)
  All others, n.e.c.

50–59 per cent
  Beer, ale
  Grain

Under 50 per cent
  Cotton

Over-all per cent = 88.3.

TABLE 35

FREQUENCY DISTRIBUTION OF CREDIT SALES AS PER CENT
OF TOTAL NET SALES OF REPORTING MANUFACTURERS'
SALES BRANCHES, BY PRINCIPAL KINDS OF BUSINESS:
UNITED STATES, 1948

95–100 per cent
  Coffee, tea, spices
  Wines, distilled spirits
  Drugs, drug sundries (specialty lines)
  Industrial chemicals
  Tobacco and products (except leaf)
  Clothing, furnishings, footwear
  Furniture (household, office)
  Home furnishings, floor coverings
  Stationery, office supplies
  Other paper products
  Electrical wiring supplies, etc.
  Plumbing, heating equipment, sup-
    plies
  Other construction materials
  Construction machinery, equipment
  Industrial machinery, equipment,
    supplies
  Professional machinery, equipment,
    supplies
  Service estab., machinery, equipment,
    supplies
  Transportation (except auto.) ma-
    chinery, equipment, supplies
  Iron, steel and products
  Nonferrous metals, metalwork
  Books, periodicals, newspapers
  Coal, coke

90–94.9 per cent
  Confectionery
  Meats, meat products
  Canned foods
  Paints, varnishes
  Garage equipment, tools
  Lumber, millwork
  Hardware
  Farm supplies
  Petroleum products
  All others, n.e.c.

85–89.9 per cent
  Drygoods, piece goods, notions
  Automotive parts, accessories
  Farm-dairy machinery, equipment

80–84.9 per cent
  Flour
  Misc. grocery, foods
  Electrical appliances, specialties
  Commercial machines, equipment
  Jewelry

70–79.9 per cent
  Beer, ale

60–69.9 per cent
  Farm products (edible dairy)

Over-all per cent = 84.6.

ventories are sold have a significant effect on the length of the collection period. Of the 24 businesses listed, only 5 had median collection periods of less than 20 days, while 13 averaged 40 to 58 days.

The second aspect reflects the range within each business between
the upper quartile and the lower quartile. Baked-goods businesses
had the lowest with only 6 days, while women's wear, coats, suits, and
dresses had the highest with 59 days. This range was equal to, or
higher than, the median number of days for the fresh-fruits and produce, men's furnishings, and women's wear groups.

TABLE 36

COLLECTION PERIOD FOR 24 KINDS OF WHOLESALE BUSINESS IN 1958*

Kind of Business	No. of Businesses	No. of Days			Difference
		Upper Quartile	Median	Lower Quartile	Upper and Lower Quartile
Automobile parts and accessories	196	32	38	49	17
Baked goods	48	9	12	15	6
Cigars, cigarettes, tobacco	76	13	17	24	11
Confectionery	21	20	23	32	12
Drugs and drug sundries	73	22	33	45	23
Dry goods	155	38	54	65	27
Electrical parts and supplies	130	38	44	57	19
Fruits (fresh) and produce	51	12	17	31	19
Furnishings (men's)	31	28	49	77	49
Gasoline, fuel oil, lubrication oil	42	29	34	54	25
Groceries	253	11	16	25	14
Hardware	191	31	41	50	19
Hosiery and underwear	38	44	50	76	32
Household appliances, elec.	101	34	49	60	26
Iron and steel and products	62	29	39	47	18
Lumber	92	34	44	54	20
Lumber and building materials	104	26	40	61	35
Meat and poultry	39	9	11	14	5
Paints, varnishes and lacquers	31	31	40	59	28
Paper	133	31	38	51	20
Plumbing-heating supplies	161	39	49	63	24
Shoes, men's, women's, children's	54	41	58	76	35
Wines and liquors	46	21	41	54	33
Women's wear, coats, suits, dresses	31	31	57	90	59

Source: "14 Important Ratios in 24 Wholesale Lines," *Dun's Review and Modern Industry* (November 1959), pp. 56–57 (Dun & Bradstreet data).

* *Definition of collection period:* The number of days that the total of trade accounts and notes receivable (including assigned accounts and discounted notes, if any), less reserves for bad debts, represents when compared with annual net credit sales. *Formula:* Divide the annual net credit sales by 365 days to obtain the average credit sales per day. Then divide the total accounts and notes receivable (plus any discounted notes receivable) by the average credit sales per day to obtain the average collection period.

Selected credit and collection policies

The selling on credit used by most types of wholesale middlemen has its basis in the use of open-account or book credit. This involves some investigation of the customer as to his ability to pay, and then establishing the amount and the applicable time limits. No formal security is usually required. In other instances, the wholesale middleman may use promissory notes; sight or time drafts drawn by him against the buyer or his bank; or, in the case of certain types of agent middlemen, guaranteeing the credit of his customer to his principal.

Where products are either of high unit value, or very new in terms of their length of appearance in the channel, the wholesale middleman (especially the manufacturer-controlled types) may sell on a consignment basis. Thus, the inventory in the hands of the buyer is financed initially by the seller; and the buyer liquidates this debt only if and when he is able to liquidate such inventories.

Bromell[24] distinguishes between wholesale middlemen's credit policies which reflect "conservative," "liberal," and "middle-of-the-road" viewpoints. The conservative viewpoint has the following characteristics:

1. The retailer should have adequate capital with which to finance his current operations, and if he has adequate capital he does not need liberal credit. If he does not have adequate capital, he is not entitled to liberal credit.
2. A credit policy that is too loose results in excessive bad debts, and these, in turn, result in high operating costs and high prices to customers.
3. Liberal credit to retailers tends to make them box in their own credit policies, resulting in excessive bad-debt losses and possibly in insolvency.
4. Very liberal credit gets little additional desirable trade, for retailers who are able to pay do not object to doing so promptly.
5. Unlimited credit may cause ill-will. The customer who has lackadaisical tendencies in paying may strongly resent the suggestion that he send a check.
6. Credit to retailers is not a wholesale function. It is the wholesaler's function to finance the goods from the time they are received from the manufacturer to the time they are sold to the retailer, and the retailer's function to finance them from the time he gets them to the time they are sold to the consumer.[25]

While these arguments have been applied by Bromell to the wholesaler-retailer credit relationship, they can be applied as well with little change to other wholesale middlemen's credit relationships with other types of customers.

[24] John R. Bromell, *Dry Goods Wholesalers' Operations* (Washington, D. C.: U. S. Government Printing Office, 1949), pp. 152–54.
[25] *Ibid.*, p. 152.

The characteristics of the liberal view may be stated as follows:

1. Credit is a service to retailers, and too little is offered by most wholesalers.
2. Liberal credit enables the retailers to expand volume on limited capital, thereby increasing their purchases from wholesalers.
3. The increased volume realized through liberal credit tends to offset any increase in bad-debt losses resulting from such a policy.
4. A credit policy that is too strict drives trade to wholesalers who offer more liberal credit. Therefore, a liberal credit policy will take trade from competitors who are too strict.[26]

The differences between the conservative and liberal viewpoints are those which are present in all arguments about credit policies. Critics of the liberal viewpoint typically argue that concentration of responsibility for credits and collections in the sales division will tend to lead to loose administration of policies, higher costs, and higher losses. Concentration of authority in the financial branch, it is argued in opposite fashion, may well lead to overcautious administration, and the loss of profitable business. In actuality, regardless of the type of organizational allocation of responsibility, the competitive pressures undoubtedly will lead to the introduction of the principle of exceptions in the administration of maximum credit limits or, else, to a policy of nonadherence. It would be expected that the more important large-scale customers—as measured by purchases—would be to a given wholesale middleman, the greater would be their bargaining power in attempting to liberalize their credit limits.

The review of customers for credit by the wholesale middleman depends upon that middleman's sales size; the extent to which credit sales are made; and the availability of specialists. Some establishments may hold the salesman solely and completely responsible for screening the credit eligibility of each and every customer serviced. Where the middleman uses the factor, however, the responsibility, as noted above, is transferred to the factor. In other instances, the accounting department may assume the function. But, for most wholesale middlemen of any sales size and importance, reliance will have to be placed on credit and collection departments. In these cases, procedures must be developed whereby orders can be processed rapidly as soon as received while protecting the framework of the credit evaluation and decision made for each customer. To facilitate this, lists of "problem" accounts usually are given to the order fillers as one easy method by which to spot the problem customers.

Various methods may be used by wholesale middlemen to collect

[26] *Ibid.*, pp. 152–53.

amounts due from credit customers. Where the salesman has been given responsibility for extending credit, it follows that the salesmen may have, also, complete responsibility for collections. In other cases, a special collection unit may be used, in which bills are mailed to customers, with remittances to be returned by mail. Salesmen or professional collection agencies may be used only after each account reaches a stipulated delinquent position. Where factors assume control of accounts receivable, their personnel obviously become responsible for collections.

It should be noted, in conclusion, that these credit policies relate closely to price policies, especially in the matter of using and granting the types of discounts and other terms of sale as discussed earlier.

QUESTIONS AND PROBLEMS

1. Explain the "universality or pervasiveness" of the financing function in the wholesaling sector.
2. What is meant by the "network of credit interrelationships" in the wholesaling sector?
3. How does direct financing differ from indirect financing in the credit network?
4. What types of financing situations are found in the wholesaling sector?
5. Of what value are the "flow of funds" data in understanding the position of financing in the wholesaling sector?
6. How does the extension of credit in the wholesaling sector distribute itself with respect to the funnel concept and channel structure?
7. Differentiate between the definitions of field warehousing included in the chapter.
8. Of what value is field warehousing to the wholesaling sector?
9. Do you believe that field warehousing has increased in importance since 1930? What is the basis for your answer?
10. For what kinds of business is field warehousing important? Why?
11. What reasons may be advanced for the transformation of the factor from primarily a type of wholesale middleman to the present status as a special form of financing agency?
12. What are the present-day functions of the factor?
13. Compare and contrast factoring with accounts-receivable financing.
14. What is meant by the "internal credit-granting aspects of wholesale middlemen's operations"?
15. What conclusions can you reach from the data of Table 36?
16. How do you explain the wide variations in the importance of credit sales between the various kinds of merchant wholesalers' businesses? of sales branches?
17. Differentiate between "conservative," "liberal," and "middle-of-the-road" viewpoints towards wholesale middlemen's credit policies.

19

Managerial Control of Marketing Costs and Profits

Given the wide variations in policies, functions, and product assortments among the various types of wholesale middlemen operating in various kinds of business, some discussion needs to be directed toward the effects of variations on marketing costs and profits. In addition some attention must be given to the effects of the channel structure.

The Nature and Complexity of the Problem

Before beginning the technical discussion of marketing costs, within the context of the topic coverage listed, some difficulties need to be presented and discussed. Without a clear-cut picture of these difficulties, the reader may be misled in two directions: (1) in assuming that there is a single widely accepted conceptual base on which all marketing cost analyses of the wholesaling sector are anchored and, (2) in assuming that marketing costs are exact, accurate, unvarying measurements stemming from the conceptual base in (1), and utilizing the tools and techniques of distribution cost accounting.

Thus, by introducing materials dealing with the nature and complexity of the problem at the very outset of this chapter, it is to be hoped that the reader will keep in mind that there are varying

acceptable conceptual bases on which the analysis of marketing costs
is founded; and that such costs are estimates having varying ranges
of accuracy and pertinency. The latter aspect is highly significant
since, in addition, variations are introduced in part by the purposes
for which the determination and classification of marketing costs are
designed. These variations in purposes will be introduced and discussed at appropriate places in the remainder of the chapter.

Difficulties in the conceptual framework

Not only are there significant differences of ideas as to the definition of cost *per se,* but there are sharp differences as to what is meant
by marketing costs, and which costs are significant in cost analyses.
Dean[1] has focused sharp attention on some of these conceptual difficulties in the following excerpt:

The word "cost" has many meanings in different settings. The kind of
cost concept to be used in a particular situation depends upon the business
decision to be made. There is a widespread and unfortunate notion that
financial accounting costs are universally practical for all kinds of business
decisions because they are "actual" in the sense of being routinely recorded
somewhere. Cost considerations enter into almost every business decision, and
it is important, though sometimes difficult, to use the right kind of cost.

The costs reported by orthodox financial accounts provide an impeccable
pecuniary history that is admirably suited to the legal and financial purposes
for which it was designed. But for business decision-making, the relevant
cost concept will usually be quite different from "actual full costs" reported
by conventional accounting. Hence an understanding of the meaning of various
concepts is essential for clear business thinking. One way of getting clear-cut
distinctions among different notions of cost is to set up several alternative bases
of classifying costs and show the relevance of each for different kinds of
problems. . . .[2]

The other aspect of the conceptual difficulty arises out of the habit
of management to include anything and everything as cost, especially
for income tax purposes. A very articulate and pointed statement
(even if somewhat too cynical) of what is involved is contained in
the following:

. . . Yet this is substantially what has happened to "cost" in economic
literature where it has simply become an expense that is incurred on the
books of the entrepreneur under circumstances where he may not readily, in
the short run at least, avoid the outlay. On current showing—I have seen no
vigorous protest to the contrary—it may even include taxes of any sort,

[1] Joel Dean, *Managerial Economics* (Englewood Cliffs, N. J.: Prentice-Hall,
Inc., 1951), pp. 257–58.

[2] Dean's classification will be presented in a later section together with other
alternatives.

not to mention advertising, lobbying for laws to eliminate competition, etc., as well as any and all unearned income. A quarter of a century ago an economist in a position to know referred to his kind as singers of the "canticles of commerce" or the "troubadors of trade."[3]

Difficulties inherent in the present stage of development of distribution cost accounting

Building upon the conceptual difficulties already noted, there are those, in addition, inherent in the framework of distribution cost accounting in its present stage of development.[4] One of the difficulties originates from the overemphasis placed on past costs rather than on forecasted or projected costs. A second limitation arises from the utilization of conservative as opposed to progressive methods of allocating fixed and joint costs categories where such allocation is necessary. A final difficulty arises from the close—perhaps too close —relationship which has existed since 1936 between such methods, on the one hand, and what is acceptable as cost justification under certain types of legislation, on the other hand, especially the Robinson-Patman Act and the unfair trade practices acts.

Frequently, in addition to, and often building upon, the deficiences noted above, distribution cost accounting has introduced into the framework of the analysis of marketing costs the same difficulties encountered in production cost accounting, namely, the use or overuse of standard costs. If one agrees with the thesis that (a) marketing consists of, or *should* consist of, maximizing the alternatives that are open in the marketing organization to consumers (intermediate and final), then it follows (b) that the use of standard costs interferes with that thesis, especially by codifying cost-accounting procedure used by management so as to reduce the likelihood of visualizing more than one acceptable framework of decision.[5] Recognizing that it is always easier to criticize than to make constructive suggestions, later sections will take the positive view and offer what it is hoped are more fruitful approaches. However, one final criticism may be offered here; namely, that distribution cost accounting frequently uses bases for allocating difficult categories of costs, which are, in turn, significantly influenced by these allocation procedures.

[3] Robert A. Brady, review of K. William Kapp, *The Social Costs of Private Enterprise* (Cambridge, Mass.: Harvard University Press, 1950), in *The American Economic Review,* **XLI** (June 1951), 435.

[4] In the statements which follow, the reader should not infer that all distribution-cost accounting is being tarred with the same brush, but rather with several brushes.

[5] A legitimate use will be offered later.

Difficulties arising out of the joint nature of marketing costs

The problem of joint costs has been well recognized in connection with manufacturing operations. But the complexity and pervasiveness of joint costs in marketing activities have been far too often either minimized, assumed away, or completely overlooked. Yet, these joint costs are at the root of many of the complexities to be discussed later in this chapter. The various types of joint costs may arise from the variety of products handled by the middleman; by the operation of multiunit establishments; by the combination of types of operation at one or more than one channel level; by variations in functions performed, especially in multiple-type operations; by geographical considerations; and by other factors. The complexity of the joint cost problem is increased when the channel view is taken rather than only that of the individual establishment.

But even more important than a recognition of the sources of joint costs is the full recognition of the problem of managerial philosophy in the choice of bases for allocation. The more rigid the belief that the allocation process leads to exact costs rather than estimates, on whatever allocation base may be used, the greater the damage that may result so far as the value of such costs for making decisions. In addition, the greater the use made of allocation bases which are influenced, in turn, by the allocation process, the greater will be the additional damage that will (or may) be done to the decision-making process. One of the important objectives toward which this chapter is directed is the achievement of allocation bases which stimulate and do not stifle the relationship to the accuracy with which the marketing alternatives can be and are perceived. This is merely stating in another way what has been already noted above—that the determination of costs is not an end in itself but mainly a tool for managerial policy formulation and decision making.

Difficulties inherent in integrated and multitype
wholesale middlemen operations

Apart from those difficulties arising out of joint cost relationships as previously discussed, there are additional difficulties to be noted. One has to do with a recognition of the incidence of certain costs among more than one establishment and/or more than one managerial unit. A second has to do with the relationship of cost structures and the allocation of the component cost element of such structures to the managerial struggle for control of the channel. A third difficulty is related to the complicated problem of defining and measuring the efficiency of the marketing system. A final difficulty is once again related to certain problems of requirements of certain government regulations, especially those relating to the channel.

Stemming from these very considerable additional difficulties is the effect of such cost allocation bases as may be used in these conditions on channel competition—actual and potential. This effect is particularly significant if the product assortments move in part or entirely through nonintegrated channels as well, or through various combinations of semiintegrated and integrated channels. The same type of problem exists where a management unit conducts multitype operations in a single establishment. In addition, within the framework of existing legislation, cost allocations may serve either to hinder or to enhance managerial flexibility. Finally, intermediate and final consumers may find, as a result of such joint cost allocations, that their range of alternatives in the marketing system may be increased or reduced.

Basic Characteristics of Wholesale Middlemen's Operating Costs: 1954

Chapter 3 included some data of wholesale middlemen's operating costs (census data) by types of wholesale middleman operations, kind of business, and, for merchant wholesalers' establishments, by sales-size groups. This section will present more detailed analyses of additional types of census data for 1954.

Definition and types of operating expenses

The census definition of wholesale middlemen's operating expenses states:

Total operating expenses, sometimes referred to as "overhead," includes all expenses incurred during the Census year by the reporting establishment. It includes payroll as well as other overhead expenses, but not the cost of merchandise sold, nor does it include withdrawals by owners of unincorporated businesses. For agents, brokers, and commission bulk stations the entries under the heading "operating expenses" represent the amount of brokerage or commissions received rather than overhead expenses incurred.[6]

These data include all of the difficulties noted above, and reflect variations between establishments as to the distribution cost accounting methods used. Since for the agent and broker group the data do not reflect operating expenses, no analyses will be included.[7]

[6] Although this definition is based on the *Census of Business—Wholesale Trade* for 1948, it is equally applicable to 1954 and 1958 Census data.

[7] The actual percentages for each type of agent and broker are shown in Chapter 3.

Operating expenses, as thus defined in the census, may be subdivided into the following groups: administrative; selling; shipping and delivery; warehouse; occupancy; and others. *Administrative expenses* include those items which are not charged directly to any one division or function of the business. It includes the following: executives' and officers' salaries and expenses; office employees' salaries; office supplies and stationery; office postage; telephone and telegraph; professional services; depreciation on office furniture, fixtures and machines; dues, subscriptions, and donations; account collection expenses, etc.

Selling expenses include all of the direct expenses incurred in selling merchandise, except that delivery expenses are classified separately (as shown below). The following items are included: salesmen's salaries, commissions, and bonuses; salesmen's traveling expenses and allowances; advertising; and insurance and depreciation on salesmen's automobiles. *Shipping and delivery expenses* include all cost items incurred by the wholesale middleman in transferring merchandise sold from place of storage to the customers' locations. Included are: delivery employees' salaries and wages; out-freight; express and parcel post; contract delivery; trucking; and depreciation on delivery equipment (where applicable).

Where wholesale middlemen take physical possession of product assortments, *warehouse expenses* include the costs incurred in *operating* the warehouse or stockroom. Included, principally, are the salaries and wages of the warehouse employees, and boxing and packing costs. *Occupancy* expenses originate from the use and maintenance of the physical facilities of the wholesale middlemen, not excluding related business fixtures and equipment. Included as items are maintenance, labor, heat, light, power, and water costs. If the middleman does not own his premises, rent would be included. For the middleman owning his premises, there would be included: building repairs and supplies; insurance and taxes on the building; and depreciation.[8] Other expenses, not elsewhere classified, include interest on bank loans and losses from bad debts.

Operating expenses of multiunit firms

Data are available that show the relationship of operating expenses to the numbers of establishments operated by each firm, for each type-of-operation group. In addition, the average sales per establishment are included. For the merchant wholesalers group, operating expenses increase from the single-unit firm to the 2–3-establishment firms; and then decline gradually until the 25–49-establishment group

---

[8] Some of these items frequently are confused with warehouse expenses.

is reached.   There is a significant decline between the 25–49-establish-ment and 50–99-establishment groups, with an increase, once again, for the 100-or-more-establishment group.

Because the data of manufacturers' sales branches are combined with those for sales offices, there is no pattern of regularity in the direction of change in operating expense ratios, by the combined multiunit groups.   Similar conclusions can be stated for the petroleum bulk station (plant) and assemblers groups.   Within the framework of the number of establishments per firm, there is no systematic relationship between the average sales size per establishment and the size of the operating expense ratio; that is, operating expenses as a per cent of sales do not decrease regularly with the increase in average sales size.

Variations in merchants wholesalers' operating expense ratios, by geographical divisions

The general picture of merchant wholesalers' operating expense ratios was discussed in Chapter 3.   Table 37 indicates geographical variations in these ratios, for the important kind-of-business groups, with the division as the geographic unit.   The establishments in the East South Central States had the lowest average operating expense ratios, whereas those in the East North Central States had the highest average.   In addition to the East South Central States, below-average ratios were found for the establishments located in the Middle Atlantic, West North Central, and West South Central States.   Variations in the proportionate importance of limited-function versus full-service merchant wholesalers and of the kinds of business, coupled with regional variations in wage rates and occupancy costs, are among the important determinants of these variations.   Additionally, sharp vari-ations exist between these geographical divisions in terms of numbers of establishments and their proportionate distribution, according to both sales size per establishment and by the number of establishments per firm.

Variations in distribution of merchant wholesalers' operating expense ratios, by detailed kinds of business

Data were available from the 1954 Census which showed the operat-ing expense ratios for 208 kinds of merchant wholesalers' businesses. Table 38 shows the range and clustering of kinds of business by such expense groups.   With an average expense ratio of 13.2 per cent for all establishments engaged in all kinds of business, it will be seen from the data that more kinds of business (30 or 14.4 per cent) clus-

TABLE 37

DISTRIBUTION OF MERCHANT WHOLESALERS' 1954 OPERATING EXPENSE RATIOS,
BY SIZE GROUPS AND GEOGRAPHIC DIVISIONS, FOR MAJOR KINDS OF BUSINESS

Ratios, Per Cent	New England	Middle Atlantic	East North Central	West North Central	South Atlantic	East South Central	West South Central	Mountain	Pacific
3.0–3.9	0	0	1	1	0	1	0	0	0
4.0–4.9	0	0	0	0	0	0	1	1	1
5.0–5.9	0	2	0	1	1	1	1	0	2
6.0–6.9	2	2	1	0	1	0	0	2	0
7.0–7.9	0	4	1	1	1	2	2	0	2
8.0–8.9	6	4	3	2	1	3	2	1	2
9.0–9.9	0	2	2	3	3	3	2	3	0
10.0–10.9	2	3	2	0	1	3	3	0	1
11.0–11.9	1	3	3	5	2	4	2	3	2
12.0–12.9	5	4	4	4	3	6	4	1	5
13.0–13.9	5	4	7	7	9	3	9	4	5
14.0–14.9	6	3	4	5	6	4	3	7	5
15.0–15.9	5	4	2	1	6	4	8	8	4
16.0–16.9	6	7	6	6	3	7	3	7	5
17.0–17.9	5	4	8	6	8	5	4	8	9
18.0–18.9	4	4	4	4	5	2	7	4	1
19.0–19.9	3	3	0	4	4	2	2	4	7
20.0–20.9	2	5	4	2	2	6	5	1	4
21.0–21.9	4	3	6	4	1	1	1	1	4
22.0–22.9	5	2	0	3	4	3	3	5	1
23.0–23.9	1	3	2	5	2	3	1	2	1
24.0–24.9	2	2	2	2	3	2	2	1	3
25.0–25.9	2	0	3	1	1	1	3	1	1
26.0–26.9	3	1	2	1	3	3	0	2	4
27.0–27.9	0	0	2	1	0	0	1	1	0
28.0–28.9	1	1	1	0	0	1	1	0	0
29.0–29.9	1	0	0	1	1	1	0	0	0
30 and over	0	0	1	1	1	0	1	1	2
Total	71	71	71	71	72	70	71	68	71
Average ratio	14.3	12.2	14.4	12.5	13.9	11.4	12.4	14.3	14.1

TABLE 38

FREQUENCY DISTRIBUTION OF MERCHANT WHOLESALERS'
AVERAGE OPERATING EXPENSE RATIOS, FOR 208 KINDS
OF BUSINESS: UNITED STATES 1954

Operating Expense Ratio, Per Cent	Kinds of Business	
	No.	Per Cent
Less than 1.0	0	0
1.0–2.9	1	0.5
3.0–4.9	7	3.4
5.0–6.9	6	2.9
7.0–8.9	10	4.8
9.0–10.9	19	9.1
11.0–12.9	14	6.7
13.0–14.9	21	10.1
15.0–16.9	30	14.4
17.0–18.9	16	7.7
19.0–12.9	25	12.0
21.0–22.9	12	5.8
23.0–24.9	21	10.1
25.0–26.9	11	5.3
27.0–28.9	5	2.4
29.0–30.9	2	1.0
31.0–32.9	5	2.4
33.0–34.9	1	0.5
35.0–36.9	2	1.0
Total	208	100.0

tered in the 15–16.9 per cent group. The next most important operating expense ratio groups were those with 19–20.9 per cent, 13–14
per cent, 23–24.9 per cent, and 9–10.9 per cent in declining order.
Once again, the diversity of the wholesaling sector, as discussed
earlier in various aspects, is reflected in the wide range of operating
expense ratios. This range will be even more apparent from the data
presented in a later section.

Variations in manufacturers' sales offices and sales branches operating expense ratios, by kinds of business

The census data give separate operating ratios for manufacturers'
sales offices as compared with sales offices for only 21 kinds of business.
In addition, ratios for combined sales offices and sales branches were
available for 77 kinds of business (see Table 39). On an over-all

TABLE 39

FREQUENCY DISTRIBUTION OF MANUFACTURERS' SALES
OFFICES AND SALES BRANCHES AVERAGE OPERATING
EXPENSE RATIOS, BY KINDS OF BUSINESS:
UNITED STATES 1954

Operating Expense Ratios, Per Cent	Sales Branches	Sales Offices	Sales Branches and Sales Offices
Less than 1.0	0	0	0
1.0–2.9	0	3	3
3.0–4.9	1	3	5
5.0–6.9	3	7	16
7.0–8.9	2	5	15
9.0–10.9	3	1	14
11.0–12.9	3	0	5
13.0–14.9	2	0	4
15.0–16.9	2	0	8
17.0–18.9	4	1	4
19.0–20.9	0	0	0
21.0–22.9	0	0	1
23.0–24.9	0	0	0
25.0–26.9	0	0	1
27.0–28.9	0	0	0
29.0–30.9	0	0	0
31.0–32.9	1	1	0
33.0–34.9	0	0	0
35.0–36.9	0	0	1
Total	21	21	77

basis, the average ratio for sales branches alone was 10.5 per cent
compared with only 4.5 per cent for sales offices, and 7.7 per cent for
the combined group. For 19 of the 21 kinds of business for which
separate data were available, operating expense ratios of sales offices
were less than 11 per cent, as compared with only 9 kinds of business
for sales branches. The clustering of the ratios for the 77 kinds of
business in the combined group was between 5 and 11 per cent. The
single most important variable explaining the differences in operating
expense ratios between sales offices and sales branches is the absence
of physical possession of inventories by sales offices. However, as
was noted in Chapter 3, sales offices in the furniture and fixture, paper
and allied products, and rubber products kinds of business had higher
ratios than did the sales branches. Of some importance, also, is the

general tendency of sales offices to have higher average sales per establishment than do sales branches.

Variations in operating expense ratios within each merchant wholesaler's kind of business

Previous discussions have described some of the characteristics of variations in operating expense ratios between kinds of business. But these data were based upon frequency distributions of the average ratio for all establishments within each kind-of-business group. The present discussion emphasizes the range of operating expense ratios between establishments within the same kind-of-business group. By relating the number of establishments in each expense ratio-size group for each kind of business to the total for all kinds of business, an excellent cross-sectional picture is obtained of the varying operating cost situation for all merchant wholesalers' establishments. Of the groups listed, three may be classified in the low-expense group, 14 in the average-expense group, 11 in the high-expense group, and two in the very-high-expense group.

Every kind-of-business group had establishments which operated in every operating-expense ratio size group. But the variations in the relative clustering are significant for understanding the complex cost structure of merchant wholesalers. By relating the percentage of each kind-of-business establishments in any ratio group to the percentage of all establishments, the pattern of significant variations can best be detected. Thus, the grocery-confectionery-meats group, which accounted for one-eighth of all merchant wholesalers' establishments in 1954, had significantly higher proportions of the establishment in the low-cost groups (5 to 9 per cent). On the other hand, automobile wholesalers, with 9.4 per cent of all establishments, had significantly higher percentages in the 20–35 per cent group.

Another way of visualizing the data is to measure the spread between the lowest and highest percentages found for the expense ratio groups. The widest ranges were found for the following kinds-of-business groups: grocery, confectionery, meats (from 5.25 to 25.97); farm products—edible (from 1.32 to 11.63); beer, wine, distilled spirits (from 0.88 to 8.95); tobacco (from 0.08 to 11.15); farm products—raw materials (from 0.7 to 12.43); automotive (from 2.24 to 19.54); hardware, plumbing-heating goods (from 0.94 to 6.96); service establishment, supply houses (from 0.67 to 6.18); and scrap, waste materials (from 1.71 to 8.67). These ranges are the main determinants of the varied average operating expense ratios discussed in earlier sections.

The Analysis and Control of Costs: Internal Management Aspects

Given the above perspective of operating costs of wholesale middle-men, the discussion may now move to an investigation of some more meaningful aspects of costs from the point of view of sharpening the usefulness of such data for individual policy formulation and decision making. Of most significance will be the discussion of such topics as the alternative useful classification of costs; bases for allocating costs; special forms of marketing cost analyses for managerial use; and the interpretation and use of the results of such marketing cost anaylses.

Classification of marketing costs for analytical purposes— external marketing function emphasis

The census classification of wholesale middlemen's operating expenses has been outlined above. This classification scheme has little usefulness, however, from the point of view of sharpening individual managerial analysis. Accordingly, a discussion may be in order at this point of existing classification schemes, and of a proposed basis which will meet the individual managerial analysis needs.[9]

The first classification group is based upon the subdivision of marketing functions as developed in some of the existing basic marketing literature. The major categories of functions are as follows:

I. *Costs Based Upon Marketing Functions*
    A. *Functions of exchange;* merchandising strategy; buying and selling tactics.
    B. *Functions of physical distribution;* transportation and storage.
    C. *Facilitating functions;* marketing finance, marketing risks, standardization and communication; and marketing communication.

II. *The Vaile-Grether-Cox Adaptation*[10]
    A. Physical transfer of goods.
    B. Ownership transfer of goods.

[9] It is a pleasure to acknowledge my debt here, regarding the next several sections, to a former student's writing:

John S. Bull, "Marketing Costs and Management Decisions," unpublished B.A. 299 (M.B.A.) Report (Berkeley, Calif.: University of California Library, June 1952).

In several places I have paraphrased his ideas. The responsibility for the accuracy of such statements, accordingly, is mine and not his.

[10] R. Vaile, E. T. Grether, R. Cox, *Marketing in the American Economy* (New York: The Ronald Press Co., 1952), Chapter 7.

    C. Promoting transfer of goods.

    D. Ordering goods.

    E. Payment for goods.

    F. Negotiation for transfer of goods.

    G. Financing the transfer of goods.

    H. Risk bearing.

        1. Prior to transfer of goods.

        2. After transfer of goods.

III. *The McGarry Classification*[11]

    A. Contactual function.

        1. Costs to search out the market.

        2. Media analysis.

        3. Buyer and seller analysis.

        4. Distribution channel analysis.

    B. Merchandising function.[12]

        1. Adjustment of merchandise offered for sale to the force of customer demand.

        2. Quality determination, packaging, branding, display.

        3. All buying and selling activities (*excluding* pricing and sales promotion).

    C. Pricing function: determination of reservation, offering, and acceptance prices.

    D. Propaganda function.

        1. Methods used by buyers to have sellers sell to them.

        2. Methods used by sellers to have buyers buy from them.

    E. Physical distribution function.

        1. Transportation.

        2. Storage.

    F. Terminating function.

        1. Agreement on quality, quantity, and price.

        2. Agreement on terms of sale, and legal actions necessary to transferring of title (or leasing).

If all of the component elements of the orthodox marketing function classification are kept in mind, together with the component elements of the Duddy-Revzan concept of merchandising strategy, it is very difficult to see any unique advantages offered in either the Vaile-Grether-Cox or the McGarry reclassification schemes.

[11] Edmund D. McGarry, "Some Functions of Marketing Reconsidered," in Cox and Alderson (eds.), *Theory in Marketing* (Homewood, Ill.: Richard D. Irwin, Inc., 1950), Chapter 16.

[12] The concept as developed by McGarry should be compared with the Duddy and Revzan use (see Duddy and Revzan, *Marketing: An Institutional Approach*, 2nd ed. (New York: McGraw-Hill Book Co., Inc., 1953), Chapter III.

Classification of marketing costs for analytical purposes—
internal management emphasis

In the adaptation of the basic functional marketing cost categories outlined above to the marketing cost treatment for particular firms, certain modifications need to be made. These modifications are illustrated in the three separate classification schemes given below:

I. *The Sevin Classification*[13]
  A. Maintenance.
    1. Investment in finished goods.
    2. Storage of finished goods.
    3. Inventory control of finished goods.
  B. Movement.
    1. Order assembly: warehousing, receiving, packing, etc.
    2. Transportation.
  C. Contact.
    1. Promotion: sales solicitation, advertising.
    2. Order entry.
    3. Collections: credit extension, billing, accounts receivable.
II. *The Federal Trade Commission Classification*[14]
  A. Selling and sales promotional costs.
    1. Sales supervisory and sales office costs.
    2. Salesmen's salaries and sales office costs.
    3. Advertising.
  B. Warehousing costs.
    1. Storage space costs.
    2. Stock-handling costs.
  C. Transportation and delivery costs.
    1. Common carrier costs.
    2. Local delivery costs.
  D. Office order-handling costs.
  E. Credit and collection costs.
    1. Credit investigation, correspondence, and approval.
    2. Assembling and filing credit data.
    3. Collecting overdue accounts.

---

[13] Charles H. Sevin, "Some Aspects of Distribution Cost Analysis," *The Journal of Marketing,* XII (July 1947), 92.

[14] Federal Trade Commission, *Case Studies in Distribution Cost Accounting for Manufacturing and Wholesaling* (Washington, D. C.: U. S. Government Printing Office, 1941). This study was developed in relationship to the Robinson-Patman Act, and more will be said about it in connection with Chapter 22.

F. General administrative costs, not included in (A) through (E).
   1. Donations and contributions.
   2. Professional service fees.
   3. Subscriptions and dues.
   4. Hospitalization and welfare.
   5. Executive salaries and office expense.
   6. Group life insurance.
   7. Taxes.
   8. All others, n.e.c.

These classification categories are merely suggestive of various proposals prepared by accountants, trade associations, marketing specialists, and government agencies. All have their individual merits and weaknesses. They have the common bases of being founded in functional origins; and some add categories of costs which are not allocable, in and of themselves, to other functional categories.

Because these classification schemes have primarily a functional orientation, another framework is needed which, as Dean has stated,[15] will meet certain decision-making criteria:

Financial records aim at describing what was, whereas the useful decision-making concepts of cost aim at projecting what will happen under alternative courses of action. These special-purpose costs differ from "actual costs" in content as well as viewpoint. Different combinations of cost ingredients are appropriate for various kinds of management problems.

Based upon this point of view, he has prepared the following classification which deviates quite markedly from these which have been presented:[16]

   I. *Nature of the Sacrifice*
      A. Opportunity costs.
      B. Outlay costs.
   II. *Degree of Anticipation*
      A. Past costs.
      B. Future costs.
   III. *Degree of Adaptation to Present Output*
      A. Short-run costs.
      B. Long-run costs.
   IV. *Degree of Variation with Output Rate*
      A. Variable costs.
      B. Constant costs.

[15] Dean, *op. cit.*, p. 258.
[16] *Ibid.*, pp. 259-272. This discussion includes complete definitions and other aspects of the cost concepts as outlined here.

    V. *Traceability to Unit Operations*
       A. Traceable costs.
       B. Common costs.
   VI. *Immediacy of Expenditures*
       A. Out-of-pocket costs.
       B. Book costs.
  VII. *Relation to Added Activity*
       A. Incremental costs.
       B. Sunk costs.
 VIII. *Relation to Retrenchment*
       A. Escapable costs.
       B. Unvariable costs.
   IX. *Controllability*
       A. Controllable costs.
       B. Noncontrollable costs.
    X. *Timing of Valuation*
       A. Replacement costs.
       B. Historical costs.

A suggested classification scheme for internal management purposes

After an exhaustive and critical survey of the literature, Bull[17] has developed a set of eight criteria of a satisfactory classification scheme of marketing costs:

1. It must be of value both to executive and administrative management as a controlling check as well as a tool for future guidance of operational marketing activities, and marketing strategies and major policies.
2. It must embody all of the best techniques for examination of marketing costs discussed in Chapter II ("Present Approaches to Marketing Cost Analysis").
3. It must attempt to differentiate between those which may be considered the "labor" productive factors of marketing and those which may be considered the "psychological" productive factors.
4. It must consider those marketing costs which are incurred in order to increase the firm's sales volumes, and those differential or constant costs which result from this increased volume, or which may be independent of it.

[17] Bull, *op. cit.*, pp. 94–5. Some slight editorial changes have been made in Bull's language, but these changes do not alter the basically direct quotation aspect of the statement.

5. It must make workable the task of discovering which marketing costs are controllable and which are uncontrollable by both principal segments of management.

6. It must be a classification which disturbs the general accounting expense classifications as little as possible, and yet is one to which the marketing cost analyst may allocate natural costs on as objective a basis as possible.

7. It must be one which can be applied to all business firms engaging in marketing operations with almost equal utility if it is to be of significance to business as a whole.

8. Finally, it must differentiate between those marketing costs which "bear fruit" during the same accounting period in which they are incurred; and those which must await another period before the "harvest may be reaped."

On the basis of these criteria, Bull then develops a two-divisional classification scheme consisting of projectional marketing costs and facilitational marketing costs.[18]

I. *Projectional Marketing Costs*
    A. Advertising.
        1. Space and time media costs.
        2. Direct mail and catalog costs.
        3. Media research costs.
        4. All other advertising costs, n.e.c.
    B. Personal selling.
        1. Direct salesmen solicitation costs.
        2. Floor selling and over-the-counter sales costs.
        3. Salesmen's demonstrations and lecture costs.
    C. Point-of-sale and intrinsic product promotion.
        1. Display costs.
        2. Give-away folder costs.
        3. Packaging costs.
        4. Product embellishment costs.
    D. Special promotional devices.
        1. Premiums and sample costs.
        2. Contest costs.
    E. Competitive price promotions.
        1. Loss-leaders merchandise costs.
        2. Above-average dealer margin costs.
        3. Unprofitable customer discount costs.
        4. Excessive credit risk costs.

[18] *Ibid.,* pp. 95–114.

  F. Special customer services.
    1. Above normal delivery costs.
    2. Other promotional customer service costs.
  G. Public relations.
    1. Donations.
    2. Other public relations costs.
    3. Purchase order routine costs.
  H. Normal trade customer services.
    1. Alteration and repair costs.
    2. Price lists to established customers.
    3. Returned goods costs.
    4. Installation and service costs.
    5. Rest rooms, lounges, and other customer conveniences and service costs.
 II. *Facilitational Marketing Costs*
  A. Storage and warehousing.
    1. Factory storage of finished goods costs.
    2. Stockkeeping and stock control costs.
    3. Cleaning, heating, and special storage costs.
    4. Warehouse and stockroom equipment costs.
  B. Physical handling.
    1. Grading, assembling, and sorting costs.
    2. Packing and crating costs.
    3. Intra-Firm handling of finished goods costs.
    4. Handling equipment costs.
    5. Wrapping and marking costs.
    6. Receiving and shipping costs.
  C. Transportation.
    1. Common carrier freight costs.
    2. Delivery costs.
    3. Costs incurred by salesmen time spent in personal delivery of orders.
    4. Special in transit costs.
  D. Order filling routine.
    1. Costs incurred by salesmen time spent in invoicing and order notifications.
    2. Branch and sales office order routine costs.
  E. Payment collections.
    1. Branch and head office accounts receivable activity costs.
    2. Salesmen time spent in collecting accounts.
    3. Customary bad debt and credit risk costs.

    F. Buying and purchasing.
       1. Accounts payable office costs.
       2. Buyers and purchasing agent salaries.
       3. Purchase order routine costs.
    G. Normal customer services in the trade.
       1. Alteration and repair costs.
       2. Price lists to known customers.
       3. Returned goods costs.
       4. Installation and continual service costs.
       5. Rest room, lounging and convenience services to customers.
    H. Miscellaneous facilitational costs.
III. *Miscellaneous* (n.e.c.)

Projectional marketing costs are those which project the firm's products, services, and personality (the equivalent of the presently overused concept of the "corporate image") into the market for the purpose of realizing management's objectives as to sales, market penetration, and good will. These costs have the following important characteristics: (1) They *always cause* an increase in sales volume but *never result* from such increases; (2) they are concerned primarily with affecting directly and indirectly customers' buying habits and motives; (3) they are incurred in the anticipation of future sales, so that very often, in a present accounting time period, they cannot be charged against sales actually recorded in the same time period; (4) they are homogeneous in nature, vary in proportion to each other, and have a high marginal rate of substitutability; (5) they are the competitive fighting costs of the firm, and, accordingly, "are very much dependent upon the intuitive and experienced judgment of management for analysis and control;" (6) they cannot be analyzed, except to a very limited extent, by such approaches as engineering and time-and-duty analyses; and (7) they do not lend themselves easily to concepts of standard costs and efficiency.

Facilitational marketing costs are incurred, on the other hand, as a result of marketing activities designed to place the firm's products and related services in the "right" physical time and locational proximity to buyers or their representatives. These expense categories occur in an organization either because of results already in existence by virtue of projectional marketing activities or because these results may be expected. The following characteristics of these costs are important: (1) They have only a very *indirect* effect upon sales volumes, and increases result mainly from increases in short-run sales volume; (2) they are more nearly a function of engineering-type activity; (3) they are, in the main, a function of sales volume during the same period in which they are realized; (4) they do not vary significantly in proportion to each other because they are heterogeneous in composition as to subclasses; (5) they do not have to depend upon managerial intuition, since more automatic control and analytical methods are available; (6) they readily are adaptable to such studies as engineering and motion-and-time, and the elements of standard distribution cost accounting; and (7) they tend to be more repetitive in nature and routinized in operation.

Use of projectional and facilitational function costs in a complete analysis of marketing costs for the firm

Finally, Bull[19] presents a five-step proposal for a complete analysis of marketing costs for the firm. Space will permit only an abbreviated statement of each step here (see, also, Figure 12).

Step 1. Make the necessary classification of the firm's marketing costs into administrative, supervisory, and operational categories.

Step 2. Allocate these categories wherever possible to subfunctional classifications of projectional function costs and facilitational function costs, as defined above. If the firm has newly incurred costs which cannot be so classified, they should be grouped together into an "uncertain function cost" heading. After first allocations have been made and standards of performance determined, these should be then divided into projectional and facilitational headings.

Step 3. Determine which of the projectional function costs are anticipation costs and which are current costs. Determine, also, which of the facilitational function costs are volume costs and which are capacity costs.

Step 4. Allocate all of the categories in step 3, so far as possible, to the various management decision bases, as shown in Figure 12. The residual, while they need not be allocated, must be accountable in some fashion.

Step 5. The contents of this can best be presented in Bull's language.[20]

We have faced the problem of joint costs, unallowable costs, controllable and uncontrollable costs (from administrative management's viewpoint), current and future costs, necessary and unnecessary costs, and attempted to get, by the process of classification, a clearer picture for management of what is going on behind the marketing scene. Now the problem of future planned costs, and efficiency must be tackled.

[19] *Ibid.,* Chapter V, pp. 126–43.
[20] *Ibid.,* pp. 134–35.

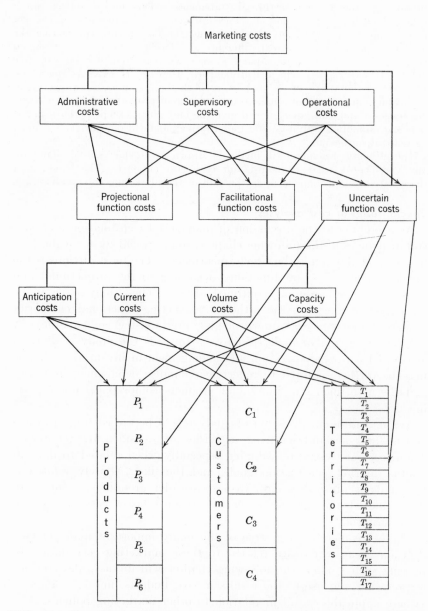

FIG. 12. Functional allocational procedure graphically explained. *Source:* Bull, *op. cit.*, p. 127.

To do this, we must start at the opposite end of the scale, and examine the product, customer, and territorial statements. This means setting up a flexible budget for every one of these statements . . . standards and budget figures should be set by investigation from the bottom up, considering the level of capacity operations at different sales levels. Capacity costs should change very little over the capacity range, whereas volume costs will give differential cost levels which will tend to decrease as capacity increases. Engineering methods can be used to set both these standards. However, in the realm of standards for anticipation and current proportional costs, marketing research and sales analysis will give the only clues, except perhaps in the personal promotion activities, and the intuitive judgment of management must be relied upon heavily.

The ultimate statement will finally be drawn up to show actual, standard, and variances (actual—standard) for each cost entailed. The handling of these variances will depend upon the skill of the marketing cost analyst. . . .

Special forms of cost analyses

As a prelude to the discussion of managerial coordination and control of policies in the following chapter, some special forms of marketing costs analyses may be briefly mentioned. The most obvious is the breakdown of costs, by functions, according to the projectional and facilitational subgroupings outlined above. These may have to be regrouped further into the orthodox marketing functional categories to permit more general interfirm and interindustry comparisons. A different direction of analysis may be towards the analysis of costs associated with the possession and management of inventories. These may be further required to reflect merchandise department activities and the assortments of individual products comprising each department.

Again, a different direction of analysis will be the costing of order-getting and account-servicing activities of salesmen by territories. These cost analyses are valuable especially when related to data of quotas, market penetration goals, and the like. Closely related is the analysis of similar data by size-of-order groupings, in order to determine whether or not to service accounts below certain size and profit criteria.

These are merely suggestive of the many important management-decision areas which are related to these marketing cost data. In making such studies, the following chapter will discuss, also, the interpretation and use of the results in cost budgets, in cost standards (where applicable), and in relation to other marketing policies.

The Analysis of Channel Cost Structures—A Case Study[21]

Apart from the use of cost justification studies by management as defenses in Robinson-Patman Act cases, there is an increasing awareness of the necessity, by such management personnel, to analyze their marketing costs in channels-of-distribution context. The greatest motivation for such studies originates, naturally, with manufacturers. In making these studies, their objectives may be: (a) a desire to compare business-getting cost ratios and profit contributions resulting from alternative channel arrangements already in use; (b) comparisons of such costs and profits via existing channels in relation to costs and profits from new channels, especially the manufacturer-controlled types; (c) the use of the channel cost framework against which to compare product and salesmen's performances, and market penetration objectives; and (d) a desire, perhaps, to measure the "efficiency" of the marketing structure use by the company.

The following discussion presents a statement of a plan presently in use by a large manufacturer.[22] Throughout this discussion, the reader should keep in mind the important and unique role played by the Marketing Research Department of the company in executing the special studies referred to in making the necessary cost allocations.

Basic policy considerations

The entire cost analysis procedure to be outlined was based upon the fundamental top management policy of identifying, on a continuous basis, the majority of the important variables which affect the marketing profitability of the company's operations as between: (a) territories; (b) classes of trade customers; (c) product lines; and (d) methods (channels) of distribution. In trying to attain these basic policies, the company instituted the pattern of analysis as follows:

1. Analyses were secured on an extensive and comprehensive basis of delivery invoices for a representative period of time. These

---

[21] One of the most unique and imaginative approaches to this subject is contained in Ralph F. Breyer, *Quantitative Systemic Analysis and Control: Study No. 1—Channel and Channel Group Costing* (Philadelphia: College Offset Press, 1949). Because of its length and complexity, any attempt at condensation here would be a disservice to Professor Breyer.

[22] Because of the nature of the case, the author has agreed not to identify the company, the products handled, the nature of the customers serviced, and the types of channels utilized. As a result, the discussion has excluded some cost categories because they would help in identifying the particular manufacturer.

studies will be referred to from time to time in the sections which follow.

2. A complete analysis of these invoices resulted in the following types of data for each channel in each area, for each product group, for each trade customer class designation.

a. Average size, in physical units, of each delivery.

b. Extent and effects of multiple product deliveries.

c. Average composition of deliveries as to type of delivery, and kind of package.

d. Types of delivery vehicles used.

Other types of special studies were made in addition to these; e.g., the average distance of each type of customer from the locational point of the product's stock storage, and the methods of receiving products.

The sections which follow discuss in detail the allocation procedures developed for each of the important cost categories,[23] based upon these studies.

Allocation of depreciation, maintenance, rent, and taxes

The investment in shipping plant facilities were classified into two groups: (1) those facilities designed for receiving, storing, and handling bulk products; and (2) those facilities designed for receiving, storing, and handling packaged products. Such expenses as were to be allocated, were divided, accordingly, on the basis of this division in investment. Bulk storage records were summarized, in addition, in order to determine the total storage capacity, in physical units, for each product group. The expenses applicable to this group were then allocated to each product line on the basis of the ratio of its bulk storage capacity to the total bulk storage capacity. Similarly, the expenses applicable to the packaged products were allocated to each product line on the basis of the volume handled in packages as determined by sales analysis covering a representative period. The allocation to trade customer classes, for each product group, was made on a volume basis.

Because of the high unit value of shipping containers, depreciation was allocated to products, trade customer classes, and channels on the basis of the quantities handled and sold in these containers, as revealed from the special analysis of sales.

---

[23] The cost categories are: depreciation, maintenance, rent, and taxes; wholesale distributor commissions; solicitation and branch supervision; special customer expenses; delivery expenses, field and division administration; advertising; product research; and home office overheads.

Allocation of wholesale distributors' commissions

The allocation procedures consisted of the following: (1) Commission payments covering a representative period were summarized and analyzed to develop average rates for each product group; (2) where variances occurred in (1), average rates were developed for each trade customer class and channel; (3) the average base rates determined in (1) and (2) were then applied against current actual wholesale distributors' sales volumes; and (4) where the calculated total in (3) differed from the actual, the difference was prorated on the basis of calculated dollars.

Allocation of solicitation and branch supervision expenses

The detailed procedure used for allocating these expenses consisted of the following components:

1. Each employee engaged in these activities periodically maintained a time log for one month.
2. The following data were recorded in the time log:
   a. Time spent with customers, or on activities identified with specific products and trade customer classes, coded to identify the customer's trade class, the product group or groups solicited, and the channel of distribution servicing the customer or trade class.
   b. Supervision time.
   c. Work with customers other than on products.
   d. Such miscellaneous and general functions as travel time, meetings, civic duties, etc.
3. Allocation of expenses to channels, product groups, and trade customer classes involved as follows:
   a. *Direct solicitation*—allocated on the basis of time logged from (2a) above.
   b. *Supervision*—allocated on the basis of the direct expenses of the functions supervised.
   c. *Other customer work*—allocated to trade customer classes on the number of, or time involved in, such activities, and to products on the basis of sales value.
   d. *Miscellaneous and general*—allocated on the basis of the combined distribution of (a), (b), and (c).

Allocation of special customer expenses

In most cases, the trade class customer is known, and, also, the product or products involved. For such cases, the allocation can be made on a direct basis. Where the trade customer class, or the product class, or both may be identifiable, the allocation was made on the basis of company investment or on physical volume bases.

Allocation of delivery expenses

Because the company assumed direct responsibility for delivery, and because the delivery procedures were both complicated and expensive, an elaborate allocation procedure was developed, as outlined below.

1. Delivery expenses were divided into travel time expenses and expenses originating from time spent at the customers' place of business.
2. Operating costs per mile and per minute were established for each *type* of delivery vehicle based on current salaries and current truck rental rates.
3. Data, as listed, were obtained from special studies of delivery invoices, classified by type of truck:
   a. Ratio of deliveries, by product and trade customer classes.
   b. Average size of delivery.
   c. Effect of multiple product deliveries.
4. The allocation of travel time was then made in the following manner:
   a. Flat cents per gallon per mile basis.
   b. Truck operating cost per mile for each type of truck was converted to a cost per gallon per mile based upon truck capacity.
   c. Develop average miles traveled for the trade customer class involved, adjusted to reflect the average of all types of trucks used.
5. The allocation of customer stop time involved the following:
   a. Fixed stop time costs (cents per unit) were developed for each product and trade customer class by: (i) determining the total stop time cost per stop based on the average number of minutes per stop, and truck operating costs per minute, and (ii) total fixed cost per delivery was divided by the average size of delivery, and (iii) where the invoice analysis showed that the product was delivered in combination with other products, appropriate adjustments were made.
   b. Variable cost time per unit was obtained by dividing truck operating cost per minute by unloading time for each truck, or on a combination of trucks and/or type of package delivered.
   c. The combined fixed and variable time rates were applied against total sales volume for product and trade customer

class involved; and any difference between the totals of calculated distribution and actual expense dollars was prorated on the basis of calculated costs.

Allocation of field and direct administrative expenses

These expenses were allocated to product groups, trade customer classes, and channels on the basis of the expenses directly allocated under the "plant," "delivery," "wholesale distributor's commissions," and "solicitation" categories.

Allocation of advertising expenses

Four types of allocation situations were covered. *First*, where the intent of the advertising was clearly to promote the sales of specific products to particular trade customer classes, the allocation was made directly to the product and trade customer class affected. *Second*, where the intent of the advertising was to promote general services, or where the expense could not be directly identified with a particular product or trade customer class, such expenses were allocated on a sales realization basis. *Third*, the Advertising Department's overhead expenses were prorated to all product and trade customer classes on the basis of the direct advertising expenses involved in the preceding. *Fourth*, segregation of advertising expenses, by company regions, was made on the basis of: (*a*) the advertising agency's survey of newspaper and magazine circulation, radio and TV coverage, etc.; and (*b*) the advertising department's analysis of advertising expenditures according to where they were made and the areas affected.

Allocation of product research expenses

Since the research and development expenses attached to new and existing products were known on a current and continuing basis, under normal accounting procedures, the allocation was made to each trade customer class, thereafter, on a straight volume basis.

Allocation of home office overhead expenses

The allocation procedure was subdivided into those expenses that could be assigned to wholesale sales accounts, those that could be applied to retail sales accounts, and the "other" expense categories.

For *wholesale sales* accounts, the following components were involved:

1. All employees that could allocate their time to specific products and trade customer classes did so on appropriate questionnaire

forms. Then, where product or trade classes *only* (*not both*) could be identified, allocation was made upon the basis of value of sales.

2. A portion that could be identified only with wholesale distributor operations was allocated on the basis of distribution of commission expense as outlined above.

3. The remainder was allocated on the basis of the portion previously allocated.

4. This expense, as well as all other Home Office expense elements *except* advertising, was allocated to all areas and to all channels on a volume basis.

For *retail sales,* the allocation of Home Office expenses to trade customer class and to product class was based on questionnaire forms filled in by all employees who could make a definite time division. Expenses that could not be directly assigned were allocated on the basis of that portion allocated directly from the information contained in the questionnaire forms.

Other Home Office expenses were segregated into Credit Division expenses and "other." The Credit Division expenses were allocated to trade customer classes on the basis of departmental estimates, and to product classes on the basis of the value of products sold to each trade customer classification. The "other" category was prorated to products and trade customer classes on the basis of the combined totals of the prior distribution of all other Region, Division, and Home Office expenses.

Final note

It should be kept in mind, as a final note, that these allocation procedures would be modified based upon the results obtained from additional studies of the types mentioned.

Although this case study is based upon an example of a large manufacturer-oriented and partially integrated channel of distribution situation, many elements of the analytical situation as well as the problems encountered are pertinent, in part or in whole, to other types of channel arrangements. In addition to what has been mentioned, reference will be made to other uses of these data in management coordinated and control of policies in the next chapter.

QUESTIONS AND PROBLEMS

1. What exactly is the nature and complexity of the marketing costs problem?
2. Explain exactly the bases of the conceptual difficulties discussed by Dean.

3. What are the sources of some of the conceptual difficulties of marketing costs?

4. Indicate the categories of wholesale middlemen's operating costs included in the census data.

5. What generalizations can you advance as to the effect on operating costs of the following: (a) type of operation? (b) the operation of multi-unit firms? (c) geographic location? and (d) kind of business?

6. Compare and contrast the various classifications of marketing costs which may be used for analytical purposes. What are the main differences between the external and the internal management emphasis?

7. What do you think of Bull's criteria of a satisfactory marketing costs classification scheme?

8. Differentiate clearly between projectional and facilitational marketing costs. Give clear-cut examples of each.

9. How may projectional and facilitational costs be used in marketing costs analysis and control?

10. Describe and discuss the main features of the case study included in the chapter.

CHAPTER INTEGRATING ASSIGNMENT

In one sense, marketing costs of an individual wholesale middleman are the net resultant of all of the policy and functional activities discussed in the previous chapters. In a budgetary sense, the reverse relationship may ensue. This two-way view of the firm's marketing costs underlies many of the complexities discussed in this chapter. You are asked, in this integrating assignment, to discuss the relationship of this view to the competitive position of the individual middleman in the channel.

20

Management Coordination and Control of Policies

The concept of the wholesaling sector in all of its complexity, which has been emerging from all of the discussion in the preceding chapters, has introduced such a wide scope of management policies, and problem and operational areas related to such policies, that of necessity some discussion of coordination and control is needed. The sharply varying sizes of wholesale middlemen establishments, combined with the managerial complexities introduced by the struggle for control of the channel by producer, wholesale middlemen, and retail middlemen management levels, further bring the role of executive coordination and control of policies sharply into focus. The wide variations both in the types and composition of the policies, as discussed in the preceding chapters, serve to accentuate the importance attached to coordination and control.

Thus, every managerial unit which is related either directly or indirectly to the wholesaling sector, and to the channel within the wholesaling sector, has a direct stake in policy coordination and control if it is large enough, organizationally speaking, to have any basis for establishing significant policies.[1] Any management failure to pursue and achieve coordination and control, within the framework developed in this chapter, could very well mean that the individual policies might

[1] The last two sections of Chapter 8 should be reviewed at this point, and related to this entire chapter.

lead to cross purposes one against the other or, actually, to have their separate and combined effectiveness sharply reduced. Additionally, the management units which are manufacturers or which, through integration, control manufacturing units, must remember the close relationship of the marketing policies to production policies.

Much of what has been discussed in the chapters dealing with policies, leads to the inescapable conclusion, once again, *that the channel becomes the battleground in which the marketing successes of products, middlemen's policies, and managerial strategy are determined.* Product identification, market penetration ratios, and profits, as examples, thus stem from successful policy coordination and control. Similarly, the entire concept of an individual middleman's marketing power may or may not be realized, depending, in part, on how successfully the policy coordination and control is executed. This coordination and control importance is emphasized especially in the ever-changing patterns of marketing through the channel.

The Meaning of Policy Coordination and Control

The concept of managerial policy coordination and control has two component elements. The first element connotes that the individual policies, as discussed in previous chapters, constitute a series of targets, the realization of which when accomplished together and in harmony leads to the achievement, in turn, of a marketing campaign. The control aspects emphasize achievement in terms of stipulated cost and profit goals, analytically established which, for reasons which can be detected, may be analyzed, understood, and related to previous expected reasons. In addition, coordination may assume the perspective of achieving a balanced relationship between the individual policies, as such, and some type of forward-looking marketing plan (in either the formal or informal meaning of "plan").[2]

From the viewpoint of the personnel in an organizational unit, coordination and control connote a balanced viewpoint of assigning functional roles to each person related to the over-all marketing plan, and the additional factor of holding each responsible for the successful achievement of such functional role as it relates directly or indirectly to a given policy. These assignments and balancing have the importance, in terms of the above meaning, of trying to achieve teamwork (that elusive *ésprit de corps*) without which the necessary degree and quality of coordination cannot be attained.

[2] One meaning of "plan" will be illustrated in a later case example.

Thus, policy coordination is, in the last analysis, the blending together of the ideas inherent in the policy into a harmonious whole, and the parallel blending of the ideas and activities of the personnel most directly (but, to some extent, also those involved indirectly) related to the formulation and execution of such policies. The control feature, by measuring the degree and quality of success in execution, becomes a measure of the quality of the organizational structure and of the personnel assigned to various levels of authority and responsibility within such structure.

The concepts presented above must not be interpreted in a too rigid and oversimplified mental framework. To begin with, there is no implication in what has been presented of only one meaning of coordination and control. Much depends on the number of personnel in the organization, the number and personality of the top executives, and the number and complexity of the policies which must be coordinated and controlled. And, as the next sections will indicate, there is no single assortment of management tools available with which to achieve the necessary coordination and control. The nature and abilities of the top management—whether a single executive or a team of executives—take on, once again, considerable importance. Of significance, also, is whether the policy coordination and control involve only a single management unit at one business level or a series of units operating by means of integration at various levels in the channel.

Specific Management Devices: The Over-All Plan

Although the succeeding sections will discuss particular management coordinating and controlling devices, the logical starting point is a discussion of the over-all plan as a management device.[3] A current example of an over-all plan is that reported for Westinghouse Electric Corporation, involving a time period extending beyond 20 years.[4] This long-range plan has two sales goals: to yield increased sales volumes for the company's consumers' goods division; and the more important goal of increasing the use of Westinghouse turbines, generators, and transformers. Stemming from these sales objectives were these addi-

---

[3] In discussing such plans in this connection, there is neither direct nor implied assumption that every company either has or needs this type of planning. Furthermore, the actual difficulties underlying planning and their fundamental weaknesses have been neither forgotten nor assumed away.

[4] "Calling the Shots for the 1980's," *Business Week* (November 28, 1959), 86 ff.; and "Utilities Get New Way to Plan," *Ibid.*, 101 ff. In addition, although not reported, the company may have five-year and ten-year plans in use.

tional objectives: (1) The long-range view of building business both for Westinghouse and the electric utility companies it services; and (2) to create a planning device with which to *coordinate* all of Westinghouse's marketing activities, with the exception of its defense products.

The long-run plan as thus conceived in these two sets of objectives was composed of the following six components.

1. *Total electric home.* This phase of longe-range planning involved the consumer products groups and divisions of Westinghouse. Obviously aimed at a home entirely energized through electricity, it then conceives of the consumer goods market in terms of increased market penetration of Westinghouse appliances and components, as well as increases in the derived demand for industrial goods. To this end, the company has established already a new integrated wholesaling unit—Westinghouse Appliance Sales—with 36 locations, and headed by highly capable executives and sales staff.[5]

2. *Powercasting.* The following quotation describes the main characteristics:

> Powercasting is a comprehensive, far-sighted method of system planning that combines the high-speed calculating ability of digital electronic computers with the mathematics of simulation and game theory. It has three main beauties for the utility man:
>
> It enables him to simulate enough different situations, very rapidly and at relatively small cost, to be sure of the impact of even the most unpredictable random variables.
>
> It makes possible comparison of numerous highly detailed alternatives.
>
> It can be updated, and corrected for actual experience, quite readily.
>
> Powercasting involves constructing two mathematical models of the system under study. One is a model of system loads, the other a model of generating capacity. Each is based on detailed study of past experience, the data accumulated by utility engineers in patterns recommended by Westinghouse.
>
> The data, naturally, is highly detailed. For the load model, it will include day-by-day loads, seasonal and cyclical variations and historical growth rates and patterns. To this you add any projection of future load growth you think wise, or even useful. . . .
>
> The generation model, similarly, is constructed from detailed observation of the operating history of every generating station of the system. . . .[6]

3. *The system concept.* This involves a shift in production and marketing philosophy from optimizing the components in utility

---

[5] Notice the immediate effects on channels of a long-range plan.

[6] *Ibid.,* pp. 101–102.

generating companies to optimizing generating systems. It involves the sale, in other words, of the entire product package from Westinghouse rather than sale of only some selected components, so that, in the future, the utility customer has a complete Westinghouse generating system.

4. *Prodac.* This package planning involves two parts: (*a*) a full-line automatic control system for operating plants in such industrial processes as power plants, or blooming mills; and (*b*) a series of computers to provide an automatic control for the automatic plant setup in (*a*).

5. *Atom guarantees.* As part of this long-range plan, Westinghouse agrees presently to guarantee plant costs, performance capability, and fuel life for two types of nuclear reactors not yet constructed. In this way, the company hopes to be in a dominant producer-supplier position when every electric utility company will generate electricity only in atomic-electric plants. Thus, the company provides the pioneering expertise and shares the costs of exploration with the utility companies (or so it believes).

6. *Up-to-date distribution.* Apart from the adjustments in channels of distribution already noted, the long-range plan has involved setting up regional supply depots for all company products at Ogden, Utah, and Columbus, Ohio, to service wholesalers. These permit reductions in the size of field inventories. In addition, the company has opened distribution centers at San Lorenzo (California), New Orleans, Charlotte, Baltimore, Syracuse, and Kansas City to service retailers, and is also planning to open 19 more centers. These distribution facilities use teletype and digital-computer equipment to expedite deliveries at reduced costs. The company claims it now can fill an order before the customer has time to cancel.

While keeping in mind the many positive aspects of such planning, especially in relation to policy coordination and control, certain "ideological" difficulties inherent in such planning should not be too easily dismissed or overlooked. One such difficulty may arise out of what might be termed "too holy organizational worship" of the plan. By this is meant the tendency for management, once it has developed such a plan, to attach too much importance to it in terms of its relationship to the entire functioning of the top management unit. A second difficulty may arise from a failure to recognize the extent to which the plan must be discounted because of the relative high effectiveness of competitors' similar planning activities.[7]   A third difficulty is related to the failure of many management units to build flexibility within the long-range planning.   Although flexibility will be discussed more fully in a later section, what is meant here is to indicate in the plan the probability of alternative courses of policy actions having equal, or at least, high degrees of applicability, and the timing points within the plan when each must be given careful consideration.   Additionally, other alternatives may develop later which could not be anticipated originally.   Finally, there is the sheer problem of the limit of the abilities of the planning group to foresee all variables and contingencies.   This emphasizes even further the importance of flexibility, as noted, and as to be discussed later.

Specific Management Tools: The Role of Accounting and Finance

Increasingly, the modern business firm operating in the wholesaling sector has available a stream of quantitative data from which to prepare analyses to help in the formulation of its business policies and in their subsequent coordination and control.   These data most importantly originate from within the company's own operations.   But important, also, are the data external to the business firm (already compiled or to be specially collected), which need to be related by the firm to its own past, present, and future.   In the framework of this discussion, we are not interested in these data, as such, but rather in the analytical tools available to management, and in brief illustrations of some of these types of analyses.

The contributions of accounting and finance to the budget

In addition to providing the data contained in the balance sheet and profit-and-loss statement, accounting and finance contribute heavily to the development and use of budgets.   Given a long-range plan such as that just described for Westinghouse, it follows that the next step in its administration is to translate this plan into estimated sales goals, the financial requirements necessary for the attainment of these goals, and the estimated expenses associated with the realization of these expected sales revenue goals.

[7] This is increasingly true, as will be noted in a later section, when high-speed electronic computers and increasingly complicated research methods are available to produce ever-widening streams of data and analyses in record-breaking times.

The research arm of the firm, using methods to be discussed later, can participate in one aspect of the preparation of the budget by providing: (1) estimates of the economic dimensions of the national economy which will have pertinency for future sales; (2) estimates of the company's financial, production, and marketing position as such, wherever pertinent; and (3) estimates of the product assortments which will best help to achieve the estimated sales goals. The financial arm can then translate these into capital requirements for the various company facilities needed. The accounting arm, working the types of cost data described in Chapter 19, can then provide the best estimate of costs.

From the point of view of the discussion of the wholesaling sector, this budget can then be subdivided into as many meaningful components as are required by the kind of middleman operation within the particular kind of business. The more natural subdivisions pertain to the following:

1. The breakdown of sales, costs, and expected profit lines by (a) product lines and (b) channels of distribution.
2. Further subdivision of (1) by class of customer, including order size data.
3. Additional subdivisions of (1) by salesmen and territorial groupings.
4. Subdivision of (1) by new versus established products.
5. Analysis of the data in (1) through (4) by pertinent time periods.
6. Introduction into (1) through (5) of a range based on stipulated contingencies.
7. Statement of qualitative factors which may affect the validity and accuracy of the estimates.

Once these subdivisions of data and related materials are provided, then the next phase of budgeting takes place; namely, provision for collection of the actual results of company operations so that comparisons can be made between such results and the estimates contained in the budgets. These comparisons must be analyzed in order to develop full explanations for such relationships as are found. From these analyses must then come the final decision as to whether the budgetary targets must be revised, marketing policies and operations changed, or a combination of both provided. These cycles of management review and action must be repeated for each subsequent budget planning period.

In addition to its role in the preparation and administration of the budget, the financial arm can be of much value, as discussed earlier, in the preparation and analyses based on ratios derived from accounting and financial statements. This division of the organization also has an important role to play in the creation and administration of credit and collection policies and operations, especially because of the significant relationship to the marketing division.

Some additional aspects of the role of accounting in marketing costs control

In addition to the wide range of the discussion of marketing costs in Chapter 19, some additional remarks need to be included about the use of accounting in cost analyses particularly as these facilitate and improve policy coordination and control. The following features have been presented as essential in an accounting plan where control of marketing costs is one of the prime objectives.

1. A system of responsibility for costs by marketing operations.
2. A statement of functions for each responsibility.
3. Determination of the size of the operating unit in relation to the accounting plan.
4. Provision for the necessary natural accounts in which to catalog and allocate correctly the costs determined for each function.[8]

Accounting cost control—order-getting activities

Within the essentials of the accounting plan as outlined above, certain detailed accounting control aspects may be noted. The first of these refers to cost control in relation to order-getting activities in which four characteristics of such costs affect their control by accounting.[9]

1. Order-getting activities are a cause rather than an effect of sales and therefore control of order-getting costs cannot be based on a simple and direct relationship to the current volume of sales orders received on shipments made.
2. The effectiveness of advertising, sales promotion, and selling is very difficult to measure in terms of sales orders obtained because relationships are obscured by a multitude of influences which cannot be controlled or separated.
3. Because advertising and sales promotion appropriations are based on the plans made for realization of a sales goal, control proceeds by spending the appropriated funds according to plan.

[8] This list was developed by E. W. Kelley, and is contained in "Cost Control for Marketing Operations—General Considerations," *N.A.C.A. Bulletin,* **XXXV,** Research Series No. 25, Section 3 (April 1954), 1070.

[9] Cost Control for Marketing Operations—Order Getting, *Ibid.,* Research Series No. 26, Section 3 (June 1954), 1352.

4. Control of order-getting costs involves a greater dependence upon the judgment of the persons spending the money than it does with order-filling and manufacturing costs. In field selling, this may carry down to the individual salesman who must be relied upon to decide when, where, and how to spend money for getting sales orders.

Based upon the above, the components of the control system are: (1) Classification of advertising and sales promotion costs; (2) preparation of the advertising and sales promotion cost budgets; (3) establishment of written records of current commitments; (4) comparisons of actual expenditures with the budgeted amounts on a weekly, monthly, and cumulative year (or season)-to-date; (5) measurement of the effectiveness of advertising and sales promotion; (6) a series of steps similar to (1) to (5), for selling costs; and (7) preparation of an expense budget of those marketing department administrative costs which affect order-getting activities.

Accounting cost control—other managerial decision-making aspects

Given these accounting-control arrangements, the next steps would be the assignment of costs to territories, to products, and to other management decision-making needs. These have been discussed in detail in the preceding chapter, and need not be repeated here.[10] From all these the basis is derived for the assignment of marketing costs as a tool for management decision making. In addition to the Bull approach discussed in Chapter 19, more detailed attention may be given here to the *contribution* theory of assignment.[11]

The contribution margin approach has been defined as follows:[12]

A contribution margin figure is computed by deducting from sales income those direct and indirect costs which are incurred in obtaining that sales income. It may relate to all sales income of a given period or to some

[10] The interested reader will want to refer to the following, in addition to the discussion and references in Chapter 19:

"The Assignment of Nonmanufacturing Costs to Products," *Ibid.*, XXXII, Research Series No. 20, Section 4 (August 1951), 1559–1589.

"The Assignment of Nonmanufacturing Costs to Territories and Other Segments," *Ibid.*, XXXIII, Research Series No. 21, Section 3 (December 1951), 527–547.

"Cost Control for Manufacturing Operations—Order Filling," *Ibid.*, XXXV, Research Series No. 27 (August 1954), pp. 1647–1675.

Charles H. Sevin, "Analytical Approach to Channel Policies—Marketing Cost Analysis," in R. Clewett (ed.), *Marketing Channels for Manufactured Products* (Homewood, Ill.: Richard D. Irwin, Inc., 1954), Chapter 19.

[11] The material presented here is derived from: "Assignment of Nonmanufacturing Costs for Managerial Decisions," *N.A.C.A. Bulletin*, XXXII, Section 4 (May 1951), 1135–1172.

[12] *Ibid.*, pp. 1162–1163.

segment of that sales income such as income from sales of a given product on income from sales in a designated territory. Moreover, the margin may be either that realized in a historical period or it may be a margin anticipated in the future under circumstances defined by a budget or special study.

The specific costs to be deducted are sometimes described as the costs which would not need to be incurred if the segment being costed were not present. Some writers also refer to them as direct costs or variable costs. However, specific costs chargeable against income in computing a contribution margin often include some costs which may be treated as indirect in the ordinary processes of accounting for costs . . . where a break-down between fixed and variable costs has been made, the variable costs are generally used, although an exception to this arises in special cases where volume is not an important variable in the problem. These problems usually involve a proposed change in methods, of which a study to determine whether to use owned or rented warehouse space may be cited as an example. Other terms used which cover both volume and nonvolume variables are "saveable costs" and "escapable costs." While often distinguished as those costs which could be saved if the product or territories were discontinued, elimination of the segment is usually not the question at issue.

Costs not deducted from income in computing margins are the costs which are not changed in total amount by the decision in question. The contribution margin is therefore the income balance contributed by the segment toward the unallocated costs and profits combined. As defined by Atkinson,[13] the contribution margin is the "profit contribution that each one of our 250 products contributes toward meeting company fixed expenses." Similar margins may, of course, be computed for sales territories, customers, and other segments.

The contribution margin views the individual segments as related units in an organization rather than separate businesses. Such expenditures are made for the business as a whole and the individual segments share the benefits from these expenditures. Those who use the contribution margin approach reason that any separation of these common expenses is unrealistic to the extent that they cannot be allocated on a reasonable basis. Hence they prefer to have a measure of what the individual segment contributes to these joint expenses and over-all company profits rather than a somewhat arbitrary net profit figure. Proper application of the contribution margin approach does not constitute disregard of the unallocated expenses, but instead it emphasizes the contribution which each segment makes to these expenses.

Given the comprehensive definition, it may be seen that the contribution margin approach can be used in making decisions about a wide variety of marketing policies and problems.

1. Territorial profit contribution reports which show what contributions each territory has made in relation to the contribution planned for in the budget. From this, the management can

[13] "Profit Control by Territories and Products in the Food Processing Industry," *Ibid.*, **XXX** (March 1950), 809.

analyze what situations underlie a weak territorial performance, and those elements of strength which need to be protected and extended in a strong territorial performance.

2. Accounting statements can be prepared which show the contribution margin for each product and families of products. From these, plus the analyses of strong and weak products and product lines, additional insights may be gained in studying the effects of changes in advertising; the effects of product changes on transportation costs and transportation methods; and whether or not to change prices.

3. Similar analyses can be made by class of customer, and of trade channel alternatives.

4. These data may also furnish valuable insights in the determination of whether or not to introduce new products.[14]

Specific Management Tools: Selected Research Methods

Building upon the data and analyses originating from the internal accounting and financial systems, present-day management, at any level of the channel, has available a wide array of research methods.[15] Among these, the more important for present discussion are statistical analysis, marketing research, econometric analysis, and operations research. These overlap in their research methodology and in the type of problems for which used.

In the discussion which follows of each of these methods, no attempt will be made to present the actual methods employed since each is represented by a wide variety of technical and professional literature. The main objectives will be, then, by indicating the range of problems analyzed, how staff specialists and research departments furnish top management with a stream of analyses designed to sharpen and improve the decisions pertaining to the formulation, coordination, and control of policies.

Statistical analysis

Statistical analysis is a form of scientific method which places emphasis upon the collection and analysis of phenomena in their

---

[14] See reference 11, pp. 1163–1166. This report contains a discussion of the method's advantages, and its use with the full allocation method.

[15] These should be visualized in a broad perspective as being used by specialists within the firm; as being available by the use of outside research agencies; or as being available in completed research studies.

quantitative (numerical) aspects. The main purposes of such collection and analysis are to test hypothesis and to furnish bases for making theoretical or practical decisions in those problem situations involving conditions of uncertainty.[16] Based upon this definition, statistical analysis can furnish management with studies of internal and external data involving such topics as the following: (a) Observation and measurement; (b) the statistical description of these data by such means as organizing and averaging, and by computation and interpretation of measures of variability and association; and (c) the analysis of data and the preparation of conclusions through the use of statistical inference, including such topics as randomness, probability, sampling and sampling distributions, statistical testing for reliability and significance, decision procedures, and estimation and forecasting. Other topics include: the design of the statistical research investigation; the measurement of quality; relationship between variables; and the analysis of seasonal, cyclical, secular, and random variations in time series data.

These components of statistical analysis form, in part or in their entirety, the foundations for much of the multiple research methods to be described in the remainder of this section. Because of the high degree of professional ability required for this work, most statistical analysis is conducted by specialists either in a staff unit or research department arrangement within a business unit, by professional external agencies available for consultation, or by combinations. This means that the statistical analyses used for coordination and control vary widely in professional quality depending upon the manpower and financial resources which are available.

Marketing research

The chief multiple-type research method available to top management in the coordination and control activities discussed here is marketing research. Based upon a wide range of other research methods (listed below), the definition which best indicates the breadth is the following:

Marketing research involves the critical examination (or investigation) and analysis of both quantitative and qualitative data and materials in order to seek for, or to develop, basic principles pertaining to the whole or part of the subject matter of marketing; i.e., to the

---

[16] See W. Allen Wallis and Harry V. Roberts, *Statistics: A New Approach* (Glencoe, Ill.: The Free Press, 1956), pp. 3–5.

processes and functions by which goods and services move from points of production to points of intermediate and ultimate use, both in a physical sense, and in such a manner as to facilitate the maximum satisfaction of consumers' wants.[17]

The range of component research methods included in marketing research are analogy, the case method, statistical analysis, experimental method, econometrics, historical method, contemporaneous analysis, and the geographical method. Increasingly, it has drawn from psychology in the use of motivation research and from other behavioral sciences as well.[18]

Based upon this definition, and the multiplicity of methods, and restricting the viewpoint to the individual firm, marketing research investigates all of the policy and problem areas discussed in the preceding chapters. Such research may be comprehensive in scope at any one time or may be directed towards any segment of the principal problem areas classified under the following main headings:

1. Determination of product assortments; production and marketing aspects.
2. Estimations of sales potentials—total, and by product, customer, and geographical subdivisions (for appropriate time units).
3. Analysis of actual and potential customers in terms of types, location, numbers, buying habits and motivations, product attitudes, etc.
4. Selection of locations of officers, warehouses, etc.; and determination of actual versus potential trading area boundaries.
5. Organization of marketing activities.
6. Determination of channels of distribution, investigation of channel effectiveness, and analysis of productivity of alternative channel arrangements.
7. Research in the selection, administration, and evaluation of demand creation activities (advertising and personal selling).
8. Research into prices, price policies, and terms of sales.
9. Analysis of inventories, inventory-handling methods, and order-filling activities.
10. Research in marketing costs relative to total marketing activities.
11. Analysis of postsales policies.
12. Analysis of the scope and effect of government regulations.

---

[17] This definition is the author's.

[18] See David A. Revzan, "Les Études de Marches aux États-Unis," *Revue Economique*, No. 3 (May 1954), 404–421.

13. Analysis of structural changes in the marketing environment—past, present, and anticipated—as they relate to the firm.

Any and all of the marketing research into these problem areas have important effects in management activities directed towards policy coordination and control. Part of the role of marketing research in the management of costs and the preparation of budgets has been discussed in a preceding section of this chapter and in Chapter 19. The role of marketing research to the Westinghouse type of long-range planning is self-apparent; and the literature of marketing research is filled with numerous additional examples.[19]

Econometric analysis

Of expanding applicability in making forecasts are the combination of economic theory, mathematics, and statistical analysis into the research method which comprises econometrics. One definition of econometrics states:

> Econometrics is the application of a specific method in the general field of economic science in an effort to achieve numerical results and to verify economics theorems. It consists in the application of mathematical economic theory and statistical procedures to economic data in order to establish numerical results in the field of economics and to verify economic theorems.[20]

The topics included under this definition are multivariate analysis problems, and problems in time-series analysis. Under multivariate analysis, Tintner includes, in turn: multiple regression and correlation; applications of multivariate analysis to economic data; and stocastic models. The topics included in time series analysis are: the trend; oscillatory and periodic movements; the interdependence of successive observations; and the transformation of observations.

This multiple scientific research method has value to the decision-making activities by permitting the construction of various models (in quantitative terms) of the economic environment in which the business firm has to function. These models may be static or dynamic, and emphasize the separation of variables into *endogenous* and *exogenous*, with the use of the former as the base on which to build models. They are of particular value where they furnish accurate guides to the economic weather and related environmental conditions

---

[19] See, for example, Richard D. Crisp, "Analytical Approach to Channel Policies-Sales Analyses," in Clewett (ed.), *op. cit.*, Chapter 18.

[20] Gerhard Tintner, *Econometrics* (New York: John Wiley and Sons, Inc., 1952), pp. 3–4. He goes on, in succeeding sections, to differentiate econometrics from mathematical economics and from statistical economics.

which the business firm will face in preparing its short-run, inter-mediate, and long-range plans and accompanying budgets.

Operations research

One of the newest of the multiple research methods is Operations Research (or O.R., for short). The definition, characteristics, and procedures have been summarized as follows by a leading textbook:

It has been shown that O.R. grew out of the evolution of organizations in which the management function was divided into types and levels of man-agement. The need for study of executive-type problems—those involving the interaction of the functional units of the organization—and the op-portunity for scientists to attack such problems provided by military manage-ment in World War II combined to produce O.R.

O.R. is perhaps still too young to be defined in any authoritative way. A tentative working definition has been provided:

O.R. is the application of scientific methods, techniques, and tools to problems involving the operations of a system so as to provide those in con-trol of the system with optimum solutions to the problems [italics provided].

It has been shown that by the use of teams (where members are drawn from different disciplines) a variety of scientific methods, techniques, and tools is made available. O.R. has begun to develop a method designed to be effective for the class of problems by which it is confronted. Its procedures can be broken into the following steps:

1. Formulation of the problem.
2. Construction of a mathematical model to represent the system under study.
3. Deriving a solution from the model.
4. Testing the model and the solution to be derived from it.
5. Establishing controls over the solution.
6. Putting the solution to work.

Although mixed research teams provide a variety of techniques and tools on specific problems, new techniques and tools have been developed and old ones adapted for certain recurrent classes of problems involving the following five processes: inventory, allocation, waiting-time, replacement, and com-petition.[21]

Quantitative analysis and new data-processing methods

The use of the preceding research methods has been widened by the increased availability of electronic equipment. These computers and

[21] C. West Churchman, Russell L. Ackoff, E. Leonard Arnoff (and collaborators), *Introduction to Operations Research* (New York: John Wiley and Sons, Inc., 1957), p. 18. This book deals in detail with each of the phases of O.R. and each class of problem referred to in the definition. In addition, it includes reference to game theory and linear programming (sometimes referred to as separate research methods).

data-processing machines not only increase markedly the availability of data in quantity and quality in sharply reduced time periods but also they make possible increasingly complicated analyses which could not be executed previously.

Specific Management Tools: Qualitative Analysis

The preceding discussion, emphasizing the increase in the number and complexity of quantitative analytical tools available for managerial decision making, indicates that top management now, presumably more than ever before, can base decisions upon rational methods of analysis. But the very increase so noted, raises interesting philosophical questions which can be posed here, and only partially answered: Do the numerical data furnish an accurate base sufficient to warrant always the use of such expensive and highly accurate analytical research devices?[22] Are the research experts significantly more able than nonexpert (researchwise) executives in formulating policies? Will the apparent increase in accuracy with which analyses can be made in the future narrow significantly the range of difference between competing managements in making decisions?

If the answer to all of the preceding is "yes," what are the implications for the maintenance of competition, especially so far as government policy is concerned? Are monopolies the only logical expectations in most, if not all, kinds of business? And, finally, what are the implications for accentuating reducing the maximization of alternatives in the marketing system?

The role of executive judgment

Given the content of the increasingly mathematical approach to business problems, the development of more effective psychological and other behavioral sciences research methods, and the philosophical questions posed above, it would appear that the importance of executive judgment in final decisions concerning the formulation of policies and the subsequent coordination will increase rather than decline. If all management units have at their disposal increasingly effective and accurate scientific research methods, then the problem resolves itself ultimately into an executive decision as to what additional factors to consider in order to secure the benefits to be derived for organizational innovation and flexibility. In addition, the increased role of executive

[22] Stated another way, "Are inexperienced analysts cutting butter with Swedish steel blades, instead of more simple, but equally effective, cutting edges?"

judgment will be based on the need to choose between the answers derived from one research method as compared with others investigating the same problem.

A great deal of executive judgment seems to be of the same inexplicable nature as artistic temperament, with, apparently, the little known element of understanding. Reference has been made earlier to the importance of this characteristic in the determination of merchandising strategy. In view of what has been said and posed, it may not be too much of an exaggeration to state that an overemphasis upon the role of the scientific method in policy coordination and control may actually serve to inhibit the abilities of management to outmaneuver competition through merchandising strategy.

That the role of management has not been made easier, so far as the use of executive judgment is concerned despite the increased application of high-powered mathematical and behavioral science research methods, is evident in two other respects. First, given an increased variety of research methods with which to investigate a given problem, the executive must face increasing concern—and, accordingly, greater exercise of judgment—as to whether the best method or combination of methods has been used. Second, the problem of interpretation and application, by the executive and *not* the research specialist, becomes more complicated than ever before, *unless* the executive is willing to give up a significant element of his authority and responsibility. It is apparent that the abdication to the analysts does not, in and of itself, automatically eliminate the dilemma if some of the present research fiascos (especially in the case of the ill-fated Edsel motor car, and the whole area of the "small" automobile) are kept in mind.

Organizational coordinating and control devices

Certain organizational devices exist, depending upon the size of the firm and the amount of financial resources, which may help in the executive task of policy coordination and control. One such device— the use of specialists—has been partially discussed in the decision as to whether to use the firm's research staff or outside research talent, and in the use of the firm's accounting and finance personnel. But there is another aspect of the use of specialists which needs to be mentioned here. This aspect involves the increasing need to provide the equivalent of a presidential cabinet with the recognized and assigned responsibility to make use of all internal and external resources in formulating a series of targets (policies) in relationship to an integrated system of short-run, intermediate, and long-range places in which these plans have to function. Such a cabinet could be expected to advise the "president" as to the relationships which are found between what is taking place and what was provided in the targets; and recommendation, as needed, as to future policy courses of actions.[23]

Stemming from, or in addition to, these presidential cabinets are the various liaison committees or liaison personnel used to coordinate divisional executive opinions about particular policies and problems which are the province and concern of more than one functional segment of the organization. Two such liaison areas are of especial importance to the context of this book; namely, the determination of prices and price policies, and the determination of product policies.

Finally, there are those communication devices which function between the various levels of the internal organizational structure of the firm, but importantly, also, between the managerial units which constitute the channel structure. As has been noted earlier, the internal communication devices consist of reports, training meetings, other forms of meetings, directives, executive administration, and interpersonal relationships of other types as well.

But what are overlooked are the important communication devices which exist and function horizontally and vertically in the channel structure. These may be *authoritative* in nature as in the instance of a completely vertically integrated channel (vertical and horizontal) accomplished by ownership. In such instances, the communication problem merges with the internal aspects noted above.

In the examples of channel integration not based on ownership, communication may be persuasive by means of contractual relationships; *viz.*, resale price maintenance, and exclusive franchise dealerships. In other instances, communication may be *cooperative*. The producing enterprise may furnish wholesale and retail middlemen with research results, advertising help, and salesmen's training. These middlemen may furnish producing units with reports about marketing conditions in their territories, and related information. Wholesale middlemen, as in the example of voluntary chains, may furnish managerial and other aids to affiliated retail middlemen members.[24]

[23] With the internal and/or external research specialists providing the necessary professional research as needed.

[24] See D. J. Duncan, "Co-operation with Distribution Channels," in C. F. Phillips (ed.), *Marketing by Manufacturers*, rev. ed. (Homewood, Ill.: Richard D. Irwin, Inc., 1951), Chapter XII.

The roles of flexibility and innovation

Perhaps the single most difficult problem area which exists in the coordination and control of policies is how to maintain flexibility of executive decision making and action in the fact of growing organizational rigidities stemming from growing organizational size and communication problems. *Flexibility*, in this context, refers to the rapidity with which the coordinating and controlling executive(s) can react to fundamental changes in the environment in which the policies were formulated originally; and the accuracy with which the evaluation and necessary policy changes, if any, are made. It includes, also, some notion of the time span involved in communicating these changes within the organization, and through the channel.

Innovation stems, in part, from the element of flexibility and, in part, from other factors. The importance of innovation in marketing has been stressed elsewhere especially in relation to the function of merchandising. All that needs to be emphasized here, in addition, is its increasing importance in an era when the increased use of the scientific research methods, as noted above, may narrow the range of quantitative uncertainty in executive decision making.

Some Final Observations

The complexity of the wholesaling sector is no more evident than in the wide range of policy, problem, and operational aspects which have been discussed in the section of this book beginning with Chapter 8. Wholesale middlemen run a wide gamut of financial size, integration, product assortments, and geographical outreach characteristics. As a result, the organizational structure varies from the highly informal one-or-two person type to the most complex known to the modern business world. Correspondingly, this wide range brings with it more than proportionate variations in the range and complexity of marketing problems. This generates, as has been noted, widely varying executive needs and talent so far as formal policy formulation and policy coordination and control are concerned.

It is this element of variety which underscores, on the one hand, the importance attached to the flexibility of managerial decision making, and, on the other, the importance attached to innovation as related to merchandising strategy. The preceding discussion in this chapter has outlined the ever-widening range of analytical tools and research methods available to top management in its search for increasingly scientific approaches to the policy formulation, and coordination and control activities. Yet, the ever-widening availability and use of these create, in their wake, the philosophical problems already noted which would appear, in turn, to require widened rather than narrowed qualities of executive judgment. This has, as was discussed above, certain repercussions on the extent to which the elements of flexibility and innovation increasingly are or will have to be more apparent in executive decision making. The battleground for all of these complexities will continue to be the channels of distribution.

QUESTIONS AND PROBLEMS

1. Discuss the implications which you find in the statement, "Thus, every managerial unit which is related either directly or indirectly to the wholesaling sector, and to the channel within the wholesaling sector, has a direct stake in policy coordination and control if it is large enough, organizationally speaking, to have any basis for establishing significant policies."

2. What is the relation of the individual firm's coordination and control of policies to its channel position?

3. What are the component elements inherent in the meaning of policy coordination and control?

4. To what extent is an over-all plan useful for a wholesale middleman?

5. How do middlemen's type of operation, sales size, and kind of business affect their ability to develop and use an over-all plan?

6. What are the "ideological difficulties" inherent in long-range planning?

7. What are the roles played by accounting and finance in managerial coordination and control?

8. To what extent is accounting distribution cost control helpful to management in analyzing order-getting activities from a policy point of view?

9. What is the meaning of the contribution margin approach? Of what use is it to the management of a wholesale middleman operation in decision making?

10. Of what value to management is the marketing research function so far as policy coordination and control is concerned?

11. What research tools (methods) are available to management?

12. What is meant by qualitative analysis as a specific management tool?

13. Indicate what, in your opinion, is the essence of executive judgment.

14. Do you believe that the importance of executive judgment has been increasing or declining? What are the reasons for your answer?

15. What is the nature of the organizational coordinating and control devices?

16. To what extent does coordination and control involve elements of flexibility and innovation? How are these elements initiated and sustained within an organization?

CHAPTER INTEGRATING ASSIGNMENT

Wholesale middlemen, as noted, have widely varying opportunities for simplicity or complexity in organizational structure, policy formation, and functional operations. These widely varying opportunities, in turn, create ranges of opportunities for over-all planning, and differences in the complexity of coordination and control. Discuss the nature of the problems created when these are viewed in the framework of the channel as well as from the individual firm's viewpoint. To what extent does the channel create conflicts in planning and coordination and control activities? To what extent does it introduce elements of cooperation within the "network-of-organizations" framework?

21

Government Regulation:
Over-All Analysis

Government regulation of the wholesaling sector of marketing organization takes place within the environment of government regulation of the entire marketing system. And this broader environment of regulation is, in turn, only part of the over-all system of social control.[1] However, while any discussion of government regulation must recognize these broader interrelationships, the greater emphasis in this and the following chapters will be placed on those regulations and regulatory activities which bear most heavily on the wholesaling sector. Especial attention will be given to the regulation of marketing in the channels of distribution.

In presenting this large framework, it is recognized at the outset that a compromise must be effected in detail, because of the wealth of materials, so far as the legal coverage is concerned, of each type of regulatory activity to be mentioned. The only exception, as noted, will be the detailed treatment afforded the Robinson-Patman Act. Additionally, no attempt will be made to evaluate the effects of each and every regulatory effort. In many instances, the range of the individual effects has not been determined. And for many other regu-

[1] There is such a volume of available bibliographical materials that the pertinent references included for this chapter represent only a selective sample. In addition to this sample, the interested reader will find it valuable to review the chapters on government regulation included in the basic marketing textbooks.

latory activities, the important range of results is merged in a complex of multiple variables. Accordingly, much of the discussion of effects will be treated in combined fashion under the discussion of the present dilemma of government regulation, with the exception, again, of the Robinson-Patman Act.

The Criteria of a Good System of Social Control of Business

The present system of government regulation of business, within the ideology of a democracy in the political form of a constitutional republic, is the resultant of a long series of traditions, customs, political beliefs, and diverse populational elements. These have been working, in turn, within a long-range evolution of the business economy in the United States from primarily a system of petty trade at the beginning to the present complexity of a wide range of units from small independent entrepreneurs to the giants composing the complicated large-scale integrated units. This type of evolutionary pattern does not lead, unfortunately, to systematic and orderly economic progress; nor can the pattern of government regulation, accordingly, follow a very systematic pattern. Significant time gaps ensue between the periods in which given business policies and practices originate in the market place, and the periods in which the governmental authorities make judgments about which of these are in the public interest, and those which need to be controlled or eliminated.[2] At the same time, the government complicates the whole regulatory framework increasingly by shifting from the role of umpire to one in which the agencies either take over active management of business enterprises, or become suppliers of important enterprise capital.

The criteria of a good system of social control

The complicated network of government control which will be traced in later sections of this chapter stems from four types of coordinating and controlling activities:

1. Government sets forth either implicit or explicit limits to the freedom of businessmen in the interest of protecting the general public welfare as it may be defined (or inferred) at any given period of regulatory activity.
2. In the regulatory efforts designed to maintain, or restore, equality and freedom of competition, or to restrain overly aggressive

[2] See E. A. Duddy and D. A. Revzan, *Marketing: An Institutional Approach,* 2nd ed. (New York: McGraw-Hill Book Co., Inc., 1953), pp. 538–40.

business tactics of some groups, the government may act *positively* to promote the interest of particular economic groups; or it may act in a *restraining* fashion by prohibiting overly aggressive competitive activities.

3. Government may determine areas of business activity which it decides cannot function properly under free competition, and permit these, accordingly, to operate as monopolies under sets of legal restraints and standards.

4. Finally, in some areas, the government may engage in business competition with the private citizen; or may assume control of certain monopolies.

Within this group of coordinating and controlling activities, many writers have asked, "What is a good system of social control?" One of the most persuasive answers over the years has come from J. M. Clark in the form of the following eleven criteria:[3]

1. It must be democratic. . . .
2. It should know what it wants. . . .
3. It must be powerful—powerful enough to make an unwilling minority obey the will of the majority. . . .[4]
4. It must be efficient, and at the same time it must not destroy the efficiency of the thing it is regulating.
5. It must "economize coercion."
6. It must utilize all the strongest and most persistent motives of human nature, both generous and selfish; hope of reward, fear of punishment, and those loyalties, persuasions, and suggestions which have nothing directly to do with rewards or punishments, but which rest upon the deepest fact that the individual is essentially part of a community.
7. The duties imposed must be simple enough to be understood; and this means, among other things, that social control must follow precedent a great deal of the time.
8. Control must be guided by experience or be wisely experimental.
9. It must be adaptable.
10. It must be farseeing. . . .
11. And, last, social control must be capable of progressively raising the level of mankind. . . .

Clark, in presenting these criteria, recognized at once that they included many contradictory elements. He states a series of questions representing these contradictory elements which may be paraphrased as follows: Liberty versus coordination? Liberty of the manager

---

[3] John M. Clark, *Social Control of Business* (Chicago: The University of Chicago Press, 1926), pp. 17–18. Some of the explanatory text has been omitted as indicated.

[4] Although, as will be discussed later, without infringing upon the ability to compete, innovate, and develop.

versus liberty of the managed? Over-all needs of leadership in a democracy versus class prejudices of constituent groups? Stability versus endless change? Trial-and-error methods versus planning toward goals? Requisite of only one power that can coerce versus actualities of many coercive groups? Political power organized on geographic units versus organization for control on lines of economic interests? Finally, direct rivalry of economic groups as to shares in the national dividend, power, and jurisdiction?

Classification of objectives of government regulation

Given the countless regulatory activities of city, county, state, and Federal Government agencies as they relate directly and indirectly to marketing, there is no single scheme of classification of objectives that can claim to serve all needs. The scheme presented below is that based upon the Duddy-Revzan treatment.[5]

I. *Regulatory Actions Designed to Compel Competition*
  A. Basic Policy Legislation; Interstate Commerce Act (1887); Sherman Antitrust Act (1890), and amendments thereto.
  B. Exceptions: contained in Clayton Act (1914); Webb-Pomerene Act (1918); Merchant Marine Act (1920); Transportation Act (1920); Amendments to I.C.C. Act (1921); and Capper-Volstead Act (1922).

II. *Regulation of Unfair Competitive Practices*
  Federal Trade Commission Act (1914).
  State chain store tax laws.
  Robinson-Patman Act (1936).

III. *Fair Trade and Unfair Trade Practices Acts*
  Miller-Tydings Act (1937).
  McGuire Act (1952).
  State unfair trade practices acts (minimum price, minimum mark-up laws).

IV. *Protection of Consumer*
  Pure Food and Drug Act (1910); Food, Drug, and Cosmetics Act (1938); and amendments.
  Federal Meat Inspection Act (1906).
  Cotton Standards Act (1916).
  Grain Standards Act (1916).
  Wool Products Labeling Act (1939).
  Wheeler-Lea Amendment, F.T.C. Act (1938).

[5] Duddy and Revzan, *op. cit.,* Chapter XXX.

Regulation of trading in organized commodity markets: Cotton Futures Act (1915); Grain Futures Act (1922); Commodity Exchange Regulation Act (1936); Packers and Stockyards Act (1921); Produce Agency Act (1927); and Perishable Agricultural Commodities Act (1937).
V. *Protective and Promotive Functions*
  A. Protective aspects: protective tariffs; patent laws; copyright laws; Lanham Act (1946).
  B Promotive aspects: Webb-Pomerene Act (1918); research activities; subsidies.
VI. *Cooperative Action: Planning and Control*
  A. Capper-Volstead Act (1922).
  B. Cooperative Marketing Act (1926).
  C. Agricultural Marketing Act (1929).
  D. NRA activity.
  E. Bituminous Coal Act.
  F. Sugar Control Act.
  G. Petroleum Conservation Act.
  H. Agricultural Adjustment and Marketing Agreement Acts (1933, 1937, 1938); and amendments.
VII. *Taxes, Business License Fees,* etc.

While this classification scheme is most useful for the regulation of the entire field of marketing, the special needs of the view of the wholesaling sector developed in this book suggests the classification breakdown noted at the beginning of this chapter. This three-divisional breakdown is discussed in the next sections.

Governmental Regulations: Internal Business Firm Emphasis[6]

The Contract

The contract is of basic importance as the foundation which supports all business activities and all regulatory aspects. Apart from statutory arrangements for codification of certain types of contracts to be discussed later, centuries of common law and equity provisions, coupled with hundreds of volumes of judicial decisions, have created a formidable body of the law of contracts. The principal dimensions of

---

[6] The form of organization, the sequence of topics, and the coverage of regulations which follow are based upon the treatment in Dow Votaw, *Legal Aspects of Business Administration* (Englewood Cliffs, N. J.: Prentice-Hall, Inc., 1956).

the body of law can be outlined here, but no attempt will be made to present and discuss technical legal principles. Most modern treatments of the law of contracts include the following dimensions as a minimum:

1. *General matters:* importance and nature of contracts; types (executed and executory, formal and simple, express and implied, and void, voidable, and valid); essentials of the contract; and problems of proof.
2. *Agreement:* the offer (nature, differentiation from other statements, duration, and termination); the acceptance (in unilateral and bilateral contracts); and the communication of the acceptance.
3. *Situations where consent is not real:* mistakes; fraud; undue influence; duress; and menace.
4. *Consideration.*
5. *Competent parties.*
6. *Legality of object of contracts.*
7. *Contracts which must be in writing* (under Statute of Frauds originating in England, 1677): those not performed within a year; those not to be performed within promisor's lifetime; marriage contracts; promises by executors, or administrators; contracts to meet another obligation; sale or lease of real property; agency; and sales of goods over specified amounts.
8. *Performance.*
9. *Remedies.*
10. *Contracts and third parties.*
11. *Discharge of contracts.*
12. *Interpretation and construction of contracts.*

This detailed list has been presented to underwrite the extent to which the pervasive law of contracts provides a basis for the origination, unification, and continuity of business which make possible everything else which takes place in modern business. The contract underlies every facet of business activity, and, as such, is in itself an important agency of control.

Kinds of business and forms of organization

Although freedom of entry is preached as one of the cardinal virtues of the competitive system, a moment's reflection will reveal that this is highly romantic under existing municipal and state regulations. For one thing, certain kinds of business may be simply not in the general public interest, *viz.*, sales of narcotics as such, gambling in certain states, counterfeiting, etc. In addition, certain kinds of business may be operated as municipal or state monopolies—such as liquor stores. And most municipalities, and some states as well, have certain business licenses and tax requirements to meet. One of the effects of such entry requirements may represent actual restrictions on the number of business units.[7]

In addition to these basic requirements relating to the number and kinds of business units, there are additional statutory requirements pertaining to the form of organization, and to selected organizational procedures. The partnership form, although based upon an amalgamation of legal principles originating in common law, civil law, equity, and *Law Merchant,* has had considerable codification and restatement in Uniform Partnership Acts found presently in about 31 states.[8] In addition, most states have general incorporation laws stemming from the original use of Royal Charters in England. Most states have statutes covering the organization and responsibility of limited partnerships, and many use the Uniform Limited Partnership Act as a companion enactment to the Uniform Partnership Act noted above. Finally, there are varying applications of nonstatutory and statutory provisions to business trusts, joint stock companies, and joint ventures.

Financing new businesses

Most of the financing problems of new unincorporated businesses involve arrangements which are covered by the law of contracts. But once the corporate form of organization is introduced, and common and preferred stocks are used to provide capital, more complicated regulatory devices are brought into use. If the company engages only in *intrastate* commerce, stock issues may be subject to state fraud laws; laws covering disclosures of financial data; laws requiring securities brokers and dealers to register and/or secure licenses; and laws requiring registration and/or permits for the issuance of securities. For corporations engaged in *interstate* commerce, additional and more complicated control is exercised through provisions of the Security Act (1933); the Securities and Exchange Commission; and the regulation of stock exchange and their middlemen members.

Site aspects

If the location of the business involves leasing facilities, special aspects of the law of contracts may come into operation and application. However, if the new business acquires ownership, a much wider application of regulatory powers is encountered, including real

---

[7] For example, a state may restrict the number of liquor licenses to some population base.

[8] As reported in Votaw, *op. cit.,* Chapter 4.

property laws; zoning restrictions; restrictions on site and property use by virtue of prior property deeds; provisions for laws or regulations covering the recording of deeds; and laws applying to estates and wills.

Relationships with employees

Along with the contract, the agency device is one of the most basic and pervasive device in use in modern business. By enabling a principal to extend his authority, ideas, and activities beyond the reach of his physical presence, it permits the complexities of the large-scale organization to exist, and provides as well for the existence of the various types of agent middlemen which have been classified and discussed elsewhere. Thus, the law of agency, as a special form of the contract, provides, in the uses noted above for: the creation of the agency; its operation, including the duties and liabilities of agent and principal, and third parties dealing with the agent; and termination of the agency.

A much broader employer-employee relationship involves the whole area now designated as labor relations. Only a skeleton reference can be made here to the ever-widening range of regulations. The basic employment contract is subject, first of all, to the common law and the law of contracts. Union activities, as such, are exempt from the antitrust laws by virtue of an exemption written into the Clayton Act (1914). But, beginning in 1931, an increasing volume of state and Federal legislation has poured forth governing union activities, hours of work, wages, use of child labor, etc. The most important are the National Labor Relations Act (1935), and the Taft-Hartley Act (1947) and 1959 amendments. These deal with bargaining agreements including their negotiation; execution; unfair practices under such collective agreements; regulation of strikes, picketing, etc.; and arbitration.[9]

Finally, brief mention should be made of those regulations which govern the liability of the employer for injuries to employees. These liabilities range from liability under the common law to the modern Employers' Liability and Workmen's Compensation laws. And the provisions for unemployment and insurance benefits under the Social Security Act (1935) should not be overlooked.

Sales contracts

Of primary significance to marketing organization, and covering the activities of the middleman firm in the channel, are selling activities.

---

[9] As this is being written, the termination of the record-breaking steel strike of 1959 may bring forth a host of new regulations, or, at least, amendments to existing regulations.

In a sense, sales contracts may be viewed merely as one special form of the law of contracts. But the complexities of modern marketing have made it necessary to move far from the origins in common law, equity, civil law, and the *Law Merchant* to the present-day Uniform Sales Acts and Uniform Conditional Sales Acts found in most states. In addition, some states and municipalities have found it necessary to enact Retail Installment Sales Acts.[10]

The Uniform Sales Act contains the following sections: (1) Formation of the contract, including its form and the application of the Statute of Frauds; (2) the subject matter of the contract; (3) the applicable price; (4) conditions; and express and implied warranties; (5) conditions governing the transfer of property between sellers and buyers; (6) documents of title; (7) performance of contract; (8) sellers' remedies; and (9) buyer's remedies. In addition to the types of provisions outlined above, the Uniform Conditional Sales Act provides for features of resale by sellers, redemption by buyers, statements of carrying charges, etc.[11]

Finally, provisions of the Retail Installment Sales Acts contain sections pertaining to evidence of indebtedness and security; insurance features; and financing charges, in addition to the usual sales contract provisions. In a sense, such contracts may be considered as a special form of the conditional sales contract.

Transfers of funds, facilitating credit, etc.

The general use of negotiable instruments in the United States, so far as legal requirements are concerned, has been codified under state Uniform Negotiable Instruments Acts. In addition, there are a wide variety of regulations pertaining to the various forms of financing and credit discussed in Chapter 18. Among other aspects, in addition to sales contracts discussed above, are: the regulation of liens under common law, equity and statutes (such as the Factor's Lien Statute in Massachusetts); pledges as created by contracts; mortgages under common law (title theory), and under equity (lien theory), etc.

Storage and transportation of goods; other bailment relationships

Next to sales contracts, the most pervasive activities relating to marketing have to do with the storage and transportation of goods, especially in the wholesaling sector. With respect to storage, reference has been made in earlier discussions to the creation of warehouse

[10] It is interesting to note that most parts of the British Commonwealth have enacted Sale of Goods Act.

[11] A recent (1959) stricter version in California—the Unruh Act—even stipulates the size of type face to be used in printing the conditional sales contracts.

receipts under State Uniform Warehouse Receipts Acts, and their use in relation to financing. The typical act covers the issue of warehouse receipts; obligations and rights of warehousemen upon their receipts; negotiation and transfer of receipts; criminal offenses; and interpretation. In addition, most states have licensing requirements for public merchandise warehouses; bonding requirements for warehousemen; and regulations pertaining to such special warehouses as cold storage facilities and grain elevators. Finally, the Federal Government provides for the licensing and bonding of public warehouses storing certain agricultural products (U. S. Warehouse Act, 1916, and amendments); and the bonding of warehouses in order to secure payment to the United States Treasury of certain import duties or taxes on products stored.

A complicated series of Federal and state statutes, and administrative agencies, exist to regulate types of common carrier transportation; routes and routings; rates; service; consolidations; and related topics. There exist, in addition, Uniform Bills of Lading Acts both at the Federal level (1916), and in some 33 states. They apply to bills of lading issued by *any* common carrier, and their provisions include: bills governed by these acts; essential and insertable terms; obligations and rights of carriers upon their bills of lading; negotiation and transfer of bills; criminal offenses; and interpretation.

Shifting risks

Only brief mention can be included here of devices where businessmen can shift risks either by insurance or hedging contracts. Apart from the ordinary law applicable to such contracts, additional state regulations apply to the insurance companies. The regulation of commodity markets has been indicated in the outline above, and will be discussed in a later section.

Taxes

The outline above has suggested the wide range of taxes which may be applicable to the various operations of the business firm.

Competitive practices

The regulation of the competitive practices of the firm in relation to other firms in the channel will be covered in detail in a later section.

Patents, copyrights, and brand protection

A very formal framework of regulation is available to the individual firm so far as protection of its products in the channel is concerned. If the product is unique by virtue of being a piece of writing or other form of artistic work, protection is available under existing patent and copyright laws which give the holder a legal monopoly, in effect, for a stipulated number of years.

In addition, there is available to the owner of a product (or family of products) protection of the brand name(s) selected, under both common and statutory law. At the Federal level under the Lanham Act (1948), provision is made for the kinds of identification devices which may be registered; different classes of registration; types of protection given; and remedies. Many states have parallel provisions. However, those brands which may not be protected as trade marks under existing legislation may still qualify for protection as trade names under the common law and certain statutory enactments. The range of these protective devices have important repercussions on pricing activities, on communication, and upon other aspects of marketing organization in the channel.

Termination of the business

Brief mention may be made, finally, of regulations pertaining to the termination of the individual business firm. The first set of regulations has to do with the liquidation of a business under conditions of voluntary or involuntary bankruptcy. The second set has to do with the termination of a business under the pertinent provisions of governing partnerships, corporations, or other forms of business organization, where bankruptcy is not involved. Finally, termination of a business may invoke the provisions of existing antitrust legislation, if the business is either being merged with an existing business or is being so terminated that the structure of competition is affected.

Government Regulation: Channel Competition

It is in the control of channel competition that the full range of government regulation in relation to marketing organization comes into focus. Many of the objectives outlined earlier particularly affect the rivalry of business firms in this context. Seven categories of regulatory activities will be discussed in the subdivisions which follow:

1. Regulations designed to control the number of producing units and their market control in the channel.
2. Regulations designed to control and modify producers' pricing activities either by (a) maintaining or restoring the competitive aspect or (b) introducing oligopolistic or monopolistic elements in the channel.

3. Regulations designed to affect directly the activities of wholesale middlemen.
4. Regulations designed to control the activities of organized wholesale markets.
5. Regulations designed to control integration in the channel.
6. Regulations designed to control marketing communication through the channel.
7. Government research activities.

Regulation of number of producing units and their market control

The course of government control under this heading has been highly confused. Technically, the Sherman Antitrust Act was restrictive against the formation of monopolies in the interest, first, of preserving freedom of entry into an industry, and then maintaining equality of opportunity once such entry had been achieved. Actually, the Act did not prohibit patent monopolies; nor did it affect limitation on the number of units in the transportation industry. And, under the pressure of the large-scale producing units which were developing as a result of technological forces, the Federal courts either had to outlaw every combination in restraint of trade, or to develop a "rule of reason" by which to differentiate between reasonable and unreasonable restraints. Unfortunately, the courts chose the latter, thus opening the floodgates, in part, to the dilemma of regulation to be discussed later. By 1922, several special economic groups had succeeded, in addition, in receiving the special statutory exemptions noted in the preceding outline.

In none of the basic amendments to the Sherman Act were any empirical tests of market control developed and applied. Later judicial decisions did apply such tests from time to time (as in the aluminum industry), but these applications have been neither consistent nor uniform. However, market control was being attacked from another direction; namely, by regulation of unfair competitive practices. Under the common law, and adaptations thereof, unfair competition had mainly ethical implications referring to undue advantages in marketing secured through fraud, misrepresentation, deceitful diversion of competitors' customers, misappropriations of trade secrets, or malicious interference with a competitor's business relations or operations.

Lagging far behind emerging business practices, the Federal Government regulations by 1914 began to assign new meaning to the concept of unfair competition, in addition to that noted. The emphasis shifted, in other words, from only the ethical, to a combination of the ethical and the economic. The main criterion may be paraphrased as follows: "Any method used in competition *which hinders or prevents normal results ensuing from the free operation of the principle of competition* must be adjudged unfair."[12] To implement this criterion, three pieces of Federal legislation were enacted.[13] The Federal Trade Commission Act declared as unlawful certain unfair methods of competition, and unfair or deceptive acts or practices in commerce. Enforcement was vested in the Federal Trade Commission, with power to initiate complaints and to issue cease-and-desist orders, subject to court review. Through its own actions and court review, the Commission has continually enlarged the specific content of unfair competition.

Direct attention to the channel of distribution first became evident in the Clayton Act which defined and prohibited *trade* practices which "substantially lessen competition or tend to create a monopoly." Sections (2) and (3) had two main aspects: (1) they specifically prohibited discrimination in pricing between different purchasers of like commodities; and (2) they outlawed such exclusive agencies or leasing agreements that prevent lessors or sellers from dealing in competitive goods.

As is usual in such regulations, allowances were provided for discriminations in price which originate from differences in grade; differences in quality, differences in quantities; or after making due allowances for differences in selling and/or transportation costs; or, finally, price discrimination to meet competition. Apart from difficulties encountered in establishing objective bases for proving such differences, certain trends in channels of distribution, especially the increased importance of large-scale middlemen, created a markedly changed marketing environment from that present originally in 1914. The resulting amendments were contained in the Robinson-Patman Act.

Regulations designed to control producers' pricing activities

Apart from the control of price discrimination, the confused state of government regulatory policy is no more evident than in its attitude toward the pricing freedom of non-agricultural producers. Two examples will be discussed here, namely, resale price maintenance under the Miller-Tydings and McGuire Acts, and the control of minimum

---

[12] The classic complete statement is contained in William H. S. Stevens, *Unfair Competition: A Study of Certain Practices* (Chicago: The University of Chicago Press, 1917). He discusses such devices as local price cutting; operation of bogus "independent" concerns; fighting instruments; "tying clauses," etc.

[13] The state corporate chain store tax laws must be considered a partial type of regulation under this heading.

prices and mark-ups under state "unfair" trade practices acts. Other types will be discussed later in this chapter in connection with the operation of organized wholesale markets and with the control of agricultural production and marketing.

Under the guise of protecting (a) the producer of nationally advertised and branded goods, and (b) the independent wholesale and retail middlemen against the effects of these middlemen in the channel featuring low prices, the Federal Government and many state governments have legalized resale price maintenance. Previous attempts at control had proved ineffective in the face of certain types of marketing channel development, or ran afoul of the barrier of illegal contracts under the Sherman Act. With the depression of the 1930's, the whole politico-economic environment was receptive to all sorts of regulations designed to interfere with the effectiveness of the price-determining mechanism in the competitive system.

While the language of the state acts varies from that in the Federal legislation, the general provisions are as follows: (1) Establishment of the legality of contracts between producer (or owner) and wholesale and retail middlemen in the channel, whereby the producer is permitted to stipulate the exact price at which a branded product may be sold and/or resold; (2) provisions for establishing such control over all middlemen by virtue of a contract which covers only part of the middlemen membership in the channel; (3) exemptions of such price control under certain conditions such as close-out sales; and (4) provisions for enforcement, and penalties for violations.

Whatever the merits of such legislation, it is the considered opinion of the author that the following areas of criticism far outweigh the advantages:

1. Together with the Robinson-Patman Act, there has been greater encouragement given to private brands because these private brands can be used either as price leaders or they can receive the benefits of higher margins by virtue of the "price umbrella" afforded under the legislation.
2. Even though title to covered products may pass to the wholesale and retail middlemen in the channel, these middlemen waive their independence of price decisions in the channel. This interferes sharply with the efficiency and effectiveness of the channel.
3. Prices of fair-traded products tend to be higher, and they demonstrate considerable inflexibility (stickiness) over time. In addition, they no longer reflect variations in service between the middlemen in the channel.

4. Since many producers of protected products also produce private branded merchandise, it is difficult to know to what extent the legislation may be honored in the breach.
5. Finally, instead of providing the channel stability and protection often publicized, this legislation has been a significant factor in the development of new price-cutting middlemen in the form of discount houses.

The recent rash of adverse court rulings against fair trade legislation in many states may be a harbinger of a new era, although the strength of the lobbying groups should not be underestimated. Increasingly, authorities are recommending that the Federal and state legislation be repealed.[14] In addition, many of the earliest and most fanatic of the earliest supporters of resale price maintenance (e.g., General Electric and Eastman Kodak) have recently abandoned their support.

Beginning with California in 1935, a number of states have enacted "unfair" trade practices acts aimed at the control over "loss-leader" pricing of products, not covered under resale price maintenance, by establishing floors under which prices of certain classes of products could not move in certain kinds of business. These regulations have the following characteristics: .

1. Coverage is given mainly to wholesale and retail middlemen, although manufacturers are also included in some states. In addition, all classes of products are included, regardless of whether or not they are branded.
2. Cost is variously defined, depending upon the regulation of the particular state, as the manufacturer's list price to the particular middleman, invoice cost, or replacement cost.
3. To cost in (2) is added an additional amount, ranging from 6 to 12 per cent, to cover overhead or cost of doing business.
4. The determination of costs is based on the notorious "cost surveys" of trade associations or upon data collected by some state administrative agency.

The evaluation of these laws by Bain,[15] as follows, is one of the most complete and balanced.

The actual effects of "unfair practices" or minimum-markup distributive-trade competition have not been thoroughly studied and are not too evident.

[14] See, for example, J. S. Bain, *Industrial Organization* (New York: John Wiley and Sons, Inc., 1959), pp. 564–68, 623, and 626–27.
[15] *Ibid.*, pp. 576–77.

By and large, the publicized application of such laws has been mainly in the grocery trades (where resale price maintenance is unimportant). It is also notable that the larger grocery chains (against whom this sort of legislation was initially aimed) have been prominent supporters of trade-association activity directed toward calculating and policing minimum markups under these laws.

In general, these laws do not seem to have disadvantaged chain stores. Unless the true "loss leader" were some strategic and indispensable competitive device of chain stores—which it very evidently is not, in view of their overall advantages in efficiency—there is no reason the minimum-markup laws should limit mass distributors. In fact it may help them, since if a uniform minimum retail markup is made mandatory for a whole trade, the chain stores, with generally lower costs of acquiring merchandise, begin with a lower legal retail price than their independent competitors (though this may usually be met in competition by the independents), and are in some degree protected from aggressive price competition by independent retailers. The chains have thus usually much more to gain than to lose from minimum-markup conventions, and it is not evident that they have lost at all.

So far as effects on general competition in the distributive trades are concerned, it does not appear that minimum-markup regulations have been very significant. This is in considerable part because the minimum markups established by trade associations under the law have in general been rather low (ranging from 6 to 12 per cent of inventory cost), and lower than the average markup obtained under unregulated competition. The main effect has thus been felt in traditionally fast-turnover, low-markup items within a stock in trade, where loss-leader price policies may be discouraged. Overall, price competition has been affected mainly to the extent that independent price-cutting competition with the chains has been limited, and price-cutting tactics limited in range.[16]

Although the minimum-markup laws have so far been relatively innocuous devices for restricting retail competition, it is clear that they could become dangerous to the public interest if more effectively implemented by private agencies and more vigorously enforced. And they share with the "fair trade" laws the lack of any real justification for attempted restriction of retail competition. They are, also, like the "fair trade" laws, *politically unsound in their undue delegation of legislative power to private groups, and correspondingly subject to attack on constitutional grounds.* (italics added.)

Regulations designed to control wholesale middlemen

These regulations are related closely to the regulation of organized wholesale markets to be discussed immediately following this section. Apart from regulations as to contractual obligations under the law of contracts and the law of agency, the main purpose of the regulations under consideration are the statutory provisions for policing the business ethics of the wholesale middlemen. Thus, the wholesale middlemen who buy and sell in the organized markets for agricultural

[16] Here Bain overlooks the development of the price-cutting strength of the voluntary chain and the increased incidence of the discount house in the food business.

goods must register with the Secretary of Agriculture; and, similarly, the wholesale middleman in the organized securities exchanges must register with the Securities and Exchange Commission.

Regulations designed to control trading in organized wholesale markets

Apart from requiring wholesale middlemen to register, the Federal Government has had a long history of regulation of organized wholesale markets in order to guarantee that prices determined in these markets, "reflect as fairly as possible actual supply-and-demand situations." By means of the Cotton Futures Act (1915) and the Grain Futures Act (1922), and their merger later into the Commodity Exchange Regulations Act (1936), the Federal Government attempted to correct the "abuses" of speculation, and to prevent "corners" or the existence of other large trading interests. The Act of 1936 provided more specifically for the following: application to the Secretary of Agriculture by futures markets for permission to be designated as contract markets; Federal inspection of commodities handled; provision for written records of all cash and futures transactions; provision for inclusion in membership of all financially responsible cooperatives; licensing of the trading wholesale middlemen as noted; and limitations on the amount of open contracts held by any one trading party; and the amount of speculative trading in one day. Similar provisions, so far as they are applicable, apply to organized livestock markets under the Packers and Stockyards Act (1921); and to organized wholesale fruit and vegetable markets under the Produce Agency Act (1927), and the Perishable Agricultural Commodities Act (1930).

No one can argue about the desirability of such regulations designed to curb unethical practices, to reduce buyers' or sellers' manipulations of prices, and otherwise to increase the competitive tone of these price-determining markets. Unfortunately, the government through its price stabilization, marketing agreements, and market order programs, has hampered effectively and increasingly the increased competitive efficiency so secured. These regulatory activities must be viewed in the dual environmental background of treating agriculture as a distressed industry, and the constituent farmers as a political pressure group worthy of discriminatory economic treatment.

Price stabilization currently stems from a series of regulations which became the Agricultural Adjustment Act of 1938, and which, with later amendments, is still in effect. The purpose of the Act, in addition to the conservation of natural resources, was

. . . to regulate interstate and foreign commerce in cotton, wheat, corn, tobacco, and rice to the extent necessary to provide an orderly, adequate, and balanced flow of such commodities in interstate and foreign commerce through storage of reserve supplies, loans, marketing quotas, assisting farmers to obtain in so far as practicable, parity prices for such commodities and parity income, and assisting consumers to obtain an adequate and steady supply of such commodities at fair prices.[17]

These parity prices have acted to interfere severely with the effectiveness of the organized wholesale market as a competitive price-determining institution.

Marketing orders and marketing agreements have been provided for increasingly by Federal legislation beginning with the Agricultural Marketing Agreements Act (1937). These orders and agreements represent the additional intrusion of the Federal Government into the channel for many agricultural products in order, by restraining competition, to raise the prices and thus the incomes received by the producers of the stipulated products. In the case of fresh fluid milk, the state and/or Federal Government may fix either the actual prices paid to producers, or additionally, retail prices in stores or home delivery. Further interferences with competition may arise through quantities of agricultural products permitted to be produced under the newer soil-bank programs.

Generally, apart from the damage done to the price-determining mechanism, certain broad effects may be noted:

1. Farmers' incomes may have been based upon or adjusted to levels above those that might have been expected to accrue under normal competition.
2. Questions may be raised as to whether the farmers' incomes have been increased in the most desirable economic and political manner.
3. Some doubt may be raised as to whether or not resources in the extractive industry are being used most efficiently.
4. Based on the ever-increasing surpluses accumulated under the years of Federal controls, many writers question whether the real economic diseases of agriculture are being corrected.
5. The various controls have had the positive attributes, however, of contributing to increased utilization of machines, sounder conservation measures, etc.[18]

One final ideological question may be raised: Can the farmer ever

[17] For a definition of parity, and an example of how such prices are computed, see Duddy and Revzan, *op. cit.,* pp. 555–57.

[18] This framework has been suggested by Bain, *op. cit.,* pp. 558–63.

wean himself from a position of continuous economic dependency on these regulations?[19]

Regulations designed to control integration in the channel

In general, except for such mergers and consolidations as are permitted, integration in the channel is subject to the whole *corpus* of existing antitrust legislation. As a result of court decisions made since World War II, there seems to be a tendency for the Federal Government increasingly to take a "tough" viewpoint towards either vertical or horizontal integration in the channel. In the Aluminum case,[20] certain market control criteria were introduced as a limit to horizontal integration. In several succeeding cases,[21] involving both horizontal and vertical integration, the Supreme Court has stipulated that monopoly is present when the "power exists to raise prices or to exclude competition," even though the power is not or may never be exercised.

In conclusion, reference may be made once again to Bain:[22]

Given these potentially exclusionary effects of vertical integration, what has been the attitude of the courts (under the Sherman Act) to the existence of such integration? First, the proposed doctrine that illegality is found in the practice or agreement between two divisions or subsidiaries of the same firm to the effect that one should be supplied by the other (thus excluding competitive firms from supplying the receiving stage of the integrated firm) has been conclusively and logically rejected. The illusive doctrine of "intrafirm" conspiracy thus has no more standing at law than in applied economic analysis. Second, the courts have held that the accomplishment of restraint of trade and monopolization via vertical integration is not exempt from the law as such—that vertical integration which results in specified degrees of restraint or monopolization *can* be illegal—but that vertical integration which imposes some restraint is by no means illegal *per se*. The degree and character of the restraint, and resulting monopolization is crucial. Third, in conjunction with the preceding, creation (or maintenance) of vertical integration having some restraining effect is not illegal restraint *per se* under section 1 of the Sherman Act, as a combination in restraint of trade. Instead, the criterion of reasonableness of the restraint is applicable. This puts vertical combinations having restraining effects on roughly the same footing as

[19] Note how difficult it has been either for Democrats or Republicans to originate or pass any substantial revisions, or to cope with the ever-increasing surpluses.

[20] *United States v. Aluminum Co. of America,* 148 F. 2d416 (2d Cir. 1945).

[21] See the following for example: *American Tobacco Co. v. United States,* 328 U. S. 781 (1946).

Schine Theatres, Inc. v. United States, 334 U. S. 110 (1948).

United States v. Griffith, 334 U. S. 100 (1948).

United States v. The New York Great Atlantic and Pacific Tea Co., et al., 173 F. 2d 79 (1949).

[22] Bain, *op. cit.,* pp. 516–17.

horizontal mergers having similar effects. They are not adjudged to be unreasonable combinations in restraint of trade *per se,* and the attention of the court is thus shifted, under a "rule of reason," to the character of the remaining competition in the market or markets involved, and to whether or not monopolization has been accomplished. Finally, vertical integration with inherently restraining tendencies are to be adjudged illegal only if the effect is "to unreasonably restrict the opportunities of competitors to market their product" (or to secure essential materials for production).

Regulations affecting marketing communication through the channel

Reference has been made earlier to the common law and statutory protection granted to producers' and middlemen's individual and family product brands in the channel. This protection has the obvious advantage of making possible the whole development of selective advertising and personal selling techniques in the channel. The regulation of deceptive and misleading advertising also has been referred to in connection with the Federal Trade Commission Act (1914). The Federal Communications Commission, in addition, has control over the number and geographical distribution of radio and television stations; and dictate, to some extent, the time distribution and content of commercial announcements. The quiz show and "payola" scandals in 1959 may lead to an increase in the degree and breadth of such regulations.

On a more positive competitive plane, comparative Federal-State market news services furnish one of the key devices for disseminating important data of production, prices, demand, etc., to everyone interested in the marketing of agricultural products, and especially in speculative and hedging transactions in the organized commodity exchanges. The Federal Government also makes available a wide array of materials pertaining to such matters as wholesale and retail sales, wholesale and consumers' price indexes, indexes of manufacturing and extractive industry production, national income statistics, etc. A final category of market news is contained in census publications, and in the research reports of various agencies.

A third aspect of communication stemming from governmental activities is represented by the development of grades and standards, and the application of these in the compulsory inspection of certain types of edible agricultural products. The important part of these activities for this aspect of government regulation is the extent to which the agencies involved aggressively promote these activities to every agency in the channel; or permit nongovernmental groups to do such promotional work.

A final aspect of the regulation of communication has to do with the censorship function of government. Thus, until recently, many periodicals, radio stations, and television stations could not advertise alcoholic beverages. Other aspects of censorship may deprive the general public accessibility to movies or to literature because, in the minds of the censors, they are "lewd, obscene, or otherwise immoral."[23] Fortunately, recent court decisions have reduced significantly the extent to which these censorship activities remove certain tangible and intangible products from marketing channels.[24]

Government research activities

These activities have been classified earlier. All that needs to be added here is a reference to them as a positive force which may act to increase the degree of professional knowledge needed to carry on marketing activities. Such research may be the originating factor, also, in the development of new products for subsequent distribution through the channel; or it may lead to elimination of harmful products. In many instances, as in the guided missile and atomic energy research programs, it may lead to new industries and accompanying channel structures. Finally, on a broad front, much of the government research should be expected to strengthen the competitive structure in the United States, although, unfortunately, these results do not always accrue.

Government Regulation and the Ultimate Consumer

Through the whole intricate network of goverment regulation, the ultimate consumer is affected in many direct and indirect ways. The earlier outline contained a variety of regulatory activities in which the ultimate consumer is placed under a *protective* cloak. This protective cloak may include barriers against physical injuries due directly to the use of products in the channel; barriers against economic injury resulting from false or misleading statements, false price information, etc.; and barriers against injuries arising out of the legal obligations of businessmen with whom the ultimate consumer has dealings either in buyer-seller or employer-employee relationships.

[23] These efforts are aided or stimulated by selective secular and religious groups who frequently confuse their interests or biases with the general public.

[24] It is interesting to note as an aside that, during the effective application of such censorship, subterranean channels may appear to supply a part of the demand which has been sharply increased because of the "whetting of appetite" effect of the censorship.

Governmental regulations create, on the other side, a wide range of attendant obligations for the ultimate consumer. First, there are the direct reciprocal obligations each and every consumer enters into under the law of contracts. Second, there is the whole range of personal liabilities of consumers under criminal statutes of the states and the Federal Government. And even under the rule of *caveat emptor,* the consumer assumes certain obligations (often overlooked or misunderstood) as stated in the following:

The phrase (*caveat emptor*) expresses in a shorthand fashion the common law rule that the buyer assumes the risk of getting goods of the quality and in the condition he desires if he is furnished by the seller with goods that substantially correspond to the description of the goods that were the subject matter of the contract.[25]

The Federal and state governments, finally, have established consumers' advisory services from time to time.[26] Mention has been made of special protective legislation. One aspect, frequently overlooked, is the exemption of consumers' cooperative associations from the ordinary applications of the antitrust laws, and the special treatment when consumers are members of labor unions. The consumers' cooperatives are exempt, as nonprofit organizations, from income tax coverage. And, in an important sense, every activity of the government to strengthen the competitive structure brings corresponding benefits to consumers, individually, collectively, and in their roles as active business participants.

The Dilemmas of Government Regulation[27]

Given the framework of government regulation outlined above (and the Robinson-Patman Act in Chapter 22), the whole picture represents a great dilemma, or at least a series of dilemmas. In presenting and discussing the great dilemma use will be made of the headings suggested by Hamilton: conscience and the corporation; the use of competition; the ways of regulation; and no choice between systems.

[25] Votaw, *op. cit.,* p. 389.

[26] New York and California are the most recent examples.

[27] The approach and the contents of this section were suggested by, and are based on, a reading of Walton Hamilton, *The Politics of Industry* (New York: Alfred A. Knopf, 1957) (Copyright 1957 by the Regents of the University of Michigan), especially Section V, "Salute to the Great Economy," pp. 136–39. Apart from the use of direct quotations, the author assumes full responsibility for the paraphrasing of Hamilton's ideas in the sections which follow.

Conscience and the corporation

The business organization form embodied in the corporation is an important foundation for the present-day complicated large-scale economy. It originated and developed under a code of common and statutory law rather than from a planned system based upon a political process and a constitution. As it evolved, the professional management group in the corporation has won its independence to the point where they shape corporate policy, and are able to use a process of self perpetuation to remain in office. These professional managers—while forced to take into account the interests of investors, workers and customers—must face the problem of devising and administering the best set of policies, by compromising as well as possible between competing interests and varying alternatives: In such compromises, two criteria are paramount: (1) the claims of one interest should not be given preferential treatment to the detriment of other interests; and (2) the interests of private groups must be made compatible with the general welfare. This section and others under this heading will pose some solutions to the problems raised in these criteria.

Hamilton points out that "the way of conscience is among the oldest, most honorable, and most compelling of human sanctions." While each individual has his own form of sensitivity and indifference, these must be related to a broader set of society's notions of right and wrong. He develops the evolution of the confessional of the Church into the chancel court, and from that into the court of equity. Similarly, the divine right of kings became transformed, over a long period of history, into constitutional government with courts of law handling those conflicts between individual which could not, through the control of conscience, act to prevent wrongdoing.

While in individual conflicts, under a system of constitutional government and courts of law, it became an established principle that no man could try his own case, in the affairs of the corporation this principle has not been completely applied. Thus, the professional management group discussed above, while concerned about the policies of the corporation and interests of conflicting groups, also face conflicts arising out of their personal economic goals, and the limitations of their own personalities and experience. Thus, Hamilton concludes that the "thrust of conscience varies from business to business." Personality differences, differences in sensitivity, differences in weighing the short-run against the long-run, all influence variations in this "thrust." But importantly in this context, the conscience of managerial authority is conditioned by each executive's rationalization of his personal interests.

Additional problems of conscience and conflicts of interests stem from the increased obliteration of the dividing lines between the state and the economy. This becomes most apparent in the increased use of businessmen in government service. The conflicts are accentuated by the usual limited experience of the businessmen, and their ignorance of both the objectives and operation of public service. And nowhere does this conflict become more dangerous than when the businessman is unaware of its existence, and yet is asked to participate in the government regulation of business.

An apologia for the innocence of such a conflict of interest has gone ringing down the ages. From the simple days of Joseph's corner in wheat to the confused times of the Dixon-Yates contract, the reply is "So are they all, all honorable men."[28]

The use of competition

It is in the concept of competition that the whole framework of government regulation comes sharply into focus. To begin with, the urge for gain which lies at the foundation of the force impelling men to compete, also may lead to many collusive acts of competitors such as creating artificial scarcities and acting to fix prices. Thus, Hamilton notes that as long ago as the 17th century, the English Parliament decreed that cases involving the validity of monopolies were not to be otherwise tried than by common law. In the United States, the common law doctrine has been replaced since 1890 by the complicated framework of statutory law already outlined. An interesting point made by Hamilton in connection with the Sherman Act was that, because the 1890 environment was too strongly based on *laissez faire*, reliance was placed on the force of the private suit instead of an adequate system of commercial police.

The great dilemma of statutory regulation of business stems from the following: (1) the legal process was designed to provide justice and end conflicts *instantly;* (2) it never was conceived originally to handle such problems as the channel or trade practices; and (3) a legal weapon "designed for petty trade" is being used to meet problems arising from the "great economy." Thus, in a sense, the system of law and courts has demonstrated remarkable flexibility and resourcefulness by functioning at all within the network of government regulation.

[28] Hamilton, *op. cit.,* p. 142.

Within this framework, Hamilton points out that the major problem in any antitrust suit is how to shape the remedy. An apparent dilemma is the necessity of ending those practices found to be illegal, while, at the same time, permitting the business firms involved to operate as normally as possible. Such cases as have been tried prove to be ineffective either because of the failure of courts to provide adequate relief in the first place; or where the decree is well directed, no adequate follow-up and policing are provided to make certain that the same evils do not reappear in new forms.

In this connection, there has appeared "a new mythology" as a weapon to the resistance to antitrust. This new mythology consists of the following myths:

1. *The myth of "hard" versus "soft" competition*—in which the Sherman Act (hard competition) is pitted against the Robinson-Patman Act (soft competition).
2. *"Invocation of the myth of good faith"*—in which the reduction of prices to a favored customer is permissive if made in good faith to meet the equally low prices of competitors. By *not* measuring the effects of such price discrimination either on the process of competition or the health of the economy, Hamilton concludes: *"For the administration of antitrust laws, no more uncertain and evasive standard of judgment could be found than that of good faith."*
3. *Creation of the myth of the concept of effective competition*—which makes it impossible to use standards of judgment because of the complex variables to be found. As a result, uncertainty characterizes standards, thus providing escape for many violations.

From this new mythology, Hamilton reminds us *that the objective of the antitrust laws is to provide vital competition.* Thus, the individual statute would have been one, in his opinion, "where public policy insinuates itself in a pattern of human behavior and demands formal enforcement only in exceptional cases." However, no matter how ideal the statute, one continuing and serious weakness is to be found in the failure of the administrative agencies to follow the policy stipulated by Congress in the legislation. Too often the enforcement of a piece of legislation is left almost entirely to the administrative agency. And where statutes conflict, an aroused business may invoke one agency's jurisdiction and argue that any antitrust action be shelved until the agency makes known its findings (which may delay action for one or more years).

Finally, Hamilton concludes with this very astute and penetrating observation about the role of the military:

It is notorious that the military has not been overscrupulous in taking the mandates of the antitrust laws into account in its operations. It has repeatedly accepted the plea of national defense as a justification for allowing a united front within an industry in disregard of established public policy. *In recent years the Pentagon has probably done more to promote the concentration of economic wealth and power than can be undone by the vigilant campaigns of a half dozen Antitrust Divisions* (italics added). Here is a working at cross-purposes which vividly attests the current backwardness of the political arts.[29]

The ways of regulation

Hamilton opens this section with the terse statement that *"the administrative agency is not the most brilliant of political inventions."* He then proceeds to dissect these agencies by revealing their many weaknesses, using as a norm from which to measure their performances that their responsibility is: (*a*) to correct the lapses of management from public duty, and (*b*) to direct the stream of executive conduct to stipulated or inferred legitimate goals. From the beginning, he emphasizes the problems of regulation by such agencies originating from certain lack of adequate personnel.

Building upon the preceding, Hamilton finally discusses the responsibility of the administrative agencies to selected reviewing bodies. With respect to Congress, administrative agencies act with delegated authority from that body, and are instructed, in turn, to report directly to it. In actual practice, these agencies appear to be increasingly reluctant to give Congress a full account of its actions and activities. Their annual reports fail continually to report on how (as well as how well) the agencies make the decisions they do.

With respect to the relationship of administrative agencies to the President, the first thing to note is that he generally is given authority by Congress to appoint a chairman. From this procedure has developed the rule that communication between the President and the agency is privileged and not open for Congressional inspection. Two contributions result, accordingly, to the dilemma of regulation: (1) the agency conceals to itself more and more information about regulatory legislation which appears to be too specific, too continuous, and too detailed for Congress; and (2) Congress is thus denied vital information needed by its members in order to permit proper policing of public

---

[29] *Ibid.,* p. 152. He might have added that, in addition, the advantages thus secured are used by the giant corporations to further bolster their oligopolistic or monopolistic strength in the civilian goods channels.

policy, and the adoption of any necessary recommendations for changes.

Under existing legal procedures, the Federal courts are the point of last resort in reviewing the decisions and activities of these agencies. However, the administration agencies have technical staffs available to review all of the data presented; and the courts appear willing to accept, increasingly, this display of *expertise*. As a result, the following obtain:

1. An increasing series of administrative acts follow administrative acts without judicial review.
2. Because of (1), the business interest that is being regulated, masses all of its resources and focuses them on the agency in the hope of securing the benefit of opportunistic timing.
3. Increasingly, the general public remains mute. So, Hamilton concludes: *"to repeat, the commission is not the happiest of all political inventions."*

No choice between systems

Finally, in the dilemma of regulation, Hamilton discusses the difficulty of choosing at any given time in any given country which is highly developed economically and politically between all systems of economic and political ideology. As he describes it, the power and impact of the past on any culture is cumulative and cannot be stayed. Then, by a series of brilliant questions,[30] he demonstrates the complexities and inconsistencies in what is called capitalism. Similar questions can be put to any other economic system. Finally, he demonstrates how the concept of any ideology is affected by all the verbalism by which it is presented, and the wide gap between a system in the abstract and all of the actual decisions and compromises needed to put the system into operation.

No people can this day choose the god they will serve with the firm knowledge that the chosen divinity will retain its identity.[31]

"Which Direction Is Forward?"

If problems of conscience, the use of competition, the ways of regulation, and no freedom of choice, are at the roots of the dilemma of

[30] *Ibid.*, pp. 162–64.
[31] *Ibid.*, p. 165.

regulation, then we may ask, "Which direction is forward?" The answer which Hamilton presents is given here verbatim:[32]

If for us and for others, there can be no choice between systems, it does not follow that there is no need for choice. The great crossroads of destiny are replaced by an endless series of points at which trails meet, intertwine, and go their divergent ways. At a myriad of such points a myriad of individuals make a myriad of decisions. Each of these individuals must determine and must keep on determining for himself which direction is forward. To decision each brings so much knowledge, understanding, and wisdom as he possesses. Persons differ from one another in foresight, in the values they hold, and in the balance they strike between private concern and public interest. The implications of a decision transcend the considerations which have prompted it. In the instance, the act which follows a judgment may lack significance; in the aggregate, the stream of decisions have a formidable impact upon the economy, the nation, the culture.

In a concern with public affairs the context of the moving culture must be reckoned with. It is impossible, even though it may be dull and soothing, to tell off a bill of particulars for driving the economy to its goal. A jigsaw puzzle, an exercise in Newtonian physics, or an excursion into the simplicities of the calculus invites a single right and indestructible answer. But the questions which impend and perplex are not of that kind. A host of persons on different levels, quite differently circumstanced, are responding to the challenges which beset them. The choices made must take their chances against the choices made by others. Ventures into planning have their limits in the freedom of others to plan. Each decision has its impact and in turn is compromised by a host of other decisions. And this stream of judgment takes its course within a culture which refuses to abide. There cannot be a series of enduring answers because we do not live in that kind of a world.

For us there can be no return to laissez faire. A great corpus of the law stands as proof of the incapacity of the industrial system to regulate itself. The experience distilled into its host of statutes attests the inability of an automatic system of checks and balances to hold industry to its appointed office. Nor can the magic of a new phrase like Countervailing Forces—a modern variant of the Invisible Hand—turn the trick. If kindred firms maintain a united front, countervailing forces can do no more than reflect the monopolistic structure which underlies. Nor can statecraft take on the task of economic architecture. Industrial activity is too multiple, too varied, and too changing to be reduced to an order in which each operation has its distinct function and station.

But if a blueprint is impossible, there are values to shape choice. *The great thing about the old competitive system was the strategic position which it assigned to the sole inventor, the lone enterpriser, the energetic minority* [italics added]. These pioneers had to do their work under the constant threat of lack of security and even of nonsurvival, but no man and no political authority sat in judgment and by its will decreed for them success or failure. *They were free to bring forward new ideas, to invent new products and processes, to innovate and contrive new methods of production* [italics added].

[32] *Ibid.*, pp. 165–69.

The only condition was that in the impartial and impersonal market they should make good. If they did, success was theirs, whatever might be the will of the majority of their colleagues. If they failed, others were free to try a like attempt. If they made good and turned out superior products or made a commodity available to the public at a lower price, their colleagues were compelled to imitate.

The economy of today calls for its degree of regimentation. It demands more than other economies that the gears engage, that the switches lock. It necessitates a great cooperative effort of the first magnitude, which to a considerable extent invites regulation. But in this process it is imperative that the cry of enterprise be not stilled, that the minority be allowed to have its chance, and that there be a thousand points in the larger system at which creative thought and effort may be applied. There is necessity, as there has always been, for the direction of industrial enterprises toward objectives which serve the general welfare. But there is also need that through all the industries which make it up the dynamic urge be kept alive.

Among the rights we hold dear is that of every man to take his own amateur fling in the role of deity. To that end he may formulate his own list of the fault lines and trouble spots within the economy. A short catalogue of problems is too obvious to be overlooked. Until the political arts reach a maturity they do not now possess, the question of the maintenance of competition will be insistent. As large an area of the industrial system as possible should be left to the competitive regime. Where it needs to be helped over the hard places or superseded by another method of control, the case needs to be made clear. Mergers ought not to be allowed where the technology does not lead and where the hazard of the concentration of economic power forbids. The grant of the patent should be limited to its proper office of promoting the progress of science and the useful arts. After the limited time the invention should be promptly restored to the public domain. There is need for policy in respect to the employment of letters patents which will prevent their use as sanctions for what the law forbids.

Too often the military honors public policy in the breach, by disregard of the statutes passed by the Congress. There is only confusion when Government procurement becomes the chief instrument in the creation of trends which it is the very purpose of the antitrust laws to arrest. The administrative agency presents problems not easily resolved. Its shortcomings inhere in the dualism between immediate business action and a belated public review. Until political invention contrives an adequate substitute, it will continue to harass and to confuse.

These and like problems will not be encountered in even so concrete a statement as they are given here. They will appear as terms in a host of questions concerned with every day affairs. As events take their course, each of them and others of their kind will demand repeated restatement. The way of economic control is that of eternal vigilance.

For better or for worse we are committed to the great economy. The structure and practices of petty trade are not those of a giant industrialism. In the course of its development the industrial system will, as in the past, undergo a series of mutations. In some form or other the rivalry of men will continue to be employed as an instrument of the general welfare. *It is not*

*important that the arrangements which currently are set down as the com-
petitive system will endure. It is important that the spirit of competition
shall be enhanced and not impaired. There must be an outlet for the creative
urge, free play for the dynamic drive. In a society, as in the physical world,
motion is inseparable from life* [italics added].

Some Suggested Reforms

Given the complicated matter called government regulation, can
anything be offered as suggested reforms building on the general
philosophy of Hamilton? The following are suggestive of some important avenues of action:

1. Increasing attention should be directed to the determination and
   use of economic size criteria as they pertain to business units
   at each level of the channel distribution. These criteria should
   be adapted to each kind of business in order to furnish the administrative agencies and courts with some rock bottom uniformity
   in measuring economic concentration.
2. Similarly, measures of market control and market penetration
   should be determined for each kind of business, firm by firm, at
   each level of the channel.
3. From the measures in (1) and (2) in relation to existing statutes
   and interpretations, maximum size ranges should be established
   firm by firm for each kind of business at each stage of the channel.
4. Attention should be given to formalizing requirements that each
   administrative agency be required to report annually to Congress:
   (a) such decisions as it has reached in cases under legislation
   establishing its responsibilities; (b) how and why these decisions
   were reached; and (c) whether or not these decisions have
   changed the public policy aspects of the legislation. Each agency
   should make such types of analysis, in addition, for court
   decisions.
5. Attention should be given to providing Federal courts with technical staffs similar to those in the administrative agencies. Two
   main benefits may accrue: (a) the courts will no longer have to
   accept arbitrarily the analyses prepared by the agency's technical
   staff; and (b) businessmen could no longer concentrate their legal
   and economic barrages at only one point in the regulatory process.
6. Steps should be taken to clarify primary from secondary jurisdiction in cases of overlapping legislation and related administrative agencies.

7. Codification should be provided of the concept of competition and the efficiency of the price-determining mechanism under competition. These concepts should be used to review existing legislation in order to remove conflicting sections.

8. Building upon (7), criteria should be established for determining (a) those industries in which competition cannot be expected to function properly; and (b) those industries which may be treated as temporarily or permanently distressed for purposes of receiving preferential regulatory treatment.

9. An independent and impartial research group should be formed to furnish Congress with reports of actual and expected changes which affect existing regulation of business; and whether or not any basic changes in over-all public policy and existing statutes will be required. This analysis should be made on a continuing basis.

10. Finally, consideration should be given to the creation of a Consumers' Division in the Federal Government to advise on the interests of the general public in current cases; in the preparation of decisions; and in the revision or preparation of legislation. Hamilton's idea of a corps of commercial police might very well be part of this unit.

QUESTIONS AND PROBLEMS

1. What are the attributes of a "good system of social control"?
2. So far as the marketing system and the wholesaling sector therein are concerned, what have been the objectives of government regulation?
3. What is the extent of the government regulatory impact upon the individual wholesale middleman?
4. To what extent does government regulation have significant channel competition aspects?
5. What can you say, in balance, is your considered judgment of the effects of governmental price regulations on the competitive structure of prices?
6. Do you agree with Bain's evaluation of the effects of the unfair practices acts? Be sure to support such ideas as you present.
7. How has the Federal Government acted to increase the competitive efficiency of organized wholesale markets? To impede their competitive efficiency?
8. Indicate how government regulation has dealt with channel communication.
9. Discuss critically what is implied in Hamilton's ideas of the dilemmas of government regulation.
10. What, in essence, are Hamilton's main suggestions for moving forward in government regulation in order to overcome the dilemmas he has noted?

11. Do you agree or disagree with the framework of the suggested reforms presented? Which would you eliminate? Would you include additional reforms?

CHAPTER INTEGRATING ASSIGNMENTS

To what extent does the present framework of government regulation coincide with the criteria of a good system of social control as developed by J. M. Clark? Do you believe that, in balance, the framework meets the requirements of a competitive marketing structure operating within a democratic governmental system?

22

Government Regulation:
The Robinson-Patman Act

Perhaps no piece of legislation enacted by the Federal Government pertaining to business in the last 70 years has had as turbulent a history as the Robinson-Patman Act.[1] Neither completely classifiable as a piece of antitrust legislation, nor as a price discrimination law, the R-P Act has been characterized by a range of adjectives from highly uncomplimentary to complimentary, depending upon the source. Although the printed text of the Act does not fill more than two pages, it has been the source of a large number of cases since its enactment on June 19, 1936,[2] while the writings on the subject are large enough to constitute almost a full-time specialty.

Originally conceived of as being directed at the food industry, and especially the Great A&P Company, the interpretations have expanded its applications in many directions towards objectives never conceived by the authors of the Act. The Act, furthermore, brings Federal regulation into the consideration of channels of distribution, and of market policies and practices, to a degree never before recognized. For all these reasons, then, and for more to be presented in sections which

[1] Reference to the Robinson-Patman Act hereafter in this chapter will be either as the "R-P Act" or as "the Act."

[2] By the end of 1957, some 610 formal complaints had been filed by the Federal Trade Commission, and 75 recorded lawsuits initiated by private parties. See Frederick M. Rowe, "The Evolution of the Robinson-Patman Act, a Twenty-Year Perspective," *Columbia Law Review*, **57** (December 1957), 1059–1088.

follow, separate treatment of the R-P Act is required. Fortunately, this presentation can be expanded and strengthened because of the recent appearance of two detailed studies.[3]

The Background of the R-P Act

Because of its controversial nature, the R-P Act must be discussed first of all against a backdrop of the environment in which it was originated. In presenting this environmental background, emphasis will be placed upon the economic background, shortcomings of Section 2 of the Clayton Act, the legislative environment, and some theoretical aspects.

The economic environment of the 1930's

The R-P Act was born in troubled economic times and, perhaps because of this, has always had a troubled existence. For one thing, the worst depression in the history of the United States was taking its toll of business, especially among the small independent producers, and wholesale and retail middlemen. The Federal Trade Commission had just finished its monumental study of the corporate chains (in 32 volumes), and its findings were being widely publicized, as well as furnishing the Commission with a basis for recommended legislation. At the same time, the corporate chains had reached their peak of relative importance in retail sales, especially in the grocery business.

The whole "New Deal" philosophy had developed an economic environment in which much faith was being placed by businessmen on the role of government intervention and planning in the hope of obtaining and keeping economic security. Pressure groups were expanding by leaps and bounds as a result of the stimulus given to trade associations by the NRA and its codes. Intervention had been systematized already at the state level in the form of corporate chain tax laws and resale price maintenance arrangements. Competition was alright as an abstract norm, but not in the concrete environment of a severe depression.

---

[3] Corwin D. Edwards, *The Price Discrimination Law: A Review of Experience* (Washington, D. C.: Brookings Institution, December 1959); and Herbert F. Taggart, *Cost Justification,* Michigan Business Studies, Vol. XIV, No. 3 (Ann Arbor, Michigan: Bureau of Business Research, The University of Michigan, 1959).

F. M. Rowe has summarized all of these environmental factors:[4]

The R-P Act of 1936 was the product of organized effort to preserve traditional marketing channels against the encroachment of mass distributors and chains whose low-priced appeal to consumers was enhanced during the general business recession of the 1930's.

Shortcomings of the Clayton Act, Section 2

Since the R-P Act amended Section 2 of the Clayton Act, some discussion of the shortcomings of the latter in its original version may be helpful. The consensus among experts is that the original Section 2 had been designed to curb the predatory tactics of large manufacturers in using local geographical price discrimination to drive smaller competitors out of business. Since the Clayton Act had been formulated in 1914, it had not visualized the possibilities of price discriminations and concessions taking place vertically in the channel of distribution. Furthermore, the Clayton Act, by permitting price differences based on quantity alone, was not as specific in its statement of the relation of costs to selling prices as were the later provisions in the R-P Act. And, the Clayton Act did not always prevent price discriminations before the harm to competitors was effected. Under the R-P Act changes, the regulatory arm of the Federal Government was extended to reach throughout the channel.[5] Finally, it may be stated that the escape provisions of the Clayton Act designating certain types of permissible price discriminations were so broad as to create basic questions of interpretation.[6] In view of the basic antagonism of Representative Patman against A&P, it seems obvious that he wanted to regulate large buyers in the same way that the Clayton Act controlled the predatory activities of large sellers.

The legislative environment[7]

Some outline of the legislative history of the R-P Act will help in understanding its entire origins and original motivations. Representative (now Senator) Wright Patman of Texas introduced the House version of the bill—H.R. 8442—on July 11, 1935, following hard on

[4] Rowe, op. cit., p. 1061.

[5] This is considerably more specific than the language of the Clayton Act; namely, "substantially to lessen competition or of tending to create a monopoly."

[6] The proviso states: "that nothing contained in the Act shall prevent discrimination in price on account of differences in grade, quality, or quantity sold; or which makes due allowance for differences in costs of selling or transportation; or made in good faith to meet competition."

[7] For a very detailed treatment see Edwards, op. cit., Chapter 2.

the heels of the Supreme Court's upset of the NRA. Immediately thereafter, the identical Senate version—S. 3154—was introduced by Senator Robinson. While both versions went far beyond the Federal Trade Commission's recommendations in the chain store investigation, Patman's version was by far the most far-reaching. His version contained the following four features:

1. Price discriminations, including discriminations in terms of sale, were unconditionally barred. Two important qualifications were made: (*a*) H.R. 8442 preserved functional discounts to wholesalers; and (*b*) corporate chains were permitted to receive *only* the regular retailers' functional (or trade) discounts.
2. Quantity discounts were to be limited in amount to those which corresponded with actual cost economies.
3. Brokerage fees were unconditionally prohibited to any broker affiliated with buyers.
4. Finally, the famous "proportionately equal terms" clause for advertising allowances was included.

The House Judiciary Committee submitted a favorable report on March 31, 1956, after the usual hearings attended by all facets of the food industry, as well as by other groups. Representative Celler of New York condemned the majority report, and in a vitriolic minority report made the following points: (1) The Patman bill was designed to maintain the profits of one class of trade regardless of its efficiency or lack of efficiency; (2) the consumer became the "goat," and would "pay the piper"; and (3) it deprived the consumer of obtaining the benefits of lower prices and more efficient marketing methods under free competition.

Meanwhile, the Senate Judiciary Committee had expressed grave doubts as to the constitutionality of the unconditional ban on price discriminations in the Patman bill. It proposed the addition of a clause which would prohibit price differentials only,

. . . where the effect of such discrimination may be to substantially lessen competition or tend to create monopoly in any line of commerce, *or to injure, destroy or prevent competition with any person who either grants or receives the benefits of such discrimination, or with customers of either of them* . . . .

The Senate bill, after amendments, and including the criminal provisions to be referred to later, was passed on April 30, 1936. Action in the House did not take place until May 28, when it passed its own amended version of the Patman bill. Thereupon, the Senate receiving it, eliminated the House's enacting clause, inserted its own text, and passed H.R. 8442 on June 1. Because of the differences, a conference committee had to be appointed; and, after several days of work, its report was presented and adopted by the House on June 15, and by the Senate on June 18. The R-P Act was signed by President Roosevelt, on June 19, 1936, and entered the statute books as 49 Stat. 1526, 15 U.S.C. 13.

Some theoretical aspects

In addition to the difficulties of the R-P Act which arise from its original motivations and its legislative history, and other aspects which will be discussed in a later section on evaluation, the legislation must be considered, as well, in an environment of the confused state of the economic theory of price discrimination. The conclusions of Cassady, in one of the definitive treatments of price discrimination, is pertinent in this connection:

Discriminatory pricing schemes are universal phenomena and from an economic standpoint are not necessarily to be condemned. *Discrimination does not depend upon the existence of monopoly control of a market; nor does the practice necessarily lead toward monopoly. Its practice may be completely free of any undesirable economic result. Indeed, discriminatory pricing may have certain advantageous aspects from the point of view of society* [italics added].[8]

He then classifies the purposes of price discrimination as follows:

I. *Discriminatory Pricing for Profit-Maximizing Purposes*
   a. The case of railroad freight rates.
   b. To meet only such geographical competition at any level of the channel as threatens to divert business.
   c. To extend the geographic outreach of sales.
   d. To secure the better utilization of production facilities.
   e. To secure long-run sales promotional benefits.
   f. To put competitors out of business.

II. *Discriminatory Pricing for Nonprofit Maximizing Purposes*
   a. For convenience in administering prices.
   b. For special war time situations.
   c. To promote public welfare.
   d. To secure the loyalty and patronage of company employees.
   e. For charitable purposes (e.g., clergyman's discounts).
   f. To spread the costs of service in equitable manner.

[8] Ralph Cassady, Jr., "Techniques and Purposes of Price Discrimination," *The Journal of Marketing*, XI (October 1946), 135–50. The interested reader should review critically, also, his, "Some Economic Aspects of Price Discrimination under Non-Perfect Market Conditions," *The Journal of Marketing*, XI (July 1946), 7–20.

III. *Discriminatory Pricing for a Combination of Purposes*
   a. Because of public pressures, "but with an eye to the effect on net revenue."
   b. Because of a combination of special deals for friends and/or regular patrons, and the customer's economic status.
   c. The famous example of doctors' fees differentiated on the buyer's ability to pay.

Finally, Cassady develops a comprehensive list of price discrimination techniques.[9]

I. *Direct Methods*
   a. Earnings of the customer or client.
   b. Earning power of the product for the user.
   c. Bargaining strength of individual customers.
   d. Presence of competitive bidding, or other evidence of intensity of customer demand.
II. *Semidirect Methods*
   a. Geographical location of customers, including variations in the necessity of discrimination.
   b. Age of customers.
   c. Sex of customers.
   d. Buyer's occupation.
   e. Military or nonmilitary status of the buyer.
   f. Public nature of the customer.
   g. Membership in specified organizations, etc.
   h. Status of customer; e.g., new versus established.
   i. Use to which product is put.
   j. Application of the principle of "charging what the traffic will bear."
III. *Indirect Methods*
   a. Quantity of products purchased by the customers.
   b. Size of item.
   c. Design of product.
   d. Container.
   e. Brand name.
   f. Format of binding—"paperback" versus "hard" books.
   g. Time product or service is purchased.
   h. Channel of distribution for the product.

From the above, it is apparent that the authors of the R-P Act had no conception of: (*a*) the intricacies of price discrimination; (*b*) the

[9] *Ibid.,* pp. 135–44.

varieties of goods and services to which it has been applied; or (c) the fact that government agencies as well as profit-making enterprises practice such tactics. As Cassady so well summarizes:

It can be seen from the foregoing classification that price discrimination is indeed ubiquitous. It is practiced by government, public service companies, and private enterprises. It is found in the professions, in industry, and in trade. It is utilized in the sale of commodities (everything from books and magazines to industrial machinery) as well as services (from moving picture entertainment and symphony concerts to transportation). As for methods utilized in discriminatory pricing, those falling within the semidirect and indirect categories appear to be more prevalent in most fields than those falling within the direct classification. Thus, price discrimination in practice would appear to be largely on a group rather than on a personal basis.[10]

The Original Objectives of the R-P Act

We may begin the discussion of objectives by comparing the language used in part of the reports of the House and Senate Judiciary Committees.

The House Committee's language:

The purpose of this legislation is to restore, so far as possible, equality of opportunity in business by strengthening antitrust laws and by protecting trade and commerce against unfair trade practices and unlawful price discrimination, and also against restraint and monopoly for the better protection of consumers, workers, and independent producers, manufacturers, merchants, and other businessmen.

Thus, the Committee established its guiding ideal as

. . . the preservation of equality of opportunity so far as possible to all who are usefully employed in the service of distribution and production, taking into consideration their equipment to serve the producing and consuming public with efficiency and the protection of the public from a threat of monopoly or oppression in the production and manufacture of the things it needs and the distribution of the same fairly and honestly without employment of unfair trade practices and unlawful price discrimination.[11]

The Senate Committee's language:

. . . the preservation of equal opportunity to all usefully employed in the service of distribution comportably with their ability and equipment to serve the producing and consuming public with real efficiency, and the prescription to that public of its freedom from threat of monopoly or oppression in obtaining its needs and disposing of its products.

[10] *Ibid.*, pp. 143–44. In a footnote on page 143, Cassady discusses variations in the onerousness of the burden of discrimination.

[11] As quoted in Edwards, *op. cit.*, p. 29.

. . . discriminations in excess of sound economic differences involve generally an element of loss, whether only of the necessary minimum of profits or of actual costs, that must be recouped from the business of customers not granted them.[12]

From the excerpts of these reports, and from the provisions of the Act (as presented in the following section), a summary statement of objectives may be prepared.

1. The Act is designed to prevent the types of price discrimination (as in the original Clayton Act) that may (a) lessen complication; or (b) tend to create monopolies.
2. The protection in (1) against the discriminations is extended from primarily the manufacturer's level (as in the Clayton Act) to individual competitors at all levels of the channels.
3. All customers are to be given the assurance of proportionately equal offers of certain marketing services and allowances, if such offers are made at all.
4. Certain conditions are specified under which price differentials may be made defensible.
5. Provision is made for the preservation of the competitive system, in general, and small businesses, in particular, at all levels of the channel.
6. And, finally, in its original perspective, to reduce severely the importance of corporate chains (especially A&P) in the food industry.

Thus, the R-P Act cuts across every pricing and other marketing policies and practices of every business engaged in interstate commerce at every level of the channel. This piece of legislation must be considered by every executive, accordingly, in every transaction in the channel which is in, or affects, interstate commerce, whenever and wherever prices, terms of sale, services, or facilities connected with the sale and purchase of goods are involved.

Provisions of the R-P Act

The R-P Act, as passed in 1936, consists of four sections in which the six subsections of Section 2 contain the heart of the legislation as it pertains to the wholesaling sector.[13]

---

[12] *Ibid.*, p. 30.

[13] For detailed treatment see Edwards, *op. cit.*, Chapter 3; and Cyrus Austin, *Price Discrimination and Related Problems under the Robinson-Patman,* 2nd rev. ed. (Philadelphia: American Law Institute, June 1959).

Section 1. This section amends Section 2 of the Clayton Act by adding the six subsections of Section 2, as described immediately below. Section 2 of the R-P Act as so constituted is the present Federal law regulating price discrimination and related matters. This law is administered and enforced by the Federal Trade Commission, and the system of Federal courts.

Section 2—subsection (a). In replacing the original Section 2 of the Clayton Act, this subsection has three important aspects: (1) It materially amends and extends the original prohibitions and provisos of the original Section 2; (2) keeping in mind the specific effects on competition to which the R-P Act was directed, it remains the basic prohibition of any forms of direct or indirect price discriminations leading to these effects; and (3) it provides for defense of certain price discriminations, especially by means of cost justifications (see the later discussion).

Section 2—subsection (b). This subsection is primarily of procedural significance. It provides, first of all, certain rules of evidence which are applicable to enforcement proceedings conducted by the Federal Trade Commission. Thus all respondents, accordingly, have the burden of justifying otherwise unlawful price discriminations by the defenses set up in subsection (a); or by showing that the lower prices were made "in good faith" to meet the equally low prices of competitors. Thus, it has been held in the *Standard Oil* case[14] that this "good faith" defense affords a complete defense to any charge of subsection (a) violations; and, in a limited sense, to subsection (e) proceedings.

Section 2—subsection (c). This is the famous, or infamous, "brokerage fee" section, depending on the point of view. It prohibits (a) payments by sellers of brokerage fees or commission fees to any buyer, buying agent, or any other wholesale middleman who acts for the buyer, or is subject to his control; and (b) it prohibits any but *bona fide* brokers from receiving such fees.

Section 2—subsection (d). This subsection "prohibits sellers from making *payment or allowance* to or for a customer's benefit as compensation for *merchandise services or facilities* furnished by a customer in connection with the processing, handling, sale or resale of goods, unless available 'on *proportionally equal* terms' to all competing customers."

Section 2—subsection (e). This subsection is closely related to (d). Such services or facilities as are mentioned in (d) may not be *furnished* by a seller to or for a purchaser, unless furnished to all competing purchasers on *proportionally equal* terms.

[14] *Standard Oil Co. v. F.T.C.*, 340 U. S. 231 (1951).

Section 2—subsection (f). This subsection provides: "That it shall be unlawful for any person engaged in the course of such (interstate) commerce, knowingly to induce or receive a discrimination in price which is prohibited by this section."

Section 3. This is a section of hybrid provisions. It incorporates, first, what was the Borah-VanNuys Bill, providing for criminal penalties of fines and/or imprisonment for violations. Under the criminal provisions, three specific sets of prohibitions are included which overlap Section 2 of the Clayton Act as amended:

1. Territorial price discriminations "for purpose of destroying competition or eliminating a competitor."
2. Sales at "unreasonably" low prices "for purpose of destroying competition or eliminating a competitor."
3. It is an offense for any person to be a party to or to assist in any sale which discriminates to his knowledge against competitors of the purchaser by the granting of "any discount, rebate, allowance, or advertising service charge," not available to such competitors in respect of a sale of goods of like grade, quality, and quantity.

Because this is a criminal section, its enforcement is handled by the Department of Justice, and *not* the Federal Trade Commission. The *Nashville Milk* case[15] has established that this section is *not* an antitrust law as defined by Section 1 of the Clayton Act, and, accordingly, neither the triple damages or injunctive relief provisions will apply.

Section 4. Cooperative associations are specifically exempted from R-P Act provisions under this Section. Further exemptions of purchases made by nonprofit religious, educational, and charitable institutions were provided for in P.L. 550, 75th Cong., Chapter 283.[16]

Relationship of the R-P Act to other regulatory laws

Austin has indicated the following relationships:[17]

1. Since Section 1 of the Clayton Act specifies it as one of the Federal antitrust laws, all of Section 2 of the R-P Act, as an amendment of Section 2 of the Clayton Act thus becomes a part of the antitrust laws. Thus, suits for triple damages become authorized.
2. The discriminations prohibited under the R-P Act amount to unfair methods of competition or unfair practices in commerce

[15] *Nashville Milk Co. v. Carnation Co.*, 355 U. S. 373 (1958).
[16] Austin, *op. cit.*, p. 4.
[17] *Ibid.*, pp. 11–13.

under Section 5 of the Federal Trade Commission Act. Thus, the Federal Trade Commission may issue complaints which contain parallel charges under both Acts.

3. The use of discriminatory practices by a single seller, such as local price cutting, may also be a violation of Section 2 of the Sherman Anti-Trust Act; and, also, of the Federal Trade Commission Act.

4. The use by a large buyer of its buying power and bargaining strength to secure unlawful discrimination (e.g., preferential prices, discounts, rebates, etc.) from sellers is prosecutable under the Sherman Act, or the Federal Trade Commission Act, for complaints which would constitute a violation of the Clayton Act as amended.[18]

5. The use of collusion or common understanding by two or more sellers to establish discriminatory pricing practices can be reached by the Sherman Act, in addition to possible prosecution under the Clayton Act.

6. Finally, many states have enacted statutes prohibiting price discriminations in intrastate transactions.

Weaknesses of the R-P Act

Edwards[19] had indicated several weaknesses in the R-P Act as passed. First, the law consists of many ambiguities in its basic language which have been, as will be seen later, the bases for many court battles, and for a wide range of recommendations, including outright repeal of the Act. A second difficulty indicated by Edwards stems from the fact that varying tests of illegality are applied to a range of business practices, and that these applications are nowhere coordinated. Third, despite the fact that Representative Patman indicated himself that the Act was directed mainly at the Great A&P Co., the final version seems more focused against the discriminatory conduct of sellers rather than against the power of "giant" buyers in the channel used to extract under buying advantages.

In addition, if the Act was designed to approach and deal with the problem of economic power in the channel of distribution, the pattern of attack as Edwards states it, "was oblique rather than direct." This shift was quite opposite, generally speaking, from the approach of

18 See *United States v. Great A&P Co.*, 173 F. 2d 79 (7th Circ., 1949).
19 Edwards, *op. cit.*, pp. 62–65.

the antitrust laws. There is an additional weakness stemming from the preceding. The antitrust laws prior to the R-P Act, were designed to deal with the various manifestations of monopolistic power especially at the producers' level. On the other hand, the R-P Act, by virtue of the provisions discussed above, could more often be directed toward the pygmies in the channel rather than against the giants. Finally, Edwards concludes: "The fact that the Robinson-Patman Act was designed to control trade practices and price relationships created in the statute a peculiar possibility of ambivalent results."

Cycles of Enforcement

Edwards has tabulated the types of violations under the R-P Act as found in 311 cases between 1937 and 1957 in which orders were issued (see Table 40). It will be seen immediately from the data that unlawful payments or receipt of brokerage fees under Section 2(c) accounted for the bulk of the violations—145 cases—excluding multiple violations. That this is so, would suggest as Edwards states, "a substantial distortion of focus in the administration of the law." Price discriminations by sellers under Section 2(a) were the next most common violation, consisting of 101 cases as such, and an additional 17 in combination with other types of violations. Including the multiple types of violations, then, these two groups accounted for 78.2 per cent of the total violations, and 85 per cent of the total orders during 1937–1957.[20] The methods of disposing of the 311 cases were as follows: admission answer—153; consent order—71; full trial—45; stipulation of facts—26; partial trial—16; and defaults by respondent—2.[21] During the same period, 119 complaints were discussed.

A further glance at Table 40 reveals quite irregular time distributions of the cases resulting in orders. The years 1939–1941 accounted for a total of 73 cases, or nearly one-fourth of the total of 311. After two years of comparative inactivity, there was another period of activity from 1944 to 1946 in which 58 orders were issued. This was followed, in turn, by 3 years of relative inactivity and, in turn, by increased activity in which 57 orders were issued between 1950 and 1953. Finally the period, 1955–57 was very active with a total of 68 orders.

[20] *Ibid.*, p. 70.
[21] *Ibid.*, p. 78.

TABLE 40

TYPES OF ROBINSON-PATMAN VIOLATIONS RESULTING
IN ORDERS, BY YEARS: 1937-1957

Type of Violation

Year	Sec. 2 (a)	Sec. 2 (c)	Sec. 2 (d)	Sec. 2 (e)	Sec. 2 (f)	Multiple	Total
1937	2	2	—	—	—	1 (a, f)	5
1938	7	2	—	—	—	1 (a, d, f)	10
1939	8	4	—	—	1	1 (a, d) 1 (a, f)	15
1940	4	15	1	1	—	3 (a, d)	24
1941	6	24	—	—	1	1 (a, d) 2 (a, d)	34
1942	2	7	—	—	—	1 (a, e)	10
1943	4	3	1	—	—	—	8
1944	3	9	2	1	2	1 (a, d)	18
1945	2	9	—	—	1	1 (a, d)	13
1946	1	23	—	—	—	—	24
1947	2	5	—	—	—	1 (a, d, f)	8
1948	3	3	—	—	—	—	6
1949	2	2	—	—	—	—	4
1950	5	6	—	—	2	—	13
1951	2	5	1	1	—	1 (c, d) 1 (c, f)	11
1952	9	3	3	—	—	1 (a, d) 1 (d, e)	17
1953	12	4	—	—	—	—	
1954	2	3	1	—	—	1 (d, e)	7
1955	8	5	1	—	—	1 (d, e)	15
1956	7	5	10	1	—	4 (d, e) 1 (a, e)	28
1957	10	6	7	1	—	1 (a, d)	25
Total	101	145	27	5	7	26	311

Source: Corwin D. Edwards, *The Price Discrimination Law* (Washington, D. C.: Brookings Institution, 1959), p. 679.

Rowe[22] has divided the 1937-1957 period of enforcement into three cycles: Cycle 1—the period of conservative enforcement in the early years of the R-P Act; cycle 2—the period of radical expansion in the forties; and cycle 3—the retreat of the fifties, whose ultimate direction remains to be fixed.

[22] Rowe, *op. cit.*

Cycle 1—the conservative period

As of August, 1937, the Federal Trade Commission had dismissed some 64 cases informally because of either a lack of demonstrable detriment to competition, or because the demonstrable price differences were so slight that no evidence could be produced to show any injurious effect on competition.

Between 1938 and 1940, the Commission instituted a very vigorous enforcement campaign with the resultant increase in the number of orders noted in Table 40. During this period, the Commission was able to secure a judicial interpretation of the brokerage clause which, for all practical purposes, limited the payment of brokerage fees to only those arrangements which met the narrow, orthodox interpretation under the law of agency. The A&P Co. lost its brokerage payments and, later, the joint buying offices of the voluntary chains similarly lost such brokerage payments, and were put on an equal treatment basis with the A&P.

Cycle 2—the radical expansion of the forties

Four key decisions were reached which gave rise to the characterization of this cycle of enforcement as the "radical expansion." In the *Corn Products* case,[23] it was held that promotional benefits not granted on "proportionally equal terms," were illegal *per se*, without any further inquiry into whether the market effects or other evidence indicated there was demonstration of competitive injury. In the first year, in the first of several orders in the *Standard Oil* case,[24] it was decided that the *"bona fide* meeting of competition" proviso was not available as a matter of law to justify price differentials which were found to create injury to competitors. Only after 13 years of heated and costly controversy was the principle reversed.

The Supreme Court in 1948 in the *Morton Salt* case,[25] extended the ruling noted above in the *Corn Products* case by establishing a test of competitive injury substantially as follows: in effect, any price differential among competing customers is condemned if it is, "sufficient in amount to influence their resale price." Finally, in what

[23] *Corn Products Refining Co. v. F.T.C.*, 324 U. S. 726 (1945); affirming 144 F. 2d 211 (7th Cir. 1944).

[24] *Standard Oil Co.*, 41 F.T.C. 263 (1945), order modified, 43 F.T.C. 56 (1946); further modified and affirmed, *Standard Oil Co. v. F.T.C.*, 173 F. 2d 210 (7th Cir. 1949); reversed and remanded 340 U. S. 231 (1951); order set aside *Standard Oil Co. v. F.T.C.*, 233 F. 2d 649 (7th Cir. 1956); and affirmed *F.T.C. v. Standard Oil Co.*, 355 U. S. 396 (1958).

[25] *Morton Salt Co. v. F.T.C.* 334 U. S. 37 (1948).

Rowe calls "the high water mark in *per se* illegalization," the *Minneapolis-Honeywell* case,[26] the Federal Trade Commission ruled: "that, to the extent that business is held . . . or diverted by a price differential, competition has been adversely affected within the meaning of the law." As indicated in the footnote, this ruling was reversed in 1951.

Cycle 3—the period of retreat and vacillation in the fifties

The Supreme Court's decision in the *Standard Oil* case in 1951, ended, according to Rowe, the period of radical extension of the R-P Act. Standard Oil's contention may be summarized as follows: the Federal Trade Commission's refusal to honor the *"bona fide* meeting competition" statutory defense hampered (*a*) a seller's pricing flexibility, and (*b*) the process of price competition, so severely, as to result in fostering the very price rigidities which were opposed in the antitrust laws. The Supreme Court, in reversing the Commission's position, acknowledged the existence of the latent clash between the antitrust enactments. It reaffirmed that

. . . the heart of our national economic policy long has been faith in the value of competition [and that]
. . . Congress did not seek by the Robinson-Patman Act either to abolish competition or so radically curtail it that a seller would have no substantial right of self-defense against the price raid by a competitor. [Furthermore, the Court saw no need to]
. . . reconcile, in its entirety, the economic theory which underlies the Robinson-Patman Act with that of the Sherman and Clayton Acts.[27]

A new era for competitive pricing appeared to be possible in 1953, according to Rowe, when the Supreme Court declared that overzealous enforcement of the R-P Act could "help to give rise to a price uniformity and rigidity in open conflict with the purpose of antitrust legislation.[28] A year later, in the *General Foods* case,[29] the Federal Trade Commission gave its council the duty to prove the existence of actual injury in any price discrimination proceeding, and adopted the doctrine of the Minneapolis-Honeywell case cited above. The Commission, in the *Purex* case,[30] concluded that the true test was not

26 *Minneapolis-Honeywell Regulator Co.*, F.T.C. Docket 4920, 44 F.T.C. (1948); Rev. *Minneapolis-Honeywell Regulator Co. v. F.T.C.*, 191 F. 2d 786 (7th Cir. 1951); cert. denied 12/22/52.
27 340 U. S. 231 (1951).
28 346 U. S. at 63.
29 *General Foods Corp.*, F.T.C. Docket 5675 (1954).
30 *Purex Corp.*, F.T.C. Docket 6008 (1954).

whether "an individual competitor was injured," but whether "competition was injured."

Since 1953, Rowe indicates the Commission "has oscillated between automatic inferences of competitive injury and more realistic inquiries into the market effects of challenged pricing practices."

Results of the R-P Act: Introductory Statements

Depending upon who is doing the evaluation, the opinions of the R-P Act vary from unadulterated complete criticism, to middle-of-the-road point of view represented by "on the one hand and on the other. . . ," to complete uncritical acceptance. Learned and Isaacs,[31] early in the history of the R-P Act, prepared a long list of expected secondary effects which were either not intended or foreseen by these sponsors. Oppenheim, in a recent review,[32] uses such adjectives as these:

> . . . chameleon-like Act [p. 57].
> Congress in this instance gave birth to a statute which has a duality of objectives, only some of which are susceptible to reconciliation with the "broader antitrust policies" [p. 57].
> Despite its classification as one of the antitrust laws, Robinson-Patman is a mixture of a few antitrust standards with other standards designed predominantly to regulate the level of competition among individual competitors without requiring proof of substantial impairments of market competition [p. 58].
> . . . enigmatic statute [p. 64].
> . . . controversial enactment [p. 64].
> . . . vexatious statute [p. 65].

A considerably more vitriolic evaluation is offered by Rowe, at the conclusion of his 20-year review.[33]

> As the offspring of a mixed marriage between antitrust and NRA, Robinson-Patman was manifestly destined from birth for a schizoid future. With the act approaching maturity today, twenty-one years after, the neurotic drift in its direction reflects its legal split personality.

[31] Edmund P. Learned, and Nathan Isaacs, "The Robinson-Patman Act: Some Assumptions and Expectations," *Harvard Business Review,* **XV** (Winter 1937), 137–155.

[32] S. Chesterfield Oppenheim, "Selected Antitrust Developments in the Courts and Federal Trade Commission During Past Year (1958–59)," American Bar Association, *Section on Antitrust Law,* Annual Proceedings, Vol. 15 (1959), pp. 37–73.

[33] Rowe, *op. cit.,* p. 1088.

Even as early as 1937, Learned and Isaacs had begun to detect the main aspects of criticism which are now in much bolder relief.

The Robinson-Patman Act suffers from many causes of ambiguity; it pretends to be what it is not when it puts forward a check on competition in the guise of an anti-trust law; it combines for the sake of a compromise what are really two statutes independently developed without making an effort to render them consistent; it assumes a great many general propositions about business practices, some of which are obviously untrue; and it attempts to extend the Federal power over matters which heretofore have been considered purely intrastate.

Behind all this doubt and confusion we discern a reason to remove an evil. That evil is the abuse of competitive power. In other words, the statute is based on the recognition that competition is not necessarily at all time and in all its manifestations a social good. But while serving this major purpose an experiment of this kind must be watched for its incidental results, its social and economic dislocations, its pressure upon business to seek new escapes for the purpose of avoiding if not evading new pressures. *In the case before us, the crop of these incidental aftergrowths seems to be quite likely one of major proportions.* Therefore no matter how deep our sympathy with the victims of the aggressiveness of powerful competitors, no matter how receptive business may be to the spirit of the Act, or how willing it may be to restrain itself, to refrain from troublesome litigation and take bearing or from hiding behind the words of the law, *the obligation nonetheless lies at the door of the government to put this piece of legislation in such shape as to minimize doubts* and *dangers; in a word to canalize it between safe banks* [italics added].[34]

Twenty-two years later, the Federal Government has yet to take such suggestions seriously.

Mention has been made in Chapter 21 of Hamilton's evaluation of the concept of "soft competition" created in the R-P Act as against the concept of "hard competition" in the Sherman Act. Other references have been made to his statement of the myths of the "invocation of the rhetoric of good faith" and of the "creation of the concept of effective competition." Hamilton has some additional comments to make about the provisions of the R-P Act.

1. The Act is not drawn as *exactly and tightly* as the Federal courts might wish.
2. The Act contains clauses which "make the effect on competition so minute and so hard to discover as to become unworkable."
3. The dominant purpose of the Act is still in *strict accord* with the Sherman Act.
4. The R-P Act is aimed at the "squeeze play" in the channels of distribution whereby the integrated manufacturer is both the

[34] Learned and Isaacs, *op. cit.,* pp. 154–55.

independent wholesale and/or independent retail middlemen's source of supply, and competitor as well, in such channels.

5. *"To allow the seller of goods for resale to discriminate in price is to corrupt the competitive process, to replace efficiency with favoritism, and to promote the concentration of economic wealth"* [italics added].[35]

The opinions of Edwards paraphrased from his recent study will be presented in a later section.

Results of the R-P Act: Cost Justification Rules

Any student of the Robinson-Patman Act must be indebted to Herbert F. Taggart for his labor of love in working through the volume of evidence submitted in every case in which the issue of cost justification was presented; and, in deriving from this labor of love and painstaking analysis, certain "rules of the game."[36] In summarizing these rules, he distinguishes between technical and more general precepts. Space will permit only the presentation of the basic rules in this, and in the following section, without his detailed comments.

Technical precepts

Taggart presents eight technical precepts which he states as follows:

1. The differential cost approach to cost justification is totally unacceptable.
2. A corollary to the differential cost rule is that no distinction be drawn in Robinson-Patman studies between fixed and variable costs.
3. The method of allocating overhead which has elsewhere in this volume been designated as the "bootstrap" method is unacceptable as a cost defense.
4. Cost classification and analysis methods used in the seller's regular accounting procedures are not necessarily appropriate for Robinson-Patman purposes.
5. Management estimates of major elements of cost are not acceptable, no matter how long and honorable their history of use within the company, unless they are supported by something in the way of tangible, factual background.
6. Time is the only really satisfactory basis for the allocation of the cost of personal services.

[35] Hamilton, *op. cit.*, in "The Use of Competition," pp. 142–52.
[36] H. F. Taggart, *Cost Justification,* Michigan Business Studies, Vol. XIV (Ann Arbor, Mich.: University of Michigan, 1959), Chapter 20.

7. The use of sampling is a completely acceptable method of reducing the cost and time required for analysis.
8. Relatively few positive statements can be made about the allocation or treatment of specific cost items.

More general precepts

In addition to the above eight rules which affect many technical aspects of R-P Act cost justifications, Taggart offers the following three more general precepts:

1. In no case should the problem of cost justification be turned over to the "second team" (management).
2. Every cost-justification study must be aimed at convincing the Commission accounting staff.
3. With respect to studies made subsequent to a complaint, or as a result of investigative procedures which immediately precede a complaint, the advice of the Commission accounting staff should be sought.

Results of the R-P Act: Over-All View

Apart from Taggart's exhaustive analysis of the cost justification provisions and results of the R-P Act, the two most complete appraisals have been those of Corwin Edwards,[37] and the Attorney General's Report.[38] This section will concentrate on a summarization of Edwards' findings,[39] although some reference will be made to the Attorney General's Report. Edwards' findings were organized around the following eight questions:

1. Was there a problem that justified action?
2. Did the Act meet the problem successfully?
3. Did the statute reach beyond the problem it was meant to meet?
4. Was efficiency affected?
5. Was the vigor of competition affected?
6. Did the law affect price movements?
7. Do the bad effects necessarily accompany the good ones?
8. Could a better law be enacted?

Was there a problem that justified action?

Three main pieces of evidence are supplied to indicate that there was a problem that justified Federal regulatory action. *First,* a series

---

[37] See footnote 4 in this chapter.

[38] *Report of the Attorney General's National Committee to Study the Antitrust Laws* (Washington, D. C.: U. S. Government Printing Office, March 31, 1955), Chapter IV, Section D.

[39] Edwards, *op. cit.,* Chapter 19.

of cases[40] have indicated problems of price discrimination significantly related to competition, in which there were either deliberate attempts to destroy competitors, or in which the channel power of giant buyers was demonstrated. As has been indicated earlier, one of the peculiarities of the evidence submitted by Edwards is the extent to which both small businesses and unimportant industries have been involved. *Second,* many examples have been uncovered of price structures both of dubious economic usefulness as well as of probable anticompetitive tendencies. This aspect of the R-P cases needs considerably more research. *Finally,* Edwards concludes that many cases have revealed that the problems posed by price and other forms of discrimination were considerably more complex than was ever recognized by either the sponsors of the Act, or by members of Congress.

Did the Act meet the problem successfully?

On the affirmative side, the following evidence is submitted: Effective protection has been afforded against the predatory price-cutting activities of would-be monopolists; there have been substantial reductions in the discriminatory price advantages enjoyed by the large buyers; chain stores have "practically" ceased to receive brokerage payments; allowances and services have been made available to customers on more equitable bases; sellers have increased their policing of advertising allowances to make certain that the advertising has taken place, and the allowance not used merely as a form of price concession; the price advantages formerly enjoyed by the big buyers either has been eliminated or substantially reduced; more customers appear to be eligible for discounts under revised schedules; and, finally, there has been some diminution of the pressure of big buyers for price concessions.

Despite this imposing list of apparent successes, Edwards points out four areas of failures:

1. The R-P Act has some serious gaps. Only sellers, for example, are liable for violations relating to services and allowances. The provision of the buyer's liability, where unlawful price concessions are concerned, has been badly conceived. Because of its burdensomeness, Edwards believes this provision can no longer play an important part in future proceedings. And, except for the brokerage provisions, the receiver of discriminatory concessions is hard to reach under the existing language.

---

[40] *Muller and Co. v. F.T.C.,* 142 F. 2d 511 (6th Cir. 1944); *Maryland Baking Co. v. F.T.C.,* 243 F. 2d 716 (4th Cir. 1957); *Champion Spark Plug Co.,* F.T.C. Docket 3977 (1953); and *United States v. Great A & P Co.,* 173 F. 2d 79 (7th Cir. 1949).

2. Because the R-P Act requires *separate* actions against sellers or buyers when there has been a conspiracy, the *net effect has been to discriminate in enforcement, and proved most often against sellers.*
3. As has been indicated earlier, the Act strikes mainly at *manifestation* of power rather than at the power itself. There are methods of power not covered; and one might add that the Act has stimulated undoubtedly new methods yet undiscovered. The Act has stimulated product differentiation, especially through middlemen's brands, because goods which are *not* of like grade and quality are not covered. And, the "giant" sellers and buyers may use selective tactics in the channel to secure a larger degree of channel control.
4. The R-P Act, while curbing discriminatory practices of the giants, has curbed also the practices of many smaller businesses designed to furnish marketing protection against the powerful. Thus, the capacity of the independent to protect himself has been weakened. A notable exception not mentioned by Edwards has been the growing strength of the voluntary chains even though they have run afoul of the brokerage provisions of the Act.[41]

Did the statute reach beyond the problem it was meant to meet?

Edwards points out that, under the brokerage fee provisions, certain examples of petty chiseling were prevented, and the inflexible orthodox theory of the brokerage function was enforced. Sometimes, the Federal Trade Commission enforced the use of channels which the wholesale middlemen did not want.[42]

Because of fear of prosecution under the advertising allowance provisions, certain unharmful selective advertising practices may have been inhibited. Sometimes the Commission has detected competitive injury in the channel even when the so-called "injured" customers claimed no injury. Finally, Federal regulation has become involved in many day-to-day marketing practices while losing sight of the more important problems of monopoly and oligopoly so far as concentration of economic power is concerned.

Was efficiency affected?

Edwards believes that, through the intensive application of the R-P Act, there have been realized a variety of improvements in business practices. He believes also that businesses have increasingly analyzed their price structures in order to get better relationships between cost and price differentials.[43] Finally, he suggests some respects in which

[41] See *Independent Grocers' Alliance Distributing Co. v. F.T.C.*, 203 F. 2d 941 (7th Cir. 1953).

[42] *Luxor, Ltd.*, 31 F.T.C. 658 (1940).

[43] The author believes that this is an area where considerably more evidence and research is needed.

there have been obstacles to full efficiency: (*a*) undue emphasis on proportionality of services; (*b*) adverse effects, on occasion, on channels of distribution; (*c*) *an increasing unwillingness of sellers to experiment with new methods of sale and with channels of distribution that might increase marketing efficiency;*[44] and (*d*) the "excessive sweep of the law" probably has increased expenses because of the careful legal and economic analyses required.[45]

Was the vigor of competition affected?

In Edwards' opinion, the "excessive sweep of the law" has tended to reduce the vigor of competition. Again, as has been emphasized earlier by Hamilton, sellers and buyers, when faced by the uncertainty of prosecution under the Act, tend to "play it safe." Buyers bargain less vigorously; prices are maintained by sellers for longer periods of time, and often without regard to shifting marketing conditions; once a price structure has been proved legally "safe," sellers are likely to introduce few changes; and, as a result, price changes become less frequent. Selective or localized price reductions appear to be hazardous. He concludes: "*Where diverting business from competitors is legally hazardous competition itself tends to become hazardous.*"[46]

Did the law affect price movements?

Buyers and sellers alike emphasize that the R-P Act has diminished price flexibility; and, unfortunately, all too many consider this to be one of the chief *virtues* of the Act! In political hassels over the Act, it is argued that if it serves to throttle price concessions, then everybody will tend to pay higher prices. And, if a seller can longer (or is afraid to) make special price reductions, he will only make overall price reductions when the marketing pressures assume enough strength. Edwards points out also that, in the price discrimination cases involving Federal Trade Commission orders, the price movements resulting have been neither uniformly higher or lower than the previous bases.

Do the bad effects necessarily accompany the good ones?

Edwards points out several. In his opinion, the proportionality sections should be applied equally against both sellers and buyers, and

---

[44] The reader should compare this with Hamilton's observations in Chapter 21.

[45] Of course, to the extent that these become costs of doing business, part of the burden may be transferred to the government through income tax avenues.

[46] Edwards, *op. cit.*, p. 630 (the italics are added).

not with the present exemptions for buyers. Disproportionate payments should not be considered as automatically illegal until the competitive impacts have been determined. Buyers' conduct under Section 2(f) should not be made merely corollary to a seller's conduct under Section 2(a).

Finally, he points out four other difficulties more deeply imbedded in the R-P Act: (1) Every move made by the marketing officials of buyers' and sellers' firms may require legal counsel; (2) since prosecution involves selective legal proceedings, as noted above, the first business firm investigated and made subject to a ruling is, in a sense, discriminated against; (3) cost justifications, as Taggart has indicated, are time consuming, expensive, and fraught with uncertainty; and (4) the discrimination in prosecution noted in (2) has contradictory effects on competitors, and has created, in addition, an inflexibility in R-P Act cases which has not been sufficiently the concern of those charged with responsibility for Federal regulatory policy.

Could a better law be enacted?

Although the more detailed viewpoints in answer to this will be presented in the next section, Edwards' summary statement is important here:

What has just been said implies that the Robinson-Patman Act could be amended to accomplish its purposes more successfully. There is little doubt that a bill could be drafted that would be a great improvement on the present statute.

However, whether or not such a bill could be passed is problematical. In law-making, group interests and conflicting ideas come into conflict and result in modifications of legislative proposals in the search for a compromise that will win legislative and executive assent. This is always an uncertain process. . . .[47]

Taggart states the same opinion in somewhat more colorful language in the preface to his book:

This book is not for him who thinks the Robinson-Patman Act will go away if he ignores it long enough. It is, instead, for the man, who whether he likes the Act or not, adopts the wholly safe assumption that the Act is here to stay. The only amendments which appear at all likely to stand a chance in Congress are those which are intended to strengthen the Act and to make price differentiation, in particular, still harder to defend. Intelligent compliance may be said to be the theme, then, rather than the mere implementation of defense.[48]

[47] *Ibid.*, p. 634.
[48] Taggart, *op. cit.*, "Preface," p. v.

What Can Be Done with the R-P Act?

Although the author's marketing bias leads him to conclude that the best approach would be to repeal the R-P Act and begin anew, he recognizes, also the pragmatic truth of the Edwards' and Taggart's points of view.[49] Starting then, with the ten-point program for regulatory reform outlined in Chapter 21, what can be done specifically to modify the R-P Act? Edwards suggests five areas.[50]

1. The brokerage provisions should be eliminated.
2. The same policy provisions presently included towards price discrimination should apply as well to sales aids and payments for selling services.
3. Discriminations affecting competition between first-line sellers in the channel, should be forbidden when reduction in market competition actually results. Cost justification of these should rest on the question of "good faith in accounting and forecasting."
4. Substantial revisions are needed in the treatment of discriminations likely to hurt competition in the second line.
    a. Sharp differentiation should be made between the purposes of protection of market competition and that of assurance of equality; and the latter should be eliminated.
    b. Appropriate exemptions in (a) should be provided for small businesses.
    c. Rules should be established governing buyers' conduct, and proceedings should be directed, when necessary, against buyers.
    d. The "good faith" provision of sellers should be replaced by a definition which, while assuring action against real damage to competition among buyers, does not preclude desirable buying practices.
    e. If the foregoing is not sufficient, supplementary rules governing sellers' conduct should be separately stated in order that they cover only sellers dealing with powerful buyers, and make provision for the balancing effects on competition on the two sides of the market under such cases.
5. Finally, if the supplementary rules in 4(e) are invoked, those sellers selling to powerful buyers should be required to do so in published price schedules.

[49] For a strong view supporting repeal, see Bain, *op. cit.*, pp. 572–73.
[50] Edwards, *op. cit.*, Chapter 20.

There seems to be no question but that Edwards and Taggart are probably accurate in their evaluation of the strength of the political support behind the R-P Act. This support continues unabated despite the Act's failure to achieve the sponsors' original objectives; and, despite its success in stimulating the undesirable results already noted. Further difficulties stem from the wide range of experts' ideas as to what to do with the R-P Act. This range is nowhere present more strongly than in the Attorney General's Report. These experts do have wide agreement, however, that the central philosophy concentrate on the "vigor of competition in the market rather than hardship to individual businessmen."

Consonant with these policies, the Committee recommends that analysis of the statutory "injury" center on the vigors of competition in the market rather than hardship to individual businessmen. *For the essence of competition is a contest for trade among business rivals in which some must gain while others lose, to the ultimate benefit of the consuming public* (italics added). Incidental hardships on individual businessmen in the normal course of commercial events can be checked by a price discrimination statute only at the serious risk of stifling the competitive process itself. Nor should competitive price reduction be singled out as responsible for "injury" if alternative means of access to goods at the lower price are in any event available to the buyer.[51]

One final set of comments appears to be justified. The R-P Act, however amended, needs to be incorporated in its entirety into the structure of antitrust laws in the United States. Businessmen should not be given the opportunity to pick the regulatory agency in which to pursue delaying tactics. Further, the entire set of recodified antitrust laws, in general, and an amended R-P Act, in particular, need to be specific about their regulation of unfair competition in the channels of distribution. In this way, criteria of competitive behavior at any level of a channel and for the channel as a whole can become much more meaningful.

QUESTIONS AND PROBLEMS

1. Do you agree with the statement that perhaps no piece of legislation has had as turbulent a history as the Robinson-Patman Act?
2. What are the economic-socio-political roots of the Robinson-Patman Act?
3. To what extent may price discrimination be viewed as a purely competitive device? as a device of monopolistic competition?
4. What are the major purposes of price discrimination? How are these related to the forms which price discrimination may take?
5. State concisely the original objectives of the Robinson-Patman Act.

[51] *Attorney General's Report, op. cit.,* pp. 164–65.

6. Outline the main provisions of the Robinson-Patman Act, and its relationship to other forms of regulation.

7. What weaknesses does Edwards find in the Robinson-Patman Act?

8. To what extent can cycles of enforcement be detected in the period 1937–1957? What are the principal identifying features of each cycle?

9. Evaluate the Learned-Isaacs statement in the light of the original objectives of the Robinson-Patman Act.

10. What is meant by "cost justification rules"? How do the technical precepts differ from the general precepts?

11. Summarize the Edwards findings as reported in the chapter. Do you disagree with any of these findings? If so, why?

12. Do you agree with the Taggart thesis that the Robinson-Patman Act is here to stay?

13. Do you believe that the Edwards recommendations for revisions are far enough reaching?

14. Why has the Robinson-Patman Act been so difficult to evaluate in its first twenty years of operation?

23

Selected Trends: Functions and Structures of Wholesale Markets

The discussion of changes in the wholesaling sector has been presented at various chapters throughout this book.[1] Therefore, the discussion of trends in this and the following chapter will be restricted, as the title indicates, to some selected aspects. This chapter is confined to only three sets of trends: First, changes in the functions and structures of agricultural goods, industrial goods, and manufactured consumers' goods markets, and the important reasons for such changes; and, second, the reasons for the resurgence in importance of the regular (orthodox) wholesaler. The final section will present the main changes between 1954 and 1958 based on such data as are available from the forthcoming *1958 Census of Business: Wholesale Trade*.

It was indicated at the very beginning of this book that the basic approach and underlying philosophy is compatible with the institutional approach.[2] This approach emphasizes the constancy and permanency of change in the structural organization of the market. The functional aspects have been discussed in detailed in connection with

[1] See especially Chapters 2 and 6.

[2] Edward A. Duddy and David A. Revzan, *Marketing: An Institutional Approach*, 2nd ed. (New York: McGraw-Hill Book Co., Inc., 1953), Chapter II and Appendix C.

the internal organization and policies of wholesale middlemen. Apart from trends in functions, what is being emphasized in this chapter are those trends centering around the biological aspects of the wholesale middlemen in an environment of structural relationships in wholesale markets; namely, their origins, peaks of life cycle importance, and ultimate decay or readaptation through change to begin a new organic cycle. The center of analytical viewpoint, as in all previous materials, will be the channel.

The forces making for change are quite complex and varied within this institutional approach framework, and the attempt to analyze these forces in any systematic fashion is complicated further by the necessity to study as well the varied attempts of the agencies involved to offset these, from time to time, with pressures making for stability. What can be presented here is primarily a cross-sectional view, so to speak, of some of the main currents. There are so many currents of change, so many nuances of component relationships within each current, and these vary so sharply between geographical segments, that only by concentrating on the main currents can the subject be included.

The General Pattern of Underlying Forces

This section will discuss some of the more important underlying forces of change without reference to any specific structural arrangement. The three sections which follow will then interweave these with the agricultural goods, industrial goods, and manufactured consumers' goods structural arrangements. While some duplication of presentation will be necessary, it is believed that the continuity of analysis so obtained will more than offset the disadvantages of duplication. The following sets of underlying forces will be included: technological changes; growth of consumers' goods markets; growth in industrial goods markets; changes in management policies; changes in market areas; and government regulation.

Technological changes

Perhaps the single most important force making for change in the wholesaling sector arise from a series of changes which may be grouped under the general heading of *technological*. By operating to effect changes in both the quantity and assortment aspects of what moves in, through, and out of the wholesaling funnel, these factors or changes cut across every component element of the wholesaling structure. Chapter 7 has dealt in detail with the technological factors involved in product assortments. All that remains to be done here, therefore, is to re-emphasize their relationship to: (a) the invention of new products which move through the channel, including the basic production machinery required in the evolving technological processes; (b) increases in the quantities of existing products produced, including increases arising from constantly improving productivity; and (c) increases in the varieties of existing products. A very important related effect will be discussed later under growth of industrial markets.

Growth of consumers' goods markets

The technological changes have placed pressures on the wholesaling funnel from the side of its broad opening. The growth in the consumers' goods markets places pressures on the funnel at the opposite end. One component of such pressures arises out of the purely qualitative aspects of numbers of persons. With the total population of the United States expected to reach 200 million persons on or before 1970, expansion in consumers' goods markets would be expected simply by virtue of the maintenance of existing per capita consumption levels. But, given the increases in varieties for the technological reasons noted, on the one hand, and rising economic ability by virtue of expanding incomes, on the other, then an additional multiplier effect on growth is obtained.

However these multiplier effects of changes in the numbers tend to operate, qualitative changes in the composition of the population will continue to act as important modifying influences. Perhaps the most significant of these qualitative changes is the change in the geographical structure of the population caused by the sharply shifting patterns between states; and, also, between the central city, noncentral cities and nonurban segments within each state and its component metropolitan areas. Because of the rapid migration of population into the so-called suburban fringes, we may expect within the next one to two decades a period of *recentralization;* i.e., the growth of present smaller suburban centers into cities of 100,000 or more persons each, paralleling a similar development in the 1920's.

Significant increases in the average age of the population will affect, qualitatively, the kinds of product assortments of consumers' goods. Any continuation of the present trend towards earlier family formations, and towards a rising average number of children per family, will continue to boom the sales of consumers' durable goods. Another important set of qualitative factors, obviously, arise from increases in the ratio of numbers of females to males, and in the average life span of the woman compared with the man. Any significant changes in Federal immigration policies will have important effects on the purchasing patterns in the markets where the immigrants will locate.[3]

Forecasted declines in the length of the average work week, coupled with continued improvements in the ratio of energy per person gainfully employed, will continue to boom the leisure time activities of the population. These increases in leisure time activities have obvious bullish effects on the sales of both tangible and intangible commodities. And from the travel activities there is an additional effect, already in full progress, namely, the increasing acceptance of, if not an outright insistence on, a wide range of products of foreign origin.

Growth of industrial goods markets

The growth of industrial goods markets stems, in part, from the technological factors and the growth of consumers' goods markets already discussed. But two other factors need to be noted: (1) the increasing demands of the Federal defense program; and (2) the increasing variety of institutional types of customers, other than the Federal Government. In addition, the increasing importance of the technological changes bring with them an increasing need for many auxiliary goods and services. As one example, the increased mechanization of so many operations brings into existence a whole new network of service establishments to maintain the operating efficiency, and to market necessary repair and replacement parts. One final aspect of the growth is tied in with the increasing pace of industrialization taking place in the world.

Changes in management policies

Previous chapters have dealt with the policy areas in which the managements of wholesale middlemen have to make decisions. Working within a framework of competition, especially as made effective through merchandising strategy, the decisions made by these managements serve to accentuate changes within the limits to which such decisions are the important determining factor. It should be remembered, however, that certain significant types of managerial actions are designed to preserve the status quo, rather than to initiate or accentuate changes.

Changes in market areas[4]

The pressures which result in changing the boundaries of wholesale market area boundaries stem from many sources. As a basic factor for the market areas of organized wholesale markets there are

[3] Note, for example, the "pockets" already found in the largest cities.

[4] See Duddy and Revzan, *op. cit.,* pp. 465–66.

fundamental changes in price relationships for the commodities involved. In addition, the changing relative importance of the central organized wholesale markets (to be discussed later) is an "envelope" factor based upon several contributing causes. All that needs to be emphasized here is the shift in geographical incidence as the wholesale markets move from key central city to production point locations.

A second aspect of the change in market areas is associated with the shift in the location of consumers already mentioned. Thus, for manufactured consumers' goods wholesale markets, the shifts in the location of population have meant: (a) an expansion in the rate of development of new wholesale markets in the areas of rapidly developing populations; and (b) a corresponding reduction in the relative importance of many existing wholesale centers. These differential developments, coupled with fundamental changes in the variety of available consumers' goods, serve to affect the entire geographical structure of wholesale market areas.

A final aspect of changing market areas stems from the transportation factor. This factor subdivides itself, in turn, into three components. The first of these components stems from the decentralizing effects resulting from the increased use of the motor truck. Because of the flexibility factor of the motor truck, the effects of the increased use of the motor truck include—on an oversimplified basis—the building up of the importance of the smaller and intermediate size groupings of wholesale centers, at the sales expense of the older, larger-size areas.

The second component has to do with the changing structure of freight rates, and railroad transit privileges. Apart from the effects of general increases in freights affect relationships between competing commodities and competing areas, the important effects stem from (a) the changing relationship of freight rates on raw goods and semi-processed and finished goods, most often in favor of longer movements of the latter; (b) the changing relationships between short, intermediate, and long hauls; (c) the ever widening extension of transit privileges to wholesale centers; and (d) the changing relationships between large-quantity and small-quantity movements.

Finally, the third component of the transportation factor has to do with the effect of the changing relationships in freight rates, noted above, on the incidence of where inventories are carried. Increasingly, the freight rate structures, except in special commodity cases, have encouraged a triple inventory position: production point versus key regional inventory buildup versus decentralized wholesale and/or retail inventories.

Government regulation

Chapters 21 and 22 have outlined the main effects of the evolving and changing patterns of regulatory patterns, and no further discussion need be added here.

Changes in Functions and Structures:
Agricultural Goods Wholesale Markets

Against the background of earlier discussions, and the discussion above of the pattern of underlying forces, the discussion now turns to an analysis of changes in function and structure in the three commodity groupings of wholesale markets. In each commodity grouping discussion, the pattern of presentation will be as follows: changes in functions discussed successively in terms of quantitative and qualitative aspects, as well as in terms of changes in methods of performance; changes in structure in terms of agency, area, and price; and, finally, a resumé of the underlying or controlling causes or forces.

Changes in functions: quantitative aspects

The last 40 years have seen a revolution in the functions of the wholesale agricultural goods markets, with sharp shifts from the dominance of the key organized primary markets to a combination of primary and local decentralized markets. For many farm products, as has been indicated in Chapter 5, the local markets have become more important than the primary markets. Accompanying this fundamental shift in importance has been a sharp change away from key price-determining responsibilities, to a combination of key wholesale price determination for selected farm products, and accentuated responsibility either for short-distance and time movements into processsing plants, or merely physical handling in conjunction with the pattern of the marketing processes. This shift will be discussed in a later section.

As a result of these changes in function, it is probably true to say that these wholesale markets are handling a smaller total of physical volume of products. An additional element in this reduction is the increased proportions of many edibles marketed in processed form, or through channels which by-pass the organized wholesale markets. Thus, integrated large-scale retail middlemen increasingly can and do make contractual arrangements, for example, for shipments directly from producing points to regional and local warehouses.

In lieu of price determination functions, greater emphasis has been placed for edible products on the increase in importance quantitatively of prepackaging functions by virtue of the greater impact of self service in retail stores. These prepackaging activities take place at any and every level of the channel. But this shift does not overshadow in quantitative importance, the increased importance of agricultural goods as primary and secondary raw materials in processing industries.

Even in those wholesale markets not so directly affected by the diversions in product movements noted above, there have been sharp quantitative effects on the price determination functions as a result of the parity price and other Federal government programs discussed in Chapter 21. Because of these control programs, the risk factor in the marketing of grains and other speculative commodities has been considerably reduced, affecting the hedging and speculative activities of the organized exchanges.[5]

A most argumentative aspect of the diversion of supplies of farm products from organized wholesale markets is whether or not there have been any significant effects upon the prices realized. Two ranges of possible effects should be noted:

1. Under the first situation, reductions both in the quantities offered for sale and in the range and width of quality grades should result in less systematic and more unrepresentative price distributions. Part of this result will stem from a reduction in the diversity and number of buying interests, as compared with the previous periods, because of the changes noted. And part of the result stems from the greater uncertainty as to both the quantity and the quality representativeness of the supplies offered for sale. Part of these effects may be offset by improvements in the quality of the market news and its dissemination.

2. In the second situation, if the wholesale market, after reductions in the supplies offered for sale, concentrates in marketing only the better qualities of products, it is quite possible that these better qualities of products will realize higher price premiums than formerly was the case. This would appear to be the result in fruit auctions in the sale of California oranges.

Of course, under these circumstances, the relative importance of certain types of selling and buying wholesale middlemen undergo

[5] See Fred M. Jones, "The Decline of Chicago as a Grain Futures Market," *The Journal of Marketing*, XII (July 1947), 61–65. See, also, Holbrook Working, "Whose Markets?—Evidence on Some Aspects of Futures Trading," *The Journal of Marketing*, XIX (July 1954), 1–11.

significant change. It is quite likely, also, that daily variations in prices will become more irregular because of the increased probability of exaggerated day-to-day changes in quantities offered for sale and their grade distribution. All in all, price determination in agricultural goods markets has become less competitive and more administered in nature.[6]

Qualitative changes in function

The most significant qualitative change stemming from the preceding would seem to be, first of all, a sharp increase in the importance of product assortments in the channels. One or two examples may suffice. In the case of livestock, under the centralized marketing pattern using important primary markets such as Chicago, product assortments existed by virtue of the width of available supplies offered, and the funnelling activities of a wide variety of wholesale middlemen. Animals were available for slaughtering, breeding, dairying, fattening, and reshipment. When the sharp shift took place to local markets, the restricted range of buyers in the local market makes adaptation of quality of livestock to this packer's needs much more limited. Remaining unsold supplies can be sold in other markets at satisfactory prices only if complementary demands exist, and adequate market news is available.

In the case of fresh fruit and vegetable markets, much depends upon whether the local processing plants merely process any grade of product, or use only the better quality gradations. In the latter case, the quality range available in the fresh products markets may decline, thus shifting demand more and more to processed products.

Changes in methods of performance

One type of change has been indicated above, namely, an increase in the prepackaging activities of middlemen and facilitating agencies. A second change may involve merely the reduction or elimination of the price-determining function in organized markets, and the substitution of negotiated or administered price arrangements. A third change, although unverifiable because of lack of data, may be a sharp increase in multitype activities.

Changes in agency structure

The main changes in the agency structure of the agricultural goods wholesale markets arise from the shrinking relative importance of

[6] Norman R. Collins, "Changing Role of Price in Agricultural Marketing," *Journal of Farm Economics,* XLI (August 1959), 528–34.

the wholesale markets noted above. This shrinking in importance is reflected, accordingly, in a corresponding decline in the importance of the assemblers' group. In addition, the decline in importance of the assemblers is related to the direct movement of farm products to processing plants, or because of direct sale of such products to large, integrated distributors who absorb the functions of the assemblers within their integrated organizational framework. And, despite the resurgence of the regular wholesaler, to be discussed later, only those handling raw material farm products have increased in importance.

Changes in area structure

The main directions of changes in the area structure of agricultural goods markets are as follows:

1. For livestock, a sharp shift towards supply area boundaries which are restricted to areas immediately adjacent to production areas, except for animals moving to slaughtering plants for the kosher market, or to be used for feeding and feeding purposes. This shift in areas has been most pronounced for the marketing of hogs, although there have been increasing movements as well of other species of livestock.
2. For fresh fruits and vegetables, there has been a strong continuation of the basic boundaries of supply and distribution areas for the primary central markets. Increasingly, however, supplies are moving directly from producing points to those secondary wholesale markets which formerly received substantial supplies as reshipments from the primary central markets.
3. Changes in the relative importance of the wholesale markets for edible agricultural goods collectively are related to the population and income changes discussed earlier. These changes in relative importance have effects in expanding the spatial outreach of the wholesale markets showing the greatest rate of growth.
4. The area structures for the organized commodity exchanges handling grains and related products have not been affected to the extent indicated for other categories of agricultural products, because of the different position of these markets in the wholesaling sector.
5. Because of the contraction in the outreach of many wholesale markets, it would be expected that, to that extent, there will be increased overlapping of boundaries with increase in the extent and area of zones of indifference.

Changes in price structures

Only brief reference need be made at this point to changes which have been discussed more completely in the preceding discussions of the decline in importance of systematic price structures. As a result, increasing blocs of prices are being determined either by government control or under noncompetitive, administered conditions. Although it cannot be said that price fluctuations have been eliminated during short-run time periods—except in the price-administered areas—it would appear to be accurate to say that: (1) increasingly, the prices determined in the organized wholesale markets are unrepresentative of the entire available base of product qualities, or of the sum total of available buying interests; (2) the price relationships are increasingly becoming less systematic; and (3) increasing areas of price determination are no longer made available in the Federal-state market news reports.

Resumé of underlying or controlling causes

Even to begin to relate the causes (factors) associated with the changes outlined is but to demonstrate what was meant by the statement that a myriad of causes is to be found, and that they intertwine in many ways to effect given changes. One basic cause has been the evolving technology underlying the fast frozen process, the development of dehydration processing, and the extension through chemical research of the uses of such products as soy beans. A second set of causes stems from the shift in areas of corn production, resulting, in turn, in a sharp increase in decentralized livestock slaughtering. Closely related and intertwined have been the decentralizing effects of increased use of motor truck transportation in the shipment of agricultural products.

Shifts in population have been mentioned in connection with the ever-increasing importance of new wholesale markets for the edible farm products. Changes in transportation rates and rate relationships have changed boundaries of wholesale market areas, and probably shifted long-haul movements from fresh to processed products.[7] The many factors leading to large-scale distribution of foods has fostered, in turn, large movements of fresh products direct from production points into warehouses rather than through wholesale markets. And, finally, the increased importance of government intervention into price

---

[7] This has been the case especially in livestock where changes in rates have favored the movement of the slaughtered animal as against the live animal.

determination, and the decline of competitive pricing has been mentioned more than once.

Changes in Function and Structure: Industrial Goods Wholesale Markets

Changes in functions: quantitative aspects

It is in the marketing of industrial goods that the spectacular increases both in quantity and assortment have taken place. The most obvious effect on functions has been in the direction of expansion of kinds-of-business categories in which the wholesale middlemen function. The second effect undoubtedly has been to increase the importance of physical handling. And the final aspect has been to broaden the product base on which specialization of function can take place.

The broadening of the quantity and variety has had other repercussions on the quantitative aspects of functions. For one, there has been a sharp increase in the importance of research, dollarwise, so far as the product planning functional aspect is concerned. The greatest stimulus to this increase undoubtedly originates from Federal Government spending, especially for such defense industries as atomic energy, missiles, and rockets. But an additional important stimulus arises from the cumulative effect of the search for new products on technological processes.

A final aspect of this section of quantitative change in functions has to do with an increase in the number of agencies needed to perform auxiliary or facilitating functions. These facilitating functional agencies cut across every level of the channel, and act as auxiliaries to almost every aspect of the basic functions of marketing strategy, buying and selling, and physical distribution. Indeed, an increasing number are appearing in connection with the increased emphasis placed on research, either to implement company-controlled research, or to furnish the complete function.

Changes in functions: qualitative aspects

Although no data are available, it seems reasonable to support the hypothesis that the preceding changes have had the following related qualitative aspects: (1) increased possibilities in specialization of function by concentrating on the increased numbers of more high-value types of products; (2) offsetting possibilities for widened product assortments by virtue of the appearance, also, of increased numbers of lower-value goods; (3) increased opportunities for multitype wholesale middlemen operations; and (4) greater needs for differentiation of industrial goods through advertising and sales promotion efforts. A case can be made, also, for increased nuances in combination of functions because of the widening range of products which have both industrial market and consumers' markets end uses.

Changes in methods of performance

Perhaps, the most dramatic change has been the "self-feeding" effects of the explosion in industrial goods; note, for example, the increased application of mechanization to warehousing activities. The interesting part of this self-feeding development has been not only in the dramatic change in warehousing activity, but, also, in the sale of other industrial equipment. Other dramatic changes can be noted in the increased use of electronic computers and other data-processing machines in the compilation and analysis of data, and the preparation of critical research conclusions, and the widening complementary lines spread wholesale middlemen's costs.

Changes in agency structure

It might have been expected that the sharp increases in quantities and assortments would have served to intensify direct marketing channels. But a careful analysis of available data seems to yield contrary results. The increased complexity of the expanding output of industrial goods has been more than matched by the increasing complexity in the varieties and importance of the users of such products. Thus, for certain categories of goods, the initial direct distribution is really only the first part of what may be called a multiple-phased channel arrangement. Correlated with this is the necessity for two levels of wholesale middlemen, involving both direct and indirect channels to reach various sizes and locations of customers. Because of this, and the reasons discussed in the next paragraph, the merchant wholesalers' group comes so close in importance to the manufacturers' sales branches and sales offices in marketing industrial goods.

Perhaps the most significant aspect of the change in agency structure has been the recent evidence that the incidence of direct marketing of industrial goods has been sharply overestimated. Appendix Table A1 has indicated that, while manufacturers' sales branches and sales offices accounted for 50.5 per cent of the gross industrial goods wholesale sales in 1954, the merchant wholesalers' group accounted for 41.1 per cent, and the agents and brokers group for 8.1 per cent. If the raw materials group of agricultural products and petroleum are included, then the merchant wholesalers' gross sales would exceed those of the sales offices and sales branches. Part of the explanation is to be found in the trend mentioned above; namely, the development of multi-phased channel arrangements. But a considerable part of the explanation is to be found in the resurgence of the orthodox wholesaler. This development, one of the key trends in the wholesaling sector, deserves and receives complete analysis in a separate section.

A far different aspect of agency structure change and development has been an increase in multiple-type wholesale middleman operations, especially among such types of merchant wholesalers as the industrial distributor. There is even the reverse situation in which manufacturers' sales branches and sales offices, in an ever-increasing group of businesses, handle complementary lines of other manufacturers in order to spread fixed costs, and to give salesmen more adequate total product assortments with which to attract customers.

One final segment of the change in agency structure should be noticed. Increasingly, as freight rate costs bear heavily on shipments of certain types of industrial goods, manufacturers engaging in direct distribution completely, or at least in the first phase of a multi-phase channel, find it more economical to use sales offices than sales branches. Thus, for many kinds of business, the average sales-size establishment for manufacturers' sales offices *exceeds* that for sales branches.

Changes in area structure

The rapid expansion of certain kinds of industrial goods businesses, especially of such types as electronics, has tended to accentuate the decentralization of location aspects. Part of this decentralization is due to the "footloose" locational characteristics of the industries involved. Other factors include changes in the degree of mechanization of industry, thus permitting more suburbanization; and the movement of new industrial goods industries to rapidly expanding standard metropolitan areas to keep pace with the growth in numbers and types of customers to be serviced.

On the other hand, centralization of location continues to characterize those industries in which scale and heavy capital investment are significant. A recent study of suburbanization of manufacturing activity between 1939 and 1947 concludes as follows:

In all size-groupings and in all but two of the regional groupings of S.M.A.'s (standard metropolitan areas), manufacturing was more centralized than population. Between 1939 and 1947 metropolitan manufacturing suburbanized in some parts of the nation, and centralized in other parts. Of the 13 economic regions of the United States, there was evidence of extensive suburbanization in three—the Pacific Southwest and the two regions of the Midwestern Province. There was a considerable increase in the centralization of manufacturing in another three regions—the Rocky Mountain and Inter-mountain Region, and the two economic regions (IX and X) in the extreme southern and western parts of the Southern Province. The 1939–47 pattern of growth in the other seven economic regions either showed no consistent trend toward centralization or suburbanization (for both value added and production workers), or caused almost no change in the central city-ring distribution that existed in 1939. Similar, though less marked, differences in trends were evident in the redistribution of manufacturing for groupings of S.M.A.'s by size of S.M.A., but these differences had little consistency with systematic variations in size.

Between 1939 and 1947, there was increased centralization of manufacturing activity (measured in terms of the members of production workers in 44 of the 125 principal S.M.A.'s. The change in suburbanization of the remaining 81 areas varied from negligible amounts to very marked increases in the suburbanization of manufacturing. Therefore, the analysis of factors related to the change in suburbanization of manufacturing was made separately for the 44 centralizing and 81 suburbanizing areas.

Among the 81 suburbanizing areas, the 1939–47 rate of suburbanization tended to be greater in the younger S.M.A.'s; in the S.M.A.'s which grew more rapidly during the same period but less rapidly during the preceding decade; in S.M.A.'s where a lower proportion of the labor force was engaged in manufacturing activity; and in S.M.A.'s where manufacturing suburbanized less, or centralized more, during the preceding decade. In those S.M.A.'s which centralized their manufacturing between 1939 and 1947, the rate of centralization tended to be greater in S.M.A.'s which grew more during the same period but grew less during the preceding decade.[8]

These mixed movements of centralization and suburbanization may be expected to continue to characterize the location of manufacturing activities since 1947, although service industries and offices have moved to suburbs in increasing numbers.[9] Chapter 4 contains additional data of the basic geographical structure of extractive and manufacturing production in 1954.

Changes in price structure

The structure of many of the industrial goods kinds of business favors the existence of non-competitive price policies. Patent monop-

[8] Evelyn M. Kitagawa, and Donald J. Bogue, *Suburbanization of Manufacturing Activity within Standard Metropolitan Areas,* Studies in Population Distribution No. 9 (Oxford, Ohio: Scripps Foundation, Miami University, 1955), pp. 32; 67–68.

[9] See John Christie and Melvin J. Goldberg, "Crisis of the Cities: Industry Heads for the Open," *Dun's Review and Modern Industry,* February 1960, 35–37. They mention four factors: (1) the suburbs offer more fresh air and room to grow at less cost; (2) initially lower tax rates; (3) increasing labor-force supplies because of favorable population expansion; and (4) more favorable highway transportation and parking space.

olies exist in abundance; and where these are not important, the concentration ratios accounted for by the dominant firms, industry by industry, favor monopolistic or oligopolistic structures. In addition, many of the customers have similar structural characteristics.

Apart from the effects of the Robinson-Patman Act already summarized and discussed in Chapter 22, the main changes in price structure stem from the declaration as illegal the entire basing-point system.[10] The present status of geographical pricing is everywhere in very muddled condition. Nowhere is this more evident than in the varied opinions of delivered pricing contained in the Attorney-General's Report.[11] Out of the confusion, one set of conclusions has been stated as follows which incorporate sound evaluation:

1. In the absence of demonstrable collusion, and with no evidence of price discrimination in either the antitrust laws on Robinson-Patman Act meanings, f.o.b. prices appear to be legal.
2. In the absence of demonstrable collusion, again, a pricing formula based upon point-of-production price plus actual freight to buyer's place of business seems to be safe. Under this formula, the legality of such pricing is strengthened if the buyer is given the option of purchasing at the point of production if he so desires.
3. If an individual seller occasionally absorbs freight, this practice would appear to be acceptable if such practice appears, in turn, to have no relationship to the pricing activities of competing sellers, and if those buyers who fail to receive such concessions *almost* establish damage to their competitive positions.
4. As indicated in Chapter 22, geographical price differentials are legal where made in good faith to meet the *bona fide* legal prices of competitors.
5. Blanket uniform delivered prices to all classes of buyers continues to be legal.
6. Zone uniform delivered prices may be legal if there is no evidence of collusion or injury to competition.[12] Considering the implications of the above, it can be understood why nowhere else in the wholesaling sector are Hamilton's "dilemmas of regulation" so well illustrated.

[10] See *Federal Trade Commission v. Cement Institute*, 333 U. S. 683 (1948).
[11] Attorney General's Report, *op. cit.*, pp. 209–220.
[12] Based upon R. S. Vaile, E. T. Grether, and R. Cox, *Marketing in the American Economy* (New York: The Ronald Press Co., 1952), p. 705. See, also, Corwin D. Edwards, "Doing Business Under the Present Law about Delivered Prices," *Louisiana Law Review,* XI (March 1951), 347–65; and J. S. Bain, *Industrial Organization* (New York: John Wiley and Sons, Inc., 1959).

One additional change in price structure may be mentioned; namely, the increasing significance of the military in certain types of purchases made in relation with the post-World War II defense program. Here are introduced all the intricacies of pricing under Federal Government contracts, together with the frequent disregard of the antitrust laws by the defense authorities mentioned by Hamilton.

Resumé of underlying or controlling causes

At the foundation of much of the change in functions and structure noted is the "New Industrial Revolution." This "revolution" has cut across every segment of change in the industrial goods markets—basic inventions, accessory products inventions, technological processes, and product improvements—just to mention a few. A second cause stems from the population explosion which, by increasing the demand for many types of consumers' goods, has a multiplier effect on the industrial goods need directly and indirectly by the agencies involved. A third group of causes originate with World War II—the expansion of certain defense industries accompanying the war effort, and the subsequent postwar defense needs. A fourth group of causes is found in the availability of capital resources. And, a final set of causes stem from Federal Government regulation in the antitrust laws area; the elimination of the basing-point price system; the fluctuating attitude towards mergers; the effects of the Robinson-Patman Act; and the continued protection of the patent laws.

Somewhat different, but nevertheless significant, is encompassed in that intangible which characterizes so much of present-day thinking, the worship of science and scientists. This leads, in turn, to the development of a widespread belief in the creation of continuous miracles of inventions and product improvements. And, in many cases, these miracles have appeared accentuating the rate of product and process obsolescence.

Changes in Function and Structure: Manufactured Consumers' Goods Wholesale Markets

Changes in function: quantitative aspects

The expansion of the consumers' goods wholesale markets is related closely to the basic factors enumerated at the beginning of this chapter. What needs to be emphasized here, once again, has been the expansion in the wholesale funnel needed to handle both the expanded physical volumes of existing products and the introduction of many new products. Especially significant has been the very large expansion which has taken place in consumers' durable goods. Often overlooked, however, are the expanding quantities of tangible goods needed in connection with the increasing supplies and varieties of intangible services.

But quantitative changes in function have originated, also, in response to the changing agency structural relationships to be discussed later, and to the impact of these changes upon channel patterns. Expedited market obsolescence of consumers' goods, both durable and nondurable, have had significant impacts upon how rapidly marketing functions in the wholesaling sectors, as encompassed in wholesale middlemen agencies, can push new styles into the channel, and "skim the cream" off the potential demand before obsolescence becomes significant in this connection. Thus the long-playing monaural phonographic record was no more than 10 years of age in the channel before stereophonic records and tape gave it a rude competitive thrust.

The exposure of many segments of the population to travel in foreign countries, first during their military careers and, more recently, as travelers, has placed a sharp quantitative burden on the functioning of wholesale markets to tap ever-widening sources and varieties of consumers' goods from foreign countries. Significantly, this ever-widening list is including more and more durables in sharp contrasts to previous periods of imports.

Changes in function: qualitative aspects

The combination of ever-widening quantities and assortments of consumers' goods, coupled with price rigidities induced by government regulatory activities, has served to place a continuing premium upon the qualitative aspects of functions, especially the quality of the merchandising strategy. As has been noticed in the previous discussion of the Robinson-Patman Act, there has been a sharp increase in the use of middleman-controlled brands. Furthermore, the increasing impact of scrambled marketing at the retail level has had corresponding impacts upon the functioning of old and new wholesale middlemen in the channels who must provide these scrambled assortments. Thus, in the performance of the marketing processes, continued high importance continues to be attached to the adaptation of the unit and form of purchase to the needs of the ultimate consumers.

Changes in function: method of performance

In the warehousing operations for consumers' goods, mechanization has been as significant as for industrial goods, or perhaps even more important. This mechanization includes all of the equipment and

devices discussed earlier. The continuing increase of self-service at
the retail level continues to place emphasis upon opportunities for
prepackaging at the manufacturers' and wholesale middlemen's levels.
Products ranging in physical characteristics from the highly perishable
foods to the smaller durables sold in hardware shops have been so
prepared. Increasingly, also, this prepackaging becomes evident in
the ever-widening assortments of products retailed through vending
machines which are serviced, of course, by certain types of wholesale
middlemen.

The increase in the width of assortments of consumers' goods, especially of the semidurable and durable varieties, has increased the
incidence of product servicing which must be offered through the
channel. In addition, it has had repercussions on where the inventories of such products should be carried in the channel. More and
more, the wholesaling sector embraces the possible inventory locations
in this agency tug of war.[13]

Changes in agency structure

Along with the edible farm products group, the manufactured consumers' goods channels continue to utilize the widest varieties of types
of wholesale middlemen. The resurgence of the regular (orthodox)
wholesaler is of key significance here as will be discussed shortly.
In the food field, the integrated wholesaler-retailer cooperative chains
have surpassed the corporate chains in importance. At the same time,
the rack wholesaler has appeared to service the needs of supermarkets
for selected groups of non-food products. The sharp increases in
both quantities and assortments has meant not only the appearance
of new kinds of business but increased opportunities, as well, in
existing businesses for choice between general-line and specialty operations.

Changes in area structure

The observations made about the centralization versus suburbanization of manufacturing of industrial goods also have application here.
But, because so many wholesale middlemen of manufactured consumers' goods are retailer-oriented in locations, it follows that the
geographical distribution has become more dispersed in keeping with
the shifts in population. In addition, the central cities of the older
standard metropolitan areas have begun to lose some of their relative
importance so far as wholesale trade percentages are concerned. This

---

[13] Note, in this connection, the changes in warehousing operations reported
for Westinghouse in Chapter 20.

decentralizing tendency varies according to type of middlemen's operation, and kind of business.

Changes in price structure

The general effects of the Robinson-Patman Act have greatest applicability to manufactured consumers' goods. Of great significance, also, has been the general collapse of resale price maintenance for most producer branded products to which the practice was applied. Unknown is the extent to which wholesale middlemen-discount house channel relationships become the significant factor in undermining such regulations. But it is known that the discount house has been a key development at the retail middleman level. The impact of foreign automobile competition has resulted in the introduction into the channel by domestic producers of what might be called "fighting brands."

The increased impact of distributors' brands has given the wholesale middlemen increased control in many kinds of business over prices and terms of sale. In addition, the use of cash-and-carry departments within regular wholesaler operations has given additional flexibility to the wholesale price structure. This has been offset, in part, by the general inflexibilities of price structures due, in part, to the prolonged period of inflation, and in part, as a result of the "play it safe" attitude resulting from the Robinson-Patman Act.

Resumé of underlying or controlling causes

The causes relating to these changes have worked at every level of the channel. They have stemmed, as was the case for industrial goods, from changes in the technology of production, again, by increasing both the quantity and assortments of available goods. They reflect population shifts and increases as well as increases in the incomes of such population groups. And these changes are related, also, the continuing struggle for channel control between producers, wholesale middlemen, and retail middlemen. The basic factors of changes in transportation and transportation rates are ever present and important, as well as the effects of government regulations, especially the Robinson-Patman Act and resale price maintenance laws. And, finally, the experimentations of business units with new methods of operation should not be overlooked.

The Resurgence of the Regular (Orthodox) Wholesaler

Perhaps no change in the wholesaling sector has been more spectacular or significant in the quarter century between 1929 and 1954 than the resurgence of the regular wholesaler.[14] This section, then, will discuss the evidence of the resurgence, the reasons for the resurgence, and some of the more important implications.

The evidence of the resurgence

From the long-run (25-year) point of view, there are three important pieces of evidence of the resurgence. First, the orthodox wholesaler had achieved in 1954 his 1929 level of importance as measured by his percentage of total United States sales—36.7 per cent in 1954, and 36.8 per cent in 1929. On an over-all basis, secondly, this type has improved steadily in relative sales importance and in number of establishments since the depression low in the 1930's. Third, this trend has not been duplicated either by other types of merchant wholesalers or by the agents and brokers group.

From the short-run point of view (1948 to 1954), there are additional pieces of evidence. In both 1948 and 1954, the regular wholesaler was the dominant type of wholesale middleman operation in both sales and number of establishments: (1) in terms of establishment, the percentages were 54.7 and 59.8 per cent, respectively; and (2) in terms of sales, the percentages were 34.2 and 36.7 per cent, respectively. The regular wholesaler's sales position exceeded the *combined* sales position of manufacturers' sales branches and sales offices. The regular wholesalers' sales also exceeded the *combined* sales for the agents and brokers group. And this trend holds true for all sizes of cities on a combined basis.

Reasons for the resurgence

As the most fundamental explanation of the resurgence are the same reasons which have always explained the role of the regular wholesaler —his role as the "eyes and ears" of the wholesale marketplace. This role, as discussed in Chapter 2, centers around three sets of advantages: (1) the closest approximation of the regular wholesaler to that encompassed in the over-all ideal strategic position of wholesaling; (2) the wide range of services to producers; and (3) the wide range of services to customers. The chapter mentioned has discussed these fully. The significant point, for purposes of the present discussion, is the continuing element of importance in explaining the competitive position of the regular wholesaler.

A second set of reasons represent recent internal managerial changes designed to bolster the foregoing advantages and reduce some basic

[14] Changes between 1954 and 1958, based on the new *1958 Census of Business* data are discussed in the final section of this chapter.

disadvantages. As has been discussed earlier, one part of this set of reasons has been increased efficiency in warehouses arising out of improvement in location and layout. In addition, the efficiency of such warehouses has been increased further by the widespread introduction of mechanized merchandise-handling arrangements, and the use of modern data collecting and processing equipment for inventory control purposes.

Thirdly, the regular wholesaler has begun to adopt aggressive sales promotional and other marketing strategy and tactics to his needs rather than acting, as was all too often the case, merely as an order-taker and order-filler. Because of this change in managerial philosophy, and based, also on the better marketing data and analyses obtained, the regular wholesaler is giving vigorous emphasis to the careful addition of new lines, and to the planned elimination of unprofitable lines.

Although data are not available, one may infer from many qualitative elements existing in the wholesaling sector that the regular wholesaler increasingly is making use of multiple-type operations. Three examples of such flexibility may be given: (1) The development of the rack jobber type of operation to service the drug sections of supermarkets; (2) the increasing appearance of cash-and-carry divisions or subsidiaries within the regular wholesaler's type of operation and establishments; and (3) operations by regular wholesalers of wholesaler-sponsored voluntary chain subsidiaries. Closely related to these has been the vigorous reaction of the regular wholesaler to the competition of other types of wholesale middlemen operations. In addition, better cost controls have proved beneficial.

A third set of reasons may be grouped together under the heading of *operational flexibility*. One evidence of this is represented under geographical flexibility. In 1954, the merchant wholesalers' group, of which the regular wholesaler is far and away most important, was the dominant group in all states except Delaware, Georgia, Michigan, and Ohio, and in the District of Columbia. By city size, the merchant wholesalers in 1954 accounted for 44 per cent of total wholesales in the 500,000-or-more category; 24 per cent in the 100,000–500,000 group; 14 per cent in the 25,000–100,000 group; 9 per cent in the 5,000–25,000 group; and 9 per cent in the area total in the remainder of the United States. Finally, so far as geographical flexibility is concerned, one-half of all merchant wholesaler's sales in 1954 was accounted for by establishments located in the 14 standard metropolitan areas; and 77.5 per cent by establishments located in 91 standard metropolitan areas.

A second aspect of flexibility is indicated by the range of orthodox wholesalers' operations under sales-size and multiunit characteristics. In 1954, about 1½ per cent of the establishments, each averaging $5 million or more of sales per establishment, accounted for 30 per cent of all merchant wholesalers' sales. On the other hand, over 31 per cent of the establishments each averaged less than $100,000 of sales per establishment, and collectively accounted for only 2.6 per cent of sales. Single-unit firms in 1954 accounted for 87 per cent of the establishments, but only 71.6 per cent of sales. At the opposite extreme, 1,314 firms each operated 100 or more establishments, and together these accounted for only $\frac{8}{10}$ of 1 per cent of the establishments, but 4 per cent of the sales.

The final aspect of operational flexibility is demonstrated by the fact that (a) the regular wholesaler is found in more kinds of business than any other type of wholesale middleman, and (b) there were *no* important kinds of business classifications in which there were no regular wholesalers. This should not be interpreted as meaning, however, that the regular wholesaler showed a resurgence of importance in all kinds of business. There were 11 major kinds of business groups[15] in which the regular wholesaler has shown growing relative sales importance. There were 9 major kinds of business groups[16] in which the sales of the regular wholesaler, relatively speaking, have declined. In the farm supplies, flowers-bulb-plant, and miscellaneous groups, there were no significant changes in the level of relative importance.

Finally, an important contributing factor has been the beneficial effects of the protective legislation for independent middlemen discussed in Chapters 21 and 22. Here, again, no conclusive data are available to support this inference.

Implications

It is not to be expected that this resurgence will continue unabated automatically. Much depends on the ingenuity of the managerial talent within the regular wholesaler group to continue to maximize opportunities, as they have between 1929 and 1954, for innovation and improvements. Much depends, also, on the kinds and intensity of the

[15] Beer, wine, distilled spirits; drugs, chemicals, allied products; paper and allied products; raw material farm products; electrical, electronics, etc.; lumber, construction materials; machinery; metals and metalwork; amusement, sporting goods; books, magazines, newspapers; and petroleum products.

[16] Groceries, confectionery, meats; edible farm products; tobacco; dry goods, apparel, home furnishings; automotive; hardware, plumbing, heating; scrap; waste materials; coal; and jewelry.

retaliatory tactics and strategy developed by the competitive middle-men. And, finally, much depends on the vigor with which Federal Government regulation succeeds, in the future, in restricting the growth of concentration and integration among all kinds of business at all levels of the channel.

But the resurgence of the regular wholesaler between 1929 and 1954 has deep significance in demonstrating the basic characteristics of the wholesaling sector discussed in the opening chapters; namely, the *flexibility* of the sector so far as types of operation are concerned; and the *adaptability* of the wholesaling funnel and the middlemen operations therein to the various kinds of business, the quantities involved, and the geographical aspects of encompassed product flows. Finally, this resurgence demonstrates, once again, the significance of change within the organic aspects of the institutional approach.

Resumé and Evaluation

Three significant developments are the culmination of the series of changes summarized and discussed in this chapter, and as presented at many points in the preceding chapters. First, and in many ways the most significant, has been the decline of organized wholesale markets and systematic pricing in the channel. As a result, more and more sales transactions through the wholesaling sector involve pricing arrangements in which large elements of imperfect competition are at work. In addition, the maximization of marketing alternatives is severely reduced as the pricing alternatives are reduced. And the framework of government regulation becomes complicated with networks of inconsistencies as statute after statute is supported in order to maintain existing nonsystematic pricing arrangements, or to introduce new varieties. Thus, the classic coordinating and controlling functions of price in the marketing system become only partially effective.

A second significant development has been the development of giantism among channel participants at the manufacturing and retailing levels, with all of the problems of monopolistic competition once again. As a result, the Federal Government finds itself at a crossroad in its basic antitrust policy. Either vigorous steps (as suggested in Chapter 21) must be taken to establish limits to corporate size and market strength in the channel on an individual kind-of-business approach, or more stringent regulation of the giant units will be necessary. That the marketing system fortunately has not lost all of its

vigor is manifested in the resurgence of the regular wholesaler as discussed. But even in many of these cases, as has been noted earlier,
the existence of semiformal and informal methods of integration has
deprived far too many wholesale middlemen of the independence of
policy formulation which should be expected.

Finally, in the manufactured consumers' goods channels, the existence of giant firms among all levels of the channel has meant an
increasing obliteration of the lines of demarcation between the wholesaling and retailing sectors. This obliteration, in and of itself, cannot
be viewed as harmful. What is harmful is the belief of far too many
channel participants, and of marketing experts, of the inevitability and
even preordained nature of such change. And what is of equal potential danger is the unwillingness of all concerned to recognize the need
for a constant sharpening of concepts and other analytical tools in
order to offset the possible dulling effects of such obliteration.

Stated somewhat differently, the significance of change as an organic
characteristic must be recognized. However, in the course of evaluating these changes sharp differentiation must be continually made
between those changes, such as population explosions, which are
beyond the control of any single business management, and those
changes which are the result of executive decisions within business
firms acting individually, or cooperatively, or in collusion. And what
also must be kept continually in the forefront of any discussion is the
continuous struggle between those agencies which wish to maximize
change in the marketing channels, and those which either want to
minimize the rate of change, or to maintain, so far as possible, the
status quo to their advantage. Change must be analyzed constantly,
in other words, for its potential for good or harmful results.

Selected Trends, 1954–1958: New Census Data

It would not be expected that census data of wholesale trade taken
at a four-year interval (1954–1958) would reveal quite significant
shifts, especially since the year 1958 was characterized by a business
recession. What might be expected would be shifts in the relative
importance of the various kinds of business based upon the relative
movements of the respective wholesale price levels for commodities
produced, and the rates of downturn due to recession economic conditions. These varying movements, in turn, would affect differentially
the relative importance of the wholesale middlemen's type of operations, depending on the extent of kind-of-business specialization. And,

some influence would be exerted on the geographical distribution of wholesale trade and types of middlemen as a result of the influence exerted by the underlying movements of people, industries, and businesses between the various geographical units.

The following discussion makes use of such reports of the *1958 Census of Business—Wholesale Trade* as were available at the time the book was printed. In analyzing these data, the pattern of presentation is designed to permit integration of the conclusions with the discussions given in Chapters 2–4.

General trends

Total wholesale trade in 1958 amounted to $283.8 billions compared with about $235 billions in 1954. This increase in sales of about $48.8 billions amounted to a change of about 20.8 per cent. Of this increase, nearly one-half would be due to increases in the wholesale price levels.[17] This increased volume of wholesale sales was accounted for by 285,996 establishments in 1958, compared with 252,318 establishments in 1954.

Compared with the total volume of retail sales, wholesale sales increased more rapidly. As a result, the ratio of wholesale sales to retail sales was 1.42 in 1958 compared with 1.38 in 1954. And because of the increase in number of establishments noted above, the average sales per establishment increased from $926,900 to $992,100, or only by about 6⅔ per cent.

Changes in U. S. sales by type of operation and kinds of business

The available preliminary data reveal the continued importance of the merchant wholesalers' group at about the same level of importance as in 1954, approximately 43 per cent. The sales of manufacturers' sales branches and sales offices combined increased by 26.1 per cent over 1954. As a result, their relative importance rose from 29.6 per cent in 1954 to 30.9 per cent in 1958. Sales of petroleum bulk plants and terminals increased by 25.5 per cent, resulting in a rise in relative importance from 6.8 to 7.1 per cent. Although sales of merchandise agents and brokers rose by 15.2 per cent, this rate of increase was below the increase noted in total wholesale sales. As a result, their relative importance declined sharply from 16.7 to 15.9 per cent. This may be interpreted, in part, as a diversion to increased control by the manufacturers through sales branches and/or sales offices. The only absolute decline in sales was recorded by assemblers of farm products, 0.6

---

[17] It should be remembered that the business recession of 1958 was peculiar in that no deflation of prices was experienced.

per cent, with an accompanying loss of relative strength from 3.9 to 3.2 per cent.

These changes in relative importance reflect the variable changes in sales between kinds of business, and the variable distribution in sales, in turn, between types-of-operation groups in these kinds of business. Groceries and related products continued to dominate the wholesale trade of the nation, with total sales of $48.2 billion in 1958. The next most important kind-of-business group—the raw materials farm products—was far behind with $27.9 billion. Four other kinds-of-business groups each accounted for over $20 billions of sales in 1958: machinery, equipment, supplies ($25 billion); motor vehicles, automotive equipment ($23.5 billion); metals and nonpetroleum mineral ($22.1 billion); and the petroleum group noted above ($20.1 billion). In noting these sales positions, consideration must be given, once again, to the variable price and business cycle movement of each kind of business group during the period under consideration.

Merchant wholesalers continue to be most important in the groceries and related products, machinery equipment and supplies, raw materials farm products, electrical goods, motor vehicles and automotive equipment, alcoholic beverages, and dry goods and apparel kinds-of-business groups, in order of importance. This distribution points to the continued importance of the orthodox (regular) wholesaler in a wider variety of business groups than any other type of operation.

Changes in state distribution of sales

The continued movements of people and expansion of business activities has reflected pressures on the importance of the leading states in wholesale trade. The five most important states—New York, California, Illinois, Pennsylvania, and Ohio—accounted for 48.7 per cent of 1954 sales and 47.4 per cent of 1958 sales. But California rose from third to second in importance, at the expense of Illinois, by a rise in importance from 7.9 to 9.1 per cent. Both New York and Illinois lost ground, relatively, with declines from 21.0 to 19.3 per cent, and 8.7 to 8.2 per cent, respectively. Ohio had a moderate decline.

There was no change in the rank order of importance of the next five most important states—Texas, Michigan, Missouri, Massachusetts, and New Jersey. As a group, they increased in relative importance from 18.2 per cent of 1954 sales to 18.6 per cent of 1958 sales. Texas and New Jersey had moderate increases in relative importance—from 4.7 to 5.1 per cent, and 2.5 to 3.0 per cent, respectively—offsetting moderate declines for the remaining three states.

The greatest flux in rank order was reflected in eight states—Minnesota, Georgia, Florida, Indiana, Tennessee, North Carolina, Wisconsin, and Iowa, in order of 1958 sales importance. This group accounted for 14.8 per cent of 1958 sales and 14.4 per cent of 1954 sales. Florida registered a spectacular increase from 1.45 to 1.94 per cent. The remainder showed small changes, although shifting in rank position.

Thus, although shifts in rank order of importance and in relative importance of each state have taken place as noted, the top ten states still account for nearly two-thirds of the wholesale trade in continental United States. And better than four-fifths of wholesale sales in 1958 were accounted for in the 18 states listed above. Merchant wholesalers, as a group, varied sharply in importance by states. With an average of 42.9 per cent of 1958 sales for the United States, the range was from a low of 21.8 per cent of Delaware's sales to a high of 62 per cent in New Mexico.

Changes in city distribution of sales

On a city basis, the range of changes in wholesale trade between 1954 and 1958 is much more apparent. Keeping in mind that total wholesale sales increased by 20.8 per cent during this period, increases of over 100 per cent were registered for each of the following cities:

California	— Beverly Hills and South San Francisco
Florida	— Fort Lauderdale
Illinois	— Melrose Park (with a spectacular 686 per cent) and Skokie
Indiana	— Hammond
Minnesota	— St. Louis Park
Missouri	— Clayton
New Jersey	— East Orange and Montclair
New York	— White Plains
Texas	— Dallas
Arizona	— Phoenix and Tucson
California	— Glendale, Richmond, Sacramento, San Diego, and San Jose
Florida	— Miami, Orlando, and St. Petersburg
Illinois	— Cicero and Rockford
Indiana	— South Bend
Louisiana	— Baton Rouge
New Jersey	— Camden, Elizabeth, and Union City
New York	— Mount Vernon
Texas	— Abilene and El Paso

Several cities in every section of the United States registered actual declines in wholesale sales, ranging from —0.3 per cent for Knoxville, Tennessee, to —29.6 per cent for Perth Amboy, New Jersey. The complete list of the more important cities showing declines was as follows:

California	— Bakersfield
Connecticut	— Hartford
Delaware	— Wilmington
Illinois	— Springfield
Iowa	— Cedar Rapids
Kentucky	— Louisville
Massachusetts	— Boston
Missouri	— Kansas City and St. Joseph
Mississippi	— Greenwood
New Jersey	— Perth Amboy
North Carolina	— Gastonia
Ohio	— Dayton
Pennsylvania	— Erie, Harrisburg, Philadelphia, Reading, and York
South Carolina	— Greenville
Tennessee	— Knoxville
Texas	— Waco
Virginia	— Danville
Wisconsin	— Madison[18]

QUESTIONS AND PROBLEMS

1. What is meant by the general pattern of underlying forces?

2. Compare and contrast the quantitative and qualitative aspects of functional changes in the agricultural goods, manufactured industrial goods, and manufactured consumers' goods markets.

3. Evaluate what have been the major effects, in your opinion, of the decline in importance of organized wholesale markets.

4. Compare and contrast the changes in agency structure for the three types of wholesale markets; the changes in area structure.

5. What is meant by the resurgence of the regular (orthodox) wholesaler? What is the evidence of such resurgence?

6. Why has there been the resurgence in importance of the regular wholesaler? What are the main repercussions for the wholesaling sector?

7. What main changes between 1954 and 1958 are indicated by new (1958) *Census of Business* data?

[18] For a discussion of the changes in manufacturing industrial markets, see Thomas Kenny, "Your Guide to the New Industrial Markets," *Dun's Review and Modern Industry* (July 1960), pp. 46–55.

CHAPTER INTEGRATING ASSIGNMENTS

1. Given the backdrop of the discussion of this chapter, prepare an analysis in which you present the forces making for change in the wholesaling sector (including the type of change); and the forces making for stability (including the type of stability).

2. To what extent do the agencies in the channel serve successfully to perpetuate the channel structure? To what extent do these agencies generate the forces which ultimately modify or destroy the channel?

24

Final Review

The preceding 23 chapters have presented various aspects of the wholesaling sector of marketing organization in its external and internal environment. There remains one finishing touch—to review the conceptual framework as it has evolved; to view the future of the wholesaling sector as revealed in the author's chipped and slightly elliptical crystal ball; and to indicate some needed professional developments.

A Critical Review of the Present Status of the Wholesaling Sector

If one statement had to suffice to explain the origins and basis for this book it would have to be *that the channel has been too much neglected of late in the marketing literature and in marketing research, and that this neglect is nowhere more apparent than in the study of the wholesaling sector.* It is from the stepping stone of this statement, then, that the conceptual framework has evolved as presented in the preceding chapters. In this, the concluding chapter, it may be worth while to take one long, hard, critical look at the fundamental characteristics of this conceptual framework.

The wholesaling sector is, first of all, the most significant part of the entire marketing organization. Early discussions have presented certain quantitative and qualitative measures of gross and net importance.[1] But the importance of the wholesaling sector, as developed in the conceptual framework, is much more significant to our way of

[1] See Chapter 1.

thinking than any of these quantitative and qualitative measures. For example, too many marketing textbooks and too much marketing research pay lip service to the statement that marketing is consumer-oriented. If the scope and complexity of the industrial goods market and the funnel concept are kept in mind, then it must be recognized that the consumers' goods market, as reflected in the retailing sector, becomes reduced in significance and conceptual impact.

From this characteristic there stems, next, the structure of markets within the wholesaling sector. There are several aspects to this characteristic. First, there is the key difference between organized and nonorganized markets—a theme which has pervaded many sections of this book. This difference gives rise, in turn, to: (*a*) differences between systematic and unsystematic prices and price structures; and (*b*) differences in the receptivity toward management activities which reflect the competitive norm in an enterprise economy.

The second aspect is concerned with the wholesaling sector as a series of organized and/or nonorganized wholesale markets (primary and auxiliary) functioning within the framework of the funnel concept. These markets, so arranged, have pertinence for the conceptual framework of the channel as discussed later.

The final aspect emphasizes the variable geographical structure of these wholesale markets. Depending upon the nature of the product handled, and a wide array of many other variables already discussed, these wholesale markets may be production-point oriented in location; be found at intermediate locations; or be oriented towards customers' locations. These patterns may reflect high degrees of regional concentration, or they may be found in highly diversified geographical patterns.

But the real focal point of the wholesaling sector, the center of gravity, or the competitive battleground so to speak, becomes the channel. The channel is the key structural arrangement in marketing organization within which various business units become linked in order to effect the flows of goods and services and the attendant functions of marketing. As has been discussed in Chapters 5 and 6, these channels may be variously viewed and analyzed. To the extent that they deal only with industrial goods, they fall entirely within the wholesaling sector. To the extent that they deal in consumers' goods, they involve the retailing sector as well. And some goods embrace both situations. These channels vary in complexity as to number of business units linked; the depth of business penetration; the extent of geographical outreach; and the incidence of horizontal and/or vertical integration.

A somewhat different view of the channel introduces the extent to which the channel completes the movement of goods from producer to point of final use, together with the related nonphysical functioning of the channel. Thus, differentiation can be made between one-phase, two-phase, and multiphase channel segmentation. These phases are involved inextricably with important time divisions in the movement, and interruptions to the movement, of goods and services from producing units to agencies at points of intermediate and final use.

Competition, then, in the realistic marketing sense, takes place between business units linked together into alternative channels involving particular products. Under some commodity arrangements, as has been noted, this competition becomes institutionalized within the framework of organized wholesale markets. But, whatever the organization of the wholesale markets, particular products of particular producing and marketing units compete with other products of other producing and marketing units through channel alternatives having particular geographical outreaches.

Within the plane of competition there arises, then, another form of competition; namely, that between the various agencies linked together in a channel for managerial control of that channel. The give and take of such competition may give rise, in turn, to: (*a*) attempts at blockages directed toward competitive channels; and (*b*) stimuli to those agencies either being outcompeted or on the receiving end of the blockages in (*a*) to formulate new channel arrangements or alternatives.

Using the institutional approach as the stepping stone,[2] the channel becomes, *as an organizing concept,* a way of looking at the external aspects of marketing organization in which various business units become linked together in some form of structural design. The structure of each of these business units becomes the way, in turn, of studying the internal aspects of marketing organization. As was stated in Chapter 1,

What is being emphasized here is the way in which many different kinds of individual firms and establishments array themselves in *formal,* systematic manner within various producing, buying, selling, and facilitating agencies in making possible the systematic, continuous movements of goods and services from producing to using units, together with the necessary determination of prices and terms of sale for their exchange.[3]

[2] As developed in E. A. Duddy and D. A. Revzan, *Marketing: An Institutional Approach,* 2nd ed. (New York: The McGraw-Hill Book Co. Inc., 1953), Chapter II and Appendix C.

[3] See page 17.

The wholesaling sector emphasizes, in the internal meaning, those agencies which cut across completely or partially the concept of wholesaling as presented.

The integration of the internal and external aspects of marketing organization becomes locationally solidified, in turn, through the channel structure. As was stated in Chapter 6:

> . . . Channels thus become effective as the resultant of a series of manufacturing decisions about particular products produced in locations dominated either by raw material on other locational considerations, and balanced by the locational determinants of the consuming markets on the other side of the equation. *From a geographic point of view, the channel becomes the marketing vehicle which obtains the best equilibrium of a series of individual and/or group management decisions about locational factors.*[4]

It may be observed, finally, that these concepts of the wholesaling sector operating through channel structures in the marketing organization, reflect the pervasive influence of change. There is a constant battle in the channel between the forces making for stability and those making for change in the wholesaling sector. To the extent the competitive norm is fostered by the middlemen in the channel, and preserved and strengthened by government regulation, to that extent will the forces of change be dominant. To the extent, however, that the competitive norm is hampered, distorted, or otherwise interfered with, to that extent will the forces making for stability become dominant during any time period. As was pointed out in the discussion of efficiency, the marketing organization must strive always to maximize channel alternatives for intermediary agencies in the channel, as well as the product and service alternatives for the ultimate consumers.

The Future of the Wholesaling Sector

There are many ways of viewing the future of the wholesaling sector, and any complete discussion would require, in and of itself, a complete book. The point of view taken is biased obviously by the viewers' concept of what is "good" and "desirable" in the way of the economic and political organization of society. What can be presented here are some abbreviated observations. In presenting these observations, the author has made the following assumptions: (a) that the accepted norm of economic organization is, and should continue to be, that assumed under a competitive enterprise economy; (b) that the

[4] See page 158.

present confused policy of government regulation, *vis-a-vis* this competitive norm, is likely to continue for the next 50 years; and (c) that some progress will be made, however, towards the achievement of some of the reforms in government regulation recommended in Chapters 21 and 22.

Given these assumptions, we may visualize next some of the main dimensions of change in the next 50 years; and conclude the discussion in this section with a statement of some desired changes. First, are presented some *expected* changes:

1. Continued expansion may be visualized and expected in the quantity and range of products and product assortments which will move through the wholesaling sector. No one can visualize with any absolute certainty the total dimensions of such changes. There are many who believe that the next half century will see the evolution of a new Industrial Revolution which will exceed, by far, any previous periods of change in technology and productivity.[5] These changes will continue to require quantitative and qualitative changes in the wholesaling funnel and in the channels.

2. Continued realignment of the geographical distributions of the human populations, together with increases in the total number in the continental United States to at least 225 million persons. These shifts and increases will have two important sets of impacts upon the wholesaling sector. First, corresponding shifts and expansions will have to take place in the part of the wholesaling sector responsible for the movement of consumer's goods. And, second, there will be ever-increasing repercussions on the location of manufacturing industries by virtue of the development of many new regional markets of demand strength sufficient to warrant the expansion and/or relocation of productive facilities.

3. Continued increases may be expected in the importance of foreign trade in the total composition of wholesale trade. These increases, if they materialize, will require a considerable expansion of the channels and middlemen in the wholesaling sector so oriented.

4. Expansion may be expected in the kinds of wholesale middlemen's businesses designed to keep pace with the changes in products

---

[5] See, for example, J. Frederic Dewhurst and Associates, *America's Needs and Resources: A New Survey* (New York: The Twentieth Century Fund, 1955), especially Parts V and VI.

and product assortments noted in (1). These may be expected
to develop along the lines of permitting either more opportunities
for product specialization as the size of demand grows, and for
general-line product assortments in those situations where the
size of demand is in the pioneering stage.

5. Paralleling the expansion in (4), continued changes may be expected to continue in the types of middlemen operations at both
the wholesaling and retailing sector levels. Much depends, so
far as the rate and direction changes are concerned, on whether
the developments of large-scale, integrated units in the channel is
permitted to continue unchecked. If the development is checked,
it may be expected that an expansion will take place in the number of middlemen alternatives—both in terms of numbers of
establishments and types of operation. In addition, greater use
may be expected to be made of semidirect and indirect channels.
But, in either case, additional changes may be expected so long
as (a) some freedom of entry is maintained, and (b) there is
continued improvement in the quality of management knowledge
and experience. In some respects, the large-scale units even if
they continue unchecked, will limit their own growth in channel
strength by both training sufficient managerial talent who ultimately will enter the channel themselves, and training competitors in stronger countercompetitive measures.

6. The growing population and its geographical diffusion on the
one hand, and changes in the speed of transportation, on the
other, may be expected to lead to increased overlappings of wholesale trade area boundaries. This will be magnified if recentralization is expected to take place; i.e., as noted, the blossoming
of many present-day suburbs into the medium and larger size
cities of tomorrow.

7. There are strong possibilities that the extensive growth of distributors' brands in the consumers' goods field may extend into
the industrial goods channels.

8. Improvements may be expected in managerial control and evaluation as a result of continued improvements in data collection and
processing, on the one hand, and in the research and analytical
tools on the other.

9. Finally, continued progress in the quality of the professional literature and knowledge brought to bear on marketing, in general,
and the wholesaling sector, in particular, may be expected. Some
suggestions will be included in the concluding section.

These nine areas represent, as stated, *expected* developments. Before this section is concluded, however, something needs to be said about hopes for some *needed* developments. The keystone for such hopes lies in the suggested reforms in government regulatory policies as discussed in Chapters 21 and 22. Without such reforms, the competitive norm would become increasingly a thing of the past. With such reforms actually achieved, much can be expected so far as achieving a return to the expected maximization of alternatives, the goal which constantly has been stressed.

One way of stating the alternatives was presented in a prize-winning essay on the future of wholesaling.

The outcome of whether there shall be integrated marketing combinations or whether there shall be decentralized and personalized marketing has much to do with the way of life in the United States. If integrated marketing, such as manufacturing outlets and chains, should come to dominate distribution channels, the individual would lose much of his scope of expression, both as to creative business endeavor and choice of products to consume. The history of industrial and marketing combinations in other countries is indicative that government intervention is also a definite possibility. . . . The fact is that as management of a gigantic organization becomes farther removed, it is less capable of discerning the individual wishes of the public and it is politically easy to blame for economic difficulties. There is every reason to anticipate that, should economic concentration extend throughout the marketing as well as the manufacturing field in the United States, there would be stresses and pressures which would ultimately lead to some form of government control, if not registration.

If, as is morely likely, the independent wholesaler-retailer method of distribution should continue to grow to the exclusion of marketing integration, the American way of life can continue more along its historical course of free initiative, enterprise, and expression. For thus, the ability to start a new, small business will be preserved; the competitive character of the economy will be retained; the individual will continue to have wide latitude as to what he shall purchase and what he shall do for a livelihood. The society and the economy of the United States will be decentralized, spontaneous, and human.

It is not an overstatement to conclude that every citizen in the United States has a stake in the future of wholesaling; in that future is involved, for each of us, a way of life.[6]

Reference has been made in earlier discussion to the vigorous attitude of Mund[7] toward the importance of open markets in the wholesaling sector. Much of what he advocates has been discussed in the

[6] Stahrl Edmunds, "In Wholesaling's Future—The Coming America," *The Journal of Marketing*, XIV (September 1949), 273–74. It is interesting to note that he overlooks the wide range of independent merchant and agent wholesale middlemen in both the consumers' and industrial goods' fields.

[7] Vernon Mund, *Open Markets, An Essential of Free Enterprise* (New York: Harper Bros., 1948).

recommendations included in Chapters 21 and 22, and in the suggestions for improving efficiency. His concluding remarks are of value, however, in the present context.

Most people in our country agree that they want free economic enterprise, full employment, and equal economic opportunity. Many, however, shrink from paying the necessary price for these conditions. If we believe in economic freedom, we must do what is absolutely necessary to make it possible—that is, preserve, restore, and create market competition by every means within our power. We can have economic freedom if we are willing to pay this price. Open markets once existed in the American economy, and they can be created again. The historical material shows that they are no illusory ideal.[8]

Needed Professional Developments

Before concluding, a brief mention should be made of the need for more writings and research directed towards the subject matter covered in the preceding chapters. There is no need to make a catalog of the subject topics since these are listed and classified in the tables of contents and the index. Especial emphasis needs to be placed, however, on the following: (1) The theory, nature, and functioning of primary and intermediate wholesale markets in the channel; (2) sharpening of the concepts of price-making efficiency in these markets in the wholesaling sector; (3) critical evaluations of the relative positions and strategies of each type of wholesale middleman in the channel; and (4) sharpening of the criteria for evaluating the effectiveness of the wholesaling sector and its component elements.

This book has argued long and arduously for a recognition of the importance of the wholesaling sector and the necessity for prime emphasis upon gross rather than net measures of importance. This philosophy needs to be reflected in more complete census data, especially better coverage of all types of wholesale middlemen operations. Special data are needed of multiple-type wholesale middlemen's establishments and operations. And better data are needed of the geographic structure of channels.

Finally, this book has emphasized the dual importance of the industrial goods and consumers' goods segments of the wholesaling sec-

[8] *Ibid.*, pp. 262–63. Other alternatives are discussed in the following:

John M. Clark, *Alternative to Serfdom* (New York: Alfred A. Knopf, 1948).

Herman Finer, *Road to Reaction* (Boston: Little, Brown and Co., 1945).

F. A. Hayek, *The Road to Serfdom* (Chicago: The University of Chicago Press, 1944).

Karl Polanyi *The Great Transformation: The Political and Economic Origins of Our Time* (Boston: Beacon Press, 1957).

tors. This point of view needs to be examined critically and expanded upon not only in special studies, but, more importantly, in completely integrated analyses. It is to be hoped that this book has so stimulated the imaginations of some of the readers that such studies will be forthcoming. If it acts as such a catalytic agent it will have more than fulfilled the author's hopes, and the book's *raison d'être*.

QUESTIONS AND PROBLEMS

1. Do you agree with the statement, "that the channel has been too much neglected of late in the marketing literature and in marketing research . . ."? Explain your agreement or disagreement. If you agree, why do you think this neglect has taken place?
2. Develop all the evidence you can to support the assertion that the wholesaling sector *is the most significant part of the entire marketing organization.*
3. What are the significant aspects of the structure of markets within the wholesaling sector? How does this structure relate to channel structure?
4. Comment on the channel as the center of gravity, or competitive battleground, of the wholesaling sector.
5. Re-evaluate the concept of competition in its channel context.
6. Explain what you understand to be meant by the channel as "an organizing concept."
7. Do you agree with the discussion of the future of the wholesaling sector? What changes would you make?
8. To what extent do you believe a return to Mund's idea of open markets represents a significant and needed development?

Appendix

APPENDIX TABLE A1

WHOLESALE TRADE—UNITED STATES 1954: PERCENTAGE DISTRIBUTION OF SALES, BY KINDS OF BUSINESS, AMONG FIVE TYPES OF OPERATION GROUPS

Kind of Business	Merchant Wholesalers Per Cent	Mfrs., Sales Branches, Sales Offices Per Cent	Mdse. Agents and Brokers Per Cent	Petroleum Group Per Cent	Assemblers of Farm Products Per Cent	Total Per Cent
Extractive industries						
Farm products (raw materials)	34.3	—	42.7	—	22.9	100
Cotton	61.3	—	24.0	—	14.7	100
Grain	47.8	—	13.5	—	38.7	100
Hides, skins, raw fur	59.5	—	35.9	—	4.6	100
Livestock (except horses, mules)	8.7	—	74.0	—	17.3	100
Leaf tobacco	9.0	—	31.1	—	⎱15.4	⎱100
Raw wool, wool tops, mohair	14.3	—	9.4	—	⎰	⎰
Other raw material farm products	15.7	—	5.0	—	—	100
Petroleum	7.9	—	3.1	89.0	—	100
Farm products (edible)	49.1	—	17.0	—	21.7	100
Dairy products	21.5	12.2	—	—	22.3	100
Poultry, poultry products	23.7	24.2	⎱8.3	—	⎱21.0	⎱100
Fresh fruits, vegetables	53.1	—	25.9	—	⎰	⎰
Lumber and forest products	72.9	11.3	15.9	—	—	100
Coal	40.9	29.0	30.1	—	—	100
Flowers, bulbs, plants	100	—	—	—	—	100
Total—Extractive industries	32.6	4.0	24.2	25.2	14.0	100
Manufactured industrial goods						
Machinery, equipment, supplies	49.7	39.5	10.8	—	—	100
Air conditioning, commercial refrigerator	22.5	⎱34.3	12.4	—	—	⎱100
Commercial machines equipment	30.8	⎰	—	—	—	⎰
Construction machinery, equipment	77.4	18.4	4.1	—	—	100
Farm-garden machinery, equipment	28.7	69.5	1.8	—	—	100
Industrial machinery, equipment	33.7	⎱23.1	⎱17.4	—	—	⎱100
Industrial materials supplies	25.8	⎰	⎰	—	—	⎰
Professional equipment, supplies	17.0	57.1	0.5	—	—	100
Service establishment supplies	22.0	57.1	3.5	—	—	100
Transportation equipment	24.1	60.6	15.3	—	—	100

APPENDIX TABLE A1 (Continued)

WHOLESALE TRADE—UNITED STATES 1954: PERCENTAGE DISTRIBUTION OF SALES, BY KINDS OF BUSINESS, AMONG FIVE TYPES OF OPERATION GROUPS

Kind of Business	Merchant Wholesalers Per Cent	Mfrs., Sales Branches, Sales Offices Per Cent	Mdse. Agents and Brokers Per Cent	Petroleum Group Per Cent	Assemblers of Farm Products Per Cent	Total Per Cent
Manufactured industrial goods (continued)						
Metals, metalwork (except scrap)	19.1	75.6	5.3	—	—	100
Iron, steel and products	N.A.	N.A.	N.A.	—	—	100
Nonferrous metals	N.A.	N.A.	N.A.	—	—	100
Chemicals, allied products	14.3	81.2	4.5	—	—	100
Industrial chemicals explosives	12.4	83.3	4.3	—	—	100
Paint, varnish	29.5	63.8	6.7	—	—	100
Electrical, electronics	44.5	39.8	15.8	—	—	100
Electrical apparatus, supplies	47.5	41.1	11.4	—	—	100
Electronic parts, equipment	34.0	35.3	30.7	—	—	100
Millwork, construction materials	58.0	39.1	3.0	—	—	100
Millwork	100	—	—	—	—	100
Construction materials	49.8	46.7	3.5	—	—	100
Paper, allied products	53.6	37.9	8.5	—	—	100
Plumbing-heating equipment, supplies	75.0	13.2	11.8	—	—	100
Scrap, waste materials	96.6	—	3.4	—	—	100
Iron, steel scrap	93.4	—	6.6	—	—	100
Waste materials	100	—	—	—	—	100
Farm supplies	75.0	—	15.7	—	9.3	100
Textile mill products	—	100	—	—	—	100
Rubber products (except tires, tubes)	—	100	—	—	—	100
Leather, leather products	—	100	—	—	—	100
Total—Industrial goods	41.1	50.5	8.1	—	0.3	100
Manufactured consumers' goods						
Groceries, confectionery, meats	50.4	25.5	24.1	—	—	100
General-line groceries	30.0			—	—	

APPENDIX TABLE A1 (Continued)

Fish, sea foods	2.7	20.6	28.1	—	—	100
Specialty-line groceries	18.7	31.6	18.3	—	—	100
Confectionery	50.1	44.4	8.5	—	—	100
Meat, meat products	47.1	65.8	6.5	—	—	100
Automotive	27.7	N.A.	N.A.	—	—	100
Motor vehicles	N.A.	N.A.	N.A.	—	—	100
Automotive equipment, tires, tubes	N.A.	N.A.	N.A.	—	—	100
Dry goods, apparel	48.0	7.2	44.8	—	—	100
Clothing, furnishing, footwear	38.4	18.0	43.6	—	—	100
General-line dry goods	7.1	—	—	—	—	100
Specialty-line dry goods	35.1	—	—	—	—	100
Piece goods converters	100	27.5	57.8	—	—	100
Beer, wine, distilled spirits	72.5		—	—	—	100
Beer, ale	91.6	8.4	—	—	—	100
Wine, distilled spirits	63.5	36.5	—	—	—	100
Tobacco	66.4	33.6	2.8	—	—	100
Electrical appliances, radios, TV sets	58.4	38.8	3.2	—	—	100
Drugs	49.3	47.5	3.2	—	—	100
General-line drugs	28.9			—	—	100
Specialty-line drugs	20.4			—	—	100
Furniture, home furnishings	62.3	20.6	17.1	—	—	100
Furniture (household, office)	56.6	21.6	21.8	—	—	100
Home furnishings, floor coverings	65.6	20.1	14.3	—	—	100
Hardware	84.9	5.3	9.8	—	—	100
Amusements, sporting goods, toys	70.1	11.8	18.1	—	—	100
Books, magazines, newspapers	58.0	35.6	6.4	—	—	100
Jewelry	92.4		7.6	—	—	100
Gift, art goods	100	—	—	—	—	100
Total—Consumers' goods	52.0	30.9	17.2	—	—	100
Miscellaneous products, n.e.c.	45.3	16.4	38.3	—	—	100
Total—All kinds of business	43.0	29.6	16.7	6.8	3.9	100

APPENDIX TABLE A2

WHOLESALE TRADE—UNITED STATES 1954: BY CITY SIZE, TYPE OF OPERATION
(IN PER CENT)

Type of Operation	United States Per Cent	Cities With Populations of				Remainder of U. S. Per Cent
		500,000 or More Per Cent	100,000–499,999 Per Cent	25,000–99,999 Per Cent	5,000–24,999 Per Cent	
No. of establishments						
1. Merchant wholesalers	100	34.8	20.5	15.7	14.0	15.0
2. Mfrs. sales offices and sales branches	100	39.7	32.4	16.0	7.0	4.9
3. Petroleum bulk tank stations	100	1.5	3.7	8.3	23.6	63.0
4. Mdse. agents and brokers	100	48.6	21.2	8.5	7.7	14.0
5. Assemblers, farm products	100	2.4	3.0	4.1	12.9	77.6
Total	100	30.9	18.7	13.6	13.9	22.9
Sales ($1,000)						
1. Merchant wholesalers	100	44.3	23.9	13.6	8.8	9.4
2. Mfrs. sales offices and sales branches	100	62.4	24.8	6.4	3.1	3.3
3. Petroleum bulk tank stations	100	12.5	15.0	16.1	18.8	37.6
4. Mdse. agents and brokers	100	55.2	19.3	8.2	6.7	13.1
5. Assemblers, farm products	100	7.9	9.2	8.9	16.1	57.9
Total	100	47.9	22.2	10.5	7.7	11.6

APPENDIX TABLE A3

WHOLESALE PRICES INDEXES, STAGE OF PROCESSING—SELECTED YEARS AS PER CENT OF 1947 INDEX

Stage	1947 (1947–1949 = 100)	1949	1953	1958	Peak Point Year	Peak Point Index	Low Point Year	Low Point Index
All commodities	96.4	103	114	124	1958	119.2	1947	96.4
Crude materials for further processing	98.6	95	101	101	1951	116.9	1947	96.0
Foodstuffs and feedstuffs	100.7	93	94	92	1951	112.3		
Nonfood materials except fuel	96.0	101	111	113	1951	128.1	1947	96.0
For manufacturing	96.1	101	110	111	1951	128.6	1947	96.1
For construction	93.0	113	126	149	1958	139.0	1947	93.0
Crude fuel	89.4	117	124	136	1958	121.2	1947	89.4
For manufacturing	89.3	118	124	135	1958	121.8	1947	89.3
For other uses	89.5	117	125	136	1958	120.9	1947	89.5
Intermediate materials, supplies, and components	96.2	104	119	130	1958	125.3	1947	96.2
Intermediate materials for manufacturing	96.4	103	120	132	1958	127.2	1947	96.4
For food manufacturing	102.8	89	99	99	1948	106.0	1949	91.2
For nondurable manufacturing	99.2	97	117	106	1951	116.5	1949	95.8
For durable manufacturing	91.2	116	143	169	1958	154.3	1947	91.2
Intermediate components for manufacturing	94.4	110	132	158	1958	149.5	1947	94.4
Materials and components for construction	93.3	111	129	142	1957–1958	132.9	1947	93.3
Processed fuels and lubricants	94.8	103	109	112	1957	113.0	1947	94.8
For manufacturing	95.8	102	107	110	1957	111.2	1947	95.8
For other than manufacturing	93.1	106	113	116	1957	116.0	1947	93.1
Containers, nonreturnable, for manufacturing	97.0	105	120	142	1958	137.4	1947	97.0
Supplies	99.0	98	109	116	1958	115.1	1947	99.0
For manufacturing	96.6	105	122	145	1958	139.9	1947	96.3
For other than manufacturing	100.1	96	103	103	1952	111.8	1949	95.8
Animal feeds	104.1	86	85	70	1952	108.7	1957	67.6
Other supplied	97.9	96	113	124	1958	121.2	1949	93.9
Finished goods	95.9	105	115	131	1958	120.8	1947	95.9
Consumer finished goods	96.8	102	111	117	1958	113.5	1947	96.8
Consumer foods	97.0	100	107	114	1951	111.3	1947	97.0
Crude foods	96.9	102	106	104	1952	109.9	1950	89.9
Processed foods	97.0	100	108	116	1951	112.8	1949	96.9
Consumer, other nondurable	97.4	102	110	115	1957	112.4	1947	97.4
Consumer, durable goods	94.8	110	120	132	1958	125.0	1947	94.8
Producer finished goods	92.8	114	133	162	1958	150.3	1947	92.8
For manufacturing	92.8	114	134	167	1958	155.0	1947	92.8
For other than manufacturing	92.8	114	131	158	1958	146.4	1947	92.8

Source: Calculations based on data in *Monthly Labor Review.*

References

Chapter I

Alderson, Wroe, "The Analytical Framework for Marketing," *Proceedings—Conference of Marketing Teachers from Far Western States,* University of California, Berkeley, September 8, 9, and 10, 1958 (Berkeley: University of California Press, 1959), pp. 15–28.

————, *Marketing Behavior and Executive Action: A Functionalistic Approach to Marketing Theory* (Homewood, Ill.: Richard D. Irwin, 1957).

Beckman, Theodore N., and Nathanael H. Engle, *Wholesaling: Principles and Practice,* rev. ed. (New York: The Ronald Press Co., 1949); 3rd ed., with Robert D. Buzzell (New York: The Ronald Press Co., 1959).

Breyer, Ralph F., *The Marketing Institution* (New York: McGraw-Hill Book Co., Inc., 1934).

Clark, Fred E., and Carrie P. Clark, *Principles of Marketing,* 3rd ed. (New York: The Macmillan Co., 1942).

Duddy, Edward A., and David A. Revzan, *Marketing: An Institutional Approach,* 2nd ed. (New York: McGraw-Hill Book Co., Inc., 1953).

Vaile, Roland, E. T. Grether, and Reavis Cox, *Marketing in the American Economy* (New York: The Ronald Press Co., 1952).

Chapter 2

Beckman, T. N., N. H. Engle, and R. D. Buzzell, *op. cit.,* Chapters 6–13.

Duddy, E. A., and D. A. Revzan, *op. cit.,* Chapters II, XV–XXII, and Appendix C.

Chapter 3

Copeland, Melvin T., *Principles of Merchandising* (New York: McGraw-Hill Book Co., Inc., 1929).

U. S. Bureau of the Census, *U. S. Census of Business—1954,* Vol. III, *Wholesale Trade—Summary Statistics and Warehouses;* Vol. IV, *Wholesale Trade—Area Statistics* (Washington, D. C.: U. S. Government Printing Office, 1956, 1957).

Chapter 4

Books

Creamer, Daniel B., *Is Industry Decentralizing?* (Philadelphia: University of Pennsylvania Press, 1945).

Duddy, E. A., and D. A. Revzan, *op. cit.,* Chapters II, XXIV, Appendix C.

Fetter, Frank, *The Masquerade of Monopoly* (New York: Harcourt, Brace and Co., Inc., 1931).

Friederich, Carl J. (ed.), *Alfred Weber's Theory of the Location of Industries* (Chicago: The University of Chicago Press, 1929).

Greenhut, Melvin L., *Plant Location in Theory and in Practice: The Economics of Space* (Chapel Hill, N. C.: The University of North Carolina Press, 1955).

Hoover, Edgar M., *The Location of Economic Activity* (New York: McGraw-Hill Book Co., Inc., 1948).

Isard, Walter, *Location and Space-Economy: A General Theory Relating to Industrial Location, Market Areas, Land Use, Trade, and Urban Structure* (New York: John Wiley and Sons, Inc., 1956).

Lösch, August, *The Economics of Location,* translated by W. H. Woglow and W. F. Stalper (New Haven: Yale University Press, 1954).

Ohlin, Bertil, *Interregional and International Trade,* Harvard Economic Studies, Vol. XXXIX (Cambridge, Mass.: Harvard University Press, 1933).

Articles, Monographs, etc.

Battin, Charles T., "The Economic Organization and Competitive Status of the Chicago Potato Market," *The Journal of Business of the University of Chicago,* VIII (April 1935), 111–142.

Bredo, William, and Anthony S. Rojko, *Prices and Milk-Sheds of North-Eastern Markets,* Northeast Regional Publications No. 9 (Amherst, Mass.: University of Massachusetts, Agricultural Experiment Station, *Bulletin No. 470,* August, 1952).

Bureau of Foreign and Domestic Commerce, U. S. Dept. of Commerce, *Basic Industrial Markets in the United States* (Washington, D. C.: U. S. Government Printing Office, 1937).

Duddy, Edward A., "The Competitive Supply Area of the Chicago Livestock Market," *Journal of Farm Economics,* XIII (July 1931), 410–425.

———, and David A. Revzan, "The Distribution of Grain and Grain Products from the Chicago Market," *The Journal of Business of the University of Chicago,* VIII (January 1935), 65–96.

———, *The Distribution of Livestock from the Chicago Market, 1924–1929,* Studies in Business Administration, Vol. III, No. 1 (Chicago: The University of Chicago Press, 1932).

———, *The Grain Supply Area of the Chicago Market, ibid.,* Vol. IV, No. 4 (1934).

Duddy, Edward A., *The Physical Distribution of Fruits and Vegetables, ibid.,* Vol. VII, No. 2 (1937).

———, "Potential Supply Areas of Pacific Coast Markets for Hogs," *Journal of Farm Economics,* XIV (October 1932), 586–98.

———, "The Shipment of Grain and Grain Products from Chicago, 1924–25 to 1932–33," *The Journal of Business of the University of Chicago,* VIII (April 1935), 150–87.

Fetter, Frank, "The Economic Law of Market Areas," *Quarterly Journal of Economics,* XXXVIII (May 1924), 520–29.

Freutel, Guy, "The Eighth District Balance of Trade," *Monthly Review of the Reserve Bank of St. Louis* (June 1952).

Greenhut, Melvin L., "Integrating the Leading Theories of Plant Location," *The Southern Economic Journal,* XVII (April 1952), 526–38.

Grether, E. T., "The Economics of Space: A Review Article," *The Journal of Marketing,* XXI (January 1957), 369–75.

Hyson, C. D., and W. P. Hyson, "The Economic Law of Market Areas," *Quarterly Journal of Economics,* LXIV (May 1950), 319–27.

Isard, Walter, "Regional Commodity Balances and Inter-Regional Commodity Flows," *American Economic Review,* XLIII (May 1953), 167–98; 199–202.

———, and Walter M. Capron, "The Future Locational Patterns of Iron and Steel Production in the United States," *The Journal of Political Economy,* XLII (April 1949), 118–33.

Lewis, Edwin H., "Wholesale Market Patterns," *The Journal of Marketing,* XII (January 1948), 317–326.

Lösch, August, "The Nature of Economic Regions," *Southern Economic Journal,* V (July 1938), 71–78.

Millard, J. W., *Atlas of Wholesale Grocery Territories,* Bureau of Foreign and Domestic Commerce, U. S. Dept. of Commerce, Domestic Commerce Series, No. 7 (Washington, D. C.: U. S. Government Printing Office, 1926).

Monthly Review of the Federal Reserve Bank of San Francisco, "Twelfth District Interregional Trade—1950" (Sept. 1952); and "Twelfth District Commodity Trade—1950" (June 1955).

Moulton, Elma S., *Atlas of Wholesale Dry Goods Trading Areas,* Bureau of Foreign and Domestic Commerce, U. S. Dept. of Commerce, Economic Series No. 12 (Washington, D. C.: U. S. Government Printing Office, 1941).

Perroux, Francois, "Economic Space: Theory and Applications," *Quarterly Journal of Economics,* LXIV (February 1950), 89–104.

Predohl, Andreas, "The Theory of Location in its Relation to General Economics," *The Journal of Political Economy,* XXXVI (June 1928), 371–90.

Rasmussen, E. Guy, "Hardware Wholesale Trading Centers and Trading Territories in Nine Southeastern States," *The Journal of Marketing,* VIII (October 1943), 165–71.

Shepherd, Geoffrey, "Decentralization in Agricultural Marketing—Causes and Consequences," *The Journal of Marketing,* VI (April 1942), 341–348.

Stepp, James, *The Economics of Price in the Milk Industry,* Report of the Bureau of Public Administration, Series B, No. 9 (Charlottesville, Va.: University of Virginia, 1943, mimeographed).

Tousley, Rayburn D., "Some Aspects of the Spokane Wholesale Market," *The Journal of Marketing,* XVI, Part 1 (January 1952), 321–330.

U. S. Bureau of the Census, *Location of Manufacturers, 1899–1929* (Washington, D. C.: U. S. Government Printing Office, 1933).

Wardwell, Charles A. R., *Regional Trends in the United States Economy* (Washington, D. C.: U. S. Government Printing Office, 1951).

Wellman, Harry R., "The Distribution of Selling Efforts among Geographical Areas," *The Journal of Marketing*, III (January 1939), 225–239.

Chapters 5 and 6

Breyer, Ralph F., *op. cit.*, Chapter X.

———, *Quantitative Systemic Analysis and Control: Study No. 1—Channel and Channel Group Costing* (Philadelphia: The Author, 1949).

Clewett, Richard M. (ed.), *Marketing Channels for Manufactured Products* (Homewood, Ill.: Richard D. Irwin, Inc., 1954).

Craig, David R., and Werner K. Gabler, "The Competitive Struggle for Market Control," *Annals of the American Academy of Political and Social Science*, CCIX (May 1940), 84–107.

Duddy, E. A., and D. A. Revzan, *op. cit.*, 2nd ed., Chapters XV–XXII.

Fisher, Walter D., *California Fresh Tomatoes—Marketing Channels and Gross Margins from Farm to Consumer—Summer and Fall, 1948* (Berkeley: University of California, College of Agriculture, June 1951), Mimeographed Report No. 113.

Hirsch, Werner Z., "Toward a Definition of Integration," *The Southern Economic Journal*, XVII (October 1950), 159–165.

Hovde, Howard T. (ed.), "Wholesaling in Our American Economy," *The Journal of Marketing*, XIV (September 1949), 319–361.

Vaile, R., E. T. Grether, R. Cox, *op. cit.*, Chapters 5, 7.

Chapter 7

Alderson, Wroe, *Marketing Behavior and Executive Action, op. cit.*, pp. 199–200.

Breyer, Ralph F., *Quantitative Systemic Analysis and Control, . . . op. cit.*, p. 61.

Progressive Grocer, "Facts in Grocery Distribution," 1959 ed.

U. S. Bureau of the Census, *Census of Business: 1954*, Vols. III, IV

Chapter 8

Barnard, Chester I., *The Function of the Executive* (Cambridge, Mass.: Harvard University Press, 1938).

Business Week, "Expanding in the Face of a Trend," April 20, 1957, pp. 61 ff.

Koontz, Harold, and Cyril O'Donnell, *Principles of Management: An Analysis of Managerial Functions*, 2nd ed. (New York: McGraw-Hill Book Co., Inc., 1959).

March, James G., and Herbert A. Simon, *Organizations* (New York: John Wiley and Sons, Inc., 1958).

Mooney, James D., *The Principles of Organization,* rev. ed. (New York: Harper and Bros., 1947).

Newman, William H., *Administrative Action: The Techniques of Organization and Management* (Englewood Cliffs, N. J.: Prentice-Hall, Inc., 1951).

Peterson, Elmore, and E. G. Plowman, *Business Organization and Management,* 4th ed. (Homewood, Ill.: Richard D. Irwin, Inc., 1958).

Shartle, Carroll L., *Executive Performance and Leadership* (Englewood Cliffs, N. J.: Prentice-Hall, Inc., 1956).

Chapter 9

Dun's Review and Modern Industry, February, 1959, p. 16.

Foulke, Roy A., *Practical Statement Analysis,* 4th ed. (New York: McGraw-Hill Book Co., Inc., 1957).

"What Distributors Want to Know before Taking on a Line," *Sales Management* (October 1, 1951), pp. 76 ff.

"Why Our Sales Policies Are Built Around Manufacturers' 'Reps'," *ibid.* (Oct. 1, 1950), pp. 117 ff.

Yogerst, W. M., "What Can a Manufacturer Do to Keep His Agents Prosperous and Happy?" *ibid.* (June 1, 1950), pp. 52 ff.

Chapter 10*

Duddy, Edward A., and David A. Revzan, *The Changing Relative Importance of the Central Livestock Market,* Studies in Business Administration, Vol. VIII, No. 4 (Chicago: The University of Chicago Press, August 1938).

Revzan, David A., "Locational Clusterings of Manufacturing, Retail, Service, and Wholesale Establishments," in *The Broadening Perspective of Marketing,* Proceedings of Gold Triangle Conference, American Marketing Association (Pittsburgh, June 20–22, 1956), pp. 90–96.

Chapter 11

Borden, Neil H., *The Economic Effects of Advertising* (Homewood, Ill.: Richard D. Irwin, Inc., 1942), pp. 589–602; 631–639.

Business Week

"Placing Furniture Marts" (Jan. 24, 1959), p. 71.

"Middlemen in the Plastics Trade" (Aug. 10, 1957), p. 92.

Duddy, E. A., and D. A. Revzan, *op. cit.,* 2nd ed., Chapter III.

Larson, Gustav E., *Developing and Selling New Products: A Guidebook for Manufacturers,* 2nd ed. (Washington, D. C.: U. S. Government Printing Office, 1955).

Phelps, D. M., *Planning the Product* (Homewood, Ill.: Richard D. Irwin, Inc., 1947).

* *Note:* See references to Chapter 4 in addition.

Chapters 12, 13

Aljian, George W. (ed.), *Purchasing Policies* (New York: McGraw-Hill Book Co., Inc., 1958).

Beckman, T. N., et al., *op. cit.,* Chapters 20, 25.

Churchman, C. West, Russell L. Ackoff, and E. Leonard Arnoff, *Introduction to Operations Research* (New York: John Wiley and Sons, Inc., 1957), Chapters 8, 9, 10. Pages 232–234, and pp. 273–74 contain a comprehensive bibliography.

Duddy, E. A., and D. A. Revzan, *op. cit.,* 2nd ed., Chapters XXI, XXII; pp. 79–88; and Appendix B.

Phelps, D. M., *op. cit.,* Chapter V.

Whitin, T. M., *The Theory of Inventory Management* (Princeton, N. J.: Princeton University Press, 1953).

Working, Holbrook, "Futures Trading and Hedging," *The American Economic Review,* XLII (June 1953), 314–343.

Chapter 14

Bogert, George W., and William E. Britton, *Cases on the Law of Sales,* 3rd ed. (Brooklyn: The Foundation Press, 1956).

Duffy, Ben, *Advertising Media and Markets,* 2nd ed. (Englewood Cliffs, N. J.: Prentice-Hall, Inc., 1951).

Frey, Albert W., *How Many Dollars for Advertising?* (New York: The Ronald Press Co., 1955).

Phelps, D. M., *Sales Management* (Homewood, Ill.: Richard D. Irwin, Inc., 1951).

Chapters 15, 16

Backman, Jules (ed.), *Price Practices and Price Policies* (New York: The Ronald Press Co., 1953).

Bain, Joe S., "Price and Production Policies," in Howard S. Ellis (ed.), *A Survey of Contemporary Economics* (Philadelphia: The Blakiston Co., 1948), Chapter 4.

Business Week, "Drug Probes," October 24, 1959, pp. 140–41.

Duddy, E. A., and D. A. Revzan, *op. cit.,* 2nd ed., Chapter XXV.

Edwards, Corwin D., "The Effect of Recent Basing Point Decisions upon Business Practices," *The American Economic Review,* XXXVIII (December 1948), 828–42.

Fetter, Frank A., *op. cit.*

Hansen, A. H., "Price Flexibility and the Full Employment of Resources," *The Structure of the American Economy: II. Toward Full Use of Resources* (Washington, D. C.: National Resources Planning Board, June 1940), pp. 27–34.

Kaplan, A. D. H., Joel B. Dirlam, and Robert F. Lanzillotti, *Pricing in Big*

Business; A Case Approach (Washington, D. C.: The Brookings Institution, 1958).

Lanzillotti, Robert F., "Pricing Objectives in Large Companies," *The American Economic Review*, XLVIII (December 1958), 921–940.

Lynip, B. F., *Factors Affecting the Wholesale Price Level* (San Francisco: California and Hawaiian Sugar Refining Corp., Ltd., July 1950).

Machlup, Fritz, *The Basing-Point System* (Philadelphia: The Blakiston Co., 1949).

Means, Gardiner C., *Industrial Prices and Their Relative Inflexibility*, Senate Document No. 13, 74th Congress, 1st Session (Washington, D. C.: U. S. Government Printing Office, 1935).

Mund, Vernon, *Open Markets: An Essential of Free Enterprise* (New York: Harper and Bros., 1948), Chapter i.

New York Times, "Debate on 'Administered Prices'," March 22, 1959, p. E-7.

Nourse, Edwin G., "The Meaning of Price Policy," *Quarterly Journal of Economics*, 55 (February 1941), 175–209.

———, *Price Making in a Democracy* (Washington, D. C.: The Brookings Institution, 1942).

Oxenfeldt, Alfred R., *Industrial Pricing and Market Practices* (Englewood Cliffs, N. J.: Prentice-Hall, Inc., 1951).

Revzan, David A., *The Wholesale Price Structure for Oranges, with Special Reference to the Chicago Auction Market*, Studies in Business Administration, Vol. XIV, No. 1 (Chicago: The University of Chicago Press, January 1944).

Seaver, S. K., *Economic Analysis of the Market Organization and Operation of the California Egg Industry*, Mimeographed Report No. 229 (California Agricultural Experiment Station, February 1960).

Shaw, Arch W., "Some Problems in Market Distribution," *Quarterly Journal of Economics*, XXVI (August 1912), 703–65.

Survey of Current Business, "Recent Price Developments," 32 (April 1952), 4–9.

Tannenbaum, Robert, *Cost under the Unfair Practices Acts, Studies in Business Administration*, Vol. IX, No. 2 (Chicago: The University of Chicago Press, 1939).

Wardwell, Charles A. R., "Structure and Trends of Wholesale Prices," *Survey of Current Business*, 34 (March 1954), 13–19.

Wolozin, Harold, "Wholesale Price Movements in Three Recessions," *Monthly Labor Review*, 81 (August 1958), 888–90.

Chapter 17

Beckman, T. N., et al., *op. cit.*, Chapters 23, 24.

Bromell, John R., *Dry Goods Wholesalers' Operations* (Washington, D. C.: U. S. Government Printing Office, 1949).

———, *Modernizing and Operating Grocery Warehouses*, Domestic Commerce Series, No. 26 (Washington, D. C.: U. S. Government Printing Office, 1951).

Business Week, "New-Fangled Routes Deliver the Goods—Faster and Cheaper" (November 14, 1959), pp. 108 ff.

Distribution Age, "Automatic Order-Filling—Six Million Blouses a Year" (March 1957), pp. 34 ff.

Fortune, "Materials Handling: The New Word in Industry," XXXVII (June 1948), 96 ff.

"The Push Button Warehouse," LIV (December 1956), 140 ff.

Meserole, W. M., "Organization of Wholesale Operations for Low Cost," *The Journal of Marketing,* XIV (September 1949), 192–197.

Phelps, Clyde E., "An Ancient Industry Goes Modern," *Distribution Age* (August 1956), pp. 48 ff.

U. S. Bureau of the Census, *U. S. Census of Business: 1954*—Vol. III.

Wright, Clark C., and John P. H. Perry, "The Trend to One-Storied Warehouses," *Distribution Age* (April 1948), pp. 34 ff.

Chapter 18

Dun's Review and Modern Industry, "14 Important Ratios in 24 Wholesale Lines" (November 1959), pp. 56–57.

Federal Reserve Bulletin

"Saving and Financial Flows" (August 1959), pp. 825–26.

"A Flow-of-Funds System of National Accounts Annual Estimates, 1939–54" (October 1955), pp. 1085–1124.

Frederick, John H., *Public Warehousing: Its Organization, Economic Services, and Legal Aspects* (New York: The Ronald Press Co., 1940).

Jacoby, Neil H., and Raymond J. Saulnier, *Financing Inventory on Field Warehouse Receipts* (New York: National Bureau of Economic Research, 1944).

Moore, Carroll G., "Factoring—A Unique Form of Financing and Service," *The Business Lawyer,* XIV (April 1959), 703–727.

Phelps, Clyde W., *The Role of Factoring in Modern Business Finance,* Studies in Commercial Finance No. 1 (Baltimore: Commercial Credit Co., Educational Division, 1956).

Westerfield, Ray B., "Middlemen in English Business," *Transactions of the Connecticut Academy of Arts and Sciences,* XIX (New Haven: Yale University Press, 1915).

Chapter 19

Brady, Robert A., Review of K. William Kapp, *The Social Cost of Private Enterprise* (Cambridge, Mass.: Harvard University Press, 1950), in *The American Economic Review,* XLI (June 1951), 435.

Bull, John S., "Marketing Costs and Management Decisions," unpublished B.A. 299 (M.B.A.) Report (Berkeley: University of California Library, June 1952).

Dean, Joel, *Managerial Economics* (Englewood Cliffs, N. J.: Prentice-Hall, Inc., 1951).

Duddy, E. A., and D. A. Revzan, *op. cit.,* 2nd ed., Chapter III.

Federal Trade Commission, *Case Studies in Distribution Cost Accounting for Manufacturing and Wholesaling* (Washington, D. C.: U. S. Government Printing Office, 1941).

Heckert, J. B., and Robert B. Miner, *Distribution Costs* (New York: The Ronald Press Co., 1953).

Longman, Donald R., and Michael Schiff, *Practical Distribution Cost Analysis* (Homewood, Ill.: Richard D. Irwin, Inc., 1955).

McGarry, Edmund D., "Some Functions of Marketing Reconsidered," in R. Cox and W. Alderson (eds.), *Theory in Marketing* (Homewood, Ill.: Richard D. Irwin, Inc., 1950), Chapter 16.

Sevin, Charles H., "Some Aspects of Distribution Cost Analysis," *The Journal of Marketing,* XII (July 1947), 92.

Chapter 20

Business Week

"Calling the Shots for the 1980's" (November 28, 1959), pp. 86 ff.

"Utilities Get New Ways to Plan" (November 28, 1959), pp. 101 ff.

Churchman, C. W., et al., *op. cit.*

Crisp, Richard D., "Analytical Approach to Channel Policies—Sales Analyses," in R. M. Clewett (ed.), *Marketing Channels,* Chapter 18.

Duncan, Delbert J., "Co-operation with Distribution Channels," in C. F. Phillips (ed.), *Marketing by Manufacturers,* rev. ed. (Homewood, Ill.: Richard D. Irwin, Inc., 1951), Chapter XII.

Kelley, E. W., "Cost Control for Marketing Operations—General Considerations," *N.A.C.A. Bulletin,* XXXV, Research Series No. 25, Section 3 (April 1954), 1070.

N.A.C.A. Bulletin

"Assignment of Nonmanufacturing Costs for Managerial Decisions," XXXII, Section 4 (May 1951), 1135–1172.

"The Assignment of Nonmanufacturing Costs to Products," XXXII, Research Series No. 20, Section 4 (August 1951), 1559–1589.

"The Assignment of Nonmanufacturing Costs to Territories and Other Segments," XXXII, Research Series No. 21, Section 3 (December 1951), 527–547.

"Cost Control for Manufacturing Operations—Order Filling," XXXV, Research Series No. 27 (August 1954), 1647–1675.

"Cost Control for Marketing Operations—Order Getting," XXXV, Research Series No. 26, Section 3 (June 1954), 1352.

"Profit Control by Territories and Products in the Food Processing Industry," XXX (March 1950), 809.

Revzan, David A., "Les études des marches aux Etats-Unis," *Revue Economique,* No. 3 (May 1954), pp. 404–421.

Sevin, Charles H., "Analytical Approach to Channel Policies—Marketing Cost Analysis," in R. M. Clewett (ed.), *Marketing Channels,* Chapter 19.

Tintner, Gerhard, *Econometrics* (New York: John Wiley and Sons, Inc., 1952).

Wallace, W. Allen, and Harry V. Roberts, *Statistics: A New Approach* (Glencoe, Illinois: The Free Press, 1956).

Chapters 21, 22

Austin, Cyrus, *Price Discrimination and Related Problems under the Robinson-Patman Act,* 2nd rev. ed. (Philadelphia: American Law Institute, June 1959).

Bain, Joe S., *Industrial Organization* (New York: John Wiley and Sons, Inc., 1959).

Cassady, Ralph, Jr., "Some Economic Aspects of Price Discrimination under Non-Perfect Market Conditions," *The Journal of Marketing*, XI (July 1946), 7–20.

———, "Techniques and Purposes of Price Discrimination," *The Journal of Marketing*, XI (October 1946), 135–150.

Clark, John M., *Social Control of Business* (Chicago: The University of Chicago Press, 1926), pp. 17–18.

Duddy, E. A., and D. A. Revzan, *op. cit.*, 2nd ed., Chapter XXX.

Edwards, Corwin D., *The Price Discrimination Law: A Review of Experience* (Washington, D. C.: The Brookings Institution, December 1959).

Hamilton, Walton, *The Politics of Industry* (New York: Alfred A. Knopf, 1957).

Learned, Edmund P., and Nathan Isaacs, "The Robinson-Patman Law: Some Assumptions and Expectations," *Harvard Business Review*, XV (Winter 1937), 137–55.

Oppenheim, S. Chesterfield, "Selected Antitrust Developments in the Courts and Federal Trade Commission During Past Year (1958–59)," American Bar Association, *Section on Antitrust Law*, Annual Proceedings, Vol. 15 (1959), pp. 37–73.

Report of the Attorney-General's National Committee to Study the Antitrust Laws (Washington, D. C.: U. S. Government Printing Office, March 31, 1955).

Rowe, Frederick M., "The Evolution of the Robinson-Patman Act, A Twenty-Year Perspective," *Columbia Law Review*, 57 (December 1957).

Stevens, W. H. S., *Unfair Competition: A Study of Certain Practices* (Chicago: The University of Chicago Press, 1917).

Taggart, Herbert F., *Cost Justification*, Michigan Business Studies, Vol. XIV (Ann Arbor, Michigan: Bureau of Business Research, University of Michigan, 1959).

Votaw, Dow, *Legal Aspects of Business Administration* (Englewood Cliffs, N. J.: Prentice-Hall, Inc., 1956).

Chapter 23

Christie, John, and Melvin J. Boldberg, "Crisis of the Cities: Industry Heads for the Open," *Dun's Review and Modern Industry* (February 1960), pp. 35–37.

Collins, Norman R., "Changing Role of Prices in Agricultural Marketing," *Journal of Farm Economics*, XLI (August 1959), 528–34.

Duddy, E. A., and D. A. Revzan, *op. cit.*, 2nd ed., Chapter II, Appendix C.

Edwards, Corwin D., "Doing Business under the Present Law about Delivered Prices," *Louisiana Law Review*, XI (March 1951), 347–65.

Jones, Fred M., "The Decline of Chicago as a Grain Futures Market," *The Journal of Marketing*, XII (July 1947), 61–65.

Kitagawa, Evelyn M., and Donald J. Bogue, *Suburbanization of Manufacturing Activity within Standard Metropolitan Areas*, Studies in Population Distribution, No. 9 (Oxford, Ohio: Scripps Foundation, Miami University, 1955).

Vaile, R., E. T. Grether, and R. Cox, *op. cit.*

Working, Holbrook, "Whose Markets?—Evidence on Some Aspects of Futures Trading," *The Journal of Marketing*, XIX (July 1954), 1–11.

Chapter 24

Beckman, Theodore N., "A Critical Appraisal of Current Wholesaling," *The Journal of Marketing*, **XIV** (September 1949), 307–316.

Clark, John M., *Alternatives to Serfdom* (New York: Alfred A. Knopf, 1948).

Duddy, E. A., and D. A. Revzan, *op. cit.*, 2nd ed., Chapter II, Appendix C.

Edmunds, Stahrl, "In Wholesaling's Future—The Coming America," *The Journal of Marketing*, **XIV** (September 1949), 273–74.

Finer, Herman, *Road to Reaction* (Boston: Little, Brown and Co., 1945).

Hayek, F. A., *The Road to Serfdom* (Chicago: The University of Chicago Press, 1944)

Mund, Vernon, *op. cit.*

Polanyi, Karl, *The Great Transformation: The Political and Economic Origins of Our Time*, paperback ed. (Boston: Beacon Press, 1957).

Name Index

Ackoff, Russell, 512
Alderson, Wroe, 7–10, 161 n.
Aljian, George W., 314 n.
Apparel City, 256 n., 271
Arnoff, E. Leonard, 512
Attorney General's National Committee, 575, 591
Austin, Cyrus, 558 n.

Backman, Jules, 361 n., 379 n., 391 n.
Bain, Joe S., 379 n., 533–534, 536 n., 537–538, 574 n., 591 n.
Banks for Cooperatives, 452
Barnard, Chester I., 182 n.
Beckman, Theodore N., 3, 4 n., 34 n., 323 n., 439 n., 445 n.
Bentley Automobile, 267
Bogert, George G., 355 n.
Bogue, Donald J., 589–590
Borden, Neil H., 263, 269 n.
Brady, Robert A., 470–471
Bredo, William, 100
Breyer, Ralph F., 11 n., 121 n., 146 n., 164 n., 491 n.
Britton, William E., 355 n.
Bromell, John R., 434 n., 436 n., 441, 466–467
Bull, John S., 480–481, 484–490
Bureau of Census, 2, 3, 473–474
Bureau of Labor Statistics, 377
Business Week, 390 n., 427 n.

Buzzell, Richard D., 323 n.

Cadillac Plastic & Chemical Co., 265 n.
Cassady, Ralph, Jr., 166 n., 555–557
Celler, Emanuel, 554
Christie, John, 590 n.
Chrysler Motors, 290 n.
Churchman, C. West, 512
Clark, Carrie P., 7
Clark, Fred E., 7
Clark, John M., 521–522, 613 n.
Clewett, Richard M., 151 n.
Collins, Norman R., 584 n.
Consumers' Research, 319
Consumers' Union, 319
Copeland, Melvin T., 62
Cox, Reavis, 7, 10, 110 n., 120 n., 480–481, 591 n.
Craig, David R., 146 n.
Crescent Electric Supply Co., 193 n.
Crisp, Richard D., 511 n.
Curtis Publishing Co., 104

Daggett, Stuart, 96 n.
Dean, Joel, 470, 483–484
Department of Agriculture, U. S., 319
Department of Commerce, U. S., 22, 104
Department of Justice, U. S., 560
Dewhurst, J. Frederic, 610 n.
Dirlam, Joel B., 386 n.

633

Subject Index